Durationator Copyright Files: Foundational Concepts in Usability

Other Titles in the Just Wanna Legal DIY Series

Just Wanna Trademark

A Little Bit of Copyright for Quilters

Just Wanna Quilt Notebook

Just Wanna Patent

Just Wanna Create: Copyright and Fair Use Strategies

Durationator Copyright Files

Foundational Concepts in Usability
with Cases

By

Elizabeth Townsend Gard

Just Wanna Publications

Durationator Copyright Files: Foundational Concepts with Cases

An Imprint of Limited Times Publishing House
New Orleans, LA

Editor-in-Chief, Ricardo Gonzalez
Book design/Layout, Eyeridum, LLC.

ISBN: 978-1-7341271-7-1

No warranty for accuracy is given on the legal information on this book. The book is meant as a teaching tool and is not a substitute for legal representation. This book is up-to-date with the U.S. law as of December 2020. Please consult an attorney for legal advice and guidance.

First U.S. Edition, January 2021.

All images are either used with permission or under the fair use doctrine. For more information, please contact the author. Portions of the writings were previously published in the following law journals: Mitigating Term: A Proposal, Journal of Copyright Society of the USA, Copyright Soc'y 63, 1-53 (2016), J.D. Salinger and Rule of the Shorter Term, 19 Vand. J. Ent. & Tech. 777 (2017), Creating a Last Twenty (L20) Collection: Implementing Section 108(h) in Libraries, Archives and Museums (22 UCLA J. law and Tech 1 (2018), A Tale of Two Ginsburgs: *Eldred v. Ashcroft* and *Golan v. Holder* (Depaul L.R. 2014), "*Golan* and *Prometheus* as Misfit First Amendment Cases," Cato Supreme Court Review (2012), Federalizing Pre-1972 Sound Recordings: Two Proposals, co-authored with Erin Anapol, 15 *Tulane Journal of Technology and Intellectual Property*, Fall 2012, "The Making of the Durationator®: An Unexpected Journey into Entrepreneurship," book chapter in *Entrepreneurship and Innovation in Evolving Economies: the Role of Law*, Megan Carpenter, ed., Edward Elgar Publishing, 2012, In the Trenches with Section 104A: An Evaluation of the Parties' Arguments in *Golan v. Holder* as It Heads to the U.S. Supreme Court, Vanderbilt Law Review (invited, *64 Vand L. Rev. En Banc 199 (2011)*), Copyright Law v. Trade Policy: Understanding the *Golan* Battle within the Tenth Circuit, 34 *Columbia Journal for Law and the Arts* 2 (Winter 2011), 131-199, With W. Ron Gard, The Present (User-Generated Crisis) is the Past (1909 Copyright Act): An Essay Theorizing the "Traditional Contours of Copyright" Language, 28 *Cardozo Arts and Entertainment Law Journal* 455, (455-499) (2011), "Unpublished Work and the Public Domain: The Opening of a New Frontier, "54 *J. Copyright Society of the U.S.A.* (Winter 2007), and "The Birth of the Unpublished Public Domain and the International Implications," 24 *Cardozo Arts & Ent. L.J.* (2006). Footnotes have been deleted from the articles and cases have been deleted, and alterations to the original articles have been made.

Dedicated to my father, Robert Joel Townsend (1937-2019),
who taught me how to think about the law and
to be confident in finding my place in the world.

Acknowledgments

The *Durationator* began officially in 2007, but had started a decade earlier when my father took me to the law library in Los Angeles to research fair use. I fell in love with legal research, and after completing my Ph.D., went on to law school and then a career as a law professor. Those few hours in the law library downtown changed everything.

Many people have been part of the Durationator journey -- Ron Gard, who stepped in to work with me on the entrepreneurial side of the project, and Sid, who competed for attention, learned to read, and waited patiently as we had meeting after meeting. Sid and the Durationator grew up together. Sid goes to college next year.

To the law students who have dedicated themselves to the project: Matt Miller and Jeff Pasternek, who started it all, with Justin Levy, Evan Dicharry, and Ben Varadi joining quickly thereafter.[1] Justin, Evan, and I would gather early Saturday mornings to think through the latest research challenges -- how to code a particular part of the law, until Sid, then 4 would wake and want to play. Evan would usually "challenge" her to a video game, especially "Smooth Moves" on Wii, which would give us a few hours more to think out the problem of the day. Ben made our logo, the Durationator girl, out of 19th-century ads in the public domain, and also our short video about the Durationator. He also built a book scanner (yes!).

The second wave was led by Bri Whetstone, Caroline Fischer, Greg Stein, and Zachary Christiansen, who helped with our massive research efforts to gather every copyright law in the world, and every copyright law that has ever been.[2] Greg Stein was the first to gather laws for Section 104A, and he went on to work on the entrepreneurial side as well.

[1] The first set of Research Assistant students also included Jessica Denisi, Eric Arnold, Katherine Quandar, Michael Wisen, A. Galia, Hilary Adams, Thien Hua, Jeremy Johnson, Ryan Kelly, Adriane Tracy-Drazdek, Benjamin Turpen, Charles Smith, Christy Hardegree, Patricia Guzman, Neil Mikeska, Victor Roberts, Francisco Besosa, Roger Conant, Amiel Provosty, Benjamin Feldman, Brian Dollar, Wendy Hadfield, Andrew Maragiliotta, Danie Beuke, Diana Csank, Kimberly Hart, Brandon Creekbaum, and Blake Simon.

[2] The second wave of Research Assistants also included Hilaryr Adams, Francisco Besosa, Daniel Beuke, Roger Conant, Brandon Chreebaum, Diana Csank, Brian Dollar, Elizabeth Dufour, Jessica Edmundson, William Gamble, Elizabeth Gray, Patricia Guzman, Wendy Hadfield, Courtney Halwig, Christy Hardegree, Kimberly Hart, Matthew Horton, Thien Hua, Jermey Johnson, Jacklina Len, John McNew, Nei Mikeska, Andrew Miragliotta, Jeffery Pastorek, Erin Pritchard, Amie Provosty, Victor Roberts, Andrew Sensai, Blakeys Simon, Karen Rudnkcki, Garrison Hershey, Nicholas KrienkeRoss Carlson and Benjamin Turpen.

Our third wave ramped up the coding with Dan Collier leading the team,with Toni Xu, and students who specialized in particular countries.[3] Thea Crane, along with Tulane Law School librarian Kim Glorioiso, were up to the challenge of finding the "hard ones", and John Bicknell kept us organized with an amazing chart. We also added LL.M. students that researched specific countries, including China and Haiti, among other countries.

And to Ricardo Gonzalez and Corrie Dutton, the fourth wave, who conducted research at the Frick and Library of Congress, and crunched the data from the Internet Archive.[4] They helped transform the project into something usable in this next phase, including the building of a Catalog of Copyright Entries database, and strategies for the Durationator short-cuts. And to my copyright and IP courses at Tulane Law School, who have pitched in with classroom activities for over the last decade.

John Christie, Executive Director, Technology Transfer., guided and supported this project from the beginning. Deans Ponoroff and Meyer at the law school also supported the project, as did Dean Swartz at Phyllis Taylor Center for Social Innovation and Design Thinking. And to Provosts Bernsten and Forman for their support as well.

We've had many grants for this project, including the Tulane University Research Enhancement Grant, Phase IIB; Tulane University Technology Transfer IDEA Grant; Provost Research Funds, and Paul Verkuil Faculty Research Fund. And we've had support from Thomson Reuters, Culture/Tech, Harvard University, University of Michigan, the Library of Congress, MOMA, NYPL, NOMA, the Ogden, the Internet Archive, and the Frick, among others. In particular, thanks to Kenneth Crews, Greg Cram, Peter Hirtle, Melissa Levine, Dale Nelson, Kyle Courtney, Chris Reed, and David Nimmer, among others. We have worked with entrepreneurial organizations including Idea Village, Propeller New Orleans, 52 Business, University of California Berkeley Haas School of Business, DePaul Business School, Taylor Center at Tulane University. This work has been supported by the following fellowships: Non-resident fellow at the Center for Internet and Society; Leverhulme Trust Postdoctoral Research Fellowship, London, UK; U.S. Holocaust Museum Faculty Award Curt C. and Else Silberman Seminar for Faculty; Lepage Faculty Fellow at the A.B. Freeman School of Business, Tulane; and the Jill H. and Avram A. Glazer Professorship in Social Entrepreneurship.

[3] The third wave included John Bicknell, Caroline Fischer, Alexandre De Lespinasse, Morgan Embleton, Michele Emmons, Kimberly Jemison, Jessica Johnson, Lauren Peralta, Joshua Lesser, Jessica Johnson, Michelle Emmnos, Caroline Wick, Tyler Allen, Ryan Noormanham, Elvia Zepeda, Benjamin Vanesse, Latisha Mais, and Alexandra Stork.

[4] The fourth wave also included Anjana Turner, Olatomiwa Aina, Emily Dombrowski, Christopher Blexrrud, Madeline Weisblatt, Stan Sater, Thomas Lemler, and Margaret Wilbourne.

Special thanks to Janice Sayas, who has been there every step, with every crazy request. You are my anchor and friend. And, of course, to the Quilting Army, who has taught me more about copyright than I have to them. In particular, thank you to Polly Mumma, Wilma Havenga, D. Newland, Karen Klamczynski, Wendy Starn, Sarah Myers, and Beth Bornick.

This book is about teaching the foundational texts of understanding copyright as a property right, that at some point transitions into a work that is free for all to use -- into the public domain. It turns out to sometimes be really easy to identify, and other times, a bit more complicated. The same has been true of the project itself. But it also turns out that duration leads to a whole set of other questions.

Table of Contents

Preface

On the eve of publishing this book, the Copyright Alternative in Small-Claims Enforcement Act, or CASE Act was passed into law in December 2020. The CASE Act for the first time provides a small claims opportunity for copyright. This creates new questions and issues for how copyright will be governed. Now more than ever it is essential to understand the foundational concepts of copyright so that we can understand how it changes over the next year(s) as the CASE Act is implemented. In 2018-2020 we had already seen great changes. Pre-1972 sound recordings were brought partially under Federal law. We got clarification on the importance of registration and timing in lawsuits through the U.S. Supreme Court. State sovereignty and copyright infringement was taken up by the U.S. Supreme Court. States also saw their annotated codes taken up by the U.S. Supreme Court. The public domain started to grow again after a 20 year freeze. Fair use cases abound. The Copyright Office is modernizing and beta testing a virtual card catalog. Section 108(h) for libraries is being used for the first time since its enactment in 1998, thanks to our work at Tulane Law school, in connection with the Internet Archive, the Frick Collection, and the Library of Congress. And we all are waiting for the U.S. Supreme Court decision in Google v. Oracle. Now more than ever must we understand foundational concepts in copyright, and how these new changes will impact our assumptions and working copyright system. Foundational concepts help us understand how copyright works.

The Durationator Copyright Files approaches all of these new topics and more from the perspective of usability: how the copyright law is working in practical application. To do this, we combine statutory interpretation with case law. Additionally, we'll examine materials produced by the U.S. Copyright Office to better understand copyright at this moment.

The future is here. We are ready to face it by understanding the past as well as what we currently know. Time will tell how much copyright remains within the "traditional contours" of what we have come to expect, and how much is a new frontier.

Ricardo Gonzalez
Editor-in-Chief, Just Wanna series

1: Introduction

"Can I use this work?" We've heard that question thousands of times over the last decade. Usability of an image, text, photograph, film, architecture plans, sound recording, artwork, and other creative works can be a complicated inquiry. What does "use" mean? Could it mean that one is asking whether the work is in the public domain (copyright term)? Could it mean that we are asking whether the elements I want to use are non-protectable? Could it mean we are asking the question how do I get permission from the copyright holder, and who *is* the copyright holder? Could it mean you are asking if you can incorporate part of the work into another piece of art, and does fair use apply? Can a library digitize this work? Can a teacher make a copy for a class? Can an artist use it as inspiration? This book approaches the question of "can I use that work" from a variety of angles and points of entry.

This book is designed for law students and those serious about learning advanced copyright. This is not a DIY book. Rather, this book approaches the topic as a way of learning the idea of usability from a variety of angles. We will be approaching the study of copyright from a number of angles. The reason *why* you study copyright matters. Are you a law student yearning to practice in the field? Are you a librarian tasked with understanding how copyright works? Do you want to know the law to register and protect your works? Are you an artist trying to understand fair use? Are you planning to sell fan art? All of those uses will be addressed.

Mastering a subject takes time. Learning to read how law works in a given area takes time. Understanding how the law actually is applied is a luxury that comes with practice and experience. In classrooms, we teach a subject as if you go from A to B. IIn the real world, C sometimes comes before F, long before A, and B never arrives. This book attempts to teach you a flexibility in thinking - that the starting point into a usability inquiry may start at any one of many entry points.

Copyright Law

We will be looking at copyright law from at least three vantage points: deep dive into parts of U.S. law; comparative work with the countries of the world; and the application of what we find to helpful forms for non-specialists.

Diving into US Law

We will be looking at specific aspects of US law, namely the statute plus caselaw. We will be looking at Section 302, 303, 304, 1401, 104A, 512, 107, 108, 106A, 411, 511(a), among others. The goal will be to learn how to read and analyze these parts of the statute. You will also have the opportunity to work on real-world problems. We will also be looking at Section 1401, which was recently added for pre-1972 sound recordings. We will look at fair use in depth, both historically and in the area of fan art/fan fiction and social media uses. And we will tackle the new CASE Act, the small claims court, which is the new Chapter 15 in the 1976 Copyright Act. We will also be looking at the two 2020 U.S. Supreme court cases related to state laws in relationship to federal copyright law.

Beyond U.S. Law

U.S. copyright does not exist in a vacuum. Copyright is territorial. We quickly find ourselves asking what happens outside of our U.S. borders. International copyright expert and professor Peter Yu suggests a three-tier approach to studying international copyright. First, there are the individual countries and the laws that they enact. We compare those. Second, there are the international treaties that govern behavior between countries and impact how their copyright laws are constructed. Finally, he suggests we look at the transnational aspects of copyright: how copyright operates across national boundaries, especially in the age of the Internet.[5] We will be doing just that, all three parts. We will also be looking at a number of treaties as well as copyright laws of different countries. We will be comparing the structure and content of these laws with the 1976 Copyright Act.

We also have recognized that the laws of countries interact with each other in a number of instances. The U.S. requires, for Section 104A, one look to the country of origin to determine if a work is still protected. Other countries also look to the country of origin for Rule of the Shorter Term, a concept we will discuss in detail.

We often see U.S. companies, institutions and libraries are quickly asking for information in key countries. We will be learning how to research this. Then, if you are looking at foreign copyright laws, you will have to be able to understand the structure and relationship of the internal laws, as well as the relationship of their laws to their treaty obligations and foreign laws within their own system. So, we have to get familiar and comfortable not only with U.S. laws but foreign laws and treaties as well. And

[5] Peter K. Yu, *Teaching International Intellectual Property Law*, 52 St. Louis U. L.J. 923, 928 (2008).

sometimes, even then, there will be no clear answers. We also have to get comfortable with ambiguity and uncertainty.

Concepts of Copyright

We will be exploring comparative copyright laws around the world as an introduction to more advanced copyright. Today, copyright laws around the world have merged the two systems, one from common law and the other from civil law, but we have to understand that we have two ways of thinking about copyright. In both systems, the author plays a central role.

Common Law

Common law is based on utilitarianism. The author is given certain rights to exploit the work for the benefit of society. If the author is incentivized to economically benefit from their efforts, then so too will society benefit. This is often referred to as a "copyright" tradition.

The history of common law begins in the United Kingdom with the invention of the printing press in 1476, which immediately made "pirating" copies a lot easier (than copying by hand). A system was put in place where the British Crown controlled who and what was-printed -- mostly censorship for religious reasons. A guild was created, the Stationers' Company, which comprised London's publishers and booksellers. You had to get a printing patent to print books. Authors sold their books to publishers, who then had the right to print and sell them.

Over time, this went out of favor, and the system was replaced with the first copyright act, called the Statute of Anne (1709). What was unique about this statutory change was two things: authors, not a guild of publishers controlled the right to copy, and unlike under the previous system, the government grant for exclusive rights to the author was time limited. We had the first experience of works coming into the public domain. These two concepts play significant roles in how we still approach copyright.

The U.S. enacted its first copyright act in 1790, and it mirrors the Statute of Anne in many ways. It, too, is author-based, with a focus on books, maps, and charts. Both the Statute of Anne and the 1790 Copyright Act would expand the categories with time. The protection was also limited in time.

We will look at countries that come out of the Anglo-American tradition. What this means for us is countries that were former colonies of Great Britain. Their copyright acts look a particular way. Some still use British law, even after no longer being a colony. We will be looking at this strain as part of the work we do. We will return to this subject in Chapter 6 on Comparative Copyright.

Civil Law

Civil law is based on a natural rights theory of property. The author is at the center of the system, and that means moral rights are key. This is often referred to as an "author" based tradition. Interestingly, playwriting was the first type of work protected in France. The idea is that the work comes from the author's mind, and so is an exclusive incorporeal property right that bears the "personal imprint" of the author as part of its makeup.[6] The "author's right" tradition begins in France, which ended the printing monopolies with the rise of the French Revolution. The 1791 and 1793 laws established the basic system, which stayed in place till 1957, with minimal changes. Not all civil law is the same. France and Germany approach copyright in slightly different terms. For example, in Germany, the economic and moral rights cannot be separated, believing in the doctrine of "monism." Most of the world (except the countries above) follow the civil law tradition. We will be looking at these countries. We've found in the past that grouping them together by traditions, geographies, and colonial relationships prove helpful.

Geographic areas:

- ❑ Europe
- ❑ Asia
- ❑ Middle East
- ❑ South and Central America
- ❑ Former Soviet Union Countries

We will be looking at these countries and their historical relationship in Chapter 6 Comparative Copyright.

Copyright Law as an International Economic Trading System

Traditionally, copyright law regulates trade between producers of culture. The borders were distinctly national. England protected their own works and pirated from France. U.S. protected their own works and pirated from everyone. And so, by the mid-19th century, it was clear that authors and countries wanted a way to have protection not

[6] See Goldstein and Hugenholts, International Copyright (4th), 7.

just at home but abroad. We get a history of bilateral treaties, multinational treaties, regional agreements, and more. They become part of the regulation of trade. Countries agree to alter/implement their national law in accordance with the treaties they have signed. We will be looking at key treaties, including:

- ❑ Berne Convention for the Protection of Literary and Artistic Works
- ❑ Universal Copyright Convention
- ❑ TRIPS (Agreement on Trade-Related Aspects of Intellectual Property Rights, Including Trade in Counterfeit Goods)
- ❑ European Union directives
- ❑ Bilateral treaties
- ❑ Rome Convention (Rome Convention for the Protection of Performers, Producers of Phonograms and Broadcasting Organizations)
- ❑ Geneva Convention (Convention for the Protection of Producers of Phonograms Against Unauthorized Duplication of Their Phonograms)
- ❑ Marrakesh Treaty to Facilitate Access to Published Works for Persons Who Are Blind, Visually Impaired or Otherwise Print Disabled
- ❑ WIPO Copyright Treaty

Custom versus Law

We will also be doing some work on how the law really works, as compared to what the law says. This will be true of our fan fiction and social media lessons.

The Importance of the Public Domain

Copyright law has always been seen as a bargain. In the U.S., that bargain is found with the language of the Constitution, which gives Congress the power to "promote the Progress of Science...by securing for limited Times to Authors...the exclusive Right to their respective Writings..." We see the concept of the public domain throughout the world and in our copyright treaties.

The basic utilitarian notion is that the public benefits from granting a monopoly to authors as an incentive to create new works, which the public can enjoy during the life of the copyright. Once the limited monopoly term expires, the public then benefits from the free exercise of use of the previously copyrighted work—the work comes into the public domain. As Justice Stevens noted in *Sony Corp. v. Universal City Studios*, each year the public domain grows, as new works complete their copyright term. Once in the public domain, individuals are free to use the work as they wish—reprint, create new versions (turning a novel into a movie), quote extensively, post on the Internet—anything—and all without permission of the original copyright holder. The work has entered its second life, free from copyright constraints. The *Durationator* started as a project that hunts for that transition moment. It is not always easy to puzzle out.

The copyright bargain traditionally played out as follows: a work traveled from creation to protection under federal copyright law and ultimately to the public domain. The end of the journey was seen as permanent—where once a work entered the public domain, it stayed there forever. But Congressional legislation in the mid-1990s called our assumptions into question. As part of our international obligations, millions of foreign works had copyright "restored"—works that had previously been in the public domain in the U.S. These public domain works had been used sometimes for decades without need for permission. The change in law meant these works were suddenly encumbered automatically by copyright.

Anti-circumvention, anti-bootlegging, and digital rights management all introduced new elements to copyright that potentially altered the relationship of copyright and the public domain. What if anti-circumvention devices prevent access to public domain works? What if digital watermarks trace (and report) uses long after the work is supposed to be "free as the air to common use?" What happens when the public, whose assumption had been that a work was free to use, finds the legal status of a given work has suddenly and automatically been altered? In short, are works in the public domain protectable because of their public domain status? Does the Constitution mandate a public domain? Are works in the public domain secure from privatization and federal copyright (re)protection?

In the last decades, the public domain has been the subject of great study, after having been taken for granted for most of copyright history. Some believe the public domain exists as a constitutionally-protected component of the copyright system on account of the "limited Times"-ness of the Copyright clause in the Constitution. Others see the public domain as encompassing not only works with expired copyright terms or subject matter that had not been protectable in the first place (i.e. facts, ideas, etc.), but include fair uses and other permissible uses of protected works. The discussion of the public domain, in part, comes from its seemingly precarious legal position. The idea of what is included in the public domain has been conceptually expanded by scholars like Samuelson, Benkler, Zimmerman, and Boyle, among others, partly in response to legislation and cases during the 1990s that significantly—sometimes temporarily but in other instances permanently—diminished the number of works included in the public domain.

The Pessimist/Realist View on Copyright

When does it matter that you get the copyright term right? That's part of the question you should be asking yourself. If I post a photograph of my 1972 kindergarten class, does it matter that I didn't get permission from the copyright holder? (And who is the copyright holder? The photographer? The school? and so many questions follow). Likely not. But with the CASE Act, the assumptions and expectations may change. We will have to wait and see. Smaller infractions might now be caught in the copyright net in a way they hadn't before.

Two key questions one might ask: one is about attribution, and the other is control. A third is money. Are you Netflix making a series based on a short story? Are you a library that will make available a work (precluding potentially the economic opportunity to republish the work)? Are you an artist creating Baby Yodas to take advantage of a particular craze? Part of what we must do in the real world is sort through these variables and make a decision. That's why lawyers come in so handy. They help us weigh the risks involved in our actions.

For now, we are learning the law. We will put it into context along the way. And you may feel frustrated that you have to learn complex law that no one seems to adhere to. That's part of learning copyright as well. Because you will see: just because the general public often ignores copyright, the courts do not. They like to get into the details. And so do we. And we will soon see if the claims filed in the CASE Act will too.

Readings: An Introduction to Copyright

We begin with *Eldred v. Ashcroft*, a 2003 U.S. Supreme Court case that asked the question: can copyright terms be extended? The case provides us with a little insight into the history of copyright, and how copyright works. We will then turn to excerpts from an article that again looks at what is copyright, and how does it work? In this piece we broaden out to think about why copyright looks the way it does now and why it looked different before.

Eldred v. Ashcroft 123 S.Ct. 769 (2003)

Justice GINSBURG delivered the opinion of the Court.

[note: footnotes omitted]

This case concerns the authority the Constitution assigns to Congress to prescribe the duration of copyrights. The Copyright and Patent Clause of the Constitution, Art. I, § 8, cl. 8, provides as to copyrights: "Congress shall have Power ... [t]o promote the Progress of Science ... by securing [to Authors] for limited Times ... the exclusive Right to their ... Writings." In 1998, in the measure here under inspection, Congress enlarged the duration of copyrights by 20 years. Copyright Term Extension Act (CTEA), Pub.L. 105–298, §§ 102(b) and (d), 112 Stat. 2827–2828 (amending 17 U.S.C. §§ 302, 304). As in the case of prior extensions, principally in 1831, 1909, and 1976, Congress provided for application of the enlarged terms to existing and future copyrights alike.

Petitioners are individuals and businesses whose products or services build on copyrighted works that have gone into the public domain. They seek a determination that the CTEA fails constitutional review under both the Copyright Clause's "limited Times" prescription and the First Amendment's free speech guarantee. Under the 1976 Copyright Act, copyright protection generally lasted from the work's creation until 50 years after the author's death. Pub.L. 94–553, § 302(a), 90 Stat. 2572 (1976 Act). Under the CTEA, most copyrights now run from creation until 70 years after the author's death. 17 U.S.C. § 302(a). Petitioners do not challenge the "life–plus–70–years" timespan itself. "Whether 50 years is enough, or 70 years too much," they acknowledge, "is not a judgment meet for this Court." Brief for Petitioners 14. Congress went awry, petitioners maintain, not with respect to newly created works, but in enlarging the term for published works with existing copyrights. The "limited Tim[e]" in effect when a copyright is secured, petitioners urge, becomes the constitutional boundary, a clear line beyond the power of Congress to extend. See *ibid.* As to the First Amendment, petitioners contend that the CTEA is a content-neutral regulation of speech that fails inspection under the heightened judicial scrutiny appropriate for such regulations.

[*Eldred* concerns works created under the 1909 Act. These were the works that were most affected by the extra twenty years from the CTEA.]

In accord with the District Court and the Court of Appeals, we reject petitioners' challenges to the CTEA. In that 1998 legislation, as in all previous copyright term extensions, Congress placed existing and future copyrights in parity. In prescribing that alignment, we hold, Congress acted within its authority and did not transgress constitutional limitations.

[We will see this question of whether a law reaches back to works already in existence. Note, all of these works were still under copyright; none of them had fallen into the public domain. We will see in many countries around the world that their laws are retroactive -- they restore works that had previously fallen into the public domain because the term was shorter or they did not comply with formalities. Here we do not have that situation, but we will when we discuss Section 104A that applies to foreign works in the U.S.]

I

A

We evaluate petitioners' challenge to the constitutionality of the CTEA against the backdrop of Congress' previous exercises of its authority under the Copyright Clause. The Nation's first copyright statute, enacted in 1790, provided a federal copyright term of 14 years from the date of publication, renewable for an additional 14 years if the author survived the first term. Act of May 31, 1790, ch. 15, § 1, 1 Stat. 124 (1790 Act). The 1790 Act's renewable 14–year term applied to existing works (*i.e.,* works already published and works created but not yet published) and future works alike. *Ibid.* Congress expanded the federal copyright term to 42 years in 1831 (28 years from publication, renewable for an additional 14 years), and to 56 years in 1909 (28 years from publication, renewable for an additional 28 years). Act of Feb. 3, 1831, ch. 16, §§ 1, 16, 4 Stat. 436, 439 (1831 Act); Act of Mar. 4, 1909, ch. 320, §§ 23–24, 35 Stat. 1080–1081 (1909 Act). Both times, Congress applied the new copyright term to existing and future works, 1831 Act §§ 1, 16; 1909 Act §§ 23–24; to qualify for the 1831 extension, an existing work had to be in its initial copyright term at the time the Act became effective, 1831 Act §§ 1, 16.

[That last sentence is important. To qualify for term extension, a work must still have been in its initial copyright term, that had not fallen into the public domain.]

In 1976, Congress altered the method for computing federal copyright terms. 1976 Act §§ 302–304. For works created by identified natural persons, the 1976 Act provided that federal copyright protection would run from the work's creation, not—as in the 1790, 1831, and 1909 Acts—its publication; protection would last until 50 years after the author's death. § 302(a). In these respects, the 1976 Act aligned United States copyright terms with the then-dominant international standard adopted under the Berne Convention for the Protection of Literary and Artistic Works. See H.R.Rep. No. 94–1476, p. 135 (1976), U.S. Code Cong. & Admin News 1976, p.5659. For anonymous works, pseudonymous works, and works made for hire, the 1976 Act provided a term of 75 years from publication or 100 years from creation, whichever expired first. § 302(c).

These new copyright terms, the 1976 Act instructed, governed all works not published by its effective date of January 1, 1978, regardless of when the works were created. §§ 302–303. For published works with existing copyrights as of that date, the 1976 Act granted a copyright term of 75 years from the date of publication, §§ 304(a) and (b), a 19–year increase over the 56–year term applicable under the 1909 Act.

took into account petitioners' acknowledgment that the preamble itself places no substantive limit on Congress' legislative power. 239 F.3d, at 378.

The appeals court found nothing in the constitutional text or its history to suggest that "a term of years for a copyright is not a 'limited Time' if it may later be extended for another 'limited Time.' " *Id.*, at 379. The court recounted that "the First Congress made the Copyright Act of 1790 applicable to subsisting copyrights arising under the copyright laws of the several states." *Ibid.* That construction of Congress' authority under the Copyright Clause "by [those] contemporary with [the Constitution's] formation," the court said, merited "very great" and in this case "almost conclusive" weight. *Ibid.* (quoting *Burrow–Giles Lithographic Co. v. Sarony*, 111 U.S. 53, 57, 4 S.Ct. 279, 28 L.Ed. 349 (1884)). As early as *McClurg v. Kingsland*, 1 How. 202, 11 L.Ed. 102 (1843), the Court of Appeals added, this Court had made it "plain" that the same Clause permits Congress to "amplify the terms of an existing patent." 239 F.3d, at 380. The appeals court recognized that this Court has been similarly deferential to the judgment of Congress in the realm of copyright. *Ibid.* (citing *Sony Corp. of America v. Universal City Studios, Inc.*, 464 U.S. 417, 104 S.Ct. 774, 78 L.Ed.2d 574 (1984); *Stewart v. Abend*, 495 U.S. 207, 110 S.Ct. 1750, 109 L.Ed.2d 184 (1990)).

Concerning petitioners' assertion that Congress might evade the limitation on its authority by stringing together "an unlimited number of 'limited Times,' " the Court of Appeals stated that such legislative misbehavior "clearly is not the situation before us." 239 F.3d, at 379. Rather, the court noted, the CTEA "matches" the baseline term for "United States copyrights [with] the terms of copyrights granted by the European Union." *Ibid.* "[I]n an era of multinational publishers and instantaneous electronic transmission," the court said, "harmonization in this regard has obvious practical benefits" and is "a 'necessary and proper' measure to meet contemporary circumstances rather than a step on the way to making copyrights perpetual." *Ibid.*

Judge Sentelle dissented in part. He concluded that Congress lacks power under the Copyright Clause to expand the copyright terms of existing works. *Id.*, at 380–384. The Court of Appeals subsequently denied rehearing and rehearing en banc. 255 F.3d 849 (2001).

We granted certiorari to address two questions: whether the CTEA's extension of existing copyrights exceeds Congress' power under the Copyright Clause; and whether the CTEA's extension of existing and future copyrights violates the First Amendment. 534 U.S. 1126 and 1160, 122 S.Ct. 1062 and 1170, 151 L.Ed.2d 966 and 152 L.Ed.2d 115 (2002). We now answer those two questions in the negative and affirm.

II

A

We address first the determination of the courts below that Congress has authority under the Copyright Clause to extend the terms of existing copyrights. Text, history, and precedent, we conclude, confirm that the Copyright Clause empowers Congress to prescribe "limited Times" for copyright protection and to secure the same level and duration of protection for all copyright holders, present and future.

The CTEA's baseline term of life plus 70 years, petitioners concede, qualifies as a "limited Tim[e]" as applied to future copyrights.[4] Petitioners contend, however, that existing copyrights extended to endure for that same term are not "limited." Petitioners' argument essentially reads into the text of the Copyright Clause the command that a time prescription, once set, becomes forever "fixed" or "inalterable." The word "limited," however, does not convey a meaning so constricted. At the time of the Framing, that word meant what it means today: "confine[d] within certain bounds," "restrain[ed]," or "circumscribe[d]." S. Johnson, A Dictionary of the English Language (7th ed. 1785); see T. Sheridan, A Complete Dictionary of the English Language (6th ed. 1796) ("confine[d] within certain bounds"); Webster's Third New International Dictionary 1312 (1976) ("confined within limits"; "restricted in extent, number, or duration"). Thus understood, a timespan appropriately "limited" as applied to future copyrights does not automatically cease to be "limited" when applied to existing copyrights. And as we observe, *infra,* at 783, there is no cause to suspect that a purpose to evade the "limited Times" prescription prompted Congress to adopt the CTEA.

To comprehend the scope of Congress' power under the Copyright Clause, "a page of history is worth a volume of logic." *New York Trust Co. v. Eisner,* 256 U.S. 345, 349, 41 S.Ct. 506, 65 L.Ed. 963 (1921) (Holmes, J.). History reveals an unbroken congressional practice of granting to authors of works with existing copyrights the benefit of term extensions so that all under copyright protection will be governed evenhandedly under the same regime. As earlier recounted, see *supra,* at 775, the First Congress accorded the protections of the Nation's first federal copyright statute to existing and future works alike. 1790 Act § 1. Since then, Congress has regularly applied duration extensions to both existing and future copyrights. 1831 Act §§ 1, 16; 1909 Act §§ 23–24; 1976 Act §§ 302–303; 17 U.S.C. §§ 302–304.[6]

Congress' consistent historical practice of applying newly enacted copyright terms to future and existing copyrights reflects a judgment stated concisely by Representative Huntington at the time of the 1831 Act: "[J]ustice, policy, and equity alike forb[id]" that an "author who had sold his [work] a week ago, be placed in a worse situation than the author who should sell his work the day after the passing of [the] act." 7 Cong. Deb. 424 (1831); accord, Symposium, The Constitutionality of Copyright Term Extension, 18 Cardozo Arts & Ent. L.J. 651, 694 (2000) (Prof.Miller) ("[S]ince 1790, it has indeed been Congress's policy that the author of yesterday's work should not get a lesser reward than the author of tomorrow's work just because Congress passed a statute lengthening the term today."). The CTEA follows this historical practice by keeping the duration provisions of the 1976 Act largely in place and simply adding 20 years to each of them. Guided by text, history, and precedent, we cannot agree with petitioners' submission that extending the duration of existing copyrights is categorically beyond Congress' authority under the Copyright Clause.

Satisfied that the CTEA complies with the "limited Times" prescription, we turn now to whether it is a rational exercise of the legislative authority conferred by the Copyright Clause. On that point, we defer substantially to Congress. *Sony,* 464 U.S., at 429, 104 S.Ct. 774 ("[I]t is Congress that has been assigned the task of defining the scope of the limited monopoly that should be granted to authors ... in order to give the public appropriate access to their work product.").

The CTEA reflects judgments of a kind Congress typically makes, judgments we cannot dismiss as outside the Legislature's domain. As respondent describes, see Brief for Respondent 37–38, a key factor in the CTEA's passage was a 1993 European Union (EU) directive instructing EU members to establish a copyright term of life plus 70 years. EU Council Directive 93/98, Art. 1(1), p. 11; see 144 Cong. Rec. S12377–S12378 (daily ed. Oct. 12, 1998) (statement of Sen. Hatch). Consistent with the Berne Convention, the EU directed its members to deny this longer term to the works of any non-EU country whose laws did not secure the same extended term. See Berne Conv. Art. 7(8); P. Goldstein, International Copyright § 5.3, p. 239 (2001). By extending the baseline United States copyright term to life plus 70 years, Congress sought to ensure that American authors would receive the same copyright protection in Europe as their European counterparts.[11] The CTEA may also provide greater incentive for American and other authors to create and disseminate their work in the United States. See Perlmutter, Participation in the International Copyright System as a Means to Promote the Progress of Science and Useful Arts, 36 Loyola (LA) L.Rev. 323, 330 (2002) ("[M]atching th[e] level of [copyright] protection in the United States [to that in the EU] can ensure stronger protection for U.S. works abroad and avoid competitive disadvantages vis-à-vis foreign rightholders."); see also *id.,* at 332 (the United States could not "play a leadership role" in the give-and-take evolution of the international copyright system, indeed it would "lose all flexibility," "if the only way to promote the progress of science were to provide incentives to create new works").

In addition to international concerns, Congress passed the CTEA in light of demographic, economic, and technological changes, Brief for Respondent 25–26, 33, and nn. 23 and 24, and rationally credited projections that longer terms would encourage copyright holders to invest in the restoration and public distribution of their works, *id.,* at 34–37; see H.R.Rep. No. 105–452, p. 4 (1998) (term extension "provide[s] copyright owners generally with the incentive to restore older works and further disseminate them to the public").

In sum, we find that the CTEA is a rational enactment; we are not at liberty to second-guess congressional determinations and policy judgments of this order, however debatable or arguably unwise they may be. Accordingly, we cannot conclude that the CTEA—which continues the unbroken congressional practice of treating future and existing copyrights in parity for term extension purposes—is an impermissible exercise of Congress' power under the Copyright Clause.

B

Petitioners' Copyright Clause arguments rely on several novel readings of the Clause. We next address these arguments and explain why we find them unpersuasive

1

Petitioners contend that even if the CTEA's 20–year term extension is literally a "limited Tim[e]," permitting Congress to extend existing copyrights allows it to evade the "limited Times" constraint by creating effectively perpetual copyrights through repeated extensions. We disagree.

As the Court of Appeals observed, a regime of perpetual copyrights "clearly is not the situation before us." 239 F.3d, at 379. Nothing before this Court warrants construction of the CTEA's 20–year term extension as a congressional attempt to evade or override the "limited Times" constraint.[16] Critically, we again emphasize, petitioners fail to show how the CTEA crosses a constitutionally significant threshold with respect to "limited Times" that the 1831, 1909, and 1976 Acts did not. See *supra,* at 775–776; Austin, *supra* n. 13, at 56 ("If extending copyright protection to works already in existence is constitutionally suspect," so is "extending the protections of U. S copyright law to works by foreign authors that had already been created and even first published when the federal rights attached."). Those earlier Acts did not create perpetual copyrights, and neither does the CTEA.

2

Petitioners dominantly advance a series of arguments all premised on the proposition that Congress may not extend an existing copyright absent new consideration from the author. They pursue this main theme under three headings. Petitioners contend that the CTEA's extension of existing copyrights (1) overlooks the requirement of "originality," (2) fails to "promote the Progress of Science," and (3) ignores copyright's *quid pro quo.*

Petitioners' "originality" argument draws on *Feist Publications, Inc. v. Rural Telephone Service Co.,* 499 U.S. 340, 111 S.Ct. 1282, 113 L.Ed.2d 358 (1991). In *Feist,* we observed that "[t]he *sine qua non* of copyright is originality," *id.,* at 345, 111 S.Ct. 1282, and held that copyright protection is unavailable to "a narrow category of works in which the creative spark is utterly lacking or so trivial as to be virtually nonexistent," *id.,* at 359, 111 S.Ct. 1282. Relying on *Feist,* petitioners urge that even if a work is sufficiently "original" to qualify for copyright protection in the first instance, any extension of the copyright's duration is impermissible because, once published, a work is no longer original.

Feist, however, did not touch on the duration of copyright protection. Rather, the decision addressed the core question of copyrightability, *i.e.,* the "creative spark" a work must have to be eligible for copyright protection at all. Explaining the originality requirement, *Feist* trained on the Copyright Clause words "Authors" and "Writings." *Id.,* at 346–347, 111 S.Ct. 1282. The decision did not construe the "limited Times" for which a work may be protected, and the originality requirement has no bearing on that prescription.

More forcibly, petitioners contend that the CTEA's extension of existing copyrights does not "promote the Progress of Science" as contemplated by the preambular language of the

Copyright Clause. Art. I, § 8, cl. 8. To sustain this objection, petitioners do not argue that the Clause's preamble is an independently enforceable limit on Congress' power. See 239 F.3d, at 378 (Petitioners acknowledge that "the preamble of the Copyright Clause is not a substantive limit on Congress' legislative power." Rather, they maintain that the preambular language identifies the sole end to which Congress may legislate; accordingly, they conclude, the meaning of "limited Times" must be "determined in light of that specified end." Brief for Petitioners 19. The CTEA's extension of existing copyrights categorically fails to "promote the Progress of Science," petitioners argue, because it does not stimulate the creation of new works but merely adds value to works already created.

As petitioners point out, we have described the Copyright Clause as "both a grant of power and a limitation," *Graham v. John Deere Co. of Kansas City,* 383 U.S. 1, 5, 86 S.Ct. 684, 15 L.Ed.2d 545 (1966), and have said that "[t]he primary objective of copyright" is "[t]o promote the Progress of Science," *Feist,* 499 U.S., at 349, 111 S.Ct. 1282. The "constitutional command," we have recognized, is that Congress, to the extent it enacts copyright laws at all, create a "system" that "promote[s] the Progress of Science." *Graham,* 383 U.S., at 6, 86 S.Ct. 684

We have also stressed, however, that it is generally for Congress, not the courts, to decide how best to pursue the Copyright Clause's objectives. See *Stewart v. Abend,* 495 U.S., at 230, 110 S.Ct. 1750 ("Th[e] evolution of the duration of copyright protection tellingly illustrates the difficulties Congress faces .... [I]t is not our role to alter the delicate balance Congress has labored to achieve."); *Sony,* 464 U.S., at 429, 104 S.Ct. 774 ("[I]t is Congress that has been assigned the task of defining the scope of [rights] that should be granted to authors or to inventors in order to give the public appropriate access to their work product."); *Graham,* 383 U.S., at 6, 86 S.Ct. 684 ("Within the limits of the constitutional grant, the Congress may, of course, implement the stated purpose of the Framers by selecting the policy which in its judgment best effectuates the constitutional aim."). The justifications we earlier set out for Congress' enactment of the CTEA, *supra,* at 781–782, provide a rational basis for the conclusion that the CTEA "promote[s] the Progress of Science."

On the issue of copyright duration, Congress, from the start, has routinely applied new definitions or adjustments of the copyright term to both future works and existing works not yet in the public domain.[19] Such consistent congressional practice is entitled to "very great weight, and when it is remembered that the rights thus established have not been disputed during a period of [over two] centur[ies], it is almost conclusive." *Burrow–Giles Lithographic Co. v. Sarony,* 111 U.S., at 57, 4 S.Ct. 279. Indeed, "[t]his Court has repeatedly laid down the principle that a contemporaneous legislative exposition of the Constitution when the founders of our Government and framers of our Constitution were actively participating in public affairs, acquiesced in for a long term of years, fixes the construction to be given [the Constitution's] provisions." *Myers v. United States,* 272 U.S. 52, 175, 47 S.Ct. 21, 71 L.Ed. 160 (1926). Congress' unbroken practice since the founding generation thus overwhelms petitioners' argument that the CTEA's extension of existing copyrights fails *per se* to "promote the Progress of Science."

Closely related to petitioners' preambular argument, or a variant of it, is their assertion that the Copyright Clause "imbeds a quid pro quo." Brief for Petitioners 23. They contend, in this regard, that Congress may grant to an "Autho[r]" an "exclusive Right" for a "limited Tim[e]," but only in exchange for a "Writin[g]." Congress' power to confer copyright protection, petitioners argue, is thus contingent upon an exchange: The author of an original work receives an "exclusive Right" for a "limited Tim[e]" in exchange for a dedication to the public thereafter. Extending an existing copyright without demanding additional consideration, petitioners maintain, bestows an unpaid-for benefit on copyright holders and their heirs, in violation of the *quid pro quo* requirement.

We can demur to petitioners' description of the Copyright Clause as a grant of legislative authority empowering Congress "to secure a bargain—this for that." *Id.*, at 16; see *Mazer v. Stein*, 347 U.S. 201, 219, 74 S.Ct. 460, 98 L.Ed. 630 (1954) ("The economic philosophy behind the clause empowering Congress to grant patents and copyrights is the conviction that encouragement of individual effort by personal gain is the best way to advance public welfare through the talents of authors and inventors in 'Science and useful Arts.' "). But the legislative evolution earlier recalled demonstrates what the bargain entails. Given the consistent placement of existing copyright holders in parity with future holders, the author of a work created in the last 170 years would reasonably comprehend, as the "this" offered her, a copyright not only for the time in place when protection is gained, but also for any renewal or extension legislated during that time.[21] Congress could rationally seek to "promote ... Progress" by including in every copyright statute an express guarantee that authors would receive the benefit of any later legislative extension of the copyright term. Nothing in the Copyright Clause bars Congress from creating the same incentive by adopting the same position as a matter of unbroken practice. See Brief for Respondent 31–32.

Neither *Sears, Roebuck & Co. v. Stiffel Co.*, 376 U.S. 225, 84 S.Ct. 784, 11 L.Ed.2d 661 (1964), nor *Bonito Boats, Inc. v. Thunder Craft Boats, Inc.*, 489 U.S. 141, 109 S.Ct. 971, 103 L.Ed.2d 118 (1989), is to the contrary. In both cases, we invalidated the application of certain state laws as inconsistent with the federal patent regime. *Sears*, 376 U.S., at 231–233, 84 S.Ct. 784; *Bonito*, 489 U.S., at 152, 109 S.Ct. 971. Describing Congress' constitutional authority to confer patents, *Bonito Boats* noted: "The Patent Clause itself reflects a balance between the need to encourage innovation and the avoidance of monopolies which stifle competition without any concomitant advance in the 'Progress of Science and useful Arts.' " *Id.*, at 146, 109 S.Ct. 971. *Sears* similarly stated that "[p]atents are not given as favors ... but are meant to encourage invention by rewarding the inventor with the right, limited to a term of years fixed by the patent, to exclude others from the use of his invention." 376 U.S., at 229, 84 S.Ct. 784. Neither case concerned the extension of a patent's duration. Nor did either suggest that such an extension might be constitutionally infirm. Rather, *Bonito Boats* reiterated the Court's unclouded understanding: "It is for Congress to determine if the present system" effectuates the goals of the Copyright and Patent Clause. 489 U.S., at 168, 109 S.Ct. 971. And as we have documented, see *supra*, at 779–781, Congress has many times sought to effectuate those goals by extending existing patents.

We note, furthermore, that patents and copyrights do not entail the same exchange, and that our references to a *quid pro quo* typically appear in the patent context. See, *e.g., J.E.M. Ag Supply, Inc. v. Pioneer Hi–Bred International, Inc.*, 534 U.S. 124, 142, 122 S.Ct. 593, 151 L.Ed.2d 508 (2001) ("The disclosure required by the Patent Act is 'the *quid pro quo* of the right to exclude.' " (quoting *Kewanee Oil Co. v. Bicron Corp.*, 416 U.S. 470, 484, 94 S.Ct. 1879, 40 L.Ed.2d 315 (1974))); *Bonito Boats,* 489 U.S., at 161, 109 S.Ct. 971 ("the *quid pro quo* of substantial creative effort required by the federal [patent] statute"); *Brenner v. Manson,* 383 U.S. 519, 534, 86 S.Ct. 1033, 16 L.Ed.2d 69 (1966) ("The basic *quid pro quo* ... for granting a patent monopoly is the benefit derived by the public from an invention with substantial utility."); *Pennock v. Dialogue,* 2 Pet. 1, 23, 7 L.Ed. 327 (1829) (If an invention is already commonly known and used when the patent is sought, "there might be sound reason for presuming that the legislature did not intend to grant an exclusive right," given the absence of a "*quid pro quo.*"). This is understandable, given that immediate disclosure is not the objective of, but is *exacted from,* the patentee. It is the price paid for the exclusivity secured. See *J.E.M. Ag Supply,* 534 U.S., at 142, 122 S.Ct. 593. For the author seeking copyright protection, in contrast, disclosure is the desired objective, not something exacted from the author in exchange for the copyright. Indeed, since the 1976 Act, copyright has run from creation, not publication. See 1976 Act § 302(a); 17 U.S.C. § 302(a).

Further distinguishing the two kinds of intellectual property, copyright gives the holder no monopoly on any knowledge. A reader of an author's writing may make full use of any fact or idea she acquires from her reading. See § 102(b). The grant of a patent, on the other hand, does prevent full use by others of the inventor's knowledge. See Brief for Respondent 22; *Alfred Bell & Co. v. Catalda Fine Arts,* 191 F.2d 99, 103, n. 16 (C.A.2 1951) (The monopoly granted by a copyright "is not a monopoly of knowledge. The grant of a patent does prevent full use being made of knowledge, but the reader of a book is not by the copyright laws prevented from making full use of any information he may acquire from his reading." (quoting W. Copinger, Law of Copyright 2 (7th ed.1936))). In light of these distinctions, one cannot extract from language in our patent decisions—language not trained on a grant's duration—genuine support for petitioners' bold view. Accordingly, we reject the proposition that a *quid pro quo* requirement stops Congress from expanding copyright's term in a manner that puts existing and future copyrights in parity.

3

As an alternative to their various arguments that extending existing copyrights violates the Copyright Clause *per se,* petitioners urge heightened judicial review of such extensions to ensure that they appropriately pursue the purposes of the Clause. See Brief for Petitioners 31–32. Specifically, petitioners ask us to apply the "congruence and proportionality" standard described in cases evaluating exercises of Congress' power under § 5 of the Fourteenth Amendment. See, *e.g., City of Boerne v. Flores,* 521 U.S. 507, 117 S.Ct. 2157, 138 L.Ed.2d 624 (1997). But we have never applied that standard outside the § 5 context; it does not hold sway for judicial review of legislation enacted, as copyright laws are, pursuant to Article I authorization.

Section 5 authorizes Congress to *enforce* commands contained in and incorporated into the Fourteenth Amendment. Amdt. 14, § 5 ("The Congress shall have power to *enforce*, by appropriate legislation, the provisions of this article." (emphasis added)). The Copyright Clause, in contrast, empowers Congress to *define* the scope of the substantive right. See *Sony*, 464 U.S., at 429, 104 S.Ct. 774. Judicial deference to such congressional definition is "but a corollary to the grant to Congress of any Article I power." *Graham*, 383 U.S., at 6, 86 S.Ct. 684. It would be no more appropriate for us to subject the CTEA to "congruence and proportionality" review under the Copyright Clause than it would be for us to hold the Act unconstitutional *per se*.

For the several reasons stated, we find no Copyright Clause impediment to the CTEA's extension of existing copyrights.

III

Petitioners separately argue that the CTEA is a content-neutral regulation of speech that fails heightened judicial review under the First Amendment.[23] We reject petitioners' plea for imposition of uncommonly strict scrutiny on a copyright scheme that incorporates its own speech-protective purposes and safeguards. The Copyright Clause and First Amendment were adopted close in time. This proximity indicates that, in the Framers' view, copyright's limited monopolies are compatible with free speech principles. Indeed, copyright's purpose is to *promote* the creation and publication of free expression. As *Harper & Row* observed: "[T]he Framers intended copyright itself to be the engine of free expression. By establishing a marketable right to the use of one's expression, copyright supplies the economic incentive to create and disseminate ideas." 471 U.S., at 558, 105 S.Ct. 2218.

In addition to spurring the creation and publication of new expression, copyright law contains built-in First Amendment accommodations. See *id.*, at 560, 105 S.Ct. 2218. First, it distinguishes between ideas and expression and makes only the latter eligible for copyright protection. Specifically, 17 U.S.C. § 102(b) provides: "In no case does copyright protection for an original work of authorship extend to any idea, procedure, process, system, method of operation, concept, principle, or discovery, regardless of the form in which it is described, explained, illustrated, or embodied in such work." As we said in *Harper & Row*, this "idea/expression dichotomy strike[s] a definitional balance between the First Amendment and the Copyright Act by permitting free communication of facts while still protecting an author's expression." 471 U.S., at 556, 105 S.Ct. 2218 (internal quotation marks omitted). Due to this distinction, every idea, theory, and fact in a copyrighted work becomes instantly available for public exploitation at the moment of publication. See *Feist*, 499 U.S., at 349–350, 111 S.Ct. 1282.

Second, the "fair use" defense allows the public to use not only facts and ideas contained in a copyrighted work, but also expression itself in certain circumstances. Codified at 17 U.S.C. § 107, the defense provides: "[T]he fair use of a copyrighted work, including such use by reproduction in copies ..., for purposes such as criticism, comment, news reporting, teaching (including multiple copies for classroom use), scholarship, or research, is not an infringement of copyright." The fair use defense affords considerable "latitude for scholarship and comment," *Harper & Row,* 471 U.S., at 560, 105 S.Ct. 2218, and even for parody, see *Campbell v. Acuff–Rose Music, Inc.,* 510 U.S. 569, 114 S.Ct. 1164, 127 L.Ed.2d 500 (1994) (rap group's musical parody of Roy Orbison's "Oh, Pretty Woman" may be fair use).

The CTEA itself supplements these traditional First Amendment safeguards. First, it allows libraries, archives, and similar institutions to "reproduce" and "distribute, display, or perform in facsimile or digital form" copies of certain published works "during the last 20 years of any term of copyright ... for purposes of preservation, scholarship, or research" if the work is not already being exploited commercially and further copies are unavailable at a reasonable price. 17 U.S.C. § 108(h); see Brief for Respondent 36. Second, Title II of the CTEA, known as the Fairness in Music Licensing Act of 1998, exempts small businesses, restaurants, and like entities from having to pay performance royalties on music played from licensed radio, television, and similar facilities. 17 U.S.C. § 110(5)(B); see Brief for Representative F. James Sensenbrenner, Jr., et al. as *Amici Curiae* 5–6, n. 3.

Finally, the case petitioners principally rely upon for their First Amendment argument, *Turner Broadcasting System, Inc. v. FCC,* 512 U.S. 622, 114 S.Ct. 2445, 129 L.Ed.2d 497 (1994), bears little on copyright. The statute at issue in *Turner* required cable operators to carry and transmit broadcast stations through their proprietary cable systems. Those "must-carry" provisions, we explained, implicated "the heart of the First Amendment," namely, "the principle that each person should decide for himself or herself the ideas and beliefs deserving of expression, consideration, and adherence." *Id.,* at 641, 114 S.Ct. 2445.

The CTEA, in contrast, does not oblige anyone to reproduce another's speech against the carrier's will. Instead, it protects authors' original expression from unrestricted exploitation. Protection of that order does not raise the free speech concerns present when the government compels or burdens the communication of particular facts or ideas. The First Amendment securely protects the freedom to make—or decline to make—one's own speech; it bears less heavily when speakers assert the right to make other people's speeches. To the extent such assertions raise First Amendment concerns, copyright's built-in free speech safeguards are generally adequate to address them. We recognize that the D.C. Circuit spoke too broadly when it declared copyrights "categorically immune from challenges under the First Amendment." 239 F.3d, at 375. But when, as in this case, Congress has not altered the traditional contours of copyright protection, further First Amendment scrutiny is unnecessary. See *Harper & Row,* 471 U.S., at 560, 105 S.Ct. 2218; cf. *San Francisco Arts & Athletics, Inc. v. United States Olympic Comm.,* 483 U.S. 522, 107 S.Ct. 2971, 97 L.Ed.2d 427 (1987)

IV

If petitioners' vision of the Copyright Clause held sway, it would do more than render the CTEA's duration extensions unconstitutional as to existing works. Indeed, petitioners' assertion that the provisions of the CTEA are not severable would make the CTEA's enlarged terms invalid even as to tomorrow's work. The 1976 Act's time extensions, which set the pattern that the CTEA followed, would be vulnerable as well.

As we read the Framers' instruction, the Copyright Clause empowers Congress to determine the intellectual property regimes that, overall, in that body's judgment, will serve the ends of the Clause. See *Graham*, 383 U.S., at 6, 86 S.Ct. 684 (Congress may "implement the stated purpose of the Framers by selecting the policy which *in its judgment* best effectuates the constitutional aim." (emphasis added)). Beneath the facade of their inventive constitutional interpretation, petitioners forcefully urge that Congress pursued very bad policy in prescribing the CTEA's long terms. The wisdom of Congress' action, however, is not within our province to second-guess. Satisfied that the legislation before us remains inside the domain the Constitution assigns to the First Branch, we affirm the judgment of the Court of Appeals.

It is so ordered.

Justice STEVENS, dissenting.

Writing for a unanimous Court in 1964, Justice Black stated that it is obvious that a State could not "extend the life of a patent beyond its expiration date," *Sears, Roebuck & Co. v. Stiffel Co.*, 376 U.S. 225, 231, 84 S.Ct. 784, 11 L.Ed.2d 661 (1964).[1] As I shall explain, the reasons why a State may not extend the life of a patent apply to Congress as well. If Congress may not expand the scope of a patent monopoly, it also may not extend the life of a copyright beyond its expiration date. Accordingly, insofar as the 1998 Sonny Bono Copyright Term Extension Act, 112 Stat. 2827, purported to extend the life of unexpired copyrights, it is invalid. Because the majority's contrary conclusion rests on the mistaken premise that this Court has virtually no role in reviewing congressional grants of monopoly privileges to authors, inventors, and their successors, I respectfully dissent.

[Stevens does a lot of comparison with patents]

[omitted materials]

Congress first enacted legislation under the Copyright/Patent Clause in 1790 when it passed bills creating federal patent and copyright protection. Because the content of that first legislation, the debate that accompanied it, and the differences between the initial versions and the bills that ultimately passed provide strong evidence of early Congresses' understanding of the constitutional limits of the Copyright/Patent Clause, I examine both the initial copyright and patent statutes.

Congress first considered intellectual property statutes in its inaugural session in 1789. The bill debated, House Resolution 10—"a bill to promote the progress of science and useful arts, by securing to authors and inventors the exclusive right to their respective writings and discoveries," 3 Documentary History of First Federal Congress of the United States 94 (L. de Pauw, C. Bickford, & L. Hauptman eds. 1977) (hereinafter Documentary History)—provided both copyright and patent protection for similar terms.[5] The first Congress did not pass H.R. 10, though a similar version was reintroduced in the second Congress in 1790. After minimal debate, however, the House of Representatives began consideration of two separate bills, one covering patents and the other copyrights. Because, as the majority recognizes, "congressional practice with respect to patents informs our inquiry," *ante,* at 779, I consider the history of both patent and copyright legislation.

[omitted Patent Act materials]

The Copyright Act

Congress also passed the first Copyright Act, 1 Stat. 124, in 1790. At that time there were a number of maps, charts, and books that had already been printed, some of which were copyrighted under state laws and some of which were arguably entitled to perpetual protection under the common law. The federal statute applied to those works as well as to new works. In some cases the application of the new federal rule reduced the pre—existing protections, and in others it may have increased the protection.[7] What is significant is that the statute provided a general rule creating new federal rights that supplanted the diverse state rights that previously existed. It did not extend or attach to any of those pre—existing state and common-law rights: "That congress, in passing the act of 1790, did not legislate in reference to existing rights, appears clear." *Wheaton v. Peters,* 8 Pet. 591, 661, 8 L.Ed. 1055 (1834); see also *Fox Film Corp. v. Doyal,* 286 U.S. 123, 127, 52 S.Ct. 546, 76 L.Ed. 1010 (1932) ("As this Court has repeatedly said, the Congress did not sanction an existing right but created a new one"). Congress set in place a federal structure governing certain types of intellectual property for the new Republic. That Congress exercised its unquestionable constitutional authority to *create* a new federal system securing rights for authors and inventors in 1790 does not provide support for the proposition that Congress can *extend pre-existing* federal protections retroactively.

Respondent places great weight on this first congressional action, arguing that it proves that "Congress thus unquestionably understood that it had authority to apply a new, more favorable copyright term to existing works." Brief for Respondent 12–13. That understanding, however, is not relevant to the question presented by this case—whether "Congress has the power under the Copyright Clause to extend retroactively the term of existing copyrights?" Brief for Petitioners i. Precisely put, the question presented by this case does not even implicate the

1790 Act, for that Act created, rather than extended, copyright protection. That this law applied to works already in existence says nothing about the First Congress' conception of its power to extend this newly created federal right.

Moreover, Members of Congress in 1790 were well aware of the distinction between the creation of new copyright regimes and the extension of existing copyrights. The 1790 Act was patterned, in many ways, after the Statute of Anne enacted in England in 1710. 8 Ann., c. 19; see *Fred Fisher Music Co. v. M. Witmark & Sons,* 318 U.S. 643, 647–648, 63 S.Ct. 773, 87 L.Ed. 1055 (1943). The English statute, in addition to providing authors with copyrights on new works for a term of 14 years renewable for another 14–year term, also replaced the booksellers' claimed perpetual rights in existing works with a single 21–year term. In 1735, the booksellers proposed an amendment that would have extended the terms of existing copyrights until 1756, but the amendment was defeated. Opponents of the amendment had argued that if the bill were to pass, it would "in Effect be establishing a perpetual Monopoly ... only to increase the private Gain of the Booksellers ...."[9] The authors of the federal statute that used the Statute of Anne as a model were familiar with this history. Accordingly, this Court should be especially wary of relying on Congress' creation of a new system to support the proposition that Congress unquestionably understood that it had constitutional authority to extend existing copyrights.

IV

Since the creation of federal patent and copyright protection in 1790, Congress has passed a variety of legislation, both providing specific relief for individual authors and inventors as well as changing the general statutes conferring patent and copyright privileges. Some of the changes did indeed, as the majority describes, extend existing protections retroactively. Other changes, however, did not do so. A more complete and comprehensive look at the history of congressional action under the Copyright/Patent Clause demonstrates that history, in this case, does not provide the "'volume of logic,'" *ante,* at 778, necessary to sustain the Sonny Bono Act's constitutionality.

[omitted Patent section]

Copyright legislation has a similar history. The federal Copyright Act was first amended in 1831. That amendment, like later amendments, not only authorized a longer term for new works, but also extended the terms of unexpired copyrights. Respondent argues that that historical practice effectively establishes the constitutionality of retroactive extensions of unexpired copyrights. Of course, the practice buttresses the presumption of validity that attaches to every Act of Congress. But, as our decision in *INS v. Chadha,* 462 U.S. 919, 103 S.Ct. 2764, 77 L.Ed.2d 317 (1983), demonstrates, the fact that Congress has repeatedly acted on a mistaken interpretation of the Constitution does not qualify our duty to invalidate an unconstitutional practice when it is finally challenged in an appropriate case. As Justice White pointed out in his dissent in *Chadha,* that case sounded the "death knell for nearly 200 other statutory provisions" in which Congress had exercised a " 'legislative veto.' " *Id.,* at 967, 103 S.Ct. 2764. Regardless of the effect of unconstitutional enactments of Congress, the scope of " 'the constitutional power of Congress ... is ultimately a judicial rather than a legislative question, and can be settled finally only by this Court.' " *United States v. Morrison*, 529 U.S. 598, 614, 120 S.Ct. 1740, 146 L.Ed.2d 658 (2000) (quoting *Heart of Atlanta Motel, Inc. v. United States*, 379 U.S. 241, 273, 85 S.Ct. 348, 13 L.Ed.2d 258 (1964) (Black, J., concurring)). For, as this Court has long recognized, "[i]t is obviously correct that no one acquires a vested or protected right in violation of the Constitution by long use, even when that span of time covers our entire national existence." *Walz v. Tax Comm'n of City of New York*, 397 U.S. 664, 678, 90 S.Ct. 1409, 25 L.Ed.2d 697 (1970).

It would be particularly unwise to attach constitutional significance to the 1831 amendment because of the very different legal landscape against which it was enacted. Congress based its authority to pass the amendment on grounds shortly thereafter declared improper by the Court. The Judiciary Committee Report prepared for the House of Representatives asserted that "an author has an exclusive and perpetual right, in preference to any other, to the fruits of his labor." 7 Cong. Deb., App., p. cxx (1831). The floor debate echoed this same sentiment. See, *e.g., id.*, at 424 (statement of Mr. Verplanck (rejecting the idea that copyright involved "an implied contract existing between an author and the public" for "[t]here was no contract; the work of an author was the result of his own labor" and copyright was "merely a legal provision for the protection of a natural right")). This sweat-of-the-brow view of copyright, however, was emphatically rejected by this Court in 1834 in *Wheaton v. Peters*, 8 Pet., at 661, 8 L.Ed. 1055 ("Congress, then, by this act, instead of sanctioning an existing right, as contended for, created it"). No presumption of validity should attach to a statutory enactment that relied on a shortly thereafter discredited interpretation of the basis for congressional power.[11]

In 1861, Congress amended the term of patents, from a 14–year term plus opportunity for 7–year extension to a flat 17 years with no extension permitted. Act of Mar. 2, 1861, ch. 88, § 16, 12 Stat. 249. This change was not retroactive, but rather only applied to "all patents hereafter granted." *Ibid.* To be sure, Congress, at many times in its history, has retroactively extended the terms of existing copyrights and patents. This history, however, reveals a much more heterogeneous practice than respondent contends. It is replete with actions that were unquestionably unconstitutional. Though relevant, the history is not dispositive of the constitutionality of the Sonny Bono Act.

The general presumption that historic practice illuminates the constitutionality of congressional action is not controlling in this case. That presumption is strongest when the earliest acts of Congress are considered, for the overlap of identity between those who created the Constitution and those who first constituted Congress provides "contemporaneous and weighty evidence" of the Constitution's "true meaning." *Wisconsin v. Pelican Ins. Co.*, 127 U.S. 265, 297, 8 S.Ct. 1370, 32 L.Ed. 239 (1888). But that strong presumption does not attach to congressional action in 1831, because no member of the 1831 Congress had been a delegate to the framing convention 44 years earlier.

Moreover, judicial opinions relied upon by the majority interpreting early legislative enactments have either been implicitly overruled or do not support the proposition claimed. *Graham* flatly contradicts the cases relied on by the majority and respondent for support that "renewed or extended terms were upheld in the early days." *Ante*, at 779.[12] *Evans v. Jordan*, 8 F. Cas. 872, 874 (No. 4,564)(CC Va. 1813) (Marshall, J.); *Evans v. Robinson*, 8 F. Cas. 886, 888 (No. 4,571) (CC Md. 1813); and *Blanchard v. Sprague*, 3 F. Cas. 648, 650 (No. 1,518) (CC Mass. 1839) (Story, J.), all held that private bills passed by Congress extending previously expired patents were valid. *Evans v. Jordan* and *Evans v. Robinson* both considered Oliver Evans' private bill discussed above while *Blanchard* involved ch. 213, 6 Stat. 589, which extended Thomas Blanchard's patent after it had been in the public domain for five months. Irrespective of what circuit courts held "in the early days," *ante*, at 779, such holdings have been implicitly overruled by *Graham* and, therefore, provide no support for respondent in the present constitutional inquiry.

[omitted materials]

The history of retroactive extensions of existing and expired copyrights and patents, though relevant, is not conclusive of the constitutionality of the Sonny Bono Act. The fact that the Court has not previously passed upon the constitutionality of retroactive copyright extensions does not insulate the present extension from constitutional challenge.

V

Respondent also argues that the Act promotes the useful arts by providing incentives to restore old movies. For at least three reasons, the interest in preserving perishable copies of old copyrighted films does not justify a wholesale extension of existing copyrights. First, such restoration and preservation will not even arguably promote any new works by authors or inventors. And, of course, any original expression in the restoration and preservation of movies will receive new copyright protection.[13] Second, however strong the justification for preserving such works may be, that justification applies equally to works whose copyrights have already expired. Yet no one seriously contends that the Copyright/Patent Clause would authorize the grant of monopoly privileges for works already in the public domain solely to encourage their restoration. Finally, even if this concern with aging movies would permit congressional protection, the remedy offered—a blanket extension of all copyrights—simply bears no relationship to the alleged harm.

VI

Finally, respondent relies on concerns of equity to justify the retroactive extension. If Congress concludes that a longer period of exclusivity is necessary in order to provide an adequate incentive to authors to produce new works, respondent seems to believe that simple fairness requires that the same lengthened period be provided to authors whose works have already been completed and copyrighted. This is a classic non sequitur. The reason for increasing the inducement to create something new simply does not apply to an already-created work. To the contrary, the equity argument actually provides strong support for petitioners. Members of the public were entitled to rely on a promised access to copyrighted or patented works at the expiration of the terms specified when the exclusive privileges were granted. On the other hand, authors will receive the full benefit of the exclusive terms that were promised as an inducement to their creativity, and have no equitable claim to increased compensation for doing nothing more.

One must indulge in two untenable assumptions to find support in the equitable argument offered by respondent—that the public interest in free access to copyrighted works is entirely worthless and that authors, as a class, should receive a windfall solely based on completed creative activity. Indeed, Congress has apparently indulged in those assumptions for under the series of extensions to copyrights, with the exception of works which required renewal and which were not renewed, no copyrighted work created in the past 80 years has entered the public domain or will do so until 2019. But as our cases repeatedly and consistently emphasize, ultimate public access is the overriding purpose of the constitutional provision. See, *e.g., Sony Corp.*, 464 U.S., at 429, 104 S.Ct. 774. *Ex post facto* extensions of existing copyrights, unsupported by any consideration of the public interest, frustrate the central purpose of the Clause.

VII

The express grant of a perpetual copyright would unquestionably violate the textual requirement that the authors' exclusive rights be only "for limited Times." Whether the extraordinary length of the grants authorized by the 1998 Act are invalid because they are the functional equivalent of perpetual copyrights is a question that need not be answered in this case because the question presented by the certiorari petition merely challenges Congress' power to extend retroactively the terms of existing copyrights. Accordingly, there is no need to determine whether the deference that is normally given to congressional policy judgments may save from judicial review its decision respecting the appropriate length of the term.[14] It is important to note, however, that a categorical rule prohibiting retroactive extensions would effectively preclude perpetual copyrights. More importantly, as the House of Lords recognized when it refused to amend the Statute of Anne in 1735, unless the Clause is construed to embody such a categorical rule, Congress may extend existing monopoly privileges *ad infinitum* under the majority's analysis.

By failing to protect the public interest in free access to the products of inventive and artistic genius—indeed, by virtually ignoring the central purpose of the Copyright/Patent Clause—the Court has quitclaimed to Congress its principal responsibility in this area of the law. Fairly read, the Court has stated that Congress' actions under the Copyright/Patent Clause are, for all intents and purposes, judicially unreviewable. That result cannot be squared with the basic tenets of our constitutional structure. It is not hyperbole to recall the trenchant words of Chief Justice John Marshall: "It is emphatically the province and duty of the judicial department to say what the law is." *Marbury v. Madison,* 1 Cranch 137, 177, 2 L.Ed. 60 (1803). We should discharge that responsibility as we did in *Chadha.*

I respectfully dissent.

Justice BREYER, dissenting.

The Constitution's Copyright Clause grants Congress the power to "*promote* the *Progress* of Science ... by securing for *limited* Times to *Authors* ... the exclusive Right to their respective Writings." Art. I, § 8, cl. 8 (emphasis added). The statute before us, the 1998 Sonny Bono Copyright Term Extension Act, extends the term of most existing copyrights to 95 years and that of many new copyrights to 70 years after the author's death. The economic effect of this 20–year extension—the longest blanket extension since the Nation's founding—is to make the copyright term not limited, but virtually perpetual. Its primary legal effect is to grant the extended term not to authors, but to their heirs, estates, or corporate successors. And most importantly, its practical effect is not to promote, but to inhibit, the progress of "Science"—by which word the Framers meant learning or knowledge, E. Walterscheid, The Nature of the Intellectual Property Clause: A Study in Historical Perspective 125–126 (2002).

The majority believes these conclusions rest upon practical judgments that at most suggest the statute is unwise, not that it is unconstitutional. Legal distinctions, however, are often matters of degree. *Panhandle Oil Co. v. Mississippi ex rel. Knox,* 277 U.S. 218, 223, 48 S.Ct. 451, 72 L.Ed. 857 (1928) (Holmes, J., dissenting), overruled in part by *Alabama v. King & Boozer,* 314 U.S. 1, 8–9, 62 S.Ct. 43, 86 L.Ed. 3 (1941); accord, *Walz v. Tax Comm'n of City of New York,* 397 U.S. 664, 678–679, 90 S.Ct. 1409, 25 L.Ed.2d 697 (1970). And in this case the failings of degree are so serious that they amount to failings of constitutional kind. Although the Copyright Clause grants broad legislative power to Congress, that grant has limits. And in my view this statute falls outside them.

I

The "monopoly privileges" that the Copyright Clause confers "are neither unlimited nor primarily designed to provide a special private benefit." *Sony Corp. of America v. Universal City Studios, Inc.,* 464 U.S. 417, 429, 104 S.Ct. 774, 78 L.Ed.2d 574 (1984); cf. *Graham v. John Deere Co. of Kansas City,* 383 U.S. 1, 5, 86 S.Ct. 684, 15 L.Ed.2d 545 (1966). This Court has made clear that the Clause's limitations are judicially enforceable. *E.g., Trade–Mark Cases,* 100 U.S. 82, 93–94, 25 L.Ed. 550 (1879). And, in assessing this statute for that purpose, I would take into account the fact that the Constitution is a single document, that it contains both a Copyright Clause and a First Amendment, and that the two are related.

The Copyright Clause and the First Amendment seek related objectives—the creation and dissemination of information. When working in tandem, these provisions mutually reinforce each other, the first serving as an "engine of free expression," *Harper & Row, Publishers, Inc. v.*

Nation Enterprises, 471 U.S. 539, 558, 105 S.Ct. 2218, 85 L.Ed.2d 588 (1985), the second assuring that government throws up no obstacle to its dissemination. At the same time, a particular statute that exceeds proper Copyright Clause bounds may set Clause and Amendment at cross-purposes, thereby depriving the public of the speech-related benefits that the Founders, through both, have promised.

Consequently, I would review plausible claims that a copyright statute seriously, and unjustifiably, restricts the dissemination of speech somewhat more carefully than reference to this Court's traditional Copyright Clause jurisprudence might suggest, cf. *ante*, at 780–781, and n. 10. There is no need in this case to characterize that review as a search for " 'congruence and proportionality,' " *ante*, at 788, or as some other variation of what this Court has called "intermediate scrutiny," *e.g., San Francisco Arts & Athletics, Inc. v. United States Olympic Comm.*, 483 U.S. 522, 536–537, 107 S.Ct. 2971, 97 L.Ed.2d 427 (1987) (applying intermediate scrutiny to a variant of normal trademark protection). Cf. *Nixon v. Shrink Missouri Government PAC*, 528 U.S. 377, 402–403, 120 S.Ct. 897, 145 L.Ed.2d 886 (2000) (BREYER, J., concurring) (test of proportionality between burdens and benefits "where a law significantly implicates competing constitutionally protected interests"). Rather, it is necessary only to recognize that this statute involves not pure economic regulation, but regulation of expression, and what may count as rational where economic regulation is at issue is not necessarily rational where we focus on expression—in a Nation constitutionally dedicated to the free dissemination of speech, information, learning, and culture. In this sense only, and where line-drawing among constitutional interests is at issue, I would look harder than does the majority at the statute's rationality—though less hard than precedent might justify, see, *e.g., Cleburne v. Cleburne Living Center, Inc.*, 473 U.S. 432, 446–450, 105 S.Ct. 3249, 87 L.Ed.2d 313 (1985); *Plyler v. Doe*, 457 U.S. 202, 223–224, 102 S.Ct. 2382, 72 L.Ed.2d 786 (1982); *Department of Agriculture v. Moreno*, 413 U.S. 528, 534–538, 93 S.Ct. 2821, 37 L.Ed.2d 782 (1973).

Thus, I would find that the statute lacks the constitutionally necessary rational support (1) if the significant benefits that it bestows are private, not public; (2) if it threatens seriously to undermine the expressive values that the Copyright Clause embodies; and (3) if it cannot find justification in any significant Clause-related objective. Where, after examination of the statute, it becomes difficult, if not impossible, even to dispute these characterizations, Congress' "choice is clearly wrong." *Helvering v. Davis*, 301 U.S. 619, 640, 57 S.Ct. 904, 81 L.Ed. 1307 (1937).

II

A

Because we must examine the relevant statutory effects in light of the Copyright Clause's own purposes, we should begin by reviewing the basic objectives of that Clause. The Clause authorizes a "tax on readers for the purpose of giving a bounty to writers." 56 Parl. Deb. (3d Ser.) (1841) 341, 350 (Lord Macaulay). Why? What constitutional purposes does the "bounty" serve?

The Constitution itself describes the basic Clause objective as one of "promot [ing] the Progress of Science," *i.e.,* knowledge and learning. The Clause exists not to "provide a special private benefit," *Sony, supra,* at 429, 104 S.Ct. 774, but "to stimulate artistic creativity for the general public good," *Twentieth Century Music Corp. v. Aiken,* 422 U.S. 151, 156, 95 S.Ct. 2040, 45 L.Ed.2d 84 (1975). It does so by "motivat[ing] the creative activity of authors" through "the provision of a special reward." *Sony, supra,* at 429, 104 S.Ct. 774. The "reward" is a means, not an end. And that is why the copyright term is limited. It is limited so that its beneficiaries—the public—"will not be permanently deprived of the fruits of an artist's labors." *Stewart v. Abend,* 495 U.S. 207, 228, 110 S.Ct. 1750, 109 L.Ed.2d 184 (1990).

That is how the Court previously has described the Clause's objectives. See also *Mazer v. Stein,* 347 U.S. 201, 219, 74 S.Ct. 460, 98 L.Ed. 630 (1954) ("[C]opyright law ... makes reward to the owner a secondary consideration" (internal quotation marks omitted)); *Sony,* 464 U.S., at 429, 104 S.Ct. 774 ("[L]imited grant" is "intended ... to allow the public access to the products of [authors'] genius after the limited period of exclusive control has expired"); *Harper & Row, supra,* at 545, 105 S.Ct. 2218 (Copyright is "intended to increase and not to impede the harvest of knowledge"). But cf. *ante,* at 785, n. 18. And, in doing so, the Court simply has reiterated the views of the Founders.

Madison, like Jefferson and others in the founding generation, warned against the dangers of monopolies. See, *e.g.,* Monopolies. Perpetuities. Corporations. Ecclesiastical Endowments. in J. Madison, Writings 756 (J. Rakove ed.1999) (hereinafter Madison on Monopolies); Letter from Thomas Jefferson to James Madison (July 31, 1788), in 13 Papers of Thomas Jefferson 443 (J. Boyd ed.1956) (hereinafter Papers of Thomas Jefferson) (arguing against even copyright monopolies); 2 Annals of Cong. 1917 (1791) (statement of Rep. Jackson in the First Congress, Feb. 1791) ("What was it drove our forefathers to this country? Was it not the ecclesiastical corporations and perpetual monopolies of England and Scotland?"). Madison noted that the Constitution had "limited them to two cases, the authors of Books, and of useful inventions." Madison on Monopolies 756. He thought that in those two cases monopoly is justified because it amounts to "compensation for" an actual community "benefit" and because the monopoly is "temporary"—the term originally being 14 years (once renewable). *Ibid.* Madison concluded that "under that limitation a sufficient recompense and encouragement may be given." *Ibid.* But he warned in general that monopolies must be "guarded with strictness against abuse." *Ibid.*

Many Members of the Legislative Branch have expressed themselves similarly. Those who wrote the House Report on the landmark Copyright Act of 1909, for example, said that copyright was not designed "primarily" to "benefit" the "author" or "any particular class of citizens, however worthy." H.R.Rep. No. 2222, 60th Cong., 2d Sess., 6–7 (1909). Rather, under the Constitution, copyright was designed "primarily for the benefit of the public," for "the benefit of the great body of people, in that it will stimulate writing and invention." *Id.,* at 7. And were a copyright statute not "believed, in fact, to accomplish" the basic constitutional objective of advancing learning, that statute "would be beyond the power of Congress" to enact. *Id.*, at 6–7. Similarly, those who wrote the House Report on legislation that implemented the Berne Convention for the Protection of Literary and Artistic Works said that "[t]he constitutional purpose of copyright is to facilitate the flow of ideas in the interest of learning." H.R.Rep. No. 100–609, p. 22 (1988), U.S.Code Cong. & Admin.News 1988, pp. 3706, 3727 (internal quotation marks omitted). They added:

> "Under the U.S. Constitution, the primary objective of copyright law is not to reward the author, but rather to secure for the public the benefits derived from the authors' labors. By giving authors an incentive to create, the public benefits in two ways: when the original expression is created and ... when the limited term ... expires and the creation is added to the public domain." *Id.*, at 17.

For present purposes, then, we should take the following as well established: that copyright statutes must serve public, not private, ends; that they must seek "to promote the Progress" of knowledge and learning; and that they must do so both by creating incentives for authors to produce and by removing the related restrictions on dissemination after expiration of a copyright's "limited Tim[e]"—a time that (like "a *limited* monarch") is "restrain[ed]" and "circumscribe[d]," "not [left] at large," 2 S. Johnson, A Dictionary of the English Language 1151 (4th rev. ed. 1773). I would examine the statute's effects in light of these well-established constitutional purposes.

B

This statute, like virtually every copyright statute, imposes upon the public certain expression-related costs in the form of (1) royalties that may be higher than necessary to evoke creation of the relevant work, and (2) a requirement that one seeking to reproduce a copyrighted work must obtain the copyright holder's permission. The first of these costs translates into higher prices that will potentially restrict a work's dissemination. The second means search costs that themselves may prevent reproduction even where the author has no objection. Although these costs are, in a sense, inevitable concomitants of copyright protection, there are special reasons for thinking them especially serious here.

First, the present statute primarily benefits the holders of existing copyrights, *i.e.*, copyrights on works already created. And a Congressional Research Service (CRS) study prepared for Congress indicates that the added royalty-related sum that the law will transfer to existing copyright holders is large. E. Rappaport, CRS Report for Congress, Copyright Term Extension: Estimating the Economic Values (1998) (hereinafter CRS Report). In conjunction with official figures on copyright renewals, the CRS Report indicates that only about 2% of copyrights between 55 and 75 years old retain commercial value—*i.e.*, still generate royalties after that time. Brief for Petitioners 7 (estimate, uncontested by respondent, based on data from the CRS, Census Bureau, and Library of Congress). But books, songs, and movies of that vintage still earn about $400 million per year in royalties. CRS Report 8, 12, 15. Hence, (despite declining consumer interest in any given work over time) one might conservatively estimate that 20 extra years of copyright protection will mean the transfer of several billion extra royalty dollars to holders of existing copyrights—copyrights that, together, already will have earned many billions of dollars in royalty "reward." See *id.*, at 16.

The extra royalty payments will not come from thin air. Rather, they ultimately come from those who wish to read or see or hear those classic books or films or recordings that have survived. Even the $500,000 that United Airlines has had to pay for the right to play George Gershwin's 1924 classic Rhapsody in Blue represents a cost of doing business, potentially reflected in the ticket prices of those who fly. See Ganzel, Copyright or Copywrong? 39 Training 36, 42 (Dec. 2002). Further, the likely amounts of extra royalty payments are large enough to suggest that unnecessarily high prices will unnecessarily restrict distribution of classic works (or lead to disobedience of the law)—not just in theory but in practice. Cf. CRS Report 3 ("[N]ew, cheaper editions can be expected when works come out of copyright"); Brief for College Art Association et al. as *Amici Curiae* 24 (One year after expiration of copyright on Willa Cather's My Antonia, seven new editions appeared at prices ranging from $2 to $24); Ganzel, *supra*, at 40–41, 44 (describing later abandoned plans to charge individual Girl Scout camps $257 to $1,439 annually for a license to sing songs such as God Bless America around a campfire).

A second, equally important, cause for concern arises out of the fact that copyright extension imposes a "permissions" requirement—not only upon potential users of "classic" works that still retain commercial value, but also upon potential users of *any other work* still in copyright. Again using CRS estimates, one can estimate that, by 2018, the number of such works 75 years of age or older will be about 350,000. See Brief for Petitioners 7. Because the Copyright Act of 1976 abolished the requirement that an owner must renew a copyright, such still-in-copyright works (of little or no commercial value) will eventually number in the millions. See Pub.L. 94–553, §§ 302–304, 90 Stat. 2572–2576; U.S. Dept. of Commerce, Bureau of Census, Statistical History of the United States: From Colonial Times to the Present 956 (1976) (hereinafter Statistical History).

The potential users of such works include not only movie buffs and aging jazz fans, but also historians, scholars, teachers, writers, artists, database operators, and researchers of all kinds—those who want to make the past accessible for their own use or for that of others. The permissions requirement can inhibit their ability to accomplish that task. Indeed, in an age where computer-accessible databases promise to facilitate research and learning, the permissions requirement can stand as a significant obstacle to realization of that technological hope.

The reason is that the permissions requirement can inhibit or prevent the use of old works (particularly those without commercial value): (1) because it may prove expensive to track down or to contract with the copyright holder, (2) because the holder may prove impossible to find, or (3) because the holder when found may deny permission either outright or through misinformed efforts to bargain. The CRS, for example, has found that the cost of seeking permission "can be prohibitive." CRS Report 4. And *amici,* along with petitioners, provide examples of the kinds of significant harm at issue.

Thus, the American Association of Law Libraries points out that the clearance process associated with creating an electronic archive, documenting the American South, "consumed approximately a dozen man-hours" *per work.* Brief for American Association of Law Libraries et al. as *Amici Curiae* 20. The College Art Association says that the costs of obtaining permission for use of single images, short excerpts, and other short works can become prohibitively high; it describes the abandonment of efforts to include, *e.g.*, campaign songs, film excerpts, and documents exposing "horrors of the chain gang" in historical works or archives; and it points to examples in which copyright holders in effect have used their control of copyright to try to control the content of historical or cultural works. Brief for College Art Association et al. as *Amici Curiae* 7–13. The National Writers Union provides similar examples. Brief for National Writers Union et al. as *Amici Curiae* 25–27. Petitioners point to music fees that may prevent youth or community orchestras, or church choirs, from performing early 20th-century music. Brief for Petitioners 3–5; see also App. 16–17 (Copyright extension caused abandonment of plans to sell sheet music of Maurice Ravel's Alborada Del Gracioso). *Amici* for petitioners describe how electronic databases tend to avoid adding to their collections works whose copyright holders may prove difficult to contact, see, *e.g.*, Arms, Getting the Picture: Observations from the Library of Congress on Providing Online Access to Pictorial Images, 48 Library Trends 379, 405 (1999) (describing how this tendency applies to the Library of Congress' own digital archives).

As I have said, to some extent costs of this kind accompany any copyright law, regardless of the length of the copyright term. But to extend that term, preventing works from the 1920's and 1930's from falling into the public domain, will dramatically increase the size of the costs just as—perversely—the likely benefits from protection diminish. See *infra,* at 807–808. The older the work, the less likely it retains commercial value, and the harder it will likely prove to find the current copyright holder. The older the work, the more likely it will prove useful to the historian, artist, or teacher. The older the work, the less likely it is that a sense of authors' rights can justify a copyright holder's decision not to permit reproduction, for the more likely it is that the copyright holder making the decision is not the work's creator, but, say, a corporation or a great-grandchild whom the work's creator never knew. Similarly, the costs of obtaining permission, now perhaps ranging in the millions of dollars, will multiply as the number of holders of affected copyrights increases from several hundred thousand to several million. See *supra,* at 804–805. The costs to the users of nonprofit databases, now numbering in the low millions, will multiply as the use of those computer-assisted databases becomes more prevalent. See, *e.g.*, Brief for Internet Archive et al. as *Amici Curiae* 2, 21, and n. 37 (describing nonprofit Project Gutenberg). And the qualitative costs to education, learning, and research will multiply as our children become ever more dependent for the content of their knowledge upon computer-accessible databases—thereby condemning that which is not so accessible, say, the cultural content of early 20th-century history, to a kind of intellectual purgatory from which it will not easily emerge.

The majority finds my description of these permissions-related harms overstated in light of Congress' inclusion of a statutory exemption, which, during the last 20 years of a copyright term, exempts "facsimile or digital" reproduction by a "library or archives" "for purposes of preservation, scholarship, or research," 17 U.S.C. § 108(h). *Ante,* at 789. This exemption, however, applies only where the copy is made for the special listed purposes; it simply permits a library (not any other subsequent users) to make "a copy" for those purposes; it covers only "published" works not "subject to normal commercial exploitation" and not obtainable, apparently not even as a used copy, at a "reasonable price"; and it insists that the library assure itself through "reasonable investigation" that these conditions have been met. § 108(h). What database proprietor can rely on so limited an exemption—particularly when the phrase "reasonable investigation" is so open-ended and particularly if the database has commercial, as well as noncommercial, aspects?

The majority also invokes the "fair use" exception, and it notes that copyright law itself is restricted to protection of a work's expression, not its substantive content. *Ante,* at 788–789. Neither the exception nor the restriction, however, would necessarily help those who wish to obtain from electronic databases material that is not there—say, teachers wishing their students to see albums of Depression Era photographs, to read the recorded words of those who actually lived under slavery, or to contrast, say, Gary Cooper's heroic portrayal of Sergeant York with filmed reality from the battlefield of Verdun. Such harm, and more, see *supra,* at 804–806, will occur despite the 1998 Act's exemptions and despite the other "First Amendment safeguards" in which the majority places its trust, *ante,* at 788–789.

I should add that the Motion Picture Association of America also finds my concerns overstated, at least with respect to films, because the extension will sometimes make it profitable to reissue old films, saving them from extinction. Brief for Motion Picture Association of America, Inc., as *Amicus Curiae* 14–24. Other film preservationists note, however, that only a small minority of the many films, particularly silent films, from the 1920's and 1930's have been preserved. 1 Report of the Librarian of Congress, Film Preservation 1993, pp. 3–4 (Half of all pre–1950 feature films and more than 80% of all such pre–1929 films have already been lost); cf. Brief for Hal Roach Studios et al. as *Amici Curiae* 18 (Out of 1,200 Twenties Era silent films still under copyright, 63 are now available on digital video disc). They seek to preserve the remainder. See, *e.g.,* Brief for Internet Archive et al. as *Amici Curiae* 22 (Nonprofit database digitized 1,001 public-domain films, releasing them online without charge); 1 Film Preservation 1993, *supra,* at 23 (reporting well over 200,000 titles held in public archives). And they tell us that copyright extension will impede preservation by forbidding the reproduction of films within their own or within other public collections. Brief for Hal Roach Studios et al. as *Amici Curiae* 10–21; see also Brief for Internet Archive et al. as *Amici Curiae* 16–29; Brief for American Association of Law Libraries et al. as *Amici Curiae* 26–27.

Because this subsection concerns only costs, not countervailing benefits, I shall simply note here that, with respect to films as with respect to other works, extension does cause substantial harm to efforts to preserve and to disseminate works that were created long ago. And I shall turn to the second half of the equation: Could Congress reasonably have found that the extension's toll-related and permissions-related harms are justified by extension's countervailing preservationist incentives or in other ways?

C

What copyright-related benefits might justify the statute's extension of copyright protection? First, no one could reasonably conclude that copyright's traditional economic rationale applies here. The extension will not act as an economic spur encouraging authors to create new works. See *Mazer,* 347 U.S., at 219, 74 S.Ct. 460 (The "economic philosophy" of the Copyright Clause is to "advance public welfare" by "encourag[ing] individual effort" through "personal gain"); see also *ante,* at 785, n. 18 ("[C]opyright law serves public ends by providing individuals with an incentive to pursue private ones"). No potential author can reasonably believe that he has more than a tiny chance of writing a classic that will survive commercially long enough for the copyright extension to matter. After all, if, after 55 to 75 years, only 2% of all copyrights retain commercial value, the percentage surviving after 75 years or more (a typical pre-extension copyright term)—must be far smaller. See *supra,* at 804; CRS Report 7 (estimating that, even after copyright renewal, about 3.8% of copyrighted books go out of print each year). And any remaining monetary incentive is diminished dramatically by the fact that the relevant royalties will not arrive until 75 years or more into the future, when, not the author, but distant heirs, or shareholders in a successor corporation, will receive them. Using assumptions about the time value of money provided us by a group of economists (including five Nobel prize winners), Brief for George A. Akerlof et al. as *Amici Curiae* 5–7, it seems fair to say that, for example, a 1% likelihood of earning $100 annually for 20 years, starting *75 years into the future,* is worth less than seven cents today. See *id.,* App. 3a; see also CRS Report 5. See generally Appendix, Part A, *infra.*

What potential Shakespeare, Wharton, or Hemingway would be moved by such a sum? What monetarily motivated Melville would not realize that he could do better for his grandchildren by putting a few dollars into an interest-bearing bank account? The Court itself finds no evidence to the contrary. It refers to testimony before Congress (1) that the copyright system's incentives encourage creation, and (2) (referring to Noah Webster) that income earned from one work can help support an artist who " ' continue[s] to create.' " *Ante,* at 782, n. 15. But the first of these amounts to no more than a set of undeniably true propositions about the value of incentives *in general.* And the applicability of the second to *this* Act is mysterious. How will extension help today's Noah Webster create new works 50 years after his death? Or is that hypothetical Webster supposed to support himself with the extension's present discounted value, *i.e.,* a few pennies? Or (to change the metaphor) is the argument that Dumas *fils* would have written more books had Dumas *pére'* s Three Musketeers earned more royalties?

Regardless, even if this cited testimony were meant more specifically to tell Congress that somehow, somewhere, some potential author might be moved by the thought of great-grandchildren receiving copyright royalties a century hence, so might some potential author also be moved by the thought of royalties being paid for two centuries, five centuries, 1,000 years, " 'til the End of Time." And from a rational economic perspective the time difference among these periods *makes no real difference.* The present extension will produce a copyright period of protection that, even under conservative assumptions, is worth more than *99.8%* of protection *in perpetuity* (more than *99.99%* for a songwriter like Irving Berlin and a song like Alexander's Ragtime Band). See Appendix, Part A, *infra.* The lack of a practically meaningful distinction from an author's *ex ante* perspective between (a) the statute's extended terms and (b) an infinite term makes this latest extension difficult to square with the Constitution's insistence on "limited Times." Cf. Tr. of Oral Arg. 34 (Solicitor General's related concession).

I am not certain why the Court considers it relevant in this respect that "[n]othing ... warrants construction of the [1998 Act's] 20–year term extension as a congressional attempt to evade or override the 'limited Times' constraint." *Ante,* at 783. Of course Congress did not intend to act unconstitutionally. But it may have sought to test the Constitution's limits. After all, the statute was named after a Member of Congress, who, the legislative history records, "wanted the term of copyright protection to last forever." 144 Cong. Rec. H9952 (daily ed. Oct. 7, 1998) (statement of Rep. Mary Bono). See also Copyright Term, Film Labeling, and Film Preservation Legislation: Hearings on H.R. 989 et al. before the Subcommittee on Courts and Intellectual Property of the House Judiciary Committee, 104th Cong., 1st Sess., 94 (1995) (hereinafter House Hearings) (statement of Rep. Sonny Bono) (questioning why copyrights should ever expire); *ibid.* (statement of Rep. Berman) ("I guess we could ... just make a permanent moratorium on the expiration of copyrights"); *id.,* at 230 (statement of Rep. Hoke) ("Why 70 years? Why not forever? Why not 150 years?"); cf. *ibid.* (statement of the Register of Copyrights) (In Copyright Office proceedings, "[t]he Songwriters Guild suggested a perpetual term"); *id.,* at 234 (statement of Quincy Jones) ("I'm particularly fascinated with Representative Hoke's statement.... [W]hy not forever?"); *id.,* at 277 (statement of Quincy Jones) ("If we can start with 70, add 20, it would be a good start"). And the statute ended up creating a term so long that (were the vesting of 19th-century real property at issue) it would typically violate the traditional rule against perpetuities. See 10 R. Powell, Real Property §§ 71.02[2]-[3], p. 71–11 (M. Wolf ed.2002) (traditional rule that estate must vest, if at all, within lives in being plus 21 years); cf. *id.,* § 71.03, at 71–15 (modern statutory perpetuity term of 90 years, 5 years shorter than 95–year copyright terms).

In any event, the incentive-related numbers are far too small for Congress to have concluded rationally, even with respect to new works, that the extension's economic-incentive effect could justify the serious expression-related harms earlier described. See Part II–B, *supra.* And, of course, in respect to works already created—the source of many of the harms previously described—*the statute creates no economic incentive at all.* See *ante,* at 792–793 (STEVENS, J., dissenting).

Second, the Court relies heavily for justification upon international uniformity of terms. *Ante,* at 776, 781–782. Although it can be helpful to look to international norms and legal experience in understanding American law, cf. *Printz v. United States,* 521 U.S. 898, 977, 117 S.Ct. 2365, 138 L.Ed.2d 914 (1997) (BREYER, J., dissenting), in this case the justification based upon foreign rules is surprisingly weak. Those who claim that significant copyright-related benefits flow from greater international uniformity of terms point to the fact that the nations of the European Union have adopted a system of copyright terms uniform among themselves. And the extension before this Court implements a term of life plus 70 years that appears to conform with the European standard. But how does "uniformity" help to justify this statute?

Despite appearances, the statute does *not* create a uniform American–European term with respect to the lion's share of the economically significant works that it affects—*all* works made "for hire" and *all* existing works created prior to 1978. See Appendix, Part B, *infra.* With respect to those works the American statute produces an extended term of 95 years while comparable European rights in "for hire" works last for periods that vary from 50 years to 70 years to life plus 70 years. Compare 17 U.S.C. §§ 302(c), 304(a)-(b), with Council Directive 93/98/EEC of 29 October 1993 Harmonizing the Term of Protection of Copyright and Certain Related Rights, Arts. 1–3, 1993 Official J. Eur. Coms. (L290), pp. 11–12 (hereinafter EU Council Directive 93/98). Neither does the statute create uniformity with respect to anonymous or pseudonymous works. Compare 17 U.S.C. §§ 302(c), 304(a)-(b), with EU Council Directive 93/98, Art. 1, p. 11.

The statute does produce uniformity with respect to copyrights in new, post–1977 works attributed to natural persons. Compare 17 U.S.C. § 302(a) with EU Council Directive 93/98, Art. 1(1), p. 11. But these works constitute only a subset (likely a minority) of works that retain commercial value after 75 years. See Appendix, Part B, *infra.* And the fact that uniformity comes so late, if at all, means that bringing American law into conformity with this particular aspect of European law will neither encourage creation nor benefit the long-dead author in any other important way.

What benefit, then, might this partial future uniformity achieve? The majority refers to "greater incentive for American and other authors to create and disseminate their work in the United States," and cites a law review article suggesting a need to " 'avoid competitive disadvantages.' " *Ante,* at 782. The Solicitor General elaborates on this theme, postulating that because uncorrected disuniformity would permit Europe, not the United States, to hold out the prospect of protection lasting for "life plus 70 years" (instead of "life plus 50 years"), a potential author might decide to publish initially in Europe, delaying American publication. Brief for Respondent 38. And the statute, by creating a uniformly longer term, corrects for the disincentive that this disuniformity might otherwise produce.

That disincentive, however, could not possibly bring about serious harm of the sort that the Court, the Solicitor General, or the law review author fears. For one thing, it is unclear just who will be hurt and how, should American publication come second—for the Berne Convention still offers full protection as long as a second publication is delayed by 30 days. See Berne Conv. Arts. 3(4), 5(4). For another, few, if any, potential authors would turn a "where to publish" decision upon this particular difference in the length of the copyright term. As we have seen, the present commercial value of any such difference amounts at most to comparative pennies. See *supra,* at 807–808. And a commercial decision that turned upon such a difference would have had to have rested previously upon a knife edge so fine as to be invisible. A rational legislature could not give major weight to an invisible, likely nonexistent incentive-related effect.

But if there is no incentive-related benefit, what is the benefit of the future uniformity that the statute only partially achieves? Unlike the Copyright Act of 1976, this statute does not constitute part of an American effort to conform to an important international treaty like the Berne Convention. See H.R.Rep. No. 94–1476, pp. 135–136 (1976), U.S.Code Cong. & Admin. News 1976, pp. 5659, 5751–52 (The 1976 Act's life–plus–50 term was "required for adherence to the Berne Convention"); S.Rep. No. 94–473, p. 118 (1975) (same). Nor does European acceptance of the longer term seem to reflect more than special European institutional considerations, *i.e.,* the needs of, and the international politics surrounding, the development of the European Union. House Hearings 230 (statement of the Register of Copyrights); *id.,* at 396–398 (statement of J. Reichman). European and American copyright law have long coexisted despite important differences, including Europe's traditional respect for authors' "moral rights" and the absence in Europe of constitutional restraints that restrict copyrights to "limited Times." See, *e.g.,* Kwall, Copyright and the Moral Right: Is an American Marriage Possible? 38 Vand. L.Rev. 1–3 (1985) (moral rights); House Hearings 187 (testimony of the Register of Copyrights) ("limited [T]imes").

In sum, the partial, future uniformity that the 1998 Act promises cannot reasonably be said to justify extension of the copyright term for new works. And concerns with uniformity cannot possibly justify the extension of the new term to older works, for the statute there creates no uniformity at all.

Third, several publishers and filmmakers argue that the statute provides incentives to *those who act as publishers* to republish and to redistribute older copyrighted works. This claim cannot justify this statute, however, because the rationale is inconsistent with the basic purpose of the Copyright Clause—as understood by the Framers and by this Court. The Clause assumes an initial grant of monopoly, designed primarily to encourage creation, followed by termination of the monopoly grant in order to promote dissemination of already-created works. It assumes that it is the *disappearance* of the monopoly grant, not its *perpetuation,* that will, on balance, promote the dissemination of works already in existence. This view of the Clause does not deny the empirical possibility that grant of a copyright monopoly to the heirs or successors of a long-dead author could *on occasion* help publishers resurrect the work, say, of a long-lost Shakespeare. But it does deny Congress the Copyright Clause power to base its actions primarily upon that empirical possibility—lest copyright grants become perpetual, lest on balance they restrict dissemination, lest too often they seek to bestow benefits that are solely retroactive.

This view of the Clause finds strong support in the writings of Madison, in the antimonopoly environment in which the Framers wrote the Clause, and in the history of the Clause's English antecedent, the Statute of Anne—a statute which sought to break up a publishers' monopoly by offering, as an alternative, an author's monopoly of limited duration. See Patterson, Understanding the Copyright Clause, 47 J. Copyright Soc. 365, 379 (2000) (Statute of Anne); L. Patterson, Copyright in Historical Perspective 144–147 (1968) same); Madison on Monopolies 756–757; Papers of Thomas Jefferson 442–443; The Constitutional Convention and the Formation of the Union 334, 338 (W. Solberg 2d ed.1990); see also *supra,* at 803.

This view finds virtually conclusive support in the Court's own precedents. See *Sony,* 464 U.S., at 429, 104 S.Ct. 774 (The Copyright Clause is "intended ... to allow the public access ... after the limited period of exclusive control"); *Stewart,* 495 U.S., at 228, 110 S.Ct. 1750 (The copyright term is limited to avoid "permanently depriv[ing]" the public of "the fruits of an artist's labors"); see also *supra,* at 802–803.

This view also finds textual support in the Copyright Clause's word "limited." Cf. J. Story, Commentaries on the Constitution § 558, p. 402 (R. Rotunda & J. Nowak eds. 1987) (The Copyright Clause benefits the public in part because it "admit[s] the people at large, after a *short* interval, to the full possession and enjoyment of all writings ... without restraint" (emphasis added)). It finds added textual support in the word "Authors," which is difficult to reconcile with a rationale that rests entirely upon incentives given to publishers perhaps long after the death of the work's creator. Cf. *Feist Publications, Inc. v. Rural Telephone Service Co.,* 499 U.S. 340, 346–347, 111 S.Ct. 1282, 113 L.Ed.2d 358 (1991).

It finds empirical support in sources that underscore the wisdom of the Framers' judgment. See CRS Report 3 ("[N]ew, cheaper editions can be expected when works come out of copyright"); see also Part II–B, *supra.* And it draws logical support from the endlessly self-perpetuating nature of the publishers' claim and the difficulty of finding any kind of logical stopping place were this Court to accept such a uniquely publisher-related rationale. (Would it justify continuing to extend copyrights indefinitely, say, for those granted to F. Scott Fitzgerald or his lesser known contemporaries? Would it not, in principle, justify continued protection of the works of Shakespeare, Melville, Mozart, or perhaps Salieri, Mozart's currently less popular contemporary? Could it justify yet further extension of the copyright on the song Happy Birthday to You (melody first published in 1893, song copyrighted after litigation in 1935), *still in effect* and currently owned by a subsidiary of AOL Time Warner? See Profitable "Happy Birthday," Times of London, Aug. 5, 2000, p. 6.)

Given this support, it is difficult to accept the conflicting rationale that the publishers advance, namely, that extension, rather than limitation, of the grant will, by rewarding publishers with a form of monopoly, promote, rather than retard, the dissemination of works already in existence. Indeed, given these considerations, this rationale seems constitutionally perverse—unable, constitutionally speaking, to justify the blanket extension here at issue. Cf. *ante,* at 799–800 (STEVENS, J., dissenting).

Fourth, the statute's legislative history suggests another possible justification. That history refers frequently to the financial assistance the statute will bring the entertainment industry, particularly through the promotion of exports. See, *e.g.,* S.Rep. No. 104–315, p. 3 (1996) ("The purpose of the bill is to ensure adequate copyright protection for American works in foreign nations and the continued economic benefits of a healthy surplus balance of trade"); 144 Cong. Rec., at H9951 (statement of Rep. Foley) (noting "the importance of this issue to America's creative community," "[w]hether it is Sony, BMI, Disney," or other companies). I recognize that Congress has sometimes found that suppression of competition will help Americans sell abroad—though it has simultaneously taken care to protect American buyers from higher domestic prices. See, *e.g.,* Webb–Pomerene Act (Export Trade), 40 Stat. 516, as amended, 15 U.S.C. §§ 61–65; see also IA P. Areeda & H. Hovenkamp, Antitrust Law ¶ 251a, pp. 134–137 (2d ed.2000) (criticizing export cartels). In doing so, however, Congress has exercised its commerce, not its copyright, power. I can find nothing in the Copyright Clause that would authorize Congress to enhance the copyright grant's monopoly power, likely leading to higher prices both at home and abroad, *solely* in order to produce higher foreign earnings. That objective is not a *copyright* objective. Nor, standing alone, is it related to any other objective more closely tied to the Clause itself. Neither can higher corporate profits alone justify the grant's enhancement. The Clause seeks public, not private, benefits.

Finally, the Court mentions as possible justifications "demographic, economic, and technological changes"—by which the Court apparently means the facts that today people communicate with the help of modern technology, live longer, and have children at a later age. *Ante,* at 782, and n. 14. The first fact seems to argue not for, but instead against, extension. See Part II–B, *supra.* The second fact seems already corrected for by the 1976 Act's life–plus–50 term, which automatically grows with lifespans. Cf. Department of Health and Human Services, Centers for Disease Control and Prevention, Deaths: Final Data for 2000 (2002) (Table 8) (reporting a 4–year increase in expected lifespan between 1976 and 1998). And the third fact—that adults are having children later in life—is a makeweight at best, providing no explanation of why the 1976 Act's term of 50 years after an author's death—a longer term than was available to authors themselves for most of our Nation's history—is an insufficient potential bequest. The weakness of these final rationales simply underscores the conclusion that emerges from consideration of earlier attempts at justification: There is no legitimate, serious copyright-related justification for this statute.

III

The Court is concerned that our holding in this case not inhibit the broad decision making leeway that the Copyright Clause grants Congress. *Ante,* at 780–781, 783, 790. It is concerned about the implications of today's decision for the Copyright Act of 1976—an Act that changed copyright's basic term from 56 years (assuming renewal) to life of the author plus 50 years, *ante,* at 775–776. *Ante,* at 790. It is concerned about having to determine just how many years of copyright is too many—a determination that it fears would require it to find the "right" constitutional number, a task for which the Court is not well suited. See *ibid.;* but cf. *ante,* at 784, n. 17.

I share the Court's initial concern, about intrusion upon the decision making authority of Congress. See *ante,* at 781, n. 10. But I do not believe it intrudes upon that authority to find the statute unconstitutional on the basis of (1) a legal analysis of the Copyright Clause's objectives, see *supra,* at 802–804, 810–811; (2) the total implausibility of any incentive effect, see *supra,* at 807–809; and (3) the statute's apparent failure to provide significant international uniformity, see *supra,* at 808–810. Nor does it intrude upon congressional authority to consider rationality in light of the expressive values underlying the Copyright Clause, related as it is to the First Amendment, and given the constitutional importance of correctly drawing the relevant Clause/Amendment boundary. *Supra,* at 801–802. We cannot avoid the need to examine the statute carefully by saying that "Congress has not altered the traditional contours of copyright protection," *ante,* at 790, for the sentence points to the question, rather than the answer. Nor should we avoid that examination here. That degree of judicial vigilance—at the far outer boundaries of the Clause—is warranted if we are to avoid the monopolies and consequent restrictions of expression that the Clause, read consistently with the First Amendment, seeks to preclude. And that vigilance is all the more necessary in a new century that will see intellectual property rights and the forms of expression that underlie them play an ever more important role in the Nation's economy and the lives of its citizens.

I do not share the Court's concern that my view of the 1998 Act could automatically doom the 1976 Act. Unlike the present statute, the 1976 Act thoroughly revised copyright law and enabled the United States to join the Berne Convention, an international treaty that requires the 1976 Act's basic life–plus–50 term as a condition for substantive protections from a copyright's very inception, Berne Conv. Art. 7(1). Consequently, the balance of copyright-related harms and benefits there is far less one sided. The same is true of the 1909 and 1831 Acts, which, in any event, provided for maximum terms of 56 years or 42 years while requiring renewal after 28 years, with most copyrighted works falling into the public domain after that 28–year period, well before the putative maximum terms had elapsed. See *ante,* at 775–776; Statistical History 956–957. Regardless, the law provides means to protect those who have reasonably relied upon prior copyright statutes. See *Heckler v. Mathews,* 465 U.S. 728, 746, 104 S.Ct. 1387, 79 L.Ed.2d 646 (1984). And, in any event, we are not here considering, and we need not consider, the constitutionality of other copyright statutes.

Neither do I share the Court's aversion to line-drawing in this case. Even if it is difficult to draw a single clear bright line, the Court could easily decide (as I would decide) that this particular statute simply goes too far. And such examples—of what goes too far—sometimes offer better constitutional guidance than more absolute-sounding rules. In any event, "this Court sits" in part to decide when a statute exceeds a constitutional boundary. See *Panhandle Oil,* 277 U.S., at

223, 48 S.Ct. 451 (Holmes, J., dissenting). In my view, "[t]ext, history, and precedent," *ante,* at 778, support both the need to draw lines in general and the need to draw the line here short of this statute. See *supra,* at 801–804, 810–811. But see *ante,* at 778, n. 4.

Finally, the Court complains that I have not "restrained" my argument or "train[ed my] fire, as petitioners do, on Congress' choice to place existing and future copyrights in parity." *Ante,* at 775, n. 1, and 778, n. 4. The reason that I have not so limited my argument is my willingness to accept, for purposes of this opinion, the Court's understanding that, for reasons of "[j]ustice, policy, and equity"—as well as established historical practice—it is not "categorically beyond Congress' authority" to "exten[d] the duration of existing copyrights" to achieve such parity. *Ante,* at 781 (internal quotation marks omitted). I have accepted this view, however, only for argument's sake—putting to the side, for the present, Justice STEVENS' persuasive arguments to the contrary, *ante,* at 792–801 (dissenting opinion). And I make this assumption only to emphasize the lack of rational justification for the present statute. A desire for "parity" between *A* (old copyrights) and *B* (new copyrights) cannot justify extending *A* when there is no rational justification for extending *B.* At the very least (if I put aside my rationality characterization), to ask *B* to support *A* here is like asking Tom Thumb to support Paul Bunyan's ox. Where the case for extending new copyrights is itself so weak, what "justice," what "policy," what "equity" can warrant the tolls and barriers that extension of existing copyrights imposes?

IV

This statute will cause serious expression-related harm. It will likely restrict traditional dissemination of copyrighted works. It will likely inhibit new forms of dissemination through the use of new technology. It threatens to interfere with efforts to preserve our Nation's historical and cultural heritage and efforts to use that heritage, say, to educate our Nation's children. It is easy to understand how the statute might benefit the private financial interests of corporations or heirs who own existing copyrights. But I cannot find any constitutionally legitimate, copyright-related way in which the statute will benefit the public. Indeed, in respect to existing works, the serious public harm and the virtually nonexistent public benefit could not be more clear.

I have set forth the analysis upon which I rest these judgments. This analysis leads inexorably to the conclusion that the statute cannot be understood rationally to advance a constitutionally legitimate interest. The statute falls outside the scope of legislative power that the Copyright Clause, read in light of the First Amendment, grants to Congress. I would hold the statute unconstitutional.

I respectfully dissent.

The Public Domain Line is Moving Again – One Year Later

Internet Archive Blog Posted on December 13, 2019 by Lila Bailey
Guest post by Professor Elizabeth Townsend Gard

When I was about 20, I fell in love with the love of Vera and Roland, British youth that loved to chat and write about books, Oxford, and love. Roland would go to war. Vera would go to Oxford. They would meet a few times, kiss a few times, and get secretly engaged. He had leave at Christmas 1915. She waited by the phone. His sister called instead. Roland had been killed a few days earlier. Vera was never the same. She became a nurse, and she would write about Roland, her brother, and their two friends, along with her own experiences for the rest of her life. For a long time, she was the only woman recognized as writing about the Great War. I sought to find other women's stories and compare them to the stories of men. And I did. But I also ran into copyright issues that drove me to law school, to study duration of copyright, and to wait. The wait took over 20 years, but the opening of the U.S. public domain will now be in its second year. Books from 1923 came into the public domain last year, and books from 1924 come into the public domain as of 2020.

Scholars, and especially biographers, have choices: get permission from the families of copyrighted works, rely on fair use, or use public domain works. When I started my dissertation, most of the works I was using as a World War I scholar, looking at the war generation writing throughout the 20th century about their experiences (although I didn't know it), were in the public domain. But before I filed my dissertation, the world had changed. In 1996, foreign works that had previously been in the public domain were suddenly restored by the Uruguay Round Agreements Act, including most of Vera Brittain's works. In 1998, the Copyright Term Extension Act was passed, freezing the public domain for 20 years. I would finish my Ph.D. and be hooded in the Spring of 1998

When I started my work, many of the books from the 1920s had come into the public domain because they didn't have proper copyright notice, or they weren't renewed in their 27th year. But as of 1996, that was no longer true with the foreign works that were still under copyright in their home country. This included Vera who had all of her works restored, even the ones no one really cared or knew about. Most who were writing about the war had survived through 1918, and many of the great artists and authors lived until the 1970s. All of their works were restored automatically. For a European historian, the world was quite bleak. All of our source materials for the most part were restored and therefore not easily included in scholarly articles and dissertations.

Now, as of 2019, the world is moving again. Works from 1923 were released into the public domain last year. That included Vera Brittain's *The Dark Tide* (1923), published in England. And now, her second novel, *Not Without Honour* (1924) comes into the public domain in 2020. The war generation books, generally published 1925-1932 will soon be flooding our public domain. And this matters tremendously.

While Internet Archive has many books that are available through their lending system—books that we have access to and read, and while Section 108(h) allows libraries to copy and disseminate non-commercially available books in the last twenty years of their term, this does not allow scholars the freedom to use the books without fear of threats, or use of more than a judge might think acceptable under fair use. This is particularly problematic for biographers, who tend to rely on some sources in ways that families may threaten with a lawsuit (think the Schloss case with the Joyce estate) or publishers that may feel uncomfortable relying on fair use.

In the last twenty years, fair use has developed into a robust tool. Maybe that was partly because the published public domain was frozen? And we've taken strides in *Best Practices* and other means to make fair use vibrant and usable. Much of the work that I was doing would clearly be covered under fair use today. The world is very different from when I was writing about Vera Brittain and her ghosts in the 1990s. I would probably not have gone to law school. But it is still important that works come into the public domain, and that's the story we are here to tell.

And so, on the second anniversary of the opening of the public domain again, I am re-reading *The Dark Tide* and *Not Without Honour*, and looking forward to the books that should shortly come into the public domain in the future. I'm also very excited to sift through the Internet Archive collection for hidden gems – books written in 1923, 1924, and even anticipating the new additions in 2021 from 1925. Oh, the possibilities!

Here's some of the works I'm particularly excited about, that are part of the war generation, Vera's generation that I studied so long ago:

- Agatha Christie's *The Man in the Brown Suit* (1924) and *Poriot Investigates* (1924) (she learned about poisons while working as a nurse in the war, and her husband, Archie Christie flew planes);
- Winifred Holtby (Vera's best friend), *The Crowded Street* (1924),
- A.A. Milne, *When We Were Very Young* (1924) and we get the first appearance of Pooh in the poem "Teddy Bear" (1924) (Milne was also in the Great War), and
- The first novel of Ford Maddox Ford's Parade's End series, titled *Some Do Not*, to name a few.

And it's not just novels and poetry, its art. Käthe Kollwitz's *War series, 1923* also came into the public domain last year.

A Chasm: US versus the rest of the world

Because of our nutty U.S. system – for works first published before 1978, the term is 95 years from publication, many foreign works will be in the public domain for many years in the United States before they are out of copyright in their home country. Take, David Jones' "The Garden Enclosed" (1924).

Currently the photograph of David Jones' painting found on the Tate website has the following copyright information: © the estate of David Jones/Bridgeman Images. You have to license the use. But as of January 1, 2020, the work is in the public domain in the U.S., and so you do not have to get permission to use the painting or an image of the painting. It will remain under copyright in Great Britain through 2044.

But the joy of the public domain in the U.S. is more than the great works; it is also the ephemera – the photographs in newspapers, postcards, films and so much more that have been locked up because they were *restored* as foreign works. All of these works are now coming into the public domain, and it is glorious. As of January 1, 2020, any work published anywhere in the world before 1925 is in the public domain in the United States.

One of the best features of the Internet Archive is that you can add a filter to any search of the publication year. So, as you search, check "1924". It doesn't matter whether the works were published here or in the US, whether they were renewed or had proper notice. They are now in the public domain in the U.S. for all to enjoy unfettered and without restriction.

Year

Year	Count	Year	Count	Year	Count	Year	Count
2016	1	1991	295	1966	36	1941	73
2015	38	1990	273	1965	33	1940	52
2014	75	1989	260	1964	32	1939	60
2013	116	1988	234	1963	44	1938	52
2012	204	1987	261	1962	30	1937	38
2011	246	1986	245	1961	25	1936	57
2010	287	1985	253	1960	15	1935	61
2009	293	1984	227	1959	13	1934	41
2008	303	1983	249	1958	24	1933	115
2007	358	1982	237	1957	9	1932	46
2006	383	1981	193	1956	17	1931	45
2005	447	1980	177	1955	20	1930	52
2004	458	1979	191	1954	15	1929	54
2003	490	1978	182	1953	16	1928	52
2002	451	1977	155	1952	13	1927	34
2001	497	1976	171	1951	10	1926	3
2000	519	1975	126	1950	17	1925	2
1999	481	1974	121	1949	8	1924	5
1998	416	1973	112	1948	11	1923	7
1997	476	1972	163	1947	3	1922	16
1996	487	1971	91	1946	18	1921	19
1995	491	1970	104	1945	49	1920	20
1994	403	1969	67	1944	48	1919	16
1993	390	1968	65	1943	51	1918	18
1992	309	1967	43	1942	49	1917	34

1 2 3

Apply your filters

So, I encourage you to go play on the Internet Archive site and around the world in search of new public domain treasures. Just remember, these works are in the public domain in the U.S. They may be (and likely are) still under copyright in other places around the world.

Elizabeth Townsend Gard holds a Ph.D in European History from UCLA, and is a Professor of Law at Tulane University, where she focuses on the intersection of law and culture, and in particular the role of law in creativity in copyright and trademark. Her work includes the invention of the Durationator, and the host of the popular research podcast, Just Wanna Quilt, exploring the art, craft and copyright of an industry. She is currently a Lepage Entrepreneur Faculty Fellow at the A.B. Freeman School of Business, and the Greenbaum Fellow at the Newcomb Institute, both at Tulane University. For more information on the Durationator and determining copyright can be found at www.durationator.com.

A Word About Copyright Term and Time

Before we end this introduction and move on to more substantive topics, let's chat about the concept of the term of copyright. Duration is often seen as a static, impenetrable part of copyright law, where terms are too long, locking up culture for decades upon decades. The problem, of course, is that copyright terms are often dictated by treaties that have been in place for over a hundred years. Shortening the term is not an easy option, and yet long terms cause many of our orphan work problems - works still under copyright whose author cannot be found because *inter alia* the term is so long. Duration, in fact, is in part why copyright law has become such a mess, and why groups and organizations all over the country are calling and/or discussing copyright reform. Ironically, duration itself is never really part of discussion regarding solutions. This is the traditional story. Duration is impossible. We must reform. We must work around the copyright term itself. Why bother with duration?

Copyright term is more than when will it end. Term triggers the beginning of copyright -- a new work is created and copyright is granted. Time and term are part of that beginning. And throughout the life of the copyright we have relationships with all kinds of parts of the law -- fair use, idea/expression, first sale, and library uses that often have a component of time or timeliness as part of their construction. In many ways, we create works with the property boundary in part as time.

So, as we think of copyright and its temporal nature, we should also be looking for mitigating mechanisms that 1) allow others to use the work during its copyrighted term, 2) identify components that are not protectable by copyright; and 3) lessen the power of the copyright itself. Let's look quickly at an example of lessening the power of copyright in a given work.

Section 412 is an example of a mechanism that potentially *lessens* the impact of automatic protection, and in that way, lessens the impact of the property right. Section 412 requires copyright registration with the U.S. Copyright Office in order to receive statutory damages or attorney's fees. Without either of these mechanisms, damages from an infringement suit are reduced to actual damages only. The risk of infringement is dramatically reduced. Section 412 states:

> In any action under this title, other than an action brought for a violation of the rights of the author under § 106A(a), an action for infringement of the copyright of a work that has been preregistered under § 408(f) before the commencement

> of the infringement and that has an effective date of registration not later than the earlier of 3 months after the first publication of the work or 1 month after the copyright owner has learned of the infringement, or an action instituted under § 411(c), no award of statutory damages or of attorney's fees, as provided by §§ 504 and 505, shall be made for
>
> > **(1)** any infringement of copyright in an unpublished work commenced before the effective date of its registration; or
> >
> > (2) any infringement of copyright commenced after first publication of the work and before the effective date of its registration, unless such registration is made within three months after the first publication of the work.

While registration is not required as part of gaining protection or even (for foreign works) bringing an action into court, or receiving actual damages, *registration* is required for attorneys' fees and statutory damages. For copyright, this is very important. Actual damages are likely to be fairly minimal in most instances. Statutory damages are where the money is to be made, so to speak. It was statutory damages that brought huge awards for the Recording Industry Association of America (RIAA).

The standard monetary remedy for infringement is actual damages and profits. During an infringement suit, one can elect statutory damages, which range from $750 to $30,000 per infringement, with willful infringement topping at $150,000 per infringement -- the big prize. But those potential damages, even willful infringement, are only applied *if the work is registered* with the U.S. Copyright Office. Most works are not registered. Think of all of the materials not registered - everyday items, photographs, archival materials. Much of these works are now housed, curated or owned by libraries and museums, who would not have it in their best interest to register the works, or moreover the capital to do such a thing. So, the scholars working in an archive fearful of using an unknown photograph *still under copyright* but clearly not registered should be a little more daring.

An example from the Newcomb College Archive at Tulane University comes to mind. There is a set of photographs donated to the library that were taken, judging from the dress and style of the photos, from the mid-1980s. The photographer is not identified. These works may or may not be under copyright, depending on a couple of situations. But moreover, if the photographs are still under copyright, they are not registered. What is the risk of using the photographs? Fairly low.

The power of § 412 is significant.
It was a balancing mechanism within the 1976 Copyright Act that allowed for infringing activity to occur. Without statutory damages, attorney's fees and willful damages, a copyright case would have a hard time getting traction, as actual damages and profits are very difficult to prove. Section 412 can be seen as defining the interest and scope of rights in copyright law. Works not registered signal a different level of commitment. We should be more aware of, and use, this information, rather than shying away from the cues and clues given. Most archival works are not registered. Many other kinds of works are not registered. This mitigates the effect of duration, particularly when paired with statute of limitations.

Section 412 is not the only mechanism we have for lessening the impact of copyright's long terms. We will encounter others as well.

So, let's be on the lookout for understanding not only whether a work is protected by copyright, but in what circumstances is it's term mitigated? That's really what this book is about.

The original Durationator girl…created by then law student, Ben Varadi using public domain images.

Worksheet: Can I Use This Work?

In determining whether you can use a work, there are a number of questions that need to be asked. You can start in many different places, and intuitively as you learn copyright, you will learn where to begin.

- ❑ Starting with the user

  For libraries or patrons of libraries, for example, this is a good place to start. Also, if you are a major commercial user, this is a good place too, as you need to proceed cautiously and more carefully.

- ❑ Starting with the use

  For artists and scholars relying on fair use this is a good place to start, but quickly leads to a set of questions.

  - ❑ What are you using? Unprotectable? Protectable?
  - ❑ Is the work under copyright?
  - ❑ How much are you using?
  - ❑ Four-factor fair use test
    - ❑ Commercial or non-commercial use?
    - ❑ Market Replacement?
    - ❑ Transformative?
    - ❑ Nature of the original work?

      Among other questions.

- ❑ Starting with the venue

  Where is the work being displayed or used? On a social media platform? Sold online? This is more of a risk assessment approach.

- ❑ Starting with the work

  For most of the life of the Durationator, we began here. We saw the work as finite, and then we looked to the circumstances in which the question was being asked. This is still a good starting point.

- [ ] Starting with the records

  Can you find a registration record for this work at the U.S. Copyright Office? What does that tell us about the work? Can we find other records by the author/copyright holder (meaning they register only when there is potential infringement)?

2: Copyright Basics

This chapter can be skipped for those that have a background in copyright. The chapter is designed to provide a basic overview of principles in copyright, using the 1976 Copyright Act, the current law that governs copyright in the United States.

1.8.8.

Referred to as the IP clause, I.8.8 allows Congress to pass laws for regulation of patents and copyrights. Let's look at the clause:

> to promote the progress of science and useful arts, by securing for limited times, to authors and inventors, the exclusive right to their respective writings and discoveries

This is a parallel construction:

> Science = refers to copyright (science meant knowledge when this was written)
>
> Useful arts = patents

You start there, and then you see the pairs:

> Science = authors = writings
>
> Useful arts = inventors = discoveries

The clause says that Congress can enact laws for copyright and patents that will last a limited time–not perpetual rights–that will be theirs exclusively (we'll see this, with some limitations) for their creative works and inventions.

Theories of Intellectual Property

Theories are important because they tell us from what perspective someone is approaching the creation and use of intellectual property. There are three basic theories.

#1 Locke's Labor Theory

John Locke wrote *Two Treatises of Government* (1690). In it, he discussed how hypothetically, property goes from owned by the commons to private property. It remains a key text in understanding property rights, including intellectual property. His theory is called "natural rights." Here is the key passage:

> Everyman has a property in his own Person. This no body has any right to but himself. The labour of his body, and the work of his hands, we may say, are properly his. Whatsoever then he removes out of the state that nature hath provided, and left it in, he hath mixed his labour with, and joyned to it something that is his own, and thereby makes it his property. It being by him removed from the common state nature placed it in, it hath by this labour something annexed to it, that excludes the common right of other men.

#2 Personhood Theory

Personhood theory comes from Hegel and Kant, but was applied by a more contemporary scholar, Jane Radin. Sounds intimidating? Not really. The basic premise is that people develop their identity when interacting with property. Our relationship with property matters. Your wedding ring, a favorite toy, the house that has been in your family for 100 years, are all things that may define who you are, and you put a value on these things that are beyond how much they cost or how much someone would value them to replace them. They mean more to you than what money can offer.

#3 Utilitarianism

Our U.S. system is based on a utilitarian model. The government gives you exclusive rights to encourage your creativity and inventiveness. You get trademarks from the government because ownership encourages you to invest and build up businesses. This is based on the work of Jeremy Bentham (1748-1832), who was a philosopher that developed theories related to political economy. If someone is building a business of greeting cards, the law protects the greeting cards themselves, any invention in the printing methods and the logo of the company. This benefits society because the greeting card company is incentivized to make for sale their products for our benefit.

Copyright History

Technology and copyright have always gone together from the beginning. Copyright only became a legal concept after the invention of the printing press, because it was only then that copies could be easily and economically made. There became a need to develop laws to decide who could print a book and when that right expired. So, copyright is about copying. Get it? It's in the name. Copy-right. It's also about limiting who can make copies. The first copyright act was the British: the Statute of Anne (1710), and is what the first U.S. Copyright Act was based upon in 1790.

Technology played another role in copyright, particularly beginning in the 19th century. New works could be created *by* technology. Photographs, films, sound recordings, digital art, and 3D printing are examples of technology that created new forms of art. Copyright had to adjust and protect them. It did. And then, at the end of the 20th century, technology began to create new mechanisms of transmission of creative works. From the photocopier to CD burner to the Internet, reproductive technology moved quickly. And then the user-generated content hit.

Before the age of the Internet, copyright really only mattered to the big players – the publishers, the movie industry, and the recording industry. We consumed products. We made our own versions and shared them with our neighbors, family and local communities. Now, we make products for the world. We post pictures of our versions of quilts. We may watch YouTube videos, but we also may make one. We will self-publish novels. Our computers come with software to create music and movies. We are encouraged every day to create works. The dividing line between industry and consumers has become much murkier.

The Dividing Lines in Copyright

Think of copyright as distinction between private property (the copyright) and common property (the public domain). There are also times when others can *use* private property that is not their own. We'll be discussing that with library exceptions and fair uses, along with non-protectable elements. Here are some dividing lines:

- ❑ Idea/Expression Dichotomy: Ideas are not protected; only the expression of those ideas.
- ❑ Functional objects, systems, algorithms, and other scientific things are not protectable. Section 102(b) of the U.S. Copyright Act outlines what is not protected by copyright: "In no case does copyright protection for an original work of authorship extend to any idea, procedure, process, system, method of operation, concept, principle, or discovery, regardless of the form in which it is described, explained, illustrated, or embodied in such work."
- ❑ The idea is that Section 102(b) provides boundaries of what does not fall under copyright. We'll look at a couple of these before we dive into what is copyrightable.
- ❑ Merger doctrine: If there is only one way to express something, that cannot be copyrighted.
- ❑ Useful articles doctrine: We must separate the aesthetics (copyrightable) from the usefulness (the article).
- ❑ No novelty or nonobviousness requirement: unlike patents, copyright does not require novelty, and two artists that independently without knowledge of the other can gain copyright protection of the same work.
- ❑ Many elements on their own are not copyrightable, but their selection, arrangement, and coordination might be.

Let's take a more careful look at some of these concepts.

Levels of Abstraction: Idea to Expression

Ideas are not protected. Only the expression of the idea. Your version. Your selection, arrangement, and coordination of that idea. That's an expression. The question is where that boundary between an idea and expression lies. "Nobody has ever been able to fix that boundary, and nobody ever can," wrote Judge Learned Hand.

We turn to an old test by Judge Learned Hand, a famous judge from the first half of the 20th century. This is a famous quote, in which he is analyzing a play. "Upon any work, and especially upon a play, a great number of patterns of increasing generality will fit equally well, as more and more of the incident is left out. The last may perhaps be no more than the most general statement of what the play is about, and at times might consist only of its title; but there is a point in this series of abstractions where they are no longer protected, since otherwise, the playwright could prevent the use of his "ideas," to which, apart from their expression, his property is never extended." 45 F.2d 119 (2d Cir. 1930). As something goes from details to abstraction, we find that what is protectable diminishes.

The case, *Nichols v. Universal Pictures Corp*, 45 F.2d 119 (2d Cir. 1930) concerned the play "Abie's Irish Rose," by Anne Nichols and the potentially infringing film, "The Cohens and the Kellys." In both, a young Jewish man marries an Irish Catholic woman, and both fathers are against the marriage. Both are comedies. The court looks to the similarities as well as elements that were stock characters and other elements that would be available to everyone. General motifs and characters are not protectable. There is no fixed formula to tell if someone has taken more than an idea and has nudged into expression. Idea/expression can be seen as three sub-categories:

- ❑ idea/expression,
- ❑ processes/expression, and
- ❑ fact/expression.

The idea behind all of these is that copyright should not lock up building blocks (ideas, facts) and that patents and trade secrets protect functional elements (e.g. processes).

Doctrine of Functionality and the Useful Articles Doctrine

We will see doctrine of functionality both in copyright and trademark. Neither protects the inventiveness of a work -- the potentially patentable, functional aspects. For artwork (pictorial, graphic and sculptural work), we have an added doctrine: the useful articles doctrine. Copyright does not protect the usefulness of the art, and you must be able to separate the functional from the useful to obtain copyright protection.

Merger Doctrine

When directions or a set of rules can only clearly be explained in one way, the functional aspect of the expression takes over, and no copyright is granted.

Blank Forms Doctrine

Copyright sees blank, basic forms as functional: blank checks, graph paper, time cards, diaries, address books, are just a few examples.

No Novelty or Nonobviousness Requirement

The Copyright Office does not review copyright registration for novelty or nonobviousness. *Feist,* 499 U.S. at 345. "The copyright law protects "those components of a work that are original to the author," but "originality" does not require "novelty." Compendium III, Section 308.1. "The fact that a work may be novel, distinctive, innovative, or even unique is irrelevant to this analysis. *See* H.R. REP. NO. 94-1476, at 51 (1976), *reprinted in* 1976 U.S.C.C.A.N. at 5664 (stating "the standard of originality established by the courts . . . does not include requirements of novelty [or] ingenuity" and that Congress did not intend "to enlarge the standard of copyright protection" to impose these requirements).... Conversely, the fact that a work is new, innovative, or even unique does not necessarily mean that it contains a sufficient amount of creative expression to satisfy the originality requirement." Compendium III, Section 310.1.

Thinking about Copyright

So here is a way to think about copyright:

- ❑ There is a **system of copyright.** It's how we understand the world. The system is federal law (the statute) and federal cases (subject matter jurisdiction). The law is administered by the U.S. Copyright Office, which falls under the jurisdiction of the Librarian of Congress. It is with this office that you can register your copyrights for additional protection, and where studies and suggested legislation occurs. We may also refer to the *Compendium,* which is the Copyright Office's summary of their office practices, and is available online at http://www.copyright.gov/comp3. This is the third version. Patents and trademarks also have their internal office procedural guides, which are helpful as well.
- ❑ There is **enforcement of copyright.** There are varying degrees of enforcement. Enforcement becomes thinking through not only whether someone has infringed, but whether they have a legal reason to do so, how hard it will be to enforce, and how strong your copyright/case actually is. And of course, there is the brand/marketing aspect of enforcing too.

- ❑ **Non-commercial, fair and personal uses.** We have a huge space for non-commercial uses, fair use, nominative use, and personal uses of copyrighted works. So, not every violation of a copyright is actionable. And that's really important. Not everything is covered by copyright. We'll learn about that, too. There is a common pool of resources that we all can use.
- ❑ **Copyright law is a lot like speed limits.** In our world, there's the speed limit. But unless there are automatic cameras, most of the time, there's leeway. Copyright law, at the moment, has some cameras (especially on platforms like YouTube), and we may shortly be getting more. (At the time of the writing of this, the CASE Act had passed the House, but not the Senate.) If you know the rules of the road, you should be better able to understand when it's important to follow the speed limit, when no one really cares, and most importantly, what the speed limit is and how it varies. There are also the custom and community standards part, and the reality of enforcement of copyright. But, you also shouldn't speed, even if your chances of getting caught are low.
- ❑ **Copyright is territorial.** If you infringe someone's work in Canada, Canadian law applies. U.S. law applies in the U.S., for infringement for both domestic and foreign works. There are also international treaties in copyright that set minimum standards, which we will discuss briefly when we talk about duration.
- ❑ **Copyright has a strange relationship to time**. We will see that time plays the role of gatekeeper between when works are protected and when they come into the public domain. We also have factors that allow for use during the copyrighted time, which are key to the functioning of copyright.

Steps to Copyrightability

As of January 1, 1978, copyright arises automatically in the United States, as well as in most of the world (for much longer). When you create something, you automatically have a copyright. The two basic elements to create a copyrightable work are fixation and originality. Here is Section 102(a) of the 1976 Copyright Act that governs copyrightable subject matter:

> (a) Copyright protection subsists, in accordance with this title, in **original** works of **authorship fixed** in any **tangible medium of expression,** now known or later developed, from which they can be perceived, reproduced, or otherwise communicated, either directly or with the aid of a machine or device. Works of authorship include the following categories:
>
> (1) literary works;

(2) musical works, including any accompanying words;

(3) dramatic works, including any accompanying music;

(4) pantomimes and choreographic works;

(5) pictorial, graphic, and sculptural works;

(6) motion pictures and other audiovisual works;

(7) sound recordings; and

(8) architectural works

We see the following concepts that appear in Section 102(a):

- ❑ original works of authorship
- ❑ fixation in any tangible medium of expression
- ❑ categories of authorship

The Copyright Act is our guide. Copyright protects original works of authorship. The originality requirement has two parts: modicum of creativity and independent creation. Note: you do not have to be the first one to ever have thought of that particular idea of how to paint a flower. Originality is a constitutional requirement; remember, it is not a novelty requirement. The Intellectual Property clause reads that Congress can secure "for limited Times to Authors...the exclusive Right to their respective Writings." U.S. Constitution, I.8.8. We define "Writings" broadly, but we require original writings based on the creative powers of the mind.

Section 102(a) of the U.S. Copyright Act begins to delineate the constitutional clause:

> Copyright protection subsists, in accordance with this title, in original works of authorship fixed in any tangible medium of expression, now known or later developed, from which they can be perceived, reproduced, or otherwise communicated, either directly or with the aid of a machine or device.

How important is authorship and originality? Originality is "the bedrock principle of copyright" and "the very premise of copyright law... To qualify for copyright protection, a work must be original to the author," which means that the work must be "independently created by the author" and it must possesses "at least some minimal degree of creativity." *Feist Publications, Inc. v. Rural Telephone Service Co., Inc.*, 499 U.S. 340, 345, 347 (1991).

Copyright is awarded to authors. To be an author, you must have created the work and you have to be human. Compendium III, Section 306: "The copyright law only protects "the fruits of intellectual labor" that "are founded in the creative powers of the mind." *Trade-Mark Cases*, 100 U.S. 82, 94 (1879). Because copyright law is limited to "original intellectual conceptions of the author," the Office will refuse to register a work if it determines that a human being did not create the work. *Burrow-Giles Lithographic Co. v. Sarony*, 111 U.S. 53, 58 (1884)."Not copied: An author creates a work independently. Copyright is rewarding you for your creativity and creative work. How much creativity is key. *Feist*, 499 U.S. at 345.

Here is a further explanation from the Copyright Office:

> A work may satisfy the independent creation requirement "even though it closely resembles other works so long as the similarity is fortuitous, not the result of copying." *Id.* at 345. For example, if two authors created works that are similar or even identical, each work could be registered provided that the authors did not copy expressions from each other. As a general rule, the Office will accept the applicant's representation that the work was independently created by the author(s) named in the application, unless that statement is implausible or is contradicted by information provided elsewhere in the registration materials or in the Office's records or by information that is known to the registration specialist. If the specialist determines that the work was not independently created, he or she may communicate with the applicant or may refuse to register the claim. Compendium III, Section 308.1.

Human

No animals—think painting elephants or selfie-taking monkeys—may obtain copyright. Under the 1976 Copyright law in the U.S., you have to be human. If you are not human and you create a work, you will not be given copyright protection. Works created by artificial intelligence also do not gain protection. One scholar, Yvette Joy Liebesman explained that you can't recover damages against artificial intelligence, and so animals and AI are judgment proof. That's why they do not receive copyright. This also means that if you claim your work is written by God or dictated by a spirit from another planet, you will not gain copyright. Here is what the Compendium states: "The Office will not register works produced by nature, animals, or plants. Likewise, the Office cannot register a work purportedly created by divine or supernatural beings, although the Office may register a work where the application or the deposit copy(ies) state that the work was inspired by a divine spirit." Examples in the Compendium:

- ❑ A photograph taken by a monkey
- ❑ A mural painted by an elephant
- ❑ A claim based on the appearance of actual animal skin
- ❑ A claim based on driftwood that has been shaped and smoothed by the ocean
- ❑ A claim based on cut marks, defects, and other qualities found in natural stone
- ❑ An application for a song naming the Holy Spirit as the author of the work

"Similarly, the Office will not register works produced by a machine or mere mechanical process that operates randomly or automatically without any creative input or intervention from a human author." Compendium III, 313.2. Examples in the Compendium:

- ❑ Reducing or enlarging the size of a pre-existing work of authorship
- ❑ Making changes to a preexisting work of authorship that are dictated by manufacturing or materials requirements
- ❑ Converting a work from analog to digital format, such as transferring a motion picture from VHS to DVD
- ❑ Declicking or reducing the noise in a preexisting sound recording or converting a sound recording from monaural to stereo sound.
- ❑ Transposing a song from B major to C major.
- ❑ Medical imaging produced by x-rays, ultrasounds, magnetic resonance imaging, or other diagnostic equipment.

Modicum of Creativity

How much creativity do you need to have? Just a little bit, that's all. That's what modicum means. Traditionally, we believe that if it is more than alphabetizing or basic patterns, you can obtain copyright. The cases that help us understand how much creativity are *Burrow-Giles Lithographic Co. v. Sarony,* 111 U.S. 53 (1884), Bleistein v. Donaldson Lithographing Co., 188 U.S. 239 (1903), and *Feist Publications v. Rural Telephone Service,* 499 U.S. 340 (1991), written by Justice O'Connor, about competing telephone books. 499 U.S. 340 (1991).

> The *sine qua non* of copyright is originality. To qualify for copyright protection, a work must be original to the author. Original, as the term is used in copyright, means only that the work was independently created by the author (as opposed to copied from other works) and that it possesses at least some minimal degree of creativity. To be sure, the requisite level of creativity is extremely low; even a slight amount will suffice. The vast majority of works make the grade quite easily, as they possess **some creative spark**, "no matter how crude, humble, or obvious" it might be. Originality does not signify novelty; a work may be original even though it closely resembles other works so long as the similarity is fortuitous, not the result of copying...

Let's see how the Compendium interpreted *Feist:*

> An author's expression does not need to "be presented in an innovative or surprising way," but it "cannot be so mechanical or routine as to require no creativity whatsoever." A work that is "entirely typical," "garden-variety," or "devoid of even the slightest traces of creativity" does not satisfy the originality requirement. *Feist*, 499 U.S. at 362. "[T]here is nothing remotely creative" about a work that merely reflects "an age-old practice, firmly rooted in tradition and so commonplace that it has come to be expected as a matter of course." *Id.* at 363. Likewise, a work "does not possess the minimal creative spark required by the Copyright Act" if the author's expression is "obvious" or "practically inevitable." *Id.* at 363.Although the creativity standard is low, it is not limitless. *Id.* at 362. "There remains a narrow category of works in which the creative spark is utterly lacking or so trivial as to be virtually nonexistent. Such works are incapable of sustaining a valid copyright." *Id.* at 359 (citations omitted). If the Office determines that a work possesses sufficient creativity, it will register the claim and issue a certificate of registration. Conversely, if the Office determines that the work does not possess some minimal degree of creativity, it will refuse registration." Compendium III, Section 308.2.

Creative Labor

You also have to have creative labor. Just because you worked hard on something or spent a lot of money doesn't mean copyright will reward you. We call that "sweat of the brow" (This is not necessarily true in the United Kingdom, or in other parts of the world.) Copyright is about creativity, and so the labor that is protected is creative.

Fixation

In the United States, to obtain copyright, a work must be "fixed in a tangible medium of expression." 17 U.S.C 102(a). Not all countries require a physical embodiment of the creative work, but the U.S. does. Why? Fixation provides clear boundaries of what is included in the copyrighted work. This seems similar to patent law's "reduce to practice" requirement. But the Berne Convention (the international treaty on copyright) does not require fixation. What would not be covered in the U.S., but might elsewhere? Live concerts that are not recorded. A professor's lectures. A song created but not recorded or written down. Because of the gap between our fixation requirement and other countries that do not have one, and the rise of bootleg concert recordings, the U.S. enacted a different copyright law related to unfixed concerts with unauthorized recordings.

What about live broadcasts? If they are simultaneously being recorded, that qualifies as a "motion picture" or "sound recording."

Tangible Medium of Expression

The fixation must be in a "tangible medium of expression, now known or later developed, from which they can be perceived, reproduced, or otherwise communicated, either directly or with the aid of a machine or device." 17 U.S.C. Section 102(a). Why so wordy? It harkens back to a piano roll case at the end of the 19th century, where piano rolls were not covered by the Copyright Act because they weren't perceivable to the human eye. The 1976 Copyright Act didn't want to make that mistake again! The U.S. Supreme Court in *White-Smith Music Publishing Company v. Apollo Company*, 209 U.S. 1 (1908), ruled that manufacturers of music rolls for player pianos did not have to pay royalties to the composers. This was a year before the enactment of the new law, the 1909 Copyright Act, which rectified the situation with a compulsory license for musical compositions. The 1976 Copyright Act made it clear that the form of fixation does not matter: "There are countless ways that a work may be fixed in a copy or phonorecord and "it makes no difference what the form, manner, or medium of fixation may be." H.R. REP. NO. 94-1476, at 52 (1976), *reprinted in* 1976 U.S.C.C.A.N. at 5666."

Aesthetic Non-Discrimination

One more key element. The basic principle is that we don't judge the quality of the work to gain protection.

Categories of Copyrightable Works

Section 102(a) includes a list of categories of copyrightable works:

> Works of authorship include the following categories:
>
> (1) literary works;
> (2) musical works, including any accompanying words;
> (3) dramatic works, including any accompanying music;
> (4) pantomimes and choreographic works;
> (5) pictorial, graphic, and sculptural works;
> (6) motion pictures and other audiovisual works;
> (7) sound recordings; and
> (8) architectural works.

Compilations

Let's look at the key definitions from the 1976 Copyright Act:

- ❑ A "compilation" is a work formed by the collection and assembling of preexisting materials or of data that are selected, coordinated, or arranged in such a way that the resulting work as a whole constitutes an original work of authorship. The term "compilation" includes collective works. 17 U.S.C. Section 101.
- ❑ A "collective work" is "a work, such as a periodical issue, anthology, or encyclopedia, in which a number of contributions, constituting separate and independent works in themselves, are assembled into a collective whole." 17 U.S.C. Section 101.

The selection, arrangement, and coordination (SAC) of pre-existing materials is key to understanding how a copyrightable work is created. This can include copyrighted and non-copyrightable elements. As long as the SAC has a modicum of creativity, the work gains protection. Compilations can also be collective works like anthologies or books where different authors contribute independently protectable works, like short stories. *Feist* teaches us that individual parts need not be copyrightable, but the whole, with the requisite creativity can be. That the compilation is protectable does not change the status of the underlying, individual parts. 17 U.S.C Section 103. Now, not everyone believes that we should define everything we make as a compilation. I understand. But, I think it is a useful way, a shorthand, to help us identify the elements of creativity.

Derivative Work

Not everything we make becomes a derivative work. First, we will see that the copyright holder has the exclusive right to create derivative works. So, one needs permission (implied or explicit) to create derivative works. Second, merely changing the color of something does not create a derivative work. Third, in creating a derivative work (with permission), you gain certain rights to the new creation, but the underlying work still belongs to the copyright holder.

Here is the definition from the 1976 Copyright Act: "A "derivative work" is a work based upon one or more preexisting works, such as a translation, musical arrangement, dramatization, fictionalization, motion picture version, sound recording, art reproduction, abridgment, condensation, or any other form in which a work may be recast, transformed, or adapted. A work consisting of editorial revisions, annotations, elaborations, or other modifications which, as a whole, represent an original work of authorship, is a "derivative work"." 17 U.S.C. Section 101.

Let's break down the definition of a derivative work into elements:

A derivative work is

- ❑ "a work based upon one or more preexisting works." You have to have a work that is your base. So, Romeo and Juliet is a play. That's our preexisting work;
- ❑ "such as a translation, musical arrangement, dramatization, fictionalization, motion picture version, sound recording, art reproduction, abridgment, condensation, or any other form."
- ❑ "in which a work may be recast, transformed, or adapted." This is really important. The derivative work must be "recast, transformed, or adapted" in such a way as to be distinct and identifiably different from the original. There are many cases that go in depth into what qualifies as a derivative work, and whether it meets the threshold of originality required for a derivative work.

The law related to compilations and derivative works are found in Section 103:

> **(a)**The subject matter of copyright as specified by section 102 includes compilations and derivative works, but protection for a work employing pre-existing material in which copyright subsists does not extend to any part of the work in which such material has been used unlawfully.

> **(b)**The copyright in a compilation or derivative work extends only to the material contributed by the author of such work, as distinguished from the preexisting material employed in the work, and does not imply any exclusive right in the preexisting material. The copyright in such work is independent of, and does not affect or enlarge the scope, duration, ownership, or subsistence of, any copyright protection in the preexisting material.

Who is the Author?

Copyright law presumes that the creator is the author. Copyright ownership is found in Chapter 2 of the 1976 Copyright Act. The default is that the author is the owner. The author controls the exclusive rights of copyright, when to give permission, and when to sell and license the work. The copyright term is based on the author's death, or if there are joint authors, the last surviving author's death. Let's take a look:

> *17 U.S.C. Section 201(a) Initial Ownership.—*
>
> Copyright in a work protected under this title vests initially in the author or authors of the work. The authors of a joint work are co-owners of copyright in the work.

To be a joint author, there are a few requirements. First, here is the definition from the Copyright Office. "A "joint work" is a work prepared by two or more authors with the intention that their contributions be merged into inseparable or interdependent parts of a unitary whole." 17 U.S.C. Section 101. There are a couple of key points.

You must, as joint authors, believe you are joint authors at the time of creation, and intend to integrate your creative work. You also must contribute creative work, and not merely financial support or "sweat of the brow." You don't have to do equal shares, but the contribution must be substantial enough to stand on its own as copyrightable expression. The ownership is considered a "tenants in common," meaning that each joint author can exercise any and all rights without permission of the other authors, but there is a duty to account for the shares of the profits from any use or license. Joint authors must all agree to exclusive licenses or transfers/assignments of rights in writing.

You cannot after the fact decide to be joint authors. If you feel that you contributed a great deal but didn't get credit, that's not the time to claim joint authorship. It is something that is decided *jointly* at the time of creation. Who is named matters. Registering with the U.S. Copyright Office matters, as it provides a record of who is the author.

Work for Hire

Work for hire is a legal term. You may be working for hire, but not count as a "work for hire." There are two ways that your creative work can fall under work for hire: an employee in the course of their employment, or a commissioned work that falls under specific, enumerated categories in the Copyright Act. Let's take each of them for further discussion.

Employee in the course of their employment

A sculptor was hired to create a sculpture for a non-profit. He was given an idea – a statue in the form of a homeless man, woman, and child that harkened back to Mary, Joseph, and baby Jesus. But the parties did not indicate who the copyright holder was, and there was a conflict on who owned the statue. *Community for Creative Non-Violence v. Reid* is the U.S. Supreme Court case that helps us determine whether someone is an employee or an independent contractor under the meaning of the law. 490 U.S. 730 (1989). What we are trying to see is whether you do regular work, have health insurance, are covered by taxes, etc., or whether you have been hired to do a specific job (think wedding photographer) and control the means by which you do that job. Whoever is the copyright holder controls the use of that work. You may assign, transfer, or license those rights, but if you don't have those rights, you don't have the right to do anything, and may even be stopped from creating further copies or derivative works. Here is the statutory language:

> 17 U.S.C. Section 201(b) - Works Made for Hire.—
>
> In the case of a work made for hire, the employer or other person for whom the work was prepared is considered the author for purposes of this title, and, unless the parties have expressly agreed otherwise in a written instrument signed by them, owns all of the rights comprised in the copyright.

Let's look at how to determine the hiring party's right to control the manner and means by which the product is accomplished. This would mean that the hiring part was any employee, rather than an independent contract. Here are the factors:

- ❑ skills required
- ❑ source of the instrumentalities and tools
- ❑ location of the work
- ❑ duration of the relationship between the parties
- ❑ whether the hiring party has the right to assign additional projects to the hired party

- ❑ extent of the hired party's discretion over when and how long to work
- ❑ method of payment
- ❑ hired party's role in hiring and paying assistants
- ❑ whether the work is part of the regular business of the hiring party
- ❑ whether the hiring party is in business
- ❑ provision of employee benefits
- ❑ tax treatment of the hired party

The court found that the sculptor was the copyright holder. He had special skills, had his own tools, a studio where the work was done, and the relationship was only lasting as long as it took to create the sculpture. The hiring party could not assign additional tasks. The hiring party was not directing when and how long to work, and it wasn't the business of the non-profit to make sculptures. The sculptor received no employee benefits, and he was taxed as an independent contractor. Reid held the copyright; CCNV had a non-exclusive license to the sculpture.

Commissioned Works

A proper work for hire situation can also come up with commissioned works. This has to be one of nine categories defined in the Copyright Act:

- ❑ a contribution to a collective work,
- ❑ as a part of a motion picture or other audiovisual work,
- ❑ as a translation,
- ❑ as a supplementary work (supplementary work includes works for publication like introductions, conclusions, illustrations, explanations, revisions, commentary, forwards, afterward, maps, charts, tables, editorial notes, afterward, editorial notes, musical arrangements, answer material for tests, bibliographies, appendices, and indexes)
- ❑ as a compilation, as an instructional text,
- ❑ as a test,
- ❑ as an answer material for a test, or
- ❑ as an atlas.

If your work fits into one of these categories, there has to be an express, signed agreement in place as well. For most of us, our work does not fit into one of these categories.

Independent Contractor

If you are working for someone else, and your work does not fit into employee or commissioned works, you are an independent contractor. Unless there is an agreement to the contrary, you retain the copyright in the work, even though a third party paid you to make/create the work. They receive a non-exclusive license to use the work. But unless there is a contract in place, no assignment or exclusive license has been created by the act of creating it for someone else or even getting paid.

Contributions to Collective Works

Pat Sloan and Jane Davidson's *The Splendid Sampler* contains contributions from a variety of authors. Those are considered a contribution to a collective work. They are each a separate contribution to a collective work, which carry a distinct copyright from the whole. Think anthology.

17 U.S.C. Section 201(c) Contributions to Collective Works.—

> Copyright in each separate contribution to a collective work is distinct from copyright in the collective work as a whole, and vests initially in the author of the contribution. In the absence of an express transfer of the copyright or of any rights under it, the owner of copyright in the collective work is presumed to have acquired only the privilege of reproducing and distributing the contribution as part of that particular collective work, any revision of that collective work, and any later collective work in the same series.

Non-Protectable Items

We have two types of building blocks: non-protectable elements, and works that are in the public domain because their term expired. We will look at both kinds of building blocks in this chapter.

None of these are protectable by copyright. We'll go through them one by one.

- ❑ Ideas and concepts
- ❑ Procedures, methods and techniques
- ❑ Useful things: the doctrine of functionality and useful articles doctrine
- ❑ Facts
- ❑ Shapes
- ❑ Mere Change in Color
- ❑ Mere Copies
- ❑ Layout or Format

- ❏ Typeface and fonts (with exceptions)
- ❏ Letters, words, titles, and slogans
- ❏ Ingredients
- ❏ Restoration
- ❏ Stock characters/Scenes a faire/Common elements
- ❏ Expired copyrighted works now in the public domain (the next chapter)
- ❏ Works that did not meet the required level of creativity (the previous chapter)

No Ideas

Ideas are not protectable. Expression of the idea is. Your version. Your selection, arrangement, and coordination of that idea is protectable. The question is where is that boundary between an idea and expression.

Procedures and Techniques

Copyright law does not protect procedures, methods, techniques, or other ways of doing things. Patents and/or trade secrets protect functional elements, not copyright. So, the techniques you develop or learn from a YouTube video are not protectable by copyright. (The YouTube video itself, of course, is protected, in its expression.) You can use them, teach them to others, and profit from them. If, however, they are protected by patents, that is another story.

No Facts

Facts are not created. So, there is no modicum of creativity. That seems simple enough. Copyright, of course, has to complicate it. What about facts that are actually fiction? If they are presented as facts, then they are treated as facts. That comes from a famous U.S. Supreme Court case where a number of phone numbers were made up and stuck into a phone directory. The court found that the made-up, fake facts counted. What about fiction? Those are *not* facts. So the fact that Harry Potter lives under the stairs while growing up is not considered a fact. Fictional stories are not facts. What else are facts? Math. Dates. Historical information. No one owns these elements. And why? Because there is not authorship, says copyright, they just exist in the world—no one created facts. And going back to Section 102(a), you must have authorship to have a copyrightable work.

What about Shapes?

According to the U.S. Copyright Office, the Copyright Act does not protect common geometric shapes, either in two-dimensional or three-dimensional form. There are numerous common geometric shapes, including, without limitation, straight or curved lines, circles, ovals, spheres, triangles, cones, squares, squares, cubes, rectangles, diamonds, trapezoids, parallelograms, pentagons, hexagons, heptagons, octagons, and decagons." Compendium III, 906.1. The question is when does a shape become something more than a shape. An image with lots of shapes is protectable. The Compendium explains: "The registration specialist will register this claim because it combines multiple types of geometric shapes in a variety of sizes and colors, culminating in a creative design that goes beyond the mere display of a few geometric shapes in a preordained or obvious arrangement." Compendium, Section 906.1. What is considered "preordained or obvious?" No further suggestion is given. Once an author has used a familiar symbol in a "creative manner", it is then protectable. The question is what is a creative manner? Here are examples the Copyright Office provides:

> • Francis Ford created a sketch of the standard fleur de lys design used by the French monarchy. The registration specialist may refuse to register this claim if the work merely depicts a common fleur de lys.
>
> • Samantha Stone drew an original silhouette of Marie Antoinette with a backdrop featuring multiple fleur de lys designs. The registration specialist may register this work because it incorporates an original, artistic drawing in addition to the standard fleur de lys designs. Compendium, Section 906.2.

Mere Copies

Mere copies are not protectable as new things. The question is how much additional creative authorship is necessary to create a new copyright based on the "mere copy", or otherwise known as a derivative work. Exact copies of works do not gain additional protection. Examples from the Compendium:

- An exact reproduction of the Mona Lisa that cannot be distinguished from the original.
- A photocopy or scan of a photograph.
- Photocopying, scanning, or digitizing a literary work.
- A toy model that is an exact replica of an automobile, airplane, train, or other useful article where no creative expression has been added to the existing design. Compendium, 313.4(A).

Layout or Format

"As a general rule, the Office will not accept a claim to copyright in "format" or "layout." The general arrangement of the specific content that is selected and arranged in a sufficiently creative manner. The claim, however, would be limited to the selection and arrangement of that specific content, not to the selection and arrangement of *any* content in that particular manner." Circular 33, U.S. Copyright Office.

Letters, Words, Titles and Short Phrases

...are not copyrightable. If you are using the words or short phrases in commerce to identify a company, product or service, that's trademark. If you have a logo, that's logos. Logos suffer from the problem that lettering, short words, basic shapes and all the other things we've been discussing are not protectable.
What does this include?

- Title of a book or name of a company
- Domain name or URL
- Name of a character
- A catchphrase
- Mottos, slogans or other short expressions

Ingredients or Contents

The list of ingredients or contents is not protectable. An explanation in a cookbook, crafts book, or manual can be copyrightable in the selection, arrangement, and coordination, as well as the text, photos, and drawings. But the functional ingredients or directions themselves are not protectable.

Characters

Sometimes people want to copyright not just a novel, but want to copyright the character beyond the one story. Are characters in fabric, for instance, copyrightable? The Compendium explains: "The original, visual aspects of a character may be protected by copyright if they are sufficiently original. This may include the physical attributes of the character, such as facial features and specific body shape, as well as images of clothing and any other visual elements." Compendium III, Section 911. We have seen a great deal of litigation involving the Sherlock Holmes characters. We'll discuss this more later in the book.

Stock Characters and Scènes à Faire

Stock characters are not protectable. "The copyright law does not protect stock characters, settings, or events that are common to a particular subject matter or medium because they are commonplace and lack originality." The examples given in the Compendium makes one think:

- The copyright for a work about the Hindenburg would not cover elements that are "indispensable, or at least standard, in the treatment of" that topic, such as scenes that take place in a German beer hall or characters who utter common greetings of the period (citing Hoehling, 618 F.2d at 979.).
- The copyright for a work about a police station in an urban slum would not cover elements that necessarily result from the choice of that setting, such as scenes depicting drunks, prostitutes, vermin, and derelict cars, or stock themes commonly linked to the genre of police fiction, such as foot chases or the "familiar figure of the Irish cop." (citing Walker v. Time Life Films, 784 F.2d 44, 50 (2d Cir. 1986)
- The fact "[t]hat treasure might be hidden in a cave inhabited by snakes, that fire might be used to repel the snake, that birds might frighten an intruder in the jungle, and that a weary traveler might seek solace in a tavern ... [are] simply too general to be protectable." Zambito v. Paramount Pictures Corp, 613 F. Supp. 1107, 1112 (EDNY 1985).

Let's look at an example. In 2009, Vollet designed the multi-layered ceramic snowman ornament consisting of a snowman's head wearing a black, stovepipe hat with a green stripe and a raised adornment on the right side of the hat's brim; the face has a curved, carrot-like nose and is painted in a cartoonish fashion with an exaggerated smile drawn from a single black line. This ornament was granted Certificate of Registration # VA 1-785-997 with effective date of registration of August 11, 2011." MUD PIE, LLC v. Clay Chick Ceramics, LLC, No. 1:12-CV-3242-CAP, 2014 WL 11820249, at (N.D. Ga. Jan. 9, 2014).

Mud Pie designed a black-and-white ceramic collection of a Santa, reindeer and snowman. Clay Chick (Vollet) sent a cease and desist letter to Mud Pie. Here, Mud Pie argued that Clay Chick had "thin" copyright at best. "The Eleventh Circuit has recognized that "noncopyrightable material includes 'scènes à faire'—stock scenes that naturally flow from a common theme." MUD PIE, LLC v. Clay Chick Ceramics, LLC, No.

1:12-CV-3242-CAP, 2014 WL 11820249, at (N.D. Ga. Jan. 9, 2014). Mud Pie contended that the Santa Claus, Snowman, and Reindeer were stock elements of a Christmas theme. The court found that you can take stock elements and add creativity to create a copyrightable work.

Copyright Rights

Copyright gives the copyright holder *rights*: to make copies, distribute the work, make derivative works, publicly display, and publicly perform the work. There are five basic exclusive rights the copyright holder gets *automatically upon creation* (now) *without doing anything.* When I create a pattern, when I pick fabrics and make a quilt, when my kid draws a picture, when I type this book...anytime I put something into a "tangible medium of expression," there's a copyright, and for a long time.

"All rights reserved" means that the copyright holder is reserving for themselves all of the exclusive rights. You have to ask permission to do any of them. So, let's explore what these rights are. Let's look at each right to better understand what they mean.

Here is the Section 106 from the 1976 Copyright Act:

> Subject to sections 107 through 122, the owner of copyright under this title has the exclusive rights to do and to authorize any of the following:
>
> (1) to reproduce the copyrighted work in copies or phonorecords;
> (2) to prepare derivative works based upon the copyrighted work;
> (3) to distribute copies or phonorecords of the copyrighted work to the public by sale or other transfer of ownership, or by rental, lease, or lending;
> (4) in the case of literary, musical, dramatic, and choreographic works, pantomimes, and motion pictures and other audiovisual works, to perform the copyrighted work publicly;
> (5) in the case of literary, musical, dramatic, and choreographic works, pantomimes, and pictorial, graphic, or sculptural works, including the individual images of a motion picture or other audiovisual work, to display the copyrighted work publicly; and
> (6) in the case of sound recordings, to perform the copyrighted work publicly by means of a digital audio transmission.

Reproduction Right

Making copies of the original work is the basis of copyright: the right to copy. This includes literal copying and substantial similarity.

Distribution Right

The copyright holder has the right to decide when and how a work is distributed to the public. Once the sale occurs, however, the copyright holder does not control subsequent sales. This is called the First Sale Doctrine.

Public Display

The copyright holder decides where and when the work is displayed publicly.

Public Performance

Except for visual art (weird), the copyright holder controls when a work can be publicly performed during the term of the copyright.

Create Derivative Works

The copyright holder has the exclusive right to create secondary works from the original work. These are called derivative works. There are some instances (namely fair use) where others can use your work and make their own derivative works without permission.

These are the rights of copyright. Now, let's see the choices of expressing your rights in relationship to others' using your work, namely the general public. Obviously you could also create contracts and one-on-one relationships. But when you put out a product or something to the world, it is ideal to let them know how you feel about the rights and what they can or can't do with your work and in what situations. The rights statement with the copyright notice alerts the world as to the intentions of the copyright holder on what others can do. Sometimes there are additional words that communicate to the world permissible uses and restrictions on the use of the work. There are three basic kinds:

> *All Rights Reserved.* Copyright holder wants to control as much as possible. This is the default, even if you don't include the rights statement.
>
> *No Rights Reserved.* Copyright holder sends its work out into the world.

Some Rights Reserved, or a Creative Commons License. This tells anyone that comes to the work what they can and can't do, without having to ask direct permission.

What is a Creative Commons License?

In the 21st century, with the rise of the Internet, people found that "All rights reserved" was a bit too restrictive--that there were many times where the copyright holder was ok with people further distributing/sharing the work, using the work to build new things (derivative work), and even using the work commercially. Creative Commons transformed how we think about rights statements. They allow a license from the copyright holder to be placed on the work--tagged, embedded--and so anyone coming to the work already knows the permission and limitations in using the work.

- **Attribution**: you want your name/company included when someone else uses (posts, remixes, etc.) the work.
- **ShareAlike:** you allow people to use your work, but only if they share what they make too. Usually this means for free.
- **No Derivatives:** you allow people to use your work, but they can't make different versions - they can't change or add anything to your work.
- **NonCommercial**: they can't sell your work, or anything they make using your work, and they can't use it in a commercial context.
- **CCO "No Rights Reserved":** you disclaim all rights in the copyright and send it out into the world. No restrictions on how other people use the work.

You can create a Creative Commons license at their website and make a combination of these terms. See www.creativecommons.org. These tell the world what kind of license to the work you are giving them. You should still put the copyright notice in addition to these terms.

Copyright Infringement

Copyright infringement is a strange beast. We see copyright infringement occur every day: unauthorized use of someone's work. Sometimes, there is an exception of defense to the use: fair use (Section 107), library use exceptions (108), and many more that we will soon learn about. Maybe I have permission from the copyright holder? But for the most part, most infringement does not find its way to court. Copyright infringement cases are expensive and time consuming. We have developed other mechanisms: Section 512 notice-and-take down procedures with Internet Service providers, and cease-and-desist letters from lawyers that threaten an alleged infringer. We'll look at those as well. Still, we must look at infringement, both as doctrine and also to help us understand the boundaries when considering possession of artistic works.

Fair Use Basics

Fair uses are unauthorized uses by a third party that happen when the work is under copyright. Fair use is found as Section 107 of the 1976 Copyright Act (17 U.S.C. Section 107). It applies only to works potentially infringed in the U.S. Let's look at the Preamble to Section 107:

> *Preamble*
>
> Notwithstanding the provisions of sections 106 and 106A, the fair use of a copyrighted work, including such use by reproduction in copies or phonorecords or... by any other means specified by that section, for purposes such as criticism, comment, news reporting, teaching (including multiple copies for classroom use), scholarship, or research, is not an infringement of copyright. In determining whether the use made of a work in any particular case is a fair use the factors to be considered shall include—

Section 106 refers to the rights you get as a copyright holder (See Copyright Holder Rights) and Section 106A refers to moral rights for some kinds of artwork. (See Moral Rights). So, the first sentence reads, "Notwithstanding the rights given to copyright holders, the fair use of a copyrighted work is not an infringement of copyright."

The preamble gives examples of what might be included as a fair use. Making copies for *the purpose* of criticism, comment, news reporting, teaching (including multiple copies for classroom use), scholarship, or research. Note: this is a "such as" list, and therefore the purpose doesn't have to fall under one of the categories. In fact, we've seen Google use indexing under fair use, and parody (think Saturday Night Live) also falls under the purpose of fair use. Also notice that copies for classroom use falls under this. Fair use balances the copyright holder's rights with the unauthorized user's needs (some even say rights!). We call that the four-factor test. Over the years, the four-factor test has had a lot of cases that help us to understand what it means, and this is a whole area of subject for copyright scholars and attorneys. We're going to try to keep it simple.

> **First Factor:** The purpose and character of the third-party use. This is considered very important and can get complicated. There are a number of questions to ask.

Non-profit educational use? Weighs in favor of third party use. Courts are more likely to find in favor of the use when it is for non-profit or educational purposes, but again, not always.

Is it a commercial use? Weighs against third party use. (But not dispositive. Some commercial uses are ok, like parodies.) Things that are considered commercial include images used on an advertisement; on a product that someone is selling; on the cover of a book (to sell that book). We see with the new Illegal Streaming legislation that commercial is being defined more broadly. This may impact on other parts of copyright. But what is important to take away is that just because a use is found commercial does not defeat a fair use being found... (of course not). We'll see that when we get to parody.

Is it a parody? Weighs in favor of third party use. The courts give a lot of leeway to works that are parodies that make fun of, that comment and criticize the original work. This is super important to our democracy and our society. If a work is a parody, the four-factor test takes a different turn in some ways. We will see that shortly.

What is a parody? That was defined in a case *Campbell v. Acuff-Rose* by the U.S. Supreme Court. There, 2 Live Crew used Roy Orbison's Pretty Woman to make their own version, which degenerates into "big hairy woman" and other things. It has the same bits of music that we all know. The court found the band was commenting on the original and making a statement. You hold the original and the new one in your head at the same time.

Is the Use Transformative? This is a big one. Have you somehow transformed the original into something else? It is a use different from the original, and somehow you are commenting, criticizing, or transforming in the new work. This is a very important category for artists. Art often falls under transformative. When you use a pre-existing artwork in a new context, the work may fall under fair use. We'll talk more about this in the next chapter.

Second Factor: The nature of the copyrighted work.

A work of fiction has greater protection from fair uses, but we still see a lot of fan art and fiction. History, directions, and other non-fictional copyrighted works do not get as much protection under the fair use analysis. This is usually whether the original work is fact or fiction. Fictional works get more protection. Factual works get less. Artwork gets more. A photograph of the Washington Monument gets less. Factor two was easier. It usually is. Sometimes there's a question of whether something falls into fact or fiction.

You can see what the law is doing. The court believes that fictional, artistic works deserve greater protection, as opposed to facts that are available to everyone. A phone book gets less protection than a sculpture. You look to the original work--the work being used. Is it fictional or factual?

> **Third Factor:** The amount and substantiality of the portion used in relation to the copyrighted work as a whole. *How much did the third party take?* This can be complicated too. The amount is analyzed both for its qualitative and quantitative quantities.

If you take the heart of the work and there's no reason to buy the original, that's not fair to the copyright holder. There is no magic number. But think of it this way, if what you are doing is a market replacement that is not a fair use. And of course, there is an exception. If you are creating a parody (commenting on a thing in a way that conjures up the thing, again think SNL), you can take the heart of the work – because you need to conjure up the original. Then the court assumes you will take the "heart of the work," and then it is ok. The whole point is to identify an original work, and by making fun of it, comment and criticize it.

> **Fourth Factor:** The effects of the use upon the potential market for or value of the copyrighted work.

This is often seen as the most important factor. Is what the third party doing a market replacement or taking away licensing opportunities? Note: commenting, criticizing, and parody are not subject to this requirement. The thinking is that the copyright holder would never give permission to have a bad review or be made fun of. So, the fourth factor does not apply. That's the statute. Now, let's look at some examples.

Examples of fair use:

> I write a biography and use quotes from several letters and novels of my subject. I use only what I need to comment on the selections (Fair use, scholarship).

> I quote from a poem and create a quilt using the quote and my interpretation of that poem (Fair use, comment/criticism, and transformative use).

> I am a collage artist. I take bits from a variety of sources and carefully craft a message that reflects on the original sources. That is fair use.

Fair use is an important tool for artists. If you are using/incorporating someone else's work in your work, stop and think about why. Go through the factors. Does it make sense to call it a fair use? If not, are the parts that you are using in the public domain? If not, are you going to seek permission? If not, you may be infringing.

Finally, we asked our dear friend, Kenny Crews, IP lawyer and expert on fair use for his thoughts on using fair use. He gave us the example of a photograph:

"When you are making a new use, and changing the actual work, your use may be transformative. We have now a handful of photograph cases working their way through the courts. So, we are seeing that courts only are finding transformative work if they create a new work out of the artwork that is dramatically different. If it is merely a copy that substitutes for the original that will not be likely seen as fair use. But if that photograph is turned into a very different form of art, then it may be fair use. If you want to commercialize the transformative use, that gets a little bit harder. And we know that hanging a quilt in a quilt show is not considered a commercial use."

Fair use is a powerful and important tool for artists, for our culture, and for our democracy. This is meant merely as an introduction.

There's one more element: "The fact that a work is unpublished shall not itself bar a finding of fair use if such finding is made upon consideration of all the above factors." That's the last bit of the statute. This means that fair use can be applied to any work, not just ones out in the public, although courts often care whether the work had been circulated by the content owner (e.g. posted online) or kept unpublished (e.g. grandmother's diary in the attic).

We will return to fair use. For now, remember that a work has to be under copyright, and the use by a third party is unauthorized. If you have used a work that is in the public domain, you do not need to apply fair use. If you have gotten permission from the copyright holder, you do not need to rely on fair use. And fair use comes in many varieties in terms of its application. In our Internet world especially, fair use plays an important role in the functioning of our everyday life.

Next Steps

The next step is to understand how long the property right in a copyrighted work lasts. That is the focus of the next few chapters. It turns out to be sometimes a bit complicated.

3: U.S. Domestic Duration

You've created something. It passes the 102(a) and 102(b) requirements. You now have a property right in a creative work. How long does that property right last? How long do you as a copyright holder control the work?

We will be looking at how long copyright lasts from a number of angles: domestic terms (learning the basics); foreign works in the U.S.; international treaties; and comparative copyright amongst countries. This is the first of a number of lessons aimed at the basics of duration in copyrighted works. The U.S. Constitution requires copyright to last for "limited Times," meaning it is not forever. But how limited has changed over time. When a work is out of copyright, you can use it freely. So, the question is when is a work out of copyright?

We are not looking historically. We are looking practically. How do we determine the status of a work *today*? Think of duration as sorting. We have to sort by three variables: published or unpublished; date of publication (or creation in the case of unpublished works); and place of publication/creation. Once we have that sorted, we have other questions to ask, including information about the author. Sometimes we also must ask what kind of work, the category, as well. So, let's say we have a French published novel from 1932. Those are our four variables, including category. That tells us what law to look at: Section 104A. So, let's start to understand the sorting categories. Again, we are only focused right now on domestic U.S. works.

As you read, create a decision tree to help determine which elements and terms apply.

Works Created and/or Published on or after March 1, 1989

To begin, anything published or created on or after March 1, 1989, is under copyright (as long as it meets the copyrightability requirements). The basic term for current works is found under Section 302 of the U.S. Copyright Act.

Current Term of Copyright

For those that are curious, here are the current terms for copyright in the United States for works created on or after January 1, 1978, and that were published on or after March 1, 1989. Unpublished works created on or after January 1, 1978 are also included in this category.

> **Individual:** life of the author plus 70
>
> **Joint authors**: life of the last surviving author plus 70 years
>
> **Work for hire/anonymous works:** the shorter of 95 years from publication/120 from creation.

Here is Section 302. Note where we find the individual terms. Also, note what is also included in Section 302, and how does that help us understand the story of duration?

> **(a) In General.—**
>
> Copyright in a work created on or after January 1, 1978, subsists from its creation and, except as provided by the following subsections, endures for a term consisting of the life of the author and 70 years after the author's death.
>
> **(b) Joint Works.—**
>
> In the case of a joint work prepared by two or more authors who did not work for hire, the copyright endures for a term consisting of the life of the last surviving author and 70 years after such last surviving author's death.

(c) Anonymous Works, Pseudonymous Works, and Works Made for Hire.— In the case of an anonymous work, a pseudonymous work, or a work made for hire, the copyright endures for a term of 95 years from the year of its first publication, or a term of 120 years from the year of its creation, whichever expires first. If, before the end of such term, the identity of one or more of the authors of an anonymous or pseudonymous work is revealed in the records of a registration made for that work under subsections (a) or (d) of section 408, or in the records provided by this subsection, the copyright in the work endures for the term specified by subsection (a) or (b), based on the life of the author or authors whose identity has been revealed. Any person having an interest in the copyright in an anonymous or pseudonymous work may at any time record, in records to be maintained by the Copyright Office for that purpose, a statement identifying one or more authors of the work; the statement shall also identify the person filing it, the nature of that person's interest, the source of the information recorded, and the particular work affected, and shall comply in form and content with requirements that the Register of Copyrights shall prescribe by regulation.

(d) Records Relating to Death of Authors.—

Any person having an interest in a copyright may at any time record in the Copyright Office a statement of the date of death of the author of the copyrighted work, or a statement that the author is still living on a particular date. The statement shall identify the person filing it, the nature of that person's interest, and the source of the information recorded, and shall comply in form and content with requirements that the Register of Copyrights shall prescribe by regulation. The Register shall maintain current records of information relating to the death of authors of copyrighted works, based on such recorded statements and, to the extent the Register considers practicable, on data contained in any of the records of the Copyright Office or in other reference sources.

(e) Presumption as to Author's Death.—

After a period of 95 years from the year of first publication of a work, or a period of 120 years from the year of its creation, whichever expires first, any person who obtains from the Copyright Office a certified report that the records provided by subsection (d) disclose nothing to indicate that the author of the work is living, or died less than 70 years before, is entitled to the benefits of a presumption that the author has been dead for at least 70 years. Reliance in good faith upon this presumption shall be a complete defense to any action for infringement under this title.

Why are Section 302(d) and (e) important? When would they be used? Can you imagine an example?

U.S. Federal Government Works

U.S. federal works are not protected by copyright. So, that's exciting. However, there is a glitch. You have to figure out what is considered a federal government work. This can get complicated. Not all works under the federal government count, because they are created by independent contractors. (Remember that stuff?) Many wonderful sites have public domain images and are free for you to use for inspiration or copying as part of your art.

State and local government works are not included; they may or may not be in the public domain. It's up to the state or local government to decide, except for cases and law. And slogans, symbols, and seals of the Federal government may be protected either by trademark law, or special laws. Two specific characters are protected: The character "Smokey Bear" is protected by 18 U.S.C. Section 711, and "Woodsy Owl" character, name and slogan by 18 U.S.C. Section 711a.For more, go to https://www.law.cornell.edu/uscode/text/18/part-I/chapter-33.

Let's look at the statute. **Section 105**

(a) In general.—

Copyright protection under this title is not available for any work of the United States Government, but the United States Government is not precluded from receiving and holding copyrights transferred to it by assignment, bequest, or otherwise.

(b) Copyright Protection of Certain of Works.—

Subject to subsection (c),[1] the covered author of a covered work owns the copyright to that covered work.

(c) 1 Use by Federal Government.—

The Secretary of Defense may direct the covered author of a covered work to provide the Federal Government with an irrevocable, royalty-free, world-wide, nonexclusive license to reproduce, distribute,perform, or display such covered work for purposes of the UnitedStates Government.

(c) 1 Definitions.—In this section:

(1) The term "covered author" means a civilian member of the faculty of a covered institution.

(2) The term "covered institution" means the following:

(A) National Defense University.
(B) United States Military Academy.
(C) Army War College.
(D) United States Army Command and General Staff College.
(E) United States Naval Academy.
(F) Naval War College.
(G) Naval Post Graduate School.
(H) Marine Corps University.
(I) United States Air Force Academy.
(J) Air University.
(K) Defense Language Institute.
(L) United States Coast Guard Academy.

(3) The term "covered work" means a literary work produced by a covered author in the course of employment at a covered institution for publication by a scholarly press or journal.

These two categories, Section 302 and Section 105 are what governs copyright law for works created on or after March 1, 1989. Our current creative works. We will now turn to the chaos that is the rest of time, or at least the 20th century, in copyright in the U.S.

Works created between January 1, 1978-February 29, 1989

These works were required to have proper copyright notice if they were published, and if they did not, they came into the public domain. They had five years to fix missing or problematic notice, which included filing a copyright registration with the U.S. Copyright Office. Unpublished works do not require notice.

So, when you find a work from this period, the first thing to do is see if there is proper copyright, and if there is not, look at the registration records at the U.S. copyright office to see if you can find a registration record. Otherwise, these works are in the public domain. This is true *only* for domestic U.S. published works. Foreign workers are different.

The law changed in 1988 because of our joining the Berne Convention, which did not allow formalities to attach as a requirement for protection. While registration still provides benefits, it is not required to obtain copyright protection on published works. (It still is not and was never required for unpublished works).

Where do we find this in the law? You can't easily find it. Circular 3 written by the U.S. Copyright Office explains the importance of notice for this period of time. Here is an excerpt:

> Copyright notice provides information to the public regarding copyright ownership. Notice is optional for works created after March 1, 1989, but is generally required for works created before that date.
>
> Copyright notice is a statement placed on copies or phonorecords of a work to inform the public that a copyright owner is claiming ownership of it. A notice consists of three elements that generally appear as a single continuous statement:
>
> - The copyright symbol © (or for phonorecords, the symbol ℗); the word "copyright"; or the abbreviation "copr.";
> - The year of first publication of the work; and
> - The name of the copyright owner. Example: © 2017 John Doe
>
> The use of a copyright notice is the responsibility of the copyright owner and does not require permission from, or registration with, the Copyright Office. Copyright notice was required for all works first published before March 1, 1989, subject to some exceptions discussed below. If the notice was omitted or a mistake was made in using copyright notice, the work generally lost copyright protection in the United States. Copyright notice is optional for works published on or after March 1, 1989, unpublished works, and foreign works; however, there are legal benefits for including notice on your work.

https://www.copyright.gov/circs/circ03.pdf

Can you find works that do not have copyright attached that are 1) published and 2) from the 1970s-1980s time period? What kinds of questions do you start to ask? How do you know (if there is not a date) that sometime happened in 1978 and not 1977? In 1988 and not 1990? How do you know that it is published? We will soon see that these variations make a big difference in the status of the work.

Works published before January 1978

These works fall into a number of categories. This is where the messiness lives.

- Works published longer than 75 years from 1998 (or before 1923)
- Works published longer than 95 years ago
- Works published between 1923-1949
- Works published between 1950-1963
- Works published between 1964-1977
- Sound recordings 1972-1977
- Pre-1972 Sound recordings
- Works created, but not registered or published, before 1978

Add these categories to your decision tree. We will be going through pre-1972 sound recordings in a separate lesson, as well as foreign works in the U.S., and works created but not registered or published before 1978 (unpublished works) each as a separate lesson. Let's continue our backward march.

Works published longer than 95 years ago

Any work published anywhere in the world that is older than 95 years is in the public domain. Easy math. Done.

As of 2021, any work published before 1926 is in the public domain. You can use it without asking permission. A lot of people know that. This date changes every year. The formula? For this period of time, the term of copyright is no longer than 95 years from publication.

You do not need to know anything else, except to confirm that the work was published (generally circulating without restriction).

Works published before 1923

This was the date that established a frozen public domain for 20 years with the Copyright Term Extension Act (1998). Since the CTEA was enacted in 1998, work still had to be under copyright at that time. The term for works that were published before 1978 was a maximum term of 75 years. So, works published in 1922 and before did not get the extra term because they were in the public domain upon the enactment of the CTEA. That's what that date means, and a lot of charts and other information sheets have not updated their information. We are now past that frozen period where more works come into the public domain.

Domestic Works published 1926-1977

To determine the status of a domestically published work, there are a number of steps.

- ❑ **No Notice?** For works first published between 1925 and 1989, proper notice was required in order to be under copyright. If the work was published in the U.S. before 1989 and there is no © notice, the work is also in the public domain.

Works with Notice:

- ❑ **Works first published between 1924-1949:** These have to have been renewed in the 27th year from date of publication. To see if a work was renewed, you have to look at certain records that the U.S. Copyright Office does not still have in a searchable database. We built a tool as part of the Durationator.
- ❑ **Works first published between 1950-1963:** These have to be renewed in the 28th year starting on January 1. You can look to see if they were renewed at www.copyright.gov. Also, they have to have proper notice. No notice, no copyright.
- ❑ **Works first published 1964-1977:** If there is proper notice, they are protected for 95 years from first publication.

These works fall under Section 304. Let's take a look. This is can be a hard one to parse

Review Section 304 - Works Published Before January 1, 1978. Parse through all of it.

17 U.S. Code §304

(a) Copyrights in Their First Term on January 1, 1978.—

(1)

(A) Any copyright, the first term of which is subsisting on January 1, 1978, shall endure for 28 years from the date it was originally secured.

(B) In the case of—

(i) any posthumous work or of any periodical, cyclopedic, or other composite work upon which the copyright was originally secured by the proprietor thereof, or

(ii) any work copyrighted by a corporate body (otherwise than as assignee or licensee of the individual author) or by an employer for whom such work is made for hire, the proprietor of such copyright shall be entitled to a renewal and extension of the copyright in such work for the further term of 67 years.

(C) In the case of any other copyrighted work, including a contribution by an individual author to a periodical or to a cyclopedic or other composite work:

(i) the author of such work, if the author is still living,

(ii) the widow, widower, or children of the author, if the author is not living,

(iii) the author's executors, if such author, widow, widower, or children are not living, or

(iv) the author's next of kin, in the absence of a will of the author,

shall be entitled to a renewal and extension of the copyright in such work for a further term of 67 years.

(2)

(A) At the expiration of the original term of copyright in a work specified in paragraph (1)(B) of this subsection, the copyright shall endure for a renewed and extended further term of 67 years, which—

(i) if an application to register a claim to such further term has been made to the Copyright Office within 1 year before the expiration of the original term of copyright, and the claim is registered, shall vest, upon the beginning of such further term, in the proprietor of the copyright who is entitled to claim the renewal of copyright at the time the application is made; or

(ii) if no such application is made or the claim pursuant to such application is not registered, shall vest, upon the beginning of such further term, in the person or entity that was the proprietor of the copyright as of the last day of the original term of copyright.

(B) At the expiration of the original term of copyright in a work specified in paragraph (1)(C) of this subsection, the copyright shall endure for a renewed and extended further term of 67 years, which—

(i)if an application to register a claim to such further term has been made to the Copyright Office within 1 year before the expiration of the original term of copyright, and the claim is registered, shall vest, upon the beginning of such further term, in any person who is entitled under paragraph (1)(C) to the renewal and extension of the copyright at the time the application is made; or

(ii)if no such application is made or the claim pursuant to such application is not registered, shall vest, upon the beginning of such further term, in any person entitled under paragraph (1)(C), as of the last day of the original term of copyright, to the renewal and extension of the copyright.

(3)

(A) An application to register a claim to the renewed and extended term of copyright in a work may be made to the Copyright Office—

(i) within 1 year before the expiration of the original term of copyright by any person entitled under paragraph (1)(B) or (C) to such further term of 67 years; and

(ii) at any time during the renewed and extended term by any person in whom such further term vested, under paragraph (2)(A) or (B), or by any successor or assign of such person, if the application is made in the name of such person.

(B) Such an application is not a condition of the renewal and extension of the copyright in a work for a further term of 67 years.

(4)

(A) If an application to register a claim to the renewed and extended term of copyright in a work is not made within 1 year before the expiration of the original term of copyright in a work, or if the claim pursuant to such application is not registered, then a derivative work prepared under authority of a grant of a transfer or license of the copyright that is made before the expiration of the original term of copyright may continue to be used under the terms of the grant during the renewed and extended term of copyright without infringing the copyright, except that such use does not extend to the preparation during such renewed and extended term of other derivative works based upon the copyrighted work covered by such grant.

(B) If an application to register a claim to the renewed and extended term of copyright in a work is made within 1 year before its expiration, and the claim is registered, the certificate of such registration shall constitute prima facie evidence as to the validity of the copyright during its renewed and extended term and of the facts stated in the certificate. The evidentiary weight to be accorded the certificates of a registration of a renewed and extended term of copyright made after the end of that 1-year period shall be within the discretion of the court.

(b) Copyrights in Their Renewal Term at the Time of the Effective Date of the Sonny Bono Copyright Term Extension Act:

Any copyright still in its renewal term at the time that the Sonny Bono Copyright Term Extension Act becomes effective shall have a copyright term of 95 years from the date copyright was originally secured.

Unpublished Works Created but Not Published before Jan 1, 1978

You thought we were done, right? Unpublished works, created both in the U.S. and abroad, are governed by a different part of the copyright law, Section 303(a). This one is divided between unpublished works created before or after January 1, 1978.

- ❑ ***Before January 1, 1978:*** All unpublished works that were created before January 1, 1978, and not registered with the U.S. Copyright Office:

  The longer of life + 70 and 2002.

  If first published between 1978 and 2002, then the longer of life + 70 and December 31, 2047.

- ❑ ***On or After January 1, 1978:*** Section 302 applies (life plus 70; 120 for work for hire/anonymous works)

One of my favorite examples concerns Eloise, the fictional girl who lived at the Plaza Hotel. The series was written by Kay Thompson (1909–1998). In the 1960s, she wrote *Eloise Takes a Bawth* with Hilary Knight and Mart Crowley. The work was first published after 1978 but before December 31, 2002. So, the term? The longer of life of the author plus seventy years, and December 31, 2047.

Strangely, this book was not registered with the U.S. Copyright Office, and so we don't have official information on who is considered the author(s). However, the copyright notice helps: © Estate of Kay Thompson. The Illustrations by Hilary Knight are also copyrighted by the Estate of Kay Thomson. Both list 2002 as the date--that important cut-off year. The text is likely protected for 70 + 1998, or 2068, and the illustrations for 70 years from the death of Hilary Knight (b. 1926, and 94 as of 2020). If the work had been published in 1964, the term would have been through 2059.

Let's look at the statute: Section 303(a).

> (a) Copyright in a work created before January 1, 1978, but not theretofore in the public domain or copyrighted, subsists from January 1, 1978, and endures for the term provided by section 302. In no case, however, shall the term of copyright in such a work expire before December 31, 2002; and, if the work is published on or before December 31, 2002, the term of copyright shall not expire before December 31, 2047.

Charts, Diagrams and Tools (and the Durationator too)

In many ways, these are the easy formulations. When we began the Durationator, our concern was really not these works. Everyone could figure them out. Sometimes you couldn't easily find the resources to determine the status of works, especially the 1923-1949 period. But the law itself was pretty straightforward.

There are many ways to get assistance with this part. Let's look at some of the current tools, charts and maps.

- ❑ Peter Hirtle's annual duration chart: https://copyright.cornell.edu/publicdomain
- ❑ Mary Minow's Chart: http://www.librarylaw.com/DigitizationTable.htm
- ❑ Sunstein Law: http://sunsteinlaw.com/practices/copyright-portfolio-development/copyright-pointers/copyright-flowchart/
- ❑ Copyright Data: http://chart.copyrightdata.com
- ❑ Public Domain Sherpa:
- ❑ Out of Copyright: http://www.outofcopyright.eu/
- ❑ Public Domain Calculators: http://publicdomain.okfn.org/calculators/
- ❑ UC Berkeley: https://www.law.berkeley.edu/files/FINAL_PublicDomain_Handbook_FINAL(1).pdf.

Let's evaluate these. Strengths and weaknesses. And we've built a version in the Durationator. The question is how to build a better mousetrap that includes the needed records.

Social media question: when do you need to know copyright? When does it matter?

MUDS system

Copyright is complicated. Not only do you have the status of the work to determine, but there may be underlying works, or even "inserts", which have a separate copyright from the main work. All of these have to be evaluated to determine the copyright status of a work, and in part, was why Google gave up the idea of determining the status of works they had scanned and returned to a fair use argument instead.

As part of Durationator, we developed the MUDS system to catalog and distinguish main, underlying, derivative, and separate works. This helps sorts out questions when there are multiple layers of works. We will see the multiple layers in the *Happy Birthday* case as well. There is no right starting place. You start at one place and then do a relational analysis.

Main: The main work is usually the first work. Sometimes this is the work that one is focused on. For example, one may be focused upon the film, West Side Story, and so the musical version may be an underlying work. But usually, one begins with the first expression of the work, namely the short story, or the script. In this case, we are looking at the play, *The Philadelphia Story.* In the MUDS system, we label that first work, "Main." We now create relationships between the main work and the rest of the works that we are reviewing.

Underlying (U): The main work may be based on a work, and if so, you want to note that to make sure that you evaluate the copyright status of the work. Let's say you start with the film *The Philadelphia Story*, instead of the short story. The underlying work would then be the short story, and *The Philadelphia Story* would be the main work. You get to decide where to start.

Derivative (D): Derivative works that have the main work included, may have enough creativity to secure an additional copyright. The main work's term remains the same. The derivative work has a term on the new material. In the example below, the radio play may be considered a derivative work of the original, in that any new components made for the radio would be added to the original work. The performance is a derivative of the derivative radio play, with the main work's copyright still in play.

Separate (S): A separate work is a work that may be included at any stage, but carries a separate copyright term. An illustration in a book is a good example. The label "separate" helps to indicate that the term may be distinct.

Again, as part of this system, you decide where to start.

Work 1: The Philadelphia Story by Philip Barry (play)

Short Story	U	Underlying Work
Original Play	**M**	**Main**
Recorded Performance of the Play	MD1	Derivative 1 of Main
French Translation of Original Play	MD2	Derivative 2 of Main

U = Underlying work
M = Main
M+D+1 = First Derivative of Main
M+D+2 = Second Derivative of Main

Let's continue with this example

Work 2: The Philadelphia Story (film) based on Barry's play

Play	U	Underlying work of Main
Original director's cut of Film	M	Main
Remastered version of Film	MD1	Derivative 1 of Main
Original Film with Turkish subtitles	MD2	Derivative 2 of Main

Can you put the codes in?

Work 3: Twelfth Night by Shakespeare

	Durationator MUDS
Original English text	
1892 American Book Company Edition	

Microform version of 1892 American Book edition

2008 Arden Edition

Electronic text of Project Gutenberg

Spanish Translation of 1892 version

1899 Spanish translation. Revista nueva edition

Radio show of 2008 Version

Performance by the Royal Shakespeare Company

DVD of recorded live performance by RSC

Here are the answers

Work 3: Twelfth Night by Shakespeare

		Durationator MUDS
Original English text	M	Main
1892 American Book Company Edition	MD1	Derivative 1 of Main
Microform version of 1892 American Book edition	MD1	No change; copy of Derivative
2008 Arden Edition	MD2	Derivative 2 of Main

Electronic text of Project Gutenberg	MD?	Where does the text come from?
Spanish Translation of 1892 Version	MD1D D1	Derivative 1 of Derivative 1 of Main
Radio show of 2008 version	MD2D D1	Derivative 1 of Derivative 2 of Main
1928 Rivadeneyra edition	MD3	Derivative 3 of Main
Performance by the Royal Shakespeare Company of 1892 Version	MD1D D2	Derivative 2 of Derivative 1 of Main
DVD of recorded live performance by RSC of 1892 version	MD1D D2DD D1	Derivative 1 of Derivative 2 of Derivative 1 of Main

Does this make sense? Do you see why you want to identify the relationship between works? Once you know the relationship you can start to parse out the copyright status of the work.

Let's start with our first example again.

Work 1: The Philadelphia Story (film) based on Barry's play

Expression		Durationator MUD system	Copyright status
Original play	M	Main	Publication date: 1939 IC-US (through 2034) 95 years from first pub Section 304

Screenplay based on original play	MD1	Derivative 1 of Main	Publication date: 1940 (incorporated into film) IC-US (through 2035) (underlying work out of copyright 2034) 95 years from first pub Section 304
Original director's cut based on screenplay	MD1DD1	Derivative 1 of Derivative 1 of Main	Publication date: 1940 IC-US (through 2035) (underlying work out of copyright 2034) 95 years from first pub Section 304
Remastered version	MD1DD1DDD1	Derivative 1 of Derivative 1 of Main	Publication date: 2000 IC-US (through 2095) (underlying play out of copyright 2034; underlying film out of copyright 2035) Section 302
Dubbed Spanish version of 1940 film	MD1DD1DDD1 DDDDD1	Derivative 1 of Derivative 1 of Derivative 1 of Main	Publication date: 1942 IC-US (through 2037) 95 years from first pub Section 304

This is just one way to evaluate the copyright status of multi-layered works. Some works will not have more than one layer.

Let's take a look at the famous *Happy Birthday* case to see how the court applied the Section 304 analysis. Note, the court does not refer to MUDS, but you can see it at work.

Marya v. Warner/Chappell Music, Inc., 131 F. Supp. 3d 975, 979 (C.D. Cal. 2015)

[This is an important recent case that brought *Happy Birthday* confidently into the public domain. Let's follow the logic of the case. I've included headings and commentary as you read so that you don't get lost in the weeds. The question, in the end, is did the court find that *Happy Birthday* is in the public domain? Is that a knowable answer? What do you think happened with *Happy Birthday?*

I. Background

Plaintiffs Rupa Marya, Robert Siegel, Good Morning to You Productions Corp., and Majar Productions, LLC (collectively, "Plaintiffs") filed this class action to declare invalid Defendants Warner/Chappell Music, Inc. ("Warner/Chappell") and Summy–Birchard, Inc.'s ("Summy–Birchard") (collectively, "Defendants") purported copyright in the famous song *Happy Birthday To You* ("*Happy Birthday*").

Good Morning to All

The classic melody of *Happy Birthday* is the same as that of another song called *Good Morning To All* ("*Good Morning* ") (hereafter, the "*Happy Birthday/Good Morning* melody"). At some time **before 1893,** Mildred Hill and Patty Hill wrote *Good Morning*. Mildred composed the music with Patty's help, and Patty wrote the lyrics. The lyrics of *Good Morning* are similar to those of *Happy Birthday*:

In 1893, Mildred and Patty assigned their rights to the manuscript containing *Good Morning* and other songs to Clayton F. Summy ("Mr. Summy"). A copy of the assignment is not available, but the Parties do not dispute that the assignment occurred. That same year, Mr. Summy published the manuscript in, and filed for copyright registration of, a songbook titled *Song Stories for the Kindergarten* ("*Song Stories* "). After Mildred died, Jessica Hill, a third Hill sister, filed for renewal of the copyright to *Song Stories* in 1921 as one of Mildred's heirs. Under the Copyright Act of 1909, works could receive copyright protection for two consecutive 28–year terms. *See* 17 U.S.C. § 24 (1909 Act). Accordingly, copyright protection for *Song Stories,* including the song *Good Morning,* expired in 1949.

Can you follow what happened so far?

Before 1893: *Good Morning* - Music by Mildred; lyrics by Patty

1893: Sisters assigned their rights in *Good Morning* to Summy

1893: Summy files registration on *Song Stories for the Kindergarten* (which includes *Good Morning)*

1921: Renewal on *Song Stories* filed by third Sister.

1949: Copyright expires on *Good Morning* and *Song Stories for Kindergarten*. (28 years + 28 years, which was the term under the 1909 Act at the time)

This is the original version.

Happy Birthday

The origins of the lyrics to *Happy Birthday* (the "*Happy Birthday* lyrics") are less clear. The *Happy Birthday* lyrics did not appear in *Song Stories*. The first reference to them in print appeared in an article from 1901 in the *Inland Educator and Indiana School Journal*:

> A birthday among the little people is always a special occasion. The one who is celebrating is decorated with a bright flower or badge and stands in the center of the circle while the children sing "Happy birthday to you."

The full *Happy Birthday* lyrics did not appear in the article. In 1909, a prayer songbook similarly made reference to the song but did not include the lyrics.

Publication of the full *Happy Birthday* lyrics first occurred in a 1911 book titled *The Elementary Worker and His Work*. The book did not credit anyone with authorship of the lyrics, but mentioned that *Happy Birthday* and *Good Morning* shared the same tune, and noted that the latter song had been published in *Song Stories*. *The Elementary Worker and His Work* was registered for a copyright in 1911. After 1911, *Happy Birthday* appeared in other publications—*Harvest Hymns* in 1924 and *Children's Praise and Worship* in 1928. These publications similarly did not credit anyone with creating the *Happy Birthday* lyrics. *Children's Praise and Worship* was registered for a copyright at the time of publication. Next, in the early 1930s, Happy Birthday appeared in a series of movies—*Girls About Town, Bosko's Party, Strange Interlude, Baby Take a Bow, The Old Homestead,* and *'Way Down East.* (J.A. 25–26, 30, 35, 39, 41; SUF P64–65, P69, P71, P78, P94, P102.) Finally, in 1933, *Happy Birthday* was performed publically in the play *As Thousands Cheer.* (J.A. 29; SUF P77.)

Ok. Let's go through this one:

- ❑ **Music:** *Good Morning* tune (which we know expires in 1949)
- ❑ **Lyrics to Happy Birthday:** at least as old as 1911, when published in *The Elementary Worker and His Work* (without author credit)

In 1934, Jessica filed a lawsuit against the producers of *As Thousands Cheer* for copyright infringement (hereafter, the "*As Thousands Cheer* lawsuit"). Notably, the basis for her infringement claim was not that the producers had infringed any rights she allegedly held in the *Happy Birthday* lyrics. Rather, she alleged that the defendants infringed the copyright in *Good Morning,* which included the common melody for the two songs. *TIME* magazine, the *New York Times,* and the *New York Herald Tribune* all reported the *As Thousands Cheer* lawsuit. Patty and Jessica were both deposed in that action. In Patty's deposition, she claimed that she wrote the lyrics to *Happy Birthday* around the time *Good Morning* was created. The outcome of the *As Thousands Cheer* lawsuit is not clear from the record before us, but neither party claims it has any bearing on the instant action.

In 1935, the Clayton F. Summy Company ("Summy Co.") registered copyrights to two works entitled "Happy Birthday to You"—registration numbers E51988 and E51990. Defendants argue that E51990 is *the* publication that secured a federal copyright in the *Happy Birthday* lyrics, and they have staked their claim to the lyrics on that registration.

Our record does not contain any contractual agreement from 1935 or before between the Hill sisters and Summy Co. concerning the publication and registration of these works. What little information we have about the circumstances under which E51990 was published and registered comes from a federal lawsuit filed in 1942 by the Hill Foundation—an entity formed by Jessica and Patty—against Summy Co. in the Southern District of New York (hereafter, the "Hill–Summy lawsuit"). The Amended Complaint, discussed in more detail below, alleged that Summy Co. had granted licenses to movie and play producers without the Hill sisters' authorization. The Hill Foundation alleged that, in addition to an agreement between Mildred and Patty and Summy Co. concerning the copyright in *Song Stories* and *Good Morning* (the "First Agreement"), there was another agreement from 1934 and 1935 in which Jessica granted Summy Co. "a number of licenses" for "various piano arrangements of the song variously entitled 'GOOD MORNING TO ALL' or 'HAPPY BIRTHDAY TO YOU' " (the "Second Agreement"). In Summy Co.'s Answer to the Amended Complaint, it admitted that it had entered into the Second Agreement with Jessica, stating that she "assigned ... various piano arrangements of ... 'Good Morning To All' " to Summy Co. (J.A. 51 at ¶ 18.)

In 1944, the Hill sisters and Summy Co. settled the Hill–Summy lawsuit by entering into a new agreement (the "Third Agreement"). The Hill sisters, via the Hill Foundation, assigned to Summy Co. all of their rights in eleven different copyrights, including E51990, E51988, and the *Song Stories* copyright. After the Third Agreement, Summy Co. filed three lawsuits alleging copyright infringement related to *Happy Birthday.* E51990 is not mentioned in the complaints for any of these lawsuits. (*Id.*) When describing the song *Happy Birthday,* the complaints each said that "[o]ne of the songs in [*Song Stories*], entitled 'Good Morning To All', later became popularly known as 'Happy Birthday to You', the opening lines of the verses later written by Patty S. Hill for the song." None of the lawsuits asserted infringement of any purported right that Summy Co. had to the lyrics from its ownership of E51990.

On April 21, 2014, Plaintiffs filed their FACC in this action. (Dkt. 95.) Plaintiffs contend that Defendants do not own a copyright in the *Happy Birthday* lyrics and that they should be compelled to return the "millions of dollars of unlawful licensing fees" they have collected by wrongfully asserting copyright ownership in the *Happy Birthday* lyrics. We bifurcated this case on October 16, 2013. We will first determine whether Plaintiffs are entitled to a declaratory judgment invalidating Defendants' purported claim of copyright in the lyrics.

II. New Evidence

Both Parties recently sought to add new evidence to the summary judgment record after the Cross–Motions had been taken under submission. In particular, Plaintiffs seek to add evidence regarding the 1922 publication of the fourth revised edition of *The Everyday Song Book. Good Morning* and *Happy Birthday* are printed as one song called "Good Morning and Birthday Song" in the book. Below the title of the song, a caption reads: "Special permission through courtesy of The Clayton F. Summy Co." (*Id.*) Defendants do not oppose the introduction of this evidence into the record, but they dispute its significance. As Plaintiffs' request to supplement the record is unopposed, we hereby GRANT that request.

Defendants seek to introduce new evidence regarding the deposit copy of E51990. The Copyright Office no longer has the deposit copy for E51990, and Plaintiffs have argued that the *Happy Birthday* lyrics may not have even appeared in the work that was deposited. Defendants now proffer a copy of a work that was deposited with the British Museum on the same day that E51990 was registered, which they claim to have obtained recently. Plaintiffs argue that the introduction of this evidence is prejudicial because Defendants did not tell Plaintiffs that they were looking for a copy of the work from the British Museum during discovery. We do not see how Plaintiffs are prejudiced by Defendants' failure to disclose their efforts to find the British Museum copy. Plaintiffs were well aware of the dispute surrounding the deposit copy for E51990, and Defendants' disclosure of their earlier fruitless efforts would have had minimal, if any, impact on how Plaintiffs conducted discovery. Accordingly, we hereby GRANT Defendants' request to supplement the record.

[materials omitted]

V. Validity of Defendants' Copyright

Defendants claim to have a copyright in the *Happy Birthday* lyrics. As a musical work, *Happy Birthday* has at least two copyrightable elements, the music and the lyrics, and each element is protected against infringement independently. *See* 1–2 *Nimmer on Copyright* § 2.05 **The distinction between the music and the lyrics as copyrightable elements is critical in this**

case because both Parties agree that the *Happy Birthday* melody was borrowed from *Good Morning* and entered the public domain a long time ago. The Parties disagree only about the status of the *Happy Birthday* lyrics. Defendants contend, in brief, that the Hill sisters authored the lyrics to *Happy Birthday* around the turn of the last century, held onto the common law rights for several decades, and then transferred them to Summy Co., which published and registered them for a federal copyright in 1935. Plaintiffs challenge nearly every aspect of this narrative. They argue that the lyrics may have been written by someone else, the common law copyrights in the lyrics were lost due to general publication or abandonment before the lyrics were published, and the rights were never transferred to Summy Co.

[Can you identify and understand the two arguments? Make sure you understand.]

A. Presumption of Validity

Before we address the merits of the Parties' respective arguments, we must consider what evidentiary weight should be afforded to the registration certificate for E51990. The 1909 Copyright Act, which governs E51990, did not require that a work be registered to obtain a federal copyright. *See* 2–7 *Nimmer* § 7.16. But registration was nonetheless highly desirable, not only because it was a precondition to the filing of an infringement suit, but also because, once registered, the certificate of registration "shall be admitted in any court as prima facie evidence of the facts stated therein." 17 U.S.C. § 209 (1909 Act); *see also* 17 U.S.C. § 410(c) (1976 Act) Furthermore, "[a]lthough the 'facts' stated in a certificate of registration are limited to the date, name and description of the work, and name of the registration holder, a majority of courts have held that § 209 [of the 1909 Copyright Act] creates a rebuttable presumption that the certificate holder has met all the requirements for copyright validity." *Acad. of Motion Picture Arts & Scis. v. Creative House Promotions, Inc.*, 944 F.2d 1446, 1451 (9th Cir.1991). Once a claimant shows that she has a certificate of registration, the burden of proof shifts to the opposing party who must "offer some evidence or proof to dispute or deny the [claimant's] prima facie case." *United Fabrics Int'l, Inc. v. C & J Wear, Inc.*, 630 F.3d 1255, 1257 (9th Cir.2011).

[material omitted]

E51990 Registration: Piano Arrangement

Defendants claim that Summy Co. registered the *Happy Birthday* lyrics in E51990. In 1935, a certificate of copyright registration was a very simple document consisting of nothing more than a copy of the claimant's registration application and a certification statement from the Copyright Office. The registration application for E51990 stated that it was an "Application for Copyright for Republished Musical Composition with New Copyright Matter." (J.A. 48.) **In other words, E51990 was a derivative work**. *See* 17 U.S.C. § 101 (1976 Act) ("A 'derivative work' is a work based upon one or more preexisting works, such as a ... musical arrangement...."). The title of the musical composition was listed as "Happy Birthday to You." (J.A. 48.) The **author of the new copyright material** was "Preston Ware Orem, employed for hire by Clayton F. Summy Co." (*Id.*) In one blank space, the application prompted the claimant to "[s]tate exactly on what new matter copyright is claimed...." (*Id.*) For E51990, the response read: "**Arrangement as easy piano solo, with text." (*Id.*)**

Defendants contend that this registration entitles them to a presumption of validity. We disagree. Even assuming that the lyrics were printed in the deposit copy for E51990, it is unclear whether those lyrics were being registered, and therefore it is unclear whether the Copyright Office determined the validity of Summy Co.'s alleged interest in the lyrics in 1935. The "new matter" that the registration purported to cover was a **piano arrangement**—a derivative version of another melody. Defendants argue that since the arrangement was registered "with text," that meant that the *Happy Birthday* lyrics were part of the new matter being registered alongside the arrangement. But the registration clearly listed "Preston Ware Orem" as the author of the new matter. **To our knowledge, no one has ever contended that Orem wrote the *Happy Birthday* lyrics.** Defendants even admit in their pleadings that Orem did not do so. Therefore, the registration is flawed in any event. If, as Defendants assert, the new matter being registered included the lyrics, then, contrary to the registration certificate, Mr. Orem could not have been the author of the new matter. Conversely, if Mr. Orem were the author of the new matter, then the lyrics could not have been a part of the registration.

[material omitted]

Because this registration does not list any Hill sister as the author or otherwise make clear that the *Happy Birthday* lyrics were being registered, we cannot presume this registration reflects the Copyright Office's determination that Summy Co. had the rights to the lyrics to copyright them.

Given this facial and material mistake in the registration certificate, we cannot presume (1) that Patty authored the lyrics or (2) that Summy Co. had any rights to the lyrics at the time of the E51990 registration. Accordingly, Defendants must present other evidence to prove their case.

Normally, at this point, we would proceed with our analysis of the Parties' Cross–Motions by first examining the elements that Defendants must prove to establish the validity of their interest in the *Happy Birthday* lyrics, and then, if Defendants carry their burden, we would turn to Plaintiffs' affirmative defenses. However, the factual and legal issues of this case are deeply interwoven and do not lend themselves to a traditional analytical approach. The nature of this lawsuit is a dispute over the provenance of Defendants' purported interest in the lyrics. Accordingly, a chronological examination of the issues, tracing the history of the lyrics up to the point when Summy Co. supposedly acquired the rights to them, is more logical. Thus, we will begin with the **question of who wrote *Happy Birthday*,** an issue for which **Defendants have the burden of proof because they must show that their interest can be traced back to the true author of the lyrics.** Then we will consider whether the lyrics were **lost or abandoned** at some point after they were written, both of which are defenses for which Plaintiffs, who would normally be defendants in a traditional infringement suit, have the burden of proof. Finally, we will turn to the question of **whether a valid transfer of rights occurred between the Hill**

sisters and Summy Co., an issue for which Defendants again have the burden of proof because it is essential to their claim that Summy Co. is the owner of a valid copyright.

B. Who Wrote the *Happy Birthday* Lyrics?

Defendants claim that Patty wrote the lyrics to *Happy Birthday*; Plaintiffs claim someone else may have.

Since Plaintiffs do not have the burden of proof on this issue, they may discharge their initial burden on their Motion by pointing to affirmative evidence negating Defendants' authorship claim. Plaintiffs point to the many publications of the *Happy Birthday* lyrics throughout the 1920s and 1930s that did not credit Patty. References to the lyrics (without full publication) appeared in 1901 and 1909. The words were fully published in 1911, 1912, 1915, 1922, 1924, and 1928. The song was performed in several movies in the early to mid–1930s. **Furthermore, though none of these publications explicitly credited anyone with authoring the *Happy Birthday* lyrics, several of them were copyrighted, and the certificates of registration listed other authors. For instance, *The Elementary Worker and His Work*, which was published in 1911 and contained the full *Happy Birthday* lyrics, listed Alice Jacobs and Ermina Chester Lincoln as its authors in the copyright certificate.** Given that copyright certificates are normally afforded a presumption of validity, as discussed, this is at least some evidence that these two individuals may have authored the *Happy Birthday* lyrics. **Similarly, the publication and registration of the *Happy Birthday* lyrics in *Harvest Hymns* in 1924 demonstrate that its author may have written the lyrics.** (J.A. 19 (listing "Robert Henry Coleman" as author of *Harvest Hymns*).) This evidence is sufficient to shift the burden to Defendants to proffer admissible evidence to create a genuine issue for trial. *Celotex Corp.*, 477 U.S. at 324, 106 S.Ct. 2548.

Defendants' primary evidence is Patty's 1935 deposition for the *As Thousands Cheer* lawsuit. While explaining that she and her sister Mildred created *Good Morning* some time around 1893, Patty claimed to have also written the *Happy Birthday* lyrics as one of a number of lyrical variations to be sung with the familiar melody:

Q. How long would you say that you and Miss Mildred Hill worked on the particular song "Good Morning To All" before it was completed.
A. It was one of the earliest of the group and for that reason took longer to work out with the children. It would be written and I would take it into the school the next morning and test it with the little children. If the register was beyond the children we went back home at night and altered it and I would go back the next morning and try it again and again until we secured a song that even the youngest children could learn with perfect ease and while only the words "Good Morning To All" were put in the book we used it for "Good-bye to you", "Happy Journey to You", "Happy Christmas to You" and "Happy New Year to You", "Happy Vacation to You" and so forth and so on.
Q. Did you also use the words "Happy Birthday to You"?
A. We certainly did with every birthday celebration in the school.

Q. Did you write the words for this particular tune of "Good Morning To All", Miss Hill?
A. I did.
(J.A. 87 at 1007.)

Defendants have raised genuine issues of material fact for trial. **A reasonable fact finder may choose to believe that Patty wrote the lyrics in 1893 but, for whatever reason, failed to publically say so until some forty years later. But a reasonable fact finder could also find that the *Happy Birthday* lyrics were written by someone else, such as the authors of *The Elementary Worker and His Work* or *Harvest Hymns* or some unknown person who never took credit for them, and that Patty's 1935 claim to authorship was a *post hoc* attempt to take credit for the words that had long since become more famous and popular than the ones she wrote for the classic melody.**

For the same reasons, Patty's deposition testimony would not be sufficient to entitle Defendants to a directed verdict on the issue of authorship because it is contradicted by the evidence of **multiple publications of the lyrics before 1935, some of which were registered for copyrights**. We conclude there are genuine issues of material fact for trial. The Parties' Cross–Motions are DENIED on this issue.

C. Divestive Publication of the *Happy Birthday* Lyrics

Plaintiffs claim that, even if Patty wrote the *Happy Birthday* lyrics, she lost the rights to the lyrics through **divestive publication before 1935**.

Under the Copyright Act of 1909, one secured a federal copyright by **publishing a work with proper notice**. Before such publication, the work was protected by common law copyright. *See Estate of Martin Luther King, Jr., Inc. v. CBS, Inc.*, 194 F.3d 1211, 1214 (11th Cir.1999) ("Under the regime created by the 1909 Act, an author received state common law protection automatically at the time of creation of a work. This state common law protection persisted until the moment of a general publication.") If the work was published *without* notice, two things happened: the author (1) failed to obtain a federal copyright and (2) lost the common law copyright as well. *See Twin Books Corp. v. Walt Disney Co.*, 83 F.3d 1162, 1165 (9th Cir.1996) ("When a work was published for the first time, it lost state common law protection. The owner could, however, obtain federal protection for the published work by complying with the requirements of the 1909 Copyright Act. If the owner failed to satisfy the Act's requirements, the published work was interjected irrevocably into the public domain precluding any subsequent protection of the work under the 1909 Copyright Act.").

General publication, which would cause a forfeiture, occurs "when, by consent of the copyright owner, the original or tangible copies of a work are sold, leased, loaned, given away, or otherwise made available to the general public, or when an authorized offer is made to dispose of the work in any such manner, even if a sale or other such disposition does not in fact occur." 1 *Nimmer* § 4.03. By contrast, a limited publication, which does not cause a forfeiture, is when "tangible copies of the work are distributed both (1) to a 'definitely selected group,' and (2) for a limited purpose, without the right of further reproduction, distribution or sale." *Acad. of Motion Picture Arts & Scis.*, 944 F.2d at 1452. Moreover, "mere performance or exhibition of a work does not constitute a [general] publication of that work." *Am. Vitagraph, Inc. v. Levy*, 659 F.2d 1023, 1027 (9th Cir.1981).

On this affirmative defense of divestive publication, Plaintiffs have the burden of proof and must point to evidence that would entitle them to a directed verdict at trial if it were uncontroverted. While Plaintiffs emphasize heavily the evidence in the record showing that the lyrics were "published, publicly performed, and sung millions of times for more than three decades," that is insufficient to show divestive publication in this case. (Jt. Br. at 7.) **Unless the owner of the work published it personally or authorized someone else to publish it, she would not be divested of her common law copyright.** *See* 2–7 *Nimmer* § 7.03 ("[A] public distribution of copies or phonorecords will not trigger the legal consequences of a publication without notice unless it is shown that such public distribution occurred by or under the authority of the copyright owner."); *see also Holmes v. Hurst*, 174 U.S. 82, 19 S.Ct. 606, 43 L.Ed. 904 (1899) (author forfeited his work after consenting to its publication); *Egner v. E.C. Schirmer Music Co.*, 48 F.Supp. 187 (D.Mass.1942) (author lost his rights after giving others permission to publish his song); *Blanc v. Lantz*, 83 U.S.P.Q. 137, 1949 WL 4766 (Cal.Super.1949) (author lost his rights after permitting the distribution and exhibition of his work in movie theaters throughout the world).

Plaintiff's strongest evidence in support of their divestive publication defense is the publication of *Happy Birthday* in *The Everyday Song Book* in 1922. Unlike the other publications in the record, the publisher of *The Everyday Song Book* appears to have had the permission of at least Summy Co. to print *Good Morning* and *Happy Birthday*. A fact finder could reasonably infer from this that the Hill sisters authorized Summy Co. to grant the publisher permission. After all, Summy Co. and the Hill sisters were hardly strangers at the time; they had been associated with each other through the publication and distribution of *Song Stories* for decades. **If the publication was authorized, that could make it a general publication (without proper copyright notice), divesting the Hill sisters of their common law copyright.**

The publication of *The Everyday Song Book*, however, is not sufficient to entitle Plaintiffs to a directed verdict at trial. **As Defendants point out, there is no direct evidence that the Hill sisters had authorized Summy Co. to grant permission for the publication of the lyrics in *The Everyday Song Book*. It is undisputed that, in 1922, Summy Co. did not have any rights to the *Happy Birthday* lyrics; Defendants claim that the rights to the lyrics were given to Summy Co., at the earliest, in 1934 and 1935.** It is also not clear if Summy Co. gave the publisher of *The Everyday Song Book* permission to publish the *Happy Birthday* lyrics specifically or just permission to publish *Good Morning,* of which Summy Co. had been printing and selling copies on the Hill sisters' behalf at that time. Since the publication of *The Everyday Song Book* would not be sufficient to entitle Plaintiffs to a directed verdict, Plaintiffs cannot satisfy their initial burden under Rule 56. Accordingly, Plaintiffs' Motion is DENIED as to this issue.

As to Defendants' Cross–Motion, while the publication of *The Everyday Song Book* is not sufficient to entitle Plaintiffs to a directed verdict, it is at least sufficient to show that there are genuine disputes of material fact. Accordingly, Defendants' Cross–Motion is also DENIED as to this issue.

D. Abandonment of the *Happy Birthday* Lyrics

Plaintiffs argue that, even if no divestive publication occurred, Patty abandoned her rights, if any, before the publication and registration of E51990. "[A]bandonment of copyright occurs only if there is an intent by the copyright proprietor to surrender rights in his work." *A & M Records, Inc. v. Napster, Inc.*, 239 F.3d 1004, 1026 (9th Cir.2001) (internal quotation marks omitted). Under Ninth Circuit law, abandonment "must be manifested by some overt act indicative of a purpose to surrender the rights and allow the public to copy." *Hampton v. Paramount Pictures Corp.*, 279 F.2d 100, 104 (9th Cir.1960). Compared to divestive publication, "[a]bandonment ... turns on the copyright owner's intent, while forfeiture results by operation of law regardless of intent." 2 Patry, *Copyright* § 5:155.

In their supplemental briefing on abandonment, both Parties have cited numerous cases in support of their respective positions regarding abandonment. **Unfortunately, we can discern no clear rule for what does or does not constitute abandonment.** Cases from the early to mid-Twentieth Century fail to make a clear distinction between divestive publication and abandonment. *See, e.g., White v. Kimmell*, 193 F.2d 744, 745 (9th Cir.1952) (describing the plaintiff's complaint as alleging that the work was "abandoned by White to the general public by his reproducing and distributing copies ... without notice of claim of copyright"); *Nutt v. Nat'l Inst. Inc. for the Improvement of Memory*, 31 F.2d 236, 238 (2d Cir.1929) ("Only a publication of the manuscript, amounting to an abandonment of the rights of the author, will transfer it to public domain."); *Egner*, 48 F.Supp. at 189 (describing author's conduct as showing "such a tender of the song to the public generally as to imply an abandonment"). It is difficult to draw any firm conclusions about abandonment from these cases. As for the more recent cases, most involve factual circumstances that bear little resemblance to this case. *See, e.g., Hadady Corp. v. Dean Witter Reynolds, Inc.*, 739 F.Supp. 1392, 1395 n. 2, 1398–99 (C.D.Cal.1990) (abandonment found where newsletter stated it was protected by copyright only for a certain amount of time); *Pac. & S. Co. v. Duncan*, 572 F.Supp. 1186, 1196 (N.D.Ga.1983) (abandonment found where copyright owner destroyed the only copy of the work). As far as a general rule, we think the most that can be said about abandonment is that evidence of mere inaction or "lack of action" is insufficient. *Hampton*, 279 F.2d at 104. Beyond this, what does or does not constitute abandonment appears to be a highly fact-specific inquiry.

1. Overt Acts of Abandonment by Patty

Plaintiffs bear the burden of proof at trial on this affirmative defense. To prevail on their Motion, Plaintiffs must present evidence entitling them to a directed verdict if uncontradicted. They present a passage from a *TIME* magazine article reporting on the *As Thousands Cheer* lawsuit, which said:

Because the tune of "Happy Birthday to You" sounds precisely like the tune of "Good Morning to All," Sam H. Harris, producer of *As Thousands Cheer,* last week found himself the defendant in a Federal plagiarism suit asking payment of $250 for each and every performance of the song.... **Lyricist Patty Hill, who will share in the damages, if any, *had no complaint to make on the use of the words because she long ago resigned herself to the fact that her ditty had become common property of the nation.*** The clear implication from the article is that Patty told the *TIME* journalist that she had surrendered any claim she may have had to the *Happy Birthday* lyrics. **A public statement like this, if believed, is an overt act on which a reasonable fact finder could base a finding that Patty abandoned her copyright interest in the lyrics.** *See Melchizedek v. Holt,* 792 F.Supp.2d 1042, 1048, 1061 (D.Ariz.2011) (finding triable issue of fact where author made public statements indicating that he was not interested in protecting his work). However, we cannot say that this evidence is sufficient to entitle Plaintiffs to a directed verdict at trial inasmuch as it is not a direct quote from Patty. The journalist could have been paraphrasing something she said or relying on a secondary source to characterize her intentions. Accordingly, Plaintiffs' Motion on their affirmative defense of abandonment is DENIED. To the extent Defendants cross-move for summary judgment on abandonment, we conclude that this article is at least sufficient to raise triable issues of fact as to whether Patty abandoned her rights.

2. Joint Authorship

In the alternative, Defendants argue they are entitled to summary judgment on abandonment because Mildred and Patty were joint authors of the *Happy Birthday* lyrics so that Plaintiffs must at least raise triable issues of fact as to both Mildred's (or Jessica's as heir to Mildred's rights) and Patty's abandonment to survive summary judgment against them. They argue that even if there are triable issues as to Patty's abandonment, Plaintiffs have no evidence of any overt acts of abandonment by either Mildred or Jessica.

A joint work is defined as "a work prepared by two or more authors with the intention that their contributions be merged into inseparable or interdependent parts of a unitary whole." 17 U.S.C. § 101 (1976 Act); *Richlin v. Metro–Goldwyn–Mayer Pictures, Inc.,* 531 F.3d 962, 968 (9th Cir.2008) (stating that the 1976 Act's definition of joint work "incorporated the well-established case law interpreting the definition of 'joint work' under the 1909 Act"). The Ninth Circuit has articulated three factors to consider in determining joint authorship: (1) whether the "putative coauthors ma[de] objective manifestations of a shared intent to be coauthors"; (2) whether the alleged authors superintended the work by exercising control; and (3) whether "the audience appeal of the work" can be attributed to both authors, and whether "the share of each in its success cannot be appraised." *Aalmuhammed v. Lee,* 202 F.3d 1227, 1234 (9th Cir.2000) (internal quotation marks omitted).

Defendants point to Patty's deposition testimony in the *As Thousands Cheer* litigation in which she described working with Mildred in a collaborative, iterative process to create *Good Morning* and the other songs in *Song Stories.* (*See* J.A. 87 at 1007 ("It would be written and I would take it into the school the next morning and test it with the little children. If the register was beyond the children we went back home at night and altered it and I would go back the next morning and try it again and again until we secured a song that even the youngest children could learn with perfect ease ...."); *see also id.* at 1004 ("We were writing songs from 1889 to 1893."); *id.* at 1006 ("When my sister Mildred and I began the writing of these songs....").) If Mildred and Patty created the *Happy Birthday* lyrics as a part of this process, that would be evidence that Mildred and Patty intended to be co-authors and that both exercised control over the work.

It is not clear from Patty's deposition that the *Happy Birthday* lyrics were created as a part of the described collaborative process. The deposition took place in the context of a lawsuit in which Jessica was asserting infringement of the copyright to *Good Morning,* not *Happy Birthday*. Accordingly, virtually the entire deposition centered on how *Song Stories* and *Good Morning* were created. There are very few points in the transcript where one can discern any clear reference to *Happy Birthday*. A reasonable fact finder could find that Patty's discussions of her collaboration with Mildred are not relevant because she was not talking about how the *Happy Birthday* lyrics were created. If Mildred had developed the *Happy Birthday/Good Morning* melody specifically for use with the *Good Morning* lyrics but Patty decided, on her own initiative, to use other lyrics in combination with the melody, then a fact finder could find that the *Happy Birthday* lyrics belonged to Patty alone as a derivative work. In that event, Mildred would not have had the requisite intent to combine her work (the *Happy Birthday/Song Stories* melody) with the *Happy Birthday* lyrics in order to make *Happy Birthday* a "work prepared by two or more authors with the intention that their contributions be merged into inseparable or interdependent parts of a unitary whole." 17 U.S.C. § 101 (1976 Act); *see also* 1–6 *Nimmer* § 6.05 ("The requisite distinction must lie instead in the intent of each contributing author at the time her contribution is composed. If his work is written with the intention that [his] contribution ... be merged into inseparable or interdependent parts of a unitary whole, then the merger of his contribution with that of others creates a joint work. If that intention occurs only after the work has been written, then the merger results in a derivative or collective work.") (Internal quotation marks and footnotes omitted).

Both Parties also try to use the pleadings to the Hill–Summy lawsuit from 1942 to reinforce their arguments about joint or sole authorship. Defendants emphasize the fact that the Hill Foundation described *Happy Birthday* as "written and composed" by Patty and Mildred. (J.A. 50 at ¶ 11.) Plaintiffs emphasize the fact that *Good Morning* was described as being "later" entitled *Happy Birthday* by both the Hill Foundation and Summy Co. Both of these arguments are inadequate to resolve, as a matter of law, the factual questions surrounding the creation of the *Happy Birthday* lyrics.

Because neither Party is entitled to summary judgment, we need not also consider whether there are triable issues as to Mildred's or Jessica's abandonment inasmuch as that issue is dependent on the joint authorship inquiry which cannot be resolved due to triable issues of fact.

The Parties' Cross–Motions for summary judgment on the issue of abandonment are DENIED.

E. Transfer of the *Happy Birthday* Lyrics

Plaintiffs argue that, even if the Hill sisters never lost or abandoned their common law rights to the *Happy Birthday* lyrics before the publication in E51990, Defendants have no evidence that Summy Co. ever obtained those rights. They contend that the evidence shows that E51990 was merely for one of several piano arrangements that Jessica authorized Summy Co. to publish and register. This showing is sufficient to discharge Plaintiffs' initial burden under Rule 56 as the party without the burden of proof at trial. Defendants argue that one or more of the agreements between the Hill sisters/the Hill Foundation and Summy Co. raise at least a triable issue that the former had transferred rights to the *Happy Birthday* lyrics to the latter.

1. The Hill–Summy Agreements

On the record before us, there is evidence of three agreements between the Hill sisters/the Hill Foundation and Summy Co.—the First, Second, and Third Agreements. Defendants' primary argument is that Jessica transferred rights in the *Happy Birthday* lyrics to Summy Co. under the Second Agreement in 1934 and 1935. (*See, e.g.,* Jt. Br. at 35, 37; Jt. Supp. Br. at 16.) What little we know of the Second Agreement is entirely based on the pleadings filed in the Hill–Summy lawsuit in 1942. The actual agreement is not in the record; nor is there any other description of the agreement. To determine the content of Second Agreement, then, we must examine the Hill–Summy pleadings closely, and in context.

The Amended Complaint contained two relevant causes of action. In the first cause of action, the Hill Foundation alleged that Mildred and Patty entered into the First Agreement in the 1890s, granting Mr. Summy and Summy Co. the rights to publish and register various versions of *Song Stories* in return for royalties on every copy sold. (J.A. 50 at ¶¶ 4–10.) The Amended Complaint noted that "one of the songs contained in the works mentioned and described in paragraphs 'FOURTH' to 'EIGHTH' [the paragraphs describing the various published versions of *Song Stories*] is one entitled 'GOOD MORNING TO ALL' which, with words written by the said PATTY S. HILL, was later entitled 'HAPPY BIRTHDAY TO YOU' and was included among the songs copyrighted as aforesaid by the said SUMMY." (*Id.* at ¶ 10.) The Hill Foundation alleged that "said song, 'HAPPY BIRTHDAY TO YOU'," later acquired a "nation-wide popularity" and was widely performed both musically and dramatically. (*Id.* at ¶ 11.)

The Amended Complaint then alleged that, at the time of the First Agreement, "sound motion pictures were unknown commercially." (*Id.* at ¶ 15.) Therefore, the First Agreement did not "contemplate the use of the aforementioned songs in sound motion pictures or dramatic performances or in any other wise or manner except in sheet music form." (*Id.*) Accordingly, the First Agreement did not give Summy Co. "the right to grant licenses or sub-licenses to the producers of sound motion pictures or dramatic performances in respect to the use of any of said songs therein and in particular the aforesaid song 'HAPPY BIRTHDAY TO YOU.' " (*Id.*) And yet, according to the Amended Complaint, that was precisely what Summy Co. had been doing: "secretly enter [ing] into various agreements with the producers of sound motion pictures and of stage or dramatic performances ... for the sound and dialogue rights for the use of the song 'HAPPY BIRTHDAY TO YOU' and purport[ing] to hold itself out as having the right to grant licenses or sub-licenses in respect to the use of the aforesaid song." (*Id.* at ¶ 18.) This conduct, the Hill Foundation alleged, was "in violation of the rights conferred upon" the Hill sisters and the Hill Foundation "by the copyright laws of the United States of America." (*Id.* at ¶ 20.)

In the second cause of action, the Hill Foundation alleged that Jessica had entered into another agreement in 1934 and 1935—the Second Agreement—granting Summy Co. "a number of licenses for the publication, sale and performance of various piano arrangements of the song variously entitled 'GOOD MORNING TO ALL' or 'HAPPY BIRTHDAY TO YOU' " in return for further royalties. (*Id.* at ¶ 24.) In contrast to the First Agreement, the Second Agreement apparently contemplated the use of these piano arrangements in motion pictures and plays, because Jessica was entitled to 50% of any payment Summy Co. received for the "*performance* [of the works] in any country." (*Id.* at ¶ 26 (emphasis added); *see also id.* at ¶ 24 (licenses granted "for the publication, sale and *performance* of various piano arrangements") (emphasis added).) The Hill Foundation then went on to say that "by reason of [Summy Co.'s] breach of duty and wrongful conduct as alleged in the paragraphs ... 'EIGHTEENTH' to 'TWENTIETH' [the paragraphs in the first cause of action describing the secret licensing agreements granted by Summy Co. to movie and play producers]," it was electing to terminate the Second Agreement. (*Id.* at ¶ 29.)

In its Answer, Summy Co. took issue with some of the Hill Foundation's allegations, but it agreed with most of the important points. As to the First Agreement, Summy Co. denied that the Hill sisters had granted it only limited rights in the sheet music of *Song Stories,* but admitted that it had granted licenses to movie and play producers for *Happy Birthday*. (J.A. 51 at ¶¶ 9, 12.) As to the Second Agreement, Summy Co. described it as "several so-called royalty contracts wherein and whereby it was provided that the said Jessica M. Hill sold, assigned, and transferred to [Summy Co.] various piano arrangements of the said musical composition 'Good Morning To All' and all world rights (including publishing, public performance and mechanical reproduction rights) ... of said work" in return for royalties. (*Id.* at ¶ 18.) Summy Co. confirmed that Jessica was to receive 50% of any payment made to Summy Co. for the "performance of said work." (*Id.*)

Defendants argue that a fact finder could reasonably infer from these pleadings that Jessica transferred rights to the *Happy Birthday* lyrics to Summy Co. under the Second Agreement, thus raising an issue of fact for trial. We disagree. Such an inference is so implausible that no reasonable fact finder could so find. *See Matsushita,* 475 U.S. at 586, 106 S.Ct. 1348 ("When the moving party has carried its burden under Rule 56(c), its opponent must do more than simply show that there is some metaphysical doubt as to the material facts.").

First, and most importantly, an inference that the Second Agreement had something to do with the *Happy Birthday* lyrics is not supported by any explicit description of the agreement in either the Amended Complaint or the Answer. Both the Hill Foundation and Summy Co. described the agreement as transferring rights in "piano arrangements." (J.A. 50 at ¶ 24; J.A. 51 at ¶ 18.)

Obviously, pianos do not sing. Thus, it is not logical to infer that rights to "piano arrangements" would include rights to any lyrics or words as well.

Defendants argue that the lyrics must have been part of the Second Agreement because the Amended Complaint described the arrangements as based on the "song variously entitled 'GOOD MORNING TO ALL' *or* 'HAPPY BIRTHDAY TO YOU.' " (J.A. 50 at ¶ 24 (emphasis added).) But this quoted statement says nothing about the transfer of any lyrics. The *Happy Birthday* lyrics could not have been "variously entitled" "Good Morning To All." If anything, it is a reference to the fact that *Good Morning* and *Happy Birthday* have the same melody and therefore are, in that sense, the same song that formed the basis of the piano arrangements. Notably, only a few sentences later, the Hill Foundation described the content of works involved in the Second Agreement again, but this time it called them "various piano arrangements of said song 'GOOD MORNING TO ALL' " with no reference to *Happy Birthday* at all. (*Id.* at ¶ 29.) In its Answer, Summy Co. similarly described the works as "various piano arrangements of the said musical composition 'Good Morning To All' " without mentioning *Happy Birthday*. (J.A. 51 at ¶ 18.)

Second, an inference that the Second Agreement covered the lyrics is unreasonable because it would be inconsistent with the underlying legal theory behind the lawsuit. If the Second Agreement had covered the *Happy Birthday* lyrics, that would have meant that in 1934 and 1935 Jessica explicitly granted Summy Co. the right to license the lyrics to others for public performance. (J.A. 50 at ¶ 24 (Second Agreement granted Summy Co. rights to "the publication, sale and *performance* ") (emphasis added); *id.* at ¶ 26 (Second Agreement gave Jessica right to 50% of any payment Summy Co. received for the "*performance* [of the works] in any country."); J.A. 51 at ¶ 18. (Second Agreement gave Summy Co. "all world rights (including publishing, *public performance* and mechanical reproduction rights) ... of said work") (emphasis added); *id.* (Second Agreement gave Jessica rights to 50% of any payment Summy Co. received "for the mechanical reproduction or *performance*" of the work "in any country") (emphasis added).) If that were the case, there would have been no reason for the Hill Foundation to accuse Summy Co. of "secretly" entering into deals behind the Hill sisters' backs with movie and play producers, granting them permission to publically perform *Happy Birthday*. Moreover, there would have been no reason for Summy Co. not to point out in its Answer that it had acquired the public performance rights to the lyrics from Jessica under the Second Agreement, since that fact would have given the company a strong defense to the accusation that what they were doing was somehow a "secret" or was otherwise unlawful.

Third, Defendants posit that the allegations in the Amended Complaint can be read to indirectly imply that the Second Agreement covered the *Happy Birthday* lyrics. But this theory is based on a misunderstanding of what the Amended Complaint actually said. Defendants' theory appears to be that the Hill Foundation sued Summy Co. because Jessica had granted Summy Co. permission to publish and distribute copies of the *Happy Birthday* lyrics in sheet music form under the Second Agreement, but Summy Co. had exceeded the scope of that agreement by granting movie and play producers the rights to publically perform the lyrics.

(*See* Jt. Supp. Br. at 16 ("In 1934 and 1935, Jessica granted Summy the rights to publish, copyright, and sell *Happy Birthday to You* [including the lyrics] as sheet music, in exchange for a percentage of the list price for sales.... Patty and Jessica's foundation, the Hill Foundation, sued Summy in 1942. The Foundation asserted that Summy had exceeded the scope of its license to publish *Happy Birthday to You* sheet music by sublicensing the 'sound *and dialogue* rights for the use of the song'—*i.e.*, the melody *and lyrics*—in movies and plays.") (emphasis in original); *see also* Hr'g Tr. of July 29, 2015 at 52:6–62:6 (colloquy with Defendants' counsel discussing transfer theory based on the Amended Complaint); Hr'g Tr. of March 23, 2015 at 37:8–40:11 (same).)

Defendants' theory is not consistent with the allegations in the Amended Complaint. As discussed, the Second Agreement was not limited to sheet music. That was the First Agreement. Moreover, the Hill Foundation did not accuse Summy Co. of exceeding the scope of the Second Agreement. That was, again, the First Agreement. In fact, the Hill Foundation did not accuse Summy Co. of doing anything unlawful with respect to the Second Agreement. Rather, it sought termination of the Second Agreement in light of Summy Co.'s alleged unlawful conduct with respect to the First Agreement. Finally, the Hill Foundation's accusation that Summy Co. exceeded the scope of the rights it possessed had nothing to do with the *Happy Birthday* lyrics. The Hill Foundation leveled that accusation in the first cause of action in the context of discussing the First Agreement, which covered only the *Happy Birthday/Good Morning* melody, not the *Happy Birthday* lyrics.

Finally, Defendants argue that Summy Co. must have been given the rights to the *Happy Birthday* lyrics because, otherwise, the Hill Foundation would have sued Summy Co. for publishing the lyrics in sheet music form without permission in 1935, in addition to accusing the company of granting unauthorized licenses to movie producers and others for public performance of those lyrics. (*See* Hr'g Tr. of July 29, 2015 at 59:11–21 ("MR. KLAUS: Your Honor, the question I would have, Your Honor, is then why seven years after Summy had published *Happy Birthday to You* with lyrics [as E51990] and if Jessica—if Jessica Hill is complaining about the fact that you are using this in motion pictures and I don't—I don't like you using it in motion pictures and I only granted you a license with respect to a particular musical arrangement that some other people have called *Good Morning to All* and some other people call *Happy Birthday to You,* why is there no complaint by Jessica Hill or the Hill Foundation about Summy's publishing the sheet music, including the lyrics?").) This argument fails as well. The record contains no evidence that the Hill Foundation chose not to sue Summy Co. for publishing the lyrics because Jessica had authorized the company to publish them. Defendants' argument is based on unsupported speculation, which cannot create a triable issue of fact in and of itself, especially where that speculation is premised in part on a theory that, for the reasons discussed above, would be inconsistent with, and is a misreading of, the allegations in the Amended Complaint. *See LVRC Holdings LLC v. Brekka,* 581 F.3d 1127, 1136 (9th Cir.2009) ("While we must draw all reasonable inferences in favor of the non-moving party, we need not draw inferences that are based solely on speculation.").

Defendants' fall-back argument is that, even if the Hill sisters/the Hill Foundation had not granted Summy Co. any rights in the Second Agreement, the Hill Foundation did so in the Third Agreement. This argument fails as well. Unlike the First and Second Agreement, we have a copy of the Third Agreement in the record. The Third Agreement was entered into in 1944 to resolve the Hill–Summy lawsuit. (*See* J.A. 126 at ¶ g.) Under the agreement, the Hill Foundation and the Hill sisters transferred all their "right, title and interest ... in" eleven different registered copyrighted works, including all the copyrights to the various published versions of *Song Stories* and the copyrights to E51990 and four other piano-based versions of *Happy Birthday* (presumably, the "various piano arrangements" of the Second Agreement). (*Id.* at ¶¶ a, 2.) Nowhere in the agreement is there any discussion of the *Happy Birthday* lyrics; nor is there any suggestion that the Hill sisters transferred their common law rights in the *Happy Birthday* lyrics to Summy Co.

The argument that the Third Agreement transferred the *Happy Birthday* lyrics to Summy Co. is circular. The agreement could have transferred such rights only if the lyrics were within the scope of one of the eleven copyrighted works that were the subject of the agreement. But the lyrics could have been within the scope of those registered copyrights only if, at some point in the past, the Hill sisters had given Summy Co. authorization to publish and register the lyrics. As already discussed, there is no evidence showing that the Hill sisters ever did that. Other than this circular argument, the Third Agreement itself contains no reference to the transfer of the *Happy Birthday* lyrics.

One last point is that we are mindful of the fact that the Second and Third Agreements, whatever their contents, cannot be considered in a vacuum. Defendants urge us to look to the intent of the contracting parties. (Hr'g Tr. of March 23, 2015 at 41:15–22 ("COURT: I'll take another look at the 1944 assignment, but it seems to me the 1944 assignment just assigned whatever rights they may have had in those specific copyright certificates as identified. So if that's it, then your argument becomes a little bit circular. MR. KLAUS: Well, I think it was all—it's a matter of intent as to what was covered by the assignment, Your Honor.").) But Defendants cannot point to any particular evidence that would show us the intent of contracting parties, aside from the evidence that we have already discussed. There is no evidence that Patty or any of the Hill sisters ever fought to protect the *Happy Birthday* lyrics on their own such that we might infer that they would have wanted to give their rights to Summy Co. to continue to protect them. The Hill sisters never tried to obtain a copyright for *Happy Birthday* on their own, even though Patty claimed to have written the lyrics decades earlier. None of the Hill sisters ever sued anyone for infringing the lyrics. Even Summy Co.'s behavior after the Third Agreement was executed does not show that any transfer occurred. Immediately after the Third Agreement was executed, Summy Co. filed several lawsuits alleging that *Happy Birthday* had been infringed. Yet, it never asserted that E51990, or any copyright interest it purportedly held in the lyrics had been infringed in those lawsuits. Looking to the intent of the parties does nothing to help Defendants' case because there is no evidence that the intent of the parties was to transfer the rights to the lyrics.

Accordingly, Defendants' Motion is DENIED, and Plaintiffs' Motion is GRANTED as to the issue of whether Summy Co. ever received the rights to the *Happy Birthday* lyrics from the Hill sisters.

VI. Conclusion

The summary judgment record shows that there are triable issues of fact as to whether Patty wrote the *Happy Birthday* lyrics in the late Nineteenth Century and whether Mildred may have shared an interest in them as a co-author. Even assuming this is so, neither Patty nor Mildred nor Jessica ever did anything with their common law rights in the lyrics. For decades, with the possible exception of the publication of *The Everyday Song Book* in 1922, the Hill sisters did not authorize any publication of the lyrics. They did not try to obtain federal copyright protection. They did not take legal action to prevent the use of the lyrics by others, even as *Happy Birthday* became very popular and commercially valuable. In 1934, four decades after Patty supposedly wrote the song, they finally asserted their rights to the *Happy Birthday /Good Morning* melody—but still made no claim to the lyrics.

Defendants ask us to find that the Hill sisters eventually gave Summy Co. the rights in the lyrics to exploit and protect, but this assertion has no support in the record. The Hill sisters gave Summy Co. the rights to the melody, and the rights to piano arrangements based on the melody, but never any rights to the lyrics. Defendants' speculation that the pleadings in the Hill–Summy lawsuit somehow show that the Second Agreement involved a transfer of rights in the lyrics is implausible and unreasonable. Defendants' suggestion that the Third Agreement effected such a transfer is circular and fares no better. As far as the record is concerned, even if the Hill sisters still held common law rights by the time of the Second or Third Agreement, they did not give those rights to Summy Co.

In light of the foregoing, Defendants' Motion is DENIED and Plaintiffs' Motion is GRANTED as set forth above. Because Summy Co. never acquired the rights to the *Happy Birthday* lyrics, Defendants, as Summy Co.'s purported successors-in-interest, **do not own a valid copyright in the *Happy Birthday* lyrics.**

IT IS SO ORDERED.

So what happened? What allows *Happy Birthday* to be in the public domain?

4: Unpublished Works

Unpublished works are an interesting category. Unpublished works do not ever require notice. Also, under the 1909 Act, they were covered by state laws, until they were published, upon which they were then protected by federal law, if they met the formality requirements. And the 1976 Copyright Act brought unpublished works under federal protection. To do that, there was a transition period to bring unpublished works protected perpetually by state law into limited times under federal law. Let's look again at the statute for unpublished works created and not published before January 1, 1978. Let's look again at the statute: Section 303(a).

> (a)Copyright in a work created before January 1, 1978, but not theretofore in the public domain or copyrighted, subsists from January 1, 1978, and endures for the term provided by section 302. In no case, however, shall the term of copyright in such a work expire before December 31, 2002; and, if the work is published on or before December 31, 2002, the term of copyright shall not expire before December 31, 2047.

January 1, 2003, marked a historic transformation in copyright law, and by extension, in scholarship, documentary films, and culture at large. For the first time, unpublished works automatically began entering the public domain in the United States, and will now continue to do so, just as published works have for centuries, once their statutory term of copyright expires.

Section 303(a) of the Copyright Act brings a new found freedom never before experienced by those researchers, artists, and others whose work depends upon unpublished works. For the first time, users of unpublished works eventually will not have to seek copyright approval for the use of a particular letter or diary. This change may in itself seem innocuous, but it means the freedom to write, comment, criticize, and create new works without censorship from disapproving literary executors or copyright holders. It also means that once the copyright term has expired, users of unpublished works need not depend on the unreliable concept of fair use. Instead, the user may work with the text in confidence, knowing that because the unpublished work is now part of the public domain, the user is free to use the work as she wishes. Finally, by including unpublished work into federal law, unpublished works are subject to fair use, library uses, and other aspects of the 1976 Copyright Act. We even have a specific sentence in fair use that declares that it applies to unpublished works. Before 1978, unpublished works were governed by state laws. The shift to federal law mattered in so many ways. Section 303(a) opens up whole new worlds, strengthening scholarship, art, documentary filmmaking, storytelling (novels, films, television), and all of the other parts of our culture that utilize sources of our past to create new works for our future.

If an artist wants to use an unpublished Gustav Klimt sketch as the basis for a new artistic work, that is now possible without seeking approval from the copyright holder.5 If a documentary filmmaker wants to have an actor recite one of Thomas Edison's unpublished letters in its entirety, he need not worry about prohibitively high copyright fees. In some instances, such fees have become so high that they are altering the content of what gets included in anthologies.

If a scholar wants to write a biography of T.E. Lawrence, his unpublished works are now part of the public domain in the United States. Previously, that same scholar would have had to get permission from the copyright holder. Often, this meant the copyright holder was not only approving the use of primary materials, but also evaluating the argument itself. A copyright holder could easily prevent unflattering portraits by withholding the documents necessary to support the assertions. This, in fact, is what is at the heart of the *Shloss v. Joyce* copyright fair use and misuse case.

The 1976 Copyright Act brought unpublished works under the federal statutory system, giving them a limited term of protection, just as published works have had for centuries. Before the 1976 Act, unpublished works were protected by state common law copyright perpetually until publication, upon which they would then enter the federal system. The 1976 Copyright Act completely changed the nature and duration of protection for unpublished works. Section 302 of the 1976 Copyright Act created a unified system of duration whereby unpublished and published works alike carry copyright protection for the term of the life of the author plus seventy years. In order to aid the transition from a state common law perpetual system to a "limited Times" federal statutory system, the 1976 Copyright Act created two mechanisms for change. First, section 303(a) guaranteed that no work would enter the public domain until December 31, 2002, regardless of how long the author had been deceased. Second, that section provided an incentive for publication of unpublished works created before 1978. If the unpublished work was published for the first time between January 1, 1978 and December 31, 2002, the new published work would be granted further protection until December 31, 2047. This means that as of January 1, 2003, all unpublished works by authors who had been deceased longer than seventy years (deceased before January

1, 1933), became part of the public domain. Therefore, January 1, 2003, can be seen as marking the birth of the unpublished public domain. Each year, additional unpublished materials are added to the public domain. For example, as of 2021, the public domain includes unpublished works from authors deceased before 1951. However, any works that were published for the first time between January 1, 1978 and December 31, 2002 will remain under copyright until at least December 31, 2047.

Unpublished works come in all forms. We naturally think of diaries, unpublished letters, sketches for paintings, and unpublished manuscripts. A newly discovered Hemingway short story, a manuscript version of a lost Beethoven piano piece, and a grocery list from the 1900s are all examples of unpublished works. Letters sent to presidents and fan mail sent to movie stars are additional examples that come to mind. But unpublished works also include films, both home movies and those produced by Hollywood studios, unpublished photographs, unpublished comics, and scrapbooks filled with family photos. Anthony Reese has organized unpublished works into three categories: 1) private works such as letters, diaries and manuscripts; 2) preparatory works including early drafts of manuscripts and extra film footage; and 3) works performed and displayed works like radio and television, but not technically published. There is no question that January 1, 2003, brought the largest influx of materials into the public domain at one time, and yet few seemed to have been aware of this new category.

Section 303(a) of the Copyright Act looks deceptively simple: an unpublished work created before 1978 that is published for the first time between January 1, 1978, and December 31, 2002, will receive additional protection until December 31, 2047. Works that remain unpublished as of 2002 receive the same protection as published works created after January 1, 1978, that is, for the life of the author plus seventy years. In no case, however, would any unpublished materials come into the public domain under this new scheme before December 31, 2002, even if the author had been deceased more than seventy years.24 If the work was a work for hire, then the term is 120 years from creation. Section 303(a) also includes all corporate works created before 1886.

"Unpublished" Under the 1909 Act

To qualify for additional protection under section 303(a), a work must have been unpublished as of January 1, 1978.26 The definition of "unpublished" or "publication," therefore, is governed by the 1909 Act. However, the 1909 Act did not define "publication." This is further complicated by the fact that the 1909 Act had stiff penalties for improper execution of the copyright formalities required upon publication.

The 1909 Act required that when a work was published, an accompanying © symbol be attached to the work, along with the name of the copyright holder and the date, and that the work be properly deposited and registered with the Copyright Office. If any of these elements was missing, the newly published work immediately became part of the public domain. Courts mitigated this harsh penalty by creating the concept of "limited" versus "general" publication, whereby if a work was published in a limited context, it technically remained unpublished, and therefore was not subject to the formal requirements for federal copyright protection.29 Consequently, we must include in the category of "unpublished works" not only those works that were never distributed, but also those works that received limited publication under the 1909 Act and therefore also qualify as unpublished for the purpose of section 303(a) of the 1976 Copyright Act.

A "limited" publication was technically considered unpublished, and was not required to meet deposit, registration, or other formalities required of published works under the 1909 Act. For instance, an early Supreme Court case, *American Tobacco Co. v. Werckmeister*, determined that the display of a painting in a gallery did not constitute general publication. General publication occurred only when the work was sold, distributed, or loaned to the general public, without restrictions, qualifications, or limitations. An example of this is the sale of a book in a bookstore.

In contrast, only "limited" publication occurred if circulation satisfied a three-part test. First, the work was only communicated to a select group; second, the work was communicated to the select group for limited purposes; and third, those to whom the work had been communicated had no additional distribution rights to the work. A restricted archival collection that permits scholars access only for personal use and requires them to sign an agreement that the copies will not be further distributed is a classic example of limited publication.

One important example of how courts used the limited versus general publication doctrine to avoid inadvertent injection of a work into the public domain concerned Martin Luther King, Jr.'s "I Have a Dream" speech. The question was whether the fact that the speech was delivered before a wide audience and that copies of it were distributed to the news media without formal copyright notice and registration with the Copyright Office caused the "I Have a Dream" speech to come into the public domain. In 1963, a Southern District of New York Court, relying on precedent, found that the public performance of a work did not constitute publication. Regarding the distribution of the speech news media, the court concluded, "[t]here is nothing to suggest that copies of the speech were ever offered to the public; the fact is clear that the 'advance text' was given to the press only."

A second case addressing the same speech arose thirty years later, and the court reached the same conclusions. Once again, in Estate of Martin Luther King, Jr., Inc. v. CBS, Inc., the court decided that even though the speech was broadcast to a large, general audience, and copies of the speech were given out to the news media, this did not constitute general publication under the 1909 Copyright Act.43. The court reiterated that:

> [a] performance, no matter how broad the audience, is not a publication; to hold otherwise would be to upset a long line of precedent. This conclusion is not altered by the fact that the Speech was broadcast live to a broad radio and television audience and was the subject of extensive contemporaneous news coverage. We follow the above cited case law indicating that release to the news media for contemporary coverage of a newsworthy event is only a limited publication.44 The King rulings make sense because film, television, and radio shows were also considered unpublished in the "limited" publication sense.

"Limited" publication broadens the category of unpublished works to include not only traditional unpublished works like diaries, letters, and photographs, but also the nightly news, portraits displayed at museums, films, radio shows, and even Martin Luther King Jr.'s "I Have a Dream" speech. This means that many more unpublished works have potentially come into the public domain, as long as they remained unpublished through December 31, 2002, and their authors have been deceased for over seventy years, or in the case of a corporate work or a work for hire, 120 years from the creation have passed.

Unpublished Registered Works

One category of unpublished works disqualified from the additional protection afforded under section 303(a) is that of unpublished works registered under the 1909 Act. Section 12 of the 1909 Copyright Act set out an enumerated list of works that could be registered under the federal system. The category included lectures, dramatic or musical compositions, motion-picture photoplays, photographs, motion pictures, stills from motion pictures, and artistic works or drawings. If the copyright holder registered these works, these works would not qualify for the additional term of protection under section 303(a), even if the registered unpublished work was published between 1978 and 2002, as their copyright term is determined under the 1909 Copyright Act for published works.

Unpublished Works (specific categories)

To make matters more complicated, there are two categories of works that do not quite follow the rules set out above: visual art and sound recordings. Like unpublished works, sound recordings were protected by state common law copyright, with a perpetual term of protection, but they are protected in a slightly different manner in terms of a transition period to a federal statutory term. As of 2018, we now have new terms for pre-1972 sound recordings that we will look at in another chapter.

Art works present an even more complicated matter. Under the 1909 Act, a piece of art work was considered unpublished prior to any sale. Under this Act, courts determined that if the work was sold or offered for sale, the work should be considered published. Some courts also ruled that an art piece was published if the work was exhibited to the public without any copying restrictions. This makes the category of whether an art work was unpublished as of January 1, 1978 a little narrower.

"Published" Under the 1976 Copyright Act

Once it is determined that a work was considered "unpublished" under the 1909 Act, the next task is to determine whether the work was "published" between 1978 and 2002. The 1976 Copyright Act incorporated the case law developed under the 1909 Act with regard to publication and the distinction between limited and general publication. But in general, publication is less complicated under the 1976 Act, especially since there are no longer formality requirements upon publication.

By Whose Authority Did the Publication Take Place? Another significant question that arises is whether a publication "counts" if it is not authorized by the copyright holder. Copyright law forbids the unauthorized copying, distribution, public display or performance of a copyrighted work, as well as the unauthorized creation of a derivative work. Circular 22 from the Copyright Office states that "[u]nauthorized publication without the copyright notice, or with a defective notice, does not affect the validity of the copyright in the work." So, even if someone benevolently publishes unpublished works to get the additional protection, unless he is authorized to do so by the copyright holder, these efforts do not count as a publication.

Getting it Right

Section 303(a) gets it right. Why? The change gave copyright holders warning (notice) that the law was changing. The change also gave copyright holders twenty-five years to continue to exploit and exert copyright control over the works. It encouraged copyright holders to publish the unpublished works to gain more protection. But in the end, the goal was radically new for unpublished works. Regardless of the efforts of copyright holders, all unpublished works come into the public domain in the U.S. This had never happened before. Assumptions surrounding our relationship with unpublished works are significantly altered. In short, Section 303(a) of the 1976 Copyright Act brought unpublished works into the federal copyright system, and provided a transition period for copyright holders to further their economic opportunities to make unpublished works available to the public through publication, in return for forty-five more years of copyright protection.

Let's look at the example of British writer Vera Brittain (1893-1970). Her literary estate did just what they should have. In 1981, an edited collection of her diaries was published, followed by two more volumes in 1983 and 1989. This meant that the copyright was extended from the end of 2040 (life plus 70) to the end of 2047. More dramatically is the case of her brother and friends killed in the Great War—all British citizens killed in France or Italy. Her brother Edward Brittain, her fiancé Roland Leighton, and her friends, Victor Richardson and Geoffrey Thurlow all died between 1915 and 1918. Even though this is greater than seventy years, all of their unpublished letters were protected in the U.S. by federal statute through December 31, 2002, regardless of whether the copyright holder(s) elected to publish the letters. In this case, an edited collection of their letters was published in 1999, and therefore the published portions of the boys' letters are now protected through December 31, 2047—around 130 years after their deaths. This is how the system was supposed to work.

While the "traditional contours" of unpublished works being protected by state common law might have changed, the underlying notion of an incentive system did not. Also, there seems to be a nice balance of the public interest and the copyright holder. The public had twenty-five years to prepare for a work to be in the public domain, but knew from the beginning that at any time during that twenty-five year period, the copyright holder had one last shot at obtaining additional copyright protection. It was a transparent transition for all. Moreover, it retained the concept of balance—the essential element we are all taught when it comes to the IP clause.

For a scholar using these materials, Section 303(a) provides certainty and continuity—one will know when a work will be in the public domain. Before Section 303(a), unpublished works could be protected forever, unless they were published. Now, there is a time when that term ends.

Second, even if an unpublished work is published within the allotted time, we still have access to an interesting number of sources right now without asking permission. For example, in the Brittain example, only the portion of the boys' letters that were published are now protected through 2047. All of the unpublished scraps are now in the public domain, after December 31, 2002. This provides an incentive for scholars publishing works in the U.S. to use versions not previously published (because no permission is needed for those portions), which gets into circulation more materials most would not have access.

Again, Section 303(a) gets it right—providing incentives to copyright holders and to third parties.Section 303(a) incentivized copyright holders to make more available through publication of previously unpublished works. Section 303(a) in combination with 104(a) incentivizes scholars to look at new works, to sift through the unpublished versions, to do what scholars do...uncover hidden treasures not previously known.

5: Foreign Works in the U.S.

Beginning in 1790, we did not extend copyright protection to foreign authors for over 100 years. Many British and French authors saw this as deeply unfair including Charles Dickens and others. But the U.S. happily made available upon publication these works and countless others. No copyright protection means that works upon publication came into the public domain. The U.S. market was flooded with copies of British authors like Austen, Dickens, Bronte, and others. The Berne Convention, passed in 1888, was, in part, an attempt to get the U.S. to be more of a team player. The U.S. wouldn't join the team until 1989 – a hundred years later, and even then it would take till 1996 for the U.S. to be compliant and fair to foreign works. And it wouldn't be until Jan 1, 1996 that we would make amends for the treatment of foreign works properly.

There were two incremental steps that allowed for foreign works to gain copyright protection in the U.S. prior to 1989. First, in 1891, the Chase Act provided that as long as there was a bilateral treaty in place, authors of that foreign country could meet all of the formality requirements within the U.S. (and there were a few hurdles) to obtain protection. That same protection would be lost if there were missteps or the author did not renew within the 27th year. Then, in the 1950s came the Universal Copyright Convention, a multinational treaty. See the U.S. Copyright Office 38A Circular, International Copyright Relations of the United States, https://www.copyright.gov/circs/circ38a.pdf. However, both alternatives suffered from the renewal problem that required foreign authors to renew their works in the 28th year, and most did not.

The U.S.'s bad behavior caught up with it. As a country, we joined a few copyright treaties and were finally forced to treat foreign works properly. On January 1, 1996, millions of foreign works were restored automatically. Of course, the law is complicated. So, rule of thumb? Try not to use foreign works when you can. If you do, most are under copyright from 1925 to the present. Some may be out of copyright, but you have to check with a system like www.durationator.com.

Let's look at Section 104A. Can you sort out the requirements for automatic protection?

17 U.S. Code §104A

(a) Automatic Protection and Term.—

"(1) Term.—

"(A) Copyright subsists, in accordance with this section, in restored works, and vests automatically on the date of restoration.

"(B) Any work in which copyright is restored under this section shall subsist for the remainder of the term of copyright that the work would have otherwise been granted in the United States if the work never entered the public domain in the United States.

"(2) Exception.—Any work in which the copyright was ever owned or administered by the Alien Property Custodian and in which the restored copyright would be owned by a government or instrumentality thereof, is not a restored work.

"(b) Ownership of Restored Copyright.—A restored work vests initially in the author or initial rightholder of the work as determined by the law of the source country of the work.

"(c) Filing of Notice of Intent to Enforce Restored Copyright Against Reliance Parties.—On or after the date of restoration, any person who owns a copyright in a restored work or an exclusive right therein may file with the Copyright Office a notice of intent to enforce that person's copyright or exclusive right or may serve such a notice directly on a reliance party. Acceptance of a notice by the Copyright Office is effective as to any reliance parties but shall not create a presumption of the validity of any of the facts stated therein. Service on a reliance party is effective as to that reliance party and any other reliance parties with actual knowledge of such service and of the contents of that notice.

"(d) Remedies for Infringement of Restored Copyrights.—

"(1) Enforcement of copyright in restored works in the absence of a reliance party.—As against any party who is not a reliance party, the remedies provided in chapter 5 of this title shall be available on or after the date of restoration of a restored copyright with respect to an act of infringement of the restored copyright that is commenced on or after the date of restoration.

"(2) Enforcement of copyright in restored works as against reliance parties.—As against a reliance party, except to the extent provided in paragraphs (3) and (4), the remedies provided in chapter 5 of this title shall be available, with respect to an act of infringement of a restored copyright, on or after the date of restoration of the restored copyright if the requirements of either of the following subparagraphs are met:

"(A)(i) The owner of the restored copyright (or such owner's agent) or the owner of an exclusive right therein (or such owner's agent) files with the Copyright Office, during the 24-month period beginning on the date of restoration, a notice of intent to enforce the restored copyright; and

"(ii)(I) the act of infringement commenced after the end of the 12-month period beginning on the date of publication of the notice in the Federal Register;

"(II) the act of infringement commenced before the end of the 12-month period described in subclause (I) and continued after the end of that 12-month period, in which case remedies shall be available only for infringement occurring after the end of that 12-month period; or

"(III) copies or phonorecords of a work in which copyright has been restored under this section are made after publication of the notice of intent in the Federal Register.

"(B)(i) The owner of the restored copyright (or such owner's agent) or the owner of an exclusive right therein (or such owner's agent) serves upon a reliance party a notice of intent to enforce a restored copyright; and

"(ii)(I) the act of infringement commenced after the end of the 12-month period beginning on the date the notice of intent is received;

"(II) the act of infringement commenced before the end of the 12-month period described in subclause (I) and continued after the end of that 12-month period, in which case remedies shall be available only for the infringement occurring after the end of that 12-month period; or

"(III) copies or phonorecords of a work in which copyright has been restored under this section are made after receipt of the notice of intent.

"In the event that notice is provided under both subparagraphs (A) and (B), the 12-month period referred to in such subparagraphs shall run from the earlier of publication or service of notice.

"(3) Existing derivative works.—(A) In the case of a derivative work that is based upon a restored work and is created—

"(i) before the date of the enactment of the Uruguay Round Agreements Act, if the source country of the restored work is an eligible country on such date, or

"(ii) before the date on which the source country of the restored work becomes an eligible country, if that country is not an eligible country on such date of enactment,

"a reliance party may continue to exploit that derivative work for the duration of the restored copyright if the reliance party pays to the owner of the restored copyright reasonable compensation for conduct which would be subject to a remedy for infringement but for the provisions of this paragraph.

"(B) In the absence of an agreement between the parties, the amount of such compensation shall be determined by an action in United States district court, and shall reflect any harm to the actual or potential market for or value of the restored work from the reliance party's continued exploitation of the work, as well as compensation for the relative contributions of expression of the author of the restored work and the reliance party to the derivative work.

"(4) Commencement of infringement for reliance parties.—For purposes of section 412, in the case of reliance parties, infringement shall be deemed to have commenced before registration when acts which would have constituted infringement had the restored work been subject to copyright were commenced before the date of restoration.

"(e) Notices of Intent to Enforce a Restored Copyright.—

"(1) Notices of intent filed with the copyright office.—(A)(i) A notice of intent filed with the Copyright Office to enforce a restored copyright shall be signed by the owner of the restored copyright or the owner of an exclusive right therein, who files the notice under subsection (d)(2)(A)(i) (hereafter in this paragraph referred to as the "owner"), or by the owner's agent, shall identify the title of the restored work, and shall include an English translation of the title and any other alternative titles known to the owner by which the restored work may be identified, and an address and telephone number at which the owner may be contacted. If the notice is signed by an agent, the agency relationship must have been constituted in a writing signed by the owner before the filing of the notice. The Copyright Office may specifically require in regulations other information to be included in the notice, but failure to provide such other information shall not invalidate the notice or be a basis for refusal to list the restored work in the Federal Register.

"(ii) If a work in which copyright is restored has no formal title, it shall be described in the notice of intent in detail sufficient to identify it.

"(iii) Minor errors or omissions may be corrected by further notice at any time after the notice of intent is filed. Notices of corrections for such minor errors or omissions shall be accepted after the period established in subsection (d)(2)(A)(i). Notices shall be published in the Federal Register pursuant to subparagraph (B).

"(B)(i) The Register of Copyrights shall publish in the Federal Register, commencing not later than 4 months after the date of restoration for a particular nation and every 4 months thereafter for a period of 2 years, lists identifying restored works and the ownership thereof if a notice of intent to enforce a restored copyright has been filed.

"(ii) Not less than 1 list containing all notices of intent to enforce shall be maintained in the Public Information Office of the Copyright Office and shall be available for public inspection and copying during regular business hours pursuant to sections 705 and 708.

"(C) The Register of Copyrights is authorized to fix reasonable fees based on the costs of receipt, processing, recording, and publication of notices of intent to enforce a restored copyright and corrections thereto.

"(D)(i) Not later than 90 days before the date the Agreement on Trade-Related Aspects of Intellectual Property referred to in section 101(d)(15) of the Uruguay Round Agreements Act enters into force with respect to the United States, the Copyright Office shall issue and publish in the Federal Register regulations governing the filing under this subsection of notices of intent to enforce a restored copyright.

"(ii) Such regulations shall permit owners of restored copyrights to file simultaneously for registration of the restored copyright.

"(2) Notices of intent served on a reliance party.—(A) Notices of intent to enforce a restored copyright may be served on a reliance party at any time after the date of restoration of the restored copyright.

"(B) Notices of intent to enforce a restored copyright served on a reliance party shall be signed by the owner or the owner's agent, shall identify the restored work and the work in which the restored work is used, if any, in detail sufficient to identify them, and shall include an English translation of the title, any other alternative titles known to the owner by which the work may be identified, the use or uses to which the owner objects, and an address and telephone number at which the reliance party may contact the owner. If the notice is signed by an agent, the agency relationship must have been constituted in writing and signed by the owner before service of the notice.

"(3) Effect of material false statements.—Any material false statement knowingly made with respect to any restored copyright identified in any notice of intent shall make void all claims and assertions made with respect to such restored copyright.

"(f) Immunity From Warranty and Related Liability.—

"(1) In general.—Any person who warrants, promises, or guarantees that a work does not violate an exclusive right granted in section 106 shall not be liable for legal, equitable, arbitral, or administrative relief if the warranty, promise, or guarantee is breached by virtue of the restoration of copyright under this section, if such warranty, promise, or guarantee is made before January 1, 1995.

"(2) Performances.—No person shall be required to perform any act if such performance is made infringing by virtue of the restoration of copyright under the provisions of this section, if the obligation to perform was undertaken before January 1, 1995.

"(g) Proclamation of Copyright Restoration.—Whenever the President finds that a particular foreign nation extends, to works by authors who are nationals or domiciliaries of the United States, restored copyright protection on substantially the same basis as provided under this section, the President may by proclamation extend restored protection provided under this section to any work—

"(1) of which one or more of the authors is, on the date of first publication, a national, domiciliary, or sovereign authority of that nation; or

"(2) which was first published in that nation.

"The President may revise, suspend, or revoke any such proclamation or impose any conditions or limitations on protection under such a proclamation.

"(h) Definitions.—For purposes of this section and section 109(a):

"(1) The term "date of adherence or proclamation" means the earlier of the date on which a foreign nation which, as of the date the WTO Agreement enters into force with respect to the United States, is not a nation adhering to the Berne Convention or a WTO member country, becomes—

"(A) a nation adhering to the Berne Convention;

"(B) a WTO member country;

"(C) a nation adhering to the WIPO Copyright Treaty;

"(D) a nation adhering to the WIPO Performances and Phonograms Treaty; or

"(E) subject to a Presidential proclamation under subsection (g).

"(2) The "date of restoration" of a restored copyright is—

"(A) January 1, 1996, if the source country of the restored work is a nation adhering to the Berne Convention or a WTO member country on such date, or

"(B) the date of adherence or proclamation, in the case of any other source country of the restored work.

"(3) The term "eligible country" means a nation, other than the United States, that—

"(A) becomes a WTO member country after the date of the enactment of the Uruguay Round Agreements Act;

"(B) on such date of enactment is, or after such date of enactment becomes, a nation adhering to the Berne Convention;

"(C) adheres to the WIPO Copyright Treaty;

"(D) adheres to the WIPO Performances and Phonograms Treaty; or

"(E) after such date of enactment becomes subject to a proclamation under subsection (g).

"(4) The term "reliance party" means any person who—

"(A) with respect to a particular work, engages in acts, before the source country of that work becomes an eligible country, which would have violated section 106 if the restored work had been subject to copyright protection, and who, after the source country becomes an eligible country, continues to engage in such acts;

"(B) before the source country of a particular work becomes an eligible country, makes or acquires 1 or more copies or phonorecords of that work; or

"(C) as the result of the sale or other disposition of a derivative work covered under subsection (d)(3), or significant assets of a person described in subparagraph (A) or (B), is a successor, assignee, or licensee of that person.

"(5) The term "restored copyright" means copyright in a restored work under this section.

"(6) The term "restored work" means an original work of authorship that—

"(A) is protected under subsection (a);

"(B) is not in the public domain in its source country through expiration of term of protection;

"(C) is in the public domain in the United States due to—

"(i) noncompliance with formalities imposed at any time by United States copyright law, including failure of renewal, lack of proper notice, or failure to comply with any manufacturing requirements;

"(ii) lack of subject matter protection in the case of sound recordings fixed before February 15, 1972; or

"(iii) lack of national eligibility;

"(D) has at least one author or rightholder who was, at the time the work was created, a national or domiciliary of an eligible country, and if published, was first published in an eligible country and not published in the United States during the 30-day period following publication in such eligible country; and

"(E) if the source country for the work is an eligible country solely by virtue of its adherence to the WIPO Performances and Phonograms Treaty, is a sound recording.

"(7) The term "rightholder" means the person—

"(A) who, with respect to a sound recording, first fixes a sound recording with authorization, or

"(B) who has acquired rights from the person described in subparagraph (A) by means of any conveyance or by operation of law.

"(8) The "source country" of a restored work is—

"(A) a nation other than the United States

"(B) in the case of an unpublished work—

"(i) the eligible country in which the author or rightholder is a national or domiciliary, or, if a restored work has more than 1 author or rightholder, of which the majority of foreign authors or rightholders are nationals or domiciliaries; or "(ii) if the majority of authors or rightholders are not foreign, the nation other than the United States which has the most significant contacts with the work; and

"(C) in the case of a published work—

"(i) the eligible country in which the work is first published, or

"(ii) if the restored work is published on the same day in 2 or more eligible countries, the eligible country which has the most significant contacts with the work."

104A Walkthrough

Not all foreign works required restoring. Many had renewed their term through the U.S. Copyright Office in the 28th year, and so the copyright had been continuous since the year of publication. But many foreign works had not met the formality requirements under the 1909 Copyright Act, and therefore, had fallen into the public domain in the U.S. The question was how a work would qualify for restoration under Section 104A. Using British author Vera Brittain's *Testament of Youth* (1936), let's walk through the steps.

To be a "restored work," Section 104A requires seven elements.

1. Original Work of Authorship

   First, the work must be an original work of authorship. This is a constitutional requirement for protection in the US, and requires only a modicum of creativity. Most works would meet this requirement, but some works in foreign countries would not meet the U.S. originality requirement, as it also requires fixation. But for most, this is not a difficult hurdle.

Take, for example, Vera Brittain's *Testament of Youth*. The memoir would have no problem meeting the originality and fixation requirement. Note, registration of the work also served to create a prima facie presumption of a valid copyright, "and hence, of originality," and since *Testament of Youth* was registered, it would also be presumed to meet the originality requirement.

2. Under Copyright in the Source Country

Second, the work must not be in the public domain in the source country through "expiration of term of protection". Using Vera Brittain as an example, we would have to determine whether *Testament of Youth* was still under copyright in the United Kingdom. Under UK copyright law, the work is under copyright for the life of the author plus seventy years, or through 2040, as Vera Brittain passed away in 1970. *Testament of Youth* therefore meets the second requirement.

The key here is that you must look to the law *at the time of measuring*, rather than the current law. And that may be difficult to determine. Take for instance, the United Kingdom. If the measuring date is the date of enactment of the URAA, which is the legislation that implemented Section 104A, it would be December 8, 1994, and the term in the UK was life plus 50. If it is when the work is restored, January 1, 1996, then the term would be life plus 70. The earlier date is more likely, but there is no consensus. In the case of Brittain's works, the difference doesn't matter.

3. An Eligible Source Country

The source country must have joined one of the following: the WTO, Berne, WIPO Copyright Treaty, WIPO Performances and Phonogram Treaty, or Presidential proclamation. This means that not all foreign works are eligible. Notably, countries without intellectual property treaties are not eligible for restoration, nor are countries that have only joined the Universal Copyright Convention. In the case of Brittain's *Testament of Youth*, was first published in the UK. The UK was a member of all of the treaties listed, and so her work was eligible for protection.

4. Public Domain in the United States

The fourth requirement is that the work must have gone into the public domain in the United States because of one of three of the following situations:

(i) noncompliance with formalities imposed at any time by United States copyright law, including failure of renewal, lack of proper notice, or failure to comply with any manufacturing requirements;

(ii) lack of subject matter protection in the case of sound recordings fixed before February 15, 1972; or

(iii) lack of national eligibility

In the case of Vera Brittain, we are focused on the first situation—noncompliance with formalities imposed at any time by United States copyright law. It looks like from the record that she was unaware that she needed to renew her work in the 27th year, as the first significant pieces – *Testament of Youth, Poems of the War and After* and *Testament of Friendship* were the first of her U.S. revisions to need renewing, and all three were not renewed, falling into the public domain in the U.S. in their 28th year of copyright (or for works published during or after 1950, after their 28th year).

After that, she and/or her family promptly renewed the works in the 27th year for those works that had been published in the U.S. Eleven of Brittain's works had been renewed; three had not. Had Vera Brittain known about the renewal requirement, there is no doubt in my mind that she would have renewed *Testament of Youth*, as it was her seminal life's work, but also brought great economic security to her and her family. The work was very popular in the U.S., and again, was a source of income and fame.

Section 104A was designed to restore works that suffered from just such a mistake in formalities, and to allow the author to reap the benefit of the copyright for the term as if it had not fallen into the public domain. The copyright page on the Penguin classic version of Testament of Youth seems to confirm this as well. It would appear that before Section 104A, *Testament of Youth* (1933), *The Poems of the War and After* (1934), and *Testament of Friendship* (1940) all entered the public domain due to lack of renewal, and remained free for all to use in the U.S. twenty-eight years after their publication. *Testament of Youth* had been in the public domain in the U.S. since 1961, or for thirty-seven years. In that time, a number of editions had been published, including the Penguin edition that had included a forward by her daughter, Shirley Williams. Interestingly, the Penguin version had not been registered with the Copyright Office. It was also published as a Penguin Classic in 1994. Then 104A was enacted.

PENGUIN BOOKS
Published by the Penguin Group
Penguin Books USA Inc., 375 Hudson Street,
New York, New York 10014, U.S.A.
Penguin Books Ltd, 27 Wrights Lane, London W8 5TZ, England
Penguin Books Australia Ltd, Ringwood, Victoria, Australia
Penguin Books Canada Ltd, 10 Alcorn Avenue,
Toronto, Ontario, Canada M4V 3B2
Penguin Books (N.Z.) Ltd, 182–190 Wairau Road,
Auckland 10, New Zealand

Penguin Books Ltd, Registered Offices:
Harmondsworth, Middlesex, England

First published in Great Britain by Victor Gollancz Limited 1933
First published in the United States of America
by The Macmillan Company 1933
This edition first published in Great Britain
by Virago Press Limited 1978
Published in Penguin Books 1989
Reissued in Penguin Books 1994

10

Copyright vera Brittain, 1933
Preface copyright © Shirley Williams, 1978
All rights reserved

Testament of Youth is now back under copyright in the U.S.

A second category is sound recordings. Sound recordings were not protected under federal copyright law in the U.S. until 1972. Before 1972, sound recordings were protected by state common law as unpublished works. A short window exists where sound recordings required proper notice to be considered published, and therefore, works without proper notice between 1972 and 1989 may have fallen into the public domain. But what is strange about Section 104A is that sound recordings, even though not protected by federal protection before 1972, remain under copyright and not in the public domain. They do not qualify for the next step. Only works in the public domain may be restored. Foreign works created before 1972 remain under state common law. The addition of this category is particularly peculiar and suspicious. A good deal of the legislative hearings discussed the need to protect U.S. works abroad, particularly sound recordings. In fact, the first TRIPS case the U.S. would submit to the WTO dispute resolution would be against Japan.

The 2012 U.S. Supreme Court case, *Golan v. Holder,* 565 U.S. 302 (2012*),* case concerned the third situation—works that had not been protected because no treaties existed between the U.S. and the source country. Russian paintings and classical music, for instance, had been in the public domain in the U.S. from their inception because the U.S. did not have treaty relations with Russia until May 27, 1973, when the Soviet Union joined the Universal Copyright Convention. Russian works in the public domain in the U.S. included literature by Alexander Block, Sergei Yesenin, Marina Tsvetaeva, Vladmiir Mayakovsky, Maxim Gorky, Vladimir Nabokov, Mikhail Sholokhov Mikhail Blugakov and Alexsandr Solzhenitsyn; and music by Prokofiev, Shostakovich, and Issak Dunayevsky. Section 104A automatically restored all of these works, as long as they met the other requirements.

5. Work must have gone into the public domain in the United States prior to ...

Strangely, the measuring date of when a work is in the public domain is not settled. The URAA enacts Section 104A as of December 8, 1994. So, that could be the measuring date. But works were not restored until January 1, 1996. Can you figure out a solution? Also, countries could join required treaties later. That would be the date of joining.

6. National or Domiciliary of Source Country other than the United States

At least one of the authors of the work must be a national or a domiciliary of the source country.

Vera Brittain was a citizen of the UK and resided in London during this particular period in the 1930s (and for most of her life).

7. First Published in a Source Country Other than the U.S.

Seventh, the first publication must have taken place in a country other than the U.S.

Here, *Testament of Youth* was first published in the UK in August 1933, and then later published in the U.S. around October 10, 1933, the U.S. *Testament of Youth*, therefore would qualify under its UK publication.

8. Limitation of Simultaneous Publication

The eighth requirement is that when the work was published, it must first have been published in the source country, and not published in the United States during the 30-day period following publication in such eligible country.

The 30-day period adopts the concept of "simultaneous" publication from the Berne Convention. "Simultaneous publication" had previously been used as a back-door method of gaining the protection of Berne in a non-Berne member country, particularly useful for Americans, as the U.S. did not join Berne until 1988. So, if in 1980, an American author published a work simultaneously in the US and Canada, that American author's work obtained Berne protection, as Canada is a member of Berne, even though the U.S. was not a party to Berne.

Now, simultaneous publication under Section 104A is being used a limitation on copyright restoration. Since "back door" Berne was used mostly by U.S. authors, this limitation means that Section 104A does not apply to U.S. works. But, we might see instances where the U.S. and foreign publication (for other reasons other than "back door" Berne protection) may have been published within 30 days. In that case, the foreign work's copyright would not be restored.

Term of Protection

If a work met all of the 104A requirements, then the work was restored under U.S. law, with the term according to its category, usually ninety-five years under Section 304, but potentially 302. Note: unpublished works are not covered by Section 104A. That would be covered by Section 104(a), Section 303(a) and Section 302.

104A in Action

Sandra Scheiber Johnson had an idea to take artist's Robert Delaunay's "Rythme Sans Fin," or "Endless Rhythm" painting and reproduce it in a quilt. She began researching the copyright status of the work. She contacted the Legal Department at Tate Museum, where the work was located. She got a response: "As far as we are concerned, as owners of the object, you may proceed happily as planned, perhaps referencing (when possible) the underlying work is in Tate's collection.' She had permission from the owners of the object. It is not clear that they also held the copyright (two separate things). But after Sandra contacted me, we decided to do a Durationator analysis to determine the status *in the U.S.* Even though the painting is located in London, Sandra would be making and displaying in the United States.

The 1934 painting was a foreign work. Robert Delauney was a French artist, who co-founded the Orphism art movement. He died in 1941. The work is out of copyright throughout the world including Europe, Canada, and Australia. The question was whether it was out of copyright in the U.S. as well. We did a Section 104A analysis. The work did not qualify for restoration. Therefore, the work is in the public domain in the United States. We provided a full Durationator report to Sandra.

Robert Delaunay, Endless Rhythm, 1934 (owned by the Tate Museum, https://www.tate.org.uk/art/artworks/delaunay-endless-rhythm-t01233)

Sandra's version is on the right.

Now, you may be asking, if a work is out of copyright, did she need to ask permission from the owner? Access to the object is different from copyright. It was a nice courtesy of her to reach out. But works in the public domain do not require permission. You may still need to ask permission for access, if that had been an issue. In this case, the image was on Tate's website. So, access was not an issue. Also, does it matter if the coloring is different?

The Twin Books problem in the 9th Circuit

> "It has never been clearly established whether a work only published abroad is to be treated as a published work for purposes of duration under U.S. law or should be treated as unpublished for these purposes."
>
> Paul Edward Geller, International Copyright Law and Practice.

Section 104A concerned only published or registered works. Unpublished works, as already discussed, are governed by Section 303(a). The question, then, is when is a foreign work considered published for the purposes of Section 104A? While the case law surrounding the 1909 Act had a great deal of commentary and opinion on what constituted general and limited publication, a strange line of cases has arisen concurrent to Section 104A case law. We turn once again to the case of Vera Brittain to better understand what is called the *Twin Books* problem.

Vera's first publication was a slim volume of poems entitled, *Verses of the V.A.D*, in 1918. The work was only published in the UK. All works published before 1923 are in the public domain in the US, with Section 104A having no bearing. But duration is never that simple, in this case because the work is of foreign origin. Moreover, and depending on if one is in the Ninth circuit, one may have to contend with a different result, thanks to the *Twin Books* case, and the 2006 decision of *Societe Civile Succession Richard Guino v. Beseder*.

The question is whether *Twin Books* stands for the proposition that if a work was published in a foreign country without formalities is the work considered unpublished, and how does that work with Section 104A? That is, would the *Verses of a V.A.D.* published without proper notice in 1918 qualify for protection under Section 303(a) or Section 104A? If Section 104A applies, the work is in the public domain. If Section 303(a) applies, the work could be under copyright through 2047.

Twin Books v. Disney was a 1996 Ninth Circuit case that involved the children's classic, *Bambi, a Life in the Woods*, a work which was first published in Germany in 1923 without a copyright notice, or as the court wrote,the work "contained no notice to the world that Mr. Salten (the author) intended to protect the young German fawn. Therefore, Bambi was fair game to any deer hunter in the world outside Germany." The court continues, "However, in 1926, Salten must have realized this potential danger, and therefore, he republished the German language *Bambi: A Life in the Woods* in Germany, this time with a notice of United States Copyright, in an attempt to afford Bambi some protection from the dangerous American hunters." The 1926 version was timely registered in the US in early 1927, which was then properly renewed in 1954. In 1993, Salten's heirs assigned all of the rights in Bambi to Twin Books.

Disagreements arose related to agreements made in 1958, and Twin Books brought this lawsuit. Disney moved for summary judgment, claiming that Bambi fell into the public domain in 1923 because there had not been proper copyright notice on the original German version.Without proper copyright notice, a work would fall into the public domain.

The case then relied on *Heim v. Universal Pictures*. Heim held that U.S. copyright began with publication overseas without the notice prescribed by U.S. law (a position the Copyright Office later rejected), but at least U.S. protection was coterminous with the facts of publication and term began and could end based on those facts, say by failure to renew. *Twin Books* however held that U.S. copyright did not begin until publication with notice in the U.S., that is, in 1926.

So what then of the status of the work in 1923–1925? The court held that within that period, anyone in the U.S. could have used the work without liability. But that makes no sense: if the work was not "published" within the meaning of the U.S. copyright before 1926, then it was "unpublished." There is no third category. If it was unpublished, it was protected in the U.S. and no one could use it. The Court of Appeals thus created a new category of work never before seen or dreamed of, even by Walt. Using *Heim* as a basis, the court found that the 1923 version had not placed Bambi in the public domain in Germany. "Therefore, we find the 1923 publication did not preclude the author from subsequently obtaining copyright protection in the United States by complying with the 1909 Copyright Act." Using the doctrine of territoriality, the court reasoned that US copyright was not secured until 1926, when "it was published with a United States copyright notice."

In 2006, the US District Court in Arizona applied the *Twin Books* decision in *Société Civile Succession Richard Guino v. Beseder Inc.*, F.Supp.2d 2006 WL 2917349 (D. Ariz) (October 6, 2006, (not reported)). At dispute were works of art created by Pierre-Auguste Renoir. Among the issues was the question of "determining the appropriate copyright term for the works." The works in question were sculptures created between 1913 and 1917 by Renoir and Richard Guino. The sculptures were published in 1917 in France as works by Renoir, and then published as Renoir-Guino works in 1974, again in Paris. The original district court determined that the works were first published in 1983 using Renoir and Guino's name. The Plaintiff, a French trust for Guino, registered the copyright of the sculptures with the US Copyright Office in 1984. Neither the 1917 publication, nor the 1974 contained proper copyright notice, even though the 1974 work would have come under the Universal Copyright Convention (UCC) requirements.

The question the court was faced with was whether the works were considered unpublished, and therefore gained protection in the US through Section 303(a) or whether Section 104A applied. If the 1917 work was considered published, the sculpture was not eligible for protection; if the work was unpublished, it would be protected by Section 303(a).

Here again was a foreign work that did not comply with the US copyright formalities. Was it therefore an unpublished work or was it considered improperly published, and therefore in the public domain? The court turned to *Twin Books*, controlling law in the Ninth Circuit: "The Ninth Circuit has held "that publication without a copyright notice in a foreign country [does] not put the work in the public domain in the United States."'

The court went on to follow *Twin Books*, but not before criticizing it. First, the court found that the *Twin Books* court had misread *Heim*. *Heim* really stood for the "rule that foreign publication without a copyright notice can commence the term of an American copyright, not the rule that foreign publication cannot place a work in the public domain in the United States, which the Ninth Circuit adopted in *Twin Books*." The court explained that the proper reading means that formalities are waived for foreign works; the *Twin Books* reading means the copyright term does not begin for a foreign work until proper copyright notice is affixed.

The court then followed the reasoning of *Twin Books* to its logical conclusion, namely that foreign works created before January 1, 1978 and published with improper or no copyright notice would be considered unpublished, and therefore would be protected by Section 303(a). These foreign works, because they were not considered published in the U.S. (and then in the public domain because, for instance, because of lack of formalities), would not be eligible for Section 104A. Thus, the court saw the *Twin Books* decision as limiting the scope of Section 104A with regard to foreign works. Not all foreign works would be eligible for 95 years from publication, even though the statute itself explicitly includes improper notice as a reason a foreign work would have been in the public domain in the U.S.

Twin Books actually makes the implication of what is included under copyright far more expansive. Under Section 104A, only foreign works published after 1922 are eligible. In contrast, any foreign work that was published without copyright notice or with improper copyright notice would be eligible for additional protection of life of the author, or until December 31, 2002, and if the work was published (1976 definition of published) for the first time between 1978 and 2002, then the work would be granted protection through December 31, 2047.

What is interesting is that the court did not get the law right on Section 303(a), only applying the "life of the author plus seventy years" to the last surviving author. If the first two publications—in 1917 and 1974—do not count for "publication" in the US, then the first publication occurred in 1983.

Moreover, the court did not apply the terms of the UCC, which allowed for copyright protection of 28 years for a foreign work with proper UCC notice. In this case, that would mean the work published in 1974 in France would have received an automatic term, and after 1964, renewal occurred automatically. The question was whether the work had proper UCC notice. The work would have been under copyright, and not in need of Section 104A, until ninety-five years after the 1974 publication, or 2069. Instead, the court found the original work in 1917 was unpublished, and therefore based the term of seventy years from the death of the life of the last surviving author, or until 2043—losing four years granted by Section 303(a) for the publication in 1983.

The Renoir court never took into account that the works had been first published as Renoir-Guino works in 1983 and registered in 1984, qualifying for additional protection through December 31, 2047. However, it appears from the registration record, the Estate of Guino was claiming the work to be unpublished. In December 2008, the Ninth circuit reviewed the Renoir case. The Ninth circuit posed the question as follows: "Whether the sculptures are protected by §§ 303(a) or 104A turns on whether the sculptures passed into the public domain in the United States." Applying Twin Books, the Ninth circuit found that the works had not passed into the public domain, and therefore were not eligible for copyright restoration under Section 104A. The Ninth circuit continued with the strange conclusion: "For the years between 1917 and 1978, therefore, the sculptures were neither protected by copyright nor injected into the public domain." Does this mean that they were unpublished and protected by state common law?

The court then analyzes the sculptures under Section 303(a). I quote in full, because like the District Court, the Ninth circuit gets it wrong!

> Section 303(a) of the 1976 Act applies because the sculptures were "created before January 1, 1978, but not theretofore in the public domain or copyrighted." 17 U.S.C. § 303(a). The sculptures were created between 1913 and 1917. Pursuant to *Twin Books*, the sculptures have not passed into the public domain, 83 F.3d at 1167, and were not protected by copyright after foreign publication without notice, see id. at 1168. The sculptures were not copyrighted until 1984. Section 303(a) provides protection for the term provided by § 302, which is a term seventy years after the death of the last surviving author. Because Guino passed away in 1973, the sculptures are entitled to protection until 2043, which the district court properly held. If the first publication took place in 1984, the term of protection is not life of the author plus seventy years, but in this case, the longer term of through December 31, 2047.

First, the public sale in 1917, if constituting publication, would mean the sculptures were not eligible for 104A protection. If only the 1974 date counted, then the UCC may have applied. Moreover, the required publication under Section 303(a) must have occurred between 1978 and 2002 for the additional protection. If the original publications counted for Section 303(a), meaning that the sculptures would not be eligible for protection because they were published before 1978, then *Twin Books* wouldn't apply—that is they would be considered published and then be analyzed for restoration under Section 104A. This would inject the 1917 version into the public domain and would only cover the additional alterations (if original enough to qualify as a derivative work) of any subsequent version.

Back to Brittain

To merely end the discussion with a rehashing of the case law would not further our inquiry, and Vera Brittain provides a perfect example of the *Twin Books* problem. *Verses of a VAD* was published in the UK in 1918. At the time, the Chase Act and a British/UK Treaty that had been put in place not long before, allowed UK authors copyright protection of their work, as long as they met the formality and manufacturing requirements under the 1909 Act.

So, the first question to ask was whether the slim volume of poems was ever protected by US copyright law? The answer appears to be no, as only the UK version was published. In this case, the work was considered in the public domain in the US from its time of publication in the UK in 1918 because Brittain had not met the publication and formalities requirements needed for copyright protection in the US, and the work had been in general circulation.

Therefore, the poems were in the public domain in the US since 1918, or were they? Are they still? *Verses of a VAD* would not qualify under 104A, because the work was published before 1923. However, the work might still qualify for protection in at least three different instances: under *Twin Books*, by restoration of the 1934 poetry collection through Section 104A, or through Section 303(a) upon republication by the Imperial War Museum.

To determine whether *Twin Books* applies, we must look at the original copyright notice on the work. The work was published by Erskine MacDonald (listed on the title page), and on the following page, we find "All rights reserved. First published August 1918." Does this count for US Copyright? The formalities in the US required under 1909 was revised to consist of the word "Copyright," or the abbreviation "Copr.," accompanied by the name of the copyright proprietor. The date of first publication was required for printed literary, musical, or dramatic works." This would mean that under *Twin Books*, the 1918 version would not qualify as a published work, and therefore, it would seem, was considered unpublished.

Are there cases that allow this kind of citation? If the work was considered published, then the work would have automatically fallen into the public domain in 1918. It would also mean that it would not meet the qualifications for Section 104A, because it was published before 1923. So, the work would have been in the public domain continuously since 1918.

However, if *Twin Books* applies and improper notice is found, then the work may still be under copyright—because its status from 1918 until present is now categorized as unpublished. Section 303(a) then applies. In 1995, The Imperial War Museum reissued *Verses of a VAD* in 1995 with a new introduction by Mark Bostridge and Paul Berry, the authors of her authorized biography. The new introduction is now under copyright in the US, and under the duration rules for joint authorship, protected seventy years after the death of Mark Bostridge, as Berry died in 1999, and Bostridge is still living.

What about the poems? With the *Twin Books*, it could be that the work was considered unpublished, which leads to two possible scenarios. First, if it was unpublished, then *Verses of a VAD* qualified for additional protection under Section 303(a), the work had been protected by US federal copyright law since 1978, and would not have been in the public domain any earlier than 2040 (life plus seventy). However, the 1995 publication by the Imperial War Museum with permission from the Estate of Vera Brittain (which is credited on the copyright page of the work), would qualify the work for protection through December 31, 2047. A work that would have been in the public domain since its inception is now protected (and seemingly had always been protected) as an unpublished work, and now is under copyright through 2047, or 129 years from its original publication.

Vera would include some of the poems from Verses of a VAD in a collection of poems entitled Poems of the War and After, published in the US and UK in 1934. The new poems and the compilation are protected by the term that began in 1934. This was one of the works that Vera Brittain had obtained U.S. registration but had failed to renew. These poems would be restored under Section 104A for a period of 95 years, or through 2029. The *Poems of the War and After* fell into the public domain because of lack of renewal in 1962, and then was restored with Section 104A in 1996. How did this alter the status of the original versions? Was this considered the first publication of the poem, because the copyright notice had been improper on the 1918 versions?

Traditionally (that is without *Twin Books*), one believed, no new copyright is given to the already individual published poems published in 1918. There were now two problems to work out. First, if *Verses of a VAD* did not count as a publication, then all of the poems in *The Poems of the War and After* would be eligible for copyright protection. If *Verses of a VAD* did count as a publication, and was therefore in the public domain, then only the new poems and the compilation itself would be protected, and not the original poems from *Verses of a VAD*. Second, we needed to know the copyright status of *The Poems of the War and After.* Were the poems included from *Verses of a VAD* then first published with *Poems of the War and After* (because the original publication did not count), and therefore now carry the term through 2029, or were those poems in the public domain, and therefore do not have their copyright revived because publication occurred before 1923? Finally, how is one to sort out—if Section 303(a) applies—that some of the poems in *Poems of the War and After* carry the term through December 31, 2047 (because of *Twin Books*) or carry a term of copyright through December 31, 2029?As yet, there appears to be no set answer. As a Vera Brittain scholar, I would like to know if I can use the poems from *Verses of a VAD*. In fact, this was how this long journey began—with an unsolicited email inquiry from someone who wanted to put Brittain's poems to music and wanted to know their copyright status. Answer?

Twin Books does not merely affect works before 1923. In fact, *Bambi*, the text at issue in *Twin Books* was originally published in 1923. *Twin Books* applies potentially to any work that has either improper or no notice. This means that to determine the status of a work—in the Ninth circuit—one must not only have the bibliographic information, but an actual copy of the book. Were any of the Brittain UK-Only works published without proper U.S. copyright notice? This requires further investigation. Moreover, it seems to contradict Section 104A, which includes "improper notice" as a category. So, how is one to determine whether *The Dark Tide* carries a term of 95 years under 104A, or a term through December 31, 2047, under Section 303(a)? *Twin Books* has brought enormous uncertainty and great legal contradictions to play in a world that had previously been rather stable. There is no easy way to read *Twin Books* and 104A together.

The U.S. Supreme court took up the question of Section 104A in *Golan v. Holder*. In many ways, this is a companion case to *Eldred*. We are also pleased that the Durationator was cited by the dissent, as well as a second mention of Townsend Gard's work as well.

Golan v. Holder, 609 F. 3d 1076 (2012)

Justice GINSBURG delivered the opinion of the Court.

The Berne Convention for the Protection of Literary and Artistic Works (Berne Convention or Berne), which took effect in 1886, is the principal accord governing international copyright relations. Latecomer to the international copyright regime launched by Berne, the United States joined the Convention in 1989. To perfect U. S. implementation of Berne, and as part of our response to the Uruguay Round of multilateral trade negotiations, Congress, in 1994, gave works enjoying copyright protection abroad the same full term of protection available to U. S. works. Congress did so in §514 of the Uruguay Round Agreements Act (URAA), which grants copyright protection to preexisting works of Berne member countries, protected in their country of origin, but lacking protection in the United States for any of three reasons: The United States did not protect works from the country of origin at the time of publication; the United States did not protect sound recordings fixed before 1972; or the author had failed to comply with U. S. statutory formalities (formalities Congress no longer requires as prerequisites to copyright protection).

The URAA accords no protection to a foreign work after its full copyright term has expired, causing it to fall into the public domain, whether under the laws of the country of origin or of this country. Works encompassed by §514 are granted the protection they would have enjoyed had the United States maintained copyright relations with the author's country or removed formalities incompatible with Berne. Foreign authors, however, gain no credit for the protection they lacked in years prior to §514's enactment. They therefore enjoy fewer total years of exclusivity than do their U. S. counterparts. As a consequence of the barriers to U. S. copyright protection prior to the enactment of §514, foreign works "restored" to protection by the measure had entered the public domain in this country. To cushion the impact of their placement in protected status, Congress included in §514 ameliorating accommodations for parties who had exploited affected works before the URAA was enacted.

Petitioners include orchestra conductors, musicians, publishers, and others who formerly enjoyed free access to works §514 removed from the public domain. They maintain that the Constitution's Copyright and Patent Clause, Art. I, §8, cl. 8, and First Amendment both decree the invalidity of §514. Under those prescriptions of our highest law, petitioners assert, a work that has entered the public domain, for whatever reason, must forever remain there.

In accord with the judgment of the Tenth Circuit, we conclude that §514 does not transgress constitutional limitations on Congress' authority. Neither the Copyright and Patent Clause nor the First Amendment, we hold, makes the public domain, in any and all cases, a territory that works may never exit.

I

A

Members of the Berne Union agree to treat authors from other member countries as well as they treat their own. Berne Convention, Sept. 9, 1886, as revised at Stockholm on July 14, 1967, Art. 1, 5(1), 828 U. N. T. S. 221, 225, 231–233. Nationals of a member country, as well as any author who publishes in one of Berne's 164 member states, thus enjoy copyright protection in nations across the globe. Art. 2(6), 3. Each country, moreover, must afford at least the minimum level of protection specified by Berne. The copyright term must span the author's lifetime, plus at least 50 additional years, whether or not the author has complied with a member state's legal formalities. Art. 5(2), 7(1). And, as relevant here, a work must be protected abroad unless its copyright term has expired in either the country where protection is claimed or the country of origin. Art. 18(1)–(2).

A different system of transnational copyright protection long prevailed in this country. Until 1891, foreign works were categorically excluded from Copyright Act protection. Throughout most of the 20th century, the only eligible foreign authors were those whose countries granted reciprocal rights to U. S. authors and whose works were print ed in the United States. See Act of Mar. 3, 1891, §3, 13, 26 Stat. 1107, 1110; Patry, The United States and International Copyright Law, 40 Houston L. Rev. 749, 750 (2003).[2] For domestic and foreign authors alike, protection hinged on compliance with notice, registration, and renewal formalities.

The United States became party to Berne's multilateral, formality-free copyright regime in 1989. Initially, Congress adopted a "minimalist approach" to compliance with the Convention. H. R. Rep. No. 100–609, p. 7 (1988) (hereinafter BCIA House Report). The Berne Convention Implementation Act of 1988 (BCIA), 102 Stat. 2853, made "only those changes to American copyright law that [were] clearly required under the treaty's provisions," BCIA House Report, at 7. Despite Berne's instruction that member countries—including "new accessions to the Union"—protect foreign works under copyright in the country of origin, Art. 18(1) and (4), 828 U. N. T. S., at 251, the BCIA accorded no protection for "any work that is in the public domain in the United States," §12, 102 Stat. 2860. Protection of future foreign works, the BCIA indicated, satisfied Article 18. See §2(3), 102 Stat. 2853 ("The amendments made by this Act, together with the law as it exists on the date of the enactment of this Act, satisfy the obligations of the United States in adhering to the Berne Convention ...."). Congress indicated, however, that it had not definitively rejected "retroactive" protection for pre- existing foreign works; instead it had punted on this issue of Berne's implementation, deferring consideration until "a more thorough examination of Constitutional, commercial, and consumer considerations is possible." BCIA House Report, at 51, 52.[3]

The minimalist approach essayed by the United States did not sit well with other Berne members.[4] While negotiations were ongoing over the North American Free Trade Agreement (NAFTA), Mexican authorities complained about the United States' refusal to grant protection, in accord with Article 18, to Mexican works that remained under copyright domestically. See Intellectual Property and International Issues, Hearings before the Subcommittee on

Intellectual Property and Judicial Administration, House Committee on the Judiciary, 102d Cong., 1st Sess., 168 (1991) (statement of Ralph Oman, U. S. Register of Copyrights).[5] The Register of Copyrights also reported "questions" from Turkey, Egypt, and Austria. *Ibid.* Thailand and Russia balked at protecting U. S. works, copyrighted here but in those countries' public domains, until the United States reciprocated with respect to their authors' works. URAA Joint Hearing 137 (statement of Ira S. Shapiro, General Counsel, Office of the U. S. Trade Representative (USTR)); *id.*, at 208 (statement of Professor Shira Perlmutter); *id.*, at 291 (statement of Jason S. Berman, Recording Industry Association of America (RIAA)).

Berne, however, did not provide a potent enforcement mechanism. The Convention contemplates dispute resolution before the International Court of Justice. Art. 33(1). But it specifies no sanctions for noncompliance and allows parties, at any time, to declare themselves "not ... bound" by the Convention's dispute resolution provision. Art. 33(2)–(3) 828 U. N. T. S., at 277. Unsurprisingly, no enforcement actions were launched before 1994. D. Gervais, The TRIPS Agreement 213, and n. 134 (3d ed. 2008). Although "several Berne Union Members disagreed with [our] interpretation of Article 18," the USTR told Congress, the Berne Convention did "not provide a meaningful dispute resolution process." URAA Joint Hearing 137 (statement of Shapiro). This shortcoming left Congress "free to adopt a minimalist approach and evade Article 18." Karp, Final Report, Berne Article 18 Study on Retroactive United States Copyright Protection for Berne and other Works, 20 Colum.-VLA J. L. & Arts 157, 172 (1996).

The landscape changed in 1994. The Uruguay round of multilateral trade negotiations produced the World Trade Organization (WTO) and the Agreement on Trade-Related Aspects of Intellectual Property Rights (TRIPS).[7] The United States joined both. TRIPS mandates, on pain of WTO enforcement, implementation of Berne's first 21 articles. TRIPS, Art. 9.1, 33 I. L. M. 1197, 1201 (requiring adherence to all but the "moral rights" provisions of Article 6*bis*). The WTO gave teeth to the Convention's requirements: Noncompliance with a WTO ruling could subject member countries to tariffs or cross-sector retaliation. See Gervais, *supra*, at 213; 7 W. Patry, Copyright §24:1, pp. 24–8 to 24–9 (2011). The specter of WTO enforcement proceedings bolstered the credibility of our trading partners' threats to challenge the United States for inadequate compliance with Article 18. See URAA Joint Hearing 137 (statement of Shapiro, USTR) ("It is likely that other WTO members would challenge the current U. S. implementation of Berne Article 18 under [WTO] procedures.").

Congress' response to the Uruguay agreements put to rest any questions concerning U. S. compliance with Article 18. Section 514 of the URAA, 108 Stat. 4976 (codified at 17 U. S. C. §104A, 109(a)), extended copyright to works that garnered protection in their countries of origin, but had no right to exclusivity in the United States for any of three reasons: lack of copyright relations between the country of origin and the United States at the time of publication; lack of subject-matter protection for sound recordings fixed before 1972; and failure to comply with U.S. statutory formalities (*e.g.*, failure to provide notice of copyright status, or to register and renew a copyright). See §104A(h)(6)(B)–(C).

Works that have fallen into the public domain after the expiration of a full copyright term—either in the United States or the country of origin—receive no further protection under §514. *Ibid.* Copyrights "restored" under URAA §514 "subsist for the remainder of the term of copyright that the work would have otherwise been granted ... if the work never entered the public domain." §104A(a)(1)(B). Prospectively, restoration places foreign works on an equal footing with their U. S. counterparts; assuming a foreign and domestic author died the same day, their works will enter the public domain simultaneously. See §302(a) (copyrights generally expire 70 years after the author's death). Restored works, however, receive no compensatory time for the period of exclusivity they would have enjoyed before §514's enactment, had they been protected at the outset in the United States. Their total term, therefore, falls short of that available to similarly situated U.S. works.

The URAA's disturbance of the public domain hardly escaped Congress' attention. Section 514 imposed no liability for any use of foreign works occurring before restoration. In addition, anyone remained free to copy and use restored works for one year following §514's enactment. See 17 U. S. C. §104A(h)(2)(A). Concerns about §514's compatibility with the Fifth Amendment's Takings Clause led Congress to include additional protections for "reliance parties"—those who had, before the URAA's enactment, used or acquired a foreign work then in the public domain. See §104A(h)(3)–(4). Reliance parties may continue to exploit a restored work until the owner of the restored copyright gives notice of intent to enforce—either by filing with the U. S. Copyright Office within two years of restoration, or by actually notifying the reliance party. §104A(c), (d)(2)(A)(i), and (B)(i). After that, reliance parties may continue to exploit existing copies for a grace period of one year. §104A(d)(2)(A)(ii), and (B)(ii). Finally, anyone who, before the URAA's enactment, created a "derivative work" based on a restored work may indefinitely exploit the derivation upon payment to the copyright holder of "reasonable compensation," to be set by a district judge if the parties cannot agree. §104A(d)(3).

B

In 2001, petitioners filed this lawsuit challenging §514. They maintain that Congress, when it passed the URAA, exceeded its authority under the Copyright Clause and transgressed First Amendment limitations. The District Court granted the Attorney General's motion for summary judgment. *Golan* v. *Gonzales*, No. Civ. 01–B–1854, 2005 WL 914754 (D. Colo., Apr. 20, 2005). In rejecting petitioners' Copyright Clause argument, the court stated that Congress "has historically demonstrated little compunction about removing copyrightable materials from the public domain." *Id.*, at 14. The court next declined to part from "the settled rule that private censorship via copyright enforcement does not implicate First Amendment concerns." *Id.*, at 17.

The Court of Appeals for the Tenth Circuit affirmed in part. *Golan* v. *Gonzales*, 501 F. 3d 1179 (2007). The public domain, it agreed, was not a "threshold that Congress" was powerless to "traverse in both directions." *Id.*, at 1187 (internal quotations marks omitted). But §514, as the Court of Appeals read our decision in *Eldred* v. *Ashcroft*, 537 U. S. 186 (2003), required further First Amendment inspection, 501 F. 3d, at 1187. The measure " 'altered the traditional contours of copyright protection,' " the court said—specifically, the "bedrock principle" that once works enter the public domain, they do not leave. *Ibid.* (quoting *Eldred*, 537 U. S., at 221). The case was remanded with an instruction to the District Court to address the First Amendment claim in light of the Tenth Circuit's opinion.

On remand, the District Court's starting premise was uncontested: Section 514 does not regulate speech on the basis of its content; therefore the law would be upheld if "narrowly tailored to serve a significant government interest." 611 F. Supp. 2d 1165, 1170–1171 (Colo. 2009) (quoting *Ward* v. *Rock Against Racism*, 491 U. S. 781, 791 (1989)). Summary judgment was due petitioners, the court concluded, because §514's constriction of the public domain was not justified by any of the asserted federal interests: compliance with Berne, securing greater protection for U.S. authors abroad, or remediation of the inequitable treatment suffered by foreign authors whose works lacked protection in the United States. 611 F. Supp. 2d, at 1172–1177.

The Tenth Circuit reversed. Deferring to Congress' predictive judgments in matters relating to foreign affairs, the appellate court held that §514 survived First Amendment scrutiny. Specifically, the court determined that the law was narrowly tailored to fit the important government aim of protecting U.S. copyright holders' interests abroad. 609 F. 3d 1076 (2010).

We granted certiorari to consider petitioners' challenge to §514 under both the Copyright Clause and the First Amendment, 562 U. S. ___ (2011), and now affirm.

II

We first address petitioners' argument that Congress lacked authority, under the Copyright Clause, to enact §514. The Constitution states that "Congress shall have Power ...[t]o promote the Progress of Science ... by securing for limited Times to Authors .. the exclusive Right to their ... Writings." Art. I, §8, cl. 8. Petitioners find in this grant of authority an impenetrable barrier to the extension of copyright protection to authors whose writings, for whatever reason, are in the public domain. We see no such barrier in the text of the Copyright Clause, historical practice, or our precedents.

A

The text of the Copyright Clause does not exclude application of copyright protection to works in the public domain. Symposium, Congressional Power and Limitations Inherent in the Copyright Clause, 30 Colum. J. L. & Arts 259, 266 (2007). Petitioners' contrary argument relies primarily on the Constitution's confinement of a copyright's lifespan to a "limited Tim[e]." "Removing works from the public domain," they contend, "violates the 'limited [t]imes' restriction by turning a fixed and predictable period into one that can be reset or resurrected at any time, even after it expires." Brief for Petitioners 22.

Our decision in *Eldred* is largely dispositive of petitioners' limited-time argument. There we addressed the question whether Congress violated the Copyright Clause when it extended, by 20 years, the terms of existing copyrights. 537 U. S., at 192–193 (upholding Copyright Term Extension Act (CTEA)). Ruling that Congress acted within constitutional bounds, we declined to infer from the text of the Copyright Clause "the command that a time prescription, once set, becomes forever 'fixed' or 'inalterable.' " *Id.*, at 199. "The word 'limited,' " we observed, "does not convey a meaning so constricted." *Ibid.* Rather, the term is best understood to mean "confine[d] within certain bounds," "restrain[ed]," or "circumscribed." *Ibid.* (internal quotation marks omitted). The construction petitioners tender closely resembles the definition rejected in *Eldred* and is similarly infirm.

The terms afforded works restored by §514 are no less "limited" than those the CTEA lengthened. In light of *Eldred*, petitioners do not here contend that the term Congress has granted U. S. authors—their lifetimes, plus 70 years—is unlimited. See 17 U. S. C. §302(a). Nor do petitioners explain why terms of the same duration, as applied to foreign works, are not equally "circumscribed" and "confined." See *Eldred*, 537 U. S., at 199. Indeed, as earlier noted, see *supra*, at 2, 10, the copyrights of restored foreign works typically last for fewer years than those of their domestic counterparts.

The difference, petitioners say, is that the limited time had already passed for works in the public domain. What was that limited term for foreign works once excluded from U. S. copyright protection? Exactly "zero," petitioners respond. Brief for Petitioners 22 (works in question "received a specific term of protection ... sometimes expressly set to zero"; "at the end of that period," they "entered the public domain"); Tr. of Oral Arg. 52 (by "refusing to provide any protection for a work," Congress "set[s] the term at zero," and thereby "tell[s] us when the end has come"). We find scant sense in this argument, for surely a "limited time" of exclusivity must begin before it may end.[16]

Carried to its logical conclusion, petitioners persist, the Government's position would allow Congress to institute a second "limited" term after the first expires, a third after that, and so on. Thus, as long as Congress legislated in installments, perpetual copyright terms would be achievable. As in *Eldred*, the hypothetical legislative misbehavior petitioners posit is far afield from the case before us. See 537 U. S., at 198–200, 209–210. In aligning the United States with other nations bound by the Berne Convention, and thereby according equitable treatment to once disfavored foreign authors, Congress can hardly be charged with a design to move stealthily toward a regime of perpetual copyrights.

B

Historical practice corroborates our reading of the Copyright Clause to permit full U. S. compliance with Berne. Undoubtedly, federal copyright legislation generally has not affected works in the public domain. Section 514's disturbance of that domain, petitioners argue, distin guishes their suit from Eldred's. In adopting the CTEA, petitioners note, Congress acted in accord with "an unbroken congressional practice" of granting pre-expiration term extensions, 537 U.S., at 200. No comparable practice, they maintain, supports §514.

On occasion, however, Congress has seen fit to protect works once freely available. Notably, the Copyright Act of 1790 granted protection to many works previously in the public domain. Act of May 31, 1790 (1790 Act), §1, 1 Stat. 124 (covering "any map, chart, book, or books already printed within these United States"). Before the Act launched a uniform national system, three States provided no statutory copyright protection at all. Of those that did afford some protection, seven failed to protect maps; eight did not cover previously published books; and all ten denied protection to works that failed to comply with formalities. The First Congress, it thus appears, did not view the public domain as inviolate. As we have recognized, the "construction placed upon the Constitution by [the drafters of] the first [copyright] act of 1790 and the act of 1802 . . . men who were contemporary with [the Constitution's] formation, many of whom were members of the convention which framed it, is of itself entitled to very great weight." *Burrow-Giles Lithographic Co.* v. *Sarony*, 111 U. S. 53, 57 (1884).

Subsequent actions confirm that Congress has not understood the Copyright Clause to preclude protection for existing works. Several private bills restored the copyrights of works that previously had been in the public domain. See Act of Feb. 19, 1849 (Corson Act), ch. 57, 9 Stat. 763; Act of June 23, 1874 (Helmuth Act), ch. 534, 18 Stat. 618; Act of Feb. 17, 1898 (Jones Act), ch. 29, 30 Stat. 1396. These bills were unchallenged in court.

Analogous patent statutes, however, were upheld in litigation.[22] In 1808, Congress passed a private bill restoring patent protection to Oliver Evans' flour mill. When Evans sued for infringement, first Chief Justice Marshall in the Circuit Court, *Evans* v. *Jordan*, 8 F. Cas. 872 (No. 4,564) (Va. 1813), and then Justice Bushrod Washington for this Court, *Evans* v. *Jordan*, 9 Cranch 199 (1815), upheld the restored patent's validity. After the patent's expiration, the Court said, "a general right to use [Evans'] discovery was not so vested in the public" as to allow the defendant to continue using the machinery, which he had constructed between the patent's expiration and the bill's passage. *Id.*, at 202. See also *Blanchard* v. *Sprague*, 3 F. Cas. 648, 650 (No. 1,518) (CC Mass. 1839) (Story, J.) ("I never have entertained any doubt of the constitutional authority of congress" to "give a patent for an invention, which ... was in public use and enjoyed by the community at the time of the passage of the act.").

This Court again upheld Congress' restoration of an invention to protected status in *McClurg* v. *Kingsland*, 1 How. 202 (1843). There we enforced an 1839 amendment that recognized a patent on an invention despite its prior use by the inventor's employer. Absent such dispensation, the employer's use would have rendered the invention unpatentable, and therefore open to exploitation without the inventor's leave. *Id.*, at 206–209.

Congress has also passed generally applicable legislation granting patents and copyrights to inventions and works that had lost protection. An 1832 statute authorized a new patent for any inventor whose failure, "by inadvertence, accident, or mistake," to comply with statutory formalities rendered the original patent "invalid or inoperative." Act of July 3, §3, 4 Stat. 559. An

1893 measure similarly allowed authors who had not timely deposited their work to receive "all the rights and privileges" the Copyright Act affords, if they made the required deposit by March 1, 1893. Act of Mar. 3, ch. 215, 27 Stat. 743. And in 1919 and 1941, Congress authorized the President to issue proclamations granting protection to foreign works that had fallen into the public domain during World Wars I and II. See Act of Dec. 18, 1919, ch. 11, 41 Stat. 368; Act of Sept. 25, 1941, ch. 421, 55 Stat. 732.

Pointing to dictum in *Graham* v. *John Deere Co. of Kansas City*, 383 U. S. 1 (1966), petitioners would have us look past this history. In *Graham*, we stated that "Congress may not authorize the issuance of patents whose effects are to remove existent knowledge from the public domain, or to restrict free access to materials already available." *Id.*, at 6; *post*, at 15. But as we explained in *Eldred*, this passage did not speak to the constitutional limits on Congress' copyright and patent authority. Rather, it "addressed an invention's very eligibility for patent protection." 537 U. S., at 202, n. 7.

Installing a federal copyright system and ameliorating the interruptions of global war, it is true, presented Congress with extraordinary situations. Yet the TRIPS accord, leading the United States to comply in full measure with Berne, was also a signal event. See *supra*, at 7–8; cf. *Eldred*, 537 U. S., at 259, 264–265 (Breyer, J., dissenting) (acknowledging importance of international uniformity advanced by U.S. efforts to conform to the Berne Convention). Given the authority we hold Congress has, we will not second-guess the political choice Congress made between leaving the public domain untouched and embracing Berne unstintingly. Cf. *id.*, at 212–213.

C

Petitioners' ultimate argument as to the Copyright and Patent Clause concerns its initial words. Congress is empowered to "promote the Progress of Science and useful Arts" by enacting systems of copyright and patent protection. U.S. Const., Art. I, §8, cl. 8. Perhaps counterintuitively for the contemporary reader, Congress' copyright authority is tied to the progress of science; its patent authority, to the progress of the useful arts. See *Graham*, 383 U.S., at 5, and n. 1; *Evans*, 8 F. Cas., at 873 (Marshall, J.).

The "Progress of Science," petitioners acknowledge, refers broadly to "the creation and spread of knowledge and learning." Brief for Petitioners 21; accord *post*, at 1. They nevertheless argue that federal legislation cannot serve the Clause's aim unless the legislation "spur[s] the creation of ... new works." Brief for Petitioners 24; accord *post*, at 1–2, 8, 17. Because §514 deals solely with works already created, petitioners urge, it "provides no plausible incentive to create new works" and is therefore invalid. Reply Brief 4.

The creation of at least one new work, however, is not the sole way Congress may promote knowledge and learning. In *Eldred*, we rejected an argument nearly identical to the one petitioners rehearse. The *Eldred* petitioners urged that the "CTEA's extension of existing copyrights categorically fails to 'promote the Progress of Science,' . . . because it does not stimulate the creation of new works." 537 U. S., at 211–212. In response to this argument, we held that the Copyright Clause does not demand that each copyright provision, examined discretely, operate to induce new works. Rather, we explained, the Clause "empowers Congress to determine the intellectual property regimes that, overall, in that body's judgment, will serve the ends of the Clause." *Id.*, at 222. And those permissible ends, we held, extended beyond the creation of new works. See *id.*, at 205–206 (rejecting the notion that " 'the only way to promote the progress of science [is] to provide incentives to create new works' " (quoting Perlmutter, Participation in the International Copyright System as a Means to Promote the Progress of Science and Useful Arts, 36 Loyola (LA) L. Rev. 323, 332 (2002))).[26]

Even were we writing on a clean slate, petitioners' argument would be unavailing. Nothing in the text of the Copyright Clause confines the "Progress of Science" exclusively to "incentives for creation." *Id.*, at 324, n. 5 (internal quotation marks omitted). Evidence from the founding, moreover, suggests that inducing *dissemination*—as opposed to creation—was viewed as an appropriate means to promote science. See Nachbar, Constructing Copyright's Mythology, 6 Green Bag 2d 37, 44 (2002) ("The scope of copyright protection existing at the time of the framing," trained as it was on "publication, not creation," "is inconsistent with claims that copyright must promote creative activity in order to be valid." (Internal quotation marks omitted)). Until 1976, in fact, Congress made "federal copyright contingent on publication[,] [thereby] providing incentives not primarily for creation," but for dissemination. Perlmutter, *supra*, at 324, n. 5. Our decisions correspondingly recognize that "copyright supplies the economic incentive to create *and disseminate* ideas." *Harper & Row, Publishers, Inc.* v. *Nation Enterprises*, 471 U.S. 539, 558 (1985) (emphasis added). See also *Eldred*, 537 U.S., at 206.

Considered against this backdrop, §514 falls comfortably within Congress' authority under the Copyright Clause. Congress rationally could have concluded that adherence to Berne "promotes the diffusion of knowledge," Brief for Petitioners 4. A well-functioning international copyright system would likely encourage the dissemination of existing and future works. See URAA Joint Hearing 189 (statement of Professor Perlmutter). Full compliance with Berne, Congress had reason to believe, would expand the foreign markets available to U.S. authors and invigorate protection against piracy of U.S. works abroad, S. Rep. No. 103–412, pp. 224, 225 (1994); URAA Joint Hearing 291 (statement of Berman, RIAA); *id.*, at 244, 247 (statement of Smith, IIPA), thereby benefitting copyright-intensive industries stateside and inducing greater investment in the creative process.

The provision of incentives for the creation of new works is surely an essential means to advance the spread of knowledge and learning. We hold, however, that it is not the sole means Congress may use "[t]o promote the Progress of Science." See Perlmutter, *supra*, at 332 (United States would "lose all flexibility" were the provision of incentives to create the exclusive way to promote the progress of science).[28] Congress determined that exemplary adherence to Berne would serve the objectives of the Copyright Clause. We have no warrant to reject the rational judgment Congress made.

III

A

We next explain why the First Amendment does not inhibit the restoration authorized by §514. To do so, we first recapitulate the relevant part of our pathmarking decision in *Eldred*. The petitioners in *Eldred*, like those here, argued that Congress had violated not only the "limited Times" prescription of the Copyright Clause. In addition, and independently, the *Eldred* petitioners charged, Congress had offended the First Amendment's freedom of expression guarantee. The CTEA's 20-year enlargement of a copyright's duration, we held in *Eldred*, offended neither provision.

Concerning the First Amendment, we recognized that some restriction on expression is the inherent and intended effect of every grant of copyright. Noting that the "Copyright Clause and the First Amendment were adopted close in time," 537 U. S., at 219, we observed that the Framers regarded copyright protection not simply as a limit on the manner in which expressive works may be used. They also saw copyright as an "engine of free expression[:] By establishing a marketable right to the use of one's expression, copyright supplies the economic incentive to create and disseminate ideas." *Ibid.* (quoting *Harper & Row*, 471 U.S., at 558 (internal quotation marks omitted)); see *id.*, at 546 ("rights conferred by copyright are designed to assure contributors to the store of knowledge a fair return for their labors").

We then described the "traditional contours" of copyright protection, *i.e.*, the "idea/expression dichotomy" and the "fair use" defense. Both are recognized in our jurisprudence as "built-in First Amendment accommodations." *Eldred*, 537 U.S., at 219; see *Harper & Row*, 471 U.S., at 560 (First Amendment protections are "embodied in the Copyright Act's distinction between copyrightable expression and uncopyrightable facts and ideas," and in the "latitude for scholarship and comment" safeguarded by the fair use defense). The idea/expression dichotomy is codified at 17 U. S. C. §102(b): "In no case does copyright protec[t] ... any idea, procedure, process, system, method of operation, concept, principle, or discovery ... described, explained, illustrated, or embodied in [the copyrighted] work." "Due to this [idea/expression] distinction, every idea, theory, and fact in a copyrighted work becomes instantly available for public exploitation at the moment of publication"; the author's expression alone gains copyright protection. *Eldred*, 537 U. S., at 219; see *Harper & Row*, 471 U. S., at 556 ("idea/expression dichotomy strike[s] a definitional balance between the First Amendment and the Copyright Act by permitting free communication of facts while still protecting an author's expression" (internal quotation marks omitted)).

The second "traditional contour," the fair use defense, is codified at 17 U. S. C. §107: "[T]he fair use of a copyrighted work, including such use by reproduction in copies . . . , for purposes such as criticism, comment, news reporting, teaching (including multiple copies for classroom use), scholarship, or research, is not an infringement of copyright." This limitation on exclusivity "allows the public to use not only facts and ideas contained in a copyrighted work, but also [the author's] expression itself in certain circumstances." *Eldred*, 537 U. S., at 219; see *id.*, at 220 ("fair use defense affords considerable latitude for scholarship and comment, ... even for parody" (internal quotation marks omitted)).

Given the "speech-protective purposes and safeguards" embraced by copyright law, see *id.*, at 219, we concluded in *Eldred* that there was no call for the heightened review petitioners sought in that case.[30] We reach the same conclusion here.[31] Section 514 leaves undisturbed the "idea/expression" distinction and the "fair use" defense. Moreover, Congress adopted measures to ease the transition from a national scheme to an international copyright regime: It deferred the date from which enforcement runs, and it cushioned the impact of restoration on "reliance parties" who exploited foreign works denied protection before §514 took effect. See *supra,* at 10–11 (describing 17 U. S. C. §104A(c), (d), and (h)). See also *Eldred*, 537 U. S., at 220 (describing supplemental allowances and exemptions available to certain users to mitigate the CTEA's impact).

B

Petitioners attempt to distinguish their challenge from the one turned away in *Eldred*. First Amendment interests of a higher order are at stake here, petitioners say, because they—unlike their counterparts in *Eldred*—enjoyed "vested rights" in works that had already entered the public domain. The limited rights they retain under copyright law's "built-in safeguards" are, in their view, no substitute for the unlimited use they enjoyed before §514's enactment. Nor, petitioners urge, does §514's "unprecedented" foray into the public domain possess the historical pedigree that supported the term extension at issue in *Eldred*. Brief for Petitioners 42–43.

However spun, these contentions depend on an argument we considered and rejected above, namely, that the Constitution renders the public domain largely untouchable by Congress. Petitioners here attempt to achieve under the banner of the First Amendment what they could not win under the Copyright Clause: On their view of the Copyright Clause, the public domain is inviolable; as they read the First Amendment, the public domain is policed through heightened judicial scrutiny of Congress' means and ends. As we have already shown, see *supra,* at 13–19, the text of the Copyright Clause and the historical record scarcely establish that "once a work enters the public domain," Congress cannot permit anyone—"not even the creator—[to] copyright it," 501 F. 3d, at 1184. And nothing in the historical record, congressional practice, or our own jurisprudence warrants exceptional First Amendment solicitude for copyrighted works that were once in the public domain.[32] Neither this challenge nor that raised in *Eldred*, we stress, allege Congress transgressed a generally applicable First Amendment prohibition; we are not faced, for example, with copyright protection that hinges on the author's viewpoint.

The Tenth Circuit's initial opinion determined that petitioners marshaled a stronger First Amendment challenge than did their predecessors in *Eldred*, who never "possessed unfettered access to any of the works at issue." 501 F. 3d, at 1193. See also *id.*, at 1194 ("[O]nce the works at issue became free for anyone to copy, [petitioners] had vested First Amendment interests in the expressions, [thus] §514's interference with [petitioners'] rights is subject to First

Amendment scrutiny."). As petitioners put it in this Court, Congress impermissibly revoked their right to exploit foreign works that "belonged to them" once the works were in the public domain. Brief for Petitioners 44–45.

To copyright lawyers, the "vested rights" formulation might sound exactly backwards: Rights typically vest at the *outset* of copyright protection, in an author or rightholder. See, *e.g.*, 17 U. S. C. §201(a) ("Copyright in a work protected ... vests initially in the author ..."). Once the term of protection ends, the works do not revest in any rightholder. Instead, the works simply lapse into the public domain. See, *e.g.*, Berne, Art. 18(1), 828 U. N. T. S., at 251 ("This Convention shall apply to all works which ...have not yet fallen into the public domain ..."). Anyone has free access to the public domain, but no one, after the copyright term has expired, acquires ownership rights in the once-protected works.

Congress recurrently adjusts copyright law to protect categories of works once outside the law's compass. For example, Congress broke new ground when it extended copyright protection to foreign works in 1891, Act of Mar. 3, §13, 26 Stat. 1110; to dramatic works in 1856, Act of Aug. 18, 11 Stat. 138; to photographs and photographic negatives in 1865, Act of Mar. 3, §1, 13 Stat. 540; to motion pictures in 1912, Act of Aug. 24, 37 Stat. 488; to fixed sound recordings in 1972, Act of Oct. 15, 1971, 85 Stat. 391; and to architectural works in 1990, Architectural Works Copyright Protection Act, 104 Stat. 5133. And on several occasions, as recounted above, Congress protected works previously in the public domain, hence freely usable by the public. See *supra,* at 15–19. If Congress could grant protection to these works without hazarding heightened First Amendment scrutiny, then what free speech principle disarms it from protecting works prematurely cast into the public domain for reasons antithetical to the Berne Convention?

Section 514, we add, does not impose a blanket prohibition on public access. Petitioners protest that fair use and the idea/expression dichotomy "are plainly inadequate to protect the speech and expression rights that Section 514 took from petitioners, or . . . the public"—that is, "the unrestricted right to perform, copy, teach and distribute the *entire* work, for any reason." Brief for Petitioners 46–47. "Playing a few bars of a Shostakovich symphony," petitioners observe, "is no substitute for performing the entire work." *Id.*, at 47.

But Congress has not put petitioners in this bind. The question here, as in *Eldred*, is whether would-be users must pay for their desired use of the author's expression, or else limit their exploitation to "fair use" of that work. Prokofiev's Peter and the Wolf could once be performed free of charge; after §514 the right to perform it must be obtained in the marketplace. This is the same marketplace, of course, that exists for the music of Prokofiev's U. S. contemporaries: works of Copland and Bernstein, for example, that enjoy copyright protection, but nevertheless appear regularly in the programs of U.S. concertgoers.

Before we joined Berne, domestic works and some foreign works were protected under U.S. statutes and bilateral international agreements, while other foreign works were available at an artificially low (because royalty-free) cost. By fully implementing Berne, Congress ensured that most works, whether foreign or domestic, would be governed by the same legal regime. The phenomenon to which Congress responded is not new: Distortions of the same order occurred with greater frequency—and to the detriment of both foreign and domestic authors—when, before 1891, foreign works were excluded entirely from U.S. copyright protection. See Kampelman, The United States and International Copyright, 41 Am. J. Int'l L. 406, 413 (1947) ("American readers were less inclined to read the novels of Cooper or Hawthorne for a dollar when they could buy a novel of Scott or Dickens for a quarter."). Section 514 continued the trend toward a harmonized copyright regime by placing foreign works in the position they would have occupied if the current regime had been in effect when those works were created and first published. Authors once deprived of protection are spared the continuing effects of that initial deprivation; §514 gives them nothing more than the benefit of their labors during whatever time remains before the normal copyright term expires.

Unlike petitioners, the dissent makes much of the so-called "orphan works" problem. See *post*, at 11–14, 23–24. We readily acknowledge the difficulties would-be users of copyrightable materials may face in identifying or locating copyright owners. See generally U.S. Copyright Office, Report on Orphan Works 21–40 (2006). But as the dissent concedes, see *post*, at 13, this difficulty is hardly peculiar to works restored under §514. It similarly afflicts, for instance, U.S. libraries that attempt to catalogue U.S. books. See *post*, at 12. See also Brief for American Library Association et al. as *Amici Curiae* 22 (Section 514 "exacerbated," but did not create, the problem of orphan works); U. S. Copyright Office, *supra,* at 41–44 (tracing orphan-works problem to Congress' elimination of formalities, commencing with the 1976 Copyright Act).[36]

Nor is this a matter appropriate for judicial, as opposed to legislative, resolution. Cf. *Authors Guild* v. *Google, Inc.*, 770 F. Supp. 2d 666, 677–678 (SDNY 2011) (rejecting proposed "Google Books" class settlement because, *inter alia*, "the establishment of a mechanism for exploiting unclaimed books is a matter more suited for Congress than this Court" (citing *Eldred*, 537 U.S., at 212)). Indeed, the host of policy and logistical questions identified by the dissent speak for themselves. *Post*, at 12. Despite "longstanding efforts," see *Authors Guild*, 770 F. Supp. 2d, at 678 (quoting statement of Marybeth Peters), Congress has not yet passed ameliorative orphan-works legislation of the sort enacted by other Berne members, see, *e.g.*, Canada Copyright Act, R. S. C., 1985, c. C–42, §77 (authorizing Copyright Board to license use of orphan works by persons unable, after making reasonable efforts, to locate the copyright owner). Heretofore, no one has suggested that the orphan-works issue should be addressed through our implementation of Berne, rather than through overarching legislation of the sort proposed in Congress and cited by the dissent. See *post,* at 23–24; U. S. Copyright Office, Legal Issues in Mass Digitization 25–29 (2011) (discussing recent legislative efforts). Our unstinting adherence to Berne may add impetus to calls for the enactment of such legislation. But resistance to Berne's prescriptions surely is not a necessary or proper response to the pervasive question, what should Congress do about orphan works.

IV

Congress determined that U.S. interests were best served by our full participation in the dominant system of international copyright protection. Those interests include ensuring exemplary compliance with our international obligations, securing greater protection for U.S. authors abroad, and remedying unequal treatment of foreign authors. The judgment §514 expresses lies well within the ken of the political branches. It is our obligation, of course, to determine whether the action Congress took, wise or not, encounters any constitutional shoal. For the reasons stated, we are satisfied it does not. The judgment of the Court of Appeals for the Tenth Circuit is therefore

Affirmed.

Justice KAGAN took no part in the consideration or decision of this case.

Justice BREYER, with whom Justice ALITO joins, dissenting.

In order "[t]o promote the Progress of Science" (by which term the Founders meant "learning" or "knowledge"), the Constitution's Copyright Clause grants Congress the power to "secur[e] for limited Times to Authors ... the exclusive Right to their ... Writings." Art. I, § 8, cl. 8. This "exclusive Right" allows its holder to charge a fee to those who wish to use a copyrighted work, and the ability to charge that fee encourages the production of new material. In this sense, a copyright is, in Macaulay's words, a "tax on readers for the purpose of giving a bounty to writers"—a bounty designed to encourage new production. As the Court said in *Eldred,* " '[t]he economic philosophy behind the [Copyright] [C]lause ... is the conviction that encouragement of individual effort by personal gain is the best way to advance public welfare through the talents of authors and inventors.' " *Eldred v. Ashcroft,* 537 U.S. 186, 212, n. 18, 123 S.Ct. 769, 154 L.Ed.2d 683 (2003) (quoting *Mazer v. Stein,* 347 U.S. 201, 219, 74 S.Ct. 460, 98 L.Ed. 630 (1954)). See T. Macaulay, Speeches on Copyright 25 (E. Miller ed.1913); E. Walterscheid, The Nature of the Intellectual Property Clause: A Study in Historical Perspective 125–126 (2002) (hereinafter Walterscheid).

The statute before us, however, does not encourage anyone to produce a single new work. By definition, it bestows monetary rewards only on owners of old works—works that have already been created and already are in the American public domain. At the same time, the statute inhibits the dissemination of those works, foreign works published abroad after 1923, of which there are many millions, including films, works of art, innumerable photographs, and, of course, books—books that (in the absence of the statute) would assume their rightful places in computer-accessible databases, spreading knowledge throughout the world. See *infra,* at 904–906. In my view, the Copyright Clause does not authorize Congress to enact this statute. And I consequently dissent.

I

The possibility of eliciting new production is, and always has been, an essential precondition for American copyright protection. The Constitution's words, "exclusive Right," "limited Times," "Progress of Science," viewed through the lens of history underscore the legal significance of what the Court in *Eldred* referred to as the "economic philosophy behind the Copyright Clause." 537 U.S., at 212, n. 18, 123 S.Ct. 769 (brackets omitted). That philosophy understands copyright's grants of limited monopoly privileges to authors as private benefits that are conferred for a public reason—to elicit new creation.

Yet, as the Founders recognized, monopoly is a two-edged sword. On the one hand, it can encourage production of new works. In the absence of copyright protection, anyone might freely copy the products of an author's creative labor, appropriating the benefits without incurring the nonrepeatable costs of creation, thereby deterring authors from exerting themselves in the first place. On the other hand, copyright tends to restrict the dissemination (and use) of works once produced either because the absence of competition translates directly into higher consumer prices or because the need to secure copying permission sometimes imposes administrative costs that make it difficult for potential users of a copyrighted work to find its owner and strike a bargain. See W. Landes & R. Posner, The Economic Structure of Intellectual Property Law 68–70, 213–214 (2003). Consequently, the original British copyright statute, the Constitution's Framers, and our case law all have recognized copyright's resulting and necessary call for balance.

At the time the Framers wrote the Constitution, they were well aware of Britain's 18th-century copyright statute, the Statute of Anne, 8 Anne, ch. 19 (1710), and they were aware of the legal struggles that produced it. That statute sought in part to control, and to limit, pre-existing monopolies that had emerged in the book trade as a result of the Crown's having previously granted special privileges to royal favorites. The Crown, for example, had chartered the Stationers' Company, permitting it to regulate and to censor works on the government's behalf. The Stationers had thereby acquired control over the disposition of copies of published works, from which emerged the Stationers' copyright—a right conferred on company members, not authors, that was deemed to exist in perpetuity. See L. Patterson, Copyright in Historical Perspective 1–16, 114–150 (1968) (hereinafter Patterson); Walterscheid 59–65; Gómez-Arostegui, The Untold Story of the First Copyright Suit Under the Statute of Anne in 1710, 25 Berkeley Tech. L.J. 1247, 1250–1256 (2010).

To prevent the continuation of the booksellers' monopoly and to encourage authors to write new books, Parliament enacted the Statute of Anne. It bore the title: "An Act for the Encouragement of Learning, by vesting the Copies of printed Books in the Authors or Purchasers of such Copies, during the Times therein mentioned." And it granted authors (not publishers) and their assignees the "sole Right and Liberty of printing" their works for limited periods of time *in order to encourage them "to compose and write useful Books."* 8 Anne, ch. 19, § 1 (emphasis added). As one historian has put it: "The central plank of the ... Act was ... a cultural *quid pro quo.* To encourage 'learned Men to compose and write useful Books' the state would provide a guaranteed, if temporally limited, right to print and reprint those works." Deazley,

The Myth of Copyright at Common Law, 62 Camb. L.J. 106, 108 (2003). At first, in their attempts to minimize their losses, the booksellers argued that authors had a perpetual common-law copyright in their works deriving from their natural rights as creators. But the House of Lords ultimately held in *Donaldson v. Beckett*, 1 Eng. Rep. 837 (1774), that the Statute of Anne had transformed any such perpetual common-law copyright into a copyright of a limited term designed to serve the public interest. Patterson 15–16, 153, 158–179; Deazley, *supra*, at 114–126.

Many early colonial copyright statutes, patterned after the Statute of Anne, also stated that copyright's objective was to encourage authors to produce new works and thereby improve learning. See U.S. Copyright Office, Copyright Enactments, Bulletin No. 3, pp. 1, 6, 10, 11, 17, 19 (rev.1963) (statutes of Connecticut, New Jersey, Pennsylvania, South Carolina, Georgia, and New York); Walterscheid 74–75; Bracha, The Adventures of the Statute of Anne in the Land of Unlimited Possibilities: The Life of a Legal Transplant, 25 Berkeley Tech. L.J. 1427, 1444–1450 (2010).

At least, that was the predominant view expressed to, or by, the Founders. Patterson 93. Thomas Jefferson, for example, initially expressed great uncertainty as to whether the Constitution should authorize the grant of copyrights and patents at all, writing that "the benefit even of limited monopolies is too doubtful" to warrant anything other than their "suppression." Letter from Thomas Jefferson to James Madison (July 31, 1788), in 13 Papers of Thomas Jefferson 440, 443 (J. Boyd ed.1956). James Madison also thought that "Monopolies ... are justly classed among the greatest nu [i]sances in Government." Letter from James Madison to Thomas Jefferson (Oct. 17, 1788), in 14 *id.*, at 16, 21 (J. Boyd ed.1958). But he argued that "in certain cases" such as copyright, monopolies should "be granted" ("with caution, and guarded with strictness against abuse") to serve as "*compensation for a benefit actually gained to the community* ... which the owner might otherwise withhold from public use." Monopolies. Perpetuities. Corporations. Ecclesiastical Endowments., in J. Madison, Writings 756 (J. Rakove ed.1999) (emphasis added). Jefferson eventually came to agree with Madison, supporting a limited conferral of monopoly rights but only "*as an encouragement to men to pursue ideas which may produce utility*." Letter from Thomas Jefferson to Isaac McPherson (Aug. 13, 1813), in 6 Papers of Thomas Jefferson, at 379, 383 (J. Looney ed.2009) (emphasis added).

This utilitarian view of copyrights and patents, embraced by Jefferson and Madison, stands in contrast to the "natural rights" view underlying much of continental European copyright law—a view that the English booksellers promoted in an effort to limit their losses following the enactment of the Statute of Anne and that in part motivated the enactment of some of the colonial statutes. Patterson 158–179, 183–192. Premised on the idea that an author or inventor has an inherent right to the fruits of his labor, it mythically stems from a legendary 6th-century statement of King Diarmed " 'to every cow her calf, and accordingly to every book its copy.' " A. Birrell, Seven Lectures on the Law and History of Copyright in Books 42 (1899). That view, though perhaps reflected in the Court's opinion, *ante*, at 893, runs contrary to the more utilitarian views that influenced the writing of our own Constitution's Copyright Clause. See S.

Ricketson, The Berne Convention for the Protection of Literary and Artistic Works: 1886–1986, pp. 5–6 (1987) (The first French copyright laws "placed authors' rights on a more elevated basis than the Act of Anne had done," on the understanding that they were "simply according formal recognition to what was already inherent in the 'very nature of things' "); S. Stewart, International Copyright and Neighbouring Rights 6–7 (2d ed.1989) (describing the European system of *droit d'auteur*).

This utilitarian understanding of the Copyright Clause has long been reflected in the Court's case law. In *Mazer,* for example, the Court refers to copyright as embodying the view that "*encouragement of individual effort by personal gain* is the best way to advance public welfare through the talents of authors and inventors." 347 U.S., at 219, 74 S.Ct. 460 (emphasis added). In *Twentieth Century Music Corp. v. Aiken,* 422 U.S. 151, 95 S.Ct. 2040, 45 L.Ed.2d 84 (1975), the Court says that underlying copyright is the understanding that "*[c]reative work is to be encouraged and rewarded, but private motivation must ultimately serve the cause of promoting broad public availability of literature, music, and the other arts.*" *Id.,* at 156, 95 S.Ct. 2040 (emphasis added). And in *Sony Corp. of America v. Universal City Studios, Inc.,* 464 U.S. 417, 104 S.Ct. 774, 78 L.Ed.2d 574 (1984), the Court, speaking of both copyrights and patents, points out that the "monopoly privileges that Congress may authorize are ... [not] primarily designed to provide a special private benefit. Rather, the limited grant is a means by which an important public purpose may be achieved. It is intended *to motivate the creative activity of authors ... by the provision of a special reward.*" *Id.,* at 429, 104 S.Ct. 774 (emphasis added); see also, *e.g., Graham v. John Deere Co. of Kansas City,* 383 U.S. 1, 6, 86 S.Ct. 684, 15 L.Ed.2d 545 (1966) (The "constitutional command ... '[to] promote the Progress [of Science]' ... is the *standard* expressed in the Constitution and it may not be ignored"); *Fox Film Corp. v. Doyal,* 286 U.S. 123, 127, 52 S.Ct. 546, 76 L.Ed. 1010 (1932) ("The sole interest of the United States ... lie[s] in the general benefits derived by the public from the labors of authors").

Congress has expressed similar views in congressional Reports on copyright legislation. Thus, for example, an 1892 House Report states:

> "The object to be attained and the reason for the constitutional grant of power are imbedded in the grant itself. They are 'to promote the progress of science and the useful arts.' ... [The Clause says] nothing ... about any desire or purpose to secure to the author or inventor his 'natural right to his property.' " H.R.Rep. No. 1494, 52d Cong., 1st Sess., 2.

Similarly, the congressional authors of the landmark 1909 Copyright Act wrote:

> "The Constitution ... provides that Congress shall have the power to grant [copyrights] ... [n]ot primarily for the benefit of the author, ... but because the policy is believed to be for the benefit of the great body of people, *in that it will stimulate writing and invention,* to give some bonus to authors and inventors." H.R.Rep. No. 2222, 60th Cong., 2d Sess., 7 (1909).

And they went on to say:

> "Congress must consider ... two questions: First, how much will the legislation stimulate the producer and so benefit the public; and, second, how much will the monopoly granted be detrimental to the public? The granting of such exclusive rights, under the proper terms and conditions, confers a benefit upon the public that outweighs the evils of the temporary monopoly." *Ibid.*

The upshot is that text, history, and precedent demonstrate that the Copyright Clause places great value on the power of copyright to elicit new production. Congress in particular cases may determine that copyright's ability to do so outweighs any concomitant high prices, administrative costs, and restrictions on dissemination. And when it does so, we must respect its judgment. See *Eldred,* 537 U.S., at 222, 123 S.Ct. 769. But does the Clause empower Congress to enact a statute that withdraws works from the public domain, brings about higher prices and costs, and in doing so seriously restricts dissemination, particularly to those who need it for scholarly, educational, or cultural purposes—all *without providing any additional incentive* for the production of new material? That is the question before us. And, as I have said, I believe the answer is no. Congress in this statute has exceeded what are, under any plausible reading of the Copyright Clause, its permissible limits.

II

The Act before us says that it "restores" American copyright to a set of works, which, for the most part, did not previously enjoy American copyright protection. These works had fallen into America's public domain, but as of the "restoration" date, they had not yet fallen into the public domain of the foreign country where they originated.

The statute covers works originating almost anywhere outside the United States. See 17 U.S.C. § 104A(h)(3) (setting out eligibility criteria); U.S. Copyright Office, Circular No. 38A: International Copyright Relations of the United States (2010). The relevant set of works consists primarily of works originating abroad that did not obtain, or at some point lost, American copyright protection because (1) the author failed to comply with applicable American copyright formalities (such as notice or renewal), or (2) the nation in which they were first published then lacked copyright relations with the United States, or (3) they are sound recordings fixed before February 15, 1972. § 104A(h)(6)(C). A work must also satisfy other technical requirements: It must have had a rightholder who was a national or resident of an eligible country on the day it was created; and it cannot have been published in the United States within 30 days of its first publication. § 104A(h)(6)(D). The Act grants these works a copyright that expires at the time it would have expired had the author obtained a full American copyright term starting from the date on which the work was first published (in the foreign country). § 104A(a)(1)(B).

The Act mainly applies to works first published abroad between 1923 and 1989. It does not apply significantly to earlier works because any work published before 1921 would have fallen into the public domain before 1977 had it received a full American copyright term, while works published between 1921 and 1923 obtained a "restored" copyright that expired before the 1998 Sonny Bono Copyright Term Extension Act, and so could have lasted two years at most. See Tit. I, § 101, 90 Stat. 2574 (extending the copyright term of works still under copyright in 1977 to 75 years); 17 U.S.C. § 304(b) (extending the copyright term of works still under copyright in 1998 to 95 years). It has less impact on more recent works because in 1989 the United States became a Berne member, abolished the copyright notice requirement, and thenceforth provided prospective copyright protection throughout the Berne Union. See R. Schechter & J. Thomas, Intellectual Property: The Law of Copyrights, Patents and Trademarks 75–77 (2003); § 7, 102 Stat. 2857–2858 (codified as amended at 17 U.S.C. §§ 401–406).

Despite these temporal limitations, the Act covers vast numbers of works. The first category includes works published in countries that had copyright relations with the United States during this time period, such as most of Western Europe and Latin America, Australia, and Japan, see Circular No. 38A, at 2–10, whose authors did not satisfy American copyright formalities, perhaps because the author, who may not have sought an American copyright, published the book abroad without proper American notice, or perhaps because the author obtained a valid American copyright but failed to renew it.

The second category (works that entered the public domain due to a lack of copyright relations) includes, among others, all works published in Russia and other countries of the former Soviet Union before May 1973 (when the U.S.S.R. joined the Universal Copyright Convention (UCC)), all works published in the People's Republic of China before March 1992 (when bilateral copyright relations between the People's Republic and the United States were first established), all South Korean works published before October 1987 (when South Korea joined the UCC), and all Egyptian and Turkish works published before March 1989 (when the United States joined Berne). See *id.*, at 878 – 883, and 883, nn. 2, 5, 6.

The third category covers all sound recordings from eligible foreign countries published after February 15, 1972. The practical significance of federal copyright restoration to this category of works is less clear, since these works received, and continued to receive, copyright protection under state law. See 17 U.S.C. § 301(c).

Apparently there are no precise figures about the number of works the Act affects, but in 1996 the then-Register of Copyrights, Marybeth Peters, thought that they "probably number in the millions." The Year in Review: Accomplishments and Objectives of the U.S. Copyright Office, 7 Ford. Intellectual Property Media & Entertainment L.J. 25, 31 (1996).

A

The provision before us takes works from the public domain, at least as of January 1, 1996. See § 104A(h)(2)(A) (setting "restoration" dates). It then restricts the dissemination of those works in two ways.

First, "restored copyright" holders can now charge fees for works that consumers previously used for free. The price of a score of Shostakovich's Preludes and Fugues Op. 87, for example, has risen by a multiple of seven. Brief for Conductors Guild et al. as *Amici Curiae* 11. And, as the Court recognizes, an orchestra that once could perform "Peter and the Wolf ... free of charge" will now have to buy the "right to perform it ... in the marketplace." *Ante*, at 893. But for the case of certain "derivative" works, § 104A(d)(3), the "restored copyright" holder, like other copyright holders, can charge what the market will bear. If a school orchestra or other nonprofit organization cannot afford the new charges, so be it. They will have to do without—aggravating the already serious problem of cultural education in the United States. See Brief for Conductors Guild et al. as *Amici Curiae* 4–5, 7–8 (describing the inability of many orchestras to pay for the rental of sheet music covered by "restored copyright[s]").

Second, and at least as important, the statute creates administrative costs, such as the costs of determining whether a work is the subject of a "restored copyright," searching for a "restored copyright" holder, and negotiating a fee. Congress has tried to ease the administrative burden of contacting copyright holders and negotiating prices for those whom the statute calls "reliance part[ies]," namely those who previously had used such works when they were freely available in the public domain. § 104A(h)(4). But Congress has done nothing to ease the administrative burden of securing permission from copyright owners that is placed upon those who want to use a work that they did not previously use, and this is a particular problem when it comes to "orphan works"—older and more obscure works with minimal commercial value that have copyright owners who are difficult or impossible to track down. Unusually high administrative costs threaten to limit severely the distribution and use of those works—works which, despite their characteristic lack of economic value, can prove culturally invaluable.

There are millions of such works. For example, according to European Union figures, there are 13 million orphan books in the European Union (13% of the total number of books in copyright there), 225,000 orphan films in European film archives, and 17 million orphan photographs in United Kingdom museums. A. Vuopala, Assessment of the Orphan Works Issue and Costs for Rights Clearance 19, 25 (2010), online at http://ec.europa.eu/information_society/activities/digital_libraries/doc/reports_orphan/anna_report.pdf (all Internet materials as visited Jan. 13, 2012, and available in Clerk of Court's case file). How is a university, a film collector, a musician, a database compiler, or a scholar now to obtain permission to use any such lesser known foreign work previously in the American public domain? Consider the questions that any such individual, group, or institution usually must answer: Is the work eligible for restoration under the statute? If so, who now holds the copyright—the author? An heir? A publisher? An association?A long-lost cousin? Whom must we contact? What is the address? Suppose no one answers? How do we conduct a negotiation?

To find answers to these, and similar, questions costs money. The cost to the University of Michigan and the Institute of Museum and Library Services, for example, to determine the copyright status of books contained in the Hathi Trust Digital Library that were published in the

United States from 1923 to 1963 will exceed $1 million. Brief for American Library Association et al. as *Amici Curiae* 15.

It is consequently not surprising to learn that the Los Angeles Public Library has been unable to make its collection of Mexican folk music publicly available because of problems locating copyright owners, that a Jewish cultural organization has abandoned similar efforts to make available Jewish cultural music and other materials, or that film preservers, museums, universities, scholars, database compilers, and others report that the administrative costs associated with trying to locate foreign copyright owners have forced them to curtail their cultural, scholarly, or other work- preserving efforts. See, *e.g.*, Comments of the Library Copyright Alliance in Response to the U.S. Copyright Office's Inquiry on Orphan Works 5 (Mar. 25, 2005), online at http://www.arl.org/bm~doc/1cacomment0305.pdf; Comments of Creative Commons and Save The Music in Response to the U.S. Copyright Office's Inquiry on Orphan Works (Mar. 25, 2005), online at http://www.copyright.gov/orphan/comments/OW0643–STM–CreativeCommons.pdf; General Agreement on Tariffs and Trade (GATT): Intellectual Property Provisions, Joint Hearing before the Subcommittee on Intellectual Property and Judicial Administration of the House Committee on the Judiciary and the Subcommittee on Patents, Copyrights and Trademarks of the Senate Committee on the Judiciary, 103d Cong., 2d Sess., 131, 273 (1994) (hereinafter Joint Hearing) (statement of Larry Urbanski, Chairman of the Fairness in Copyright Coalition and President of Moviecraft, Inc.); Brief for American Library Association et al. as *Amici Curiae* 6–23; Brief for Creative Commons Corp. as *Amicus Curiae* 7–8; Brief for Project Petrucci, LLC, as *Amicus Curiae* 10–11.

These high administrative costs can prove counterproductive in another way. They will tempt some potential users to "steal" or "pirate" works rather than do without. And piracy often begets piracy, breeding the destructive habit of taking copyrighted works without paying for them, even where payment is possible. Such habits ignore the critical role copyright plays in the creation of new works, while reflecting a false belief that new creation appears by magic without thought or hope of compensation.

B

I recognize that ordinary copyright protection also comes accompanied with dissemination-restricting royalty charges and administrative costs. But here the restrictions work special harm. For one thing, the foreign location of restored works means higher than ordinary administrative costs. For another, the statute's technical requirements make it very difficult to establish whether a work has had its copyright restored by the statute. Gard, In the Trenches With § 104A: An Evaluation of the Parties' Arguments in *Golan* v. *Holder* as It Heads to the Supreme Court, 64 Vand. L.Rev. En Banc 199, 216–220 (2011) (describing difficulties encountered in compiling the information necessary to create an online tool to determine whether the statute applies in any given case).

Worst of all, "restored copyright" protection removes material from the public domain. In doing so, it reverses the payment expectations of those who used, or intended to use, works that they thought belonged to them. Were Congress to act similarly with respect to well-established property rights, the problem would be obvious. This statute analogously restricts, and thereby diminishes, Americans' pre-existing freedom to use formerly public domain material in their expressive activities.

Thus, while the majority correctly observes that the dissemination-restricting harms of copyright normally present problems appropriate for legislation to resolve, *ante,* at 893 – 894, the question is whether the Copyright Clause permits Congress seriously to exacerbate such a problem by taking works out of the public domain without a countervailing benefit. This question *is* appropriate for judicial resolution. Indeed, unlike *Eldred* where the Court had to decide a complicated line-drawing question—when is a copyright term too long?—here an easily administrable standard is available—a standard that would require works that have already fallen into the public domain to stay there.

The several, just mentioned features of the present statute are important, for they distinguish it from other copyright laws. By removing material from the public domain, the statute, in literal terms, "abridges" a pre-existing freedom to speak. In practical terms, members of the public might well have decided what to say, as well as when and how to say it, in part by reviewing with a view to repeating, expression that they reasonably believed was, or would be, freely available. Given these speech implications, it is not surprising that Congress has long sought to protect public domain material when revising the copyright laws. See *infra,* at 909 (listing instances). And this Court has assumed the particular importance of public domain material in roughly analogous circumstances. See *Graham,* 383 U.S., at 6, 86 S.Ct. 684 ("Congress may not authorize the issuance of patents whose effects are to remove existent knowledge from the public domain"); *Kewanee Oil Co. v. Bicron Corp.,* 416 U.S. 470, 484, 94 S.Ct. 1879, 40 L.Ed.2d 315 (1974) (trade secret protection is not incompatible with "policy that matter once in the public domain must remain in the public domain"); *Cox Broadcasting Corp. v. Cohn,* 420 U.S. 469, 496, 95 S.Ct. 1029, 43 L.Ed.2d 328 (1975) (First Amendment prohibits sanctioning press for publishing material disclosed in public court documents); see also *Dastar Corp. v. Twentieth Century Fox Film Corp.,* 539 U.S. 23, 33, 123 S.Ct. 2041, 156 L.Ed.2d 18 (2003) ("The right to copy ... once a copyright has expired ... passes to the public" (internal quotation marks omitted)).

Moreover, whereas forward-looking copyright laws tend to benefit those whose identities are not yet known (the writer who has not yet written a book, the musician who has not yet composed a song), when a copyright law is primarily backward looking the risk is greater that Congress is trying to help known beneficiaries at the expense of badly organized unknown users who find it difficult to argue and present their case to Congress. In *Eldred,* I thought this problem was severe. See generally 537 U.S., at 243–266, 123 S.Ct. 769 (dissenting opinion). And in light of the fact that Congress, with one minor exception, heard testimony only from the representatives of existing copyright holders, who hoped that passage of the statute would enable them to benefit from reciprocal treatment of American authors abroad, *infra,* at 910, I cannot say that even here the problem, while much diminished, was nonexistent.

I agree with the majority that, in doing so, this statute does not discriminate among speakers based on their viewpoints or subject matter. *Ante,* at 891 – 892. But such considerations do not exhaust potential First Amendment problems. Cf. *Sorrell v. IMS Health Inc.,* 564 U.S. 552, 566, 131 S.Ct. 2653, 2663, 180 L.Ed.2d 544 (2011) (finding First Amendment problem in statute that prohibits drug manufacturers from using publicly available prescriber-identifying information in their marketing efforts in part because it "disfavor[ed] specific speakers"); *Turner Broadcasting System, Inc. v. FCC,* 512 U.S. 622, 659, 114 S.Ct. 2445, 129 L.Ed.2d 497 (1994) ("Regulations that discriminate among media, or among different speakers within a single medium, often present serious First Amendment concerns").

Taken together, these speech-related harms (*e.g.,* restricting use of previously available material; reversing payment expectations; rewarding rent-seekers at the public's expense) at least show the presence of a First Amendment interest. And that is enough. For present purposes, I need not decide whether the harms to that interest show a violation of the First Amendment. I need only point to the importance of interpreting the Constitution as a single document—a document that we should not read as setting the Copyright Clause and the First Amendment at cross-purposes. Nor need I advocate the application here of strict or specially heightened review. I need only find that the First Amendment interest is important enough to require courts to scrutinize with some care the reasons claimed to justify the Act in order to determine whether they constitute reasonable copyright-related justifications for the serious harms, including speech-related harms, which the Act seems likely to impose.

C

1

This statute does not serve copyright's traditional public ends, namely the creation of monetary awards that "motivate the creative activity of authors," *Sony,* 464 U.S., at 429, 104 S.Ct. 774, "encourag[e] individual effort," *Mazer,* 347 U.S., at 219, 74 S.Ct. 460, and thereby "serve the cause of promoting broad public availability of literature, music, and the other arts," *Twentieth Century Music,* 422 U.S., at 156, 95 S.Ct. 2040. The statute grants its "restored copyright[s]" *only* to works *already produced.* It provides no monetary incentive to produce anything new. Unlike other American copyright statutes from the time of the Founders onwards, including the statute at issue in *Eldred,* it lacks any significant copyright-related *quid pro quo.*

The majority seeks to avoid this awkward fact by referring to past congressional practice that mostly suggests that Congress may provide new or increased protection *both* to newly created *and* to previously created works. *Ante,* at 885 – 886, 886 – 887; Act of May 31, 1790, § 1, 1 Stat. 124 (conferring its new federal copyright on new works as well as old); Act of July 3, 1832, § 3, 4 Stat. 559 (authorizing new patents for past and future inventors who inadvertently failed to comply with applicable statutory formalities); *McClurg v. Kingsland,* 1 How. 202, 11 L.Ed. 102 (1843) (applying an act deeming a past or future inventor's patent valid despite it being briefly used by, for example, the inventor's employer). I do not dispute that copyright power. Insofar as such a statute does the former, *i.e.,* extends protection to newly created material, it embodies copyright's traditional justification—eliciting new production. And I do not doubt that Congress may then also include existing works within the scope of, say, increased protection for equitable and administrative reasons. See *Eldred,* 537 U.S., at 204, 214–215, 123 S.Ct. 769 (describing equitable reasons for applying newly extended copyright terms to future and existing copyrights alike). The statute before us, however, does not directly elicit any new production. Compare *id.,* at 204–208, 123 S.Ct. 769 (majority opinion) (noting that statute's extended term would apply to newly created material, and finding that the determination of the likelihood of its eliciting new production in practice was a matter for Congress to determine), with *id.,* at 243–267, 123 S.Ct. 769 (BREYER, J., dissenting) (expressing the view that there is little likelihood, in practice, that the statute would elicit new material). See also Walterscheid 219 (the 1790 Congress likely thought it was substituting federal protection for pre-existing state common-law protections); Maher, Copyright Term, Retrospective Extension, and the Copyright Law of 1790 in Historical Context, 49 J. Copyright Soc. USA 1021, 1023–1024, and n. 8 (2002) (numerical estimate suggesting that 1790 Act removed only a small number of books from public domain).

The other statutes to which the majority refers are private bills, statutes retroactively granting protection in wartime, or the like. *Ante,* at 885 – 887; Act of Feb. 19, 1849, ch. 57, 9 Stat. 763 (Levi Corson); Act of June 23, 1874, ch. 534, 18 Stat., pt. 3, p. 618 (Tod Helmuth); Act of Feb. 17, 1898, ch. 29, 30 Stat. 1396 (Judson Jones); Act of Dec. 18, 1919, ch. 11, 41 Stat. 368; Act of Sept. 25, 1941, ch. 421, 55 Stat. 732; see also *Evans v. Jordan,* 9 Cranch 199, 3 L.Ed. 704 (1815) (upholding a private bill restoring patent protection to a flour mill). But special circumstances, like wars, hurricanes, earthquakes, and other disasters, prevent the realization in practice of a reasonable expectation of securing or maintaining a pre-existing right. Private bills are designed to provide special exceptions for comparable equitable reasons. See also Act of Mar. 3, 1893, ch. 215, 27 Stat. 743 (similar, as far as I can tell). To find in these laws an important analogy to the present law, which for the most part covers works that the author did not expect to protect in America (and often did not particularly want to protect), seems somewhat farfetched.

In fact, congressional practice shows the contrary. It consists of a virtually unbroken string of legislation preventing the withdrawal of works from the public domain. See, *e.g.,* Berne Convention Implementation Act of 1988, § 12, 102 Stat. 2860 (the Act "does not provide copyright protection for any work that is in the public domain in the United States"); Copyright Act of 1976, Tit. I, § 101, 90 Stat. 2573 (declining to extend copyright protection to any work that is in the public domain prior to the Act taking effect); Copyright Act of 1909, § 7, 35 Stat. 1077

("[N]o copyright shall subsist in the original text of any work which is in the public domain, or in any work which was published in this country or any foreign country prior to the going into effect of this Act and has not been already copyrighted in the United States"); Act to Amend the Several Acts Respecting Copy Rights § 16, 4 Stat. 439 (the Act "shall not extend to any copyright heretofore secured, the term of which has already expired"); see also H.R.Rep. No. 1742, 87th Cong., 2d Sess., 3 (1962) (expressing concern that because "it is not possible to revive expired terms of copyright, it seems to the committee to be desirable to suspend further expiration of copyright for a period long enough to enable the working out of remaining obstacles to the overall revision of the copyright law").

2

The majority makes several other arguments. First, it argues that the Clause does not require the "creation of at least one new work," *ante,* at 888, but may instead "promote the Progress of Science" in other ways. And it specifically mentions the "dissemination of existing and future works" as determinative here. *Ante,* at 887 – 890, and n. 25. The industry experts to whom the majority refers argue that copyright protection of already existing works can help, say, music publishers or film distributers raise prices, produce extra profits, and consequently lead them to publish or distribute works they might otherwise have ignored. But ordinarily a copyright—since it is a *monopoly* on copying—*restricts* dissemination of a work once produced compared to a competitive market. And simply making the industry richer does not mean that the industry, when it makes an ordinary *forward-looking* economic calculus, will distribute works not previously distributed. The industry experts might mean that temporary extra profits will lead them to invest in the development of a market, say, by advertising. But this kind of argument, which can be made by distributers of all sorts of goods, ranging from kiwi fruit to Swedish furniture, has little if anything to do with the nonrepeatable costs of initial creation, which is the special concern of copyright protection. See *supra,* at 878 – 879.

Moreover, the argument proves too much. It is the kind of argument that the Stationers' Company might well have made and which the British Parliament rejected. Cf. Patterson 154–155 (describing failed booksellers' bill seeking protection from foreign competition through an extension of the copyright term). It is the kind of argument that could justify a legislature's withdrawing from the public domain the works, say, of Hawthorne or of Swift or for that matter the King James Bible in order to encourage further publication of those works; and, it could even more easily justify similar action in the case of lesser known early works, perhaps those of the Venerable Bede. The Court has not, to my knowledge, previously accepted such a rationale—a rationale well removed from the special economic circumstances that surround the nonrepeatable costs of the initial creation of a "Writing." *Supra,* at 878. And I fear that doing so would read the Copyright Clause as if it were a blank check made out in favor of those who are not themselves creators.

It is not surprising that the copyright holders' representatives who appeared before Congress did not emphasize this argument. (With one minor exception only those representatives appeared, see generally Joint Hearing; the Copyright Office did not testify, *id.*, at 239.) Rather, they focused on the Berne Convention itself. By that time, Congress had already protected all *new* works of Berne members. But it had not provided additional protection to pre-existing foreign works that were then in the American public domain. Industry witnesses testified that withdrawing such works from the American public domain would permit foreign copyright owners to charge American consumers more for their products; and that, as a result, the United States would be able to persuade foreign countries to allow American holders of pre-existing copyrights to charge foreign customers more money for their products. See *id.*, at 241 (statement of Eric Smith, Executive Director and General Counsel, International Intellectual Property Alliance) ("[F]ailure to [comply with Article 18] will ... undermine the ability of the United States to press other countries to implement the same sort of protection in their implementing legislation currently pending in many legislatures around the globe"); *id.*, at 253 (statement of Matt Gerson, Vice President for Congressional Affairs, Motion Picture Assn. of America) (similar). See also *id.*, at 85 (statement of Xavier Becerra, House Judiciary Committee member) ("[R]etroactivity ... is probably the best way to ensure that some of our older American works, anything from Motown, to 'Star Trek,' to 'The Hardy Boys' get the protection in some of these emerging foreign markets. It is important to ensure that countries no longer use our U.S. law as an excuse for not extending retroactive copyright protections to some of our own works"). But see *id.*, at 272–279 (statement of Larry Urbanski, Chairman of the Fairness in Copyright Coalition and President of Moviecraft Inc.) (testifying against restoration on grounds similar to those set out, *supra*, at 882 – 884).

This argument, whatever its intrinsic merits, is an argument that directly concerns a private benefit: how to obtain more money from the sales of existing products. It is not an argument about a public benefit, such as how to promote or to protect the creative process.

Third, the majority points out that the statute "gives [authors] nothing more than the benefit of their labors during whatever time remains before the normal copyright term expires." *Ante*, at 893. But insofar as it suggests that copyright should in general help authors obtain greater monetary rewards than needed to elicit new works, it rests upon primarily European, but not American, copyright concepts. See *supra*, at 879 – 880.

Fourth, the majority argues that this statutory provision is necessary to fulfill our Berne Convention obligations. *Ante*, at 879 – 881. The Treaty, in Article 18, says that the "Convention shall apply to all works which, at the moment of its coming into force [*i.e.*, 1989 in the case of the United States] have not yet fallen into the public domain in the country of origin through the expiry of the term of protection." Berne Convention for the Protection of Literary and Artistic Works, Art. 18(1), Sept. 9, 1886, as revised at Stockholm on July 14, 1967, 828 U.N.T.S. 221, 251. The majority and Government say that this means we must protect the foreign works at issue here. And since the Berne Convention, taken as a whole, provides incentives for the creation of new works, I am willing to speculate, for argument's sake, that the statute might indirectly encourage production of new works by making the United States' place in the international copyright regime more secure.

Still, I cannot find this argument sufficient to save the statute. For one thing, this is a dilemma of the Government's own making. The United States obtained the benefits of Berne for many years despite its failure to enact a statute implementing Article 18. But in 1994, the United States and other nations signed the Agreement on Trade–Related Aspects of Intellectual Property Rights, which enabled signatories to use World Trade Organization dispute resolution mechanisms to complain about other members' Berne Convention violations. And at that time the Government, although it successfully secured reservations protecting other special features of American copyright law, made no effort to secure a reservation permitting the United States to keep some or all restored works in the American public domain. Indeed, it made no effort to do so despite the fact that Article 18 explicitly authorizes countries to negotiate exceptions to the Article's retroactivity principle. See Art. 18(3), *ibid.* ("The application of [the retroactivity] principle *shall be subject to any provisions contained in special conventions to that effect* existing or to be concluded between countries of the Union" (emphasis added)); Gervais, *Golan* v. *Holder* : A Look at the Constraints Imposed by the Berne Convention, 64 Vand. L.Rev. En Banc 147, 151–152 (2011); Gard, 64 Vand. L.Rev. En Banc, at 206.

For another thing, the Convention does not require Congress to enact a statute that causes so much damage to public domain material. Article 18(3) also states that "the respective countries shall determine, each in so far as it is concerned, *the conditions of application of this principle.*" 18 U.N.T.S., at 251 (emphasis added). Congress could have alleviated many of the costs that the statute imposes by, for example, creating forms of compulsory licensing, requiring "restored copyright" holders to provide necessary administrative information as a condition of protection, or insisting upon "reasonable royalties." Cf. S. 2913, 110th Cong., 2d Sess. (2008) (legislation that would have limited judicial remedies against users of orphan works); H.R. 5889, 110th Cong., 2d Sess. (2008) (House version of same); American Society of Composers, Authors and Publishers, http://www.ascap.com/licensing/termsdefined.aspx (society of music copyright owners offering blanket licenses that give users the unlimited right to perform any of its members' songs for a fixed fee, thus reducing negotiation and enforcement costs).

To say this is not to criticize the Convention or our joining it. Rather, it is to argue that the other branches of Government should have tried to *follow* the Convention and in particular its provisions offering compliance flexibility. The fact that the statute has significant First Amendment costs is relevant in this respect, for that Amendment ordinarily requires courts to evaluate less restrictive, alternative possibilities. Doing so here reveals that neither Congress nor the Executive took advantage of less restrictive methods of compliance that the Convention itself provides. And that fact means that the Convention cannot provide the statute with a constitutionally sufficient justification that is otherwise lacking.

III

The fact that, by withdrawing material from the public domain, the statute inhibits an important pre-existing flow of information is sufficient, when combined with the other features of the statute that I have discussed, to convince me that the Copyright Clause, interpreted in the light of the First Amendment, does not authorize Congress to enact this statute.

I respectfully dissent from the Court's contrary conclusion.

A Note on *Golan:*

We were particular proud to be cited for our work at Tulane *twice* in the Breyer dissent:

> "I recognize that ordinary copyright protection also comes accompanied with dissemination-restricting royalty charges and administrative costs. But here the restrictions work special harm. For one thing, the foreign location of restored works means higher than ordinary administrative costs. For another, the statute's technical requirements make it very difficult to establish whether a work has had its copyright restored by the statute. Gard, In the Trenches with § 104A: An Evaluation of the Parties' Arguments in *Golan v. Holder* as It Heads to the Supreme Court, 64 Vand. L.Rev. En Banc 199, 216-220 (2011) (describing difficulties encountered in compiling the information necessary to create an online tool to determine whether the statute applies in any given case)."
>
> "Still, I cannot find this argument sufficient to save the statute. For one thing, this is a dilemma of the Government's own making. The United States obtained the benefits of Berne for many years despite its failure to enact a statute implementing Article 18. But in 1994, the United States and other nations signed the Agreement on Trade-Related Aspects of Intellectual Property Rights, which enabled signatories to use World Trade Organization dispute resolution mechanisms to complain about other members' Berne Convention violations. But at that time the Government, although it successfully secured reservations protecting other special features of American copyright law, made no effort to secure a reservation permitting the United States to keep some or all restored works in the American public domain. And it made no effort to do so despite the fact that Article 18 explicitly authorizes countries to negotiate exceptions to the Article's retroactivity principle. See Art. 18(3), *ibid.* ("The application of [the retroactivity] principle *shall be subject to any provisions contained in special conventions to that effect* existing or to be concluded between countries of the Union" (emphasis added)); Gervais, *Golan v. Holder*: A Look at the Constraints

Imposed by the Berne Convention, 64 Vand. L.Rev. En Banc 147, 151-152 (2011); Gard, 64 Vand. L.Rev. En Banc, at 206."

A Tale of Two Ginsburgs: Traditional Contours in *Eldred* and *Golan*

Introduction

Born in 2003 as a simple, off-handed phrase, "traditional contours of copyright protection" was the creation of Justice Ginsburg in *Eldred v. Ashcroft*. The phrase never quite developed, at least until Judge Henry in *Golan v. Gonzales* took an interest in the phrase in his Tenth Circuit opinion. But in 2012, in *Golan v. Holder*, not only did Justice Ginsburg disapprove of Judge Henry's interpretation of her phrase, she very much tried to limit its usefulness entirely. "Traditional contours" lived a short, unloved, and troubled life. And yet, the potential for greatness was there.

"Traditional contours of copyright protection"--what was it exactly? Did it define the underlying system of copyright itself? Did it mean only the parameters of safeguards that triggered First Amendment analysis? Did it only apply to copyright law, or were there "traditional contours" in other areas of intellectual property (IP) law, for instance patents (sharing the same origin point in the Copyright Clause), or even law in general? Was it a poor man's "text, precedent, and history," and therefore redundant and unnecessary? In the end, was it a mistake of birth, never wanted, its life shortened before being fully defined? Or is it a phrase we should take more seriously? Could "traditional contours" have been an analytic mechanism to keep in check the balance of our copyright system in changing times?

I did not intend to write about "the tale of two Ginsburgs." I already explored Golan in its pre-Supreme Court days and extensively examined the statute connected to the case, § 104A of the Copyright Act of 1976 (1976 Act), both in writing and in practice. I also explored in detail the theoretical underpinnings of the phrase as articulated by Judge Henry in the Tenth Circuit, again in two separate pieces. I had seen my work as complete. I was happy to move on to other topics, and in fact I had.

Then, Justice Ginsburg delivered her opinion in *Golan v. Holder.* The contradictions with *Eldred* and the tone of Justice Ginsburg's *Golan v. Holder* opinion, combined with the dismissive footnote regarding Judge Henry's work, all surprised me. Her whole opinion seemed out of sorts. I found myself back in the thicket of "traditional contours," this time seeking to understand the differences between Justice Ginsburg in 2003 with *Eldred* and Justice Ginsburg in 2012 with *Golan*. Justice Ginsburg instilled meaning into the phrase twice. What did she mean by "traditional contours" each time? But it also goes further.

In all my years of study, I had in some ways danced around the phrase. For instance, the practical side of my work looked into the components of § 104A, while the more theoretical work looked to understand the continuity and differences in triggering federal protection for copyright works under the Copyright Act of 1909 (1909 Act) and the 1976 Act. I held the belief that traditional contours existed, and that it was only a matter of working out the details--what is tradition? What is a contour? But Justice Ginsburg in 2012 upset that apple cart. This development called for returning to *Eldred* as the origin point and comparing it with the new incarnation of traditional contours. Indeed, Justice Ginsburg seemed to question whether the phrase had any use at all.

In the aftermath of *Golan v. Holder*, I delved deep into the research, looking at every piece of scholarship written on *Eldred*, as well as the cases following Eldred. How had scholars written about *Eldred*, and what other complimentary work would help illuminate what Justice Ginsburg meant in 2003? How had that changed in 2012? I looked to other areas of intellectual property. I looked into First Amendment literature. I was on a quest: What does the phrase "traditional contours" mean? So many scholars had written that Justice Ginsburg in *Eldred* left "traditional contours of copyright protection" undefined. I had always believed that to be true. But as I revisited the opinion itself, I began to disagree. The question was how to read the two decisions, the two mappings of traditional contours of copyright protection.

In the process of researching traditional contours, my research has taken many unexpected turns. My doctoral chair long ago told me that an article is only the tip of an iceberg of discarded research and many drafts. That is certainly true of this piece, which at one point had a full section devoted to patent law and traditional contours. In the end, however, I think the goal has become understanding the two words "traditional contours" as used by Justice Ginsburg in 2003, debated for ten years, and then used again by Justice Ginsburg. Ultimately, this piece has very modest goals. But I also felt an obligation. It is likely that no one will spend as much time as I have with these two words--no one should.

The analysis of copyright through the lens of traditional contours forces us to look into what makes us who we are--why we function the way we do and how our underlying expectations inform the choice we must make in the moment. It requires a serious look at history--not as a simple question of what the founders did, but an investigation of what really informs our laws and the origins of what we believe (and whether it is presently applicable). Traditional contours had the opportunity to spawn a doctrine that employed a strategic plan, with bedrock principles and a larger vision of what the system means and why or how it should function beyond the issue at hand.

Few ever really embraced the phrase. Many seemed embarrassed or even downright angered by it. So, in the aftermath of *Golan v. Holder,* those who believed in traditional contours are left to wonder where to go next. In fact, we see evidence of traditional contours having seeped into our consciousness. Moreover, unconsciously, we may all be practicing traditional contours as we struggle to understand our place of what we know and expect in an ever-changing world.

The Birth of Traditional Contours

"Traditional contours of copyright protection" originated with the 2003 Supreme Court case *Eldred v. Ashcroft*. Justice Ginsburg summed up her analysis that First Amendment scrutiny of the Copyright Term Extension Act (CTEA) was unnecessary by noting that the amendments to the 1976 Act did not "alter[ ] the traditional contours of copyright protection." Her placement of that phrase was curious, significant, and potentially forceful, at least until 2012.

After extensive research, it appears from the record that the phrase originated with Justice Ginsburg herself. First, the phrase had not been used in any previous Supreme Court or other federal court cases. Second, neither the *Eldred* plaintiff's brief nor the government included "traditional contours" as a phrase. The government, however, discussed "Congress's traditional authority to extend copyright terms," and the government referred to "traditional copyright considerations" and "traditional safeguards of free speech." If Justice Ginsburg had adopted either of these statements, the implication of the term "traditional contours" would be far more limited. One would have to identify the traditional safeguards for free speech, and whether idea/expression and fair use satisfied the needed traditional safeguards. The discussion would be over. But Justice Ginsburg used the phrase "traditional contours of copyright protection." Surely, this distinction was not meaningless.

Eldred considered whether the twenty-year extension of the copyright term for existing published works was constitutional. From the beginning, Justice Ginsburg framed the argument as a constitutional question: "This case concerns the authority the Constitution assigns to Congress to prescribe the duration of copyrights." Justice Ginsburg concluded that "Congress acted within its authority and did not transgress constitutional limitations." She explained that **text, history, and precedent** "confirm that the Copyright Clause empowers Congress to prescribe 'limited Times' for copyright protection and to secure the same level and duration of protection for all copyright holders, present and future." To this point, there is nothing unusual in the opinion.

The second half of the *Eldred* opinion turned to the First Amendment argument raised by the petitioners. It is in this portion of the opinion that Justice Ginsburg mentioned "traditional contours of copyright protection." Justice Ginsburg began by noting that the adoption of the Copyright Clause and the First Amendment came close in time. Because of this timing and their location in the same larger document, they must somehow work together, rather than be in conflict. This is the starting point for most discussions regarding the relationship between the First Amendment and copyright law. Again, this is not unusual or new.

Then Justice Ginsburg turned her attention to *Harper & Row Publishers, Inc. v. Nation Enterprises*, another oft-cited starting point for analyzing copyright and the First Amendment. She quoted, "'[T]he Framers intended copyright itself to be the engine of free expression. By establishing a marketable right to the use of one's expression, copyright supplies the economic incentive to create and disseminate ideas."' Here, the idea is that copyright provides protection to authors that create works, and therefore provides protection of the author's First Amendment rights. The underlying system protects an author's right to speak and not have her words purloined.

The opinion then took a structural turn to how copyright protects others' First Amendment rights in relation to a copyrighted work through safeguards, specifically the idea/expression dichotomy. These safeguards assure that third parties can use parts of the work, even while the work is protected by copyright. Thus, third parties and the copyright holder are both protected. According to Justice Ginsburg, safeguards are not limited to fair use and idea/expression. She provided two examples: (1) a library's ability to create preservation, scholarship, or research copies of works in the last twenty years of the copyright if no commercial copy is available; and (2) the restaurant "homestyle" exception, which allows restaurants and other establishments to play copyrighted music under certain conditions without the requirement of a license. These seem like two very arbitrary choices--one was added with the CTEA, and the other is merely part of the 1976 Act. However, they stand as two very different examples of additional safeguards to the First Amendment interests of third parties in copyrighted works.

Justice Ginsburg's opinion could be read to suggest that the copyright system itself takes the First Amendment into account in its very structure. For example, § 106, which grants exclusive rights to authors, gives authors the freedom to create, and authors have a remedy for infringement under section 501. The 1976 Act, however, balances the needs of both the author and the public. Section 102(b) contains a non-exhaustive list of elements that are non-copyrightable, limiting the subject matter of any particular copyright, and sections 107-122 contain the exemptions from and defenses to infringement for activities that are allowable without permission from the copyright holder during the life of the copyright. What is strange is that Justice Ginsburg called the library and home-style exception "supplements to the traditional First Amendment safeguards" of fair use and idea/expression. She described sections 102(b) and 107 as "traditional" safeguards, and then included two examples from sections 108-122 as additional supplements to the safeguards.

The Court then considered the CTEA, and the twenty-year extension of the copyright term to existing and future works. Here, the Court found that no one was being forced to reproduce speech: "Instead, [the CTEA] protects authors' original expression from unrestricted exploitation. Protection of that order does not raise the free speech concerns present when the government compels or burdens the communication of particular facts or ideas." The Court explained, "The First Amendment securely protects the freedom to make--or decline to make--one's own speech; it bears less heavily when speakers assert the right to make other people's speeches."

Justice Ginsburg then scolded the D.C. Circuit: "We recognize that the D.C. Circuit spoke too broadly when it declared copyrights 'categorically immune from challenges under the First Amendment.'" This led to the grand finale: **"But when, as in this case, Congress has not altered the traditional contours of copyright protection, further First Amendment scrutiny is unnecessary."**

Justice Ginsburg provided a clue as to what she meant by altering traditional contours in the two citations that follow the phrase. *Harper & Row* addressed a purloined manuscript written by President Ford. The Court found that President Ford had the right to determine when and where to publish his work, and thus another magazine's preemptive publication was not a fair use. President Ford had the right to speak when he wished, and the First Amendment protection came in the form of copyright law's "right of first publication." This follows the traditional scope of what we think a copyright does and how it protects the copyright holder.

In the other case she cited, *San Francisco Arts & Athletics v. United States Olympic Committee*, the Supreme Court found that the First Amendment did not prohibit granting an exclusive use to the word "Olympic." The case concerned the Amateur Sports Act of 1978, which authorized the U.S. Olympic Committee (USOC) "to prohibit certain commercial and promotional uses of the word "Olympic." "Petitioner was a California nonprofit that wanted to use the term "Gay Olympic Games" for a nine-day event in San Francisco. The Court reviewed the legislative history and found that the statute was meant to give exclusive control of the word "Olympic" to the USOC, "without regard to whether use of the word tends to cause confusion." The Court noted that the protection of "Olympic" differed from normal trademark protection because the statute did not require likelihood of confusion, so the normal trademark defenses were not available.

The question then became whether the restriction of the use of the word "Olympic" restricted expressive speech, and "whether [these] incidental restrictions on First Amendment freedoms [were] greater than necessary to further a substantial governmental interest." The government interests advanced included the promotion and participation of amateur athletes, along with international goodwill. "Section 110 primarily applies to all uses of the word 'Olympic' to induce the sale of goods or services." Congress is not limited to the terms of the Lanham Act, but can enact what it deems necessary, which in this case included restricting unauthorized commercial uses and promotional uses of athletic or theatrical events.

What clues does this send regarding traditional contours? We learn from her examples that (1) an alteration of traditional contours appears to be when Congress goes outside the normal expectations of the system (locking up the word "Olympics," for example); (2) copyrights, trademarks, and, presumably, patents all appear to have traditional contours; and (3) Congress has powers beyond a particular statute to enact laws that affect a particular area of IP. While a First Amendment analysis might be necessary if Congress alters the traditional contours of copyright protection, the alteration itself does not preclude the new amendments or addition to the law.

It was only after many years of working on traditional contours that I could clearly see the work that Justice Ginsburg had done. Justice Ginsburg's opinion contained all of the elements needed to understand that she was trying to preserve the system itself, to explain that copyright law worked by balancing the author's rights on the one hand and third-party rights as safeguards on the other. When an alteration, inside or outside of copyright law, violates this balance, only then should the judiciary step in to evaluate its effect on First Amendment interests.

For Justice Ginsburg in *Eldred,* traditional contours referred to the system itself--how one protects an author's work and safeguards a third party's use of the work during the life of the copyright. A First Amendment analysis is triggered only when the basic structure of the system is violated. No such violation occurred with the enactment of the CTEA. Extending the term of copyright an additional twenty years did not violate the "limited Times" clause of the Constitution because the term is not perpetual and the system had been used to extend terms many times in its history. As she laid out in *Eldred*, extensions of terms have frequently been applied for both future works and existing works.

Justice Ginsburg concluded *Eldred* by referencing the Framers: "As we read the Framers' instruction, the Copyright Clause empowers Congress to determine the intellectual property regimes that, overall, in that body's judgment, will serve the ends of the Clause." This harkens back to Justice Ginsburg's earlier discussion in the opinion, in which she explained, "The 'constitutional command,' we have recognized, is that Congress, to the extent it enacts copyright laws at all, create[s] a 'system' that 'promote[s] the Progress of Science.'" Again, the system is the traditional contours and the First Amendment comes into play only when Congress alters that traditional system. When Congress ventures beyond its duties prescribed in the Copyright Clause, the judiciary will step in. Traditional contours then could be an analysis of the boundaries for legislation in the Copyright Clause context.

In the months and years surrounding Eldred, scholars began to discuss traditional contours. In September 2003, Michael Birnhack wrote, "As copyright law continues to expand into new territories and in unpredictable ways, and as new bills are introduced at a staggering rate to further the scope of the rights of copyright owners, it is crucial that we study the contours of copyright law." A year after *Eldred*, Marshall Leaffer wrote,

> In my opinion, the First Amendment issue in Eldred ultimately may have more impact on the future of copyright law than the Court's status quo, inherently deferential reading of Article I.... [W]hat Justice Ginsburg said about the interplay of copyright and the First Amendment indicates real constraints on the scope of copyright law.

For Leaffer, Justice Ginsburg's "traditional contours of copyright protection" phrase was potentially powerful in the future, and "may be the most important feature of the Court's opinion on future developments in copyright law." He was compelled to ask, "When does legislation alter those 'traditional contours?'" Many would ask the same question. Brett Frischmann acknowledged that the phrase could be interpreted in many ways: "Traditionally, it at least evokes historical consideration. But of what exactly?

What are the relevant contours?" Moreover, how would we apply a traditional contours analysis to the problems of the day?

Scholars recognized some potential importance but, like me, did not see the simplicity and utter beauty of the phrase. Few took on the task of defining traditional contours over the following ten years, and confusion set in--did it mean the system itself, or did it somehow relate only to the First Amendment? But Justice Ginsburg had given us the map: her traditional contours preserved the copyright system itself, which was created to support patents and copyrights under the IP Clause in the Constitution.

To summarize, *Eldred* is a starting point where traditional contours referred to (1) the subject matter protected by the area of IP; (2) the exclusive rights given to the author or holder of the right; (3) the safeguards for third party use of the system; and (4) the duration of the limited monopoly requirement. As long as the expectations fell in line with what was traditionally considered part of the system, no First Amendment analysis was necessary.

"Traditional contours" is the copyright system itself, the Copyright Clause in action. When an alteration affects the balance or strays from these categories, the First Amendment steps in as a tool to evaluate the two-hundred-year-old balance of copyright protection and free speech. As long as the traditional contours are not altered, the 1976 Act renders First Amendment analysis unnecessary. What might fall outside of the system? Many have speculated. Anti-circumvention, safeguards for online service providers, and anti-bootlegging legislation all operate outside our traditional expectations of the system. Under Justice Ginsburg's system, one would look to see if the built-in safeguards or additional safeguards specific to the issue address First Amendment concerns. If not, then the Court would evaluate the issue, as in San Francisco Arts & Athletics. One wonders what she would have thought of the new small claims court.

Golan's Version(s) of "Traditional Contours"

Two cases would be brought to challenge section 514 of the Uruguay Round Agreements Act (URAA), a statutory amendment that restored copyright protection to foreign works that had entered the public domain in the United States, but were still under copyright in their home country. The first was *Luck's Music Library v. Gonzales* in the D.C. Circuit, and the second was *Golan v. Holder,* which was heard before the Supreme Court. Section 514 was enacted as part of the implementing legislation for the

United States joining the World Trade Organization (WTO) and appears in the 1976 Act as section 104A.

Section 104A creates an interesting conflict. On the one hand, because the United States has a duty to fulfill treaty obligations, it was required as a new member to the Berne Convention to restore works covered under copyright in the country of origin. Joining Berne required two major areas of restoration: works for which no treaty relationship had existed, as in the case of Russia, and works that had not met the very complicated formality requirements in the United States, including notice and renewal. For instance, Russian paintings and music from the 1940s, for example, were in the public domain in the United States because Russia and the United States had no treaty relations until 1972, yet these works were restored by the URAA.

On the other hand, restoring works was something very strange to our system; suddenly works that had been in the public domain and free to use for sometimes ninety years or more were re-copyrighted, with new restrictions. The plaintiffs in *Golan v. Gonzales* and *Luck's Music* claimed that recopyrighting works violated the First Amendment by ***altering the traditional contours***--the traditional expectations--of copyright protection.

The district court in *Luck's Music* found section 514 of the URAA to be within the traditional contours of copyright protection because the amendment contained built-in safeguards for those who had previously used the work when it was in the public domain, creating a class of users known as reliance parties. Further, the district court found that § 104A did not overstep congressional power or violate the First Amendment, and therefore granted the defendant's motion to dismiss. Because Justice Ginsburg's actions in *Golan v. Holder* nearly a decade later paralleled those of the district court in *Luck's Music*, it is useful to review the structure of the district court's argument.

The district court began by noting the need to implement Article 18 of the Berne Convention. So too would Justice Ginsburg in *Golan v. Holder.* The court noted that section 514 not only restores works as required by Article 18 but also includes additional safeguards for those who relied on the work when it was in the public domain. The court then turned to the specifics of the plaintiffs' arguments in *Luck's Music.*

Luck's Music, a family business, sold and repackaged public domain classical orchestral sheet music "to more than 7,000 orchestras ranging from elementary to operatic and to

12,000 individuals worldwide." A good deal of their catalog included works whose authors had not been eligible for copyright protection due to lack of treaty relations, namely Russia before 1972. Luck's Music received 200-300 notices of Intent to Enforce restored copyrights and had one year, according to the statute, to sell off its inventory before they were subject to a lawsuit for copyright infringement. Luck's Music, however, was unable to sell all of its inventory during the one-year period. Moviecraft, the other plaintiff in *Luck's Music*, was in the same situation: a family business that operated a film archive of public domain works, including foreign works that had not met formality requirements. These works, which Moviecraft had preserved, were now restored and unusable without permission from the copyright holder.

The court addressed the legal standard for interpreting the Copyright Clause, particularly in light of *Eldred*, including the fact that the judiciary "defers substantially to Congress for its policy decisions on [c]opyright law." Next the court considered its analysis of section 514. The defendants argued that Congress had restored works before, while the plaintiffs argued that any restoration of works was an unusual case. To sort these arguments out, the court turned to history and tradition. The court conducted a historical analysis and discovered an "unbroken practice of granting retroactive copyrights and removing works from the public domain since the founding of the Constitution." This is an interesting way of framing the issue. It presupposed that restoration of works is the norm, and that the plaintiffs had the burden of proving that it was not an "unbroken practice." As a result, we see this new phrase entering into the traditional contours framework. The court's analysis of the historical practices of restoration in the United States was the first of its kind.

In some ways, determining what constitutes an unbroken practice or traditional contour becomes a battle of history. First, the court examined the Copyright Act of 1790 (1790 Act) and wrote, "The plaintiffs' interpretation that the 1790 Act merely codified existing copyright law requires the assumption that either all states had copyright statutes enacted or that a common-law of copyright existed in the United States." Again, this is an interesting position: the plaintiffs had to prove that the 1790 Act did not retroactively restore copyright.

> If neither of these bodies of law existed, then Congress' implementation of the 1790 Act would have created copyright law and granted retroactive copyrights to works already in the public domain. A review of state statutes before the ratification of the Constitution and the enactment of the 1790 Act reveals that the plaintiffs' argument is flawed.

The court then delved into state copyright laws and the Articles of Confederation. Because the Articles of Confederation did not vest Congress with the power to enact intellectual property laws, the task fell to each state. Three states did not enact copyright laws: Delaware, Maryland, and Pennsylvania. Because no copyright protection existed for works in those states, "Congress' actions with the enactment of the 1790 Act created retroactive copyrights for works published by the citizens of these three states." The court, citing *Wheaton v. Peters*, also found that a common law copyright did not exist in states without copyright statutes. The court wrote,

> In *Wheaton*, the Court interpreted the words "by securing" in the IP clause to mean that the Constitution gave Congress the power to create a new right through the 1790 Act. The Court explained that "securing" had to refer to the creation of a new right, since the Constitution includes both copyright and patent law in the same clause, and patent law had no existing common law equivalent in England. The Court further reasoned that any other interpretation would render the IP clause mere surplusage because the result would be a "vest[ing] of a right already vested." Thus, "Congress, ... by [the 1790 Act], instead of sanctioning an existing right[,] created it." Because not every state had a copyright statute and because no common law right to copyright existed, the plaintiffs' argument that the 1790 Act merely codified existing common law fails.

The court then turned to the 1919 and 1941 amendments, which allowed foreigners from specific countries extra time to retroactively register works published during the war years. The court found that both amendments further demonstrated a practice of restoring works. "For instance, Presidents Wilson and Harding issued proclamations in 1920 and 1922 respectively that effectively restored copyright to British and German works published during World War I." A similar restoration occurred after World War II, which included Australia, Austria, Finland, Germany, and the United Kingdom.

The turn to history becomes a battle of interpretation. But this is not the best use of a traditional contours argument--one should not simply reach back to the past, and say, "See, they did it this way before." But in *Luck's Music*, the court exemplified this problem. It found that the evidence showed that restoration had previously occurred. Nonetheless, *Luck's Music* presents a clear articulation of one way to look at history.

The court found that the Copyright Clause itself did not impose a limitation on the public domain, and that the nature of patents is so different that patent law cases in this area do not transfer to copyright. Again, this issue of when patent law and copyright law can support one another is a larger question, but we have evidence that courts do rely on copyright law to support patent law and vice versa. Here, however, the court explicitly rejected the application of a patent decision to copyright.

Next, the court considered the First Amendment issue. The plaintiffs argued that "Section 514 violates the First Amendment because it restricts the freedom of expression of works already in the public domain." The next sentence is one of the more interesting in the opinion: "The defendants argue-- and the Court agrees--that Eldred bars this argument."

The court relied on *Eldred* to explain that when copyright protection "raises First Amendment concerns, copyright law contains built-in accommodations for First Amendment speech such as through the idea/expression dichotomy and the fair use doctrine." The court then reiterated the famous phrase: "When Congress has not altered the traditional contours of copyright protection, further First Amendment scrutiny is unnecessary." Gone is the reference to San Francisco Arts & Athletics, Inc.; traditional contours were thus narrowed.

Luck's Music is a case of reliance--one year was too short to sell off merchandise, and restoring the works from the public domain dramatically altered the business itself. In other words, the expectations associated with copyright law were changed, which economically impacted a way of life, a business entity, and a family. This was entirely ignored. Instead, the court wrote that section 514 failed to encroach on fair use or idea/expression and included additional "protections" (but not the word "safeguards" as used in Eldred), therefore, no additional scrutiny under the First Amendment was necessary.

Luck's Music is a disappointment on a number of levels: the court did a poor job of using history, traditional contours itself was not analyzed, and the safeguards at issue were not actually discussed. *Luck's Music* comes closer to Justice Ginsburg's opinion in *Golan v. Holder* than her own opinion in *Eldred*. It is the first indication that this version of history would prevail, and that traditional contours would continue to remain an undeveloped, simple concept. The D.C. Circuit affirmed the *Luck's Music* decision without further discussion. The district court in Golan also did not find any violation of traditional contours of copyright protection with regard to section 514 of the URAA, but the Tenth Circuit took up the same question and came to the opposite conclusion.

The Game-Changing Tenth Circuit Decision

A decade in the making, Golan, in all its versions, gives us the most thorough vision of traditional contours, adding the functional ("contours") and historical (the modifier "traditional" to contours) elements. Ten years later, the Supreme Court would again be confronted with the question of "traditional contours of copyright law" in *Golan v. Holder*.

Judge Henry, in the Tenth Circuit, found that Section 104A had violated the traditional contours of copyright protection, and, therefore, he remanded the case for First Amendment scrutiny. It was a big moment for traditional contours, and one could argue that, had Judge Henry not stepped down from the bench to enter academia, we might have had a different ending to the traditional contours story, at least at the appellate level. Judge Henry took seriously the question of what constitutes "traditional contours of copyright protection," finding that restoring foreign works from the public domain altered the traditional contours of copyright protection. Thus, while Congress has the power to enact such legislation, First Amendment scrutiny was necessary. The court engaged in a two-part analysis. First, Congress had the authority to enact the URAA. Judge Henry wrote,

> We agree it would be troubling if Congress adopted a consistent practice of restoring works in the public domain in an effort to confer perpetual monopolies. But this argument is similar to one the Eldred plaintiffs raised, and, like the Eldred Court, we are mindful that "a regime of perpetual copyrights is clearly not the situation before us.

Here, the works restored had "limited Times" in that their new copyright had an expiration date. The plaintiffs relied on *Graham v. John Deere Co. of Kansas City* for the proposition that works in the public domain cannot be patented or, in this case, copyrighted. The court then invoked *Luck's Music*, which distinguished patents from copyrights: "The Court concludes that plaintiffs have thrust onto Graham a burden it was never intended to bear. We decline to read Graham as standing for the proposition that, in the context of copyright, the public domain is a threshold that Congress may not 'traverse in both directions.'" It is interesting that Judge Henry was not willing to go so far as to preclude Congress from recopyrighting public domain works, rejecting the opportunity to apply Graham. "Here, we do not believe that the decision to comply with the Berne Convention, which secures copyright protections for American works abroad, is so irrational or so unrelated to the aims of the Copyright Clause that it exceeds the reach of congressional power."

But Judge Henry did not stop there: "Nevertheless, legislation promulgated pursuant to the Copyright Clause must still comport with other express limitations of the Constitution. Thus, even if Congress has not exceeded its Article I authority, § 514 may still be subject to First Amendment review." Here is the crux of the distinction: Article I powers of Congress versus the relationship between copyright and the First Amendment. Thus, while Congress may have the authority to enact section 514, the law may still be subject to First Amendment review. This is the second prong of his analysis and is an interesting structural move. The First Amendment comes into play as another area of law, separate from Congress's authority, which creates an external hurdle to copyright law. It may be that the laws enacted by Congress and interpreted by the courts comport with the Copyright Clause but do not comport with the First Amendment.

Judge Henry began the heart of his analysis regarding traditional contours with the heading "Congress's Removal of Works from the Public Domain Alters the Traditional Contours of Copyright Protection and Requires First Amendment Scrutiny." He began again with Eldred: "[W]e address the Eldred Court's holding that the CTEA's extension of existing copyrights did not require First Amendment scrutiny and discuss the Court's suggestion that an act of Congress would only be subject to First Amendment review if it 'altered the traditional contours of copyright protection.'" 'Based on the Eldred Court's analysis, we examine the bedrock principle of copyright law that works in the public domain remain there and conclude that § 514 alters the traditional contours of copyright protection by deviating from this principle." Thus, while Congress can create laws, they still may violate the traditional contours and require additional scrutiny.

Judge Henry noted that *Eldred* did not define "traditional contours," and that it did not appear in any other federal authority. This raised an interesting point. Justice Ginsburg seemed to set out "the traditional contours" as a system that included scope of protection, exclusive rights, and safeguards. She did not concentrate on defining "traditional contours" as a phrase in its own right, but Judge Henry set that as his task.

Judge Henry recognized that "the term seems to refer to something broader than copyright's built-in free speech accommodations." He then identified both a functional and historical component to traditional contours. First, he referenced the dictionary definition for "contours," finding it to mean "outline" or "the general form of something." This is reminiscent of *Eldred*, in which Justice Ginsburg found an underlying "system" based on the requirements of the Copyright Clause. Here, "contours" fulfills the same requirement. "Because the term copyright refers to a process as well as a form of intellectual property rights, we assess whether removing a work from the public domain alters the ordinary procedure of copyright protection." Judge Henry then turned to the word "traditional," which modifies "contours." He believed this phrasing "suggest[ed] that Congress's historical practice with respect to copyright and the public domain must inform [the court's] inquiry." **Judge Henry concluded "that the traditional contours of copyright protection includes the principle that works in the public domain remain there and that § 514 transgresses this critical boundary."**

Eldred and *Golan* both concerned a **question of time**--when are works protected by copyright and when are they in the public domain? In *Eldred*, the question was whether extending a term of copyright protection violated traditional contours, to which the Court answered no. Then the *Golan* court was asked whether restoring copyright protection to works currently in the public domain violated traditional contours and expectations. The concept of the public domain, then, fits as part of the fourth element of traditional contours.

Justice Ginsburg gave us an outline for the traditional contours of copyright, then Judge Henry started to give us a way to evaluate when those traditional contours might have been altered by reviewing the phrase "traditional contours" itself. He focused his attention on the fourth element of traditional contours: duration and what he refers to as the copyright sequence.

Judge Henry first took up the contours by looking at the functional aspects of duration and the idea of a copyright sequence. The process of copyright begins when an author creates a work. Whether under previous systems or the 1976 Act,

> Until § 514, every statutory scheme preserved the same sequence. A work progressed from (1) creation; (2) to copyright; (3) to the public domain. Under § 514, the copyright sequence no longer necessarily ends with the public domain: indeed, it may begin there. Thus, by copyrighting works in the public domain, the URAA has altered the ordinary copyright sequence.

The contours of the system had been upset. This is a fairly underappreciated portion of Judge Henry's argument. While most will later concentrate on the "traditional," he began with the contours, the functional. Justice Ginsburg argued that just because it has been the usual sequence, it does not have to be. Judge Henry would likely agree; where they differ is that Judge Henry believed, based on Eldred, that when what has been usual--the traditional contours--is altered, then one takes the next step and analyzes the change through First Amendment scrutiny.

Next, Judge Henry analyzed the idea of the "public domain." He looked to the copyright sequence in combination with the principle of the public domain. Judge Henry wrote, "The significance of the copyright sequence, combined with the principle that no individual may copyright a work in the public domain, is that ordinarily works in the public domain stay there." Otherwise, the removal of a work from the public domain contravenes the contours of the system.

After reviewing the "contours," Judge Henry turned to the modifier "traditional." He wrote, "The history of American copyright law reveals no tradition of copyrighting works in the public domain." To evaluate the tradition of the principle, Judge Henry used the past practices of Congress and the Framers, but after reviewing the 1790 Act he agreed with the plaintiff that preexisting works had been protected by state common law and thus were not removed from the public domain when they were federalized under the new system. This would become a key point debated between parties and amicus briefs when the case headed to the Supreme Court in 2011. According to Judge Henry, although we cannot know the Framers' view on removing works from the public domain, "[g]iven the scarcity of historical evidence, we cannot conclude that the Framers viewed removal of works from the public domain as consistent with the copyright scheme they created. Nor do we discern at the dawn of the Republic any burgeoning tradition of removing works from the public domain."

It appears, then, according to Henry, that once a court identifies a principle, it should analyze how the principle works both functionally and within the past practices. History then becomes the question: Has this been done before? If it has, no alteration has occurred. If it is new to the system, First Amendment analysis is required.
Judge Henry then examined the history of congressional grants of copyright protection to works in the public domain, where he noted that a "series of private bills" restored copyright in a few cases:

> But "[t]hese private bills do not support the [government's] historical gloss, but rather significantly undermine the historical claim." Far from providing evidence that copyrighting works in the public domain is within the traditional contours of copyright protection, the fact that individuals were

> forced to resort to the uncommon tactic of petitioning Congress demonstrates that this practice was outside the normal practice.

Wartime acts also point to restoration as being out of the normal system or practice: "[A] review of the historical record reveals that these emergency wartime bills, passed in response to exigent circumstances, merely altered the means by which authors could comply with the procedural rules for copyright; these bills were not explicit attempts to remove works from the public domain." Judge Henry continued, "The statutory context of these acts reveals that they were, at most, a brief and limited departure from a practice of guarding the public domain." He noted that the 1919 Wartime exception allowed Americans to use the work:

> Congress emphasized that it was not attempting to interfere with the rights of Americans who had relied on the foreign works... [T]he 1919 Act stated that "nothing herein contained shall be construed to deprive any person of any right which he may have acquired by the republication of such foreign work in the United States prior to approval of this Act." One of the Acts to which the 1919 Act referred was the 1909 Copyright Act. That Act made clear that "no copyright shall subsist in the original text of any work which is in the public domain." He concluded that removal of works from the public domain was an exception rather than a traditional contour.
>
> In sum, by extending a limited monopoly to expressions historically beyond the pale of such privileges, the URAA transformed the ordinary process of copyright protection and contravened a bedrock principle of copyright law that works in the public domain remain in the public domain. Therefore, under both the functional and historical components of our inquiry, § 514 has altered the traditional contours of copyright protection.

Once he established that section 514 altered the traditional contours of copyright protection, Judge Henry turned to the plaintiff's First Amendment interests. Here, we find the effect of the principle and how altering the principle affects ownership issues. We see a change in how we might think about authorship.

First, "works in the public domain belong to the public," giving the plaintiff a nonexclusive right and a First Amendment interest in the unrestrained and unrestricted use of the work. Judge Henry confirmed:

> Once a work has entered the public domain, however, neither the author nor the author's estate possesses any more right to the work than any

> member of the general public. Because § 514 bestows copyrights upon works in the public domain, these built-in safeguards are not adequate to protect plaintiffs' First Amendment interests.

Judge Henry then turned to idea/expression: "The idea/expression dichotomy is simply not designed to determine whether Congress's grant of a limited monopoly over an expression in the public domain runs afoul of the First Amendment." As with idea/expression, fair use is not a safeguard that is appropriate once a work is in the public domain, as the public is entitled to use all of a work without seeking permission. These two safeguards concern works that are still under copyright, not works in the public domain.

Judge Henry remanded the case to the district court to determine whether to apply a content-neutral or content-based standard of review. On remand, Judge Babcock, who had decided the first district court decision upholding the statute, found that the URAA's provision for restoration was broader than necessary to achieve the government's interest. To date--and even after Justice Ginsburg's opinion in *Golan v. Holder*--Judge Babcock's opinion stands as the first and only attempt at applying a First Amendment analysis to § 104A.

After reviewing the Tenth Circuit's understanding of the relationship between copyright and the First Amendment, Judge Babcock explained that, because the traditional contours were altered, the Tenth Circuit asked how the alterations impacted the plaintiff. Judge Babcock explained that before the works were removed from the public domain, the plaintiffs

> had, subject to constitutionally permissible restraints, a non-exclusive right to "unrestrained artistic use of these works" that was protected by the First Amendment.... "[O]nce the works at issue became free for anyone to copy, plaintiffs in this case had vested First Amendment interests in the expressions, and § 514's interference with plaintiff's rights is subject to First Amendment scrutiny."

Section 514 interfered with that right by restoring copyright to public domain works and, in some cases, "by making the cost of using the works prohibitive."
Judge Babcock then noted that neither the built-in First Amendment protections nor specific supplemental section 514 safeguards adequately addressed the problem.

Judge Babcock then began the First Amendment analysis--the first court to actually engage in such analysis within a "traditional contours of copyright protection" framework. He quickly agreed with the parties that the restriction was content neutral: "Here, the speech restricted is a general category of speech--namely, speech created by foreign authors. The justification for the restriction lies in the protection of the authors' interests in the expressions themselves, not the ideas the works encompass." Because the restriction was content neutral, the next determination was whether the restriction advanced an important government interest, and whether the restriction was broader than necessary to protect that interest, which was the focus of the remainder of the opinion. To determine whether the restriction was overbroad, Judge Babcock weighed the government's interests against the plaintiff's. He found that section 514 violated the First Amendment because the government's interests were not well supported and the amendment was broader than necessary to protect those interests. Therefore, the amendment violated the First Amendment.

Here, we see, for the first time, what occurs if there is a violation or alteration of the traditional contours of copyright protection. The actual First Amendment analysis plays a sideline role in the Golan case, and is not included in Justice Ginsburg's opinion, because, as in *Luck's Music*, she did not find an alteration of traditional contours, and, therefore, a First Amendment analysis was not necessary.

On appeal, the Tenth Circuit did not analyze or even mention "traditional contours," but instead focused on the second part of the First Amendment analysis from the district court--whether there was a legitimate government interest to support the regulation, which the Court found there was.

The U.S. Supreme Court

The Briefs

The Supreme Court granted certiorari in *Golan v. Holder* in 2011. The petitioners' brief framed the *Golan v. Holder* traditional contours argument by starting with *Eldred*.

> The Court reasoned that although statutes conforming to "historical contours" may be presumed constitutional because of that historical compatibility, substantial deviations from those "traditional contours"

> cannot be presumed constitutional on that basis, and must be assessed under ordinary First Amendment review.

The use of "historical" is interesting: what comes before requires no First Amendment review. This seems to be a weaker place to begin, privileging the past over the present. It could be read as cautioning against change: when change occurs we need the First Amendment's help. This, perhaps, is the most basic understanding of traditional contours--a deviation from the past.

The petitioners then asserted two elements of the argument. First, restoring foreign works from the public domain deviates from tradition and history, and second, in doing so, restoration violates a "bedrock principle" of copyright that once works enter the public domain, they remain there. The petitioners explained, "The 'federal right to copy and use' material in the public domain is not simply a 'traditional contour of copyright protection.' It is a defining feature of American copyright law, and an essential safeguard that ensures copyright remains 'compatible with free speech principles.'" Here, we see the petitioners attempting to define the sanctity of the public domain as a safeguard of the system. "Section 514 departs from the time-honored tradition of leaving the public domain intact, and dismantles the speech protections that tradition provided to both petitioners and the public. It cannot escape First Amendment scrutiny." The petitioners asserted that the public domain itself is a safeguard.

One could also see Judge Henry's reorientation at play in the petitioners' brief, of traditional contours being protectable, copyrightable materials and public domain materials.

In sum, the petitioners reiterated Judge Henry's notion of a "bedrock" principle that is included in traditional contours of copyright protection and argued that section 514 of the URAA violated that principle, thus triggering First Amendment scrutiny. The petitioners looked to history and tradition--the expectations associated with copyright for over two hundred years--as a way to define traditional contours.

The government responded that the appellate court erred when it found section 514 violated the traditional contours of copyright protection. "Section 514 does not alter the traditional balance between protected and prohibited conduct that is built into the Copyright Act. The idea/expression dichotomy and the 'fair use' defense apply fully to exploitation of restored works subject to Section 514."

The petitioners' reply brief approached the question of how *Eldred* should be interpreted head on: "The government tries to avoid First Amendment scrutiny by insisting the only 'traditional contours' that trigger it are the fair use doctrine and the 'idea/expression dichotomy."' The petitioners' brief continued:

> But Eldred implies no such limitation. It recognized these doctrines represent two "built-in First Amendment accommodations" or "safeguards" that are "generally adequate" to address First Amendment concerns. It does not say or suggest these are the only "accommodations" or "safeguards," or that any specific set of "accommodations" or "safeguards" exhaust the "traditional contours of copyright protection."

The petitioners' reply explained that *Eldred* concentrated on the limits necessary when works are still under copyright protection.

> The public's right to copy and use works in the public domain is a third safeguard that attaches once that period ends, and is designed to provide complete and permanent protection for all First Amendment interests. Copyright's protection of First Amendment interests has always progressed from partial protection to complete protection of those interests. The government's suggestion that Congress can reverse that sequence at will is precisely the departure from tradition that triggers First Amendment scrutiny.

Here we see Judge Henry's distinction of protectable work and public domain at play, and we also see Judge Henry's idea of principles regarding the copyright sequence, specifically in relation to the public domain. The nature of the safeguards changes when a work crosses over to the public domain. Each area has its own traditional contours--traditional contours of an idea, traditional contours of copyright protection, and traditional contours of the public domain. Each may include principles about the public domain, but the public domain itself, as a category, presents unique needs and safeguards.

As to the amici briefs, some mentioned "traditional contours of copyright protection," but most did not analyze what that would entail. Tomas Gomez-Arostegui and Tyler Ochoa did not directly address traditional contours, but framed the question more narrowly as whether there was precedent for removing works from the public domain. This seems to indirectly speak to the traditional contours question on the historical side of the argument, and perhaps maybe even the functional. Has Congress done this before, and how did they do it? The Google amicus brief stated that the power asserted by Congress in enacting section 514 "goes far outside the 'traditional contours' of copyright law." One wonders why more careful attention is not paid to "traditional contours" at this opportune moment.

Justice Ginsburg's *Golan* Opinion

On January 18, 2012, Justice Ginsburg delivered the opinion in *Golan v. Holder*, a 6-2 decision, with Justice Kagan taking no part. Justice Ginsburg's *Golan v. Holder* opinion is fascinating when compared to her opinion in *Eldred*, and slightly troubling because the entire basis of her decision is built on faulty law.

In *Eldred*, Justice Ginsburg did not leave us with a clear map of "traditional contours of copyright protection," but she left clues. She considered the fair use and idea/expression dichotomy as built-in mechanisms to protect the First Amendment, and she identified other safeguards, including library exceptions and the homestyle music exception for restaurants. That was in 2003. From her construction and discussion, one could frame traditional contours into four elements: subject matter, exclusive rights for authors, safeguards, and duration. Nearly a decade later, in *Golan v. Holder*, we see a different Justice Ginsburg--one anxious to put the traditional contours discussion back into Pandora's Box. It is as if she sought to turn back time--to revise *Eldred*. She had not meant to start "traditional contours of copyright protection." In *Golan v. Holder*, she tried to stop it.

Justice Ginsburg began her opinion with a discussion of the Berne Convention, and stated that the URAA did not "transgress constitutional limitations of Congress' authority." But with her next conclusion, Justice Ginsburg dramatically altered the traditional contours of copyright protection: "Neither the Copyright and Patent Clause nor the First Amendment, we hold, makes the public domain, in any and all cases, a territory that works may never exit."

In both the party briefs and amicus briefs, the fight in *Golan v. Holder* had been over history--whether we had previously seen the removal of works in the public domain. Each side had vigorously shown how history sided with their version. They were reacting to the "tradition" in traditional contours and asking what history could tell us about removal. Justice Ginsburg took a far more radical approach, extending herself further than necessary to uphold the law. She could have traveled the path of the government's brief to find that the removal was necessary and, therefore, did not violate the First Amendment. Or she could have limited her decision to exceptions that had occurred throughout history--with the first U.S. Copyright Act in 1790 (if you believe that version of history), after wars, and now in harmonizing global copyright. But she chose neither of these more limited routes. Nor did she "kill" the concept of "traditional contours of copyright protection."

Discussing Congress's authority to remove works from the public domain, Justice Ginsburg wrote, "Installing a federal copyright system and ameliorating the interruptions of global war, it is true, presented Congress with extraordinary situations." Following this line of thinking, a traditional contour is removal for extraordinary situations. Nonetheless, she did not follow this line of reasoning: "Yet the TRIPS accord, leaving the United States to comply in full measure with Berne, was also a signal event. Given the authority we hold Congress has, we will not second-guess the political choice Congress made between leaving the public domain untouched and embracing Berne unstintingly." This would have been a sufficient argument, but she did not stop there.

She then directed her argument to the Tenth Circuit's "bedrock principle that once works enter the public domain, they do not leave." Justice Ginsburg had a number of choices. She could have found that the government had satisfied its burden to overcome the First Amendment. She could have found that § 104A had enough protection for reliance parties, similar to *Luck's Music*. She could have found that "traditional contours" did not apply because most of the issues involved in Golan v. Holder were procedural, rather than substantive, as in *Kahle*. She could have found that the balance between author and society had not been altered, as in the *Silver* dissent.

Instead, she wrote, "We next explain why the First Amendment does not inhibit the restoration authorized by § 514." She began with an analysis of Eldred: "We then described the 'traditional contours' of copyright protection, i.e., the 'idea/expression dichotomy' and the 'fair use' defense." Both are recognized in our jurisprudence as "built-in First Amendment accommodations." The language is interesting. Why does she quote "traditional contours" and not the "traditional contours of copyright protection"--the complete phrase from *Eldred?* I would suggest that she is signaling something about "traditional contours." Moreover, she used "i.e.," which translates to "that is." She has limited "traditional contours" to mean idea/expression and fair use. But she had not done so in *Eldred*. In that opinion, as we have already learned, she included "other safeguards" as well. Why the shift? What happened to the 2003 Justice Ginsburg?

In *Golan v. Holder,* Justice Ginsburg seemed to limit "traditional contours" to idea/expression and fair use, and did not mention the other two safeguards. But in the next instance, she turned to what she was now calling "the transitional elements" of section 514--the protections for reliance parties. She noted that they are included, but with no follow-up commentary. We are left to wonder if they protect traditional contours too. This feels more like *Luck's Music* than the fuller discussions in the lower courts' *Golan* opinions. The petitioner, in line with the remanded district court opinion, argued that once a work enters the public domain, the public gains "vested rights," and that idea/expression and fair use are "no substitute for the unlimited use they enjoyed before § 514's enactment." Justice Ginsburg disagreed and wrote that the public domain is not untouchable by Congress, and that the "vested rights" argument is "backwards."

> Rights typically vest at the outset of copyright protection, in an author or a rightholder. Once the term of protection ends, the works do not revest in any rightholder. Instead, the works simply **lapse** into the public domain. Anyone has free access to the public domain, but no one, after the copyright term has expired, acquires ownership rights in the once-protected works.

What is interesting is that Justice Ginsburg in *Golan v. Holder* would use additional subject matter as an example of how Congress can expand copyright law, and for her, this did not require First Amendment scrutiny. But all of the examples that Justice Ginsburg gave had no retroactive protection. For instance, the inclusion of architectural buildings as copyrightable subject matter not only was not retroactive--it applied only to buildings created after the enactment of the amendment--but additional safeguards were also put in place. For example, a third party can take a photograph of a building without resulting infringement if the building can be seen from a public space. This fits into the framework Justice Ginsburg set up in *Golan v. Holder.* When new elements are added to the copyright system, one should make sure the system is still in balance, and that is done, I suggest, through a traditional contours analysis.

Justice Ginsburg belittled the petitioners' argument that fair use and idea/expression are very different than using an entire work, and that equity requires foreigners to not have their work available at "an artificially low (because royalty-free) cost." She wrote that we have moved away from a "traditional contours" argument entirely: "By fully implementing Berne, Congress ensured that most works, whether foreign or domestic, would be governed by the same legal regime." This is simply not true. Foreign works and domestic works of the same era are now treated dramatically different for the same reason in some cases--failure to follow formalities.

Traditional Contours After *Golan v. Holder*

Justice Ginsburg's opinion in *Golan v. Holder* is a disappointment because she did not actually engage in the discussion set out by the petitioners, the Tenth Circuit, or even the government. Her views focused on the Berne Convention, but without much depth, even ignoring in some instances the fact that the law actually does not implement the Berne Convention's requirements. The Berne Convention required that works be restored to the minimum term of life plus fifty. The majority of works restored in the United States under § 104A were restored under the anti-Berne Convention (pro-Universal Copyright Convention) system based on the publication date, rather than the life of the author. This restoration, then, is still in noncompliance with the Berne Convention, and the United States is still subject to a WTO dispute. The fears of noncompliance that Justice Ginsburg discussed are still very much alive. This seems careless. She should have addressed the problem in the opinion if she was going to rely and concentrate on the need to comply with Article 18 of the Berne Convention as the justification. It seems faulty reasoning to uphold a statute that did not actually fix the problem, but rather kept the United States in noncompliance.

What is most disturbing is her neglect and carelessness regarding traditional contours. Perhaps that was not intentional. She may not want traditional contours growing into a viable doctrine, and she seems to try to muffle it without the courage to kill it entirely. But she cannot let go of it--she uses it herself for justification. In that sense, "traditional contours," as she wrote in *Golan v. Holder,* or "traditional contours of copyright protection," as she wrote in *Eldred,* lives on.

Justice Ginsburg in 2012, however, was also significantly narrower. She first noted that copyright law has some restrictions on expression. In *Golan v. Holder,* she limited safeguards to sections 102(b) and 107. Then she included "transitional measures from a national scheme to an international copyright scheme," the reliance party provisions in section 104A. What is interesting is that the "transitional measures" in this case were for international adjustments, but Justice Ginsburg also discussed transitional measures for the CTEA, presumably the library exceptions. However, that leaves section 110(5), the home-style exception, completely unaccounted for. Transitional measures are meant to protect First Amendment interests when the new amendment comes into effect.

In charting her opinion, we see a dramatic change in structure. Now, the focus is the First Amendment itself, rather than traditional contours, with the first step being restriction on expression as embodied in sections 102(a) (copyrightable subject matter) and 106 (exclusive rights) of the 1976 Act. We then look to the safeguards of the system, namely traditional contours of idea/expression and fair use on the one hand and transitional measures on the other. It is a tool that focuses only on applying the questions to a particular part of the system--the issue at hand. Traditional contours does not account for the whole system, as it did in *Eldred*. It focused on the First Amendment requirements that copyright must meet, while in *Eldred* it had been a self-contained system that only looked outward to the First Amendment when the system itself had encountered significant deviation from expected norms.

Justice Ginsburg in 2012 seemed to have had a very different scheme in mind indeed. She reoriented what is needed to protect First Amendment interests, while her *Eldred* opinion seemed to focus on identifying traditional contours itself.

Justice Breyer's Dissent: Traditional Contours Versus "Text, History, and Precedent"

The dissent, written by Justice Breyer, did not directly discuss traditional contours. However, he once again employed the phrase, "text, history, and precedent," the exact phrase used in his *Bilski v. Kappas* [patent] concurrence. He also asserted, "By removing material from the public domain, the statute, in literal terms, 'abridges' a preexisting freedom to speak," an argument discussed in the patent case, *Mayo Collaborative Services v. Prometheus Laboratories, Inc*. It will be interesting to see if courts in future years will pick up on this line of thinking--the "freedom to speak" and the "freedom to think." It appears that increased property rights in patents and copyrights put these questions at the forefront.

Breyer begins with the Constitutional clause, which allows authors to charge a fee for copyrighted works, creating a reading tax that encourages new works, a utilitarian theory of incentivizing creation. "The statute before us, however, does not encourage anyone to produce a single new work. By definition, it bestows monetary rewards only on owners of old works--works that have already been created and already are in the American public domain." And that's the heart of Breyer's argument. "The upshot is that text, history, and precedent demonstrate that the Copyright Clause places great value on the power of copyright to elicit new production." Breyer believes Congress has exceed "any plausible reading of the Copyright Clause..." He turns to Section 104A.

He explains Section 104A. Then he turns to the implact. School orchestras will no longer be able to offer restored music. Administrative costs on obtaining permission is unusually high. And the orphan work problem skyrocketed --where owners cannot be found for (now) copyrighted works. And libraries cannot make collections available now because they are restored. And of course, my favorite, Breyer recognizes "the statute's technical requirements makes it difficult to establish whether a work has had its copyright restored." And he cites Gard, In the Trenches with §104A: An Evaluation of the Parties' Arguments in Golan v. Holder as It Heads to the Supreme Court, 64 Vand. L. Rev. En Banc 199, 216–220 (2011) (describing difficulties encountered in compiling the information necessary to create an online tool to determine whether the statute applies in any given case). And worst of all, the statute removes materials from the public domain.

The question is how is he going to address the requirements of Article 18 of the Berne Convention. That's why we enacted Section 104A. So, does he address this? He writes that the Article 18 obligations are not "sufficient to save the statute." He explains that the U.S did not restore works from 1989-1994, so why now? And why didn't the U.S. government in negotiation the WTO secure reservations to protect special features of American copyright law, which they could have done under Article 18? The problem is made by the United States who "made no effort [secure reservations for the U.S. public domain] despite the fact that Article 18 explicitly authorizes countries to negotiate exceptions to the Article's retroactivity principle. See Art. 18(3), ibid. ("The application of [the retroactivity] principle shall be subject to any provisions contained in special conventions to that effect existing or to be concluded between countries of the Union" (emphasis added)); Gervais, Golan v. Holder: A Look at the Constraints Imposed by the Berne Convention, 64 Vand. L. Rev. En Banc 147, 151–152 (2011); Gard, 64 Vand. L. Rev. En Banc, at 206." Note that our work at Tulane was cited again for this principle.

Breyer continues: "For another thing, the Convention does not require Congress to enact a statute that causes so much damage to public domain material. Article 18(3) also states that 'the respective countries shall determine, each in so far as it is concerned, the conditions of application of this principle.' 18 U. N. T. S., at 251 (emphasis added). Congress could have alleviated many of the costs that the statute imposes by, for example, creating forms of compulsory licensing, requiring 'restored copyright' holders to provide necessary administrative information as a condition of protection, or insisting upon "reasonable royalties.'"

Breyer makes a point that he is not criticizing the Berne Convention, but that "other branches of Government should have tried to follow the Convention and in particular its provisions offering compliance flexibility. The fact that the statute has significant First Amendment costs is relevant in this respect, for that Amendment ordinarily requires courts to evaluate less restrictive, alternative possibilities. Doing so here, reveals that neither Congress nor the Executive took advantage of less-restrictive methods of compliance that the Convention itself provides. And that fact means that the Convention cannot provide the statute with a constitutionally sufficient justification that is otherwise lacking." He does not believe in the form that it was drafted that Congress had the authorization to enact Section 104A. It's interesting that Breyer shifts the burden in this way.

Evaluating Justice Ginsburg

I would suggest that one could read *Golan v. Holder* as the clash between traditional contours of U.S. law and the introduction of a different set of contours from the Berne Convention. The question becomes what is going to give. I think there is less of a clash than Justice Ginsburg's opinion suggests, and she did not have to dramatically alter the traditional contours of copyright protection within the U.S. system to achieve compliance internationally.

First, Justice Ginsburg could have limited the opinion to the actual requirements of Article 18. Restoration under Article 18 is designed to be a "one-time" compliance adjustment and not the notion that works can come and go in the public domain. She could have written that the traditional contours of copyright protection must adjust to the pressures of joining an international treaty long in progress.

Second, Ginsburg could have analyzed section 104A itself. Did it achieve the proposed goals? It did not. We are still *not* in compliance with Article 18 of the Berne Convention, nor are we in compliance with in-copyright works (not restored) by foreign authors. We are still figuring out the term on a publication date-based system for pre-1978 works, and this violates the Berne Convention for foreign works. I think this is the most disappointing aspect of the opinion. Justice Ginsburg championed the Berne Convention, and yet section 104A does not bring the United States into compliance.

Third, Justice Ginsburg could have continued to structure traditional contours in the same manner as *Eldred* without refocusing and restricting the term. The new structure contradicts *Eldred* without providing additional usefulness. Only if idea/expression or fair use are somehow impeded would traditional contours even potentially come into play. The *Golan* opinion takes what could have been a very useful doctrine in sorting out new technologies and global questions, and restricts its usefulness almost entirely. For someone who has studied traditional contours for a long time, this was the most disappointing and unnecessary part of the opinion.

In many ways, Justice Ginsburg's opinion in *Eldred* stood as a pure, accessible way to understand traditional contours. She set up the notion of a copyright system, and only when something did not fit within the traditional expectations of that system would one evaluate the change against the First Amendment. In Justice Ginsburg's world, the system is based on exclusive rights and safeguards. As long as the issues lie within the traditional categories of copyright, traditional contours have not been altered. But there is an inherent problem: when does something alter the traditional contours? How are we to know when something does not fit within the system? It is the idea of principles that may help.

And so what are the traditional contours of copyright protection? We begin with the Copyright Clause. How has the copyright system been devised to support the requirements of this Clause? What principles can we extract from the system(s) created over time? This informs why the system is in place, and helps us measure when new areas threaten the basic principles of the system. If a new legislative amendment or judge-made doctrine alters the traditional expectations or traditional contours of copyright protection, only then do we turn to a First Amendment analysis.

Traditional contours, however, is bigger than Justice Ginsburg. Traditional contours defines the battles of our times over how we want our system to look and what can fall by the wayside as times change. As the world continues to change-new amendments, new technologies, and new international issues-it places tangible pressure on domestic systems. Traditional contours allows us to pull back from the specifics of the issue (the text, history, and precedent) and think about what our system is and why it is that way. It does not force us to stay with the past, but does require us to at least think about why the system looks the way it does. Traditional contours, however, was never popular, and *Golan v. Holder* may be its last moment of discussion. It had the promise of including deeper theoretical discussion and more significant cultural and historical analysis as part of the legal process, especially in the context of dramatic changes. Traditional contours reminds us that there is a common language, a system, a reasoning. Traditional contours gives us pause to stop and think in this ever-changing world

6: Comparative Copyright

How does U.S. law compare to other laws around the world? We are all mostly governed by the Berne Convention to set minimum standards. We'll be looking at the structure and content of laws around the world. We will also be looking at specific areas of the Berne Convention and general concepts in depth:

In particular look at the following in detail:

Section 7 of the Berne Convention
Section 18 of the Berne Convention
Section 104 of the 1976 Copyright Act (not 104A)

And the concepts:

Retroactivity and Restoration
Rule of the Shorter Term
Qualifying for Protection

Common Copyright Concepts

- Copyright is based on authorship in all countries. We will see that some countries designate some works to the category "neighboring rights", which they see as not necessarily having a human author, like broadcasts of sound recordings.
- Copyright is about creativity. We will see that in some countries fixation is required and in others it is not. The idea of what counts as creativity may also differ, particularly with applied art.
- Most jurisdictions have moral rights. We'll look at that separately.
- Countries divide copyright into idea/expression, protecting expression and not ideas. They also all have a public domain and do not protect basic building blocks.
- Fair use (and fair dealings) varies around the world.
- Most countries do not have work for hire.

- Most copyright acts are structured very similarly. We will explore that more as an exercise.
- Most copyright acts are governed by the Berne Convention, which sets minimum (not maximum) standards.

Key International Concepts

- Territoriality Principle: copyright is bounded by the national boundaries of the country in which the law originates. Sometimes it gets messy and complicated.
- National Treatment: foreign works will not be discriminated against, and will enjoy no less favorable protection than domestic works. They can have better protection (as we see with Section 104A in the US), but they have to have at least as good as domestic works.
- Country of Origin: a work will be protected if the author is a national or domiciliary of a member country, or if the work was published in a member country.
- Point of Attachment: this is where we measure whether the work qualifies.
- Rule of the Shorter Term: if the foreign country has a shorter term of copyright, that is applied instead of the longer term in the country where protection is sought. (We're going to go in depth on this shortly.)
- Neighbouring Rights: technology-based works in civil law countries are often called neighbouring rights. These include performance, sound recordings, broadcasts, and sometimes photography. The term is often based on fixation, creation or publication, rather than the author's life.

Treaties

- Starting in 1891 with the Chase Act, the U.S. allowed for bilateral treaties with individual countries.
- Key multinational treaties:
    - Berne Convention (dominant)
    - Universal Copyright Convention
    - WIPO Copyright Treaty
    - TRIPS (connected to the WTO)
    - Rome Convention
    - Geneva Phonograms Convention
    - WIPO Performance and Phonograms Treaty
- There are many regional treaties and directives, with the EU having some of the most powerful, and free trade agreements.

We will be focused on the Berne Convention and individual countries' copyright laws.

Berne Convention

The Berne Convention is the gold standard and the main treaty we use amongst countries. The Berne Convention has a long and lovely history that starts in the mid-19th century, and it has evolved over time. The Berne Convention provides minimums that countries must include in the copyright acts.

As you read the Berne Convention, pay particular attention to the following articles: 1-20. We will not be diving into developing countries or other elements beyond Article 20.

Article 1

Establishment of a Union [2]

The countries to which this Convention applies constitute a Union for the protection of the rights of authors in their literary and artistic works.

Article 2

Protected Works:

1. "Literary and artistic works"; 2. Possible requirement of fixation; 3. Derivative works;

4. Official texts; 5. Collections; 6. Obligation to protect; beneficiaries of protection;

7. Works of applied art and industrial designs; 8. News

(1) The expression "literary and artistic works" shall include every production in the literary, scientific and artistic domain, whatever may be the mode or form of its expression, such as books, pamphlets and other writings; lectures, addresses, sermons and other works of the same nature; dramatic or dramatico-musical works; choreographic works and entertainments in dumb show; musical compositions with or without words; cinematographic works to which are assimilated works expressed by a process analogous to cinematography; works of drawing, painting, architecture, sculpture, engraving and lithography; photographic works to which are assimilated works expressed by a process analogous to photography; works of applied art; illustrations, maps, plans, sketches and three-dimensional works relative to geography, topography, architecture or science.

(2) It shall, however, be a matter for legislation in the countries of the Union to prescribe that works in general or any specified categories of works shall not be protected unless they have been fixed in some material form.

(3) Translations, adaptations, arrangements of music and other alterations of a literary or artistic work shall be protected as original works without prejudice to the copyright in the original work.

(4) It shall be a matter for legislation in the countries of the Union to determine the protection to be granted to official texts of a legislative, administrative and legal nature, and to official translations of such texts.

(5) Collections of literary or artistic works such as encyclopaedias and anthologies which, by reason of the selection and arrangement of their contents, constitute intellectual creations shall be protected as such, without prejudice to the copyright in each of the works forming part of such collections.

(6) The works mentioned in this Article shall enjoy protection in all countries of the Union. This protection shall operate for the benefit of the author and his successors in title.

(7) Subject to the provisions of Article 7(4) of this Convention, it shall be a matter for legislation in the countries of the Union to determine the extent of the application of their laws to works of applied art and industrial designs and models, as well as the conditions under which such works, designs and models shall be protected. Works protected in the country of origin solely as designs and models shall be entitled in another country of the Union only to such special protection as is granted in that country to designs and models; however, if no such special protection is granted in that country, such works shall be protected as artistic works.

(8) The protection of this Convention shall not apply to news of the day or to miscellaneous facts having the character of mere items of press information.

Article 2*bis*

Possible Limitation of Protection of Certain Works:

1. Certain speeches; 2. Certain uses of lectures and addresses; 3. Right to make collections of such works

(1) It shall be a matter for legislation in the countries of the Union to exclude, wholly or in part, from the protection provided by the preceding Article political speeches and speeches delivered in the course of legal proceedings.

(2) It shall also be a matter for legislation in the countries of the Union to determine the conditions under which lectures, addresses and other works of the same nature which are delivered in public may be reproduced by the press, broadcast, communicated to the public by

wire and made the subject of public communication as envisaged in Article 11*bis*(1) of this Convention, when such use is justified by the informatory purpose.

(3) Nevertheless, the author shall enjoy the exclusive right of making a collection of his works mentioned in the preceding paragraphs.

Article 3

Criteria of Eligibility for Protection:

1. Nationality of author; place of publication of work; 2. Residence of author;

3: "Published" works; 4. "Simultaneously published" works

(1) The protection of this Convention shall apply to:

> *(a)* authors who are nationals of one of the countries of the Union, for their works, whether published or not;
>
> *(b)* authors who are not nationals of one of the countries of the Union, for their works first published in one of those countries, or simultaneously in a country outside the Union and in a country of the Union.

(2) Authors who are not nationals of one of the countries of the Union but who have their habitual residence in one of them shall, for the purposes of this Convention, be assimilated to nationals of that country.

(3) The expression "published works" means works published with the consent of their authors, whatever may be the means of manufacture of the copies, provided that the availability of such copies has been such as to satisfy the reasonable requirements of the public, having regard to the nature of the work. The performance of a dramatic, dramatico-musical, cinematographic or musical work, the public recitation of a literary work, the communication by wire or the broadcasting of literary or artistic works, the exhibition of a work of art and the construction of a work of architecture shall not constitute publication.

(4) A work shall be considered as having been published simultaneously in several countries if it has been published in two or more countries within thirty days of its first publication.

Article 4

Criteria of Eligibility for Protection of Cinematographic Works, Works of Architecture and Certain Artistic Works

The protection of this Convention shall apply, even if the conditions of Article 3 are not fulfilled, to:

> *(a)* authors of cinematographic works the maker of which has his headquarters or habitual residence in one of the countries of the Union;
>
> *(b)* authors of works of architecture erected in a country of the Union or of other artistic works incorporated in a building or other structure located in a country of the Union.

Article 5

Rights Guaranteed:

1. and 2. Outside the country of origin; 3. In the country of origin; 4. "Country of origin"

(1) Authors shall enjoy, in respect of works for which they are protected under this Convention, in countries of the Union other than the country of origin, the rights which their respective laws do now or may hereafter grant to their nationals, as well as the rights specially granted by this Convention.

(2) The enjoyment and the exercise of these rights shall not be subject to any formality; such enjoyment and such exercise shall be independent of the existence of protection in the country of origin of the work. Consequently, apart from the provisions of this Convention, the extent of protection, as well as the means of redress afforded to the author to protect his rights, shall be governed exclusively by the laws of the country where protection is claimed.

(3) Protection in the country of origin is governed by domestic law. However, when the author is not a national of the country of origin of the work for which he is protected under this Convention, he shall enjoy in that country the same rights as national authors.

(4) The country of origin shall be considered to be:

> *(a)* in the case of works first published in a country of the Union, that country; in the case of works published simultaneously in several countries of the Union which grant different terms of protection, the country whose legislation grants the shortest term of protection;
>
> *(b)* in the case of works published simultaneously in a country outside the Union and in a country of the Union, the latter country;

(c) in the case of unpublished works or of works first published in a country outside the Union, without simultaneous publication in a country of the Union, the country of the Union of which the author is a national, provided that:

(i) when these are cinematographic works the maker of which has his headquarters or his habitual residence in a country of the Union, the country of origin shall be that country, and

(ii) when these are works of architecture erected in a country of the Union or other artistic works incorporated in a building or other structure located in a country of the Union, the country of origin shall be that country.

Article 6

Possible Restriction of Protection in Respect of Certain Works of Nationals of Certain Countries Outside the Union:

1. In the country of the first publication and in other countries; 2. No retroactivity; 3. Notice

(1) Where any country outside the Union fails to protect in an adequate manner the works of authors who are nationals of one of the countries of the Union, the latter country may restrict the protection given to the works of authors who are, at the date of the first publication thereof, nationals of the other country and are not habitually resident in one of the countries of the Union. If the country of first publication avails itself of this right, the other countries of the Union shall not be required to grant to works thus subjected to special treatment a wider protection than that granted to them in the country of first publication.

(2) No restrictions introduced by virtue of the preceding paragraph shall affect the rights which an author may have acquired in respect of a work published in a country of the Union before such restrictions were put into force.

(3) The countries of the Union which restrict the grant of copyright in accordance with this Article shall give notice thereof to the Director General of the World Intellectual Property Organization (hereinafter designated as "the Director General") by a written declaration specifying the countries in regard to which protection is restricted, and the restrictions to which rights of authors who are nationals of those countries are subjected. The Director General shall immediately communicate this declaration to all the countries of the Union.

Article 6*bis*

Moral Rights:

1. To claim authorship; to object to certain modifications and other derogatory actions;

2. After the author's death; 3. Means of redress

(1) Independently of the author's economic rights, and even after the transfer of the said rights, the author shall have the right to claim authorship of the work and to object to any distortion, mutilation or other modification of, or other derogatory action in relation to, the said work, which would be prejudicial to his honor or reputation.

(2) The rights granted to the author in accordance with the preceding paragraph shall, after his death, be maintained, at least until the expiry of the economic rights, and shall be exercisable by the persons or institutions authorized by the legislation of the country where protection is claimed. However, those countries whose legislation, at the moment of their ratification of or accession to this Act, does not provide for the protection after the death of the author of all the rights set out in the preceding paragraph may provide that some of these rights may, after his death, cease to be maintained.

(3) The means of redress for safeguarding the rights granted by this Article shall be governed by the legislation of the country where protection is claimed.

Article 7

Term of Protection:

1. Generally; 2. For cinematographic works; 3. For anonymous and pseudonymous works;

4. For photographic works and works of applied art; 5. Starting date of computation;

6. Longer terms; 7. Shorter terms; 8. Applicable law; "comparison" of terms

(1) The term of protection granted by this Convention shall be the life of the author and fifty years after his death.

(2) However, in the case of cinematographic works, the countries of the Union may provide that the term of protection shall expire fifty years after the work has been made available to the public with the consent of the author, or, failing such an event within fifty years from the making of such a work, fifty years after the making.

(3) In the case of anonymous or pseudonymous works, the term of protection granted by this Convention shall expire fifty years after the work has been lawfully made available to the public.

However, when the pseudonym adopted by the author leaves no doubt as to his identity, the term of protection shall be that provided in paragraph (1). If the author of an anonymous or pseudonymous work discloses his identity during the above-mentioned period, the term of protection applicable shall be that provided in paragraph (1). The countries of the Union shall not be required to protect anonymous or pseudonymous works in respect of which it is reasonable to presume that their author has been dead for fifty years.

(4) It shall be a matter for legislation in the countries of the Union to determine the term of protection of photographic works and that of works of applied art in so far as they are protected as artistic works; however, this term shall last at least until the end of a period of twenty-five years from the making of such a work.

(5) The term of protection subsequent to the death of the author and the terms provided by paragraphs (2), (3) and (4) shall run from the date of death or of the event referred to in those paragraphs, but such terms shall always be deemed to begin on the first of January of the year following the death or such event.

(6) The countries of the Union may grant a term of protection in excess of those provided by the preceding paragraphs.

(7) Those countries of the Union bound by the Rome Act of this Convention which grant, in their national legislation in force at the time of signature of the present Act, shorter terms of protection than those provided for in the preceding paragraphs shall have the right to maintain such terms when ratifying or acceding to the present Act.

(8) In any case, the term shall be governed by the legislation of the country where protection is claimed; however, unless the legislation of that country otherwise provides, the term shall not exceed the term fixed in the country of origin of the work.

Article 7*bis*

Term of Protection for Works of Joint Authorship

The provisions of the preceding Article shall also apply in the case of a work of joint authorship, provided that the terms measured from the death of the author shall be calculated from the death of the last surviving author.

Article 8

Right of Translation

Authors of literary and artistic works protected by this Convention shall enjoy the exclusive right of making and of authorizing the translation of their works throughout the term of protection of their rights in the original works.

Article 9

Right of Reproduction:

1. Generally; 2. Possible exceptions; 3. Sound and visual recordings

(1) Authors of literary and artistic works protected by this Convention shall have the exclusive right of authorizing the reproduction of these works, in any manner or form.

(2) It shall be a matter for legislation in the countries of the Union to permit the reproduction of such works in certain special cases, provided that such reproduction does not conflict with a normal exploitation of the work and does not unreasonably prejudice the legitimate interests of the author.

(3) Any sound or visual recording shall be considered as a reproduction for the purposes of this Convention.

Article 10

Certain Free Uses of Works:

1. Quotations; 2. Illustrations for teaching; 3. Indication of source and author

(1) It shall be permissible to make quotations from a work which has already been lawfully made available to the public, provided that their making is compatible with fair practice, and their extent does not exceed that justified by the purpose, including quotations from newspaper articles and periodicals in the form of press summaries.

(2) It shall be a matter for legislation in the countries of the Union, and for special agreements existing or to be concluded between them, to permit the utilization, to the extent justified by the purpose, of literary or artistic works by way of illustration in publications, broadcasts or sound or visual recordings for teaching, provided such utilization is compatible with fair practice.

(3) Where use is made of works in accordance with the preceding paragraphs of this Article, mention shall be made of the source, and of the name of the author if it appears thereon.

Article 10*bis*

Further Possible Free Uses of Works:

1. Of certain articles and broadcast works; 2. Of works seen or heard in connection with current events

(1) It shall be a matter for legislation in the countries of the Union to permit the reproduction by the press, the broadcasting or the communication to the public by wire of articles published in newspapers or periodicals on current economic, political or religious topics, and of broadcast works of the same character, in cases in which the reproduction, broadcasting or such communication thereof is not expressly reserved. Nevertheless, the source must always be clearly indicated; the legal consequences of a breach of this obligation shall be determined by the legislation of the country where protection is claimed.

(2) It shall also be a matter for legislation in the countries of the Union to determine the conditions under which, for the purpose of reporting current events by means of photography, cinematography, broadcasting or communication to the public by wire, literary or artistic works seen or heard in the course of the event may, to the extent justified by the informatory purpose, be reproduced and made available to the public.

Article 11

Certain Rights in Dramatic and Musical Works:

1. Right of public performance and of communication to the public of a performance;

2. In respect of translations

(1) Authors of dramatic, dramatico-musical and musical works shall enjoy the exclusive right of authorizing:

> (i) the public performance of their works, including such public performance by any means or process;
>
> (ii) any communication to the public of the performance of their works.

(2) Authors of dramatic or dramatico-musical works shall enjoy, during the full term of their rights in the original works, the same rights with respect to translations thereof.

Article 11*bis*

Broadcasting and Related Rights:

1. Broadcasting and other wireless communications, public communication of broadcast by wire or rebroadcast,

public communication of broadcast by loudspeaker or analogous instruments;

2. Compulsory licenses; 3. Recording; ephemeral recordings

(1) Authors of literary and artistic works shall enjoy the exclusive right of authorizing:

> (i) the broadcasting of their works or the communication thereof to the public by any other means of wireless diffusion of signs, sounds or images;
>
> (ii) any communication to the public by wire or by rebroadcasting of the broadcast of the work, when this communication is made by an organization other than the original one;
>
> (iii) the public communication by loudspeaker or any other analogous instrument transmitting, by signs, sounds or images, the broadcast of the work.

(2) It shall be a matter for legislation in the countries of the Union to determine the conditions under which the rights mentioned in the preceding paragraph may be exercised, but these conditions shall apply only in the countries where they have been prescribed. They shall not in any circumstances be prejudicial to the moral rights of the author, nor to his right to obtain equitable remuneration which, in the absence of agreement, shall be fixed by competent authority.

(3) In the absence of any contrary stipulation, permission granted in accordance with paragraph (1) of this Article shall not imply permission to record, by means of instruments recording sounds or images, the work broadcast. It shall, however, be a matter for legislation in the countries of the Union to determine the regulations for ephemeral recordings made by a broadcasting organization by means of its own facilities and used for its own broadcasts. The preservation of these recordings in official archives may, on the ground of their exceptional documentary character, be authorized by such legislation.

Article 11*ter*

Certain Rights in Literary Works:

1. Right of public recitation and of communication to the public of a recitation; 2. In respect of translations

(1) Authors of literary works shall enjoy the exclusive right of authorizing:

(i) the public recitation of their works, including such public recitation by any means or process;

(ii) any communication to the public of the recitation of their works.

(2) Authors of literary works shall enjoy, during the full term of their rights in the original works, the same rights with respect to translations thereof.

Article 12

Right of Adaptation, Arrangement and Other Alteration

Authors of literary or artistic works shall enjoy the exclusive right of authorizing adaptations, arrangements and other alterations of their works.

Article 13

Possible Limitation of the Right of Recording of Musical Works and Any Words Pertaining Thereto:

1. Compulsory licenses; 2. Transitory measures;

3. Seizure on importation of copies made without the author's permission

(1) Each country of the Union may impose for itself reservations and conditions on the exclusive right granted to the author of a musical work and to the author of any words, the recording of which together with the musical work has already been authorized by the latter, to authorize the sound recording of that musical work, together with such words, if any; but all such reservations and conditions shall apply only in the countries which have imposed them and shall not, in any circumstances, be prejudicial to the rights of these authors to obtain equitable remuneration which, in the absence of agreement, shall be fixed by competent authority.

(2) Recordings of musical works made in a country of the Union in accordance with Article 13(3) of the Conventions signed at Rome on June 2, 1928, and at Brussels on June 26, 1948, may be reproduced in that country without the permission of the author of the musical work until a date two years after that country becomes bound by this Act.

(3) Recordings made in accordance with paragraphs (1) and (2) of this Article and imported without permission from the parties concerned into a country where they are treated as infringing recordings shall be liable to seizure.

Article 14

Cinematographic and Related Rights:

1. Cinematographic adaptation and reproduction; distribution;

public performance and public communication by wire of works thus adapted or reproduced;

2. Adaptation of cinematographic productions; 3. No compulsory licenses

(1) Authors of literary or artistic works shall have the exclusive right of authorizing:

> (i) the cinematographic adaptation and reproduction of these works, and the distribution of the works thus adapted or reproduced;
>
> (ii) the public performance and communication to the public by wire of the works thus adapted or reproduced.

(2) The adaptation into any other artistic form of a cinematographic production derived from literary or artistic works shall, without prejudice to the authorization of the author of the cinematographic production, remain subject to the authorization of the authors of the original works.

(3) The provisions of Article 13(1) shall not apply.

Article 14*bis*

Special Provisions Concerning Cinematographic Works:

1. Assimilation to "original" works; 2. Ownership; limitation of certain rights of certain contributors;

3. Certain other contributors

(1) Without prejudice to the copyright in any work which may have been adapted or reproduced, a cinematographic work shall be protected as an original work. The owner of copyright in a cinematographic work shall enjoy the same rights as the author of an original work, including the rights referred to in the preceding Article.

(2)

(a) Ownership of copyright in a cinematographic work shall be a matter for legislation in the country where protection is claimed.

(b) However, in the countries of the Union which, by legislation, include among the owners of copyright in a cinematographic work authors who have brought contributions to the making of the work, such authors, if they have undertaken to bring such contributions, may not, in the absence of any contrary or special stipulation, object to the reproduction, distribution, public performance, communication to the public by wire, broadcasting or any other communication to the public, or to the subtitling or dubbing of texts, of the work.

(c) The question whether or not the form of the undertaking referred to above should, for the application of the preceding subparagraph (b), be in a written agreement or a written act of the same effect shall be a matter for the legislation of the country where the maker of the cinematographic work has his headquarters or habitual residence. However, it shall be a matter for the legislation of the country of the Union where protection is claimed to provide that the said undertaking shall be in a written agreement or a written act of the same effect. The countries whose legislation so provides shall notify the Director General by means of a written declaration, which will be immediately communicated by him to all the other countries of the Union.

(d) By "contrary or special stipulation" is meant any restrictive condition which is relevant to the aforesaid undertaking.

(3) Unless the national legislation provides to the contrary, the provisions of paragraph (2)(b) above shall not be applicable to authors of scenarios, dialogues and musical works created for the making of the cinematographic work, or to the principal director thereof. However, those countries of the Union whose legislation does not contain rules providing for the application of the said paragraph (2)(b) to such director shall notify the Director General by means of a written declaration, which will be immediately communicated by him to all the other countries of the Union.

Article 14*ter*

"Droit de suite" in Works of Art and Manuscripts:

1. Right to an interest in resales; 2. Applicable law; 3. Procedure

(1) The author, or after his death the persons or institutions authorized by national legislation, shall, with respect to original works of art and original manuscripts of writers and composers, enjoy the inalienable right to an interest in any sale of the work subsequent to the first transfer by the author of the work.

(2) The protection provided by the preceding paragraph may be claimed in a country of the Union only if legislation in the country to which the author belongs so permits, and to the extent permitted by the country where this protection is claimed.

(3) The procedure for collection and the amounts shall be matters for determination by national legislation.

Article 15

Right to Enforce Protected Rights:

1. Where author's name is indicated or where pseudonym leaves no doubt as to author's identity;

2. In the case of cinematographic works; 3. In the case of anonymous and pseudonymous works;

4. In the case of certain unpublished works of unknown authorship

(1) In order that the author of a literary or artistic work protected by this Convention shall, in the absence of proof to the contrary, be regarded as such, and consequently be entitled to institute infringement proceedings in the countries of the Union, it shall be sufficient for his name to appear on the work in the usual manner. This paragraph shall be applicable even if this name is a pseudonym, where the pseudonym adopted by the author leaves no doubt as to his identity.

(2) The person or body corporate whose name appears on a cinematographic work in the usual manner shall, in the absence of proof to the contrary, be presumed to be the maker of the said work.

(3) In the case of anonymous and pseudonymous works, other than those referred to in paragraph (1) above, the publisher whose name appears on the work shall, in the absence of proof to the contrary, be deemed to represent the author, and in this capacity he shall be entitled to protect and enforce the author's rights. The provisions of this paragraph shall cease

to apply when the author reveals his identity and establishes his claim to authorship of the work.

(4)

> *(a)* In the case of unpublished works where the identity of the author is unknown, but where there is every ground to presume that he is a national of a country of the Union, it shall be a matter for legislation in that country to designate the competent authority which shall represent the author and shall be entitled to protect and enforce his rights in the countries of the Union.
>
> *(b)* Countries of the Union which make such designation under the terms of this provision shall notify the Director General by means of a written declaration giving full information concerning the authority thus designated. The Director General shall at once communicate this declaration to all other countries of the Union.

Article 16

Infringing Copies:

1. Seizure; 2. Seizure on importation; 3. Applicable law

(1) Infringing copies of a work shall be liable to seizure in any country of the Union where the work enjoys legal protection.

(2) The provisions of the preceding paragraph shall also apply to reproductions coming from a country where the work is not protected, or has ceased to be protected.

(3) The seizure shall take place in accordance with the legislation of each country.

Article 17

Possibility of Control of Circulation, Presentation and Exhibition of Works

The provisions of this Convention cannot in any way affect the right of the Government of each country of the Union to permit, to control, or to prohibit, by legislation or regulation, the circulation, presentation, or exhibition of any work or production in regard to which the competent authority may find it necessary to exercise that right.

Article 18

Works Existing on Convention's Entry Into Force:

1. Protectable where protection not yet expired in country of origin;

2. Non-protectable where protection already expired in country where it is claimed;

3. Application of these principles; 4. Special cases

(1) This Convention shall apply to all works which, at the moment of its coming into force, have not yet fallen into the public domain in the country of origin through the expiry of the term of protection.

(2) If, however, through the expiry of the term of protection which was previously granted, a work has fallen into the public domain of the country where protection is claimed, that work shall not be protected anew.

(3) The application of this principle shall be subject to any provisions contained in special conventions to that effect existing or to be concluded between countries of the Union. In the absence of such provisions, the respective countries shall determine, each in so far as it is concerned, the conditions of application of this principle.

(4) The preceding provisions shall also apply in the case of new accessions to the Union and to cases in which protection is extended by the application of Article 7 or by the abandonment of reservations.

Article 19

Protection Greater than Resulting from Convention

The provisions of this Convention shall not preclude the making of a claim to the benefit of any greater protection which may be granted by legislation in a country of the Union.

Article 20

Special Agreements Among Countries of the Union

The Governments of the countries of the Union reserve the right to enter into special agreements among themselves, in so far as such agreements grant to authors more extensive rights than those granted by the Convention, or contain other provisions not contrary to this

Convention. The provisions of existing agreements which satisfy these conditions shall remain applicable.

Article 21

Special Provisions Regarding Developing Countries:

1. Reference to Appendix; 2. Appendix part of Act

(1) Special provisions regarding developing countries are included in the Appendix.

(2) Subject to the provisions of Article 28(1)(b), the Appendix forms an integral part of this Act.

Article 22

Assembly:

1. Constitution and composition; 2. Tasks;

3. Quorum, voting, observers; 4. Convocation; 5. Rules of procedure

(1)

(a) The Union shall have an Assembly consisting of those countries of the Union which are bound by Articles 22 to 26.

(b) The Government of each country shall be represented by one delegate, who may be assisted by alternate delegates, advisors, and experts.

(c) The expenses of each delegation shall be borne by the Government which has appointed it.

(2)

(a) The Assembly shall:

(i) deal with all matters concerning the maintenance and development of the Union and the implementation of this Convention;

(ii) give directions concerning the preparation for conferences of revision to the International Bureau of Intellectual Property (hereinafter designated as "the International Bureau") referred to in the Convention Establishing the World

Intellectual Property Organization (hereinafter designated as "the Organization"), due account being taken of any comments made by those countries of the Union which are not bound by Articles 22 to 26;

(iii) review and approve the reports and activities of the Director General of the Organization concerning the Union, and give him all necessary instructions concerning matters within the competence of the Union;
(iv) elect the members of the Executive Committee of the Assembly;
(v) review and approve the reports and activities of its Executive Committee, and give instructions to such Committee;

(vi) determine the program and adopt the biennial budget of the Union, and approve its final accounts;

(vii) adopt the financial regulations of the Union;

(viii) establish such committees of experts and working groups as may be necessary for the work of the Union;
(ix) determine which countries not members of the Union and which intergovernmental and international non-governmental organizations shall be admitted to its meetings as observers;

(x) adopt amendments to Articles 22 to 26;

(xi) take any other appropriate action designed to further the objectives of the Union;

(xii) exercise such other functions as are appropriate under this Convention;

(xiii) subject to its acceptance, exercise such rights as are given to it in the Convention establishing the Organization.

(b) With respect to matters which are of interest also to other Unions administered by the Organization, the Assembly shall make its decisions after having heard the advice of the Coordination Committee of the Organization.

(3)

(a) Each country member of the Assembly shall have one vote.

(b) One-half of the countries members of the Assembly shall constitute a quorum.

(c) Notwithstanding the provisions of subparagraph (b), if, in any session, the number of countries represented is less than one-half but equal to or more than one-third of the

countries members of the Assembly, the Assembly may make decisions but, with the exception of decisions concerning its own procedure, all such decisions shall take effect only if the following conditions are fulfilled. The International Bureau shall communicate the said decisions to the countries members of the Assembly which were not represented and shall invite them to express in writing their vote or abstention within a period of three months from the date of the communication. If, at the expiration of this period, the number of countries having thus expressed their vote or abstention attains the number of countries which was lacking for attaining the quorum in the session itself, such decisions shall take effect provided that at the same time the required majority still obtains.

(d) Subject to the provisions of Article 26(2), the decisions of the Assembly shall require two-thirds of the votes cast.

(e) Abstentions shall not be considered as votes.

(f) A delegate may represent, and vote in the name of, one country only.

(g) Countries of the Union not members of the Assembly shall be admitted to its meetings as observers.

(4)

(a) The Assembly shall meet once in every second calendar year in ordinary session upon convocation by the Director General and, in the absence of exceptional circumstances, during the same period and at the same place as the General Assembly of the Organization.

(b) The Assembly shall meet in extraordinary session upon convocation by the Director General, at the request of the Executive Committee or at the request of one-fourth of the countries members of the Assembly.

(5) The Assembly shall adopt its own rules of procedure.

Article 23

Executive Committee:

1. Constitution; 2. Composition; 3. Number of members; 4. Geographical distribution; special agreements;

5. Term, limits of re-eligibility, rules of election; 6. Tasks;

7. Convocation; 8. Quorum, voting; 9. Observers; 10. Rules of procedure

(1) The Assembly shall have an Executive Committee.

(2)

> *(a)* The Executive Committee shall consist of countries elected by the Assembly from among countries members of the Assembly. Furthermore, the country on whose territory the Organization has its headquarters shall, subject to the provisions of Article 25(7)(b), have an ex officio seat on the Committee.
>
> *(b)* The Government of each country member of the Executive Committee shall be represented by one delegate, who may be assisted by alternate delegates, advisors, and experts.
>
> *(c)* The expenses of each delegation shall be borne by the Government which has appointed it.

(3) The number of countries members of the Executive Committee shall correspond to one-fourth of the number of countries members of the Assembly. In establishing the number of seats to be filled, remainders after division by four shall be disregarded.

(4) In electing the members of the Executive Committee, the Assembly shall have due regard to an equitable geographical distribution and to the need for countries party to the Special Agreements which might be established in relation with the Union to be among the countries constituting the Executive Committee.

(5)

> *(a)* Each member of the Executive Committee shall serve from the close of the session of the Assembly which elected it to the close of the next ordinary session of the Assembly.
>
> *(b)* Members of the Executive Committee may be re-elected, but not more than two-thirds of them.

(c) The Assembly shall establish the details of the rules governing the election and possible re-election of the members of the Executive Committee.

(6)

(a) The Executive Committee shall:

(i) prepare the draft agenda of the Assembly;

(ii) submit proposals to the Assembly respecting the draft program and biennial budget of the Union prepared by the Director General;

(iii) [*deleted*]

(iv) submit, with appropriate comments, to the Assembly the periodical reports of the Director General and the yearly audit reports on the accounts;

(v) in accordance with the decisions of the Assembly and having regard to circumstances arising between two ordinary sessions of the Assembly, take all necessary measures to ensure the execution of the program of the Union by the Director General;

(vi) perform such other functions as are allocated to it under this Convention.

(b) With respect to matters which are of interest also to other Unions administered by the Organization, the Executive Committee shall make its decisions after having heard the advice of the Coordination Committee of the Organization.

(7)

(a) The Executive Committee shall meet once a year in ordinary session upon convocation by the Director General, preferably during the same period and at the same place as the Coordination Committee of the Organization.

(b) The Executive Committee shall meet in extraordinary session upon convocation by the Director General, either on his own initiative, or at the request of its Chairman or one-fourth of its members.

(8)

(a) Each country member of the Executive Committee shall have one vote.

(b) One-half of the members of the Executive Committee shall constitute a quorum.

(c) Decisions shall be made by a simple majority of the votes cast.

(d) Abstentions shall not be considered as votes.

(e) A delegate may represent, and vote in the name of, one country only.

(9) Countries of the Union not members of the Executive Committee shall be admitted to its meetings as observers.

(10) The Executive Committee shall adopt its own rules of procedure.

Article 24

International Bureau:

1. Tasks in general, Director General; 2. General information; 3. Periodical;

4. Information to countries; 5. Studies and services; 6. Participation in meetings;

7. Conferences of revision; 8. Other tasks

(1)

(a) The administrative tasks with respect to the Union shall be performed by the International Bureau, which is a continuation of the Bureau of the Union united with the Bureau of the Union established by the International Convention for the Protection of Industrial Property.

(b) In particular, the International Bureau shall provide the secretariat of the various organs of the Union.

(c) The Director General of the Organization shall be the chief executive of the Union and shall represent the Union.

(2) The International Bureau shall assemble and publish information concerning the protection of copyright. Each country of the Union shall promptly communicate to the International Bureau all new laws and official texts concerning the protection of copyright.

(3) The International Bureau shall publish a monthly periodical.

(4) The International Bureau shall, on request, furnish information to any country of the Union on matters concerning the protection of copyright.

(5) The International Bureau shall conduct studies, and shall provide services, designed to facilitate the protection of copyright.

(6) The Director General and any staff member designated by him shall participate, without the right to vote, in all meetings of the Assembly, the Executive Committee and any other committee of experts or working group. The Director General, or a staff member designated by him, shall be ex officio secretary of these bodies.

(7)

(a) The International Bureau shall, in accordance with the directions of the Assembly and in cooperation with the Executive Committee, make the preparations for the conferences of revision of the provisions of the Convention other than Articles 22 to 26.

(b) The International Bureau may consult with intergovernmental and international non-governmental organizations concerning preparations for conferences of revision.

(c) The Director General and persons designated by him shall take part, without the right to vote, in the discussions at these conferences.

(8) The International Bureau shall carry out any other tasks assigned to it.

Article 25

Finances:

1. Budget; 2. Coordination with other Unions; 3. Resources;

4. Contributions; possible extension of previous budget; 5. Fees and charges;

6. Working capital fund; 7. Advances by host Government; 8. Auditing of accounts

(1)

(a) The Union shall have a budget.

(b) The budget of the Union shall include the income and expenses proper to the Union, its contribution to the budget of expenses common to the Unions, and, where applicable, the sum made available to the budget of the Conference of the Organization.

(c) Expenses not attributable exclusively to the Union but also to one or more other Unions administered by the Organization shall be considered as expenses common to

the Unions. The share of the Union in such common expenses shall be in proportion to the interest the Union has in them.

(2) The budget of the Union shall be established with due regard to the requirements of coordination with the budgets of the other Unions administered by the Organization.

(3) The budget of the Union shall be financed from the following sources:

(i) contributions of the countries of the Union;

(ii) fees and charges due for services performed by the International Bureau in relation to the Union;

(iii) sale of, or royalties on, the publications of the International Bureau concerning the Union;

(iv) gifts, bequests, and subventions;

(v) rents, interests, and other miscellaneous income.

(4)

(a) For the purpose of establishing its contribution towards the budget, each country of the Union shall belong to a class, and shall pay its annual contributions on the basis of a number of units fixed as follows :

Class I 25

Class II 20

Class III 15

Class IV 10

Class V 5

Class VI 3

Class VII 1

(b) Unless it has already done so, each country shall indicate, concurrently with depositing its instrument of ratification or accession, the class to which it wishes to belong. Any country may change class. If it chooses a lower class, the country must

announce it to the Assembly at one of its ordinary sessions. Any such change shall take effect at the beginning of the calendar year following the session.

(c) The annual contribution of each country shall be an amount in the same proportion to the total sum to be contributed to the annual budget of the Union by all countries as the number of its units is to the total of the units of all contributing countries.

(d) Contributions shall become due on the first of January of each year.

(e) A country which is in arrears in the payment of its contributions shall have no vote in any of the organs of the Union of which it is a member if the amount of its arrears equals or exceeds the amount of the contributions due from it for the preceding two full years. However, any organ of the Union may allow such a country to continue to exercise its vote in that organ if, and as long as, it is satisfied that the delay in payment is due to exceptional and unavoidable circumstances.

(f) If the budget is not adopted before the beginning of a new financial period, it shall be at the same level as the budget of the previous year, in accordance with the financial regulations.

(5) The amount of the fees and charges due for services rendered by the International Bureau in relation to the Union shall be established, and shall be reported to the Assembly and the Executive Committee, by the Director General.

(6)

(a) The Union shall have a working capital fund which shall be constituted by a single payment made by each country of the Union. If the fund becomes insufficient, an increase shall be decided by the Assembly.

(b) The amount of the initial payment of each country to the said fund or of its participation in the increase thereof shall be a proportion of the contribution of that country for the year in which the fund is established or the increase decided.

(c) The proportion and the terms of payment shall be fixed by the Assembly on the proposal of the Director General and after it has heard the advice of the Coordination Committee of the Organization.

(7)

(a) In the headquarters agreement concluded with the country on the territory of which the Organization has its headquarters, it shall be provided that, whenever the working capital fund is insufficient, such country shall grant advances. The amount of these

advances and the conditions on which they are granted shall be the subject of separate agreements, in each case, between such country and the Organization. As long as it remains under the obligation to grant advances, such country shall have an ex officio seat on the Executive Committee.

(b) The country referred to in subparagraph (a) and the Organization shall each have the right to denounce the obligation to grant advances, by written notification. Denunciation shall take effect three years after the end of the year in which it has been notified.

(8) The auditing of the accounts shall be effected by one or more of the countries of the Union or by external auditors, as provided in the financial regulations. They shall be designated, with their agreement, by the Assembly.

Article 26

Amendments:

1. Provisions susceptible of amendment by the Assembly; proposals;

2. Adoption; 3. Entry into force

(1) Proposals for the amendment of Articles 22, 23, 24, 25, and the present Article, may be initiated by any country member of the Assembly, by the Executive Committee, or by the Director General. Such proposals shall be communicated by the Director General to the member countries of the Assembly at least six months in advance of their consideration by the Assembly.

(2) Amendments to the Articles referred to in paragraph (1) shall be adopted by the Assembly. Adoption shall require three-fourths of the votes cast, provided that any amendment of Article 22, and of the present paragraph, shall require four-fifths of the votes cast.

(3) Any amendment to the Articles referred to in paragraph (1) shall enter into force one month after written notifications of acceptance, effected in accordance with their respective constitutional processes, have been received by the Director General from three-fourths of the countries members of the Assembly at the time it adopted the amendment. Any amendment to the said Articles thus accepted shall bind all the countries which are members of the Assembly at the time the amendment enters into force, or which become members thereof at a subsequent date, provided that any amendment increasing the financial obligations of countries of the Union shall bind only those countries which have notified their acceptance of such amendment.

Article 27

Revision:

1. Objective; 2. Conferences; 3. Adoption

(1) This Convention shall be submitted to revision with a view to the introduction of amendments designed to improve the system of the Union.

(2) For this purpose, conferences shall be held successively in one of the countries of the Union among the delegates of the said countries.

(3) Subject to the provisions of Article 26 which apply to the amendment of Articles 22 to 26, any revision of this Act, including the Appendix, shall require the unanimity of the votes cast.

Article 28

Acceptance and Entry Into Force of Act for Countries of the Union:

1. Ratification, accession; possibility of excluding certain provisions; withdrawal of exclusion;

2. Entry into force of Articles 1 to 21 and Appendix; 3. Entry into force of Articles 22 to 38

(1)

> *(a)* Any country of the Union which has signed this Act may ratify it, and, if it has not signed it, may accede to it. Instruments of ratification or accession shall be deposited with the Director General.
>
> *(b)* Any country of the Union may declare in its instrument of ratification or accession that its ratification or accession shall not apply to Articles 1 to 21 and the Appendix, provided that, if such country has previously made a declaration under Article VI(1) of the Appendix, then it may declare in the said instrument only that its ratification or accession shall not apply to Articles 1 to 20.
>
> *(c)* Any country of the Union which, in accordance with subparagraph (b), has excluded provisions therein referred to from the effects of its ratification or accession may at any later time declare that it extends the effects of its ratification or accession to those provisions. Such declaration shall be deposited with the Director General.

(2)

(a) Articles 1 to 21 and the Appendix shall enter into force three months after both of the following two conditions are fulfilled:

(i) at least five countries of the Union have ratified or acceded to this Act without making a declaration under paragraph (1)(b),

(ii) France, Spain, the United Kingdom of Great Britain and Northern Ireland, and the United States of America, have become bound by the Universal Copyright Convention as revised at Paris on July 24, 1971.

(b) The entry into force referred to in subparagraph (a) shall apply to those countries of the Union which, at least three months before the said entry into force, have deposited instruments of ratification or accession not containing a declaration under paragraph (1)(b).

(c) With respect to any country of the Union not covered by subparagraph (b) and which ratifies or accedes to this Act without making a declaration under paragraph (1)(b), Articles 1 to 21 and the Appendix shall enter into force three months after the date on which the Director General has notified the deposit of the relevant instrument of ratification or accession, unless a subsequent date has been indicated in the instrument deposited. In the latter case, Articles 1 to 21 and the Appendix shall enter into force with respect to that country on the date thus indicated.

(d) The provisions of subparagraphs (a) to (c) do not affect the application of Article VI of the Appendix.

(3) With respect to any country of the Union which ratifies or accedes to this Act with or without a declaration made under paragraph (1)(b), Articles 22 to 38 shall enter into force three months after the date on which the Director General has notified the deposit of the relevant instrument of ratification or accession, unless a subsequent date has been indicated in the instrument deposited. In the latter case, Articles 22 to 38 shall enter into force with respect to that country on the date thus indicated.

Article 29

Acceptance and Entry Into Force for Countries Outside the Union:

1. Accession; 2. Entry into force

(1) Any country outside the Union may accede to this Act and thereby become party to this Convention and a member of the Union. Instruments of accession shall be deposited with the Director General.

(2)

> *(a)* Subject to subparagraph (b), this Convention shall enter into force with respect to any country outside the Union three months after the date on which the Director General has notified the deposit of its instrument of accession, unless a subsequent date has been indicated in the instrument deposited. In the latter case, this Convention shall enter into force with respect to that country on the date thus indicated.
>
> *(b)* If the entry into force according to subparagraph (a) precedes the entry into force of Articles 1 to 21 and the Appendix according to Article 28(2)(a), the said country shall, in the meantime, be bound, instead of by Articles 1 to 21 and the Appendix, by Articles 1 to 20 of the Brussels Act of this Convention.

Article 29*bis*

Effect of Acceptance of Act for the Purposes of Article 14(2) of the WIPO Convention

Ratification of or accession to this Act by any country not bound by Articles 22 to of the Stockholm Act of this Convention shall, for the sole purposes of Article 14(2) of the Convention establishing the Organization, amount to ratification of or accession to the said Stockholm Act with the limitation set forth in Article 28(1)(b)(i) thereof.

Article 30

Reservations:

1. Limits of possibility of making reservations;

2. Earlier reservations; reservation as to the right of translation; withdrawal of reservation

(1) Subject to the exceptions permitted by paragraph (2) of this Article, by Article 28(1)(b), by Article 33(2), and by the Appendix, ratification or accession shall automatically entail acceptance of all the provisions and admission to all the advantages of this Convention.

(2)

(a) Any country of the Union ratifying or acceding to this Act may, subject to Article V(2) of the Appendix, retain the benefit of the reservations it has previously formulated on condition that it makes a declaration to that effect at the time of the deposit of its instrument of ratification or accession.

(b) Any country outside the Union may declare, in acceding to this Convention and subject to Article V(2) of the Appendix, that it intends to substitute, temporarily at least, for Article 8 of this Act concerning the right of translation, the provisions of Article 5 of the Union Convention of 1886 [4], as completed at Paris in 1896, on the clear understanding that the said provisions are applicable only to translations into a language in general use in the said country. Subject to Article I(6)(b) of the Appendix, any country has the right to apply, in relation to the right of translation of works whose country of origin is a country availing itself of such a reservation, a protection which is equivalent to the protection granted by the latter country.

(c) Any country may withdraw such reservations at any time by notification addressed to the Director General.

Article 31

Applicability to Certain Territories:

1. Declaration; 2. Withdrawal of declaration; 3. Effective date;

4. Acceptance of factual situations not implied

(1) Any country may declare in its instrument of ratification or accession, or may inform the Director General by written notification at any time thereafter, that this Convention shall be applicable to all or part of those territories, designated in the declaration or notification, for the external relations of which it is responsible.

(2) Any country which has made such a declaration or given such a notification may, at any time, notify the Director General that this Convention shall cease to be applicable to all or part of such territories.

(3)

(a) Any declaration made under paragraph (1) shall take effect on the same date as the ratification or accession in which it was included, and any notification given under that paragraph shall take effect three months after its notification by the Director General.

(b) Any notification given under paragraph (2) shall take effect twelve months after its receipt by the Director General.

(4) This Article shall in no way be understood as implying the recognition or tacit acceptance by a country of the Union of the factual situation concerning a territory to which this Convention is made applicable by another country of the Union by virtue of a declaration under paragraph (1).

Article 32

Applicability of this Act and of Earlier Acts:

1. As between countries already members of the Union;

2. As between a country becoming a member of the Union and other countries members of the Union;

3. Applicability of the Appendix in Certain Relations

(1) This Act shall, as regards relations between the countries of the Union, and to the extent that it applies, replace the Berne Convention of September 9, 1886, and the subsequent Acts of revision. The Acts previously in force shall continue to be applicable, in their entirety or to the extent that this Act does not replace them by virtue of the preceding sentence, in relations with countries of the Union which do not ratify or accede to this Act.

(2) Countries outside the Union which become party to this Act shall, subject to paragraph (3), apply it with respect to any country of the Union not bound by this Act or which, although bound by this Act, has made a declaration pursuant to Article 28(1)(b). Such countries recognize that the said country of the Union, in its relations with them:

(i) may apply the provisions of the most recent Act by which it is bound, and

(ii) subject to Article I(6) of the Appendix, has the right to adapt the protection to the level provided for by this Act.

(3) Any country which has availed itself of any of the faculties provided for in the Appendix may apply the provisions of the Appendix relating to the faculty or faculties of which it has availed itself in its relations with any other country of the Union which is not bound by this Act, provided that the latter country has accepted the application of the said provisions.

Article 33

Disputes:

1. Jurisdiction of the International Court of Justice;

2. Reservation as to such jurisdiction; 3. Withdrawal of reservation

(1) Any dispute between two or more countries of the Union concerning the interpretation or application of this Convention, not settled by negotiation, may, by any one of the countries concerned, be brought before the International Court of Justice by application in conformity with the Statute of the Court, unless the countries concerned agree on some other method of settlement. The country bringing the dispute before the Court shall inform the International Bureau; the International Bureau shall bring the matter to the attention of the other countries of the Union.

(2) Each country may, at the time it signs this Act or deposits its instrument of ratification or accession, declare that it does not consider itself bound by the provisions of paragraph (1). With regard to any dispute between such country and any other country of the Union, the provisions of paragraph (1) shall not apply.

(3) Any country having made a declaration in accordance with the provisions of paragraph (2) may, at any time, withdraw its declaration by notification addressed to the Director General.

Article 34

Closing of Certain Earlier Provisions:

1. Of earlier Acts; 2. Of the Protocol to the Stockholm Act

(1) Subject to Article 29*bis*, no country may ratify or accede to earlier Acts of this Convention once Articles 1 to 21 and the Appendix have entered into force.

(2) Once Articles 1 to 21 and the Appendix have entered into force, no country may make a declaration under Article 5 of the Protocol Regarding Developing Countries attached to the Stockholm Act.

Article 35

Duration of the Convention; Denunciation:

1. Unlimited duration; 2. Possibility of denunciation;

3. Effective date of denunciation; 4. Moratorium on denunciation

(1) This Convention shall remain in force without limitation as to time.

(2) Any country may denounce this Act by notification addressed to the Director General. Such denunciation shall constitute also denunciation of all earlier Acts and shall affect only the country making it, the Convention remaining in full force and effect as regards the other countries of the Union.

(3) Denunciation shall take effect one year after the day on which the Director General has received the notification.

(4) The right of denunciation provided by this Article shall not be exercised by any country before the expiration of five years from the date upon which it becomes a member of the Union.

Article 36

Application of the Convention:

1. Obligation to adopt the necessary measures; 2. Time from which obligation exists

(1) Any country party to this Convention undertakes to adopt, in accordance with its constitution, the measures necessary to ensure the application of this Convention.

(2) It is understood that, at the time a country becomes bound by this Convention, it will be in a position under its domestic law to give effect to the provisions of this Convention.

Article 37

Final Clauses:

1. Languages of the Act; 2. Signature;

3. Certified copies; 4. Registration; 5. Notifications

(1)

> *(a)* This Act shall be signed in a single copy in the French and English languages and, subject to paragraph (2), shall be deposited with the Director General.

(b) Official texts shall be established by the Director General, after consultation with the interested Governments, in the Arabic, German, Italian, Portuguese and Spanish languages, and such other languages as the Assembly may designate.

(c) In case of differences of opinion on the interpretation of the various texts, the French text shall prevail.

(2) This Act shall remain open for signature until January 31, 1972. Until that date, the copy referred to in paragraph (1)(a) shall be deposited with the Government of the French Republic.

(3) The Director General shall certify and transmit two copies of the signed text of this Act to the Governments of all countries of the Union and, on request, to the Government of any other country.

(4) The Director General shall register this Act with the Secretariat of the United Nations.

(5) The Director General shall notify the Governments of all countries of the Union of signatures, deposits of instruments of ratification or accession and any declarations included in such instruments or made pursuant to Articles 28(1)(c), 30(2)(a) and (b), and 33(2), entry into force of any provisions of this Act, notifications of denunciation, and notifications pursuant to Articles 30(2)(c), 31(1) and (2), 33(3), and 38(1), as well as the Appendix.

Article 38

Transitory Provisions:

1. Exercise of the "five-year privilege";

2. Bureau of the Union, Director of the Bureau; 3. Succession of Bureau of the Union

(1) Countries of the Union which have not ratified or acceded to this Act and which are not bound by Articles 22 to 26 of the Stockholm Act of this Convention may, until April 26, 1975, exercise, if they so desire, the rights provided under the said Articles as if they were bound by them. Any country desiring to exercise such rights shall give written notification to this effect to the Director General; this notification shall be effective on the date of its receipt. Such countries shall be deemed to be members of the Assembly until the said date.

(2) As long as all the countries of the Union have not become Members of the Organization, the International Bureau of the Organization shall also function as the Bureau of the Union, and the Director General as the Director of the said Bureau.

(3) Once all the countries of the Union have become Members of the Organization, the rights, obligations, and property, of the Bureau of the Union shall devolve on the International Bureau of the Organization.

APPENDIX

SPECIAL PROVISIONS REGARDING DEVELOPING COUNTRIES

Article I

Faculties Open to Developing Countries:

1. Availability of certain faculties; declaration; 2. Duration of effect of declaration;

3. Cessation of developing country status; 4. Existing stocks of copies;

5. Declarations concerning certain territories; 6. Limits of reciprocity

(1) Any country regarded as a developing country in conformity with the established practice of the General Assembly of the United Nations which ratifies or accedes to this Act, of which this Appendix forms an integral part, and which, having regard to its economic situation and its social or cultural needs, does not consider itself immediately in a position to make provision for the protection of all the rights as provided for in this Act, may, by a notification deposited with the Director General at the time of depositing its instrument of ratification or accession or, subject to Article V(1)(c), at any time thereafter, declare that it will avail itself of the faculty provided for in Article II, or of the faculty provided for in Article III, or of both of those faculties. It may, instead of availing itself of the faculty provided for in Article II, make a declaration according to Article V(1)(a).

(2)

(a) Any declaration under paragraph (1) notified before the expiration of the period of ten years from the entry into force of Articles 1 to 21 and this Appendix according to Article 28(2) shall be effective until the expiration of the said period. Any such declaration may be renewed in whole or in part for periods of ten years each by a notification deposited with the Director General not more than fifteen months and not less than three months before the expiration of the ten-year period then running.

(b) Any declaration under paragraph (1) notified after the expiration of the period of ten years from the entry into force of Articles 1 to 21 and this Appendix according to Article 28(2) shall be effective until the expiration of the ten-year period then running. Any

such declaration may be renewed as provided for in the second sentence of subparagraph (a).

(3) Any country of the Union which has ceased to be regarded as a developing country as referred to in paragraph (1) shall no longer be entitled to renew its declaration as provided in paragraph (2), and, whether or not it formally withdraws its declaration, such country shall be precluded from availing itself of the faculties referred to in paragraph (1) from the expiration of the ten-year period then running or from the expiration of a period of three years after it has ceased to be regarded as a developing country, whichever period expires later.

(4) Where, at the time when the declaration made under paragraph (1) or (2) ceases to be effective, there are copies in stock which were made under a license granted by virtue of this Appendix, such copies may continue to be distributed until their stock is exhausted.

(5) Any country which is bound by the provisions of this Act and which has deposited a declaration or a notification in accordance with Article 31(1) with respect to the application of this Act to a particular territory, the situation of which can be regarded as analogous to that of the countries referred to in paragraph (1), may, in respect of such territory, make the declaration referred to in paragraph (1) and the notification of renewal referred to in paragraph (2). As long as such declaration or notification remains in effect, the provisions of this Appendix shall be applicable to the territory in respect of which it was made.

(6)

(a) The fact that a country avails itself of any of the faculties referred to in paragraph (1) does not permit another country to give less protection to works of which the country of origin is the former country than it is obliged to grant under Articles 1 to 20.

(b) The right to apply reciprocal treatment provided for in Article 30(2)(b), second sentence, shall not, until the date on which the period applicable under Article I(3) expires, be exercised in respect of works the country of origin of which is a country which has made a declaration according to Article V(1)(a).

Article II

Limitations on the Right of Translation:

1. Licenses grantable by competent authority; 2. to 4. Conditions allowing the grant of such licenses;

5. Purposes for which licenses may be granted; 6. Termination of licenses; 7. Works composed mainly of illustrations;

8. Works withdrawn from circulation; 9. Licenses for broadcasting organizations

(1) Any country which has declared that it will avail itself of the faculty provided for in this Article shall be entitled, so far as works published in printed or analogous forms of reproduction are concerned, to substitute for the exclusive right of translation provided for in Article 8 a system of non-exclusive and non-transferable licenses, granted by the competent authority under the following conditions and subject to Article IV.

(2)

(a) Subject to paragraph (3), if, after the expiration of a period of three years, or of any longer period determined by the national legislation of the said country, commencing on the date of the first publication of the work, a translation of such work has not been published in a language in general use in that country by the owner of the right of translation, or with his authorization, any national of such country may obtain a license to make a translation of the work in the said language and publish the translation in printed or analogous forms of reproduction.

(b) A license under the conditions provided for in this Article may also be granted if all the editions of the translation published in the language concerned are out of print.

(3)

(a) In the case of translations into a language which is not in general use in one or more developed countries which are members of the Union, a period of one year shall be substituted for the period of three years referred to in paragraph (2)(a).

(b) Any country referred to in paragraph (1) may, with the unanimous agreement of the developed countries which are members of the Union and in which the same language is in general use, substitute, in the case of translations into that language, for the period of three years referred to in paragraph (2)(a) a shorter period as determined by such agreement but not less than one year. However, the provisions of the foregoing sentence shall not apply where the language in question is English, French or Spanish. The Director General shall be notified of any such agreement by the Governments which have concluded it.

(4)

(a) No license obtainable after three years shall be granted under this Article until a further period of six months has elapsed, and no license obtainable after one year shall be granted under this Article until a further period of nine months has elapsed

(i) from the date on which the applicant complies with the requirements mentioned in Article IV(1), or

(ii) where the identity or the address of the owner of the right of translation is unknown, from the date on which the applicant sends, as provided for in Article IV(2), copies of his application submitted to the authority competent to grant the license.

(b) If, during the said period of six or nine months, a translation in the language in respect of which the application was made is published by the owner of the right of translation or with his authorization, no license under this Article shall be granted.

(5) Any license under this Article shall be granted only for the purpose of teaching, scholarship or research.

(6) If a translation of a work is published by the owner of the right of translation or with his authorization at a price reasonably related to that normally charged in the country for comparable works, any license granted under this Article shall terminate if such translation is in the same language and with substantially the same content as the translation published under the license. Any copies already made before the license terminates may continue to be distributed until their stock is exhausted.

(7) For works which are composed mainly of illustrations, a license to make and publish a translation of the text and to reproduce and publish the illustrations may be granted only if the conditions of Article III are also fulfilled.

(8) No license shall be granted under this Article when the author has withdrawn from circulation all copies of his work.

(9)

(a) A license to make a translation of a work which has been published in printed or analogous forms of reproduction may also be granted to any broadcasting organization having its headquarters in a country referred to in paragraph (1), upon an application made to the competent authority of that country by the said organization, provided that all of the following conditions are met:

(i) the translation is made from a copy made and acquired in accordance with the laws of the said country;

(ii) the translation is only for use in broadcasts intended exclusively for teaching or for the dissemination of the results of specialized technical or scientific research to experts in a particular profession;

(iii) the translation is used exclusively for the purposes referred to in condition

(ii) through broadcasts made lawfully and intended for recipients on the territory of the said country, including broadcasts made through the medium of sound or visual recordings lawfully and exclusively made for the purpose of such broadcasts;

(iv) all uses made of the translation are without any commercial purpose.

(b) Sound or visual recordings of a translation which was made by a broadcasting organization under a license granted by virtue of this paragraph may, for the purposes and subject to the conditions referred to in subparagraph (a) and with the agreement of that organization, also be used by any other broadcasting organization having its headquarters in the country whose competent authority granted the license in question.

(c) Provided that all of the criteria and conditions set out in subparagraph (a) are met, a license may also be granted to a broadcasting organization to translate any text incorporated in an audio-visual fixation where such fixation was itself prepared and published for the sole purpose of being used in connection with systematic instructional activities.

(d) Subject to subparagraphs (a) to (c), the provisions of the preceding paragraphs shall apply to the grant and exercise of any license granted under this paragraph.

Article III

Limitation on the Right of Reproduction:

1. Licenses grantable by competent authority; 2. to 5. Conditions allowing the grant of such licenses;

6. Termination of licenses; 7. Works to which this Article applies

(1) Any country which has declared that it will avail itself of the faculty provided for in this Article shall be entitled to substitute for the exclusive right of reproduction provided for in Article 9 a system of non-exclusive and non-transferable licenses, granted by the competent authority under the following conditions and subject to Article IV.

(2)

(a) If, in relation to a work to which this Article applies by virtue of paragraph (7), after the expiration of

(i) the relevant period specified in paragraph (3), commencing on the date of first publication of a particular edition of the work, or
(ii) any longer period determined by national legislation of the country referred to in paragraph (1), commencing on the same date, copies of such edition have not been distributed in that country to the general public or in connection with systematic instructional activities, by the owner of the right of reproduction or with his authorization, at a price reasonably related to that normally charged in the country for comparable works, any national of such country may obtain a license to reproduce and publish such edition at that or a lower price for use in connection with systematic instructional activities.

(b) A license to reproduce and publish an edition which has been distributed as described in subparagraph (a) may also be granted under the conditions provided for in this Article if, after the expiration of the applicable period, no authorized copies of that edition have been on sale for a period of six months in the country concerned to the general public or in connection with systematic instructional activities at a price reasonably related to that normally charged in the country for comparable works.

(3) The period referred to in paragraph (2)(a)(i) shall be five years, except that

(i) for works of the natural and physical sciences, including mathematics, and of technology, the period shall be three years;
(ii) for works of fiction, poetry, drama and music, and for art books, the period shall be seven years.

(4)

(a) No license obtainable after three years shall be granted under this Article until a period of six months has elapsed

(i) from the date on which the applicant complies with the requirements mentioned in Article IV(1), or
(ii) where the identity or the address of the owner of the right of reproduction is unknown, from the date on which the applicant sends, as provided for in Article IV(2), copies of his application submitted to the authority competent to grant the license.

(b) Where licenses are obtainable after other periods and Article IV(2) is applicable, no license shall be granted until a period of three months has elapsed from the date of the

dispatch of the copies of the application.

(c) If, during the period of six or three months referred to in subparagraphs (a) and (b), a distribution as described in paragraph (2)(a) has taken place, no license shall be granted under this Article.

(d) No license shall be granted if the author has withdrawn from circulation all copies of the edition for the reproduction and publication of which the license has been applied for.

(5) A license to reproduce and publish a translation of a work shall not be granted under this Article in the following cases:

(i) where the translation was not published by the owner of the right of translation or with his authorization, or

(ii) where the translation is not in a language in general use in the country in which the license is applied for.

(6) If copies of an edition of a work are distributed in the country referred to in paragraph (1) to the general public or in connection with systematic instructional activities, by the owner of the right of reproduction or with his authorization, at a price reasonably related to that normally charged in the country for comparable works, any license granted under this Article shall terminate if such edition is in the same language and with substantially the same content as the edition which was published under the said license. Any copies already made before the license terminates may continue to be distributed until their stock is exhausted.

(7)

(a) Subject to subparagraph (b), the works to which this Article applies shall be limited to works published in printed or analogous forms of reproduction.

(b) This Article shall also apply to the reproduction in audio-visual form of lawfully made audio-visual fixations including any protected works incorporated therein and to the translation of any incorporated text into a language in general use in the country in which the license is applied for, always provided that the audio-visual fixations in question were prepared and published for the sole purpose of being used in connection with systematic instructional activities.

Article IV

Provisions Common to Licenses Under Articles II and III:

1. and 2. Procedure; 3. Indication of author and title of work;

4. Exportation of copies; 5. Notice; 6. Compensation

(1) A license under Article II or Article III may be granted only if the applicant, in accordance with the procedure of the country concerned, establishes either that he has requested, and has been denied, authorization by the owner of the right to make and publish the translation or to reproduce and publish the edition, as the case may be, or that, after due diligence on his part, he was unable to find the owner of the right. At the same time as making the request, the applicant shall inform any national or international information center referred to in paragraph (2).

(2) If the owner of the right cannot be found, the applicant for a license shall send, by registered airmail, copies of his application, submitted to the authority competent to grant the license, to the publisher whose name appears on the work and to any national or international information center which may have been designated, in a notification to that effect deposited with the Director General, by the Government of the country in which the publisher is believed to have his principal place of business.

(3) The name of the author shall be indicated on all copies of the translation or reproduction published under a license granted under Article II or Article III. The title of the work shall appear on all such copies. In the case of a translation, the original title of the work shall appear in any case on all the said copies.

(4)

> *(a)* No license granted under Article II or Article III shall extend to the export of copies, and any such license shall be valid only for publication of the translation or of the reproduction, as the case may be, in the territory of the country in which it has been applied for.
>
> *(b)* For the purposes of subparagraph (a), the notion of export shall include the sending of copies from any territory to the country which, in respect of that territory, has made a declaration under Article I(5).
>
> *(c)* Where a governmental or other public entity of a country which has granted a license to make a translation under Article II into a language other than English, French or Spanish sends copies of a translation published under such license to another

country, such sending of copies shall not, for the purposes of subparagraph (a), be considered to constitute export if all of the following conditions are met:

(i) the recipients are individuals who are nationals of the country whose competent authority has granted the license, or organizations grouping such individuals;

(ii) the copies are to be used only for the purpose of teaching, scholarship or research;

(iii) the sending of the copies and their subsequent distribution to recipients is without any commercial purpose; and

(iv) the country to which the copies have been sent has agreed with the country whose competent authority has granted the license to allow the receipt, or distribution, or both, and the Director General has been notified of the agreement by the Government of the country in which the license has been granted.

(5) All copies published under a license granted by virtue of Article II or Article III shall bear a notice in the appropriate language stating that the copies are available for distribution only in the country or territory to which the said license applies.

(6)

(a) Due provision shall be made at the national level to ensure

(i) that the license provides, in favour of the owner of the right of translation or of reproduction, as the case may be, for just compensation that is consistent with standards of royalties normally operating on licenses freely negotiated between persons in the two countries concerned, and

(ii) payment and transmittal of the compensation: should national currency regulations intervene, the competent authority shall make all efforts, by the use of international machinery, to ensure transmittal in internationally convertible currency or its equivalent.

(b) Due provision shall be made by national legislation to ensure a correct translation of the work, or an accurate reproduction of the particular edition, as the case may be.

Article V

Alternative Possibility for Limitation of the Right of Translation:

1. Regime provided for under the 1886 and 1896 Acts;

2. No possibility of change to regime under Article II;

3. Time limit for choosing the alternative possibility

(1)

(a) Any country entitled to make a declaration that it will avail itself of the faculty provided for in Article II may, instead, at the time of ratifying or acceding to this Act:

(i) if it is a country to which Article 30(2)(a) applies, make a declaration under that provision as far as the right of translation is concerned;
(ii) if it is a country to which Article 30(2)(a) does not apply, and even if it is not a country outside the Union, make a declaration as provided for in Article 30(2)(b), first sentence.

(b) In the case of a country which ceases to be regarded as a developing country as referred to in Article I(1), a declaration made according to this paragraph shall be effective until the date on which the period applicable under Article I(3) expires.

(c) Any country which has made a declaration according to this paragraph may not subsequently avail itself of the faculty provided for in Article II even if it withdraws the said declaration.

(2) Subject to paragraph (3), any country which has availed itself of the faculty provided for in Article II may not subsequently make a declaration according to paragraph (1).

(3) Any country which has ceased to be regarded as a developing country as referred to in Article I(1) may, not later than two years prior to the expiration of the period applicable under Article I(3), make a declaration to the effect provided for in Article 30(2)(b), first sentence, notwithstanding the fact that it is not a country outside the Union. Such declaration shall take effect at the date on which the period applicable under Article I(3) expires.

Article VI

Possibilities of applying, or admitting the application of, certain provisions of the Appendix before becoming bound by it:

1. Declaration; 2. Depository and effective date of declaration

(1) Any country of the Union may declare, as from the date of this Act, and at any time before becoming bound by Articles 1 to 21 and this Appendix:

(i) if it is a country which, were it bound by Articles 1 to 21 and this Appendix, would be entitled to avail itself of the faculties referred to in Article I(1), that it will apply the provisions of Article II or of Article III or of both to works whose country of origin is a country which, pursuant to (ii) below, admits the application of those Articles to such works, or which is bound by Articles 1 to 21 and this Appendix; such declaration may, instead of referring to Article II, refer to Article V;

(ii) that it admits the application of this Appendix to works of which it is the country of origin by countries which have made a declaration under (i) above or a notification under Article I.

(2) Any declaration made under paragraph (1) shall be in writing and shall be deposited with the Director General. The declaration shall become effective from the date of its deposit.

[1] This Table of Contents is added for the convenience of the reader. It does not appear in the original (English) text of the Convention.

[2] Each Article and the Appendix have been given titles to facilitate their identification. There are no titles in the signed (English) text.

[3] The Governing Bodies of WIPO and the Unions administered by WIPO adopted with effect from January 1, 1994, a new contribution system that replaces the contribution system set forth in Article 25(4)(a), (b) and (c) of the Berne Convention. Details concerning that system may be obtained from the International Bureau of WIPO.

[4] The text in English of Article 5 of the Berne Convention of 1886, as completed at Paris in 1896 is as follows: "Authors who are nationals of any of the countries of the Union, or their successors in title, shall enjoy in the other countries the exclusive right of making or authorizing the translation of their works throughout the term of their right in the original work. Nevertheless, the exclusive right of translation shall cease to exist if the author shall not have availed himself of it, during a term of ten years from the date of the first publication of the original work by publishing or causing to be published, in one

of the countries of the Union a translation in the language for which protection is to be claimed."

Parsing out Rule of the Shorter Term

J.D. Salinger and his estate are no strangers to copyright litigation. In the mid-1980s, a biographer's failed attempt to publish Salinger's letters added to the debate over the applicability and extent of fair use in unpublished works. Two decades later, the Second Circuit ruled again in favor of Salinger in a case about an unauthorized derivative work--a sequel to *Catcher in the Rye* called *60 Years Later: Coming Through the Rye* by John David California. Both court rulings had a long-term impact on copyright law. In the first case, after the court found that unpublished works were not covered by fair use, Congress amended the Copyright Act to include unpublished works under Section 107. The second case confirmed standards of injunctions to copyright that had been developed in the patent arena.

In 2015, the Salinger Estate again found itself in court, this time with a small publisher, Devault-Graves, who wanted the court to declare that three short stories in the public domain in the United States were also in the public domain around the world when a particular country applied "Rule of the Shorter Term" (RST). If this case followed suit, this new litigation would have done for RST what the previous cases did for injunctions, fair use, and unpublished works: provided a concrete standard by which to measure, in this case, the duration of a work's copyright term around the world. This case, however, would be dropped before that could occur.

But let's take up the topic: **the relationship between the status of a public domain work in the United States and its status around the world in countries that apply RST.** That simple request by the plaintiffs turns out actually to be an extraordinarily difficult and misguided quest. The Salinger Estate was right: you must make an accurate determination of a country-by-country analysis, and just because a work is in the public domain in the United States, does not mean that is its status in any other country. The complicated process of determining the term of a U.S. work abroad requires an understanding of U.S. domestic law, laws of each foreign country, treaty analysis, and even interpretation from the World Intellectual Property Organization (WIPO).

This is the story of why clear and succinct RST analysis remains elusive and thus I suggest ways to tame this unruly doctrine through a three-part process. Salinger's works, as in past Salinger litigation, turn out to be the perfect platform upon which to discuss duration calculations in both international and domestic contexts.

How long a copyright lasts is key in defining the property boundaries of a work. Many think copyright terms are straightforward measurements: life plus fifty years, or publication plus ninety-five years. However, a number of mechanisms exist that make determining the copyright status of a work more complicated. One of those mechanisms is the "Rule of the Shorter Term," (RST) or "Comparison of Terms." RST is a mechanism found in copyright treaties that helps to negotiate the differing lengths of term between one or more countries. The Berne Convention's Section 7(8) is the most famous version of it.

What is the "Rule of the Shorter Term" (RST)?

The Rule of the Shorter Term (RST) states that a country is permitted to shorten the length of protection for foreign works if the work's country of origin has a shorter term than the country in question. For example, if Country A provides one hundred years of protection, but Country B provides only ten years, Country A need only provide, under the RST, ten years of protection to a Country B work in Country A, not one hundred.

Many countries have adopted RST as part of their domestic law, but many more countries remain silent as to whether they observe it. These latter countries are members of the Berne Convention, which established RST as the default, but left unclear whether RST applies directly through the treaty to domestic law or whether it must affirmatively be adopted *because* it is often not clear if the Berne Convention (or other treaties) are directly applicable. Other elements--bilateral treaties, for example, or Free Trade Agreements--further complicate the question as to whether RST applies. So, without clear answers, we are actually left wondering if the term for the hypothetical Country B work in Country A is ten years or one hundred. We are left with nothing more than a best guess that it is likely to apply.

Some may think RST is old fashioned and passé, and that the Salinger case is an anomaly. The Salinger case, and a brief mention in the Trans-Pacific Partnership (TPP), show that RST is relevant and debate about it continues. In order to establish a concrete applicability standard for RST, we must know *when* and *under what circumstances* RST applies.

Salinger and RST

The latest Salinger case began after members of publisher Devault-Graves saw a documentary on writer J.D. Salinger (1919-2010), an American author most famously known for the iconic classic 1951 novel *Catcher in the Rye*. The Devault-Graves Agency specializes in republishing public domain works: "No good book deserves to fall into obscurity. We search for titles that deserve a presence in the digital age, and we bring them back to life for the enjoyments of today's readers." The owners of the publishing company, after seeing the documentary, began to wonder if they could find J.D. Salinger works that had come into the public domain. Finding such gems is the goal of re-publishers. It is how copyright law is supposed to work; once a work is in the public domain, anyone else is free to republish it. The publishers found three short stories.

How Devault-Graves found the stories remains unclear, but it found three Salinger works from the 1940s whose copyright terms were not renewed. For domestic works from this era to be protected, the works' copyrights needed to have been renewed at the US Copyright Office during their twenty-seventh year. Since they were not renewed, Devault-Graves set about publishing the stories as a collection of works titled *Three Early Stories.*

From Devault-Graves's Amended Complaint, it appears the Salinger Trust did not take kindly to the Devault-Graves re-publication. It eventually conceded that the three short stories were, indeed, in the public domain due to lack of proper renewal. Devault-Graves, however, was looking beyond U.S. re-publication. Since the stories were out of copyright in the United States, the publishers wanted to take advantage of the little-known component of copyright law, RST. They believed that if the work was out of copyright in the United States, that work would also be out of copyright in other countries, thanks to RST.

Pursuing international publication, Devault-Graves contacted a German publisher, claiming the work was out of copyright due to RST--and the Salinger Estate fought back. It is not clear why Devault-Graves chose Germany to republish and sell the short stories. In fact, there could not have been a worse country to choose. A German court found that RST did not apply to these three short stories. The same resulted when Devault-Graves sought to publish in Italy. So far, the re-publisher's plan of globally exploiting the three stories had been foiled. Devault-Graves felt harassed and bullied by the Salinger Estate, so it filed suit in the Western District of Tennessee to obtain a declaratory judgment. In its complaint, Devault-Graves claimed that "[d]efendants [the Salinger Estate]--acting without any legal basis ... have attempted to thwart Devault-Graves from exploiting [Devault-Graves's republication rights], including by tortiously interfering with Devault-Graves's contractual agreements with foreign publishers." The publisher wanted the court to declare that, since the stories were in the public domain in the United States, the works were also in the public domain in any country where RST applied.

Why did Devault-Graves believe the stories were in the public domain outside the United States while a German court and the Salinger Estate believed otherwise? To understand the answer to that question, we must look more closely at domestic and foreign copyrights in an international context.

Rule of the Shorter Term Explained

RST has been part of copyright law from the beginning, or nearly so. Germany's 1870 copyright law included RST, for instance. Germany had unified that year and with that came a copyright law applying to works in the North German Confederation:

> Those works by foreign authors which have been published in a place that is geographically situated within the boundaries of the former German Confederation, but not within those of the North German Confederation, shall enjoy the protection of this law, provided that the legislation of the state concerned gives works which come out in the North German Confederation the same level of protection as works by native authors; however, the term of protection *shall not exceed that which is valid in that state itself*. The same applies to unpublished works by authors who are not citizens of the North German Confederation, but who do come from the territory of the former German Confederation.

It would be through treaties, though, that RST would make its mark--notably the Berne Convention, the dominant copyright treaty around the world. RST found its beginning with the first version of the Berne Convention. In fact, RST predates the requirement of minimum terms in the Berne Convention by sixty years. During the first round of negotiations, and in the first version of the Berne Convention, no term of copyright was agreed upon, but RST was.

Early in the debates surrounding the Berne Convention, the Germans supported the principle of *lex loci*, applying the law of the author's own country to determine the term of a work in a foreign country. *Lex loci* allowed for a single term (that from the country of origin) applied throughout the Berne Member countries. In contrast, national treatment, or *lex fori*, was also proposed. *Lex fori* allowed for a single term within a particular country to control both foreign and domestic works. According to Professor Sam Ricketson, the leading scholar on the Berne Convention, the delegates at the 1884

Conference preferred *lex fori*, but they also wanted to make sure that only countries with comparatively long terms got the benefit. By a vote of six to three, RST was included: "[T]he advantages of national treatment were only to be reciprocally assured to authors belonging to a country of the Union 'during the existence of their rights in their country of origin.'" Ricketson explains, "All it meant was that a work should not be protected for any longer than it was protected in its country of origin." This limitation only applied to the duration of a copyright's term.

Years later, the question of how a term should be measured was revisited at the Berlin Conference for revision of the Berne Convention. The Germans then suggested a *lex fori* approach, without regard to the term in the country of origin. This was known as a principle of independence of protection. But the Union countries favored a standard minimum term and did not like the idea of abandoning material reciprocity. A compromise was reached, with RST once again playing a prominent role; a minimum term was encouraged as fifty years *post mortem auctoris (pma)*-- after the author's death--but if countries would not adopt the minimum term, the protection "must not exceed the term fixed in the country of origin of work." The 1908 Berlin version of the Berne Convention finally adopted a suggested term of protection of fifty *pma*, with RST in place to allow for maintaining shorter terms.

In 1948, the Brussels version of the Berne Convention finally applied fifty *pma* as mandatory, but continued to include RST. The 1967 Stockholm revision included the minimum term of fifty *pma* and RST. The 1971 Paris version continued both, with no changes in the RST language from the 1971 version. The 1979 version again held no changes.

The Berne Convention is not the only treaty to utilize RST. The Buenos Aires Copyright Convention of 1910, which required copyright protection to be obtained in the country of origin "in conformity with its laws," also applied RST. The Inter-American Convention included a RST provision, as well. This tells us that RST has long been believed to be a key element in regulating trade of copyrighted works. Outside of the Berne Convention, the most significant contemporary example of RST occurred in the European Union (EU). This is part of the reason, or so the story goes, that the United States had to extend the term of copyright from fifty to seventy years with the Copyright Term Extension Act. In Europe, RST was included in the 1993 European Union Term Directive, as part of the attempt to harmonize terms across the EU:

> Whereas, for works whose country of origin within the meaning of the Berne Convention is a third country and whose author is not a Community

> national, *comparison of terms of protection should be applied*, provided that the term accorded in the Community does not exceed the term laid down in this Directive.

Works from countries outside of the European Union receive a shorter term of protection within the EU. However, there is a caveat: "[C]omparison of terms should not result in Member States being brought into conflict with their international obligations." International obligations can include a number of elements: bilateral treaties and free trade agreements must be reviewed to see if RST is compliant with their specific terms and that special arrangements have not been made between countries. One further question is whether a bilateral treaty in place with, say, Germany, which does not follow RST, is sufficient to prohibit application of RST in all of the other countries in Europe, as well.

Determining the Term in the Country of Origin

Under RST, we look to the country of origin to determine the length of the original term. Devault-Graves assumed that the term for the three early Salinger works was twenty-eight years because the works were not renewed. It then likely compared the term to other current terms around the world, usually life of the author plus seventy years, and believed that the three stories were in the public domain. Simple math. But copyright is rarely that simple. Devault-Graves's mistake was believing that the actual term of the US domestic works was indeed proper means for the measuring term abroad for RST.

The Term When the United States Is the Country of Origin

U.S. works published in or before 1978 had to satisfy a number of formalities in order to obtain an initial term of protection and more hurdles to renew protection for additional years. Under the 1909 Copyright Act, a work had to meet certain requirements in order to gain federal protection. First, works could have come into the public domain upon publication because they failed to meet the formality requirements under the 1909 Copyright Act. Second, works that met the formality requirements under the 1909 Copyright Act and gained an initial twenty-eight years of protection but were not promptly renewed between the twenty-seventh and twenty-eighth years of the initial term, or, in the case of works published between 1950 and 1964, during the twenty-eighth year of the initial term, would come into the public domain. So, any work could have had a term of zero years, twenty-eight years, or ninety-five years. This was the actual term of any one work, and it was dependent on a number of events occurring or not occurring.

All of the Salinger short story works at issue were published in 1940, when renewal of the copyright term was required during the twenty-seventh year. According to the complaint, no renewal record was found. Therefore, the works should have come into the public domain twenty-eight years after their publication date. However, if formalities were not followed, they would have entered the public domain upon publication. Whatever the circumstances were, the 1940 short stories appear to have been in the public domain as of the filing of the complaint.

Potential Versus Actual Term

Most would think that if a work entered the public domain, by not meeting either the formality or renewal requirements, the work's term abroad should be measured by its actual, original term in the United States. But nothing is ever easy with copyright terms. Instead, the international community developed the concept of "expiry of term" or what we will call potential term: the optimal term under a country of origin's laws, rather than the term the country of origin actually accorded to the work. Potential term fits with the philosophy of the Berne Convention, which does not allow formalities such as those used in the United States under the 1909 Copyright Act. It also does not require fact-based searches in formalities-based countries, making it easier to determine the term for countries other than the country of origin from that of the country of origin.

Other treaties have addressed this question of the split term. The Inter-American Convention on the Rights of Authors in Literary, Scientific and Artistic Works evidences that the potential term, rather than the actual term, is the standard measurement. Article VIII of the convention sets forth the application of RST: "The duration of the copyright protection shall be governed by the law of the Contracting State in which the protection was originally obtained, but it shall not exceed the duration fixed by the law of the Contracting State in which the protection is claimed." This is another version of RST. The treaty also addresses the US split term problem: "In case the law of any Contracting State grants two successive periods of protection, the duration of the protection with respect to the State shall include, for purposes of the present Convention, the aggregate of both periods." Here we have a treaty that directly addresses the US split term problem. Both periods of protection--the initial term as well as the renewal term--are to be counted for the purposes of determining the length of the term in a Member state.

The Universal Copyright Convention (UCC) indicates a preference for the potential term over the actual term: "For the purposes of the application of the preceding provision, if the law of any Contracting State grants two or more successive terms of protection, the period of protection of that State shall be considered to be the aggregate of those terms." This means that the full two terms would apply in determining RST in the United States. The following sentence reads: "However, if a specified work is not protected by such State during the second or any subsequent term for any reason, the other Contracting States shall not be obliged to protect it during the second or any subsequent term."[8] This lack of obligation suggests that a Contracting State is not required to apply a work's potential term.

The Berne Convention itself did not address the split term or expiry of term. But the United States, upon joining the Berne Convention, called on WIPO for clarification. The letters between the United States Patent and Trademark Office (USPTO) and WIPO discussed "the correct interpretation of certain articles of the Berne Convention as they pertain to the protection of US works [that] are in the public domain in the United States because of a failure to satisfy certain formalities."

The letter addressed to Dr. Kamil Idris, Director General of WIPO, was from Robert Stoll, former USPTO Commissioner for Patents, who felt that the issue of expiry of term was a matter of "great importance to the United States." The issue was framed in relationship to Article 18, rather than Article 7(8) (Rule of the Shorter Term), of the Berne Convention. Mr. Stoll was expressing his concern that US works that have fallen into the public domain for noncompliance with formalities would be denied a full term of protection in Berne member countries. He posited that such formalities as notice, original registration, and renewal should not hold a work back from foreign protection, despite lack of protection in the United States anymore.

Here is the heart of the argument: the United States no longer penalizes foreign works in the United States for lack of formalities and, therefore, other Berne countries should not penalize US works for lacking formalities even if they have lost US protection. Stoll concludes, "We believe that under the cited articles, other Berne Union countries are obligated to extend a 'full term' of protection to such existing works, regardless of their public domain status in the United States."

Shozo Uemura, Deputy Director General, responds: "The Convention obliges the countries party to the Convention to protect all works which 'at the moment of its coming into force, have not yet fallen into the public domain in the country of origin through the expiry of the term of protection."

For works that had no copyright protection because they did not meet formality requirements under the 1909 and 1976 Copyright Acts, and therefore fell into the public domain upon publication, Uemura concludes, "It is clear that they have not fallen into the public domain ... through the expiry of the term of protection." Uemura believes that the potential term should apply regarding RST, given the consensus that the formalities should not have existed. He writes: "I believe that the answer to this question is obvious, namely that that term should be considered to be "the term fixed in the country of origin of the work" which would be applicable provided that the formalities would have been complied with (or put in another way, provided that the formalities would not have existed)." He ends with a definitive statement: "[Where] a work has fallen into the public domain through the non-compliance with formalities, the 'term fixed in the country of origin of the work' should be considered that term which would be applicable provided that the formalities would have been fulfilled (or would not have existed) ...."While an informal dialogue, this makes it clear that the potential term, or expiry of term, seems the norm regarding the Berne Convention, rather than the actual term.

Scholar Christine Angelopoulos confirmed the adoption of the WIPO position in France that the potential term ought to dictate RST. In 2009, the French court *Cour de cassation* reviewed the copyright status of the American film *His Girl Friday*. According to the case, like the Salinger short stories, the original work was published in 1940 and not renewed. However, the court found that the prohibition of formalities under Article 5(2) of the Berne Convention meant that the requirements for declining protection in France did not apply. Due to its rejection of formalities, this is the key case establishing the notion that a potential term, rather than an actual term, would be applied regarding RST.

One example of an exception to potential term application is Argentina, which does not require any kind of treaty relations in order to gain protection. However, Argentina requires that formalities in the country of origin be satisfied and that RST be applied. One could argue that renewal is a formality and, therefore, the actual term applies. But Argentina is a member of the Berne Convention, and this portion of the law--applying formalities as a condition for protection--may be seen as violating Berne. The law itself is clear, but it is unclear whether Berne overrides the law.

RST in Action

Some countries explicitly include RST in their copyright statutes. For example, Armenia and Bosnia and Herzegovina are among those with copyright provisions specifically instructing application of RST.

The United States is among those countries that does not apply RST, excluding its application in Section 104(c) of its copyright law. While not explicitly addressing RST from Article 7(8), Section 104(c) states that no rights from the Berne Convention can be directly claimed in a US copyright suit. We do see the United States use a modified version of RST in Section 104A, a restoration provision, in requiring a work still to be under copyright in its country of origin at a specified period, but then applying its own term, without regard to that of the country of origin. But in a general sense, Article 7(8) of the Berne Convention has not be replicated in the 1976 Copyright Act, and Section 104(c) makes plain that Berne is not directly applied.

The above are examples of laws that clearly address the application of RST, but the laws of many other countries remain silent, creating uncertainty as to whether RST applies to their works. Consider the countries of South America. Only Argentina and Suriname include RST. All of the other countries are silent as to whether RST applies: Brazil, Bolivia, Chile, Colombia, Ecuador, Paraguay, Peru, Venezuela, and Uruguay. The question becomes whether RST applies even when it is not included in a statute. Does one assume RST applies? Does it matter whether it is a civil law country or a common law country? That is the common distinction of when treaties are directly applied, as discussed later. How do we interpret silence?

Article 7(8) of the Berne Convention is presumed to be the norm: "In any case, the term shall be governed by the legislation of the country where protection is claimed; however, unless the *legislation of that country otherwise provides*, the term shall not exceed the term fixed in the country of origin of the work." Confirmed in 1967, RST applies unless a country proclaims otherwise.

The 1967 discussions in Stockholm on the revision of the Berne Convention included discussions regarding RST. Eighty years after those first discussions, Switzerland proposed a change because it believed RST "ran counter to the principle of assimilation." Switzerland proposed

> transposing the order of application of the principle of "comparison of terms'. Under the Swiss proposal, the term of protection would be subjected

> to the general rule of Article 4(1), i.e., to the legislation of the country in which protection was claimed, but countries of the Union would be entitled to depart from the rule contained in the Convention and declare that the law of the country of origin was applicable.

RST would not be presumed. Instead, it would be an option. The Delegation from Czechoslovakia argued in response, "[I]f this proposal [were] adopted, those *countries whose legislation contained no provision* concerning the term of protection granted to foreign works would be forced to change their national legislation." Czechoslovakia obviously read the proposal as forcing RST onto silent countries in lieu of their enacting new legislation. Thus, silence would be interpreted as adopting RST. This is important. It is a first step in understanding silence in the laws and that indeed countries expected RST to be applied, even in absence of mention in the copyright statute itself. There was good news for Czechoslovakia, however: the Swiss proposal was rejected by twenty-one votes to eight, with six abstentions. The text for RST was adopted unanimously and resides in the Berne Convention at Article 7(8).

The Berne Convention is not directly applied in the United States. Countries that remain silent regarding RST are often silent on whether Berne is applied directly to their domestic laws, as well. How does one determine, in the face of silence, whether Berne is directly applicable to the domestic law of a particular country? Paul Goldstein and Bernt Hugenholtz explain how to determine whether Berne is a self-executing treaty in a particular country in *International Copyright*:

> Most countries, including many that follow civil law tradition, will view treaties as self-executing, a directly applicable source of rights to private parties, at least so long as the treaty rules are capable of having normative effect without implementing legislation. By contrast, countries following the British and Scandinavian constitutional traditions hold that treaties are never self-executing, so that private actions must be founded on domestic legislation that implements the treaty.

While a helpful starting point, this assertion leaves us wanting for a comprehensive list of countries that do or do not hold treaties to be self-executing. We are left to wonder, indeed speculate, what the term is for many works whose country of origin has a shorter term.

Potential Term in Action: The Cases of Germany

Silence in statutes and application of the potential term are only two problems. Determining when RST applies also involves delving into bilateral treaties, multilateral treaties, and multiple domestic laws. Germany is the poster child for complexities related to RST, particularly with regard to US works. As Goldstein and Hugenholtz explain, "[t]he relationship between multilateral and bilateral treaties is chronological as well as hierarchical." It also concerns domestic law and sometimes retroactivity.

Germany and the United States have a number of treaties in place:

> (1) the 1892 US-German Bilateral Treaty,
> (2) the Universal Copyright Convention (UCC), and
> (3) the Berne Convention.

The Bilateral Treaty allowed German works to obtain protection in the United States and vice versa. It applied to literature and art, including photographs. All sources agree that the Treaty continued after World War I and World War II and is still valid today. The bilateral language makes clear that the relationship was to be that of national treatment without restrictions, with protection granted "on the same basis on which such protection is granted to subjects of the Empire." Under this treaty, U.S. works in Germany were provided with the same term of protection as German works at the time, regardless of their terms in the United States, an obvious absence of RST.

However, Germany and the United States eventually joined the UCC, which applied RST. Then, Germany subsequently enacted a new copyright law in 1965, which partially incorporated the UCC. Later still, the United States joined Berne in 1988, further complicating matters. There is, however, German case law that helps us sort through the issues of whether RST applies and, more to the point, what the term of a US work would be in Germany.

The case *Atlas Films* concerned American films by Buster Keaton that had not been renewed in the United States and therefore came into the public domain twenty years after the dates of their first publications. The plaintiff believed the films were still protected in Germany, even though their copyrights had expired in the United States. This belief was based upon reliance on the US-Germany Bilateral Treaty because the treaty did not contain any limits requiring the works still to be protected in their countries of origin; it merely provided for national treatment. Some of the films were first published in the United States, but others were initially published in Great Britain or Japan.

The films were created between 1921 and 1928, and the case sought to determine whether the Bilateral Treaty or the UCC governed protection. The court looked to Article XIX of the UCC: "[This] Convention shall not abrogate multilateral or bilateral conventions or arrangements between two or more Contracting States." The third sentence of Article XIX states that if the copyrights were acquired before the enactment of the UCC, the older rights applied. This meant that works created or published before the enactment of the UCC, September 16, 1955, would be governed by the Bilateral Treaty. Thus, US works published before this date are protected by the US-German Bilateral Treaty and treated in the same manner as a German national's publication, whereas those created or published afterward would be governed by the UCC. The court concluded that the Bilateral Treaty applied and that, therefore, RST would *not* apply in this situation because the treaty gave full national treatment to US works. *Atlas Films* gives us the chronology and hierarchy of understanding the relationship between the Bilateral Treaty and the UCC.

But that was not the end of the inquiry on the Keaton films. To qualify under the 1965 Germany law, the foreign works had to have been protected in their country of origin as of January 1, 1966. These works were, in fact, protected as of January 1, 1966, both in Germany (under the concept of national treatment through the Bilateral Treaty) and in the United States using the potential term. The films, therefore, gained the additional twenty years of protection afforded by the new 1965 law. So, in addition to seeing the Bilateral Treaty trump the UCC, we see also that the 1965 law required looking to the country of origin to assess the copyright term.

A case decided at the same time as *Atlas Films* involved Jack London's short story *White Fang*. In that case, the story (and the novel version) was published in 1905, and Jack London died eleven years later. The issue was whether the work qualified for protection under the 1965 Copyright Act in Germany. The 1935 term was a bit complicated:

> Copyright protection ends fifty years after the death of the author but in any case it will not lapse until the expiration of ten years from the date of first publication of the work. If the work is not published after [fifty] years have passed since the death of the author, it is presumed that the possessor of the work is entitled to the copyright.

In this case, Jack London died in 1916 and the work had been published within his lifetime. Therefore, the term under the previous law expired fifty years after his death, in 1966.

To qualify for the extension within the 1965 Copyright Act, the work had to possess two qualifications. First, it must have been under copyright as of January 1, 1966, in Germany, which *White Fang* satisfied. Second, the work had to have been protected in the country of origin as of January 1, 1966. In this case, the work had been published in 1905 and, as of 1966, the term of protection, even with renewal, had expired. The term for a pre-1909 work was no longer than fifty-six years or, in this case, when the work came into the public domain on January 1, 1962. Therefore, the work did not qualify for an additional twenty years of protection when the new German law came into force in 1966.

Another German case concerned *The Big Book* from Alcoholics Anonymous. *The Big Book* was registered with the US Copyright Office on April 19, 1939. However, the work had no proper copyright notice and was not renewed properly. The work was in the public domain upon first publication because formalities had not been met. But what about its status in Germany?

Like previous cases, the German court began with the 1892 Bilateral Treaty, which it found continued to apply. The UCC had been enacted as of September 16, 1955, but the 1892 treaty was found to control in light of conflicting terms and because the work had been published under the previous German copyright act, before the enactment of the UCC. The court found that the work's German term applied, even though the work was in the public domain in the United States, and chose to apply the potential term, rather than the actual term.[123] If the work were still protected by German domestic law when the Copyright Act of 1965 became active, and the period of protection had not yet expired in the country of origin, the work would benefit from the additional twenty years of protection. The court made it clear that it was reviewing the potential term: "Incidentally, it does not significantly depend on whether the concrete work in the United States was still protected by copyright. What matters is only whether the term of protection had not yet expired for works of the same description as in the United States." So, even though the work was in the public domain in actuality in the United States, the court was looking to the expiry, or potential term. The court then applied the current term, seventy years after the author's death, to the 1965 Copyright Law.

By the time of the next major case related to US works in Germany, the *Tarzan* case, the United States had joined the Berne Convention. The novel *Tarzan of the Apes* was first published in the United States on September 10, 1912, and was registered and renewed with the US Copyright Office. The copyright expired in the United States seventy-five years after the original publication, at the end of 1987. As in the previous cases of works before September 16, 1955, the inquiry followed the same steps to determine the applicability of the 1965 Copyright Act. However, the court also looked into whether the work was protected in the country of origin as of March 1, 1989, when the United States joined Berne. If so, *Tarzan* would gain the full term of protection under Germany's copyright law because Berne applies the US-Germany Bilateral Treaty as long as the work is still protected in the country of origin. The work, however, expired in the United States in 1987. The German court thus determined the copyright protection to be subject to RST in accordance with Section 121, paragraph 4, sentence 1 of the 1965 German Copyright Act.

Additionally, the court found that "[a]fter the UCC (September 16, 1955), the work accrued only the term of protection to [fifty] years."[129] The court seemed to think that the enactment of the UCC stunted or froze the copyright term for works created before the UCC's enactment to the term in place at the time:

> The term of copyright protection has indeed [been] extended by the Copyright Act of 9 September 1965, [seventy] years after the author's death. However, this extension of the right enjoys no grandfathering under Art. XIX sentence 3 WUA because they took place only after the entry into force of the Universal Copyright Convention for Germany.[130]

The work, therefore, came into the public domain in Germany as of 2001, fifty years after the death of the author.

Exemptions from RST

Bilateral Treaties

Both Germany and Italy believe their bilateral treaties afford complete national treatment without RST limitations. However, not all bilateral treaties embrace complete national treatment. The bilateral treaty between Italy and Spain, for example, explicitly includes RST. Germany and the United States agreed to national treatment without any discussion of RST. However, other German bilateral treaties have different terms and conditions. So how does one determine whether RST applies in bilateral treaties? This, unfortunately, requires a treaty-by-treaty analysis looking for mention of RST.

Free Trade Agreements

In the same way we must look at bilateral treaties, we must also review free trade agreements. Like many treaties, most free trade agreements (FTAs) are silent on whether RST applies. Given their name, FTAs should signal that national treatment *without* RST limitations applies. But many do not include information about RST--only that national treatment applies.

Canada

Canada excludes works from Mexico and the United States in its use of RST for joint authors because all three are signatories to the North American Free Trade Agreement (NAFTA), Article 1703 of which provides for national treatment without formalities or conditions for new works only.[134] Regarding copyright, NAFTA explicitly cites to Berne Article 2 for subject matter protection and also sets out minimum terms of fifty years from publication for photographs or, failing publication, fifty years from creation. Sound recordings are also required to have a minimum term of fifty years from fixation.[136] These are longer terms than Berne would provide.

Regarding protection of existing subject matter, Article 1720 of NAFTA refers back to Article 18 of the Berne Convention and reiterates that if a work is in the public domain in its country of origin, it does not gain additional protection· Annex 1705.7 specifically addresses motion pictures that have fallen into the public domain in the United States. But no explicit discussion of Section 7(8)--RST--of the Berne Convention is included. Because RST garners no mention, we must assume that national treatment trumps RST in importance.

US-Singapore Free Trade Agreement

We see more explicit mention of protection duration in the US-Singapore FTA. Article 2.1 of the treaty sets out the general national treatment requirements. The 2004 treaty sets out the terms upon which copyright is calculated: seventy years *pma*, and if not calculated on the natural life of a person, no shorter than seventy years from publication. However, if publication does not occur within fifty years of creation, then copyright applies for seventy years from the creation of the work.

FTAs

For the United States, Berne is not self-executing, so authors from member country Singapore must rely on Section 104A of the US Copyright Act and traditional means of obtaining copyright in the United States instead. On the flip side, for US works in Singapore, while the 1998 Copyright (International Protection) Regulations provide for RST in Singapore, no restoration provisions are included directly in the regulations, nor are the terms of the FTA explicitly included in the current law. So does RST apply to US works? Does the FTA override RST?

Australia's FTA with the United States, which contains the same language regarding copyright term as Singapore's mandates national treatment. Peru and Panama also have the same language: minimum terms, national treatment, and Article 18. In Oman, national treatment and Article 18 apply but the minimum terms are different. Like the bilateral treaties, each FTA must be reviewed to see if anything related to RST and Article 18 has been included, as we saw with Germany. Why was Article 18 included, but not Article 7(8)? One might come to the conclusion that RST does not apply because one term is included and the other is not.

RST Rule of Thumb for U.S. Works

If the United States has a bilateral or free trade agreement with a jurisdiction, it is prudent to review the actual agreement. It will likely be silent regarding RST, but for U.S. works abroad, it probably means that national treatment, and not RST, applies. Other intervening issues may still arise, such as Germany's inclusion of the UCC into the law that overrides the terms of bilateral agreements for certain works, whether a work is protected by its *potential term*, whether the work was protected in the United States as of March 1, 1989, when the United States joined Berne, and any additional FTAs.

For pre-UCC works, bilateral treaties protect a work under national treatment. If the UCC is included in the national law, then the UCC applies *after* its enactment, unless the domestic law is retroactive. It is unclear whether national treatment or RST applies when the UCC is not directly included in a country's law or is included as a self-executing treaty on post-1955 works. If a work is still under copyright in the United States as of March 1, 1989, the work likely obtains national treatment again. FTAs provide for national treatment, along with implementation of Article 18. So the March 1, 1989, date is likely the key to determining how the work is treated.

While RST may apply to non-U.S. works, U.S. copyright owners should not generally fear the effect of RST in forty-three countries. But this is not definitive. It is a best guess. More certain answers would require WIPO to step up and produce a list, asking each country of the world to confirm the status of RST within its laws and any limitations or exceptions that may exist. It is time we create this list. It is becoming increasingly necessary in today's world economy. Indeed, this Article, like Devault-Graves in the Salinger case, is calling on WIPO for a reliable status check regarding the applicability of RST. But until WIPO comes through in that respect, this Article proposes a three-part analysis to apply in any case raising questions of RST applicability.

RST Analysis

Rule of the Shorter Term can be complicated, but it is not impossible to discern.

A. Preliminary Questions

1. The Work: Identify the country of origin of the work. This is the country of first publication.

2. Would it make a difference if RST were applied? That is, is the country of origin's term shorter than the term of the country where protection is sought? If no, RST analysis is not necessary.

B. Does RST apply between country of origin and country where protection is being sought?

1. RST in the Copyright Statute. Does the statute of the country where protection is being sought explicitly indicate that RST applies?

a. If yes, skip to PART C.

b. If no, proceed.

2. Multilateral/Bilateral Treaties. Are both countries (the country of origin and the country where protection is being sought) members of a multilateral agreement that explicitly applies RST?

a. If yes, proceed.

b. If no, no RST.

3. Role of Treaties in Country Where Protection Is Being Sought. Is the multilateral agreement applied directly in the country; that is, is the multilateral agreement self-executing?

a. If yes, proceed.

b. If no, no RST.

Note: this question of direct application is the crux of the problem: how to determine when treaties are directly applicable when the statute is silent.

4. Role of Bilateral Treaties in Country Where Protection Is Being Sought. Are there any bilateral agreements or other treaties that exempt the country of origin from RST within the country where protection is being sought?

a. If yes, no RST.

b. If no, proceed.

5. Relationship Between National Legislation, Treaties and Bilateral Treaties. How are we to interpret competing agreements and treaties? See if there are cases or other secondary sources. Also look to the treaties themselves. Check to see any specific national legislation that would alter the results.

C. Applying RST

1. Measure the term of the country of origin (be mindful that this could either be a potential or an actual term) and then compare it to the country where protection is being sought.

a. If the origin term is shorter, apply RST. Note, "expiry" of term may be applied, rather than the actual term, as in the case of the United States.

b. If the origin term is longer or the same, do not apply RST.

c. If simultaneous publication occurred and both countries are members of Berne, the shorter term of the two countries applies. If some countries that had simultaneous publication were not members of Berne, then only the

> countries that are members of Berne apply for determining the shortest term.

What becomes clear is that anyone working through foreign works in a particular jurisdiction must come to grips with RST. Otherwise, one can end up with the wrong term for a given work and maybe even end up in messy litigation, as evidenced by Devault-Graves and its publication of the three early Salinger stories.

Devault-Graves was looking for a US court to affirm that if RST applied in a particular country, the three Salinger stories were in that country's public domain. The first judge, in Tennessee, transferred the case to New Hampshire where the Salinger Estate resides, but there was no ruling on the merits. Then, in New Hampshire, the Salinger Estate wanted the case dismissed because the kinds of questions would be too complicated, looking at each country of the world to determine whether RST applied or not. Before the New Hampshire judge could rule, Devault-Graves decided to drop the lawsuit.

An Associated Press story reported that Devault-Graves did not see this move as the end, declaring that it "is certainly no loss for us."[1] And what of the fight to publish the work around the world? The Associated Press reported representatives of Devault-Graves as saying it will "defend our right to publish in every foreign market that is legitimately open to us. It is merely a new way of looking at the equation." According to Publisher's Weekly, "[d]espite Salinger's opposition, Graves told *PW* that the publisher had licensed the book to [ten] foreign publishers, and that there are now six foreign editions in print." Perhaps the *Devault-Graves v. Salinger Estate* litigation will continue around the world, after all.

Comparative Copyright Checklist

When looking at the status of which law applies:

- ❑ Point of Attachment Analysis: domestic or foreign; if foreign, are there treaties in place? (Note: if unpublished this may not be a requirement. See, for example Section 104 in 17 U.S.C. for the U.S.)
- ❑ Subject matter: Is it protected under the country at lissueu?
- ❑ Current Law: Is it retroactive? If not, march through the laws starting with the publication/creation date.
- ❑ Rule of the Shorter Term analysis needed? If not explicit in the law, is the Berne Convention self-executing?

And if you are using the laws to determine a 104A status in the U.S., make sure to use the appropriate law (as of December 8, 1994, or for countries that joined later, that date). The current law will not apply.

For your convenience:

17 U.S.C. Section 104 (not to be confused with Section 104A)

17 U.S.C. Section 104 - **Subject matter of copyright: National origin**

(a) Unpublished Works.—
The works specified by sections 102 and 103, while unpublished, are subject to protection under this title without regard to the nationality or domicile of the author.

(b) Published Works.—The works specified by sections 102 and 103, when published, are subject to protection under this title if—

(1) on the date of first publication, one or more of the authors is a national or domiciliary of the United States, or is a national, domiciliary, or sovereign authority of a treaty party, or is a stateless person, wherever that person may be domiciled; or
(2) the work is first published in the United States or in a foreign nation that, on the date of first publication, is a treaty party; or
(3) the work is a sound recording that was first fixed in a treaty party; or
(4) the work is a pictorial, graphic, or sculptural work that is incorporated in a building or other structure, or an architectural work that is embodied in a building and the building or structure is located in the United States or a treaty party; or
(5) the work is first published by the United Nations or any of its specialized agencies, or by the Organization of American States; or
(6) the work comes within the scope of a Presidential proclamation. Whenever the President finds that a particular foreign nation extends, to works by authors who are nationals or domiciliaries of the United States or to works that are first published in the United States, copyright protection on substantially the same basis as that on which the foreign nation extends protection to works of its own nationals and domiciliaries and works first published in that nation, the President may by proclamation extend protection under this title to works of which one or more of the authors is, on the date of first publication, a national, domiciliary, or sovereign authority of that nation, or which was first published in that nation. The President may revise, suspend, or revoke any such

proclamation or impose any conditions or limitations on protection under a proclamation.

For purposes of paragraph (2), a work that is published in the United States or a treaty party within 30 days after publication in a foreign nation that is not a treaty party shall be considered to be first published in the United States or such treaty party, as the case may be.

(c) Effect of Berne Convention.—
No right or interest in a work eligible for protection under this title may be claimed by virtue of, or in reliance upon, the provisions of the Berne Convention, or the adherence of the United States thereto. Any rights in a work eligible for protection under this title that derive from this title, other Federal or State statutes, or the common law, shall not be expanded or reduced by virtue of, or in reliance upon, the provisions of the Berne Convention, or the adherence of the United States thereto.

(d) Effect of Phonograms Treaties.—
Notwithstanding the provisions of subsection (b), no works other than sound recordings shall be eligible for protection under this title solely by virtue of the adherence of the United States to the Geneva Phonograms Convention or the WIPO Performances and Phonograms Treaty.

Common Law Countries

Quite a few countries were former colonies of the United Kingdom, and they often have kept the common law as their tradition. Some even still have British copyright laws, often out of date ones. What we do see is commonalities with their copyright laws. Their copyright acts look a particular way. Some still use British law, even after no longer being a colony. We will be looking at this strain as part of the work we do. The countries include

- ❑ Antigua and Barbuda
- ❑ American Samoa
- ❑ Australia
- ❑ Bahamas
- ❑ Bangladesh
- ❑ Barbados
- ❑ Belize
- ❑ Bhutan
- ❑ British Virgin Islands
- ❑ Brunei
- ❑ Canada
- ❑ Cayman Islands
- ❑ Cyprus
- ❑ Dominica
- ❑ Fiji
- ❑ Gibraltar
- ❑ Grenada
- ❑ Ghana
- ❑ Hong Kong
- ❑ India
- ❑ Ireland
- ❑ Israel
- ❑ Jamaica
- ❑ Kenya
- ❑ Kiribati
- ❑ Liberia
- ❑ Malaysia
- ❑ Marshall Islands
- ❑ Myanmar
- ❑ Nauru
- ❑ Nepal
- ❑ New Zealand
- ❑ Nigeria
- ❑ Northern Ireland
- ❑ Palau
- ❑ Pakistan
- ❑ Philippines
- ❑ Saint Kitts and Nevis
- ❑ Saint Vincent and the Grenadines
- ❑ Sri Lanka
- ❑ Singapore
- ❑ South Africa
- ❑ Tonga
- ❑ Trinidad and Tobago
- ❑ Tuvalu
- ❑ Uganda
- ❑ United States

Civil Law Countries

Here is a list of countries that identify as a civil law tradition:

- ❑ Albania
- ❑ Angola
- ❑ Argentina
- ❑ Andorra
- ❑ Armenia
- ❑ Aruba
- ❑ Austria
- ❑ Azerbaijan
- ❑ Belarus
- ❑ Belgium
- ❑ Benin
- ❑ Bolivia
- ❑ Bosnia and Herzegovina
- ❑ Brazil
- ❑ Burkina Faso
- ❑ Burundi
- ❑ Chad
- ❑ People's Republic of China
- ❑ Republic of the Congo
- ❑ Democratic Republic of the Congo
- ❑ Cote d'Ivoire
- ❑ Cambodia
- ❑ Cape Verde
- ❑ Central African Republic
- ❑ Chile
- ❑ Colombia
- ❑ Costa Rica
- ❑ Croatia
- ❑ Cuba
- ❑ Curacao
- ❑ Czech Republic
- ❑ Denmark
- ❑ Dominican Republic
- ❑ Ecuador
- ❑ El Salvador
- ❑ Estonia
- ❑ finland
- ❑ France
- ❑ Egypt
- ❑ Equatorial Guinea
- ❑ Ethiopia
- ❑ Gabon
- ❑ Guinea
- ❑ Guinea-Bissau
- ❑ Georgia
- ❑ Germany
- ❑ Greece
- ❑ Guatemala
- ❑ Haiti
- ❑ Honduras
- ❑ Hungary
- ❑ Iceland
- ❑ Italy
- ❑ Japan
- ❑ Latvia
- ❑ Lebanon
- ❑ Lithuania
- ❑ Luxembourg
- ❑ Libya
- ❑ Macau
- ❑ Mauritius
- ❑ Mexico
- ❑ Mongolia
- ❑ Montenegro
- ❑ Mozambique

- ❑ Netherlands
- ❑ Nepal
- ❑ Norway
- ❑ Panama
- ❑ Paraguay
- ❑ Peru
- ❑ Poland
- ❑ Portugal
- ❑ Taiwan
- ❑ Romania
- ❑ Russia
- ❑ Rwanda
- ❑ Sao Tome e Principe
- ❑ Serbia
- ❑ Slovakia
- ❑ Slovenia
- ❑ South Korea
- ❑ Spain
- ❑ Suriname
- ❑ Sweden
- ❑ Switzerland
- ❑ Syria
- ❑ Timor-Leste
- ❑ Turkey
- ❑ Ukraine
- ❑ Uruguay
- ❑ Vietnam
- ❑ Venezuela

Each country has its own copyright history, its colonial relationship, and its relationship to conventions, free trade agreements, and for us, its copyright relationship to the United States.

We must also ask, how are the common law and civil law traditions similar or different? How does that impact on how we think about copyright laws, and as we do a deeper investigation. What makes one system different from the other, and how does that impact on interpretation?

7: Moral Rights

Section 106A of the 1976 Copyright Act addresses the rights of attribution and integrity for certain artists. These rights, commonly called moral rights, are distinct from the economic rights. This part of the Copyright Act is called the Visual Arts Rights Act, or VARA, as it is often referred to. They only apply to certain artistic works and have a lot of exceptions.

The United States was late to the moral rights party, and still have not implemented them for all works, as most countries have. We will be looking at four elements of moral rights: 1) Section 106A; 2) case law in the U.S.; 3) the recent study by the U.S. Copyright Office; and 4) comparative work with moral rights statutes around the world.

The concept of copyright focuses on economic rights. Moral rights concentrate on the non-economic rights associated with the personality of the author. Moral rights can include:

- right of attribution/paternity (the right to be named) and the right not to be named
- right of integrity (the right to protect one's work from reputational harm)
- right to withdraw a work if it no longer represents the author's views
- right of divulgation and disclosure
- right to pseudonymity
- right of an author to compel the completion of a commissioned work of art

Civil law countries generally have had strong moral rights systems, based on a natural rights concept of authorship. Moral rights come out of the spirit of the French Revolution and the importance of the individual creator's rights of authorship. In some cases moral rights are waivable and alienabile, but usually not. In some countries, corporations have moral rights, and in others they do not.

The requirement of moral rights of copyrighted works is found in Article 6*bis* of the Berne Convention. Let's take a look at Article 6*bis*

> (1) Independently of the author's economic rights, and even after the transfer of the said rights, the author shall have the **right to claim authorship** of the work and to **object to any distortion, mutilation or other modification of, or other**

> **derogatory action in relation to, the said work, which would be prejudicial to his honor or reputation.**
>
> (2) The rights granted to the author in accordance with the preceding paragraph shall, **after his death, be maintained, at least until the expiry of the economic rights**, and shall be exercisable by the persons or institutions authorized by the legislation of the country where protection is claimed. However, those countries whose legislation, at the moment of their ratification of or accession to this Act, does not provide for the protection after the death of the author of all the rights set out in the preceding paragraph may provide that some of these rights may, after his death, cease to be maintained.
>
> (3) The means of redress for safeguarding the rights granted by this Article shall be governed by the legislation of the country where protection is claimed.

So, what do we see with the Berne Convention? Only the right of attribution/paternity and right of integrity is required. There are also limitations. Can you identify them?

Moral rights became part of the Berne Convention in 1928.

Section 106A - Works of Visual Art in the U.S.

Let's look at Section 106A from the 1976 Copyright Act:

(a) Rights of Attribution and Integrity.—Subject to section 107 and independent of the exclusive rights provided in section 106, the author of a work of visual art—

(1) shall have the right—

(A) to claim authorship of that work, and
(B) to prevent the use of his or her name as the author of any work of visual art which he or she did not create;

(2) shall have the right to prevent the use of his or her name as the author of the work of visual art in the event of a distortion, mutilation, or other modification of the work which would be prejudicial to his or her honor or reputation; and

(3) subject to the limitations set forth in section 113(d), shall have the right—

(A) to prevent any intentional distortion, mutilation, or other modification of that work which would be **prejudicial to his or her honor or reputation,** and any intentional distortion, mutilation, or modification of that work is a violation of that right, and

(B) to prevent **any destruction of a work of recognized stature,** and **any intentional or grossly negligent destruction of that work i**s a violation of that right.

(b) Scope and Exercise of Rights.—

Only the author of a work of visual art has the rights conferred by subsection (a) in that work, whether or not the author is the copyright owner. The authors of a joint work of visual art are co-owners of the rights conferred by subsection (a) in that work.

(c) Exceptions.—

(1) The modification of a work of visual art which is a result of the passage of time or the inherent nature of the materials is not a distortion, mutilation, or other modification described in subsection (a)(3)(A).

(2) The modification of a work of visual art which is the result of conservation, or of the public presentation, including lighting and placement, of the work is not a destruction, distortion, mutilation, or other modification described in subsection (a)(3) unless the modification is caused by gross negligence.

(3) The rights described in paragraphs (1) and (2) of subsection (a) shall not apply to any reproduction, depiction, portrayal, or other use of a work in, upon, or in any connection with any item described in subparagraph (A) or (B) of the definition of "work of visual art" in section 101, and any such reproduction, depiction, portrayal, or other use of a work is not a destruction, distortion, mutilation, or other modification described in paragraph (3) of subsection (a).

(d) Duration of Rights.—

(1) With respect to works of visual art created on or after the effective date set forth in section 610(a) of the Visual Artists Rights Act of 1990, the rights conferred by subsection (a) shall endure for a term consisting of the life of the author.

(2) With respect to works of visual art created before the effective date set forth in section 610(a) of the Visual Artists Rights Act of 1990, but title to which has not, as of such effective date, been transferred from the author, the rights conferred by subsection (a) shall be coextensive with, and shall expire at the same time as, the rights conferred by section 106.

(3) In the case of a joint work prepared by two or more authors, the rights conferred by subsection (a) shall endure for a term consisting of the life of the last surviving author.

(4) All terms of the rights conferred by subsection (a) run to the end of the calendar year in which they would otherwise expire.

(e) Transfer and Waiver.—

(1) The rights conferred by subsection (a) may not be transferred, but those rights may be waived if the author expressly agrees to such waiver in a written instrument signed by the author. Such instrument shall specifically identify the work, and uses of that work, to which the waiver applies, and the waiver shall apply only to the work and uses so identified. In the case of a joint work prepared by two or more authors, a waiver of rights under this paragraph made by one such author waives such rights for all such authors.

(2) Ownership of the rights conferred by subsection (a) with respect to a work of visual art is distinct from ownership of any copy of that work, or of a copyright or any exclusive right under a copyright in that work. Transfer of ownership of any copy of a work of visual art, or of a copyright or any exclusive right under a copyright, shall not constitute a waiver of the rights conferred by subsection (a). Except as may otherwise be agreed by the author in a written instrument signed by the author, a waiver of the rights conferred by subsection (a) with respect to a work of visual art shall not constitute a transfer of ownership of any copy of that work, or of ownership of a copyright or of any exclusive right under a copyright in that work.

(Added Pub. L. 101–650, title VI, §603(a), Dec. 1, 1990, 104 Stat. 5128.)

Defining Visual Arts

Only works of visual art get moral right protection in the United States. That is *not true around the world,* where most countries have a vibrant and extensive moral rights system. The definition of a work of visual art in the United States becomes important. That is found in 17 U.S.C. Section 101:

> A "work of visual art" is—
>
> > (1) a painting, drawing, print, or sculpture, existing in a **single copy,** in a **limited edition of 200 copies or fewer that are signed and consecutively numbered by the author,** or, in the case of a sculpture, in multiple cast, carved, or fabricated sculptures of **200 or fewer** that are **consecutively numbered** by the author and **bear the signature or other identifying mark of the author**; or

(2) a **still photographic image produced for exhibition purposes only,** existing in a single copy that is signed by the author, or in a limited edition of **200 copies or fewer that are signed and consecutively numbered by the author**.

A work of visual art **does not include—**

(A)

(i) any poster, map, globe, chart, technical drawing, diagram, model, applied art, motion picture or other audiovisual work, book, magazine, newspaper, periodical, data base, electronic information service, electronic publication, or similar publication;

(ii) any merchandising item or advertising, promotional, descriptive, covering, or packaging material or container;

(iii) any portion or part of any item described in clause (i) or (ii);

(B) **any work made for hir**e; or

(C) any work **not subject to copyright protection** under this title.

A work of visual art is something unique, or 200 copies or less numbered and signed by the author. The focus seems to be on fine art and gallery art, but in recent years, graffiti cases have successfully used VARA in court.

What is not included:

- ❑ Works for hire
- ❑ Commercial art
- ❑ Non-copyrightable art
- ❑ Site-specific works
- ❑ Applied art
- ❑ Preparatory works
- ❑ Advertising and marketing materials
- ❑ Motion pictures
- ❑ books, magazines, newspapers, periodicals, databases, posters, maps, globes, charts, technical drawings, or diagrams

Works of visual arts are not mass-produced commercial works; they have to be works produced with less than 200 copies and signed. They are not practical. They are not promotional materials or advertising. They are not work made for hire. And they have to be under copyright. And not every photograph counts. VARA is a bit picky.

The Rights

If you meet the qualifications, here are the following rights you obtain under VARA.

- ❑ Right to claim authorship of the work. (The right to be named)

- ❑ Right to prevent the use of his/her name as the author of a work of visual art, which he or she did not create. (the right not to be named)

- ❑ Right to prevent use of the author's name as the author of the work of visual art in the event of a distortion, mutilation, or other modification of the work, which would be prejudicial to his or her honor or reputation. Note: there are three exceptions.

    - ❑ If the changes are a result of the passage of time or the nature of the materials.
    - ❑ changes result from conservation or public presentation (including lighting and placement)
    - ❑ modification os caused by gross negligence

- ❑ Right to prevent any destruction of a work of recognized stature

Exercise of the Rights

Only the author (whether or not the author is the copyright holder) has VARA rights. Modifications of the work that are a result of time and conservation are not considered a violation of VARA. The rights may not be transferred, but the rights may be waived by express agreement in writing by the author. The writing must identify the work, and the uses of that work to which the waiver applies. Ownership of the copyright, the work itself, and the VARA rights are each distinctly separate.

The VARA rights belong to the author, rather than the copyright holder or owner of the physical work.

Duration

The VARA term is different from the economic term of the work.

- ❑ Works created **after June 1, 1991** (when VARA was enacted): life of the author. [note this violates the requirement of Article 6*bis* of the Berne Convention that requires at least the length of the economics rights).
- ❑ Works created **before June 1, 1991** but title was not transferred from the author (meaning the original author still holds the copyright): life plus 70
    - ❑ If the title was transferred before June 1, 1991, no rights.

So what does that look like?

Let's say an author/artist dies in 2010.

- Work created after June 1: 1991. A work created in 2000 will have a term of the life of the author. The term is ends in December 31, 2010
- Works created before June 1, 1991 without transfer: The term ends December 31, 2080.
- Works created before June 1, 1991 with transfer: No moral rights.

Waiver

VARA rights cannot be transferred, but they may be waived in writing.

Remedies

You can get the same remedies as under the economic rights portion of the Copyright Act: injunctions, impounding, actual damages, statutory damages, costs, and attorney's fees. Statutory damages for moral rights begin at $500 and go up to $20,000, and if willful, $100,000. If the violation was deemed an innocent infringement, the damages can be reduced to $200.

No Registration Required

VARA does not require that a work be registered to be protected.

The Paula Nadelstern Case

Paula Nadelstern, a famous quilter, is most famous for her kaleidoscope quilts, which gained extra attention due to this lawsuit. The defendants were Couristan, the Houston Convention Center Hotel Corporation and Hilton Hotels Corporation. Couristan is a manufacturer and vendor of carpets. I think it was one of the greatest thrills of the project to chat with Paula about this very famous quilt copyright case.

Paula began experimenting with kaleidoscope quilts in 1986, and they just kept interesting her. Indeed, in 1996, she published *Kaleidoscopes & Quilts* with C & T Publishing, who registered the copyright, as they do. In 2005, Paula was attending Houston Quilt Market and Festival, a staple event for the quilt industry. A Hilton had been built that connected two floors of skywalks to the Houston George Brown Convention Center, where the Quilt, Inc. shows are held annually.

As Paula tells it, she was at a booth at the annual Quilt Market, where the quilt industry gathers each year, when people began coming up to her and congratulating her on the rugs in the new hotel's skywalk to the Convention Center. She did not know what they were referring to. "They were suggesting that the carpet looked like my work." So, she went over to see for herself. "My first response is, 'Oh, they like me! They picked mine. That's so familiar...' But my second reaction, and I think it is a very female reaction was, 'How did I let them do this to me? It's my fault.' "Now, it was my fault that a big corporation stole my designs without letting me know, and I come out of that thinking it's my fault." (Interview with Just Wanna Quilt). The first attorney she talked to didn't think she had a case. At the time, she was (and continues to be) at Benetex. "The woman who was head of the studio" asked her about her lawsuit, and she said, "I'm just going to give it up. I can't be angry about it anymore. There's nothing I can do. This is what the lawyer told me. I'm letting go." The woman suggested a lawyer that she had seen give a talk about copyright, George Gottlieb, who is a well-respected, well-known intellectual property attorney in New York. Paula wrote an email to George to appease her colleague. To her surprise, he took the case.

George informed Paula that indeed they did have a case. It began with the U.S. Copyright Registration certificate. "I never registered the copyrights in my quilts at the time. I thought it was enough for me to embroider the letter "c" with my initials and the date." explained Paula. But C & T Publishing, her publisher, did. That was important. She hadn't registered the quilts. "If they had taken a picture at a quilt show, I wouldn't have had anything. But the fact that they took the images from my first C & T book."

George set the defendants a cease and desist letter to no avail. The carpet company was in New Jersey. Paula confessed, "If they had just said, 'We're so sorry. Come on by. Come to us, and let's figure this out,' I would have settled for nothing. That's not what they did." The case went on for two years. "They went after the C & T book."

The case was filed in federal court in New York. To the infringement charge, Couristan denied needing any "permission, license or consent" with regard to the "design, manufacture and installation of the carpet at issue...because said carpet did not infringe any purported copyrights of the Plaintiff."[2] They also denied the VARA claim.

Additionally, Couristan alleged an invalid copyright registration, that the Plaintiff was not the lawful owner of the copyrights and therefore lacked standing, that the Plaintiff had committed fraud upon the Copyright Office, that the works were not substantially similar, or alternatively Couristan's use falls under fair use, and that Defendant's actions were not willful. The defendants also counterclaimed that Nadelstern used third parties' fabric designs in her quilts in order to create a kaleidoscope pattern, and thus she is infringing on the use of those fabrics. About this, Paula responded in our interview, "If they had done due diligence, th[ose] fabric companies sought me out. They sent me more fabric that I could ever need or want because they want their fabrics in a book. That's how the industry has evolved."

Turning to her 1996 book, "*Kaleidoscopes & Quilts*," third party fabrics were used throughout the book, creating derivative works of the fabrics. Here is where the fraud upon the Copyright Office comes in: the defendants claim that Nadelstern should have disclosed the third-party fabrics as pre-existing, and that she did not have permission to photograph the fabrics themselves. The defense was focused mostly on discrediting the book. Ultimately, the defendants wanted her copyright registration declared invalid and unenforceable.

In New York, cases are required to go to mediation before going to court. Recalling back to this time, Paula said, "They were so patronizing. And so was the mediator. ...He was what set me off to dig in my heels. When he came into the room, he said, 'I know nothing about quilts. If you just let them put your name on their website, you'll be famous." Paula Nadelstern was already a famous quilter. "The whole mediation, ignoring me... they all assumed the little quilter would go away," and that they could drag out the case. Most artists couldn't afford the attorney's fees, but Paula had an arrangement with George that was on a contingency basis, rather than hourly. "I was the only woman there. Everyone else was a man in a suit. My quilts were hanging but nobody looked at them and nobody cared." The day continued. The mediator had to leave.

"I got a message that the head of the carpet company wanted to talk to me alone." George thought it was ok, and the mediator said, "Yes, you can talk to anybody." Paula said, "Then I want to talk to this man, Marcus M., the head of the carpet company's design department." Marcus comes in from Dallas, dressed in shorts. In the boxes and boxes of papers they had received through discovery, there were notes that said "refer to book, refer to book with the page." George would write an article about the case for Studio Art Quilt Associates Journal. He wrote, "During the course of the investigation, as part of discovery, we were able to learn the exact number of blocks taken from Paula's quilts, that images of the carpeting appeared on the hotel's website, the size of the copied carpet, and sales figures relating to the carpeting."

Paula wanted to know how they got her book. She asked Marcus. "How did you do this to another artist?" Marcus responded, "We were told that kaleidoscopes were a generic term, and we were working through the interior decorator." The interior decorator had given them a storyboard that described what the Hilton wanted, including what the carpets would look like. "They had a picture of one of my quilts from my first C&T book. They just had it on the storyboard. When they asked what it was, they said kaleidoscopes." The President of the carpet company asked, "What would it take to settle?" This was direct evidence of access and copying. They settled that day. Included in the settlement was that her name would be added to the website, and a plaque at the Hilton hotel.

She ended the story: "So the key to my story, this was the lesson, is that copyright is not enough. I have to register my quilts. I had to register my copyright. Everybody needs to learn to register their copyright when they are making quilts, and making patterns. It's not that expensive, and you have to do it. I never use the word 'lucky'. The fact C&T Publishers registered the book, that's what made it a case. And they took everything straight from the book. And the interior decorators had a copy of my book in their Dallas library."

Currently, the Hilton has a different carpet. Throughout the years, when they had to change the carpet, they had to pay Paula a royalty. "I used to tell everyone to walk on the carpet and shuffle their feet."

Her attorneys concluded their article in SAQA Journal with the following: "One of the lessons to be learned from the case is the following: If the creator thinks he or she has a good case, he or she should meet with several different attorneys who specialize in intellectual property, and especially copyright, to find an attorney that believes that there has been an infringement. If the case is a strong one, it is possible to make a financial arrangement with the attorney whereby the artist does not have to bear the entire cost of the case until there is a settlement."

Paula Nadelstern sued for copyright infringement because C&T registered the book, and the defendants had *used the book as a model for the carpets* at the Hilton. Paula's legal team also included a VARA claim on the quilts themselves. From the original complaint: "Defendants Couristan, Hotel Corporation, and Hilton have willfully violated plaintiff's rights under Visual Artists Rights Act, 17 U.S.C. Section 106A by manufacturing, causing to be manufactured, importing, vending, distributing, selling, displaying, and/or promoting carpets which are direct copies of plaintiff's unique works of visual art (kaleidoscopic quilts)..." More specifically, the complaint asserted that the defendant violated Paula's 106A(a)(1)(A) right to claim authorship (attribution right) and 106A(a)(3)(A) right to prevent intentional distortion, mutilation or other modification...which is prejudicial to her reputation (right of integrity). Remember when Paula said she got her name on a plaque and on the website? That's settling the right of attribution claim. And replacing the rugs when they were worn and paying an additional royalty fee? Likely part of the right of integrity portion of the settlement. What is most interesting, and something to think about is that VARA did not require Paula to register the quilts. She had not registered the quilts, only the book. But she was still successful because of the way the statute is structured, to sue on VARA claims. This potentially adds statutory damages, up to $100,000 if willful. We do not know the full terms of the settlement.

Other mechanisms in U.S. Law

The United States has always claimed that there are additional mechanisms within U.S. law, including right of publicity, false attribution under the Lanham Act, state laws, fraud, misrepresentation and ironically, copyright itself. The argument against applying moral rights to more than fine art was that it would interfere with the First Amendment and fair use, which is odd since fine arts are implicated in both.

In 2017, the U.S. Copyright Office conducted a study on moral rights in the U.S. and concluded that no further federal law related to moral rights was required, and that VARA plus the patchwork laws was good enough. They believed that extending moral rights beyond fine arts might harm content industries and contracts. They believed a few changes could improve the system.

The Impact of Dastar

One argument for the U.S. not needing additional moral rights protection was that the Lanham (trademark) Act could provide protection in a moral rights-like way. Section 43(a) of the Lanham Act. Section 43(a) concerns false designation of origin:

> (1) Any person who, on or in connection with any goods or services, or any container for goods, uses in commerce any word, term, name, symbol, or device, or any combination thereof, or any false designation of origin, false or misleading description of fact, or false or misleading representation of fact, which—
>
> > (A) is likely to cause confusion, or to cause mistake, or to deceive as to the affiliation, connection, or association of such person with another person, or as to the origin, sponsorship, or approval of his or her goods, services, or commercial activities by another person, or
> >
> > (B) in commercial advertising or promotion, misrepresents the nature, characteristics, qualities, or geographic origin of his or her or another person's goods, services, or commercial activities,shall be liable in a civil action by any person who believes that he or she is or is likely to be damaged by such act.

Section 43(a) is used for unregistered trademarks and trade dress, as well as false sponsorship and endorsement, and "passing" off" or "reverse passing" off claims. It was thought that if you "passed off" something improperly that would be covered as right of attribution. See *Gilliam v. ABC*, 538 F.2d (2d 1976) where a court found that ABC had damaged Monty Python's reputation by drastically editing their work, as well as violating copyright. This was seen as the US's version of moral rights. But the U.S. Supreme Court case, *Dastar Corp. v. Twentieth Century Fox Film Corp.* ("*Dastar*") called that into question, at least for works that were no longer under copyright. Here Dastar edited older Twentieth century Fox videos that were no longer protected by copyright without attributing them to Twentieth Century Fox. Twentieth Century Fox claimed reverse passing off under Section 43(a), because Dastar did not identify the original creator. The U.S. Supreme Court decided that if the works were not copyrightable (that is in this case in the public domain), then the requirement of attribution under Section 43(a) was not required.

Moral Rights Around the World

Unlike the US., other countries have a robust moral rights system. Some of the terms parallel the economic rights. Others are perpetual. In terms of clearing copyright, the question arises what moral rights might apply, how long they last, who controls them after death, and what happens if there are no heirs - do the moral rights survive? Additionally, do moral rights apply to foreign works in the same manner (Rule of the Shorter Term).

Authors, attribution, and integrity: examining moral rights in the United States

In April 2019, the U.S. Copyright Office released, Authors, attribution, and integrity: examining moral rights in the United states, found at https://www.copyright.gov/policy/moralrights/full-report.pdf. We will divide it up and look at this in class.

Section 1202

Section 1202 may also be used as a moral rights-like mechanism. Section 1202 of the U.S. Copyright Act prohibits the removal of copyright management information in digital form. Let's take a look at the statute:

(a) **False Copyright Management Information.**—No person shall knowingly and with the intent to induce, enable, facilitate, or conceal infringement—
   (1) provide copyright management information that is false, or
   (2) distribute or import for distribution copyright management information that is false.

(b) Removal or Alteration of Copyright Management Information.—No person shall, without the authority of the copyright owner or the law—

(1) intentionally remove or alter any copyright management information,

(2) distribute or import for distribution copyright management information knowing that the copyright management information has been removed or altered without authority of the copyright owner or the law, or

(3) distribute, import for distribution, or publicly perform works, copies of works, or phonorecords, knowing that copyright management information has been removed or altered without authority of the copyright owner or the law,knowing, or, with respect to civil remedies under section 1203, having reasonable grounds to know, that it will induce, enable, facilitate, or conceal an infringement of any right under this title.

(c) Definition.—As used in this section, the term "copyright management information" means any of the following information conveyed in connection with copies or phonorecords of a work or performances or displays of a work, including in digital form, except that such term does not include any personally identifying information about a user of a work or of a copy, phonorecord, performance, or display of a work:

(1) The title and other information identifying the work, including the information set forth on a notice of copyright.
(2) The name of, and other identifying information about, the author of a work.
(3) The name of, and other identifying information about, the copyright owner of the work, including the information set forth in a notice of copyright.

(4) With the exception of public performances of works by radio and television broadcast stations, the name of, and other identifying information about, a performer whose performance is fixed in a work other than an audiovisual work.
(5) With the exception of public performances of works by radio and television broadcast stations, in the case of an audiovisual work, the name of, and other identifying information about, a writer, performer, or director who is credited in the audiovisual work.
(6) Terms and conditions for use of the work.
(7) Identifying numbers or symbols referring to such information or links to such information.
(8) Such other information as the Register of Copyrights may prescribe by regulation, except that the Register of Copyrights may not require the provision of any information concerning the user of a copyrighted work.

(d) Law Enforcement, Intelligence, and Other Government Activities.—

This section does not prohibit any lawfully authorized investigative, protective, information security, or intelligence activity of an officer, agent, or employee of the United States, a State, or a political subdivision of a State, or a person acting pursuant to a contract with the United States, a State, or a political subdivision of a State. For purposes of this subsection, the term "information security" means activities carried out in order to identify and address the vulnerabilities of a government computer, computer system, or computer network.

(e) Limitations on Liability.—

(1) **Analog transmissions.**—In the case of an analog transmission, a person who is making transmissions in its capacity as a broadcast station, or as a cable system, or someone who provides programming to such station or system, shall not be liable for a violation of subsection (b) if—
   (A) avoiding the activity that constitutes such violation is not technically feasible or would create an undue financial hardship on such person; and
   (B) such person did not intend, by engaging in such activity, to induce, enable, facilitate, or conceal infringement of a right under this title.

(2) Digital transmissions.—

   (A) If a digital transmission standard for the placement of copyright management information for a category of works is set in a voluntary, consensus standard-setting process involving a representative cross-section of broadcast stations or cable systems and copyright owners of a category of works that are intended for public performance by such stations or systems, a person identified in paragraph (1) shall not be liable for a violation of subsection (b) with respect to the particular copyright management information addressed by such standard if—

(i) the placement of such information by someone other than such person is not in accordance with such standard; and

(ii) the activity that constitutes such violation is not intended to induce, enable, facilitate, or conceal infringement of a right under this title.

(B) Until a digital transmission standard has been set pursuant to subparagraph (A) with respect to the placement of copyright management information for a category of works, a person identified in paragraph (1) shall not be liable for a violation of subsection (b) with respect to such copyright management information, if the activity that constitutes such violation is not intended to induce, enable, facilitate, or conceal infringement of a right under this title, and if—

(i) the transmission of such information by such person would result in a perceptible visual or aural degradation of the digital signal; or

(ii) the transmission of such information by such person would conflict with—

(I) an applicable government regulation relating to transmission of information in a digital signal;

(II) an applicable industry-wide standard relating to the transmission of information in a digital signal that was adopted by a voluntary consensus standards body prior to the effective date of this chapter; or

(III) an applicable industry-wide standard relating to the transmission of information in a digital signal that was adopted in a voluntary, consensus standards-setting process open to participation by a representative cross-section of broadcast stations or cable systems and copyright owners of a category of works that are intended for public performance by such stations or systems.

(3) Definitions.—As used in this subsection—

(A) the term "broadcast station" has the meaning given that term in section 3 of the Communications Act of 1934 (47 U.S.C. 153); and
(B) the term "cable system" has the meaning given that term in section 602 of the Communications Act of 1934 (47 U.S.C. 522).

So, how does Section 1202 apply to moral rights? Removing authorship and ownership information is included in Section 1202. This applies to any work, and not just visual works under VARA. But to be liable, the infringer has to know the CMI is false, and it must be done with the intent to induce, enable, facilitate or conceal infringement. This means that not all removal of CMI will be actionable.

Kelley v. Chicago Park Dist., 635 F.3d 290 (7th Cir. Feb. 15, 2011)

SYKES, Circuit Judge.

Chapman Kelley is a nationally recognized artist known for his representational paintings of landscapes and flowers—in particular, romantic floral and woodland interpretations set within ellipses. In 1984 he received permission from the Chicago Park District to install an ambitious wildflower display at the north end of Grant Park, a prominent public space in the heart of downtown Chicago. "Wildflower Works" was thereafter planted: two enormous elliptical flower beds, each nearly as big as a football field, featuring a variety of native wildflowers and edged with borders of gravel and steel.

Promoted as "living art," Wildflower Works received critical and popular acclaim, and for a while Kelley and a group of volunteers tended the vast garden, pruning and replanting as needed. But by 2004 Wildflower Works had deteriorated, and the City's goals for Grant Park had changed. So the Park District dramatically modified the garden, substantially reducing its size, reconfiguring the oval flower beds into rectangles, and changing some of the planting material.

Kelley sued the Park District for violating his "right of integrity" under the Visual Artists Rights Act of 1990 ("VARA"), 17 U.S.C. section 106A, and also for breach of contract. The contract claim is insubstantial; the main event here is the VARA claim, which is novel and tests the boundaries of copyright law. Congress enacted this statute to comply with the nation's obligations under the Berne Convention for the Protection of Literary and Artistic Works. VARA amended the Copyright Act, importing a limited version of the civil-law concept of the "moral rights of the artist" into our intellectual-property law. In brief, for certain types of visual art—paintings, drawings, prints, sculptures, and exhibition photographs—VARA confers upon the artist certain rights of attribution and integrity. The latter include the right of the artist to prevent, during his lifetime, any distortion or modification of his work that would be "prejudicial to his ... honor or reputation," and to recover for any such intentional distortion or modification undertaken without his consent. *See* 17 U.S.C. section 106A(a)(3)(A).

The district court held a bench trial and entered a split judgment. The court rejected Kelley's moral-rights claim for two reasons. First, the judge held that although Wildflower Works could be classified as both a painting and a sculpture and therefore a work of visual art under VARA, it lacked sufficient originality to be eligible for copyright, a foundational requirement in the statute. Second, following the First Circuit's decision in *Phillips v. Pembroke Real Estate, Inc.*, 459 F.3d128 (1st Cir.2006), the court concluded that site-specific art like Wildflower Works is categorically excluded from protection under VARA. The court then held for Kelley on the contract claim, but found his evidence of damages uncertain and entered a nominal award of $1. Both sides appealed.

We affirm in part and reverse in part. There is reason to doubt several of the district court's conclusions: that Wildflower Works is a painting or sculpture; that it flunks the test for originality; and that *all* site-specific art is excluded from VARA. But the court was right to reject this claim; for reasons relating to copyright's requirements of expressive authorship and fixation, a living garden like Wildflower Works is not copyrightable. The district court's treatment of the contract claim is another matter; the Park District is entitled to judgment on that claim as well.

I. Background

Kelley is a painter noted for his use of bold, elliptical outlines to surround scenes of landscapes and flowers. In the late–1970s and 1980s, he moved from the canvas to the soil and created a series of large outdoor wildflower displays that resembled his paintings. He planted the first in 1976 alongside a runway at the Dallas–Fort Worth International Airport and the second in 1982 outside the Dallas Museum of Natural History. The wildflower exhibit at the museum was temporary; the one at the airport just "gradually petered out."

In 1983 Kelley accepted an invitation from Chicago-based oil executive John Swearingen and his wife, Bonnie—collectors of Kelley's paintings—to come to Chicago to explore the possibility of creating a large outdoor wildflower display in the area. He scouted sites by land and by air and eventually settled on Grant Park, the city's showcase public space running along Lake Michigan in the center of downtown Chicago. This location suited Kelley's artistic, environmental, and educational mission; it also provided the best opportunity to reach a large audience. Kelley met with the Park District superintendent to present his proposal, and on June 19, 1984, the Park District Board of Commissioners granted him a permit to install a "permanent Wild Flower Floral Display" on a grassy area on top of the underground Monroe Street parking garage in Daley Bicentennial Plaza in Grant Park. Under the terms of the permit, Kelley was to install and maintain the exhibit at his own expense. The Park District reserved the right to terminate the installation by giving Kelley "a 90 day notice to remove the planting."

Kelley named the project "Chicago Wildflower Works I." The Park District issued a press release announcing that "a new form of 'living' art" was coming to Grant Park—"giant ovals of multicolored wildflowers" created by Kelley, a painter and "pioneer in the use of natural materials" who "attracted national prominence for his efforts to incorporate the landscape in artistic creation." The announcement explained that "[o]nce the ovals mature, the results will be two breathtaking natural canvases of Kelley-designed color patterns."

In the late summer of 1984, Kelley began installing the two large-scale elliptical flower beds at the Grant Park site; they spanned 1.5 acres of parkland and were set within gravel and steel borders. A gravel walkway bisected one of the ovals, and each flower bed also accommodated several large, preexisting air vents that were flush with the planting surface, providing ventilation to the parking garage below. For planting material Kelley selected between 48 and 60 species of self-sustaining wildflowers native to the region. The species were selected for various aesthetic, environmental, and cultural reasons, but also to increase the likelihood that the garden could withstand Chicago's harsh winters and survive with minimal maintenance. Kelley designed the initial placement of the wildflowers so they would blossom sequentially, changing colors throughout the growing season and increasing in brightness towards the center of each ellipse. He purchased the initial planting material—between 200,000 and 300,000 wildflower plugs—at a cost of between $80,000 and $152,000. In September of 1984, a battery of volunteers planted the seedlings under Kelley's direction.

When the wildflowers bloomed the following year, Wildflower Works was greeted with widespread acclaim. Chicago's mayor, the Illinois Senate, and the Illinois Chapter of the American Society of Landscape Artists issued commendations. People flocked to see the lovely display—marketed by the Park District as "living landscape art"—and admiring articles appeared in national newspapers. Wildflower Works was a hit.

For the next several years, Kelley's permit was renewed and he and his volunteers tended the impressive garden. They pruned and weeded and regularly planted new seeds, both to experiment with the garden's composition and to fill in where initial specimen had not flourished. Of course, the forces of nature—the varying bloom periods of the plants; their spread habits, compatibility, and life cycles; and the weather—produced constant change. Some wildflowers naturally did better than others. Some spread aggressively and encroached on neighboring plants. Some withered and died. Unwanted plants sprung up from seeds brought in by birds and the wind. Insects, rabbits, and weeds settled in, eventually taking a toll. Four years after Wildflower Works was planted, the Park District decided to discontinue the exhibit. On June 3, 1988, the District gave Kelley a 90–day notice of termination.

Kelley responded by suing the Park District in federal court, claiming the termination of his permit violated the First Amendment. The parties quickly settled; in exchange for dismissal of the suit, the Park District agreed to extend Kelley's permit for another year. On September 14, 1988, the Park District issued a "Temporary Permit" to Kelley and ChicagoWildflower Works, Inc., a nonprofit organization formed by his volunteers. This permit authorized them "to operate and maintain a two ellipse Wildflowers Garden Display ... at Daley Bicentennial Plaza in Grant Park" until September 1, 1989. The permit stipulated that Kelley "will have responsibility and control over matters relating to the aesthetic design and content of Wildflower Works I," and Wildflower Works, Inc. "shall maintain the Wildflower Works I at no cost to the ChicagoPark District including, without limitation, weeding and application of fertilizer." Although it did not contain a notice-of-termination provision, the permit did state that "[t]he planting material is the property of Mr. Chapman Kelley" and that Kelley "may remove the planting material" if the permit was not extended. Finally, the permit provided that "[t]his agreement does not create any proprietary interest for Chicago Wildflower Works, Inc., or Mr. Chapman Kelley in continuing to operate and maintain the Wildflower Garden Display after September 1, 1989."

The Park District formally extended this permit each succeeding year through 1994. After that point Kelley and his volunteers continued to cultivate Wildflower Works without a permit, and the Park District took no action, adverse or otherwise, regarding the garden's future. In March

2004 Kelley and Jonathan Dedmon, president of Wildflower Works, Inc., attended a luncheon to discuss the 20th anniversary of Wildflower Works. At the luncheon Dedmon asked Park District Commissioner Margaret Burroughs if Wildflower Works needed a new permit. Commissioner Burroughs responded, "You're still there, aren't you? That's all you need to do."

Three months later, on June 10, 2004, Park District officials met with Kelley and Dedmon to discuss problems relating to inadequate maintenance of the garden and forthcoming changes to Grant Park necessitated by the construction of the adjacent Millennium Park. The officials proposed reconfiguring Wildflower Works—decreasing its size from approximately 66,000 square feet to just under 30,000 square feet and remaking its elliptical flower beds into rectangles. The District's director of development invited Kelley's views on this proposal but made it clear that the District planned to go forward with the reconfiguration with or without Kelley's approval. Kelley objected to the proposed changes, but did not request an opportunity to remove his planting material before the reconfiguration took place. A week later the Park District proceeded with its plan and reduced Wildflower Works to less than half its original size. The elliptical borders became rectilinear, weeds were removed, surviving wildflowers were replanted in the smaller-scale garden, and some new planting material was added. Dedmon sent a letter of protest to the Park District.

Kelley then sued the Park District for violating his moral rights under VARA. He claimed that Wildflower Works was both a painting and a sculpture and therefore a "work of visual art" under VARA, and that the Park District's reconfiguration of it was an intentional "distortion, mutilation, or other modification" of his work and was "prejudicial to his ... honor or reputation." *See* 17 U.S.C. section 106A(a)(3)(A). He also alleged breach of contract; he claimed that Commissioner Burroughs's remark created an implied contract that the Park District had breached when it altered Wildflower Works without providing reasonable notice.[1] On the VARA claim Kelley sought compensation for the moral-rights violation, statutory damages, and attorney's fees; on the contract claim he sought the fair-market value of the planting material removed in the reconfiguration. He later quantified his damages, estimating the value of the plants at $1.5 million and requesting a staggering $25 million for the VARA violation.

The case proceeded to a bench trial, and the district court entered judgment for the Park District on the VARA claim and for Kelley on the contract claim. *See Kelley v. Chi. Park Dist.*, No. 04 C 07715, 2008 WL 4449886 (N.D.Ill. Sept. 29, 2008). The judge first concluded that Wildflower Works could be classified as both a painting and a sculpture and therefore qualified as a work of visual art under VARA. *Id.* at *4–5. But he also held that Wildflower Works was insufficiently original for copyright, a prerequisite to moral-rights protection under VARA. *Id.* at *6. Alternatively, the judge concluded that Wildflower Works was site-specific art, and following the First Circuit's decision in *Phillips,* held that VARA did not apply to this category of art. *Id.* at *6–7. On the contract claim the court construed the Chicago Park District Act, 70 ILL. COMP. STAT.. 1505/7.01, to permit individual commissioners to enter into binding contracts on the Park District's behalf. *Id.* at *7–8. The judge found that Commissioner Burroughs's statement—"You're still there, aren't you? That's all you need to do."—created an implied contract that the Park District had breached by failing to give Kelley reasonable notice before altering Wildflower Works. *Id.* But the judge also concluded that Kelley had failed to prove damages to a reasonable certainty and awarded $1 in nominal damages. *Id.* at *9.

Kelley appealed, challenging the adverse judgment on the VARA claim and the district court's treatment of the damages issue on the contract claim. The Park District cross-appealed from the judgment on the contract claim.

II. Discussion

This case comes to us from a judgment entered after a bench trial; we review the district court's factual findings for clear error and its conclusions of law de novo. *Spurgin–Dienst v. United States,* 359 F.3d 451, 453 (7th Cir.2004). In this circuit, questions of copyright eligibility are issues of law subject to independent review. *Schrock v. Learning Curve Int'l, Inc.,* 586 F.3d 513, 517 (7th Cir.2009).

A. Kelley's Moral–Rights Claim Under the Visual Artists Rights Act of 1990

1. A brief history of moral rights

That artists have certain "moral rights" in their work is a doctrine long recognized in civil-law countries but only recently imported into the United States. Moral rights are generally grouped into two categories: rights of attribution and rights of integrity. "Rights of attribution" generally include the artist's right to be recognized as the author of his work, to publish anonymously and pseudonymously, to prevent attribution of his name to works he did not create, and to prevent his work from being attributed to other artists. *Carter v. Helmsley–Spear, Inc.,* 71 F.3d 77, 81 (2d Cir.1995) (citing RALPH E. LERNER & JUDITH BRESLER, ART LAW 419–20 (1989)). "Rights of integrity" include the artist's right to prevent the modification, mutilation, or distortion of his work, and in some cases (if the work is of recognized stature), to prevent its destruction. *Id.*at 81–82 (citing ART LAW at 420–21).

Originating in nineteenth-century France, moral rights—*le droit moral*—are understood as rights inhering in the artist's personality, transcending property and contract rights and existing independently of the artist's economic interest in his work. *See* 3 MELVILLE B. NIMMER & DAVID NIMMER, NIMMER ON COPYRIGHT section 8D.01[A] (2010); 5 WILLIAM F. PATRY, PATRY ON COPYRIGHT section 16:1, 16:3 (2010); John Henry Merryman, *The Refrigerator of Bernard Buffet,* 27 HASTINGS L.J. 1023, 1023–28 (1976). American copyright law, on the other hand, protects the economic interests of artists; Article I of the Constitution authorizes Congress "To Promote the Progress of Science and useful Arts, by securing for limited Times to Authors and Inventors the exclusive Right to their respective Writings and Discoveries." U.S. CONST. art. 1, section 8, cl. 8. Unlike other intellectual-property rights, moral rights are unrelated to the artist's pecuniary interests and are grounded in philosophical ideas about the intrinsic nature and cultural value of art rather than natural-property or utility justifications.[3] *See Carter,* 71 F.3d at 81 (describing moral rights as "rights of a spiritual, non-economic and personal nature [that] ... spring from a belief that an artist in the process of creation injects his spirit into the work and that the artist's personality, as well as the integrity of the work, should therefore be protected and preserved"). VARA introduced a limited version of this European doctrine into American law, but it is not an easy fit.

VARA was enacted as a consequence of the United States' accession to the Berne Convention for the Protection of Literary and Artistic Works. After many years of resistance, the Senate ratified the treaty in 1988, bringing the United States into the Berne Union effective the following year. *See* 4 NIMMER section 17.01[C][2] (2010); 5 PATRY sections 16:1, 16:3. The Berne Convention dates to 1886, when seven European nations (plus Haiti and Tunisia) joined together to extend copyright protection across their borders. *See* 4 NIMMER section 17.01[B][1] nn. 10 & 17 (2002). During the course of the next century, many other nations joined, and the treaty underwent periodic revisions, most notably for our purposes in 1928 when Article *6bis*was added, incorporating the concept of moral rights. *See* 3 *id.* section 8D.01[B] (2004); 5 PATRY sections 16:1, 16:3. Article *6bis*provides:

(1) Independently of the author's economic rights, and even after the transfer of the said rights, the author shall have the right to claim authorship of the work and to object to any distortion, mutilation or other modification of, or other derogatory action in relation to, the said work, which would be prejudicial to his honor or reputation.

....

(3) The means of redress for safeguarding the rights granted by this Article shall be governed by the legislation of the country where protection is claimed.

Berne Convention for the Protection of Literary and Artistic Works, art. *6bis,* Sept. 9, 1886, *as revised at* Paris on July 24, 1971, S. TREATY DOC. NO.. 99–27 (1986).

When the United States joined the Berne Union in 1989, the concept of moral rights was largely unknown in American law. *See Lee v. A.R.T. Co.,* 125 F.3d 580, 582 (7th Cir.1997) ("[I]t was accepted wisdom [before VARA] that the United States did not enforce any claim of moral rights."); *see also Weinstein v. Univ. of Ill.,* 811 F.2d 1091, 1095 n. 3 (7th Cir.1987) (The Continental principle of *le droit moral* is a doctrine that "no American jurisdiction follows as a general matter."); Merryman, *The Refrigerator of Bernard Buffet,* 27 HASTINGS L.J. at 1035–36 ("The moral right of the artist, and in particular that component called the right of integrity of the work of art, simply does not exist in our law."). Article *6bis* was a major obstacle to Berne ratification. *See Martin v. City of Indianapolis,* 192 F.3d 608, 611 (7th Cir.1999) (The treaty's moral-rights concept "was controversial in this country" and was embraced post-Berne only "in a very limited way."); *Carter,* 71 F.3d at 82–83 ("The issue of federal protection of moral rights was a prominent hurdle in the debate over whether the United States should join the Berne Convention...."); *see also* 3 NIMMER section 8D.02[A]-[D] (2004); 5 PATRY sections 16:1, 16:3; Roberta Rosenthal Kwall, *How Fine Art Fares Post VARA,* 1 MARQ. INTELL. PROP. L.REV.V. 1, 1–4 (1997).

American unease with European moral-rights doctrine—more particularly, the obligations imposed by Article *6bis*—persisted beyond Berne ratification. Indeed, Congress initially took the position that domestic law already captured the concept in existing copyright and common-law doctrines and in the statutory law of some states. *See* Berne Convention Implementation Act of 1988, Pub.L. No. 100–568, sections 2(2), (3), 102 Stat. 2853; 3 NIMMER section 8D.02[D][1] (2009); 5 PATRY section 16:3. This was seen as an implausible claim. *See* 3 NIMMER section 8D.02[D][1] ("Th[e] Congressional finding flies in the face of numerous judicial and scholarly pronouncements...."); 5 PATRY section 16:3 (The American position that existing federal and state laws satisfied minimum Berne obligations created "a web of fictional compliance."). "[A] question of international credibility existed," and "some Berne co-Unionists ... expressed doubts regarding the accuracy or sincerity of the U.S. declaration that its law already afforded a degree of moral rights protection equivalent to Berne standards." Jane C. Ginsburg, *Copyright in the 101st Congress: Commentary on the Visual Artists Rights Act and the Architectural Works Copyright Protection Act of 1990,* 14 COLUM.-VLA J.L. & ARTS 477, 478–79 (1990). VARA was enacted to fill this perceived gap, but its moral-rights protection is quite a bit narrower than its European counterpart.

2. *VARA's scope*

VARA amended the Copyright Act and provides a measure of protection for a limited set of moral rights falling under the rubric of "rights of attribution" and "rights of integrity"—but only for artists who create specific types of visual art. 17 U.S.C. section 106A(a). The statutory coverage is limited to paintings, drawings, prints, sculptures, and photographs created for exhibition existing in a single copy or a limited edition of 200 or less. *See id.* section 101 (defining "work of visual art"). The rights conferred by the statute exist independently of property rights; the artist retains them even after he no longer holds title to his work. *Id.* section 106A(a).

More specifically, VARA's attribution and integrity rights are as follows:

(a) Rights of attribution and integrity. Subject to section 107 and independent of the exclusive rights provided in section 106, *the author of a work of visual art*—

(1) shall have the right—

(A) to claim authorship of that work, and

(B) to prevent the use of his or her name as the author of any work of visual art which he or she did not create;

(2) shall have the right to prevent the use of his or her name as the author of the work of visual art in the event of distortion, mutilation, or other modification of the work which would be prejudicial to his or her honor or reputation; and

(3) subject to the limitations set forth in section 113(d), *shall have the right*—

(A) *to prevent any intentional distortion, mutilation, or other modification of that work which would be prejudicial to his or her honor or reputation, and any intentional distortion, mutilation, or modification of that work is a violation of that right,* and

(B) to prevent any destruction of a work of recognized stature, and any intentional or grossly negligent destruction of that work is a violation of that right.

17 U.S.C. section 106A(a) (emphasis added). At issue here is the right of integrity conferred by subsection (a)(3)(A), which precludes any intentional modification or distortion of a work of visual art that "would be prejudicial to [the artist's] honor or reputation."

A qualifying "work of visual art" is defined as:

(1) *a painting,* drawing, print, *or sculpture,* existing in a single copy, in a limited edition of 200 or fewer that are signed and consecutively numbered by the author, or, in the case of a sculpture, in multiple cast, carved, or fabricated sculptures of 200 or fewer that are consecutively numbered by the author and bear the signature or other identifying mark of the author; or

(2) a still photographic image produced for exhibition purposes only, existing in a single copy that is signed by the author, or in a limited edition of 200 copies or fewer that are signed and consecutively number by the author.

Id. section 101 (emphasis added). This definition also contains a number of specific exclusions: e.g., posters, maps, and globes; books, newspapers, magazines, and other periodicals; "motion picture[s] or other audiovisual work [s]"; merchandising and promotional materials; "any work made for hire"; and "any work not subject to copyright protection under this title." *Id.*

This last exclusion simply reinforces the point that VARA supplements general copyright protection; to qualify for moral rights under VARA, a work must first satisfy basic copyright standards. Under the Copyright Act of 1976, copyright subsists in "original works of authorship fixed in any tangible medium of expression, now known or later developed, from which they can be perceived, reproduced, or otherwise communicated." *Id.* section 102(a). "Works of authorship" include "pictorial, graphic, and sculptural works." *Id.* section 102(a)(5). VARA's definition of "work of visual art" is limited to a narrow subset of this broader universe of "pictorial, graphic, and sculptural works" that are otherwise eligible for copyright; only a select few categories of art get the extra protection provided by the moral-rights concept. 5 PATRY section 16:7 (2010) ("Protected 'works of visual art' is a narrower subcategory of 'pictorial, graphic, and sculptural works,' protected in section 102(a)(5).").

Several exceptions limit the scope of the rights granted under the statute:

(c) Exceptions. (1) The modification of a work of visual art which is a result of the passage of time or the inherent nature of the materials is not a distortion, mutilation, or other modification described in subsection (a)(3)(A).

(2) *The modification of a work of visual art which is the result of conservation, or of the public presentation, including lighting and placement,* of the work *is not a destruction, distortion, mutilation, or other modification* described in subsection (a)(3) *unless the modification is caused by gross negligence.*

17 U.S.C. section 106A(c) (emphasis added). The second of these—the "public presentation" exception—is at issue here. Another exception invoked by the Park District is found in a different section of the Copyright Act that defines the scope of a copyright owner's rights:

(d)(1) *In a case in which—*

(A) *a work of visual art has been incorporated in or made part of a building* in such a way that removing the work from the building will cause the destruction, distortion, mutilation, or other modification of the work as described in section 106A(a)(3), and

(B) the author consented to the installation of the work in the building either before the effective date set forth in section 610(a) of the Visual Artists Rights Act of 1990, or in a written instrument executed on or after such effective date that is signed by the owner of the building and the author and that specifies that installation of the work may subject the work to destruction, distortion, mutilation, or other modification, by reason of its removal,

then the rights conferred by paragraphs (2) and (3) of section 106A(a) shall not apply.

Id. section 113 (emphasis added). This is known as the "building exception."

VARA rights cannot be transferred or assigned, but they can be waived in a writing signed by the artist and "specifically identify[ing] the work, and uses of that work, to which the waiver applies." *Id.* section 106A(e)(1). Absent a written waiver, the artist retains VARA rights during his lifetime even if he transfers ownership of the work or assigns his copyright. *Id.* section 106A(d)(1), (e)(2).

3. Is Wildflower Works a painting or sculpture?

The district court held that Wildflower Works was both a painting and a sculpture but was insufficiently original to qualify for copyright. Alternatively, the court concluded that it was site-specific art and held that all site-specific art is implicitly excluded from VARA. Other arguments—in particular, whether Wildflower Works satisfies additional threshold requirements for copyright and whether VARA's public-presentation or building exceptions applied—were not reached.

On appeal Kelley contests the district court's conclusions regarding originality and site-specific art. The Park District defends these holdings and also reiterates the other arguments it made in the district court, except one: The Park District has not challenged the district court's conclusion that Wildflower Works is a painting and a sculpture.

This is an astonishing omission. VARA's definition of "work of visual art" operates to narrow and focus the statute's coverage; only a "painting, drawing, print, or sculpture," or an exhibition photograph will qualify. These terms are not further defined, but the overall structure of the statutory scheme clearly illuminates the limiting effect of this definition. Copyright's broad general coverage extends to "original works of authorship," and this includes "pictorial, graphic, and sculptural works." 17 U.S.C. section 102(a)(5). The use of the adjectives "pictorial" and "sculptural" suggests flexibility and breadth in application. In contrast VARA uses the specific nouns "painting" and "sculpture." To qualify for moral-rights protection under VARA, Wildflower Works cannot just be "pictorial" or "sculptural" in some aspect or effect, it must actually *be* a "painting" or a "sculpture." Not metaphorically or by analogy, but *really.*

That Kelley considered the garden to be both a painting and a sculpture—only rendered in living material—is not dispositive. He also characterized it as an experiment in environmental theory, telling a reporter he was trying to "figure out the economic and ecological impact of introducing wildflowers into cities." In promoting Wildflower Works, Kelley variously described the project as a "living wildflower painting," a "study on wildflower landscape and management," and "a new vegetative management system that beautifies [the] landscape economically with low-maintenance wildflowers."

Kelley's expert, a professor of art history, reinforced his view that Wildflower Works was both a painting and a sculpture, but the district court largely disregarded her testimony as unhelpful. *Kelley,* 2008 WL 4449886, at *5. For its part the Park District initially marketed Wildflower Works as "living art," but this adds little to the analysis. VARA plainly uses the terms "painting" and "sculpture" as words of *limitation.* Even assuming a generous stance on what qualifies, *see* 5 PATRY section 16:7 (suggesting a "liberal attitude toward what may be considered a painting, drawing, print, or sculpture"), the terms cannot be read coextensively with the broader categories of "pictorial" and "sculptural" works that are generally eligible for copyright under section 102(a)(5). If a living garden like Wildflower Works really counts as both a painting and a sculpture, then these terms do no limiting work at all.

The district judge worried about taking "too literalist an approach to determining whether a given object qualifies as a sculpture or painting." *Kelley,* 2008 WL 4449886, at *4. His concern was the "tension between the law and the evolution of ideas in modern or avant garden art; the former requires legislatures to taxonomize artistic creations, whereas the latter is occupied with expanding the definition of what we accept to be art." *Id.* We agree with this important insight. But there's a big difference between avoiding a literalistic approach and embracing one that is infinitely malleable. The judge appears to have come down too close to the latter extreme.

In short, this case raises serious questions about the meaning and application of VARA's definition of qualifying works of visual art—questions with potentially decisive consequences for this and other moral-rights claims. But the Park District has not challenged this aspect of the district court's decision, so we move directly to the question of copyrightability, which is actually where the analysis should start in the first place.

4. Is Wildflower Works copyrightable?

To merit copyright protection, Wildflower Works must be an "original work [ ] of authorship fixed in a[ ] tangible medium of expression ... from which [it] can be perceived, reproduced, or otherwise communicated." 17 U.S.C. section 102(a). The district court held that although Wildflower Works was both a painting and a sculpture, it was ineligible for copyright because it lacked originality. There is a contradiction here. As we have explained, VARA supplements general copyright protection and applies only to artists who create the specific subcategories of art enumerated in the statute. VARA-eligible paintings and sculptures comprise a discrete subset of otherwise copyrightable pictorial and sculptural works; the statute designates these works of fine art as worthy of special protection. If a work is so lacking in originality that it cannot satisfy the basic requirements for copyright, then it can hardly qualify as a painting or sculpture eligible for *extra* protection under VARA. *See* Cronin, *Dead on the Vine,* 12 VAND. J. ENT. & TECH. L.. at 239 ("[I]f a work does not evince sufficient original expression to be copyrightable, the work should belong in a category other than 'visual art' as this term is contemplated under VARA.").

That point aside, the district court's conclusion misunderstands the originality requirement. Originality is "the touchstone of copyright protection today," an implicit constitutional and explicit statutory requirement. *Feist Publ'ns, Inc. v. Rural Tel. Serv. Co.,* 499 U.S. 340, 347, 346, 111 S.Ct. 1282, 113 L.Ed.2d 358 (1991) ("Originality is a constitutional requirement."); *id.* at 355 (The Copyright Act of 1976 made the originality requirement explicit.); *see also Schrock,* 586 F.3d at 518–19 ("As a constitutional and statutory matter, '[t]he *sine qua non* of copyright is originality.' " (quoting *Feist,* 499 U.S. at 345, 111 S.Ct. 1282)). Despite its centrality in our copyright regime, the threshold for originality is minimal. *See Feist,* 499 U.S. at 345, 111 S.Ct. 1282; *Am. Dental Ass'n v. Delta Dental Plans Ass'n,* 126 F.3d 977, 979 (**7th Cir.**1997) ("The necessary degree of 'originality' is low...."). The standard requires "only that the work was independently created by the author (as opposed to copied from other works), and that it possesses at least some minimal degree of creativity." *Feist,* 499 U.S. at 345, 111 S.Ct. 1282 (citation omitted). The "requisite level of creativity is extremely low; even a slight amount will suffice. The vast majority of works make the grade quite easily, as they possess some creative spark." *Id.* (citation omitted).

The district court took the position that Wildflower Works was not original because Kelley was not "the first person to ever conceive of and express an arrangement of growing wildflowers in ellipse-shaped enclosed area [s]." *Kelley,* 2008 WL 4449886, at *6. This mistakenly equates originality with novelty; the law is clear that a work can be original even if it is not novel. *Feist,*

499 U.S. at 345, 111 S.Ct. 1282 ("Originality does not signify novelty; a work may be original even though it closely resembles other works so long as the similarity is fortuitous, not the result of copying."). No one argues that Wildflower Works was copied; it plainly possesses more than a little creative spark.

The judge was also at a loss to discover "what about the exhibit is original. Is it the elliptical design? The size? The use of native instead of non-native plants? The environmentally-sustainable gardening method to which 'vegetative management system' apparently refers?" *Kelley,* 2008 WL 4449886, at *6. It is true that common geometric shapes cannot be copyrighted. *See* U.S. COPYRIGHT OFFICE, COMPENDIUM II: COPYRIGHT OFFICE PRACTICES section 503.02(a)-(b) (1984); 2 PATRY section 4:17 (2010). And "[i]n no case does copyright protection for an original work of authorship extend to any idea, procedure, process, system, method of operation, concept, principle, or discovery, regardless of the form in which it is described, explained, illustrated, or embodied in such a work." 17 U.S.C. section 102(b).

The Park District suggests that Wildflower Works is an uncopyrightable "method" or "system," and is also ineligible because its design uses simple elliptical shapes. The first of these arguments is not well-developed; the second is misplaced. Although Wildflower Works was designed to be largely self-sustaining (at least initially), it's not really a "method" or "system" at all. It's a garden. And Kelley is seeking statutory protection for the garden itself, not any supposed "system" of vegetative management encompassed within it. Regarding the use of elliptical shapes, an author's expressive combination or arrangement of otherwise noncopyrightable elements (like geometric shapes) may satisfy the originality requirement. *Roulo v. Russ Berrie & Co.,* 886 F.2d 931, 939 (**7th Cir.**1989); 2 PATRY section 4:17 (Geometric shapes or symbols cannot themselves be protected, but an original creative arrangement of them can be.).

The real impediment to copyright here is not that Wildflower Works fails the test for originality (understood as "not copied" and "possessing some creativity") but that a living garden lacks the kind of authorship and stable fixation normally required to support copyright. Unlike originality, authorship and fixation are *explicit* constitutional requirements; the Copyright Clause empowers Congress to secure for "authors" exclusive rights in their "writings." U.S. CONST. art 1, section 8, cl. 8; *see also* 2 PATRY section 3:20 (2010) ("[T]he Constitution uses the terms 'writings' and 'authors;' 'originality' is not used."); *id.* section 3:22 (2010); 1 NIMMER section 2.03[A]-[B] (2004). The originality requirement is implicit in these express limitations on the congressional copyright power. *See Feist,* 499 U.S. at 346, 111 S.Ct. 1282 (The constitutional reference to "authors" and "writings" "presuppose[s] a degree of originality."). The Supreme Court has "repeatedly construed all three terms in relation to one another [or] perhaps has collapsed them into a single concept"; therefore, "[w]ritings are what authors create, but for one to be an author, the writing has to be original." 2 PATRY section 3:20.

"Without fixation," moreover, "there cannot be a 'writing.' " *Id.* section 3:22. The Nimmer treatise elaborates:

Fixation in tangible form is not merely a statutory condition to copyright. It is also a constitutional necessity. That is, unless a work is reduced to tangible form it cannot be regarded as a "writing" within the meaning of the constitutional clause authorizing federal copyright legislation. Thus, certain works of conceptual art stand outside of copyright protection.1 NIMMER section 2.03[B]. A work is "fixed" in a tangible medium of expression "when its embodiment in a copy or phonorecord ... is sufficiently permanent or stable to permit it to be perceived, reproduced, or otherwise communicated for a period of more than transitory duration." 17 U.S.C. section 101. As William Patry explains:

Fixation serves two basic roles: (1) easing problems of proof of creation and infringement, and (2) providing the dividing line between state common law protection and protection under the federal Copyright Act, since works that are not fixed are ineligible for federal protection but may be protected under state law. The distinction between the intangible intellectual property (the work of authorship) and its fixation in a tangible medium of expression (the copy) is an old and fundamental and important one. The distinction may be understood by examples of multiple fixations of the same work: A musical composition may be embodied in sheet music, on an audio-tape, on a compact disc, on a computer hard drive or server, or as part of a motion picture soundtrack. In each of the fixations, the intangible property remains a musical composition. 2 PATRY section 3:22 (internal quotation marks omitted).

Finally, "authorship is an entirely human endeavor." *Id.* section 3:19 (2010). Authors of copyrightable works must be human; works owing their form to the forces of nature cannot be copyrighted. *Id.* section 3:19 n. 1; *see also* U.S. COPYRIGHT OFFICE, COMPENDIUM II: COPYRIGHT OFFICE PRACTICES section 503.03(a) ("[A] work must be the product of human authorship" and not the forces of nature.) (1984); *id.* section 202.02(b).

Recognizing copyright in Wildflower Works presses too hard on these basic principles. We fully accept that the artistic community might classify Kelley's garden as a work of postmodern conceptual art. We acknowledge as well that copyright's prerequisites of authorship and fixation are broadly defined. But the law must have some limits; not all conceptual art may be copyrighted. In the ordinary copyright case, authorship and fixation are not contested; most works presented for copyright are unambiguously authored and unambiguously fixed. But this is not an ordinary case. A living garden like Wildflower Works is neither "authored" nor "fixed" in the senses required for copyright.*See Toney v. L'Oreal USA, Inc.*, 406 F.3d 905, 910 (7th Cir.2005) ("A person's likeness—her persona—is not authored and it is not fixed."); *see also*Cronin, *Dead on the Vine*, 12 VAND. J. ENT. & TECH. L.. at 227–39.

Simply put, gardens are planted and cultivated, not authored. A garden's constituent elements are alive and inherently changeable, not fixed. Most of what we see and experience in a garden—the colors, shapes, textures, and scents of the plants—originates in nature, not in the mind of the gardener. At any given moment in time, a garden owes most of its form and appearance to natural forces, though the gardener who plants and tends it obviously assists. All this is true of Wildflower Works, even though it was designed and planted by an artist.

Of course, a human "author"—whether an artist, a professional landscape designer, or an amateur backyard gardener—determines the initial arrangement of the plants in a garden. This is not the kind of authorship required for copyright. To the extent that seeds or seedlings can be considered a "medium of expression," they originate in nature, and natural forces—not the intellect of the gardener—determine their form, growth, and appearance. Moreover, a garden is simply too changeable to satisfy the primary purpose of fixation; its appearance is too inherently variable to supply a baseline for determining questions of copyright creation and infringement. If a garden can qualify as a "work of authorship" sufficiently "embodied in a copy," at what point has fixation occurred? When the garden is newly planted? When its first blossoms appear? When it is in full bloom? How—and at what point in time—is a court to determine whether infringing copying has occurred?

In contrast, when a landscape designer conceives of a plan for a garden and puts it in writing—records it in text, diagrams, or drawings on paper or on a digital-storage device—we can say that his intangible intellectual property has been embodied in a fixed and tangible "copy." This writing is a sufficiently permanent and stable copy of the designer's intellectual expression and is vulnerable to infringing copying, giving rise to the designer's right to claim copyright. The same cannot be said of a garden, which is not a fixed copy of the gardener's intellectual property. Although the planting material is tangible and can be perceived for more than a transitory duration, it is not stable or permanent enough to be called "fixed." Seeds and plants in a garden are naturally in a state of perpetual change; they germinate, grow, bloom, become dormant, and eventually die. This life cycle moves gradually, over days, weeks, and season to season, but the real barrier to copyright here is not *temporal* but *essential.* The essence of a garden is its vitality, not its fixedness. It may endure from season to season, but its nature is one of dynamic change.

We are not suggesting that copyright attaches *only* to works that are static or fully permanent (no medium of expression lasts forever), or that artists who incorporate natural or living elements in their work can *never* claim copyright. Kelleycompares Wildflower Works to the Crown Fountain, a sculpture by Spanish artist Jaume Plensa that sits nearby in Chicago's Millennium Park. The surfaces of Plensa's fountain are embedded with LED screens that replay recorded video images of the faces of 1,000 Chicagoans. *See* http://www.explorechicago.org/city/en/things_see_do/attractions/dca_ tourism/Crown_Fountain.html (last visited Feb. 10, 2011). But the Copyright Act specifically contemplates works that incorporate or consist of sounds or images that are broadcast or transmitted electronically, such as telecasts of sporting events or other live performances, video games, and the like. *See* 17 U.S.C. section 101 (defining "fixed" as including a "work consisting of sounds, images, or both, that are being transmitted ... if a fixation of the work is being made simultaneously with its transmission"); *see also Balt. Orioles, Inc. v. Major League Baseball Players Ass'n,* 805 F.2d 663, 675 (7th Cir.1986); *Midway Mfg. Co. v. Artic Int'l, Inc.,* 704 F.2d 1009, 1013–14 (7th Cir.1983). Wildflower Works does not fit in this category; the Crown Fountain is not analogous.

Though not addressing the requirement of fixation directly, the district court compared Wildflower Works to "[t]he mobiles of Alexander Calder" and "Jeff Koons' 'Puppy,' a 43–foot flowering topiary." *Kelley,* 2008 WL 4449886, at *4. These analogies are also inapt. Although the aesthetic effect of a Calder mobile is attributable in part to its subtle movement in response to air currents, *see* http://en.wikipedia.org/wiki/Alexander_Calder (last visited Feb. 10, 2011), the mobile itself is obviously fixed and stable. In "Puppy" the artist assembled a huge metal frame in the shape of a puppy and covered it with thousands of blooming flowers sustained by an irrigation system within the frame. *See*http://en.wikipedia.org/wiki/Jeff_Koons (last visited Feb. 10, 2011). This may be sufficient fixation for copyright (we venture no opinion on the question), but Wildflower Works is quite different. It is quintessentially a garden; "Puppy" is not.

In short, Wildflower Works presents serious problems of authorship and fixation that these and other examples of conceptual or kinetic art do not. Because Kelley's garden is neither "authored" nor "fixed" in the senses required for basic copyright, it cannot qualify for moral-rights protection under VARA.

5. Site-specific art, and the public-presentation and building exceptions

This case also raises some important questions about the application of VARA to site-specific art, as well as the statute's public-presentation and building exceptions. Though we need not decide these questions, we do have a few words of caution about the district court's treatment of the issue of VARA and site-specific art. The court classified Wildflower Works as a form of site-specific art; we see no reason to upset this factual finding. The court then adopted the First Circuit's holding in *Phillips* that site-specific art is categorically excluded from VARA. This legal conclusion is open to question.

Phillips involved a VARA claim brought by artist David Phillips in a dispute over a display of 27 of his sculptures in Boston's Eastport Park across from Boston Harbor. *Phillips v. Pembroke Real Estate, Inc.*, 459 F.3d 128, 130 (1st Cir.2006). A planned redesign of the park called for the removal and relocation of Phillips's sculptures; he sought an injunction under VARA, claiming the removal of his sculptures would violate his right of integrity. *Id.* at 131. The district court held that although the sculptures qualified as a single integrated work of visual art, park administrators were entitled to remove them under VARA's public-presentation exception. *Id.* at 138–39. The First Circuit affirmed on alternative grounds, holding that VARA does not apply to *any* site-specific art.

The court based this holding on a perceived irreconcilable tension between the public-presentation exception and the purpose of site-specific art: "By definition, site-specific art integrates its location as one of its elements. Therefore, the removal of a site-specific work from its location necessarily destroys that work of art." *Id.* at 140. Under the public-presentation exception, a modification of a work of visual art stemming from a change in its "public presentation, including lighting or placement," is not actionable unless it is caused by gross negligence. If VARA applied to site-specific art, the First Circuit reasoned, then the statute would "purport[ ] to protect site-specific art" but also "permit its destruction by the application" of the public-presentation exception. *Id.* The court held that "VARA does not protect site-specific art and then permit its destruction by removal from its site pursuant to the statute's public presentation exception. VARA does not apply to site-specific art at all." *Id.* at 143.

There are a couple of reasons to question this interpretation of VARA. First, the term "site-specific art" appears nowhere in the statute. Nothing in the definition of a "work of visual art" either explicitly or by implication excludes this form of art from moral-rights protection. Nor does application of the public-presentation exception operate to eliminate *every* type of protection VARA grants to creators of site-specific art; the exception simply narrows the scope of the statute's protection for all qualifying works of visual art. The exception basically provides a safe harbor for ordinary changes in the public presentation of VARA-qualifying artworks; the artist has no cause of action unless through gross negligence the work is modified, distorted, or destroyed in the process of changing its public presentation.

Second, *Phillips*'s all-or-nothing approach to site-specific art may be unwarranted. Site-specific art is not *necessarily* destroyed if moved; modified, yes, but not always utterly destroyed. Moreover, some of VARA's protections are unaffected by the public-presentation exception. An artist's right of integrity can be violated in ways that do not implicate the work's location or manner of public presentation; site-specific art—like any other type of art—can be defaced and damaged in ways that do not relate to its public display. And the public-presentation exception does nothing to limit the right of attribution, which prevents an artist's name from being misappropriated.

Then there is the matter of the building exception, which applies to works "incorporated in or made part of a building in such a way that removing the work from the building will cause the destruction, distortion, mutilation, or other modification of the work." 17 U.S.C. section 113(d)(1)(A). These works do not get moral-rights protection if the artist: (1) consented to the installation of his work in the building (if pre-VARA); or (2) executed a written acknowledgment that removal of the work may subject it to destruction, distortion, mutilation, or modification (if post-VARA). *Id.* section 113(d)(1)(B). On its face this exception covers a particular kind of site-specific art. Its presence in the statute suggests that site-specific art is not categorically excluded from VARA.

These observations are of course general and not dispositive. Because we are resolving the VARA claim on other grounds, we need not decide whether VARA is inapplicable to site-specific art.

B. The Park District's Cross–Appeal on the Contract Claim

The Park District challenges the judgment against it for breach of contract even though damages were assessed at a nominal $1. The district court held that Commissioner Burroughs's casual remark—"You're still there, aren't you? That's all you need to do."—created an implied-in-fact contract requiring the Park District to give Kelley reasonable notice before reconfiguring Wildflower Works.

Although factual findings about the existence of a contract are reviewed for clear error, *ReMapp Int'l Corp. v. Comfort Keyboard Co.*, 560 F.3d 628, 633 (7th Cir.2009), there is a threshold legal question here about the commissioner's unilateral authority to bind the Park District to a contract. Our review is de novo. *See Manning v. United States,* 546 F.3d 430, 432 (7th Cir.2008).

Two statutes guide our analysis. The first is the Chicago Park District Act, which provides in relevant part that "[t]he commissioners of [the Park District] constitute the corporate authorities thereof, and have full power to manage and control all the officers and property of the district, and all parks, driveways, boulevards and parkways maintained by such district or committed to its care and custody." 70 ILL. COMP. STAT.. 1505/7.01. The district court noted the statute's use of the plural "commissioners" and "authorities" and concluded from this that each individual commissioner was a separate corporate "authority" with the power to unilaterally bind the Park District.

This conclusion strains the statutory language and ignores how public bodies customarily operate. It also contradicts another provision in the Illinois Park District Code, which applies to all Illinois park districts and must be read in conjunction with the Chicago Park District Act. The Illinois Park District Code states: "No member of the board of *any* park district ... shall have power to create any debt, obligation, claim or liability, for or on account of said park district ... *except with the express authority of said board* conferred at a meeting thereof and duly recorded in a record of its proceedings." 70 ILL. COMP. STAT.. 1205/4–6 (emphasis added). When read together, these statutes confirm that there is only one corporate authority of the Chicago Park District—its Board of Commissioners—and that individual commissioners cannot unilaterally bind the Park District's Board to a contract without express Board approval.

There is no evidence that the Park District's Board of Commissioners authorized Commissioner Burroughs to enter into a contract with Kelley. Moreover, Illinois law provides that ultra vires contracts entered into by municipal corporations are invalid, *see, e.g., McMahon v. City of Chicago,* 339 Ill.App.3d 41, 273 Ill.Dec. 447, 789 N.E.2d 347, 350 (2003), so Commissioner Burroughs's offhand remark cannot have created a valid implied-in-fact contract. The judgment for Kelley on the contract claim was premised on legal error; the Park District was entitled to judgment on this claim.

For the foregoing reasons, we AFFIRM the judgment in favor of the Park District on the VARA claim; we REVERSE the judgment in favor of Kelley on the contract claim and REMAND with instructions to enter judgment for the Park District.

Cohen v. G&M Realty L.P., 320 F.Supp. 3d 421 (SDNY 2018)

This marks the latest chapter in the ongoing saga of what has commonly become known as the 5Pointz litigation. Plaintiffs, 21 aerosol artists, initiated this lawsuit over four years ago by seeking a preliminary injunction under the Visual Artists Rights Act of 1990 ("VARA"), 17 U.S.C. section 106A, against defendants Gerald Wolkoff ("Wolkoff") and four of his real estate entities to prevent the planned demolition by Wolkoff of his warehouse buildings in Long Island City and consequent destruction of plaintiffs' paintings on the walls of the buildings.

I

On November 12, 2013, after a hearing, the Court issued an order denying preliminary injunctive relief and stating that "a written opinion would soon be issued." ECF No. 34. Rather than wait for the Court's opinion, which was issued just eight days later on November 20th, Wolkoff destroyed almost all of the plaintiffs' paintings by whitewashing them during that eight-day interim.

In its extensive opinion the Court initially noted that Wolkoff's buildings "had become the repository of the largest collection of exterior aerosol art ... in the United States" and that this litigation "marks the first occasion that a court has had to determine whether the work of an exterior aerosol artist—given its general ephemeral nature—is worthy of any protection under the law." Cohen v. G & M Realty L.P., 988 F.Supp.2d 212, 214 (E.D.N.Y. 2013) ("Cohen I"). In denying the plaintiffs' application for preliminary injunctive relief, the Court recognized that the rights created by VARA were at tension with conventional notions of property rights and tried to balance these rights. It did so by not interfering with Wolkoff's desire to tear down the warehouses to make way for high-rise luxury condos, but cautioned that "defendants are exposed to potentially significant monetary damages if it is ultimately determined after trial that the plaintiffs' works were of 'recognized stature' " under VARA. Cohen I, 988 F.Supp.2d at 227.

The trial has now happened. It lasted three weeks. At plaintiffs' insistence, it was tried before a jury, but just prior to summations, plaintiffs—with defendants' consent—waived their jury rights. Rather than summarily dismiss the jury after it had sat through the entire trial, the Court converted it to an advisory jury. During its charge, the Court carefully explained the parties' rights and obligations under VARA, including the plaintiffs' entitlement to substantial statutory damages if the jury determined that Wolkoff had violated plaintiffs' VARA rights and that he had acted willfully. On a 98–page verdict sheet, the jury found liability and made various damage awards in respect to 36 of plaintiffs' 49 works of art that were the subject of the lawsuit. In every case they found that Wolkoff had acted willfully.

Although the Court does not agree with all of the jurors' findings, it does agree that Wolkoff willfully violated plaintiffs' VARA rights in respect to those 36 paintings. The Court further finds that liability and willfulness should attach to an additional nine works.
Given the abject nature of Wolkoff's willful conduct, the Court awards the maximum statutory damages under VARA for each of the 45 works of art wrongfully and willfully destroyed in the combined sum of $6,750,000.

II

A. The Relevant Statutory Framework

As the Court explained in Cohen I, "VARA amended existing copyright law to add protections for two 'moral rights' of artists: the rights of attribution and integrity." Cohen I, 988 F.Supp.2d at 215. VARA has codified the right to integrity to provide "the author of a work of visual art" the right

> (A) to prevent any intentional destruction, mutilation, or other modification of that work which would be prejudicial to his or her honor or reputation, and any intentional distortion, mutilation, or modification of that work is a violation of that right, and
> (B) to prevent any destruction of a work of recognized stature, and any intentional or grossly negligent destruction of that work is a violation of that right.
> 17 U.S.C. section 106A(a)(3).

Thus, in Cohen I, the Court held that plaintiffs' aerosol art comes under VARA's protection as works of "visual art", Cohen I, 988 F.Supp.2d at 216, and that, under section 106A(a)(3)(B), VARA "gives the 'author of a work of visual art' the right to sue to prevent the destruction of [the] work if it is one of 'recognized stature,' " Cohen I, 988 F.Supp.2d at 215. VARA also permits the artist to seek monetary damages under section 106A(a)(3)(A) if the work was distorted, mutilated, or otherwise modified to the prejudice of the artist's honor or reputation. Section 113(d)(1) of VARA provides that

In a case in which—

> (A) a work of visual art has been incorporated in or made part of a building in such a way that removing the work from the building will cause the destruction, distortion, mutilation, or other modification of the work as described in section 106A(a)(3), and
> (B) the author consented to the installation of the work in the building either before the effective date set forth in section 610(a) of the Visual Artists Rights Act of 1990, or in a written instrument executed on or after such effective date that is signed by the owner of the building and the author and that specifies that installation of the work may subject the work to destruction, distortion, mutilation, or other modification, by reason of its removal, then the rights conferred by paragraphs (2) and (3) of section 106A(a) shall not apply.

Section 113(d)(2) provides, in part, that

> If the owner of a building wishes to remove a work of visual art which is a part of such building and which can be removed from the building without the destruction, mutilation, or other modification of the work as described in section 106A(a)(3), the author's rights under paragraphs (2) and (3) of section 106A(a) shall apply unless—
> (A) the owner has made a diligent, good faith attempt without success to notify the author of the owner's intended action affecting the work of visual art, or
> (B) the owner did provide such notice in writing and the person so notified failed, within 90 days after receiving such notice, either to remove the work or to pay for its removal.
>
> Thus, section 113(d) provides for two possibilities when a protected work of art has been integrated into a building subsequent to June 1, 1991, VARA's effective date. "Section 113(d)(1) deals with works of visual art that cannot be removed without causing destruction, mutilation, or other modifications to the work. Section 113(d)(2) deals with works of visual art that can be removed without causing such harm." 5 William F. Patry, Patry on Copyright section 16:32 (2017) ("Patry") (emphasis added).

Under section 113(d)(1), if a work is not removable without destroying, mutilating, distorting, or otherwise modifying the work, the artist's VARA right of integrity under section 106A(3) attaches, and the artist may sue to prevent the destruction of the work unless the right is waived "in a written instrument ... that is signed by the owner of the building and the author and that specifies that installation of the work may subject the work to destruction, distortion, mutilation, or other modification, by reason of its removal." section 113(d)(1)(B) (emphasis added).

Under section 113(d)(2), if a work is removable without destroying, mutilating, distorting, or otherwise modifying it, VARA gives the artist the opportunity to salvage the work upon receipt of a 90 days' written notice from the building owner of the owner's "intended action affecting the work of visual art." 17 U.S.C. sections 113(d)(2)(A)–(B). If the artist fails to remove or pay for the removal of the works within the 90 days —or if the owner could not notify the artist after making a "good faith effort," 17 U.S.C. section 113(d)(2)(A)—the artist's VARA rights are deemed waived for the removable work, and the owner may destroy them without consequences.

Damages that may be awarded for the violation of the artist's rights of attribution and integrity under section 106A(a)(3) are the same that apply for copyright infringement, namely actual (including profits) and statutory. 17 U.S.C. section 504(a). As the House Judiciary Committee Report explained:

> Section 6(a) of the bill simply amends section 501(a) of title 17 to add those authors covered by new section 106A.... It thereby makes all title 17 remedies [except criminal

> sanctions] available to those authors.... [VARA] thereby provides for monetary damages, and for injunctive relief to prevent future harm. The same standards that the courts presently use to determine whether such relief is appropriate for violations of section 106 rights will apply to violations of section 106A rights as well. H.R. Rep. No. 101–514, at 21–22 (1990)

There is no limit to the amount of actual damages for each work, but statutory damages for each may be "not less than $750 or more than $30,000 as the court considers just." 17 U.S.C. section 504(c)(1). If, however, the plaintiff "sustains the burden of proving, and the court finds, that infringement was committed willfully, the court in its discretion may increase the award of statutory damages" for each work "to a sum of not more than $150,000." 17 U.S.C. section 504(c)(2). The plaintiff is not entitled to both actual and statutory damages but must elect one or the other "before final judgment is rendered[.]" 17 U.S.C. section 504(c)(1).

B. The Advisory Jury

"A proper demand [for a jury trial] may be withdrawn only if the parties consent." Fed. R. Civ. P. 38(d). Here the defendants, through counsel, consented to submitting the case to the Court. Under the federal rules, where the right to a jury trial does not attach, "the court, on motion or on its own: (1) may try any issue with an advisory jury[.]" Fed. R. Civ. P. 39(c). "Because advisory juries permit community participation and may incorporate the public's views of morality and changing common law, their use is particularly appropriate in cases involving community-based standards." NAACP v. Acusport Corp., 226 F.Supp.2d 391, 398 (E.D.N.Y. 2002) (Weinstein, J.)."[A district court] is not bound by the findings of the advisory jury, which it is free to adopt in whole or in part or to totally disregard[.]" Ragin v. Harry Macklowe Real Estate Co., 6 F.3d 898, 907 (2d Cir. 1993) (quoting Sheila's Shine Prods., Inc. v. Sheila Shine, Inc., 486 F.2d 114, 122 (5th Cir. 1973)). "[T]he court retains the ultimate responsibility for findings of fact and conclusions [of law] ... in reliance upon the advisory jury's verdict if the court so chooses, and to explain how it arrived at those findings and conclusions." DeFelice v. Am. Int'l Life Assurance Co. of New York, 112 F.3d 61, 65 (2d Cir. 1997).

Under these principles, the Court will take the jury's verdicts under advisement in making its independent findings of fact and conclusions of law, especially on issues that require judgment of the community.

The Court would be remiss if it did not pause to acknowledge the extraordinary work of the eight jurors. Rarely were they late during the course of the extensive trial, and the Court was impressed with their rapt attention to the difficult task that awaited them in having to assess the defendants' liability in respect to each of the 49 works of art. Since the jurors had spent the better part of a month in anticipation of deliberating, the Court was disinclined to summarily dismiss them when, at the veritable 11th hour, the plaintiffs suddenly decided to convert the case to a bench trial. Moreover, since 5Pointz had achieved worldwide community recognition, the Court was keen to learn whether the jurors, as members of the community, would view the works as having achieved recognized stature under VARA. To enhance the integrity of their verdicts, the Court decided it best not to tell the jurors that their findings would only be advisory.

The complexity of the litigation did not deter the jurors from making individualized findings in respect to each of the 21 artists and their 49 works on the 98–page verdict sheet. They were tasked with having to determine whether each destroyed work was of recognized stature and/or was mutilated, distorted, or otherwise modified to the prejudice of the artist's honor or reputation by the whitewashing. They found that 28 of the 49 destroyed works had achieved recognized stature, and eight more had been mutilated, distorted, or otherwise modified to the prejudice of the artists' honor or reputation. Each of the 21 plaintiffs were adversely affected in one way or the other, and the jury had to individually assess whether actual and statutory damages were warranted in regard to each work. It awarded a total of $545,750 in actual damages and $651,750 in statutory damages.

C. The Witnesses and Evidentiary Landscape

Each of the 21 plaintiffs/artists testified; they were respectful, articulate and credible. Folios for each were admitted into evidence collectively containing their professional achievements and recognition in the form of an impressive array of fellowships, residences, public and private commissions, teaching positions, media coverage, and social media presence. Not surprisingly, each of the 21 Folios contained beautiful color prints of the artists' respective aerosol works of art which are the subject of the lawsuit. They are appended to this opinion. It is apparent that they reflect striking technical and artistic mastery and vision worthy of display in prominent museums if not on the walls of 5Pointz. The Folios also contain photos showing how almost all of these works of art were partially or wholly whitewashed by Wolkoff.

5Pointz was an egalitarian place. The artists came from many backgrounds. Some of the plaintiffs testified via Skype from international residences. Many who live in New York had immigrated from other countries to join the 5Pointz community. One artist flew from London to testify; another came of age in rural West Virginia. Some artists came from highly prestigious art schools; others were self-taught. Some were fixtures in elite, traditional art circles; others were simply dedicated to street and community art. The Court was impressed with the breadth of the artists' works and how many of the works spoke to the social issues of our times.

The principal testimony about the advent, evolution and demolition of 5Pointz came from plaintiff Jonathan Cohen, one of the world's most accomplished aerosol artists. Wolkoff had designated Cohen as 5Pointz's de facto curator, appointing him to run the site and pick the works he thought were of merit: "I gave him permission, plain, Jonathan, you are in charge, bring whoever you think is right to come and display their work on my building." Tr. at 2025:4–8.

In addition to the artists, three experts testified for the plaintiffs. Renee Vara, a certified art appraiser, former head fine art expert at Chubb Insurance and art professor at New York University, testified to the quality and recognized stature of the works; Elizabeth Littlejohn, an art appraiser certified through the Appraisers Association of America, testified to their appraisal value; and Harriet Irgang Alden, the chief paintings conservator at Art Care NYC, testified as to the removability of each of the artworks from the 5 Pointz walls.

Plaintiffs also called two fact witnesses. Angelo Madrigale, Vice President and Director of Contemporary Art at Doyle New York, an auction house, wrote a letter upon which Vara relied in formulating her report. He testified to the artistic importance of the works. Lois Stavsky developed a 5Pointz exhibit for Google Arts and Culture and testified to the creation of that exhibit and why Google believed that 5Pointz was a culturally significant site.

Wolkoff was the defendants' principal witness. He testified to his rise from a poor childhood to become a successful real estate developer and explained his role in the advent and success of 5 Pointz. He was adamant that the artists knew that the day would come when the warehouse buildings bearing their works of art would come down and be replaced by high-rise residential condos.

Although the Court believes that Wolkoff in the main testified truthfully, he was a difficult witness. He frequently ignored or challenged instructions by the Court. He was argumentative and prone to tangents and non-responsive answers. Eliciting coherent testimony was a chore and was only achieved after the Court threatened to hold him in contempt. See, e.g., Tr. at 2033:18–2034:2; 2036:19–2037:24; 2045:23–2047:6; 2087:22–2088:13; 2092:13–22.

In addition to Wolkoff, two experts testified for the defendants. Erin Thompson, a professor of art history at the City University of New York and practicing art lawyer, testified as to the issue of recognized stature, and Christopher Gaillard, a fine art appraiser with the art appraisal and acquisition firm Gurr Johns, testified as to the works' appraisal value.

The story of 5Pointz that follows comes primarily from the lips of Cohen and Wolkoff.

III

A. The Advent and Evolution of 5Pointz

What became 5Pointz originated as Phun Phactory in the early 1990s. The warehouses were largely dilapidated and the neighborhood was crime infested. There was no control over the artists who painted on the walls of the buildings or the quality of their work, which was largely viewed by the public as nothing more than graffiti. This started to change in 2002 when Wolkoff put Cohen in charge. Cohen and several other artists also rented studio space in the warehouse buildings. Collectively, they worked to improve conditions. As Cohen explained:

> We took it upon ourselves to clean the loading dock.... The dumpsters were overflowing. We took it upon ourselves, we hired his employees, we paid for the lighting. We put motion sensors up so that when you came to the loading dock it was inviting. It actually drew you in as opposed to scaring you away.Id. at 1448:20–1449:3.

Wolkoff recognized the merit of the art. As he acknowledged: "I liked it and they did more and more and I thought it was terrific. They were expressing themselves." Id. at 2082:4–5.

And he approved of the job Cohen did in curating the art: "I have no feelings even today against Jonathan Cohen. I thought he was terrific handling my building.... Anything to do with art I left up to Jonathan. He had good taste in the artists that came there." Id. at 2086:13–17.
Until Wolkoff decided over a decade later that the economic climate was ripe to convert the site into luxury condos, he and Cohen had a copacetic relationship.

But nothing was ever reduced to writing and Wolkoff only verbally laid out three rules for what could be put on the walls: no pornography, no religious content, and nothing political. In his role, Cohen established a system of rules for both the creation and curation of the art, spending seven days a week without pay to bring 5Pointz to fruition.

Cohen oversaw the site, kept it clean and safe, allotted wall space, and explained the site's rules and norms to new artists. Over time, crime in the neighborhood dropped and the site became a major attraction drawing thousands of daily visitors, including busloads of tourists, school trips, and weddings. Movie, television, and music video producers came; it was used for the 2013 motion picture Now You See Me, starring Jesse Eisenberg and Mark Ruffalo, and was the site of a notable tour for R & B singer Usher.

As the plaintiff Castillo explained, "street art became a new form," which "now has become an industry." Tr. at 202:6, 202:10. And 5Pointz became "this outdoor museum where kids can touch the wall, and .. you can't do that at a museum. You can't go and touch a Van Gogh or like a Mona Lisa." Id. at 202:2–5.

Wolkoff had nothing to do with day-to-day operations. Under Cohen's control, he witnessed his buildings emerge as a mecca for the world's largest collection of quality outdoor aerosol art.

B. The Walls

1. Covering

5Pointz was a site of creative destruction; most artworks had short lifespans and were repeatedly painted over by successive artists. The rules behind covering were important; as virtually every artist testified, "going over" someone else's piece without permission was a sign of disrespect that could cause conflicts. Going over another piece partially or sloppily was another insult. As Cohen explained:

> [Y]ou respect your wall, you clean up when you're done, you cover what you go over completely. If you do not cover what you went over, you do not last. That was rule number one. Respect in our game is everything, and if you don't have respect then you don't get respect. Tr. at 1443:15–22.

As a result, Cohen established an elaborate system of rules and norms governing how long pieces would remain and when a piece could be covered by a new artwork. As he testified:

> THE COURT: Let me ask you a question. Can anybody paint over your paintings without your permission, aside from vandalism?
>
> A: No. Everything was done with permission and there was a system that grew over the period of time I was there. You know, we perfect as we go along.
> Id. at 1423:18–23.

2. Short–Term Rotating Walls vs. Long–Standing Walls

5Pointz was organized into short-term rotating walls and long-standing walls. The short-term walls would change on a daily or weekly basis. As Cohen explained: "There were allocated spaces that were for straight beginners that had no idea how to paint. And those, I would say you could utilize the space, but it more than likely will be gone tomorrow or the next day or whatever." Id. at 1441:18–22. "Short-term rotating walls, it was communicated up front so they'd know you could have several weeks or whatever." Id. at 1444:13–15. On the other hand, pieces on long-standing walls were more permanent, although a high-quality piece could achieve permanence even if not initially placed on a long-standing wall; but an artist's reputation was not sufficient to secure long-standing status. As Cohen further explained:

> [T]he prime real estate that faces the train were the most sought after spots to paint and those went to more advanced writers. You've got to understand, as well, because you are an advanced writer doesn't mean that you are going to perform on an advanced level. You may just want to blow off steam one afternoon, but that doesn't mean your piece should last a long time. And you could be a beginner and do the performance of your lifetime and produce a piece that is so amazing that it's decided it will stay.Id. at 1441:22–7.

While Cohen had the final say as to the duration of the pieces, he always spoke with the artists about their planned lifespan and eventual replacement. As he testified: "For long term productions, where people invested time and money, I would communicate with them. I would reach out to them. In some instances, I would tell them to come back and actually egg them on to do something real better. As the bar got raised, everybody performed better." Id. at 1444:14–19.

In other words, 5Pointz operated not just as a creative space, but a competitive place. Artists would compete to outdo one another and earn prominent placement on a long-standing wall. In addition to the walls facing the passing 7 train, which were seen by millions of commuters, the artists prized the walls near the loading docks, which had the most foot traffic, and the walls inside the buildings, which were generally long-standing. While as many as 10,000 works were destroyed while Cohen was in charge, it was not anarchy. Most of the best works by the best artists achieved permanent or semi-permanent placements on the long-standing walls.

C. The Planned Demolition

Starting in 2011, rumors that Wolkoff had plans to shut down 5Pointz and turn it into luxury condos began to concern the artists. In May 2013, the rumors became reality: Cohen learned that Wolkoff had started to seek the requisite municipal approvals for his condos.
Hoping to save 5Pointz, Cohen filed an application with the City Landmark Preservation Commission to preserve the site as one of cultural significance. It was denied because the artistic work was of too recent origin. See Letter from NYC Landmarks Preservation Commission, August 20, 2013, ECF No. 31.

Cohen also sought funding to buy the property, which had been valued at $40 million. However, this fell through in October 2013 when Wolkoff obtained a necessary variance, instantly raising the property value to more than $200 million. The higher price was out of reach of Cohen's potential investors. Plaintiffs then initiated this litigation to enjoin Wolkoff from destroying 5Pointz.

D. The Whitewashing

As soon as the Court denied the plaintiffs' application for preliminary injunction, Wolkoff directed the whitewashing of virtually all the artwork on the 5Pointz site with rollers, spray machines, and buckets of white paint.

The whitewashing was inconsistent. Some works were completely covered in white paint. Others were only partially covered. Some were fully covered, but by such a thin layer of paint that the artwork was easily visible beneath the paint. What was consistent was that none of the covered works was salvageable. And plaintiffs were no longer allowed on the site, even to recover the scattered remnants of their ruined creations.

Since their works were effectively destroyed, plaintiffs were relegated to seeking monetary relief under VARA.

IV

A. Temporary Works of Art

Defendants' overarching contention is that plaintiffs knew that the day would come when the buildings would be torn down and that, regardless, the nature of the work of an outdoor aerosol artist is ephemeral. They argue, therefore, that VARA should not afford plaintiffs protection for their temporary works.

VARA does not directly address whether it protects temporary works. However, in the context of works on buildings, it is clear from 17 U.S.C. section 113(d) that temporary works are protected. Moreover, relevant case law conceptually supports this conclusion. In short, there is no legal support for the proposition that temporary works do not come within VARA's embrace.

First, section 113(d)(1) specifies that an unremovable work incorporated in a building is protected by VARA unless the artist waives his or her rights in a writing signed by both the artist and the building owner. If the building owner could orally inform the artist that the building is coming down someday, and thereby convert the work into an unprotected temporary work, the written consent provision would be rendered nugatory. As the House Judiciary Committee Report explains: "The purpose of [the written waiver] is to ensure that the author is made fully aware of the circumstances surrounding the installation and potential removal of the work and has nevertheless knowingly subjected the work to possible modifications that would otherwise be actionable under section 106A." H.R. Rep. No. 101–514, at 21. And as Patry adds: "In light of this provision's purpose of ensuring that artists be made aware fully of the circumstances surrounding installation and potential destructive removal, it should be strictly construed." Patry section 16:33.

Second, section 113(d)(2), specifying that artists are entitled to 90 days' written notice to allow them to salvage their removable works, contemplates that such works may be temporarily on the side of a building. Thus, VARA resolves the tension between the building owners' rights and the artists' rights through section 113(d), not by excluding temporary works from protection.

Of the limited available case law, Board of Managers of Soho International Arts Condominium v. City of New York, 2003 WL 21403333 (S.D.N.Y. June 17, 2003) perhaps best illustrates this point. There, an artist sought to prevent his work from being permanently removed from the wall of a condo under VARA. There was conflicting testimony as to whether the work was intended to be kept on the wall permanently or temporarily. Nonetheless, the Court, in denying summary judgment, held VARA only allowed the artist to remove the mural, not keep it in its place. The court rejected the artist's argument that removal was "tantamount to the Work's destruction" as "[n]owhere in the [dictionary] definition of 'remove' does the temporality of the act of removal arise." Id., at *10. Therefore, it was "clear to the Court that what Congress intended in bifurcating section 113(d)'s protections was to separate removal situations based not on the temporality of the removal but on the consequences of the removal." Id.

Thus, VARA draws no distinction between temporary and nontemporary works on the side of a building, particularly when all that makes a work temporary is the building owner's expressed intention to remove or destroy it. VARA protects such works; how it protects them is governed by the carefully crafted provisions of section 113(d) based on the removability of the works, not their permanence.

Also supporting the conclusion that VARA applies to temporary works is 17 U.S.C. section 106A(c)(1), which provides that modifications that are "the result of the passage of time or the inherent nature of the materials" are not violations of VARA.

This exception was applied in Flack v. Friends of Queen Catherine Inc., 139 F.Supp.2d 526 (S.D.N.Y. 2001), where the court dismissed a VARA claim because the head of a statue was exposed to the elements, causing the clay to deteriorate, but there was no evidence that the defendant otherwise directly damaged the work. 139 F.Supp.2d at 534–35. The exception is not applicable here. The whitewashing was not caused by the "passage of time" or the "inherent nature of the materials"; it was caused by Wolkoff throwing paint on the works.
Thus, Congress chose to exclude protection for the passage of time and natural deterioration but not for other types of temporary works. Under the principle of statutory interpretation expressio unius est exclusio alterius (the expression of one thing implies the exclusion of others), this choice lends support to the conclusion that there is no categorical exception for temporary works.

Moreover, the First Circuit has held that VARA protects unfinished works. Mass. Museum of Contemporary Art Found., Inc. v. Buchel, 593 F.3d 38, 65 (1st Cir. 2010). An unfinished work is inherently in a temporary state since the ultimate goal is always to finish the work; thus, VARA protects the interim, unfinished work even though it is only temporarily in that form.
Analogy to traditional copyright law is also relevant. Under the Copyright Act—of which VARA is a part—a work is " 'created' when it is fixed in a copy or phonorecord for the first time[.]" 17 U.S.C. section 101. And a work is " 'fixed' in a tangible medium of expression when its embodiment in a copy or phonorecord, by or under the authority of the author, is sufficiently permanent or stable to permit it to be perceived ... for a period of more than transitory duration." Id. (emphasis added). For copyright protection, therefore, fixation for even a short period will suffice.

Thus, in Cartoon Network LP, LLLP v. CSC Holdings, Inc., 536 F.3d 121 (2d Cir. 2008), the Second Circuit held that copies of television programs were not capable of being perceived "for a period of more than transitory duration" when they existed in the defendant's data buffers for only 1.2 seconds. 536 F.3d at 129. However, the court suggested that a work would exist for "more than transitory duration" if it was embodied in the data buffers for "at least several minutes." Id. at 128. With no indication to the contrary, it is reasonable to assume that Congress intended to apply the same minimal fixation requirement to works of visual art under VARA. Cf. Buchel, 593 F.3d at 51 (applying section 101's fixation requirement to conclude that unfinished works are protected under VARA).

In sum, section 113(d) contemplates temporary works, section 106A(c) excludes only a narrow category of temporary works unrelated to this case, and analogous case law is consistent with the conclusion that temporary works are protected under VARA.

B. Works of Recognized Stature

As the Court stated in Cohen I, the district court's decision in Carter v. Helmsley–Spear, Inc., 861 F.Supp. 303 (S.D.N.Y. 1994) ("Carter I"), aff'd in part, vacated in part, rev'd in part, 71 F.3d 77 (2d Cir. 1995) ("Carter II") remains the seminal case interpreting the phrase "recognized stature"—which is not defined in VARA—to require "a two-tiered showing: (1) that the visual art in question has 'stature,' i.e. is viewed as meritorious, and (2) that this stature is 'recognized' by art experts, other members of the artistic community, or by some cross-section of society." 861 F.Supp. at 325.

The Second Circuit on appeal never had occasion to address the correctness of this formulation since, in reversing, it held that the work did not qualify for VARA protection because it was made for hire. Carter II, 71 F.3d at 85–89. But one circuit court did thereafter embrace and apply the district court's standard for evaluating whether a work of visual art is of "recognized stature."

As explained in Cohen I, the Seventh Circuit in Martin v. City of Indianapolis, 192 F.3d 608, 612 (7th Cir. 1999), noted that the Carter I test "may be more rigorous than Congress intended," id. at 612, but nonetheless affirmed the district court's grant of summary judgment and its award of damages for a sculpture that had been destroyed, under the Carter Itest utilized by the district court. In doing so, it noted that "plaintiff offered no evidence of experts or others by deposition, affidavit or interrogatories," but nonetheless established the work's recognized stature via "certain newspaper and magazine articles, and various letters, including a letter from an art gallery director and a letter to the editor of The Indianapolis News, all in support of the sculpture." Id.

The circuit court's decision in Martin appropriately recognizes, therefore, that expert testimony is not the sine qua non for establishing that a work of visual art is of recognized stature, and indeed the district court in Carter cautioned that plaintiffs need "not inevitably ... call expert witnesses to testify before the trier of fact." 861 F.Supp. at 325. This is in keeping with Congress's expansive recognition of the moral rights of attribution and integrity of the visual artist and the consequent need to create "a climate of artistic worth and honor that encourages the author in the arduous act of creation." Carter II, 71 F.3d at 83 (quoting H.R. Rep. No. 101–514, at 5). As the Second Circuit noted in Carter II, therefore, the courts "should use common sense and generally accepted standards of the artistic community in determining whether a particular work" is a work of visual art since "[a]rtists may work in a variety of media, and use any number of materials in creating their works." Id.

The same common sense should be utilized in assessing whether the visual work is of recognized stature since "[b]y setting the standard too high, courts risk the destruction of the unrecognized masterwork; by setting it too low, courts risk alienating those ... whose legitimate property interests are curtailed." Christopher J. Robinson, The "Recognized Stature" Standard in the Visual Artists Rights Act, 68 Fordham L. Rev 1935, 1968 (2000). Thus, as one court has held, even inferred recognition from a successful career can be considered in determining whether a visual artist's work has achieved recognized stature. See Lubner v. City of Los Angeles, 45 Cal. App. 4th 525, 531, 53 Cal.Rptr.2d 24 (1996).

In the present case, the Court need not dwell on the nuances of the appropriate evidentiary standard since the plaintiffs adduced such a plethora of exhibits and credible testimony, including the testimony of a highly regarded expert, that even under the most restrictive of evidentiary standards almost all of the plaintiffs' works easily qualify as works of recognized stature.

To begin, that Jonathan Cohen selected the handful of works from the thousands at 5Pointz for permanence and prominence on long-standing walls is powerful, and arguably singular, testament to their recognized stature. They were walls that spanned multiple stories, walls visible to millions on the passing trains; walls near the entrances. Many of these works had survived for years. As 5Pointz's curator, Cohen considered them outstanding examples of the aerosol craft. And as Wolkoff himself acknowledged, Cohen was qualified to assess the artistic merits of the works since "he had good taste in the artists that came there." Tr. at 2086:17. They were 5Pointz's jewels.

Wolkoff's faith in Cohen was not unwarranted. The multitude of artists painting on the walls marched to Cohen's beat. He called the shots and had the respect of his artistic community. That it was he who chose the works that are worthy of VARA protection in this litigation speaks volumes to their recognized stature.

But there is so much more. All of the plaintiffs had also achieved artistic recognition outside of 5Pointz. And in their Folios they collectively presented over a thousand exhibits in support of their claims that their works at 5Pointz had achieved recognized stature. The Folios covered the highlights of their careers, as well as evidence of the placement of their works at 5Pointz in films, television, newspaper articles, blogs, and online videos, in addition to social media buzz.

And plaintiffs' highly qualified expert, Vara, provided detailed findings as to the skill and craftsmanship of each of the 49 works, the importance of 5Pointz as a mecca for aerosol art, the academic and professional interest of the art world in the works, and her professional opinion that they were all of recognized stature. The Court finds Vara highly credible and affords great weight to her testimony, although, as explained infra, it finds that four of the 49 works do not qualify as having achieved recognized stature.

Defendants' expert Thompson's testimony had two fatal flaws: First, she used an unduly restrictive interpretation of recognized stature that was more akin to a masterpiece standard. Second, she relied heavily on her inability to find the works on social media or in academic databases; but, as effectively drawn out by plaintiffs' counsel on cross-examination, her search methodology was unduly restrictive and almost designed to avoid finding results. Tellingly, her searches did not even uncover many of plaintiffs' social media exhibits, demonstrating the weakness of her approach. Her final conclusion that none of the works had achieved recognized stature defies credibility. If not a single one of these works meet the recognized stature standard, it is hard to imagine works that would, short of a Caravaggio or Rembrandt.

1. Recognized Stature of Individual Artworks

The Court now turns to making the requisite individualized findings as to each of the 49 works:

a. The Long–Standing Works
The Court finds that 37 works on long-standing walls all achieved recognized stature by virtue of their selection by Cohen for these highly coveted spaces, as reinforced by the supportive evidence in the plaintiffs' Folios and Vara's compelling expert testimony as to their artistic merit and embrace by the artistic community. They are:

- Jonathan Cohen's Eleanor RIP, 7–Angle Time Lapse, Patience, Character, Clown with Bulbs, Meres Outdoor Wildstyle, and Inside Wildstyle
- Sandra Fabara's Green Mother Earth
- Luis Lamboy's Blue Jay Wall, Inside 4th Floor, World Traveler, Logo for Clothing Brand aka Monopoly Man, and Electric Fish
- Esteban Del Valle's Beauty and the Beast
- Christian Cortes's Skulls Cluster, Jackson Avenue Skulls, Up High Blue Skulls, and Up High Orange Skulls
- Carlos Game's Geisha, Marilyn, Red, Denim Girl, and Black and White 5Pointz Girl
- James Rocco's Bull Face, Lord Paz, and Face on Jackson
- Steven Lew's Crazy Monsters
- Nicholai Khan's Dos Equis Man
- James Cochran's Subway Rider
- Luis Gomez's Inside King Kong
- Richard Miller's Monster I
- Jonathan Cohen and Maria Castillo's Love Girl and Burner
- Jonathan Cohen and Akiko Miyakami's Underwater Fantasy
- William Tramontozzi, Jr. and James Rocco's Jimi Hendrix Tribute
- Akiko Miyakami and Carlos Game's Japanese Fantasy
- Bienbenido Guerra and Carlo Nieva's Return of New York
- Jonathan Cohen, Luis Lamboy, and Thomas Lucero's Angry Orchard

b. Other Works

Ten works on the walls were of recent origin; two were not on walls at all. For these 12 works, the Court "adopt[s] in whole" the jurors' findings. Ragin, 6 F.3d at 907. As representatives of the community and a "cross-section of society," Carter, 861 F.Supp. at 325, their input as an advisory jury was of value to the Court, "particularly ... in cases [such as this one] involving community-based standards." NAACP v. Acusport Corp., 226 F.Supp.2d at 398.

The jury found recognized stature for Rodrigo Henter de Rezende's Fighting Tree, Thomas Lucero's Black Creature, Akiko Miyakami's Manga Koi, Francisco Fernandez's Dream of Oil, Nicholai Khan's Orange Clockwork, Kenji Takabayashi's Starry Night, Richard Miller's Monster II, and Jonathan Cohen and Akiko Miyakami's Save 5Pointz. These eight works garnered third party attention, social media presence, and/or promises from Cohen that they would be long-standing.

The jury did not find recognized stature for Jonathan Cohen's Drunken Bulbs, Akiko Miyakami's Japanese Irish Girl, Carlos Game's Faces on Hut, and Jonathan Cohen and Rodrigo Henter de Rezende's Halloween Pumpkins. Drunken Bulbs and Japanese Irish Girl were gifts to the Shannon Pot Bar. They were not part of the curated 5Pointz collection. Furthermore, neither attracted significant third-party attention or social media buzz during their short life spans, Faces on Hut was not on a 5Pointz wall; it was on a tin shack near the loading dock. As its creator, Carlos Game testified: "[N]obody wanted to paint on it because it was a tin shack, you know, and it was rusted out...." Tr. at 794:12–13. Game also did not adduce any social media coverage or commentary regarding the work. Halloween Pumpkins was created in very late October 2013, less than a month before the whitewash, and did not achieve any third party recognition. Moreover, because it was Halloween-themed, it was unlikely to have survived the holiday season. In sum, the Court finds 45 of the 49 works achieved recognized stature. Drunken Bulbs, Japanese Irish Girl, Faces on Hut, and Halloween Pumpkins did not.

C. Mutilation and Prejudice to Honor or Reputation

As noted, even if a work is not of "recognized stature," VARA also protects works from "intentional distortion, mutilation, or other modification ... [that] would be prejudicial to [the artist's] honor or reputation." 17 U.S.C. section 106A(a)(3)(A). "[I]n determining whether 'intentional distortion, mutilation, or modification' of [a] Work would be 'prejudicial to [plaintiffs'] honor or reputation,' [a court should] consider whether such alteration would cause injury or damage to plaintiffs' good name, public esteem, or reputation in the artistic community." Carter I, 861 F.Supp. at 323.

This concept is inherently murky. Carter I held that an artist's honor or reputation may be harmed if the artwork "present[ed] to viewers an artistic vision materially different from that intended by [the artist]." Id. In Massachusetts Museum of Contemporary Art Foundation, Inc. v. Buchel, 593 F.3d 38 (1st Cir. 2010), the circuit court held that changes made to an unfinished art installation by a museum against the artist's wishes were sufficient to raise a question of fact as to whether the artist's honor or reputation were injured. The court focused on evidence that newspapers covering the exhibit after the changes had a negative opinion of the altered work.

Here, the question is academic in respect to the 45 works of recognized stature since the Court is not awarding any actual damages, as explained infra, and only one statutory damages award may be awarded per artwork "for all infringements involved in the action." 17 U.S.C. section 504(c)(1). Thus, whether defendants are additionally liable under this second prong is not of any practical consequence.

Of the remaining four, Japanese Irish Girl was destroyed and therefore not "distorted, mutilated, or otherwise modified." Faces on Hut was not destroyed until the demolition of the building and apparently survived the whitewash. Therefore, it too was not "distorted, mutilated, or otherwise modified."

Drunken Bulbs was only partially whitewashed; the outlines of the bulbs are dimly visible underneath the white paint. However, these vague outlines are unrecognizable as Cohen's original work. Nobody looking at the work would know that it was his. Therefore, the Court holds this distortion did not prejudice his honor or reputation.

Halloween Pumpkins was almost entirely covered in black paint, but Cohen's "wild style" contribution to the painting was apparently left untouched. However, Cohen testified that he was able to recover this portion of the work, and once the piece was removed, the final result was a black wall; the original artwork was not visible at all under the black paint, except for one purple cloud at the top of the wall, a minor detail in the painting. Therefore, the Court holds this distortion also did not prejudice the artists' honor or reputation.

Having determined that the defendants have violated plaintiffs' rights by intentionally destroying their works of "recognized stature," the Court now turns to damages.

V

A. Actual Damages

As for actual damages, the parties presented dueling experts as to the valuation of the destroyed works. Plaintiffs' expert, Elizabeth Littlejohn, testified that the works were worth from $50,000 to $80,000 per artwork. She arrived at this number through a complicated formula that began with the sale price of a Banksy piece and awarded each artwork a percentage of that value based on the artist's reputation, the merit of the work, and other factors.

The Court finds this methodology flawed. First, it does not account for the removal costs of the works, which plaintiffs' own removal expert, Alden, testified could run in the hundreds of thousands of dollars. Second, there is no evidence that these artists have ever achieved a fraction of Banksy's sales history; most testified that they had never sold a work for more than a

few thousand dollars. Third, Littlejohn's method did not account for the unique problems in selling artwork that is the size of a wall of a building.
The Court finds defendants' appraisal expert, Christopher Gaillard, credible. Gaillard testified that because of the unique challenges and costs of selling those artworks at 5Pointz which were the size of a building wall, they did not have a provable market value. The Court agrees and holds that plaintiffs failed to establish a reliable market value for their works.
Therefore, the Court does not award actual damages.

B. Statutory Damages

The Copyright Act affords the trial court "wide discretion ... in setting the amount of statutory damages." Fitzgerald Pub. Co., Inc. v. Baylor Pub. Co., Inc., 807 F.2d 1110, 1116 (2d Cir. 1986). Statutory damages are "not fixed or readily calculable from a fixed formula." Feltner v. Columbia Pictures Television, Inc., 523 U.S. 340, 352–53, 118 S.Ct. 1279, 140 L.Ed.2d 438 (1998) (citation omitted). "Even for uninjurious and unprofitable invasions of copyright the court may, if it deems it just, impose a liability within statutory limits to sanction and vindicate the statutory policy." F.W. Woolworth Co. v. Contemporary Arts, 344 U.S. 228, 233, 73 S.Ct. 222, 97 L.Ed. 276 (1952). There need not be a correlation between statutory damages and actual damages. Psihoyos v. John Wiley & Sons, Inc., 748 F.3d 120, 127 (2d Cir. 2014). "To suggest otherwise is to ignore the various other factors a court may consider and the purposes of statutory damages in the willful infringement context." Id. "Statutory damages exist in part because of the difficulties in proving—and providing compensation for—actual harm in copyright infringement actions." Lowry's Reports, Inc. v. Legg Mason, Inc., 302 F.Supp.2d 455, 460 (D. Md. 2004).

As such, statutory damages are particularly appropriate "when no actual damages are proven or they are difficult to calculate." Warner Bros. Inc. v. Dae Rim Trading, Inc., 877 F.2d 1120, 1126 (2d Cir. 1989). They are "not meant to be merely compensatory or restitutionary. The statutory award is also meant 'to discourage wrongful conduct.' " Yurman Design, Inc. v. PAJ, Inc., 262 F.3d 101, 113 (2d Cir. 2001) (rejecting defendant's argument that statutory damages award should be overturned because it "bears little relationship" to actual damages) (citation omitted).

As previously explained, the factfinder may award between $750 and $30,000 per work, unless the infringement was committed willfully; if so, the award may be as high as $150,000 per work. Review of a statutory damages award made after a finding of willfulness "is even more deferential than abuse of discretion." Superior Form Builders, Inc. v. Dan Chase Taxidermy Supply Co., Inc., 74 F.3d 488, 496 (4th Cir. 1996) (citing Douglas v. Cunningham, 294 U.S. 207, 210, 55 S.Ct. 365, 79 L.Ed. 862 (1935)). "Within [the statutory] limitations the court's discretion and sense of justice are controlling...." D.C. Comics Inc. v. Mini Gift Shop, 912 F.2d 29, 34 (2d Cir. 1990) (quoting L.A. Westermann v. Dispatch Printing Co., 249 U.S. 100, 106, 39 S.Ct. 194, 63 L.Ed. 499 (1919)).

1. Willfulness

"A copyright holder seeking to prove that a copier's infringement was willful must show that the infringer 'had knowledge that its conduct represented infringement or ... recklessly disregarded the possibility.' " Bryant v. Media Right Prods., 603 F.3d 135, 143 (2d Cir. 2010) (quoting Twin Peaks Prods., Inc. v. Publ'ns Int'l, Ltd., 996 F.2d 1366, 1382 (2d Cir. 1993)). "This knowledge may be 'actual or constructive.' " N.A.S. Import, Corp. v. Chenson Enters., Inc., 968 F.2d 250, 252 (2d Cir. 1992). "In other words, it need not be proven directly but may be inferred from the defendant's conduct." Id.

The jury found that in each case Wolkoff acted willfully. The Court could not agree more. Wolkoff knew from the moment the lawsuit was initiated that the artists were pressing their VARA claims. He admitted as much at trial:

> Q: And you were aware that the artists were trying to apply under the Visual Artists Rights Act?
> A: Yes.
> ...
> THE COURT: You heard about VARA at that time?
> A: Yes.
> THE COURT: You have a generalized view—
> A: At that time, yes.
> ...
> Q: And you had hired Mr. Ebert's law firm at the time; correct?
> A: Yes.
> Q: You had a general counsel—an in-house lawyer advising you on legal matters; correct?
> A: Yes.
> Tr. at 2016:24–2017:22.

As previously explained, under VARA, Wolkoff could have given the plaintiffs 90 days' notice to allow them the opportunity to salvage their works. And indeed, plaintiffs' expert conservator, Alden, convincingly testified that curation techniques had evolved to the point where removal of works of art from the wall of a building was feasible and had been done. As an example, she referenced the Berlin Wall, from which hundreds of works of graffiti on the wall have been preserved and sold, auctioned, or given as gifts, including five works which were successfully transported to New York City. Alden also testified that she had personally successfully removed a mural from a building.

And in respect to the plaintiffs' works at 5Pointz, Alden explained that many could have been totally or partially removed by the artists, at little cost, because the works were on "siding or plywood or sheetrock" or they "incorporated doors or windows from the building [which] could have been easily removed," Tr. at 1971:23–1972:4; and many others could be removed by a conservator and contractors. See Exhibit 1270 (identifying 12 "Works for Which Artists' Removal

Was Possible"; 9 "Works Which Artists Were Able to Partially Remove," and 28 "Works Which Could Only Have Been Removed by Conservator and Contractors"). But Wolkoff could care less. As he callously testified:

> I decided—I alone decided to hire people to whitewash[ ] it in one shot instead of waiting for three months and them going to do something irrational again and getting arrested. I will go and end it and whitewash it. I decided to do that. It was pretty much a spur-of-the-moment thing.Tr. at 2059:1–6 (emphasis added).

Wolkoff's reference to the artists doing "something irrational again and getting arrested" is fanciful and unfounded. Plainly, the evidence does not support the notion that he cared much for what was best for the artists. After the whitewash, he refused to let them onto his property to recover what had survived and even attempted to have them arrested when they tried to do so.

And his claim that he was worried that the plaintiffs may do something reckless and illegal is also belied by the evidence. The plaintiffs operated within the law in attempting to protect their works: They sought legal advice, filed a claim with the Landmark Preservation Commission, sought to generate public pressure to preserve the site, raised money, and filed this lawsuit. Wolkoff's only justification for his concern that the plaintiffs may attempt to break the law to preserve their work is that he heard nonspecific "rumblings." Id. at 2042:5. But he could not identify any particular source of the rumblings, nor had he ever personally had a problem with the artists:

> Q: So this information that you received that the artists could be emotional is from someone you cannot identify; correct?
> A: Yes.
> Q: The artists were never violent; correct?
> A: Correct.
> Q: They always followed the law when then were on your property; correct?
> A: Yes.
> Q: You have never had any problems with the artists; right?
> A: Absolutely correct.
> Tr. at 2047:13–23.

As Cohen confirmed: "I followed the rules from day one. I went by my lawyer and he did not." Id. at 1464:2–3. Wolkoff's recalcitrant behavior was consistent with the manner by which he testified in court. He was bent on doing it his way, and just as he ignored the artists' rights he also ignored the many efforts the Court painstakingly made to try to have him responsively answer the questions posed to him.

From his testimony, the only logical inference that the Court could draw from Wolkoff's precipitous conduct as soon as the Court denied the artists' preliminary injunction application

was that it was an act of pure pique and revenge for the nerve of the plaintiffs to sue to attempt to prevent the destruction of their art. This was the epitome of willfulness.
It remains for the Court to fix the amount of statutory damages.

2. The Statutory Factors

"When determining the amount of statutory damages to award for copyright infringement, courts consider: (1) the infringer's state of mind; (2) the expenses saved, and profits earned, by the infringer; (3) the revenue lost by the copyright holder; (4) the deterrent effect on the infringer and third parties; (5) the infringer's cooperation in providing evidence concerning the value of the infringing material; and (6) the conduct and attitude of the parties." Bryant, 603 F.3d at 144.21 Wolkoff rings the bell on each relevant factor.

a. The Infringer's State of Mind

Because Wolkoff acted willfully in destroying the works of art, this factor weighs in favor of a high statutory damages award. As noted, Wolkoff's two alleged justifications for the whitewash—that it would be better for the plaintiffs to lose their works quickly, and that he was concerned the plaintiffs might do something reckless and illegal in an attempt to save the works—are implausible.

The whitewash did not end the conflict in one go; the effects lingered for almost a year. The sloppy, half-hearted nature of the whitewashing left the works easily visible under thin layers of cheap, white paint, reminding the plaintiffs on a daily basis what had happened. The mutilated works were visible by millions of people on the passing 7 train. One plaintiff, Miyakami, said that upon seeing her characters mutilated in that manner, it "felt like [she] was raped." Tr. at 1306:24–25. It is simply untenable that a rational person could view the whitewashing as being in the best interest of the artists.

b. The Expenses Saved, and Profits Earned, by the Infringer
This factor is not a clean fit for VARA since, unlike a traditional copyright infringement case, Wolkoff did not sell the plaintiffs' art; hence, there were no direct profits. However, he indirectly profited when the value of the site increased from $40 million to $200 million as soon as the variance was obtained. Destroying 5Pointz allowed Wolkoff to realize this gain. He also charged licensing fees to film at the site that netted him hundreds of thousands of dollars. Because Wolkoff realized significant profits by violating VARA, this factor cuts in favor of a high statutory damages award.

c. Revenue Lost by the Copyright Holder

While the plaintiffs were never able to place a dollar figure on how the whitewash of 5Pointz impacted their careers, it often had a negative effect. As plaintiff Takabayashi testified: "I would actually have clients ... come by and observe the work to get an idea of what they would be getting if I was going to execute a mural on their property.... There were possibilities—there was business that I probably lost because of the fact that the artwork was eliminated." Tr. at 315:23–316:4. And plaintiff Del Valle testified: "It definitely took away a lot of opportunities that I would have had. I was consistently getting contacted about opportunities ... all coming from me building my career from [5Pointz]." Id. at 131:15–22. Furthermore, as Cohen testified, the salvageable artwork at 5Pointz "could have adorned a museum, a full wing of a museum.... I don't think you guys really get a full idea of the picture of this building and its property.... It was eight stories tall. We could have filled a wing, if not more, of a museum." Id. at 1466:18–23.

The value of 5Pointz to the artists' careers was significant, and its loss, though difficult to quantify, precluded future opportunities and acclaim. Therefore, this factor also supports a significant statutory damages award.

d. The Deterrent Effect on the Infringer and Third Parties

This is perhaps the most important factor in this case. Without a significant statutory damages award, the preservative goals of VARA cannot be met. If potential infringers believe that they can violate VARA at will and escape liability because plaintiffs are not able to provide a reliable financial valuation for their works, VARA will have no teeth. It will simply be cost-effective for infringers to violate the statute. This would not further its preservative goals.

Wolkoff has been singularly unrepentant. He was given multiple opportunities to admit the whitewashing was a mistake, show remorse, or suggest he would do things differently if he had another chance. He denied them all:

> Q: Let me ask you a hypothetical question. Let's go back in time.
> A: Yes.
> Q: Would you have done it again?
> A: Yes.
> Tr. 2052:25–2053:4.
> A: But that was the decision I made. I would make the same decision today if that happened today.
> Id. at 2056:2–3.

Thus, Wolkoff remains undeterred, and unrepentant that his thoughtless act violated the law and had a devastating impact on people he claims he was trying to help. This factor could not cut more strongly in favor of a high statutory damages award.

e. The Conduct and Attitude of the Parties

The Court has discussed at length the problematic conduct of Wolkoff during the whitewashing and on the witness stand. Needless to say, he has not helped his case. On the other hand, the plaintiffs have conducted themselves with dignity, maturity, respect, and at all times within the law. Therefore, this factor also cuts heavily in favor of a high statutory damages award.

3. The Statutory Damages Award

Collectively, all five relevant factors support the maximum award of statutory damages. Therefore, the Court awards $150,000 for each of the 45 works, for a total statutory damages award of $6,750,000.

If not for Wolkoff's insolence, these damages would not have been assessed. If he did not destroy 5Pointz until he received his permits and demolished it 10 months later, the Court would not have found that he had acted willfully. Given the degree of difficulty in proving actual damages, a modest amount of statutory damages would probably have been more in order.

The shame of it all is that since 5Pointz was a prominent tourist attraction the public would undoubtedly have thronged to say its goodbyes during those 10 months and gaze at the formidable works of aerosol art for the last time. It would have been a wonderful tribute for the artists that they richly deserved.

CONCLUSION

Judgment will be entered for each individual plaintiff in the following amounts:

Artist	**Total Award**
Jonathan Cohen	$1,325,000.00
Sandra Fabara	$150,000.00
Luis Lamboy	$800,000.00
Estaban Del Valle	$150,000.00
Rodrigo Henter de Rezende	$150,000.00
Thomas Lucero	$200,000.00
Akiko Miyakami	$375,000.00
Christian Cortes	$600,000.00
Carlos Game	$825,000.00
James Rocco	$525,000.00
Steven Lew	$150,000.00
Francisco Fernandez	$150,000.00
Nicholai Khan	$300,000.00
James Cochran	$150,000.00
Luis Gomez	$150,000.00
Richard Miller	$300,000.00
Kenji Takabayashi	$150,000.00
Maria Castillo	$75,000.00
William Tramontozzi	$75,000.00
Carlo Nieva	$75,000.00
Bienbenido Guerra	$75,000.00
Total	$6,750,000.00

8: Fair Use

Fair use is a complicated, important, and a particular way of thinking. We will be looking at fair use from a number of angles. But first, let's remember that fair use only applies to works that are under copyright.

We're going to look at fair use from a number of angles:

- History of Fair Use
- Before the 1976 Copyright Act
- By Category
- Through Best Practices and Strategies

Fair use is a concept, but it is also a tool for making artist and business decisions, both that have serious impact. The reliance is real. So, can we create a framework that helps us understand the likelihood of success?

Fair use encompasses many areas: from technology to political commentary. How stable is fair use, and can we create a decision tree that helps us predict its outcome? \

Note: because of the sheer amount of cases regarding fair use, we will not be including them in the text, but you may be assigned or asked to read them independently. This chapter is meant to give an overview of the issues of fair use as we work through them as a class.

The Beginning of fair Use: Folsom v. Marsh

In 1841, Justice Storey penned a decision in the United States Circuit Court for the District of Massachusetts. 9 F. Sas. 342 (C.C.D. Mass. 1841). This is the origin point of what would become fair use, and ironically, the case involves the biography of President George Washington.

Folsom v. Marsh, 9 F. Sas. 342 (C.C.D. Mass. 1841)

The U.S. Supreme Court Cases

The U.S. Supreme Court has weighed in on fair use four times. Twice fair use was found, and in the other two cases, it was not.

- **Campbell v. Acuff-Rose Music, Inc., 510 U.S. 569 (1994)**
- **Stewart v. Abend, 495 U.S. 207 (1990)**
- **Harper & Row Publishers, Inc. v. Nation Enters., 471 U.S. 539 (1985)**
- **Sony Corp. of Am. v. Universal City Studios, Inc., 464 U.S. 417 (1984)**

Let's look at these to understand our foundation. What do each of these cases tell us? Note: fair use was defined by the U.S. Supreme Court within a ten year period. Also, remember that the 1976 Copyright Act, which incorporated fair use, was enacted in 1978. So, within six years, the U.S. Supreme Court was weighing in.

What did we learn from the Supreme Court about fair use?

Modern Cases

Let's start to see how fair use has changed. Two cases are useful, and then we will look at the Fair Use Index, and the most recent 9th circuit case related to Dr. Suess.

The Prince Dancing Baby Case

Traditionally, fair use came after a court found infringement, as a defense to the behavior. But in the new age of the Internet, *Lenz v. Universal Music Corp.*, 801 F.3d 1126 (2015), often referred to as the Prince Dancing Baby case, changed all that. Now copyright holders are required, in some instances like filing a notice-and-takedown with an Internet service provider (think YouTube, Facebook, etc.) to do an analysis to confirm that there would be no exceptions or potential defenses to the infringement. That happened because of this cute baby in the picture above.

The dancing baby who caused all the fuss.

Stephanie Lenz took a 29-second video of her toddler in a walker, who is bouncing and walking to Prince's "Let's Go Crazy." It's heard faintly in the background. Universal, who owned the rights to the song, asked YouTube to take down the video through Section 512 notice-and-takedown procedures. Stephanie fought back, turning to the Electronic Frontier Foundation, a non-profit that helps people with copyright issues. In the end, the Appeals court ruled that copyright holders have to take into consideration whether there are any fair uses before filing a notice and takedown of something online. Meaning, that it was OK for Stephanie to post the video of the baby with the incidental Prince music in the background. The court found the use to be *de minimis*. This raises the bar for copyright holders filing notice-and-takedown complaints on platforms like Pinterest, Instagram, Facebook, and of course YouTube against other parties' using their copyrighted works, and brings more balance to the system.

The burden shifted a bit with fair use. And fair use, some believe, became more than a defense. And finally, we are introduced to Section 512, which regulates much of our life on platforms and Internet Service Providers.

The Impact of the Mattel Case

One other key element is Kosinzski's *Barble Girl* case, Mattel v. MCA Records, 296 F.3d 894 (9th Cir. 2002).

The case, written by Judge Kozinski, starts out with this sentence: "If this were a sci-fi melodrama, it might be called Speech-Zilla meets Trademark Kong." Konzinski is known for his *creative* writing in opinions. We're going to work our way through this case, because it touches upon a lot of the key elements for artists using other people's/company's trademarks.

Kozinski begins with Barbie, the doll, describing her origins in the 1950s as an adult collector's item, and then turning into the mega toy that she is. "Barbie has been labeled both the ideal American woman and a bimbo...She remains a symbol of American girlhood, a public figure who graces the aisles of toy stores throughout the country and beyond. With Barbie, Mattel created not just a toy, but a cultural icon."

Aqua is a Danish band that "as yet, only dreamed of attaining Barbie-like status." (And who says court cases are dry and boring!). Aqua created a song called "Barbie Girl" on their album *Aquarium*. The song is about Barbie's life, with the band members acting out the parts of Ken and (high-pitched singing) Barbie. The song made it to the Top 40 list (and anyone who was a teenager at that time can probably still sing the lyrics!). Mattel sued in 2002.[7]

Kosinski gets down to analyzing the case. "A trademark is a word, phrase, or symbol that is used to identify a manufacturer or sponsor of a good or the provider of a service," explains the Judge. The question is how the First Amendment interacts with the property right awarded by the United States Patent and Trademark Office (USPTO) to the trademark holder. Some marks become part of our language, like "the Rolls Royce of its class," or "What else is a quick fix, but a Band Aid?" We use the mark to express concepts; they have become part of our vocabulary. They are not, in this case, being used as a source identifier, but we recognize the qualities of the mark to describe something else. "Simply put, the trademark owner does not have the right to control public discourse whenever the public imbues his mark with meaning beyond its source-identifying function." Kozinski then turns back to the Mattel case.

Here, Aqua used Mattel's mark, both as the title of the song, and as the subject of the song. "The song pokes fun at Barbie and the values that Aqua contends she represents.... The song does not rely on the Barbie mark to poke fun at another subject but targets Barbie herself." This sounds a lot like the copyright case, *Campbell v. Acuff-Rose,* right? He cites this and other cases.

Kozinski relied upon the *Rogers* case. He explains "The Second Circuit has held that "in general [the Trademark Act] should be construed to apply to artistic works only when the public interest in avoiding consumer confusion outweighs the public interest in free expression." Rogers v. Grimaldi, 875 F.2d 994, 999. This phrase became known as the *Rogers* test. Konzinski would apply it with "Barbie Girl. Let's take a look at *Rogers*.

Ginger Rogers sued over Federico Fellini's film *Ginger and Fred* for using her name in the title, and believed the film gave a false impression that she had endorsed the film; therefore, violated her right of publicity, and defamed her by presenting her in a negative light. The film was about "two Italian cabaret performers who made a living by imitating Ginger Rogers and Fred Astaire." Rogers was not happy. She believed that people would see the title and subject matter of the film as an endorsement from her. "This appeal presents a conflict between Rogers' right to protect her celebrated name and the right of others to express themselves freely in their own artistic work. Specifically, we must decide whether Rogers can prevent the use of the title Ginger and Fred for a fictional movie that only obliquely relates to Rogers and Astaire."

[7] You can listen to and see the video on YouTube here: https://www.youtube.com/watch?v=ZyhrYis509A {last accessed 1/11/2020}.

Kozinski explains the result. "At first glance, Rogers certainly had a point. Ginger was her name, and Fred was her dancing partner. If a pair of dancing shoes had been labeled Ginger and Fred, a dancer might have suspected that Rogers was associated with the shoes (or at least one of them), just as Michael Jordan has endorsed Nike sneakers that claim to make you fly through the air. But Ginger and Fred was not a brand of shoe; it was the title of a movie...and [should] be treated differently."

Titles communicate a message, but rarely identify the publisher or producer. Moreover, when an artist uses a title, very rarely would the public think that the artist is connected to the brand. He gives the example that when you see a *painting* of Campbell soup can, "we're unlikely to believe that Campbell's has branched into the art business. Nor, upon hearing Janis Joplin croon 'Oh Lord, won't you buy me a Mercedes-Benz?," would we suspect that she and the carmaker had entered into a joint venture."

The *Rogers* case found that "literary titles do not violate the [Trademark Act] 'unless the title had no artistic relevance to the underlying work whatsoever, or if it has some artistic relevance, unless the title explicitly misleads as to the source or the content of the work." (*Rogers* at 999, cited by *Mattel). Rogers* became known for a two-part test for analyzing whether someone's artistic use of a trademark work was infringing.

1. Is the use relevant to the underlying work?
2. Does the use explicitly mislead as to the source of the work?

The *Rogers* case was quickly adopted and expanded.

Kozinski applied the *Rogers* case. Aqua's use of the title "Barbie" was not trademark infringement. The use of the word "Barbie" in the title was relevant to the underlying work, and the song does not explicitly mislead as to the source of the work. After the Mattel case, another Barbie case took up the issue: Mattel v. Walking Mountain Productions (353 F.3d 792 (9th Cir. 2003)). Artist Tom Forsythe uses nude Barbies in different cooking positions: "Barbies in a Blender", "Enchilada Barbie", "Fondue a la Barbie", etc. The court applied the *Rogers* test, finding the use of the mark was a parody, and that the mark was not explicitly misleading. (Forsythe would win a $1.8 million award against Mattel).

The Fair Use Index

The U.S. Copyright Office has compiled a fair use index of a summary of nearly every

copyright case from the beginning. Fair use has been used in all kinds of instances -- from news reporting, to the Google book scanning project to artists' use of others' works. We will be looking at this more in depth and developing a greater understanding of the common principles and distinctions among categories. How has fair use evolved over time? Can we understand basic principles? And can we predict how it will be used now that the CASE Act has become law?
The link to the U.S. Copyright Office Fair Use Index:
https://www.copyright.gov/fair-use/.

The latest case

Where does the latest fair use case fit within the structure of fair use? Could you have predicted the outcome?

Dr. Seuss Enterprises v. ComicMix, (9th Cir, December 18, 2020)

McKEOWN, Circuit Judge:

In Dr. Seuss's classic book, *Oh, the Places You'll Go!* (*Go!*), the narrator counsels the protagonist on a path of exploration and discovery. The book closes with this note of caution:

> I'm sorry to say so
> But, sadly it's true
> That Bang-ups
> And Hang-ups
> Can happen to you.

If he were alive today, Dr. Seuss might have gone on to say that **"mash-ups can happen to you."**

Enter *Oh, the Places You'll Boldly Go!* (*Boldly*). Authored by *Star Trek* episodes author David Gerrold, illustrated by Ty Templeton, and edited by fellow Trekkie Glenn Hauman (collectively, ComicMix), *Boldly* is a mash up that borrows liberally—graphically and otherwise—from *Go!* and other works by Dr. Seuss, and that uses Captain Kirk and his spaceship *Enterprise* to tell readers that "life is an adventure but it will be tough." The creators thought their *Star Trek* primer would be "pretty well protected by parody," but acknowledged that "people in black robes" may disagree. Indeed, we do.

The question we consider is whether *Boldly*'s use of Dr. Seuss's copyrighted works is fair use and thus not an infringement of copyright. Because all of the fair use factors \favor Dr. Seuss, we reverse the district court's summary judgment in favor of ComicMix on the copyright infringement claim. We affirm, however, the Rule 12(c) dismissal and the grant of summary judgment in favor of ComicMix on the trademark claim.

BACKGROUND

Go! was the final book written by the late Theodor S. Geisel, better known by his pseudonym, "Dr. Seuss." Many of the dozens of books Dr. Seuss authored and illustrated were wildly popular when they were published and have remained so throughout the decades. "Dr. Seuss" was the top licensed book brand of 2017. Notably, *Go!* has been "the **number-one book on *The New York Times* Best Sellers list"** "[e]very year during graduation season." The other Dr. Seuss works that are at issue—*How the Grinch Stole Christmas!* (*Grinch*) and *The Sneetches and Other Stories* (*Sneetches*)—also remain well-recognized. For simplicity, we refer to the relevant Dr. Seuss works collectively as *Go!*.

Today, **Dr. Seuss Enterprises, L.P.** (Seuss) owns the intellectual property in Dr. Seuss's works, including the copyrights in his books and the trademarks in his brand. Seuss markets the books to children and adults. Seuss also publishes reissues of the books, such as anniversary editions. And Seuss licenses and oversees the creation of new works under the Dr. Seuss brand. Seuss carefully vets the many licensing requests it receives and works closely with the licensees and collaborators to produce works based on Dr. Seuss's books.

The myriad licensed works that proliferate in the market include fine art, toys, video games, stage productions, motion pictures, and books that incorporate elements of Dr. Seuss's iconic works. *Go!* alone is the basis for several authorized derivative works such as the following books: *Oh, the Things You Can Do that Are Good for You!*; *Oh, the Places I'll Go! By ME, Myself*; *Oh, Baby, the Places You'll Go!*; and *Oh, the Places I've Been! A Journal*. Seuss has also entered into various collaborations to create new works that target the audiences of Seuss and its collaborators. In one well-known collaboration, The Jim Henson Company and Seuss produced a television and book series called *The Wubbulous World of Dr. Seuss*, featuring "muppetized" Dr. Seuss characters.

***Boldly* is not a licensed work of Seuss.** Nor is it a collaboration or an otherwise authorized work. Nevertheless, in May 2016, David Gerrold (author of *Star Trek* episodes) and Glenn Hauman (Vice President of the publishing company ComicMix LLC) decided to send the *Enterprise* crew to a new literary world. Gerrold and Hauman agreed to create a "Star Trek Primer"—a mash-up of *Star Trek* and another well-known primer. A mash-up is "something created by combining elements from two or more sources," such as "a movie or video having characters or situations from other sources." *Mash-up*, Merriam-Webster Dictionary, https://www.merriam webster.com/dictionary/mash-up.

After considering *Pat the Bunny* and other primers, Gerrold and Hauman decided to use *Go!* and to place the *Enterprise* crew in a colorful Seussian landscape full of wacky arches, mazes, and creatures—a world that is familiar to Dr. Seuss readers but a strange new planet for Captain Kirk's team. They hired Ty Templeton, an experienced illustrator. ComicMix purposely crafted *Boldly* so that the title, the story, and the illustrations "evoke" *Go!*. ComicMix planned to publish and sell *Boldly*. An ecommerce retailer, ThinkGeek, agreed to handle the distribution and merchandizing of *Boldly*, and placed a conditional order for 5,000 copies. In August 2016, ComicMix started a successful crowdsourcing campaign on **Kickstarter to pay for production and other costs, eventually raising close to $30,000.** The campaign also drew the attention of an editor at Andrews McMeel Publishing, who proposed doing a direct sale publication of *Boldly*.

The fundraising effort raised more than eyebrows when the Seuss organization became aware of *Boldly*. **In September and October of 2016, Seuss sent ComicMix a cease-and-desist letter and two follow-up letters.** ComicMix responded that *Boldly* was a fair use of *Go!*. Seuss also sent Kickstarter a takedown notice under the Digital Millennium Copyright Act; Kickstarter took down the campaign and blocked the pledged funds. ***Boldly* remains unpublished**.

Seuss filed suit against Hauman, Gerrold, Templeton, and ComicMix LLC in November 2016 for copyright infringement, trademark infringement, and unfair competition. The district court granted ComicMix's Rule 12(c) motion and dismissed Seuss's trademark infringement claim as it relates to the title of *Boldly*. The parties then filed cross-motions for summary judgment on the copyright claim, and ComicMix moved for summary judgment on the remainder of the trademark infringement claim. The district court granted ComicMix's summary judgment motion and denied Seuss's motion, holding that *Boldly* was a fair use of *Go!* and that the remainder of Seuss's trademark infringement claim failed.

ComicMix does not dispute that it tried to copy portions of *Go!* As accurately as possible. Templeton urged the team to "keep to [*Go!*'s] sentiment" that "life is an adventure but it WILL be tough and there WILL be setbacks, and you should not despair of them." As for the text of *Boldly*, Hauman created a side-by-side chart comparing the texts of *Go!* and *Boldly* in order to "match the structure of *Go!*." *Boldly* also closely mimics many illustrations in *Go!*, as a result of what ComicMix called "slavish[] copy[ing] from Seuss." In one instance, Templeton took "about seven hours" to copy a single illustration because he "painstakingly attempted to make" the illustration in *Boldly* "nearly identical" to its Seussian counterpart.

The issue in this appeal is not whether *Boldly* infringed *Go!*, but whether *Boldly!* was a fair use of *Go!*. Gerrold and Hauman thought they could either get a license or create a parody, and concluded that *Boldly* "come[s] down well on the side of parody" and does not infringe Seuss's copyright. Templeton agreed. Despite being "slightly concerned," ComicMix did not consult a lawyer or pursue the option of a license. This failure led to this lawsuit.

ANALYSIS

I. *Boldly* Does Not Make Fair Use of *Go!*

The fair use doctrine first took root in a case involving the biography of our first president. Justice Story asked whether copying the writings of President George Washington for a biography was "a justifiable use of the original materials, such as the law recognizes as no infringement of the copyright . . . ." *See Folsom v. Marsh*, 9 F. Cas. 342, 348 (C.C.D. Mass. 1841). Although fair use was not codified until 1976, American copyright law has always counterbalanced the exclusive rights of a copyright with a fair use backstop. Under the statute, "fair use of a copyrighted work . . . is not an infringement of copyright." 17 U.S.C. § 107. "The fair use defense permits courts to avoid rigid application of the copyright statute when, on occasion, it would stifle the very creativity which that law is designed to foster." *Dr. Seuss Enters., L.P. v. Penguin Books USA, Inc.*, 109 F.3d 1394, 1399 (9th Cir. 1997) (quotation marks and citation omitted).

The factors that determine fair use have changed little since Justice Story first announced them in *Folsom* and now are reflected in § 107 of the Copyright Act of 1976 as the following four non-exclusive factors:

> (1) the purpose and character of the use, including whether such use is of a commercial nature or is for nonprofit educational purposes;
>
> (2) the nature of the copyrighted work;
>
> (3) the amount and substantiality of the portion used in relation to the copyrighted work as a whole; and
>
> (4) the effect of the use upon the potential market for or value of the copyrighted work. 17 U.S.C. § 107(1)–(4); *accord Folsom*, 9 F. Cas. at 348.

Congress codified these factors without intending to disrupt "the common-law tradition of fair use adjudication." *Campbell v. Acuff-Rose Music, Inc.*, 510 U.S. 569, 577 (1994) (citing H.R. Rep. No. 94-1476, p. 66 (1976)). The fair use defense remains an "equitable rule of reason." *Sony Corp. of Am. v. Universal City Studios, Inc.*, 464 U.S. 417, 448 (1984) (quoting H.R. Rep. No. 94-1476, p. 65). Fair-use analysis, like the *Go!* protagonist's life journey, is "a Great Balancing Act." All four factors are "to be explored, and the results weighed together, in light of the purposes of copyright." *Campbell*, 510 U.S. at 578. The Supreme Court teaches that we should eschew "bright-line rules" and "categories of presumptively fair use," and instead engage in a "case-by-case analysis." *Id.* at 577, 584. As we have observed, fair use analysis can be elusive to the point of "approaching 'the metaphysics of the law, where the distinctions are . . . very subtle and refined, and, sometimes, almost evanescent.'" *Monge v. Maya Mags., Inc.*, 688 F.3d 1164, 1171 (9th Cir. 2012) (quoting *Folsom*, 9 F. Cas. at 344). Not so with this case. Because all of the statutory factors decisively weigh against ComicMix and no countervailing copyright principles counsel otherwise, we conclude that *Boldly* did not make fair use of *Go!*.

A. The Purpose and Character of *Boldly* Weigh Against Fair Use

The first statutory factor examines "the purpose and character of the use, including whether such use is of a commercial nature or is for nonprofit educational purposes." 17 U.S.C. § 107(1). This factor has taken on a heightened significance because it influences the lens through which we consider two other fair use factors. The third factor—the amount and substantiality of use—"will harken back" to the first factor. *See Campbell*, 510 U.S. at 586. And the fourth factor, relating to market harm, is influenced by whether the commercial use was transformative. *See Monge*, 688 F.3d at 1181.

Although a commercial use is no longer considered presumptively unfair, the nature of the work remains "one element of the first factor enquiry." *Campbell*, 510 U.S. at 584–85. **As explained below, *Boldly* is not transformative, and its indisputably commercial use of *Go!* counsels against fair use.** *See Penguin Books*, 109 F.3d at 1401 (commerciality "further cuts against the fair use defense" when there is "no effort to create a transformative work").

The term "transformative" does not appear in § 107, yet it permeates copyright analysis because in *Campbell*, the Court interpreted the "central purpose" of the first-factor inquiry as determining "whether and to what extent the new work is 'transformative.'" *Campbell*, 510 U.S. at 579. Transformative use of the original work can tip the first factor in favor of fair use.

A transformative work "adds something new, with a further purpose or different character, altering the first with new expression, meaning, or message." *Id.* On the other hand, a work that "merely supersedes the objects of the original creation" is not transformative. *Id.* (quotation marks omitted). While the analysis of the first fair use factor "may be guided by the examples given in the preamble to § 107," i.e., criticism, comment, news reporting, teaching, scholarship, and research, *id.* at 578–79, not even these works compel "a per se finding of fair use," *Monge*, 688 F.3d at 1173. Thus, we do not ask whether mash-ups can be fair use—they can be—but whether *Boldly* is a transformative work.

The purpose and character of a parody fits squarely into preamble examples—particularly "criticism" and "comment"—and has "an obvious claim" to transformative use. *Campbell*, 510 U.S. at 579. By definition, a parody must "use some elements of a prior author's composition to create a new one that, at least in part, comments on that author's works." *Id.* at 580. The need "to mimic an original to make its point" is the essence of parody. *Id.* at 580–81; *see Penguin Books*, 109 F.3d at 1400 (a parody must "conjure up" at least a part of "the object of [the] parody"). In short, a parody is a spoof, send-up, caricature, or comment on another work. A great example of a parody is the book ***The Wind Done Gone*, which parrots portions of *Gone with the Wind* to offer a critical take on the book.** *See Suntrust Bank v. Houghton Mifflin Co.*, 268 F.3d 1257, 1270–71 (11th Cir. 2001) ("It is hard to imagine" how a parody that attempts to "strip the romanticism" of slavery in *Gone with the Wind* can be made "without depending heavily upon copyrighted elements of that book."). On the other hand, if the commentary has no critical bearing on the substance or style of the original composition, which the alleged infringer merely uses to get attention or to avoid the drudgery in working up something fresh, the claim to fairness in borrowing from another's work diminishes accordingly (if it does not vanish), and other factors, like the extent of its commerciality, loom larger. *Campbell*, 510 U.S. at 580.

***Boldly* is not a parody.** ComicMix does not seriously contend that *Boldly* critiques or comments on *Go!*. Rather, it claims *Boldly* is a parody because it situated the "violent, sexual, sophisticated adult entertainment" of *Star Trek* "in the context of [Dr. Seuss]" to create a "funny" book. We considered and rejected this very claim in an appeal involving another well-known book by Dr. Seuss—*The Cat in the Hat* (*Cat*). The retelling of the O.J. Simpson double murder trial in the world of *Cat*—in a book titled *The Cat NOT in the Hat! A Parody by Dr. Juice* (*Not*)—was not a parody of *Cat*. *Penguin Books*, 109 F.3d at 1396, 1401. We explained that "broadly mimic[king] Dr. Seuss'[s] characteristic style" is not the same as "hold[ing] *his style* up to ridicule," and that without a critique of *Cat*, all *Not* did was "simply retell the Simpson tale" using the expressive elements of *Cat* "to get attention or maybe even to avoid the drudgery in working up something fresh." *Id.* at 1401 (quotation marks and citation omitted).

Boldly's claim to a parody fares no better. Although elements of *Go!* are featured prominently in *Boldly*, the juxtapositions of *Go!* and *Star Trek* elements do not "hold [*Seussian*] *style*" up to ridicule. *Id.* From the project's inception, **ComicMix wanted *Boldly* to be a *Star Trek* primer that "evoke[s]" rather than "ridicule[s]" *Go!*.** Similarly, *Boldly*'s use of the other Seuss works does not conjure up a critique of *Go!*. *Boldly*'s replacement of *Grinch*'s "'Whos from Who-ville' with the diverse crew and Kirk's 'lovers of every hue,'" the redrawing of "a *Sneetches* machine to signify the *Enterprise* transporter," and the rendering of "the 'lonely games' played in *Go!*" as a "contemplative chess match between two Spocks" were all used to tell the story of the *Enterprise* crew's adventures, not to make a point about *Go!*. Lacking "critical bearing on the substance or style of" *Go!*, *Boldly* cannot be characterized as a parody. *Campbell*, 510 U.S. at 580.

We also reject as "completely unconvincing" ComicMix's "post-hoc characterization of the work" as criticizing the theme of banal narcissism in *Go!*. *Penguin Books*, 109 F.3d at 1403; *see also Castle Rock Ent., Inc. v. Carol Publ'g Grp., Inc.*, 150 F.3d 132, 142 (2d Cir. 1998) (ignoring similar "post hoc rationalizations"). The effort to treat *Boldly* as lampooning *Go!* or mocking the purported self-importance of its characters falls flat.

Nor is *Boldly* otherwise transformative. ComicMix argues that even if *Boldly* is not a parody, *Boldly* is transformative because it replaced Seuss characters and other elements with *Star Trek* material. Again, the *Cat* case repudiates ComicMix's position. There, efforts to leverage Dr. Seuss's characters without having a new purpose or giving Dr. Seuss's works new meaning similarly fell short of being transformative. The copyists "merely use[d]" what Dr. Seuss had already created—*e.g.*, "the Cat's stove-pipe hat, the narrator ("Dr. Juice"), and the title (*The Cat NOT in the Hat!*)"—and overlaid a plot about the O.J. Simpson murder trial without altering *Cat* "with 'new expression, meaning or message.'" *Penguin Books*, 109 F.3d at 1401 (quoting *Campbell*, 510 U.S. at 578). For the same reasons, ComicMix's efforts to add *Star Trek* material on top of what it meticulously copied from *Go!* fail to be transformative.

Notably, *Boldly* lacks the benchmarks of transformative use. These telltale signs of transformative use are derived from the considerations laid out in *Campbell*, our north star, and *Seltzer v. Green Day, Inc.* from our circuit: (1) "further purpose or different character" in the defendant's work, i.e., "the creation of new information, new aesthetic, new insights and understanding"; (2) "new expression, meaning, or message" in the original work, i.e., the addition of "value to the original"; and (3) the use of quoted matter as "raw material," instead of repackaging it and "merely supersed[ing] the objects of the original creation." *See Campbell*, 510 U.S. at 579; *Seltzer v. Green Day, Inc.*, 725 F.3d 1170, 1176 (9th Cir. 2013) (quoting Leval, *Toward a Fair Use Standard*, 103 Harv. L. Rev. 1105, 1111 (1990)). ***Boldly* possesses none of these qualities; it merely repackaged *Go!*.**

Boldly's claim to transformative use rests on the fact that it has "extensive new content." But the addition of new expression to an existing work is not a get-out-of-jail-free card that renders the use of the original transformative. The new expression must be accompanied by the benchmarks of transformative use. *See, e.g., Seltzer*, 725 F.3d at 1177–78; *Cariou v. Prince*, 714 F.3d 694, 706 (2d Cir. 2013); *Blanch v. Koons*, 467 F.3d 244, 251–52 (2d Cir. 2006).

Instead of possessing a further purpose or different character, *Boldly* paralleled *Go!*'s purpose. In propounding the same message as *Go*, *Boldly* used expression from *Go!* to "keep to [*Go!*'s] sentiment." Absent new purpose or character, merely recontextualizing the original expression by "plucking the most visually arresting excerpt[s]" of the copyrighted work is not transformative. *L.A. News Serv. v. CBS Broad., Inc.*, 305 F.3d 924, 938–39 (9th Cir. 2002). By contrast, reconstituting copyrighted expression was for a new, transformative purpose when a "seven-second clip of

Ed Sullivan's introduction of the [band] Four Seasons on *The Ed Sullivan Show*" was used in the musical *Jersey Boys*, not to introduce the band's performance, but to serve "as a biographical anchor" about the band. *SOFA Ent., Inc. v. Dodger Prods., Inc.*, 709 F.3d 1273, 1276, 1278 (9th Cir. 2013).

***Boldly* also does not alter *Go!* with new expression, meaning, or message.** A "'transformative work' is one that alters the original work." *Perfect 10, Inc. v. Amazon.com, Inc.*, 508 F.3d 1146, 1164 (9th Cir. 2007) (quoting *Campbell*, 510 U.S. at 579). While *Boldly* may have altered *Star Trek* by sending Captain Kirk and his crew to a strange new world, that world, the world of *Go!*, remains intact. *Go!* was merely repackaged into a new format, carrying the story of the *Enterprise* crew's journey through a strange star in a story shell already intricately illustrated by Dr. Seuss. Unsurprisingly, *Boldly* does not change *Go!*; as ComicMix readily admits, it could have used another primer, or even created an entirely original work. *Go!* was selected "to get attention or to avoid the drudgery in working up something fresh," and not for a transformative purpose. *Campbell*, 510 U.S. at 580.

Most telling is ComicMix's repackaging of *Go!*'s illustrations. The *Star Trek* characters step into the shoes of Seussian characters in a Seussian world that is otherwise unchanged. ComicMix captured the placements and poses of the characters, as well as every red hatch mark arching over the handholding characters in *Grinch*'s iconic finale scene, then plugged in the *Star Trek* characters. (The Seuss images always appear to the left of the *Boldly!* images juxtaposed in this opinion.)

ComicMix copied the exact composition of the famous "waiting place" in *Go!*, down to the placements of the couch and the fishing spot. To this, ComicMix added *Star Trek* characters who line up, sit on the couch, and fish exactly like the waiting place visitors they replaced. *Go!* continues to carry the same expression, meaning, or message: as the *Boldly* text makes clear, the image conveys the sense of being stuck, with "time moving fast in the wink of an eye."

ComicMix also copied a scene in *Sneetches*,[4] down to the exact shape of the sandy hills in the background and the placement of footprints that collide in the middle of the page. Seussian characters were replaced with Spocks playing chess, making sure they "ha[d] similar poses" as the original, but all ComicMix really added was "the background of a weird basketball court."

ComicMix likewise repackaged *Go!*'s text. Instead of using the *Go!* story as a starting point for a different artistic or aesthetic expression, Hauman created a side-by-side comparison of the *Go!* and *Boldly* texts in order "to try to match the structure of *Go!*." This copying did not result in the *Go!* story taking on a new expression, meaning, or message. Because *Boldly* "left the inherent character of the [book] unchanged," it was not a transformative use of *Go!*. *Monge*, 688 F.3d at 1176.

Although ComicMix's work need not boldly go where no one has gone before, its repackaging, copying, and lack of critique of Seuss, coupled with its commercial use of *Go!*, do not result in a transformative use. The first factor weighs definitively against fair use.

B. The Nature of *Go!* Weighs Against Fair Use

The second statutory factor considers the "the nature of the copyrighted work." 17 U.S.C. § 107(2). This factor "recognizes that creative works are 'closer to the core of intended copyright protection' than informational and functional works, 'with the consequence that fair use is more difficult to establish when the former works are copied.'" *Penguin Books*, 109 F.3d at 1402 (quoting *Campbell*, 510 U.S. at 586). Hence, *Boldly*'s copying of a creative and "expressive work[]" like *Go!* tilts the second factor against fair use. *Campbell*, 510 U.S. at 586.

This factor also considers whether the copied work is unpublished, a consideration that is not relevant for the Seuss works. "[T]he unpublished nature of a work is a key, though not necessarily determinative, factor tending to negate a defense of fair use," because a copyist's initial publication of the work undermines "the author's right to control the first public appearance of his undisseminated expression." *Harper & Row, Publishers Inc. v. Nation Enter.*, 471 U.S. 539, 554–55 (1985) (quotation marks omitted). But the converse is not necessarily true; neither *Harper & Row* nor any principle of fair use counsels that the publication of the copyrighted work weighs in favor of fair use. *See* 4 William F. Patry, *Patry on Copyright* § 10:139.30 (2020) (explaining that "the fact that a work is published does not mean that the scope of fair use is per se broader").

Mindful that the second factor "typically has not been terribly significant in the overall fair use balancing," *Penguin Books*, 109 F.3d at 1402, we conclude that the creative nature of *Go!* weighs against fair use.

C. The Amount and Substantiality of the Use of *Go!* Weigh Against Fair Use

The third statutory factor asks whether "the amount and substantiality of the portion used in relation to the copyrighted work as a whole" favor fair use. 17 U.S.C. § 107(3). We consider both "the quantitative amount and qualitative value of the original work used in relation to the justification for that use." *Seltzer*, 725 F.3d at 1178. This factor circles back to the first factor because "the extent of permissible copying varies with the purpose and character of the use." *Campbell*, 510 U.S. at 586–87.

The quantitative amount taken by *Boldly* is substantial. To be sure, we understand that "[t]he inquiry under this factor is a flexible one, rather than a simple determination of the percentage of the copyrighted work used." *Monge*, 688 F.3d at 1179. That said, ComicMix's copying was considerable—it copied "14 of *Go!*'s 24 pages," close to 60% of the book, and significant "illustrations from *Grinch* and two stories in *Sneetches*." Crucially, ComicMix did not merely take a set of unprotectable visual units, a shape here and a color patch there. For each of the highly imaginative illustrations copied by ComicMix, it replicated, as much and as closely as possible from *Go!*, the exact composition, the particular arrangements of visual components, and the swatches of well-known illustrations.

ComicMix's claim that it "judiciously incorporated just enough of the original to be identifiable" as Seussian or that its "modest" taking merely "alludes" to particular Seuss illustrations is flatly contradicted by looking at the books. During his deposition, *Boldly* illustrator Templeton detailed the fact that he "stud[ied] the page [to] get a sense of what the layout was," and then copied "the layout so that things are in the same place they're supposed to be." The result was, as Templeton admitted, that the illustrations in *Boldly* were "compositionally similar" to the corresponding ones in *Go!*. In addition to the overall visual composition, Templeton testified that he also copied the illustrations down to the last detail, even "meticulously try[ing] to reproduce as much of the line work as [he could]."

Again, we turn to *Boldly* itself for illustrative examples. Here, ComicMix replicated the overall composition and placement of the shapes, colors and detailed linework.

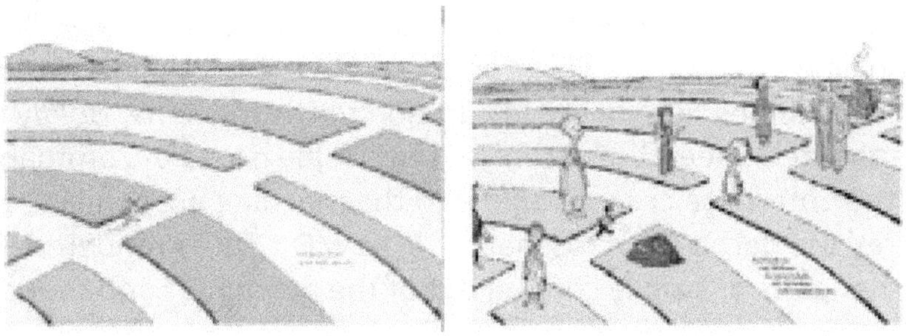

ComicMix also took the overall composition of a Seuss illustration—the placement of the tree, the hills, and the white space surrounding these elements. The trees in both versions have the same exact number, bends, and lengths of branches, with the same branch in both versions hoisting a dangling figure. ComicMix's "'verbatim' copying of the original" weighs against fair use. *Campbell*, 510 U.S. at 589.

The qualitative value used by *Boldly* is also substantial. The qualitative analysis often asks if the copyist took the "heart," that is, "the most valuable and pertinent portion," of the work. *L.A. News Serv.*, 305 F.3d at 940. Taking "the 'heart' of each individual copyrighted picture," tilts the third factor against fair use. *Monge*, 688 F.3d at 1178.

ComicMix took the heart of Dr. Seuss's works. For example, ComicMix's copying of a *Sneetches* illustration exhibits both the extensive quantitative and qualitative taking by ComicMix. *Sneetches* is a short Seuss story about two groups of Sneetches: the snooty star-bellied Sneetches and the starless ones. The story's plot, the character, and the moral center on a highly imaginative and intricately drawn machine that can take the star-shaped status-symbol on and off the bellies of the Sneetches. Different iterations of the machine, the heart of *Sneetches*, appear in ten out of twenty two pages of the book. *See Penguin Books*, 109 F.3d at 1402 (the element that "appear[s] in nearly every image of [*Cat*]" is "the highly expressive core of Dr. Seuss'[s] work").

ComicMix took this "highly expressive core" of *Sneetches*. Templeton testified that "the machine in the Star Bellied Sneetches story" was "repurposed to remind you of the transporter" in *Star Trek*. Drawing the machine "took . . . about seven hours" because Templeton tried to "match" the drawing down to the "linework" of Seuss. He "painstakingly attempted" to make the machines "identical." In addition to the machine, *Boldly* took "the poses that the Sneetches are in" so that "[t]he poses of commander Scott and the Enterprise crew getting into the machine are similar." *Boldly* also captured the particular "crosshatch" in how Dr. Seuss rendered the machine, the "puffs of smoke coming out of the machine," and the "entire layout."

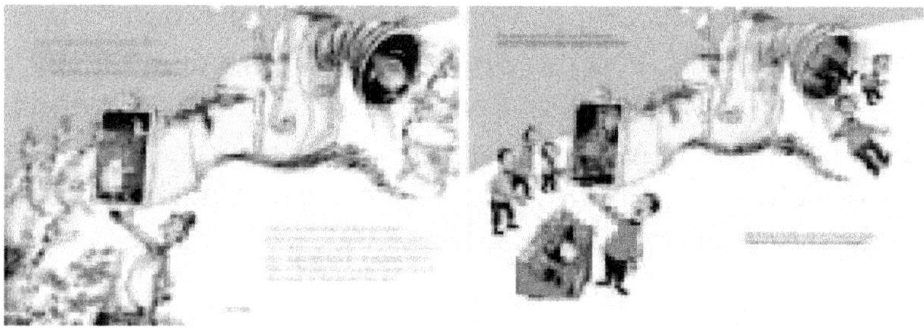

Finally, we cannot countenance ComicMix's argument that the amount taken is not substantial because ComicMix used only five out of almost sixty Dr. Seuss books. This is **fake math** that distorts the result because ComicMix has identified the wrong denominator; the third factor looks at "the amount and substantiality of the portion used *in relation to the copyrighted work as a whole*," not to the entire corpus of the author. 17 U.S.C. § 107(3) (emphasis added). Under ComicMix's theory, the more prolific the creator, the greater license a copyist would have to copy and imitate the original works. Nothing supports that argument.

Given the absence of a parody or a transformative work, ComicMix offers no justification for the commercial exploitation and the extensive and meticulous copying of *Go!*. In fact, after the case was initiated, Gerrold offered to "replace the stuff that's too dead on," demonstrating that the mash-up "based on Dr. Seuss's artwork" could have been created without wholesale copying of the work. The third factor weighs decisively against fair use.

D. The Potential Market for or Value of Seuss Weighs Against Fair Use

The fourth and final fair use factor considers "the effect of the use upon the potential market for or value of the copyrighted work." 17 U.S.C. § 107(4). Courts must address "not only the extent of market harm caused by the particular actions of the alleged infringer, but also 'whether unrestricted and widespread conduct of the sort engaged in by the defendant would result in a substantially adverse impact on the potential market' for the original" and "the market for derivative works." *Campbell*, 510 U.S. at 590 (quotation marks and citations omitted). Having found that *Boldly* was transformative—a conclusion with which we disagree—the district court also erred in shifting the burden to Seuss with respect to market harm. That shifting, which is contrary to *Campbell* and our precedent, led to a skewed analysis of the fourth factor.

Mindful of the Court's directive to "eschew[] presumptions under this factor, we refrain from presuming harm in the potential market" for commercial uses and "determine it in the first instance." *Monge*, 688 F.3d at 1181. Still, we recognize that ComicMix's non-transformative and commercial use of Dr. Seuss's works likely leads to "cognizable market harm to the original." *Campbell*, 510 U.S. at 591; *see Penguin Books*, 109 F.3d at 1403 ("Because, on the facts presented, [the defendants'] use of [the *Cat*] original was nontransformative, and admittedly commercial, we conclude that market substitution is at least more certain, and market harm may be more readily inferred.").

Not much about the fair use doctrine lends itself to absolute statements, but the Supreme Court and our circuit have unequivocally placed the burden of proof on the proponent of the affirmative defense of fair use. ComicMix tries to plow a new ground in contending that fair use is not an affirmative defense and that the burden shifts to Seuss to prove potential market harm. *Campbell* squarely forecloses this argument: "[s]ince fair use is an affirmative defense, its proponent would have difficulty carrying the burden of demonstrating fair use without favorable evidence about relevant markets." *Campbell*, 510 U.S. at 590 (footnote omitted); *see also Harper & Row*, 471 U.S. at 561. We have echoed that principle. "[F]air use is an affirmative defense," thus requiring the defendant to "bring forward favorable evidence about relevant markets." *Penguin Books*, 109 F.3d at 1403; *see Monge*, 688 F.3d at 1170 ("As with all affirmative defenses, . . . the defendant bears the burden of proof" on fair use.).

In an effort to distinguish controlling precedent, ComicMix argues that in *Lenz v. Universal Music Corp.*, we deviated from our precedent construing fair use as an affirmative defense. 815 F.3d 1145 (9th Cir. 2016). This view misreads *Lenz*, which involved fair use in a different corner of the copyright law, the safe harbor for Internet service providers under the Digital Millennium Copyright Act (DMCA). We held that to avoid liability under 17 U.S.C. § 512(f), a copyright holder must "consider the existence of fair use before sending a takedown notification." *Id.* at 1151, 1153; *see* 17 U.S.C. § 512(c)(3)(A). More pointedly, we examined the nature of fair use emphatically "for the purposes of the DMCA," and explicitly went on to note that in *that* context, "fair use is uniquely situated in copyright law so as to be treated differently than traditional affirmative defenses." *Lenz*, 815 F.3d at 1153. In no way did we deviate from our characterization of fair use as an affirmative defense under § 107. To the contrary, in addition to clarifying that, unlike copyright misuse and laches, fair use is not an excuse to copyright infringement, we reiterated that "the burden of proving fair use is always on the putative infringer." *Id.* at 1152–53 (quoting *Bateman v. Mnemonics, Inc.*, 79 F.3d 1532, 1542 n.22 (11th Cir. 1996)).

Hence, ComicMix, as the proponent of the affirmative defense of fair use, "must bring forward favorable evidence about relevant markets." *Penguin Books*, 109 F.3d at 1403. Because ComicMix's position is that it does not bear the burden of proof, it does not argue the adequacy of its scant evidence. ComicMix principally relies on the expert report of Professor Joshua Gans. The entire report is premised on *Boldly* being transformative, which it is not, and on the expert's misunderstanding about fair use and U.S. copyright law. But even if we put aside the false premises of the report, and, for the sake of argument, credit its methodology and conclusions, the report fails to account for key fourth-factor considerations. We conclude that ComicMix did not meet its burden on the fourth factor.

First, ComicMix sidesteps the fact that it intentionally targeted and aimed to capitalize on the same graduation market as *Go!*. The planned release date for the first publication of *Boldly* was scheduled to launch "in time for school graduations." ComicMix acknowledged that *Boldly*'s use of *Go!* will "resonate so much, especially as a graduation gift for folks who grew up reading Seuss." The assertion that the two works target different age groups is undermined by ComicMix's own admission that *Boldly* is "safe" for five-year-olds and "a perfect gift for children and adults of all ages."

Nor does ComicMix address a crucial right for a copyright holder—the derivative works market, an area in which Seuss engaged extensively for decades. *See* 17 U.S.C. § 106(2). A relevant derivative works market includes "those that creators of original works would in general develop or license others to develop." *Campbell*, 510 U.S. at 592. Seuss has already vetted and authorized multiple derivatives of *Go!*, including the following books: *Oh, The Things You Can Do That Are Good For You!*; *Oh, the Places I'll Go! By ME, Myself*; *Oh, Baby, the Places You'll Go!*; and *Oh, the Places I've Been! A Journal*. Recently, Seuss announced that it has partnered with Warner Animation Group to adapt *Go!* into an animated motion picture, scheduled for theatrical release in 2027. *See* Dave McNary, *Dr. Seuss' 'Cat in the Hat' Spinoff and 'Oh, The Places You'll Go' Getting Movie Adaptations*, Variety (Oct. 1, 2020).

Works like *Boldly* would curtail *Go!*'s potential market for derivative works. This is not a case where the copyist's work fills a market that the copyright owner will likely avoid, as is true for "a lethal parody" or "a scathing theater review." *Campbell*, 510 U.S. at 591–92. In fact, ComicMix hoped to get to one of the potential markets for Seuss's derivative works before Seuss, believing that Seuss would "want to publish it themselves and give [ComicMix] a nice payday."

Crucially, ComicMix does not overcome the fact that Seuss often collaborates with other creators, including in projects that mix different stories and characters. Seuss routinely receives requests for collaborations and licenses, and has entered into various collaborations that apply Seuss's works to new creative contexts, such as the television and book series entitled *The Wubbulous World of Dr. Seuss*, a collaboration with The Jim Henson Company, famous for its puppetry and the creation of other characters like the Muppets. Other collaborations include a digital game called *Grinch Panda Pop*, that combines Jam City's Panda character with a *Grinch* character; figurines that combine Funko Inc.'s toy designs with Seuss characters; and a clothing line that combines Comme des Garçons' heart design with *Grinch* artwork.

ComicMix takes issue with Seuss's apparent choice not to license a mash-up based on Dr. Seuss's works sans Dr. Seuss's characters. We say "apparent" because ComicMix only infers, from Seuss's style guide for its licensees, that Seuss will not license a Seuss–*Star Trek* mash-up. But, of course, that claim is speculative because ComicMix never asked for a license or permission. Also, the law does not limit the scope of the relevant market to products that are already made or in the pipeline. "The potential market . . . exists independent of the [copyright owner]'s present intent." *Monge*, 688 F.3d at 1181. Seuss certainly has the right to "the artistic decision not to saturate those markets with variations of their original," *Castle Rock Ent.*, 150 F.3d at 146, and it has the right "to change [its] mind," *Worldwide Church of God v. Phila. Church of God, Inc.*, 227 F.3d 1110, 1119 (9th Cir. 2000).

Finally, ComicMix does not address a central aspect of market harm set out in *Campbell*—"whether unrestricted and widespread conduct of the sort engaged in" by ComicMix would undermine Seuss's potential market. 510 U.S. at 590 (quotation marks and citation omitted). This aspect is particularly significant here because of Seuss's strong brand. ComicMix's effort to use Seuss's success against it falls flat. As noted by one of the amici curiae, the unrestricted and widespread conduct of the sort ComicMix is engaged in could result in anyone being able to produce, without Seuss's permission, *Oh the Places* Yoda'*ll Go!*, *Oh the Places You'll* Pokemon *Go!*, *Oh the Places You'll* Yada Yada Yada*!*, and countless other mash-ups. Thus, the unrestricted and widespread conduct of the sort engaged in by ComicMix could "create incentives to pirate intellectual property" and disincentivize the creation of illustrated books. *Monge*, 688 F.3d at 1182. This is contrary to the goal of copyright "[t]o promote the Progress of Science." U.S. Const. art. I, § 8, cl. 8.

The bottom line is that ComicMix created, without seeking permission or a license, a non-transformative commercial work that targets and usurps *Go!*'s potential market. ComicMix did not carry its burden on the fourth factor. Based on our weighing of the statutory factors "in light of the purposes of copyright," we conclude that ComicMix cannot sustain a fair use defense. *See Campbell*, 510 U.S. at 578. The district court erred in granting summary judgment in favor of ComicMix.

II. Seuss Does Not Have a Cognizable Trademark Infringement Claim Against ComicMix

Seuss also claims that ComicMix infringed its registered and common law trademarks in the title of *Go!*, as well as common law trademarks in the "Seussian style of illustration" and "the Seussian font." We do not express a view as to whether the Seussian style of illustration and font are valid common law trademarks, because Seuss's trademark infringement claim fails as a matter of law.

The allegedly infringing use of trademarks in an expressive work like *Boldly* raises the threshold question of whether the Lanham Act applies. **The *Rogers* test,** first articulated by the Second Circuit and later adopted by our court, balances artistic free expression and trademark rights to determine whether the Lanham Act applies. *See Rogers v. Grimaldi*, 875 F.2d 994, 999 (2d Cir. 1989); *Mattel, Inc. v. MCA Records, Inc.*, 296 F.3d 894, 902 (9th Cir. 2002) (adopting the *Rogers* test); *E.S.S. Entm't 2000, Inc. v. Rock Star Videos, Inc.*, 547 F.3d 1095, 1099 (9th Cir. 2008) (expanding the *Rogers* test from the use of a trademark in a *title* to the *body* of the expressive work). **Under the *Rogers* test, the trademark owner does not have an actionable Lanham Act claim unless the use of the trademark is "either (1) not artistically relevant to the underlying work or (2) explicitly misleads consumers as to the source or content of the work."** *VIP Prods. LLC v. Jack Daniel's Props., Inc.*, 953 F.3d 1170, 1174 (9th Cir. 2020) (quotation marks omitted). Neither of these prongs is easy to meet.

As to the first prong, any artistic relevance "above zero" means the Lanham Act does not apply unless the use of the trademark is explicitly misleading. *Twentieth Century Fox Television v. Empire Distribution, Inc.*, 875 F.3d 1192, 1198 (9th Cir. 2017) (citing *E.S.S. Entm't*, 547 F.3d at 1100); *see also Brown v. Elec. Arts, Inc.*, 724 F.3d 1235, 1245 (9th Cir. 2013) (explaining that "even the slightest artistic relevance" is enough). *Boldly* easily surpasses this low bar: as a mash up of *Go!* And *Star Trek*, the allegedly valid trademarks in the title, the typeface, and the style of *Go!* are relevant to achieving *Boldly*'s artistic purpose.

Nor is the use of the claimed *Go!* trademarks "explicitly misleading," which is a high bar that requires the use to be "an 'explicit indication,' 'overt claim,' or 'explicit misstatement'" about the source of the work. *Brown*, 724 F.3d at 1245. Thus, although titling a book "Nimmer on Copyright," "Jane Fonda's Workout Book," or "an authorized biography" can explicitly misstate who authored or endorsed the book, a title that "include[s] a well-known name" is not *explicitly* misleading if it only "*implicitly* suggest[s] endorsement or sponsorship." *Rogers*, 875 F.2d at 999–1000 (emphasis added).

Boldly is not explicitly misleading as to its source, though it uses the Seussian font in the cover, the Seussian style of illustrations, and even a title that adds just one word—*Boldly*—to the famous title—*Oh, the Places You'll Go!*. Seuss's evidence of consumer confusion in its expert survey does not change the result. The *Rogers* test drew a balance in favor of artistic expression and tolerates "the slight risk that [the use of the trademark] might implicitly suggest endorsement or sponsorship to some people." *Id.* at 1000.

A contrary result is not compelled by our recent decision in *Gordon v. Drape Creative, Inc.*, involving a registered trademark for, among other things, greeting cards. 909 F.3d 257 (9th Cir. 2018). The mark—"Honey Badger Don't Care"—is a popular comical statement that represents an "aggressive assertion of apathy." *Id.* at 268–69. The defendant created greeting cards featuring, on the front, a honey badger and an indication of the occasion the card is designed for (birthday, Halloween, etc.), and on the inside, the punchline: "Honey Badger Don't Care." *Id.* at 260–62. *Gordon* "demonstrate[d] *Roger*'s outer limits," where the defendant's expressive work consisted of the mark and not much else. *Id.* at 261, 268–69. Under this scenario, the court concluded that there was a triable issue of fact as to whether the mark was explicitly misleading. *Id.* at 271.

Boldly does not test the "outer limits" of *Rogers*. We reiterated in *Gordon* that because "use of a trademark alone" is not necessarily determinative, two "more relevant consideration[s]" weigh in evaluating whether the mark is explicitly misleading: (1) "the degree to which the junior user uses the mark in the same way as the senior user" and (2) "the extent to which the junior user has added his or her own expressive content to the work beyond the mark itself." *Gordon*, 909 F.3d at 270–71 (quoting *E.S.S. Entm't*, 547 F.3d at 1100) (citing *Rogers*, 875 F.2d at 999). Here, ComicMix has used the marks in an illustrated book just as Seuss did, but unlike with the greeting cards in *Gordon*, ComicMix has "added . . . expressive content to the work beyond the mark itself." *Id.* at 270. Also, the cover conspicuously lists David Gerrold and Ty Templeton, not Dr. Seuss, as authors, and *Boldly* states that it is "not associated with or endorsed by" Seuss. In consideration of "all the relevant facts and circumstances," the alleged use of Seuss's trademarks is not explicitly misleading. *Id.* at 269 (quoting *Rogers*, 875 F.2d at

1000 n.6). We affirm the district court's denial of Seuss's trademark claim because the Lanham Act does not apply here.

CONCLUSION

This appeal involves two different contexts in which an author's expression collides with the intellectual property rights in existing works. Here, the results for the copyright and the trademark claims diverge. Although *Boldly* did not make fair use of the copyrighted expression in *Go!*, *Boldly*'s use of *Go!* trademarks was permitted under the *Rogers* test. Accordingly, we affirm the district court's Rule 12(c) dismissal and summary judgment in favor of ComicMix as to the trademark infringement claim, but reverse and remand the district court's grant of summary judgment in favor of ComicMix as to copyright fair use.

AFFIRMED in PART; REVERSED and REMANDED in PART for proceedings consistent with this opinion.

Each party shall pay its own costs on appeal.

9: Library Exceptions and Issues

Libraries and archives are special places in our culture – a place to discover new worlds, research complex problems, and even sometimes learn a new skill or craft. From the time we are young, we are read to by librarians, and as we grow, we work on research papers and hunt for key sources. Some of us continue to rely on libraries and archives for our work. In this lesson, we will tell the story of how libraries and archives are able to operate within the world of copyright, and why we give them special privileges to do their job to help us learn and grow. We will also investigate one small part of the 1976 Copyright Act that allows libraries and archives to copy and distribute to the general public certain copyrighted works in the last twenty years of their term, through Section 108(h), allowing greater access to works for research, scholarship and preservation purposes.

One should think of the resources in a library as a duality. At once, there are laws for the library or archives itself, and then those that apply to patrons. Sometimes these are the same laws. In other instances, because the use is different, they are different laws. For instance, a library may digitize a work that is crumbling and falling apart. That is allowable under one part of the copyright act. That same work may be used by a scholar, quoted and commented upon, which is another part of the 1976 Copyright Act. In both instances in our hypothetical, the work is still under copyright, and yet both actors are able to use the work for different purposes and under different aspects of the law. This is because the U.S. Copyright Act provides certain limitations to the exclusive rights of copyright holders, and a whole set of these are related to a library's (and sometimes patron's) use of a work. And of course, there are the copyright holders and their relationship to libraries and archives, whose works are housed at the libraries and archives, preserved, cared for, and remembered for generations to reuse and rediscover. Copyright holders depend on libraries and archives, and in exchange the U.S. Copyright Act, provides certain limitations on the copyright holder's exclusive rights so that the libraries and archives can achieve their mission of providing access and preservation to our cultural resources.

Section 108 provides special limitations on the exclusive rights of copyright holders when it comes to libraries to reproduce copyrighted works without permission. When you go to a library and you photocopy an article, that's Section 108 at work. When your library doesn't have a copy of periodical, and another library makes a copy of a specific article for your home library, that's Section 108. When a copy of a work begins to fall apart, and the library makes a preservation copy, that's Section 108. When you go to an archive, and the archivists make copies of unpublished papers for you, that is Section 108. Most of Section 108 works seamlessly, even if it has quirks, and librarians and archivists discuss whether to reform or change the provisions.

Let's take a look at Section 108. Note, this is a complicated part of the statute, and we will be working through it below.

(a) Except as otherwise provided in this title and notwithstanding the provisions of section 106, it is not an infringement of copyright for a library or archives, or any of its employees acting within the scope of their employment, to reproduce no more than one copy or phonorecord of a work, except as provided in subsections (b) and (c), or to distribute such copy or phonorecord, under the conditions specified by this section, if—

(1) the reproduction or distribution is made without any purpose of direct or indirect commercial advantage;

(2) the collections of the library or archives are (i) open to the public, or (ii) available not only to researchers affiliated with the library or archives or with the institution of which it is a part, but also to other persons doing research in a specialized field; and

(3) the reproduction or distribution of the work includes a notice of copyright that appears on the copy or phonorecord that is reproduced under the provisions of this section, or includes a legend stating that the work may be protected by copyright if no such notice can be found on the copy or phonorecord that is reproduced under the provisions of this section.

(b) The rights of reproduction and distribution under this section apply to three copies or phonorecords of an unpublished work duplicated solely for purposes of preservation and security or for deposit for research use in another library or archives of the type described by clause (2) of subsection (a), if—

(1) the copy or phonorecord reproduced is currently in the collections of the library or archives; and

(2) any such copy or phonorecord that is reproduced in digital format is not otherwise distributed in that format and is not made available to the public in that format outside the premises of the library or archives.

(c) The right of reproduction under this section applies to three copies or phonorecords of a published work duplicated solely for the purpose of replacement of a copy or phonorecord that is damaged, deteriorating, lost, or stolen, or if the existing format in which the work is stored has become obsolete, if—

(1)the library or archives has, after a reasonable effort, determined that an unused replacement cannot be obtained at a fair price; and

(2) any such copy or phonorecord that is reproduced in digital format is not made available to the public in that format outside the premises of the library or archives in lawful possession of such copy.

For purposes of this subsection, a format shall be considered obsolete if the machine or device necessary to render perceptible a work stored in that format is no longer manufactured or is no longer reasonably available in the commercial marketplace.

(d) The rights of reproduction and distribution under this section apply to a copy, made from the collection of a library or archives where the user makes his or her request or from that of another library or archives, of no more than one article or other contribution to a copyrighted collection or periodical issue, or to a copy or phonorecord of a small part of any other copyrighted work, if—

(1)the copy or phonorecord becomes the property of the user, and the library or archives has had no notice that the copy or phonorecord would be used for any purpose other than private study, scholarship, or research; and

(2) the library or archives displays prominently, at the place where orders are accepted, and includes on its order form, a warning of copyright in accordance with requirements that the Register of Copyrights shall prescribe by regulation.

(e) The rights of reproduction and distribution under this section apply to the entire work, or to a substantial part of it, made from the collection of a library or archives where the user makes his or her request or from that of another library or archives, if the library or archives has first determined, on the basis of a reasonable investigation, that a copy or phonorecord of the copyrighted work cannot be obtained at a fair price, if—

(1) the copy or phonorecord becomes the property of the user, and the library or archives has had no notice that the copy or phonorecord would be used for any purpose other than private study, scholarship, or research; and

(2) the library or archives displays prominently, at the place where orders are accepted, and includes on its order form, a warning of copyright in accordance with requirements that the Register of Copyrights shall prescribe by regulation.

(f) Nothing in this section—

(1) shall be construed to impose liability for copyright infringement upon a library or archives or its employees for the unsupervised use of reproducing equipment located on its premises: Provided, That such equipment displays a notice that the making of a copy may be subject to the copyright law;

(2) excuses a person who uses such reproducing equipment or who requests a copy or phonorecord under subsection (d) from liability for copyright infringement for any such act, or for any later use of such copy or phonorecord, if it exceeds fair use as provided by section 107;

(3) shall be construed to limit the reproduction and distribution by lending of a limited number of copies and excerpts by a library or archives of an audiovisual news program, subject to clauses (1), (2), and (3) of subsection (a); or

(4) in any way affects the right of fair use as provided by section 107, or any contractual obligations assumed at any time by the library or archives when it obtained a copy or phonorecord of a work in its collections.

(g) The rights of reproduction and distribution under this section extend to the isolated and unrelated reproduction or distribution of a single copy or phonorecord of the same material on separate occasions, but do not extend to cases where the library or archives, or its employee—

(1)is aware or has substantial reason to believe that it is engaging in the related or concerted reproduction or distribution of multiple copies or phonorecords of the same material, whether made on one occasion or over a period of time, and whether intended for aggregate use by one or more individuals or for separate use by the individual members of a group; or

(2) engages in the systematic reproduction or distribution of single or multiple copies or phonorecords of material described in subsection (d): Provided, That nothing in this clause prevents a library or archives from participating in interlibrary arrangements that do not have, as their purpose or effect, that the library or archives receiving such copies or phonorecords for distribution does so in such aggregate quantities as to substitute for a subscription to or purchase of such work.

(h)

(1) For purposes of this section, during the last 20 years of any term of copyright of a published work, a library or archives, including a nonprofit educational institution that functions as such, may reproduce, distribute, display, or perform in facsimile or digital form a copy or phonorecord of such work, or portions thereof, for purposes of preservation, scholarship, or research, if such library or archives has first determined, on the basis of a reasonable investigation, that none of the conditions set forth in subparagraphs (A), (B), and (C) of paragraph (2) apply.

(2) No reproduction, distribution, display, or performance is authorized under this subsection if—

(A) the work is subject to normal commercial exploitation;

(B) a copy or phonorecord of the work can be obtained at a reasonable price; or

(C) **(C)** the copyright owner or its agent provides notice pursuant to regulations promulgated by the Register of Copyrights that either of the conditions set forth in subparagraphs (A) and (B) applies.

(3) The exemption provided in this subsection does not apply to any subsequent uses by users other than such library or archives.

(i) The rights of reproduction and distribution under this section do not apply to a musical work, a pictorial, graphic or sculptural work, or a motion picture or other audiovisual work other than an audiovisual work dealing with news, except that no such limitation shall apply with respect to rights granted by subsections (b), (c), and (h), or with respect to pictorial or graphic works published as illustrations, diagrams, or similar adjuncts to works of which copies are reproduced or distributed in accordance with subsections (d) and (e).

Overview

Section 108 can be complicated. Let's look at the categories contained within the statute.

First, you must qualify as a library or archive. Then, you have to balance the type of activity and the type of work to determine what a library (rather than a patron) can do with that work, even though it's under copyright. Note: if the work is out of copyright, none of Section 108 is necessary. A library *and* patron can make copies, even of the entire work, and post it online. Copyright law does not restrict public domain works.

Section 108 merely allows certain institutions to do certain activities under certain circumstances even while under copyright.

108 Eligibility: Library or Archive

You must be a library or archive to make use of Section 108. What does that mean? Section 108 (a) guides us.

> Except as otherwise provided in this title and notwithstanding the provisions of section 106, it is not an infringement of copyright for a library or archives, or any of its employees acting within the scope of their employment, to reproduce no more than one copy or phonorecord of a work, except as provided in subsections (b) and (c), or to distribute such copy or phonorecord, under the conditions specified by this section, if—
>
> **(1)** the reproduction or distribution is made without any purpose of direct or indirect commercial advantage;
>
> **(2)** the collections of the library or archives are (i) open to the public, or (ii) available not only to researchers affiliated with the library or archives or with the institution of which it is a part, but also to other persons doing research in a specialized field; and
>
> **(3)** the reproduction or distribution of the work includes a notice of copyright that appears on the copy or phonorecord that is reproduced under the provisions of this section, or includes a legend stating that the work may be protected by copyright if no such notice can be found on the copy or phonorecord that is reproduced under the provisions of this section.

So here is the list of requirements. Note: there are requirements for the actions of the library as well as how a library is defined.

A library i s defined as: a) open to the public, or b) available not only to researchers affiliated with the library or archives or with the i institution, but also to people doing research in a specialized field. **Note:** the only element of what constitutes a library is its available and openness. Not what a library actually *is*.

The rest of the definition is on behavior: the actions of copying must be without any purpose of direct or indirect commercial advantage.

And, the library has to include a sign about copyright for self-serve copying devices.

Are you a library or archive?

> The distinction between a library and a digital library has all but disappeared—at least to our patrons.
>
> - The Digital Library, Copyright Crash Course, University of Texas Libraries35

In order to qualify for applying any of Section 108, one has to be a library or archive. These are powerful exceptions – they are what allow libraries and archives to carry out their mission(s). But what exactly is a library or archive? For most of our history, a library or archives was easily identified as a brick-and-mortar space housing collections of books, papers, photographs and other physical works. But then the Internet happened. Does a library have to be something physical? How do we define exactly what is a library? The U.S. Copyright Act does not define "library" or "archives."

Aaron Perzanowski and Jason Shultz in *The End of Ownership*: *Personal Property in the Digital Economy* (MIT 2016) discuss digital libraries, and begin with the first known public library, the Library Company of Philadelphia, started in 1731 by Benjamin Franklin. (103). Individuals bought "shares", and the subscription money was used to buy books. (103). By 2016, over 9000 lending libraries existed in the United States. What about digital libraries? How many are there? How do we define them?

The American Library Association defines a library including both brick-and-mortar libraries as well as the digital library. They offer a number of definitions.

> "A library is a collection of resources in a variety of formats that is (1) organized by information professionals or other experts who (2) provide convenient physical, digital, bibliographic, or intellectual access and (3) offer targeted services and programs (4) with the mission of educating, informing, or entertaining a variety of audiences (5) and the goal of stimulating individual learning and advancing society as a whole."
>
> "Library -- from the Latin liber, meaning "book." In Greek and the Romance languages, the corresponding term is bibliotheca. A collection or group of collections of books and/or other print or nonprint materials organized and maintained for use (reading, consultation, study, research, etc.). Institutional libraries, organized to facilitate access by a specific clientele, are staffed by librarians and other personnel trained to provide services to meet user needs. By extension, the room, building, or facility that houses such a collection, usually but not necessarily built for that purpose...."

Both definitions include a professional or expert organizing a collection for access by the public with a mission of service and education.

In 2008, the Section 108 Study Group was conveyed by the U.S. Copyright Office to study and suggest changes to Section 108. When confronted with defining "library", the participants could not agree if a physical premise was required in order to take advantage of Section 108. But for our purposes, the report states: "The only provision that a virtual entity clearly could use to provide access under the current exception is subsection 108(h), relating to works in the last 20 years of their copyright term." (We like that!)

The Section 108 Study Group suggested that museums be included: "Section 108 applies to libraries and archives and their employees acting within the scope of their employment. Museums currently have the benefit of the section 108 exceptions only to the extent that they house, or are part of, a library or archives that meets the threshold requirements of subjections 108(a)." Museums without this were not included as part of Section 108. The Study Group felt that now museums, even without a library or archive, "make copies for preservation, replacement private study and research," and therefore should be included. The Study Group also explained that museums share a mission of "collection and preservation of, and access to, material of cultural and scientific importance for the purpose of furthering human understanding." In wanting to include Museums, the 108 Study Group seems to be helping us get to a definition:

> - make copies for preservation, replacement, private study and research
> - share a mission of collection and preservation of, and access to, material of cultural and scientific importance for the purpose of furthering human understanding

It seems like definitions such as these could lead to user-based libraries and archives – collections preserving materials of cultural importance by making a (digital) copy for preservation, replacement, and study/research. Think of all the internet-based collections of materials that might fit this definition. Would these dedicated hobbyists/fans qualify as a library or archives? It is something to think about – where the boundaries and definitions of Section 108(h) lead us. Interesting, the Discussion Document put out by the U.S. Copyright Office is concerned about this problem: "The proposed condition of "trained staff or volunteers [who] provide professional services normally associated with libraries, archives, or museums" seeks to exclude the hobbyist or amateur collector from the section 108 exceptions." If a group is making copies for preservation, replacement, private study and research, do they qualify as a library and/or archives? Does it require some official designation as a library or archives? On the other side from hobbyist are for-profit companies.

The 108 Study Group did agree that for-profit organizations are generally not covered by Section 108. The House Report said as much, but also in the House report, said that spontaneous copying by for-profit organizations would be ok in some instances.45 Section 108(a)(2) describes the requirement that the library or archives be open to the public or available to researchers in the specialized filed. The Study Group explains: "It is designed to exclude truly private libraries and archives, and in the analog world has served as an effective means of doing so. Personal book, music, or photo collections do not qualify under section 108 unless they are open to the public, or at least to researchers. Corporate libraries and archives are eligible only so long as they are willing to make their collections open to other researchers in the field (including, for example, employees of a competitor). In the online world, however, this condition does not effectively distinguish private collections from those that serve the public. Without any further qualification, private collections that are made available to the public through websites might be considered to qualify as "open to the public."

Note: at the moment, a library or archives need not be a non-profit. We learn from the Notes on the Committee on the Judiciary, House Report No. 94-1476, "Under this provision, a purely commercial enterprise could not establish a collection of copyrighted works, call itself a library or archive, and engage in for-profit reproduction and distribution of photocopies." (390) We also learn from the House Report, "it would not be possible for a non-profit institution, by means of contractual arrangements with a commercial copying enterprise, to authorize the enterprise to carry out copying and distribution functions that would be exempt if conducted by the non-profit institution itself." (390). In the digital age, "there is no clear reason to differentiate among these types of collecting institutions in their ability to collect, preserve, display, and provide access to their collections." So, we see that the focus of the committee notes was commercial entities taking advantage of Section 108. That is not allowed. A for-profit company cannot make a database of 108(h) eligible works and sell them to libraries, for instance.

While the 2008 108 Study Group might have struggled with Digital Libraries, it appears that by 2014 and earlier, the ALA had embraced the concept, publishing Karen Calhoun's Exploring Digital Libraries: Foundations, Practice, Prospects (ALA Neal-Schuma, 2014), a textbook.48 The work traces the history of the development of digital libraries

Karen Calhoun addressed the question of how to define what constitutes a library by looking at digital libraries. The idea of a digital library, she explains, began with a paper by Director of the US Office of Scientific Research and Development, Vannever Bush, "As We May Think" (1945) and a book, *Libraries of the Future*, by MIT computer scientist J.C.R Licklider (1965). (2) Licklider writes, "If books are intrinsically less than satisfactory for the storage, organization, retrieval, and display of information, then libraries of books are bound to be less than satisfactory also." He sought to create a system that would improve "library organization at the system level." He would be part of the ARPANET, the system that preceded the Internet. In1991, the National Science Foundation sponsored a workshop on "how to make digital libraries a reality." (1) Calhoun then describes the developments that led to thinking through what a digital library would like, from architecture to technology to organization.

She defines "digital libraries" as the following:

> 1. A field of research and practice with participants from many disciplines and professions, chiefly the computer, information and library sciences; publishing; the cultural sector; and education.
>
> 2. Systems and services, often openly available, that (a) support the advancement of knowledge and culture; (b) contain managed collections of digital content (objects or links to objects, annotations and metadata) intended to serve the needs of defined communities; (c) often use an architecture that first emerged in the computer and information science/library domain and that typically feature a repository mechanisms supporting search and other services, resource identifiers, and user interfaces (human and machine.)" (18)

So what is a digital library? Calhoun defined it as a "traditional repository-centered architecture," with additional social roles for communities they serve. She notes that over the years there have been a number of perspectives on what constitutes a digital library from a technical perspective to a space where people collaborate and share. 50 She includes a table of competing definitions. What do the definitions have in common? A focus on organizing and collecting materials for a community of users.

The IFLA/UNESCO Manifesto for Digital Libraries (2008) defined a digital library as: "an online collection of digital objects, of assured quality, that are created or collected and managed according to internationally accepted principles for collection development and made accessible in a coherent and sustainable manner, supported by services necessary to allow users to retrieve and exploit the resources."

Many of the definitions have similar elements: objects, collected and made accessible that allow users to use and retrieve. Now, Section 108(h) can also include a nonprofit educational institution that functions a library or archives, expanding the definition. The general definition requires the library or archives be open to the public or the collection available to specialists in the field. These requirements seem to correspond to the general definitions we have been finding for digital libraries.

Allowable Actions by a Library or Archive

Section 108 allows libraries and sometimes their patronos to copy works still under copyright. But there are limits to how many copies, and why the copying is occurring, along with who is doing the copying. Section 108(b), (c), (d), (e), and (f) provide specific activities that libraries can make copies and distribute them to other libraries and patrons – preservation copies, interlibrary loan, and patrons making copies on copy machines. These are all used everyday and are the backbone of the U.S. library system.

> Section 108(b): 3 copies of an unpublished work for the purpose of preservation and security, or for deposit for research use in another library or archive.
>
> Section. 108(c): up to 3 copies of a published work for replacement because the work is damaged, deteriorated, lost or stolen or the existing format is obsolete, where no replacement copy can be obtained at a fair price.
>
> Section 108(d): small portions of a copyrighted work requested by a patron or another library
>
> Section 108(e): entire work or substantial portions of a copyrighted work requested by a patron or another library
>
> 108(f): unsupervised copying by patrons

Section 108(h)

Section 108(h) provision allows a library or archive to make copies of a work for distribution (including online) and public display in the last twenty years of the work's copyright, as long as certain requirements are met. It was added to the 1976 Copyright Act in 1998, as part of the Copyright Term Extension Act. While the copyright term was extended twenty years, Congress felt that libraries and archives should be able to access, copyright, and even distribute works where no commercial activity was occurring, that the library should not have to wait twenty years to make the works available to the public. In some ways, the Last Twenty Exception could be seen as a library-specific public domain. When market failure occurs—there is no normal commercial exploitation and there are no copies available, the library can step in and make copies available to the public.

As of 2021, this means that libraries can digitally (and in analog form) make available to the public works that were first published in or before 1945, as they have entered the last twenty years of copyright. (Note: the maximum term for works published before 1978 is 95 years, but many have entered the public domain before that.) Each year new works are added. How many works might this be? A few years ago, the Internet Archive alone calculated that their collection held 279,911 textfiles/works first published between 1923-1942. This is just one example. Libraries and archives across the United States are filled with texts, photographs, audiovisual works, art works, and any other works that were published during or before 1942 that might be eligible.

Why does that matter? First, on a preservation level, Section 108(h) provides great freedom to libraries to digitize, even more than other aspects of Section 108. Second, Section 108(h) allows for reproduction *and distribution without restrictions,* as long as the purpose is for research, scholarship and preservation (along with other requirements). So, scholars would have greater access to works from the 1920s, 1930s and 1940s because even though they are still under copyright, a digital copy is made available to view. Finally, Section 108(h) was added to preserve the balance between access and an extended term caused by the Copyright Term Extension Act in 1998.

Now, there are restrictions, of course, and the greatest limitation is that Section 108(h) only applies to libraries and archives, and not the patrons/users of the materials. Just because I view a 1939 novel about pacifism doesn't mean that I have the freedom under Section 108(h) to *use the work*. But Section 107 – fair use comes into play. As a scholar, I can rely on Section 107 for quoting a work to comment and criticize, or other uses, including transformative uses. But the work would not have been even available in the same way without Section 108(h) potentially – for me to have known about it, or get access to the work in the first place to think, comment, criticize, and to reject or add to my argument.

But libraries were wary of using it, in part because it was difficult to determine when a work was in the last twenty years of its term, and also in part because it was difficult to determine and prove that a work met the requirements: the work was not currently commercially exploited, and no reasonable copy was available. This article sets out to address both issues, and suggests practical means of implementing Section 108(h) in collections, both small and large.

During the summers of 2017 and 2018, a team of students from Tulane Law School, led by Dr. Townsend Gard, embarked on a study to understand how Section 108(h) might be implemented, both on a small scale, but also with libraries with millions of records. Was it possible to meet the requirements and utilize Section 108(h) without high transaction costs? The team worked with a number of libraries, including the Frick Collection, the New York Public Library, Columbia University, Harvard University, the Library of Congress and the Internet Archive. After numerous conversations, studies, and experiments, the following suggests an approach to Section 108(h).

Copyright law is a bargain, between the government and a copyright holder, a statutory- created limited monopoly. With a modicum of creativity and independent creation, a copyright holder receives the exclusive right to copy, make derivative works, distribute, publicly perform, and publicly display their works for a set amount of time, or "limited Times." These five exclusive rights to control a creative work for a set number of years do have exceptions during the copyright term, the most famous being fair use, but also include classroom uses and a whole list of other exceptions and exemptions. Libraries and archives are also given special exceptions found under Section 108. "It is *not an infringement*", reads section 108...,"to engage in certain reproduction activities, including reproduction and distribution of copyrighted works." (Emphasis added)33 These exceptions include making copies for preservation, interlibrary loan and copies requested by scholars for research and study. The exception also includes reproduction and distribution of a work to the general public for the purpose of research, scholarship and preservation in its last twenty years of copyright, or what we refer to as the Last Twenty exception.

Application of Section 108(h)

Section 108(h) was enacted as part of the Copyright Term Extension Act in 1998. In extending the term of copyright by twenty years, there was concern that this would detrimentally hurt libraries. In a letter to Con- gress, the Librarian of Congress explained his position. His worry about the term extension focused on new technologies as well as the balance of the public interest and the "dissemination of knowledge." He explained, "Technology now offers our hard-pressed libraries and educational institu- tions unprecedented new opportunities to allow the American people ac- cess to a wealth of information and unique historical material previously unreachable." He discussed the problem:

> Up to this point, the works we have made available electronically through the National Digital Library project are mainly those in the public do- main: either works by the U.S. Government or those whose copyright term has expired. The proposed extension of the period of copyright pro- tection means that material from the mid-twentieth century, which would otherwise have passed into the public domain and become available for use by libraries and other education institutions, would not now be available to be freely shared with schools and libraries. This restriction very clearly would limit the range of historical coverage into the 20th century, from which schoolchildren will be able to learn.
>
> One has to be concerned that too often today copyright is seen only as an economic concept, rather than one which also fosters the growth of learn- ing and culture for public welfare. Our economic future clearly depends on the education and intellectual advancement of the American people who our copyright system seeks to advance; even as it seeks to reward authors and creators. *Copyright Term, Film Labeling, and Film PreservationLegislation, Hearings before Subcomm. of Courts and Intellectual Property of the Comm. on the Judiciary, House of Representatives on H.R. 989, H.R. 1248, and H.R. 1734, at 578 (1995) (letter from James Billington, Librarian of Congress, to Chairman Henry J. Hyde (July 12, 1995).*

His words and thoughts are very reasoned. He writes, "I understand the equity and foreign policy reasons for copyright extension.. . . At the same time, I believe that, in conjunction with this legislation, we should start to search for ways to ease the unintended negative impacts that this legislation in its present form would predictably have on libraries, educa- tion institutions and archives." Others agreed. In 1995, Robert Oakley, on behalf of the American Association of Law Libraries, the Medical Library Association, Special Li- braries Association, and the American Library Association, wrote:

> Term extension exacerbates the problem libraries face when trying to de- cide if they may legally save a deteriorating work. Legislation that ex- pands copyright protection for twenty years leaves preservationists exposed to claims of infringement for a longer period. That is unfair to the dedicated researchers in our nation's libraries and is contrary to the goal of maintaining the rich array of information accessible to our schol- ars, youths and others for education and research. A balance should be struck in this legislation which ensures that libraries may lawfully and cost-effectively protect important cultural resources,

> no matter the format in which they are stored or the period for which they are copyrighted.

A 1996 Report makes clear the tensions between librarians on the one side and content owners on the other. The two paragraphs are included in their entirety:

> The Committee is not unaware of the concern that a 20-year term exten- sion may not take into account those institutions that depend on legal, noncommercial use of protected copyright material. Current law permits libraries and archives to make limited copies or phonorecords of a work under certain circumstances, such as for preservation purposes, or for limited nonsystematic uses for patrons, which the "reproduction or distribution is made without any purpose of direct or indirect commercial advantage." (citing 17 U.S.C. 108(a)(1) (1992).
>
> The Committee is also cognizant, however, of the competing concern of copyright owners, who have expressed their belief that non-commercial users often bypass acquiring such works through readily available commercial means or can compete with the copyright owner's uses. The Committee sought to address both of these concerns by amending current copyright law to permit qualified libraries, archives and nonprofit educational institutions to reproduce or distribute a copy of a protected work in the last 20 years of its term for limited noncommercial purposes, that is, for purposes of presentation, scholarship, teaching or research, and under certain conditions, including a reasonable investigation that a work is neither subject to normal commercial exploitation nor obtainable at a reasonable price. Furthermore, the legislation provides copyright owners an opportunity to notify the Copyright Office when these conditions are not met. The Committee recognizes the fact that representatives of copyright owners and the nonprofit institutions covered by this provision are in the process of negotiating mutually agreeable terms that may differ from those adopted by the Committee. Should further agreement be reached by these parties, it is the intent of the Committee that the precise terms of this provision be subject to further modification in light of such an agreement

The Committee on the Judiciary report favoring the passage of the bill, "Section 4. Reproduction by Libraries and Archives" is described in a paragraph:

> This section is designed to permit libraries and archives to make certain uses of copyrighted material, including in digital form, during the 20-year extension, in certain circumstances. This is an exemption for libraries and archives, or other

> nonprofit educational institutions, allowing them to reproduce, distribute, display or perform a copy of a work or pho- norecord for purposes of preservation, scholarship or research. However, the exemption applies only where the entity has determined after reasonable investigation, that none of the following conditions apply: **1)** that the work is subject to normal commercial exploitation, 2) a copy of the work can be obtained at a reasonable price, and **3)** the copyright owner or its agents have provided notice that either of the first two conditions apply. This exemption would allow library users the benefit of access to published works that are not commercially exploited or otherwise reasonably available during the extended time.

And so, Section 108(h) was included as part of the CTEA. The next step was implementation. The key question was implementing a procedure at the Copyright Office for notice that a work was commercially available at a reasonable price.

Eldred and Golan's Use of 108(h)

Both Ginsburg for the majority and Breyer in the dissent of *Eldred v. Ashcroft* in 2003 speak directly to section 108(h). In *Eldred,* Ginsburg uses section 108(h) as an example of First Amendment safeguards to the extension of the copyright term by the CTEA. Breyer, in contrast, Sees Section 108(h) as a failure to achieve its goals because of its limitations and complexities, and because it does not apply to commercial database proprietors.

Digital Spaces and Section 108(h)

We see digital libraries and archives identified *as a library*. The Internet Archive "is a non- profit library of millions of free books, movies, software, music, websites and more." The library behaves like a library – even with lending of books. It has a staff and is well organized. In its "Terms," the IA states, "Access to the Archive's Collections is provided at no cost to you and is granted for scholarship and research purposes only." We see digital libraries as part of brick-and- mortar libraries, like the Digital Library at the Smithsonian, for example, that includes books online, collections and exhibitions. And we see platforms that aggregate digital content more efficiently for libraries, such as the Digital Public Library of America. "The Digital Public Library of America (DPLA) is an all-digital library that aggregates metadata — or information describing an item — and thumbnails for millions of photographs, manuscripts, books, sounds, moving images, and more from libraries, archives, and museums around the United States. DPLA brings together the riches of America's libraries, archives, and museums, and makes them freely available to the world." All three examples – Internet Archive,

Smithsonian, and DPLA *could* make use of Section 108(h), and make more works available online during the last twenty years of their copyright. The question is what would it take for large and small institutions to begin using Section 108(h) more seriously? It was what Congress envisioned.

Section 108(h) could be used even more expansively, especially if the definition for libraries and archives focuses on the conduct (collecting, preserving, etc.) rather than our traditional concepts of the library we walk to with our children to or the university stacks. What about the website cataloging, preserving, and making available old radio show recordings? Do they count as an archive? How far and wide can one take advantage of Section 108(h) and other provisions of Section 108(h)? Just as the Internet made us all creators and distributors of content, has the Internet also made us all libraries and archives, preserving culture for research and scholarship? The possibilities for Section 108(h) could be dramatic.

General Requirements of Section 108(h)

So, assuming one has met the requirement of being a library or archive, the next step is to confirm the library or archive has met the basic general requirements. To fall under Section 108, a library or archives has to first meet four general requirements:

1. No Direct or indirect commercial advantage

The purpose of the copies cannot be for direct or indirect commercial advantage.57 The notes from the Committee focus on "indirect commercial advantage" when it comes to libraries in for- profit entities like R&D in "chemical, pharmaceutical, automobile and oil corporations." (House Report, 390). The focus is prohibiting a single subscription or interlibrary loan to be copied for multiple employees, even if the employee is doing the copying. It looks to the institution, and not the reason for copying.

2. Open to the Public

"[T]he collections of the library or archives are (i) open to the public, or (ii) available not only to researchers affiliated with the library or archives or with the institution of which it is a part, but also to other persons doing research in a specialized field." Again, this is focused on prohibiting private, corporate libraries gathering information for commercial purposes from using Section 108.

3. Copyright Notice

"[T]he reproduction or distribution of the work includes a notice of copyright that appears on the copy or phonorecord that is reproduced under the provisions of this section, or includes a legend stating that the work may be protected by copyright if no such notice can be found on the copy or phonorecord that is reproduced under the provisions of this section." This is to make sure that those who receive copies recognize that the work being copied is still under copyright, because Section 108 *applies to works still under copyright*. Those works that are out of copyright do not need Section 108, because they can be copied by the libraries without restrictions. What must be included in the notice? The Copyright Office put out the exact language for display warning and an order warning.

NOTICE WARNING CONCERNING COPYRIGHT RESTRICTIONS

The copyright law of the United States (title 17, United States Code) governs the making of photocopies or other reproductions of copyrighted material.

Under certain conditions specified in the law, libraries and archives are authorized to furnish a photocopy or other reproduction. One of these specific conditions is that the photocopy or reproduction is not to be "used for any purpose other than private study, scholarship, or research." If a user makes a request for, or later uses, a photocopy or reproduction for purposes in excess of "fair use," that user may be liable for copyright infringement.

This institution reserves the right to refuse to accept a copying order if, in its judgment, fulfillment of the order would involve violation of copyright law.

The Copyright Office was specific:

(c) *Form and manner of use.*

(1) A Display Warning of Copyright shall be printed on heavy paper or other durable material in type at least 18 points in size, and shall be displayed prominently, in such manner and location as to be clearly visible, legible, and comprehensible to a casual observer within the immediate vicinity of the place where orders are accepted.

(2) An Order Warning of Copyright shall be printed within a box located prominently on the order form itself, either on the front side of the form or immediately adjacent to the space calling for the name or signature of the person using the form. The notice shall be printed in type size no smaller than that used predominantly throughout the form, and in no case shall the type size be smaller than eight points. The notice shall be printed in such manner as to be clearly legible, comprehensible, and readily apparent to a casual reader of the form.

That is very specific.

The ALA's website suggested the following: "Notice: This material may be protected by copyright law (Title 17 U.S. Code)." They suggested: "A library may choose to stamp this sentence on the first piece of each item photocopied, to attach it to the glass on the photocopying equipment so that it is automatically transferred to each sheet, to attach a sticker bearing this notice to each item photocopied, or to use some other method whereby this message is affixed to all reproductions."

4. Isolated and Unrelated Copies

The copying must be isolated and unrelated of a single copy or phonorecord. Libraries and archives, or their employees should not be aware that the library or archive is "engaging in the related or concerted reproduction or distribution of multiple copies or phonorecords of the same material, whether made on one occasion or over a period of time, and whether intended for aggregate use by one or more individuals or for separate use by the individual members of the group."

5. No systematic reproduction distribution of single or multiple copies.

The question is what does systematic apply. In footnote 15 of *Author's Guild v. HathiTrust* (SDNY), the Court writes, "plaintiffs also argue that this program is "systematic" in violation of Section 108(g). Pls.' Reply to Pls.' J. Pleadings 11. Defendants respond that "systematic" means reproducing a single work repeatedly, rather than reproducing all the works in their libraries. Defs.' Opp'n to Pls.' J. Pleadings (citing 17 U.S.C. section 108(g) (prohibiting systematic reproduction of "the same material")). I agree." Authors Guild, Inc. v. HathiTrust, 902 F. Supp. 2d 445, 456 (S.D.N.Y. 2012), aff'd in part, vacated in part, 755 F.3d 87 (2d Cir. 2014) The Second Circuit in *Author's Guild v. HathiTrust* does not discuss the point further, as the case is focused on fair use (107) and not library exceptions (108). Section 108(2) includes mention of interlibrary loans in relation to systematic copyright: interlibrary loan arrangements are exempted from this limitation, as long as the interlibrary loan requests do not substitute for obtaining a subscription or purchasing a work.

Works excluded: Apply Fair Use

Not all works fall under Section 108. In some instances, musical works, pictorial, graphic or sculptural works, motion pictures or other audiovisual works other than an audiovisual work dealing with news are not included under Section 108.68 (These exceptions are not included in Section 108(h)).

The House Report specifically discussed excluded works, but then notes that even though "musical, graphic, and audiovisual works" are excluded in some categories, they expect that fair use may be applied nonetheless. "In the case of music, for example, it would be fair use for a scholar doing musicological research to have a library supply a copy of a portion of a score or to reproduce portions of a phonorecord of a work." (393). This is really interesting. Fair use is expected to be for third party requests, even if they are not covered in Section 108 for libraries. "Nothing in section 108 [this section] impairs the applicability of the fair use doctrine to a wide variety of situations involving photocopying or other reproduction by a library of copyrighted material in its collections, where the user requests the reproduction for legitimate scholarly or research purposes." (393).

Copyright Status for Section 108(h)

Section 108(h) allows libraries and archives to digitize, make copies, and distribute – even publicly perform – works that are in the last 20 years of their copyright. To utilize Section 108(h), one has to know *when* the last twenty years of a copyright begins. That can be a difficult task, as the status of a work depends on a number of elements: whether the work is considered published or unpublished (Section 108(h) only applies to *published* works, although the suggested modifications by the U.S. Copyright Office want to expand it to both published and unpublished); the date of publication; the place of creation and/or publication, and the type of work, to name a few examples. Sometimes one must check U.S. Copyright Office renewal records to determine the status; other times one must check to see if proper notice was included. The following is not inclusive of all copyright issues related to the works currently eligible for Section 108(h), but starts to look at the complexities of copyright status.

1. Publication

The question of publication is complicated in the United States, and in particular with certain kinds of works like television shows and art works. Many cases and law reviews discuss publication. Here it is important to note that works that were distributed without restrictions. Books sold in bookshops, menus given out at restaurants, and art works offered for sale are some examples. Section 108(h) only applies to *published works*.

2. Date of Publication

To determine the status of works eligible for Section 108(h), one must know the publication date for works first published 1923-1940s. The question is what happens when there is not a date? Context clues can help. The date, for Section 108(h), is to see if it is in the window of opportunity. So, if a work is from the Great Depression, it doesn't necessarily matter if one knows whether it is 1929 or 1933. As long as the work could not have been first published after 1942 (as of 2017), one could take advantage of Section 108(h).

3. Geography

Copyright law is based on up to the two sets geographical elements: about the work, and about the use of the work. About the work: depending on the calculation, one must have the following data: author's country of origin, place of creation, and/or place of first publication. Then, one must also determine *where* the work is going to be used, that is, where potential infringement may occur. For U.S. libraries, that is generally, the United States. If a library or archives is working with a partner outside of the United States, that might alter the jurisdiction questions. In particular for pre-1978 works, the place of first publication for a status check in the United States makes a significant difference. Section 108(h) only applies to library uses in the United States. Kenneth Crews did a study on similar library exceptions around the world. (See his study).73 So, if one is working with a partner library outside of the U.S., and wanting to rely on Section 108, there will be a different set of library exceptions *and the copyright term may be different* outside of the United States.

3. Type of Work

The copyright status of the work as well as its eligibility under Section 108(h) will vary depending on the type of work. As already mentioned, audiovisual works, musical compositions, and art works are treated differently under parts of Section 108, but not Section 108(h). Most famously, pre-1972 sound recordings are determined by state law, through Feb 15, 2067.74 And the type of work may matter when determining the status of a foreign work in the U.S.75 The type of work may also come into play when a work was registered under the 1909 Copyright Act.76 Works were registered by type, and that helped explain what was protected by that copyright.77 Registration and renewal records are still relevant to determining the copyright status of works, and the registration category based on type of work continues to this day.78

Applying Section 108(h)

So, you have found that a work is still protected by copyright and even in the last twenty years of its copyright term (or soon to be and you are preparing for that moment). There are a couple of more steps you must undertake in order to use the Twenty Year exception.

The statute reads as follows:

> **(1)** For purposes of this section, during the last 20 years of any term of copyright of a published work, a library or archives, including a nonprofit educational institution that functions as such, may reproduce, distribute, display, or perform in facsimile or digital form a copy or phonorecord of such work, or portions

thereof, for purposes of preservation, scholarship, or research, if such library or archives has first determined, on the basis of a reasonable investigation, that none of the conditions set forth in subparagraphs (A), (B), and (C) of paragraph (2) apply.

(2) No reproduction, distribution, display, or performance is authorized under this subsection if—

(A) the work is subject to normal commercial exploitation;

(B) a copy or phonorecord of the work can be obtained at a reasonable price; or **(C)** the copyright owner or its agent provides notice pursuant to regulations promulgated by the Register of Copyrights that either of the conditions set forth in subparagraphs (A) and (B) applies.

(3) The exemption provided in this subsection does not apply to any subsequent uses by users other than such library or archives.

The basic requirements to implement Section 108(h) are the following:

1. Library or archives, including a nonprofit educational institution (see above)
2. Use for Preservation, Research or Scholarship

The copy and/or distribution must be for preservation, research or scholarship. This will play

an important role later when it comes to analyzing other aspects of Section 108(h). But the key is that a library or archive is making a copy of a copyrighted work for preservation, research or scholarship.

Reasonable Investigation

In order to make a copy, display, distribute or perform the work in its last twenty years of copyright, a reasonable investigation must be undertaken to determine that *all* the following conditions do not apply. The reasonable investigation has three prongs: currently no normal commercial exploitation; no copy available at a reasonable price; and no notice has been filed with the U.S. Copyright Office by the copyright holder that the work is available (normal commercial exploitation at a reasonable price). So far, since 1998 (and as of 2017), no notices by copyright holders have been filed at the U.S. Copyright Office. In fact, the Discussion Document on Section 108(h) put out by the

U.S. Copyright Office in September 2017 suggests to drop the last requirement, because for the last twenty years, no one has filed a notice.

The two remaining requirements are really about the market, and in fact, the Discussion Document calls them "market check." The idea is that if a work is accessible in the marketplace at a reasonable price, there is no need for a library to make a copy and distribute it. It makes sense. Section 108(h) had its underlying justification as an "orphan works" addition to the CTEA. If the copyright term was going to be lengthened, then orphans would be created, where works were still under copyright but no market copy was available. How does one read "normal commercial exploitation" and "reasonable copy"? Each will be discussed in detail below. One reading is that normal commercial exploitation refers to new copies, and "reasonable copy" may refer to used copies, but it is not clear, as discussed below if "reasonable copy" is new or also used.

Once a library determines that currently there is no normal commercial exploitation or a reasonably priced copy is not available, the library may make a copy (including digitizing) and distribute (including placing that work online) without restrictions. Copyright law is based on the territory of the potential infringement. So, this law applies to the U.S. only. That same work will be protected by different laws in different countries.

While neither "normal commercial exploitation" nor "reasonable copy" is defined, as the U.S. Copyright Office noted in its 2005 Orphan Work Report, "Section 108 relies expressly on the concept of reasonableness: the terms 'reasonable investigation' and 'reasonable price' are central to its operation. "

What constitutes a "reasonable search"? Orphan works legislation always talks about a "diligent search." Reasonable seems less than that. The Orphan Work Report 2005 noted: "In his dissent in Eldred v. Ashcroft, 537 U.S. 186 (2003), Justice Breyer called section 108(h) a "limited" exception, and expressed the view that the term "reasonable investigation" is "open-ended." As will be discussed later, it seems like searching major commercial sites – Amazon.com, for example, aggregates of information like ISBNDB.com or ISBNsearch.org, and informational sites like IMDB.COM (for audiovisual works, for example) would constitute a "reasonable search." Searching industry specific sites and catalogs for commercial activity would also be helpful. But it does not require a "diligent search," only reasonable.

The Orphan Work Report in 2005 and 2015 both explained what a diligent search was. In 2015, the Copyright Office "the Office recommend[ed] a framework in which liability is limited for a user who conducts a good faith diligent search for the copyright owner." How did they define a "diligent search was at a minimum, searching Copyright Office records; searching sources of copyright authorship, ownership, and licensing; using technology tools; and using databases, all as reasonable and appropriate under the circumstances..." So, a reasonable search would be less than a diligent search.

In 2017, we conducted a number of experiments to see if using Amazon.com would be sufficient for satisfying the "reasonable search" requirement. Using 158 works selected randomly from the Internet Archive, we searched to see if we could find copies available on Amazon.com. Of the 158 works that were randomly selected, 128 works were not commercially available, 30 works were commercially available; 98 works did not have a reasonable copy available, and 56 works had a reasonable copy available. For the works that were commercially available or had a reasonable copy, some of the results rendered were not the exact work that was on the Archive. Some works that were available on Amazon had different publishers or were later editions, although the works had the same title. But because commercial availability and reasonable copy are not defined in the Copyright Act, there is uncertainty as to whether the works of later editions or different publishers satisfy the 17 U.S.C. section108(h) requirement for commercial availability or reasonable copy. It seems like Amazon could be a quick way to satisfy "reasonable search." That would leave only 30 of the titles in need of further investigation.

We also ran the same titles through ISBNDB.com and ISBN search as well. These are tools that allow you to see where a book is available (new and/or used). "ISBNdb.com project is a database of books providing on-line and remote research tools for individuals, book stores, librarians, scientists, etc. Taking data from hundreds of libraries across the world ISBNdb.com is a unique tool you won't find anywhere else." They are more comprehensive than Amazon.

You can search by name, title, subject, or ISBN. So, for instance, "Testament of Youth" brought up five results. Each has a different ISBN number. They are all by Vera Brittain. You can then look at the individual works. For instance, ISBNDB.com returns the following results:

The first one returns information about the work, and lets us know that there are new and used copies of this work, which is a reprint from the 1933 version. It also provides a price history, which might be very useful for the "copy at a reasonable price" prong of the 108 reasonable investigation. Strangely, ISBNDB.com does not give us the publication date of this version. ISBNsearch.org does include the publication. Both quickly can tell you the commercial status of the work.

We did not stop here. We looked at another 300 works, again randomly chosen from the Internet Archive collection. These were all published between 1923 and 1941. We looked at both Amazon and ISBNDB.com. We did not find any instances where a work was listed on ISBNDB.com and not on Amazon. We focused on books. So, we would have to reevaluate for other forms. But for now, we feel like Amazon is a good starting point for a "reasonable search." But nothing in the law is dictating that we search Amazon or that it is sufficient for a search.

The reasonable search is two-pronged: No normal commercial exploitation and no copyright at a reasonable price found. Again, this is called a Market Search in the Discussion Paper for Section 108 put out by the U.S. Copyright Office. They propose keeping the language for both the normal commercial exploitation and a copy of the work obtained at a fair price. We found it confusing and a little bit too limiting.

Normal Commercial exploitation

Commercial exploitation is defined by Collins dictionary as "the development and use of a resource for business." Copyright law is built to incentivize commercial exploitation. As one court explained, "The Copyright Act aids commercial exploitation of copyrights by allowing the sale of particular rights ... or of the entire bundle." Section 108(h) applies when that commercial exploitation is no longer occurring. The problem is that there is no definition on when to know when that occurs. The work must not be "subject to normal commercial exploitation." The statute does not define what this means nor did the legislative history discuss "subject to normal commercial exploitation." We know that "indirect or direct commercial advantage" referred to *the entity* who is doing the copying. "Subject to normal commercial exploitation" focuses on the work itself.

We have copyright cases that look specifically at what constitutes commercial exploitation, but not in the context of Section 108(h), or even generally Section 108. Warner Bros. v. Ron Rooding differentiates between private/personal use and commercial use. Rooding planned to jump out of an airplane in a batman costume on the night of the new Batman film opening. Warner Bros and DC Comics won a restraining order to prevent Rooding from doing the activity. Because the defendant/respondent purchased the uniform and was sold the uniform for private use, he may use it privately. Because he is not franchised, licensed or privileged in any way to use it publicly, he may not use it publicly for any commercial or exploitative purpose.

A masquerade party is not a public occasion by the nature of it. A walk down the beach, if no more than that, is also a personal use. Handing out free candy at orphanages, this Court would consider to be personal. Any activity in connection with commercial circumstances, such as the opening of theaters, ballparks, parking lots, malls, swimming pools, and similar functions where the public comes for the purpose of purchase of services or goods would be considered to be under this order commercial and/or exploitative. So, normal commercial exploitation could be defined broadly as commercial circumstances...where the public comes for purpose of purchase of services of goods.

Another case, *Sega Enters. Ltd. v. MAPHIA* states that it is commercial when users download video games to avoid having to buy video game cartridges. Here the act is replacing the act of purchasing the work. It is implied that the work is available for purchase. In *Bridgeport Music, Inc. v. Still N Water Pub.*, the case concerned "music publishing, recording and distributing sound recordings, and other forms of commercial exploitation of musical copyrights." All of these activities are Section 106 rights under the Copyright Act. These rights are designed to provide legal protection and the right to exclude others from commercial exploitation of the work. The Copyright Act itself is designed to facilitate commercial exploitation. The question is whether the copyright holder is currently exploiting the work commercially. In this specific part of the statute, if they are not, and it is in the last twenty years of copyright (and meets the other two requirements of no reasonable copy and no notice from copyright holders that there is normal commercial exploitation and/or no reasonable copy), the library may make that work available *even though it is still under copyright.* Section 108(h) reflects lack of market access. One cannot just go purchase a copy. The library serves a role of making that work available because the copyright holder and the publisher have not. In some way, it's orphan work-esque in its design, and was titled "Orphan works" in its early conception.90 The modification to Section 108(h) in 2005, to allow all kinds of published works to fall under Section 108(h) was called the "Preservation of Orphan Works Act". In the Orphan Work Report of 2005, Section 108(h) was addressed. The Report noted that Section 108(h) addressed "some uses in certain situations," but noted that there were more orphans that fell outside of Section 108(h).

Patents, right of publicity, and indirectly the concept of publication in copyright may help us to understand a potential definition for "normal commercial exploitation." In order to obtain a patent, one of the qualifications is meeting the novelty requirement, and as part of the requirement, there is a limitation on time (more than one year) that a work can be in public use or for sale. The term used in the statute is "commercially exploited." 35 USC Section 102(b). How is commercial exploitation defined in patent law? For a "commercial sale" to occur, with regard to public use or sale, manufacturing of the item is not enough, but must be a transaction between a supplier and inventor. See, for example, Dorman Products v. Paccar (201 F.Supp. 3d 663)(ED Penny, 2016). (request and receipt of price quotes did not constitute "commercial offer for sale") General contract law is applied to determine if there was an actual commercial offer.

The first prong of the on-sale bar under novelty is that the work was for sale more than one year from filing. This could be a sale or offer for sale. The Supreme Court identified two elements: commercial offer and the offer must be for a patented invention. The Federal Circuit looked to the UCC to determine when an offer for sale had been made. "In order to constitute an offer for sale under section 102(b), an offer must be one "which the other party could make into a binding contract by simple acceptance (assuming consideration)." The sale must be between two separate entities.96 Attempting to sale counts. Sale of devices or technology counts. Sale and purchase agreements count.99 But, more than communication or information exchanged is required. Mere discussions are not enough.100 And preparations for sale do not count.

Right of publicity also uses commercial exploitation, in this case of identity. Nimmer in *The Right of Publicity*, distinguished between privacy and publicity doctrines: privacy focused on "solitude and privacy", while publicity focused on seeking to "profit by the commercial exploitation and control of name, photograph and likeness." H. Lee Hetherington, Direct Commercial Exploitation of Identity: A New Age for the Right of Publicity, 17 Colum.-VLA J.L. & Arts 1, 6 (1992) citing Melville B. Nimmer, The Right of Publicity, 19 Law & Contemp. Probs 203-4 (1954) (discussing the evolution of the right to privacy). Hetherington defines direct commercial exploitation as "direct in its nature and primarily commercial in its motivation." (Id at 32). He focuses on the usage and purpose, rather than manner or extent of use. Another definition is for "commercial gain".

Another place we see a division is between published and unpublished works. There, a publication, both under the 1909 Copyright Act and the 1976 Copyright Act, included distributions without restrictions. The work was available to the public. These are the normal commercial exploitations of work. So, taking this into consideration, normal commercial exploitation in the context of Section 108(h) may mean: sale or offer for sale. It would not likely include preparations for sale, mere discussions, or even requests for price lists.

This helps us in thinking about "normal commercial exploitation." It is the actual act of commercial gain, and not the contemplation. It is the act of selling, offering for sale, or demonstrating for sale. This makes the requirement visible to the public. It is not that a company may be contemplating reissuing a book. The book is for sale. What can we take away from this? Sale to the public or offer for sale likely constitutes "normal commercial exploitation" and for books, this means channels that libraries are likely to frequent.

So, how does one determine if a work is for sale? We came to believe that a "normal commercial exploitation" could mean.

- Does the work have an ISBN number?

- Is the work available in Books in Print?

- Is a new copy of the work available on Amazon?

- available from the standard sources for the industry?

W.H. Smith, the largest book retailer in Great Britain, began a means of computerizing their books, creating a Standard Book Numbering (SBN) system in 1966. This became the basis of the International system, which began in 1970, and is now used in more than 150 countries.103 The question is: what happened to works before 1970? If there is no ISBN for a work, is this a good indication that there is no "normal commercial exploitation" of the work now? Since the works we are looking at are from the 1920s, 1930s and 1940s, if they have not been reissued after 1970, they would not have an ISBN number, and so there is likely no commercial exploitation currently. (See Appendix for more on ISBN numbers).Parallel systems occur for non-books.

We found ISBNDB.com particularly helpful. At this free website, one can put in an author's name and title, and retrieve all of the places that one might find new *and used* editions of the work. We were particularly impressed that some of the results included the information about a work having an earlier publication date (that the work was a reprint). One can review the used and new copies and see the different versions, including the publication dates. It's an incredibly useful tool. Books in Print is also a good indication of whether there is currently normal commercial exploitation, as is availability at Amazon, and other sources that are industry specific.

One important caveat: just because a work is at Amazon does not mean that it qualifies as "normal commercial exploitation." We found in one study that we conducted that while a copy was found, the work was in fact in the public domain *or* it was clear that the copy we found was not authorized by the copyright holder or the original publisher. One has to really check the results to see if this is "normal commercial exploitation" by the copyright holder. The same holds true for "a reasonable copy." If there is a "reasonable copy" found is this because the work is in the public domain and many are reproducing the work. If this is the case, the library or archive is also able to reproduce the work *because the work is in the public domain*, and not under Section 108(h). Check the copyright status against your findings, and you may find hidden gems.

Reasonable Copy

The statute also requires that one cannot obtain a reasonable copy. In *Eldred v. Ashcroft*, Section 108(h) is mentioned in Dissent as a supplement to the First Amendment safeguards: "The CTEA itself supplements these traditional First Amendment safeguards. First, it allows libraries, archives, and similar institutions to "reproduce" and "distribute, display, or perform in facsimile or digital form" copies of certain published works "during the last 20 years of any term of copyright ... for purposes of preservation, scholarship, or research" if the work is not already being exploited commercially and further copies are unavailable at a reasonable price. 17 U.S.C. section 108(h)" *Eldred v. Ashcroft*, 537 U.S. 186, 220, 123 S. Ct. 769, 789, 154 L. Ed. 2d 683 (2003). Here Breyer describes the requirement as "further *copies* are unavailable at a reasonable price," and not in the singular.

How does one reasonably investigate? So, this is the heart of the work of our exploration. How does one determine whether a work is subject to "normal commercial exploitation", and how does one prove a negative – that there is no normal commercial exploitation. Second, what constitutes a reasonable copy? Does that include only new copies, or do used copies count too? What role does the first sale doctrine play in relation to reasonable copy? If reasonable copy is to benefit the copyright holder, one would assume only new copies are included.

The House Report related to Section 108 stated regarding a reasonable investigation: "The scope and nature of a reasonable investigation to determine that an unused copy cannot be obtained will vary according to the circumstances of a particular situation. It will always require recourse to commonly-known trade sources in the United States, and in the normal situation also to the publisher or other copyright owner (if the owner can be located at the address listed in the copyright registration), or an authorized reproducing service. It is further required that the copy become the property of the user, that the library or archives have no notice that the copy would be used for any purpose other than private study, scholarship, or research, and that the library or archives display prominently at the place where reproduction requests are accepted, and include on its order form, a warning of copyright in accordance with requirements that the Register of Copyrights shall prescribe by regulation."

For many works, especially archival materials, meeting the two requirements above is relatively easy. For instance, the Frick Collection has many exhibition catalogs, first published here and abroad. If the works are still under copyright (many of them are not), then the next step is a Section 108(h) analysis. In this case, they are not being commercially exploited – no one is actively selling these one-time, long forgotten works, and often the reason that they are being digitized is because they are nearly one-of-a-kind.

The other major question is whether reasonable copies are new or also used copies. There is an argument to be made on both sides. An earlier portion of Section 108, asks the library to look for unused copies at a reasonable price as a requirement before making a replacement copy: "the library or archives has, after a reasonable effort, determined that an unused replacement cannot be obtained at a fair price." The Discussion Paper from the U.S. Copyright Office on Section 108 seems to indicate that used copies count ("that a new or used copy of the work is not available at a reasonable price"). However, the statute itself is not as clear as the confident language from the Copyright Office.

Normal Commercial Exploitation and Reasonable Copy Applied

Both queries require the same search: are copies available of the work? One could see normal commercial exploitation potentially as new copies and reasonable copies as used. It is still unclear how the law approaches this, and whether reasonable copies or even just one copy suffices. Is reasonable copies new copies only? What is a reasonable copy? Does a later version count? Likely. What if the original version matters? Does that make a difference? Again, I think it goes back to intent. The goal is to provide access for research and scholarship. If a reasonable copy is available, then that seems sufficient. But the question begins again – what is a reasonable copy in a digital realm?

The Netflix Problem

How does one know when a work has not been made available for normal commercial exploitation or that a reasonable copy is not available for audiovisual works? First, as with books and periodicals, audiovisual works can be tracked with a ISBN-like number, called the International Standard Audiovisual Number (ISAN). While a voluntary system, like ISBN, the system does allow one to see if there is commercial activity on these older works. Second, the reasonable copy requirement is more easily met in some way by looking at Amazon.com or other online resources. Older films and other audiovisual works are less likely to have reasonable copies available. The real question is "normal commercial exploitation." Remember, the goal of Section 108(h) is to make available works that are not loved--that do not have copies available and are without normal commercial exploitation. As of 2017, these are works first published between 1923 and 1941.

What if a work is available on Netflix? Hmmm.... Well, that is normal commercial exploitation. But the one problem one runs into is that the works available on Netflix vary. What if there is no commercial exploitation of the work in May 2017 but there is in June, but again not in August? What if a scholar or teacher depends on a copy of the work? It seems that Netflix exploitation may not be stable enough, even though it is normal commercial exploitation. Another reading might be that it was normal commercial exploitation as of the drafting and enactment of the CTEA, in 1998. If that is the case, streaming availability by subscription was not a normal commercial exploitation.

Normal commercial exploitation also points to the library being able to purchase a copy of the work. Can a library purchase a subscription with a stable copy of the work? If not, that may not qualify as a normal commercial exploitation for the purposes of obtaining a copy to have in a library's collection.

Finally, the goal of Section 108(h), in the writer's opinion, was to rescue works that would *not* be playing on Netflix. If one can communicate with the copyright holders about their commercial exploitation, that may also be a strategy. Can the copyright holder point the library to normal commercial exploitation, which they could pass along to their patrons? Can the library buy a copy of the work?

Notice from Copyright Holders

A copyright holder may file a notice to libraries and archives of normal commercial exploitation or available at a reasonable price with the U.S. Copyright Office.106 This is the third aspect of the requirements for a library – that a notice hasn't been filed in the nearly 20 years since the law was passed in October 1998 (and there are no listed fees at the Copyright Office for doing so!) To date, no notices have ever been filed. As part of that information, the copyright holder may include information about the normal commercial exploitation or reasonable price, but is not required. However, the form must include: "A declaration made under penalty of perjury that the work identified is subject to normal commercial exploitation, or that a copy or phonorecord of the work is available at a reasonable price."107 What is interesting is no information is provided in the procedures of when the notice must be filed. What about the Compendium III, the Copyright Office practices? Nothing touches upon this process.

Once a copyright holder files a notice, the exception no longer applies. In its 2005 Orphan Work Report, the Copyright Office noted: "The provision does not provide much incentive for a copyright owner to file such a notice before it discovers that one of its works is being used under this subsection. By its terms, it appears that such a notice can be filed at any time, even after a library or archive begins use of a work it had determined to have met the criteria. Once the notice is filed, the work is no longer subject to the exception, and the library or archives would have to cease its use under section 108(h). In most cases, it would thus seem more efficient for a copyright owner to "wait and see" whether a work is being used under section 108(h) rather than to file such notices proactively."

So, should this concern libraries and archives? Well no one has filed a notice. And, in this day and age, one can take down digitizing. But I would also add that there may be some reliance on Section 108(h). If one puts resources into digitizing a work that is not commercially available and no copies are available at a reasonable price, and it is only after digitizing the work that the publisher/copyright holder then makes a copy available, one could think that the library/archive would have a case for collecting expenses from the library/archive. But at the least, the only obligation the library/archive would have would be to not use Section 108(h) as justification for making and distributing copies. Fair use, and all of the other portions of Section 108 would still apply.

Timing

When does this search for normal commercial exploitation and/or reasonable copies need to take place? Unlike Section 104A and other areas of the Copyright Act, no specifics about the timing is given. Some worry that they might have to continually be doing a search for a new or used copy of the work. We tend to view it within the context of the statute. Section 108(h) was designed to assist scholars, researchers and libraries/archives in their missions – to research and to preserve works. The reason the works are being digitized under Section 108(h) is because a reasonable copy is not found and that the work is currently not being manufactured or offered for sale as a new copy. The library/archive scans the work. The copyright holder can issue a notice that they are reasonable copies as part of the normal commercial exploitation, of course.

Registration

One additional element to consider: If a work is not registered with the U.S. Copyright Office, there is less "teeth" to the copyright. Domestic authors cannot pursue a copyright infringement case without registration, and both domestic authors and foreign authors alike cannot receive statutory damages or attorney's fees without registration.

Beyond Section 108

Libraries not only use Section 108, but they also use fair use. Kenny Crews has written extensively about fair use and libraries in *Copyright Law for Librarians and Educators* (4th ed. 2020). Two key cases related to library uses are Authors Guild, Inc. v. HathiTrust, 755 F.3d 87 (2d Cir. 2014) and

Unpublished Materials

Before 1978, unpublished materials were protected by state law, unless in rare cases they were registered with the U.S. Copyright Office, and many works were not eligible for registration. Section 303(a) of the 1976 Copyright Act changed all of that, and with it applied fair use, library exceptions and the rest of the Copyright Act to unpublished works.

We have already seen the distinction between unpublished works created before and after January 1, 1978. We also know that Section 108(h) only applies to published works. And we know that pre-1972 sound recordings are not included, that there is a separate area of the law that applies.

In section 108, we have special provisions that allow copying of unpublished works i n at least two scenarios: by the library and/or archive, and also by the user themselves.

10: Music Modernization Act

In 2018, the Music Modernization Act was signed into law. It was a combination of three bills: the Music Modernization Act, the CLASSIC Act, and the Allocation for Music Producers Act. After over a decade of discussion, the Copyright Act had new components. The Music Modernization Act (Title I) focuses on mechanical licenses and royalty payments with streaming media services, which had been the subject of much stress and disagreement. The CLASSIC Act, or the Compensating Legacy Artists for Their Songs, Service and Important Contributions to Society Act (seriously) brought pre-1972 sound recordings partially under federal protection for the first time. Sound recordings made before Feb 15, 1972 were covered only by state law, which had been a point of contention for at least a decade. The third title was the Allocation for Music Producers Act that designates SoundExchange (a non-profit) to distribute royalties on sound recordings. This chapter focuses on the CLASSICS Act.

Act II: The Classics Act

At Tulane Law School, we've been watching the status of pre-1972 sound recordings for over a decade. In this section, we are going to look at the world before the Classics Act, some of the legislation that led to the act, and finally the act itself.

Before the Classics Act, pre-1972 sound recordings were protected by a transition phase in the 1976 Copyright Act that would grant protection till Feb 15, 2067. No sound recordings -- none -- were out of copyright until that moment. Interestingly, they were not protected by federal law, but by state laws.

Everything was set to come out of state copyright on Feb 16, 2067. Now, for many works that remains true. But we will see that some works, especially older ones, will now come out as soon as 2022.

So, before the Classics Act, the Rolling Stones would have profited off their 1971 hit single "Brown Sugar" for ninety-six years (April 16, 1971 - February 16, 2067) before their song fell into the public domain. If you think that a century of copyright protection is still not long enough for one of the "500 Greatest Songs of All Time," then consider the duration of protection for the following: The Beatles' 1964 hit "A Hard Day's Night," Elvis' "Hound Dog" (1956), Bing Crosby's "White Christmas" (1942), Duke Ellington's "It Don't Mean a Thing (If It Ain't Got That Swing)" (1932), and every song ever recorded by Louis Armstrong, Jelly Roll Morton, and Sidney Bechet would not have entered the public domain until February 16, 2067. This was true not just for songs, but for every sort of sound recording, including spoken word and other sound effects. Even the very first sounds ever captured by Thomas Edison's phonograph in 1877 would not have entered the public domain until February 16, 2067 The CLASSICS Act put into place a graduated term depending on when and if the work was published.

Many people, particularly archivists and librarians, viewed the situation before the CLASSICS Act (Section 1401) as untenable, in part because pre-1972 sound recordings were not under federal law, and therefore not subject to Section 107 or 108. Addressing this criticism, in 2011, the United States Copyright Office began investigating the possibility of federalizing all pre-1972 sound recordings. The Copyright Office's investigation took the form of a study entitled "A Study on the Desirability of and Means for Bringing Sound Recordings Fixed Before February 15, 1972, Under Federal Jurisdiction." The Study consisted of a notice of inquiry, two sets of comments from the public (original and reply comments), and a roundtable discussion of several discrete issues held in Washington, D.C. Released in December 2011, the resulting final report, entitled "Federal Copyright Protection for Pre-1972 Sound Recordings," recommended federalization.

Providing federal protection for pre-1972 sound recordings required resolving many open legal issues. Though certain components of the existing federal copyright law, such as ownership, exclusive rights and fair use. In the Classics Act, they would bypass the hard questions (ownership and exclusive rights), leaving those to the state, and apply what the librarians and others wanted: fair use and library exceptions. They would also shorten the terms, at least in some categories, which are based on date of publication.

Shortening the Term

Section 1401 shortens the term of protection for pre-1972 sound recordings based on when they were published, and if not published, created.

There are four transition periods:

(i) Pre-1923 recordings.—

> In the case of a sound recording first published before January 1, 1923, the transition period described in subparagraph (A)(i)(II) shall end on December 31 of the year that is 3 years after the date of enactment of this section.

So, works first published before 1923 works come into the public domain as of January 1, 2022. This includes Thomas Edison's famous recording from 1877 presumably.

> (ii) 1923–1946 recordings.—
>
> In the case of a sound recording first published during the period beginning on January 1, 1923, and ending on December 31, 1946, the transition period described in subparagraph (A)(i)(II) shall end on the date that is 5 years after the last day of the period described in subparagraph (A)(i)(I).

This means that works come into the public domain 100 years after first publication. Duke Ellington's sound recording of "It Don't Mean a Thing (If It Ain't Got That Swing)" (1932) will be in the public domain in 2033. Bing Crosby's sound recording of "White Christmas" (1942) will be in the public domain in 2043.

Duke Ellington's 1932 recording of "It Don't Mean a Thing (If It Ain't Got That Swing)" will be protected through 2032, and Bing Crosby's 1942 recording of "White Christmas" will be protected through 2042.

> (iii) 1947–1956 recordings.—
>
> In the case of a sound recording first published during the period beginning on January 1, 1947, and ending on December 31, 1956, the transition period described in subparagraph (A)(i)(II) shall end on the date that is 15 years after the last day of the period described in subparagraph (A)(i)(I).

The term is 110 years from first publication. That means Elvis' 1956 sound recording of "Hound Dog" sound recording will be protected through 2066.

> (iv) Post-1956 recordings.—
>
> In the case of a sound recording fixed before February 15, 1972, that is not described in clause (i), (ii), or (iii), the transition period described in subparagraph (A)(i)(II) shall end on February 15, 2067.

The term is through February 15, 2067. So, the Beattles' 1964 sound recording of "A Hard Day's Night" will continue to be protected through February 15, 2067, or 103 years frorm its publication.

Section 1401 was not merely about term. Let's take a look at the whole section. Also, it is important to note that Section 1401 only applies to the sound recording, and not to the underlying musical composition or literary recording. Also, this only applies to sound recording and not audiovisual works.

Section 1401

(a) In General.—

(1) Unauthorized acts.—

Anyone who, on or before the last day of the applicable transition period under paragraph (2), and without the consent of the rights owner, engages in covered activity with respect to a sound recording fixed before February 15, 1972, shall be subject to the remedies provided in sections 502 through 505 and 1203 to the same extent as an infringer of copyright or a person that engages in unauthorized activity under chapter 12.

(2) Term of prohibition.—

(A)In general.—The prohibition under paragraph (1)—

(i)subject to clause (ii), shall apply to a sound recording described in that paragraph—

(I)through December 31 of the year that is 95 years after the year of first publication; and

(II)for a further transition period as prescribed under subparagraph (B) of this paragraph; and

(ii) shall not apply to any sound recording after February 15, 2067.

(B) Transition periods.—

(i) Pre-1923 recordings.—

In the case of a sound recording first published before January 1, 1923, the transition period described in subparagraph (A)(i)(II) shall end on December 31 of the year that is 3 years after the date of enactment of this section.

(ii) 1923–1946 recordings.—

In the case of a sound recording first published during the period beginning on January 1, 1923, and ending on December 31, 1946, the transition period described in subparagraph (A)(i)(II) shall end on the date that is 5 years after the last day of the period described in subparagraph (A)(i)(I).

(iii) 1947–1956 recordings.—

In the case of a sound recording first published during the period beginning on January 1, 1947, and ending on December 31, 1956, the transition period described in subparagraph (A)(i)(II) shall end on the date that is 15 years after the last day of the period described in subparagraph (A)(i)(I).

(iv) Post-1956 recordings.—

In the case of a sound recording fixed before February 15, 1972, that is not described in clause (i), (ii), or (iii), the transition period described in subparagraph (A)(i)(II) shall end on February 15, 2067.

(3) Rule of construction.—

For the purposes of this subsection, the term "anyone" includes any State, any instrumentality of a State, and any officer or employee of a State or instrumentality of a State acting in the official capacity of the officer or employee, as applicable.

(b) Certain Authorized Transmissions and Reproductions.—A public performance by means of a digital audio transmission of a sound recording fixed before February 15, 1972, or a reproduction in an ephemeral phonorecord or copy of a sound recording fixed before February 15, 1972, shall, for purposes of subsection (a), be considered to be authorized and made with the consent of the rights owner if—

(1) the transmission or reproduction would satisfy the requirements for statutory licensing under section 112(e)(1) or section 114(d)(2), or would be exempt under section 114(d)(1), as the case may be, if the sound recording were fixed on or after February 15, 1972; and
(2) the transmitting entity pays the statutory royalty for the transmission or reproduction pursuant to the rates and terms adopted under sections 112(e) and

114(f), and complies with other obligations, in the same manner as required by regulations adopted by the Copyright Royalty Judges under sections 112(e) and 114(f) for sound recordings that are fixed on or after February 15, 1972, except in the case of a transmission that would be exempt under section 114(d)(1).

(c) Certain Noncommercial Uses of Sound Recordings That Are Not Being Commercially Exploited.—

(1) **In general.**—Noncommercial use of a sound recording fixed before February 15, 1972, that is not being commercially exploited by or under the authority of the rights owner shall not violate subsection (a) if—

(A) the person engaging in the noncommercial use, in order to determine whether the sound recording is being commercially exploited by or under the authority of the rights owner, makes a good faith, reasonable search for, but does not find, the sound recording—

(i)in the records of schedules filed in the Copyright Office as described in subsection (f)(5)(A); and

(ii)on services offering a comprehensive set of sound recordings for sale or streaming;

(B) the person engaging in the noncommercial use files a notice identifying the sound recording and the nature of the use in the Copyright Office in accordance with the regulations issued under paragraph (3)(B); and

(C) during the 90-day period beginning on the date on which the notice described in subparagraph (B) is indexed into the public records of the Copyright Office, the rights owner of the sound recording does not, in its discretion, opt out of the noncommercial use by filing notice thereof in the Copyright Office in accordance with the regulations issued under paragraph (5).

(2) Rules of construction.—For purposes of this subsection—

(A) merely recovering costs of production and distribution of a sound recording resulting from a use otherwise permitted under this subsection does not itself necessarily constitute a commercial use of the sound recording;

(B) the fact that a person engaging in the use of a sound recording also engages in commercial activities does not itself necessarily render the use commercial; and

(C) the fact that a person files notice of a noncommercial use of a sound recording in accordance with the regulations issued under paragraph (3)(B) does not itself affect any limitation on the exclusive rights of a copyright owner described in section 107, 108, 109, 110, or 112(f) as applied to a claim under subsection (a) of this section pursuant to subsection (f)(1)(A) of this section.

(3) Notice of covered activity.—Not later than 180 days after the date of enactment of this section, the Register of Copyrights shall issue regulations that—

(A) provide specific, reasonable steps that, if taken by a filer, are sufficient to constitute a good faith, reasonable search under paragraph (1)(A) to determine whether a recording is being commercially exploited, including the services that satisfy the good faith, reasonable search requirement under paragraph (1)(A) for purposes of the safe harbor described in paragraph (4)(A); and

(B) establish the form, content, and procedures for the filing of notices under paragraph (1)(B).

(4) Safe harbor.—

(A) In general.—

A person engaging in a noncommercial use of a sound recording otherwise permitted under this subsection who establishes that the person made a good faith, reasonable search under paragraph (1)(A) without finding commercial exploitation of the sound recording by or under the authority of the rights owner shall not be found to be in violation of subsection (a).

(B) Steps sufficient but not necessary.—

Taking the specific, reasonable steps identified by the Register of Copyrights in the regulations issued under paragraph (3)(A) shall be sufficient, but not necessary, for a filer to satisfy the requirement to conduct a good faith, reasonable search under paragraph (1)(A) for purposes of subparagraph (A) of this paragraph.

(5) Opting out of covered activity.—

(A) In general.—

Not later than 180 days after the date of enactment of this section, the Register of Copyrights shall issue regulations establishing the form, content, and procedures for the rights owner of a sound recording that is the subject of a notice under paragraph (1)(B) to, in its discretion, file notice opting out of the covered activity described in the notice under paragraph (1)(B) during the 90-day period beginning on the date on which the notice under paragraph (1)(B) is indexed into the public records of the Copyright Office.

(B) Rule of construction.—

The fact that a rights holder opts out of a noncommercial use of a sound recording by filing notice thereof in the Copyright Office in accordance with the regulations issued under subparagraph (A) does not itself enlarge or diminish any limitation on the exclusive rights of a copyright owner described in section 107, 108, 109, 110, or 112(f) as applied to a claim under subsection (a) of this section pursuant to subsection (f)(1)(A) of this section.

(6) Civil penalties for certain acts.—

(A) Filing of notices of noncommercial use.—

Any person who willfully engages in a pattern or practice of filing a notice of noncommercial use of a sound recording as described in paragraph (1)(B) fraudulently describing the use proposed, or knowing that the use proposed is not permitted under this subsection, shall be assessed a civil penalty in an amount that is not less than $250, and not more than $1000, for each such notice, in addition to any other remedies that may be available under this title based on the actual use made.

(B) Filing of opt-out notices.—

(i) In general.—

Any person who files an opt-out notice as described in paragraph (1)(C), knowing that the person is not the rights owner or authorized to act on behalf of the rights owner of the sound recording to which the notice pertains, shall be assessed a civil penalty in an amount not less than $250, and not more than $1,000, for each such notice.

(ii) Pattern or practice.—

Any person who engages in a pattern or practice of making filings as described in clause (i) shall be assessed a civil penalty in an amount not less than $10,000 for each such filing.

(C) Definition.—For purposes of this paragraph, the term "knowing"—

(i) does not require specific intent to defraud; and

(ii) with respect to information about ownership of the sound recording in question, means that the person—

(I) has actual knowledge of the information;

(II) acts in deliberate ignorance of the truth or falsity of the information; or

(III) acts in grossly negligent disregard of the truth or falsity of the information.

(d)Payment of Royalties for Transmissions of Performances by Direct Licensing of Statutory Services.—

(1) In general.—

A public performance by means of a digital audio transmission of a sound recording fixed before February 15, 1972, shall, for purposes of subsection (a), be considered to be authorized and made with the consent of the rights owner if the transmission is made pursuant to a license agreement voluntarily negotiated at any time between the rights owner and the entity performing the sound recording.

(2) Payment of royalties to nonprofit collective under certain license agreements.—

(A) Licenses entered into on or after date of enactment.—To the extent that a license agreement described in paragraph (1) entered into on or after the date of enactment of this section extends to a public performance by means of a digital audio transmission of a sound recording fixed before February 15, 1972, that meets the conditions of subsection (b)—

(i) the licensee shall, with respect to such transmission, pay to the collective designated to distribute receipts from the licensing of transmissions in accordance with section 114(f), 50 percent of the performance royalties for that transmission due under the license; and

(ii) the royalties paid under clause (i) shall be fully credited as payments due under the license.

(B) Certain agreements entered into before enactment.—To the extent that a license agreement described in paragraph (1), entered into during the period beginning on January 1 of the year in which this section is enacted and ending on the day before the date of enactment of this section, or a settlement agreement with a preexisting satellite digital audio radio service (as defined in section 114(j)) entered into during the period beginning on January 1, 2015, and ending on the day before the date of enactment of this section, extends to a public performance by means of a digital audio transmission of a sound recording fixed before February 15, 1972, that meets the conditions of subsection (b)—

(i) the rights owner shall, with respect to such transmission, pay to the collective designated to distribute receipts from the licensing of transmissions in accordance with section 114(f) an amount that is equal to the difference between—

(I) 50 percent of the difference between—

(aa) the rights owner's total gross performance royalty fee receipts or settlement monies received for all such transmissions covered under the license or settlement agreement, as applicable; and

(bb) the rights owner's total payments for outside legal expenses, including any payments of third-party claims, that are directly attributable to the license or settlement agreement, as applicable; and

(II) the amount of any royalty receipts or settlement monies under the agreement that are distributed by the rights owner to featured and non-featured artists before the date of enactment of this section; and

(ii) the royalties paid under clause (i) shall be fully credited as payments due under the license or settlement agreement, as applicable.

(3) Distribution of royalties and settlement monies by collective.—

The collective described in paragraph (2) shall, in accordance with subparagraphs (B) through (D) of section 114(g)(2), and paragraphs (5) and (6) of section 114(g), distribute the royalties or settlement monies received under paragraph (2) under a license or settlement described in paragraph (2), which shall be the only payments to which featured and non-featured artists are entitled by virtue of the transmissions described in paragraph (2), except for settlement monies described in paragraph (2) that are distributed by the rights owner to featured and non-featured artists before the date of enactment of this section.

(4) Payment of royalties under license agreements entered before enactment or not otherwise described in paragraph (2).—

(A) In general.—

To the extent that a license agreement described in paragraph (1) entered into before the date of enactment of this section, or any other license agreement not as described in paragraph (2), extends to a public performance by means of a digital audio transmission of a sound recording fixed before February 15, 1972, that meets the conditions of subsection (b), the payments made by the licensee pursuant to the license shall be made in accordance with the agreement.

(B) Additional payments not required.—

To the extent that a licensee has made, or will make in the future, payments pursuant to a license as described in subparagraph (A), the provisions of paragraphs (2) and (3) shall not require any additional payments from, or additional financial obligations on the part of, the licensee.

(C) Rule of construction.—

Nothing in this subsection may be construed to prohibit the collective designated to distribute receipts from the licensing of transmissions in accordance with section 114(f) from administering royalty payments under any license not described in paragraph (2).

(e) Preemption With Respect to Certain Past Acts.—

(1) In general.—This section preempts any claim of common law copyright or equivalent right under the laws of any State arising from a digital audio transmission or reproduction that is made before the date of enactment of this section of a sound recording fixed before February 15, 1972, if—

(A) the digital audio transmission would have satisfied the requirements for statutory licensing under section 114(d)(2) or been exempt under section 114(d)(1), or the reproduction would have satisfied the requirements of section 112(e)(1), as the case may be, if the sound recording were fixed on or after February 15, 1972; and

(B) either—

(i) except in the case of a transmission that would have been exempt under section 114(d)(1), not later than 270 days after the date of enactment of this section, the transmitting entity pays statutory royalties and provides notice of the use of the relevant sound recordings in the same manner as required by regulations adopted by the Copyright Royalty Judges for sound recordings that are fixed on or after February 15, 1972, for all the digital audio transmissions and reproductions satisfying the requirements for statutory licensing under sections 112(e)(1) and 114(d)(2) during the 3 years before that date of enactment; or

(ii) an agreement voluntarily negotiated between the rights owner and the entity performing the sound recording (including a litigation settlement agreement entered into before the date of enactment of this section) authorizes or waives liability for any such transmission or reproduction and the transmitting entity has paid for and reported such digital audio transmission under that agreement.

(2) Rule of construction for common law copyright.—

For purposes of paragraph (1), a claim of common law copyright or equivalent right under the laws of any State includes a claim that characterizes conduct subject to that paragraph as an unlawful distribution, act of record piracy, or similar violation.

(3) Rule of construction for public performance rights.—

Nothing in this section may be construed to recognize or negate the existence of public performance rights in sound recordings under the laws of any State.

(f) Limitations on Remedies.—

(1) Fair use; uses by libraries, archives, and educational institutions.—

(A) In general.—

The limitations on the exclusive rights of a copyright owner described in sections 107, 108, 109, 110, and 112(f) shall apply to a claim under subsection (a) with respect to a sound recording fixed before February 15, 1972.

(B) Rule of construction for section 108(h).—

With respect to the application of section 108(h) to a claim under subsection (a) with respect to a sound recording fixed before February 15, 1972, the phrase "during the last 20 years of any term of copyright of a published work" in such section 108(h) shall be construed to mean at any time after the date of enactment of this section.

(2) Actions.—

The limitations on actions described in section 507 shall apply to a claim under subsection (a) with respect to a sound recording fixed before February 15, 1972.

(3) Material online.—

Section 512 shall apply to a claim under subsection (a) with respect to a sound recording fixed before February 15, 1972.

(4) Principles of equity.—

Principles of equity apply to remedies for a violation of this section to the same extent as such principles apply to remedies for infringement of copyright.

(5) Filing requirement for statutory damages and attorneys' fees.—

(A) Filing of information on sound recordings.—

(i) Filing requirement.—Except in the case of a transmitting entity that has filed contact information for that transmitting entity under subparagraph (B), in any action under this section, an award of statutory damages or of attorneys' fees under section 504 or 505 may be made with respect to an unauthorized use of a sound recording under subsection (a) only if—

(I) the rights owner has filed with the Copyright Office a schedule that specifies the title, artist, and rights owner of the sound recording and contains such other information, as practicable, as the Register of Copyrights prescribes by regulation; and

(II) the use occurs after the end of the 90-day period beginning on the date on which the information described in subclause (I) is indexed into the public records of the Copyright Office.

(ii) Regulations.—Not later than 180 days after the date of enactment of this section, the Register of Copyrights shall issue regulations that—

(I) establish the form, content, and procedures for the filing of schedules under clause (i);

(II) provide that a person may request that the person receive timely notification of a filing described in subclause (I); and

(III) set forth the manner in which a person may make a request under subclause (II).

(B) Filing of contact information for transmitting entities.—

(i) Filing requirement.—

Not later than 30 days after the date of enactment of this section, the Register of Copyrights shall issue regulations establishing the form, content, and procedures for the filing of contact information by any entity that, as of the date of enactment of this section, performs a sound recording fixed before February 15, 1972, by means of a digital audio transmission.

(ii)Time limit on filings.—

The Register of Copyrights may accept filings under clause (i) only until the 180th day after the date of enactment of this section.

(iii) Limitation on statutory damages and attorneys' fees.—

(I) Limitation.—An award of statutory damages or of attorneys' fees under section 504 or 505 may not be made against an entity that has filed contact information for that entity under clause (i) with respect to an unauthorized use by that entity of a sound recording under subsection (a) if the use occurs before the end of the 90-day period beginning on the date on which the entity receives a notice that—

(aa) is sent by or on behalf of the rights owner of the sound recording;

(bb) states that the entity is not legally authorized to use that sound recording under subsection (a); and

(cc)identifies the sound recording in a schedule conforming to the requirements prescribed by the regulations issued under subparagraph (A)(ii).

(II) Undeliverable notices.—

In any case in which a notice under subclause (I) is sent to an entity by mail or courier service and the notice is returned to the sender because the entity either is no longer located at the address provided in the contact information filed under clause (i) or has refused to accept delivery, or the notice is sent by electronic mail and is undeliverable, the 90-day period under subclause (I) shall begin on the date of the attempted delivery.

(C) Section 412.—

Section 412 shall not limit an award of statutory damages under section 504(c) or attorneys' fees under section 505 with respect to a covered activity in violation of subsection (a).

(6) Applicability of other provisions.—

(A) In general.—

Subject to subparagraph (B), no provision of this title shall apply to or limit the remedies available under this section except as otherwise provided in this section.

(B) Applicability of definitions.—

Any term used in this section that is defined in section 101 shall have the meaning given that term in section 101.

(g) Application of Section 230 Safe Harbor.—

For purposes of section 230 of the Communications Act of 1934 (47 U.S.C. 230), subsection (a) shall be considered to be a "law pertaining to intellectual property" under subsection (e)(2) of such section 230.

(h) Application to Rights Owners.—

(1) **Transfers.**—With respect to a rights owner described in subsection (*l*)(2)(B)—

(A) subsections (d) and (e) of section 201 and section 204 shall apply to a transfer described in subsection (l)(2)(B) to the same extent as with respect to a transfer of copyright ownership; and

(B) notwithstanding section 411, that rights owner may institute an action with respect to a violation of this section to the same extent as the owner of an exclusive right under a copyright may institute an action under section 501(b).

(2) **Application of other provisions.**—The following provisions shall apply to a rights owner under this section to the same extent as any copyright owner:

(A) Section 112(e)(2).

(B) Section 112(e)(7).

(C) Section 114(e).

(D) Section 114(h).

(i) Ephemeral Recordings.—

An authorized reproduction made under this section shall be subject to section 112(g) to the same extent as a reproduction of a sound recording fixed on or after February 15, 1972.

(j) Rule of Construction.—

A rights owner of, or featured recording artist who performs on, a sound recording under this chapter shall be deemed to be an interested copyright party, as defined in section 1001, to the same extent as a copyright owner or featured recording artist under chapter 10.

(k)Treatment of States and State Instrumentalities, Officers, and Employees.—

Any State, and any instrumentality, officer, or employee described in subsection (a)(3), shall be subject to the provisions of this section in the same manner and to the same extent as any nongovernmental entity.

(l) Definitions.—In this section:

(1) Covered activity.—

The term "covered activity" means any activity that the copyright owner of a sound recording would have the exclusive right to do or authorize under section 106 or 602, or that would violate section 1201 or 1202, if the sound recording were fixed on or after February 15, 1972.

(2)Rights owner.—The term "rights owner" means—

(A) the person that has the exclusive right to reproduce a sound recording under the laws of any State, as of the day before the date of enactment of this section; or

(B) any person to which a right to enforce a violation of this section may be transferred, in whole or in part, after the date of enactment of this section, under—

(i) subsections (d) and (e) of section 201; and

(ii) section 204.

(Added Pub. L. 115–264, title II, section 202(a)(2), Oct. 11, 2018, 132 Stat. 3728.)

Getting to Section 1401

So, how did we get here, and what does it all mean? The goal of the next section is to watch the progress of how legislation is created, at least in part.

The Copyright Office's Study was designed to explore the potential problems posed by federalization. In order to fully appreciate the issue of federalization, it is important to understand the history of copyright protection for sound recordings. Sound recordings have not always been included in the subject matter of copyright. While the phonograph was invented in 1877,[23] it was not until 1972—nearly one hundred years later—that sound recordings first received federal copyright protection. While sound recordings did not receive federal copyright protection sound recordings were not altogether unprotected; in fact, a "dual system" of copyright protection was in place. Under this dual system, both federal and state laws governed copyright, with federal law covering published works and state law covering unpublished works. Accordingly, even where federal law did not provide copyright protection, it was possible that state law could. For sound recordings, this was in fact the case. Sound recordings generally came to be considered unpublished works and were therefore eligible for state law protection. So although federal law did not provide protection against their unauthorized duplication, state laws, such as those prohibiting misappropriation and unfair competition, did.

Though state law protection was available, it proved problematic. Reliance on state law resulted in a lack of uniformity, which led to confusion and inconsistency: confusion over which state's law governed and inconsistency between federal and state law and amongst the various laws of the different states. Each state was free to create its own copyright law, and this led to ineffective enforcement and insufficient relief. The disparate treatments of sound recordings under state laws concerned copyright holders and Congress alike and served as a main justification, first, for providing federal protection for sound recordings and, later, for preemption of state copyright laws.

Reliance on state law also presented another problem: term, or duration. While Congress is bound by the Constitution's "limited times" clause, the states are not. In other words, perpetual copyright protection, while forbidden under federal law, is available under state law. But while duration presented a serious problem, the issue of perpetual protection was overshadowed by the lack of uniformity, which was itself sufficient to motivate the call for federal protection. With the dual scheme under scrutiny, Congress began the process of guaranteeing federal protection for sound recordings.

Congress had first considered adding sound recordings to the categories of federally protected subject matter in 1925. However, the idea did not gain traction until the 1960s, when Congress began preparing for the second general revision of the federal copyright law. At that time, the growing popularity of cassette tapes and the corresponding problem of piracy also contributed to the move to federal protection. The development of cassette-tape technology made the duplication of sound recordings easy and inexpensive. This led to a surge in unauthorized duplication and resale—that is, piracy. Piracy decreased record companies' profits, artists' royalties, and federal, state, and local sales tax revenues. But because sound recordings were not federally protected subject matter, piracy did not violate federal copyright law. As inconsistent state-law protections proved insufficient, the need for federal protection for sound recordings became urgent. The piracy threat became so pressing that while the general revision of the Copyright Act stalled for unrelated reasons, federal protection for sound recordings moved forward.

In 1971, with the passage of an amendment to the 1909 Act, sound recordings first received federal copyright protection. The amendment, also known as the "Sound Recordings Act of 1971," added sound recordings to the categories of protectable subject matter. Notably,however, this addition was not retroactive. Only sound recordings fixed on or after February 15, 1972—the date on which the 1971 amendment took effect—received federal copyright protection. Sound recordings fixed before February 15, 1972 remained governed by state law.

Though this split in protection seems odd today, such a division was consistent with the 1909 Act's dual system of copyright protection. Not long thereafter, in 1976, Congress passed the second general revision of the Copyright Act, which remains in effect today. The 1976 Act carried forward the 1971 amendment's protection for post-1972 sound recordings. But the 1976 Act also provided for preemption of state copyright laws. In section 301 of the 1976 Act, Congress abrogated the old dual copyright system and created a new, almost entirely federal system of copyright, without addressing the issue of pre-1972 sound recordings.

Pre-1972 sound recordings could have been subject to federal protection under section 301, which regulates preemption of state law by federal law. Instead, 301(c) specifically exempts pre-1972 sound recordings from preemption until February 15, 2067. Why were pre-1972 sound recordings, and these works only,exempted from preemption? Initial drafts of section 301 contained no exemption. However, after the Department of Justice voiced concerns that preemption would abrogate state antipiracy laws, aggravating the growing piracy problem, section 301(c) was added. With the addition of section 301(c) came the loss of federal protection for pre-1972 sound recordings. Instead, these works remain governed by state law. Section 301 of the Copyright Act preempts all state copyright laws except those governing sound recordings fixed before February 15, 1972 (pre-1972 sound recordings).

In 2009, Congress directed the Register of Copyrights to conduct a study on the desirability and means of federalizing pre-1972 sound recordings. Congress further directed the Register of Copyrights to seek comments from interested parties. On December 1, 2010, the Copyright Office launched the study by publishing a notice of inquiry. The notice called for comments on how federalization of pre-1972 recordings might affect preservation of and public access to these works, and the impact on the economic interests of parties holding the rights to these works ("rights holders"). The notice also requested comments on the best means for achieving federalization.

In addition to these general requests, the notice posed thirty specific questions. The questions fell within one of five categories: (1) Preservation of and Access to Pre-1972 Sound Recordings; (2) Economic Impact; (3) Term of Protection and Related Constitutional Considerations; (4) Partial Incorporation; and (5) Miscellaneous Questions.

Implementation of Section 1401

Part of the implementation of Section 1401 for pre-1972 sound recordings is a system that allows both copyright holders to identify works and users for non-commercial uses to also identify works. Section 1401 provides a means of registering works through a simple excel file and a fee.

Copyright holders can register their sound recordings through a special Schedule system. You must include the copyright holder's name, the title of the sound recordings, and if possible, the featured artist(s). You may do these in batches, and they are released periodically by the Copyright Office. This puts others on notice that the copyright holders are enforcing their copyrights.

Non-commercial uses must also be registered, but that is a different system.

Let's compare the two systems.
https://www.copyright.gov/rulemaking/pre1972-soundrecordings-schedules/

11: Formalities Today

Copyright arises automatically, every time we create something, for all of us--whether we are a two-year-old making art at preschool or a famous artist whose paintings are worth millions. No registration is needed. But you can get more protection if you include a copyright notice and register the work with the U.S. Copyright Office. This chapter focuses on copyright notice, the related concept of rights statements, and how to register your work at the U.S. Copyright Office.

Copyright arises automatically, it is true. But if you do not register your work, you have much MUCH less protection. In fact, without registering your work, you cannot go to court! So, while you do hold a copyright, your protection is subpar. We'll talk more about strategies for registering your work, including costs and how to group your works to save money as well.

Everyone knows what a copyright notice looks like: © 2019 Elizabeth Townsend Gard. But what does it mean, why do you include it, and what should be included? Copyright notice is the first step to let the world know you intend to enforce your property rights. The supplemental rights statement helps navigate the property rights--no commercial use, for example, or feel free to make your own version!

Rights statements are the portion usually near or after the copyright notice that tells the world what they can and can't do with the work. The most famous one is "All rights reserved." This chapter explores what that means exactly and what alternatives there are, including, "No rights reserved," and, "Some rights reserved."

This chapter navigates through both the copyright notice and rights statement, both in learning to read what a rights statement means, and also how to create one of your own. This chapter focuses on copyright notice for works published or created on or after March 1, 1989. Let's go through the basics of copyright notice, and then turn to the rights statement.

Copyright Notice

Copyright notice tells the world who the copyright holder is and when the work was created. The date and author information helps us determine how long copyright lasts.

Copyright notice is particularly important when your work is published--that is, circulating out in the public. Why? If you send something out in the world, it's a really good idea (if you care) to put your name on it and let the world know you care about the property attached to it. Now, not everyone wants this. Some want to release it out for everyone to use. Others would be happy for others to use it, but only in some instances. Before we get there, let's understand the basic components (and why) of copyright notice. **Notice should be placed on all copies that are going to be sold or distributed to the public.**

Publication

Notice is only required when a work is published, that is a work or a copy of the work is circulating out in the public without restrictions (meaning, nothing like "Draft. Do not distribute."). The legal definition has historically been complicated. Here are the basics:

· If the work is being distributed to the **public** by sale, rental, lease, lending, or transfer of ownership, the work is published. An offer to do any of these things also triggers publication. Examples: books in a bookstore or patterns sold online

· If a work is merely being displayed, this does not constitute publication, as long as there are no copies circulating to the public. So, if you have a quilt hanging in a show, that is not considered published, but if you print postcards to hand out of that quilt that would be considered published.

What about Artwork? When are works of art considered published? Sale of an original work of art (e.g. a quilt) does not constitute publication. Merely displaying the work does not constitute publication. Selling a piece of art with no intention of allowing copies doesn't seem to trigger publication. But allowing the public access to make unrestricted non-personal copies does publish the work. So, think of a one-of-a-kind art quilt. The work is still considered unpublished, and therefore would not need a copyright notice, even if it is displayed. But if patterns were made of that quilt, or the public is given unrestricted access, the work is considered published. Law scholar Deborah Gerhardt suggests the following test of whether publication has occurred:

(1) whether the copyright owner acts in a manner reflecting an intent to share the work with the public, and

(2) the availability of authorized copies

Unrestricted access is key. The Copyright Office and the courts have not been clear whether posting a work on a website constitutes publication.

Notice and Unpublished works: Notice is optional for unpublished works. It doesn't hurt to put it on your works. So, if you are making a label for a quilt, it doesn't hurt to add a copyright notice, if you care.

Notice and foreign works: Notice is also optional for foreign works--works first published outside of the U.S. Again, there are benefits to adding the notice, including preventing a claim of innocent infringement, which reduces statutory damages.

Elements of Copyright Notice

There are three elements to include on any copyright notice.

Must use one of the following: ©, Copyright, or "Copr."

It all begins with this, although the order can be different. Any of the above words can be used, but © is considered the best, particularly if your work is going to be sold or distributed internationally. What else works? (c), CO, C, %, @, [c], and c in a square. You can also misspell copyright: copyrighted, copywrite, copyritten, copy, copyr., registered U.S. copyright office, copyright applied for, copyright pending. So, you don't have to get it exactly right to still gain protection. Interestingly, "All Rights Reserved" on its own *does not work!* It has to be accompanied by "copyright" and the other requirements below in some form.

Copyright Holder

This is the name of the owner of the copyright. It can be an abbreviation too. It is the person/company with the "rights" to the copyright at the time of publication. For example,

> *Piece and Quilt with Precuts* by Christa Watson. © 2017 by Christa Watson. Even though Martingale published Christa's book, Christa holds the copyright.
>
> *Cheerful Charm Quilts*. (Note: no author list). © 2013 by Martingale and Co.

On Quiltsmart's *Mondo Bag* pattern: © 2010/2012 by Quiltsmart, Inc.

What does the name tell us? Who the copyright holder is, at least at the time of publication. It's a place to start. The copyright might have been transferred to someone else, but it is a place to begin. The name also sometimes tells us how long the copyright lasts, in combination with the date. This is important as well. When is it the author's name, and when is it the publishing company? This is based on the contractual relationship you have with your publisher, and if you are self-publishing, whether you (yourself) are the copyright holder, or you have created a company to hold the intellectual property. Sometimes copyright notices are complicated, but also help us understand which rights are held by which person. Finally, copyrights can revert back to the original owner, can be sold (assigned) or licensed. So, the copyright notice is a starting point if you want to learn more about who holds the right to grant permission.

Note: Deceased people cannot be named as the copyright holder, or register a copyright. It has to name the person, company or estate with rights. That's the point of copyright notice: to name and identify the person/company to contact should one need permission.

Date

The notice usually includes the year of publication. For pictorial, graphic or sculptural works, the year of publication is not required. This is important for quilting and crafting. This is a huge category of works--toys, dolls, useful articles, postcards, quilts, and fabric.

Placement of Notice

Where copyright notice should be placed is an important topic in the law of copyright. People have to be able to find it. It's a notice.

> **Literary works:** Ideally it would be on the title page or the page following the title page. At the beginning. If there are no more than 10 pages, the last page appears to be acceptable too.
>
> **Artistic works:** The notice can be a label either on the front or back, or on a mounting, matting, frame, or other materials where the work is durably attached.
>
>> **For fabric,** the Copyright Office has special rules, under "works consisting of sheet-like or strip material." The notice can be on the fabric

itself; the margin or selvage; the reverse side of the fabric; or on a tag or label attached to the spool or container holding the fabric. How far apart must the notice be? We have a number of cases that give a variation on how far apart the notice must be, from once every time the pattern repeats, to 19 inches to as much as 30 inches (e.g. under a yard).

The Advantages of Copyright Notice

Since March 1, 1989, copyright notice is not required in order to be protected by the U.S. Copyright Act. Why include copyright notice when it is no longer required? There are strong advantages to including proper copyright notice on works.

Mine. By putting notice on your work, it alerts the world that copyright is being claimed. In the reverse, by not putting copyright notice on your work, you are signaling that you *are not likely* to claim copyright on the work--that you are more in a sharing mood. It also helps a work from becoming an "orphan," meaning it is still under copyright but the copyright holder can't be found.

Not Innocent. If you put a notice on a work and someone uses your work anyway, s/he is no longer an innocent infringer. They knew you claimed a property right. They used it anyway. In this case, the copyright notice has to be in proper form. Not innocent means that if there is a lawsuit, it could actually be willful infringement, and then statutory damages could be significant. Innocence or willfulness deeply impacts the amount of money a court will award. Innocent infringers can have their statutory damages reduced to $200, while willful damages can be up to $150,000 per infringed work. Putting a proper copyright notice on your work makes a difference.

Identity. Because notice includes your name, it allows people to know who is claiming the property right and ideally can contact you (if necessary) for permission.

Copyright notice tells the world that you claim your property right. But to enforce that right in court, you need to register the work. You might also see your work being used without your permission and send a Cease-and-Desist notice. Or you might see your work on Facebook or other platforms, and file a Notice-and-Takedown with the platform.

Copyright Exclusive Rights and the Rights Statement

Copyright gives the copyright holder *rights*: to make copies, distribute the work, make derivative works, publicly display, and publicly perform the work. 17 U.S.C. Section 106. There are five basic exclusive rights the copyright holder gets *automatically upon creation* (now) *without doing anything.* A quick reminder of the exclusive rights.

Reproduction Right

> Making copies of the original work is the basis of copyright: the right to copy. This includes literal copying and substantial similarity.

Distribution Right

> The copyright holder has the right to decide when and how a work is distributed to the public. Once the sale occurs, however, the copyright holder does not control subsequent sales. This is called the First Sale Doctrine.

Public Display

> The copyright holder decides where and when the work is displayed publicly. This makes sense. A quilter can decide which quilt shows to enter their quilt, for example.

Public Performance

> Except for artwork (weird), the copyright holder controls when a work can be publicly performed during the term of the copyright.

Create Derivative Works

> The copyright holder has the exclusive right to create secondary works from the original work. These are called derivative works. There are some instances (namely fair use) where others can use your work and make their own works without permission.

These are the rights of copyright. Now, let's see the choices of expressing your rights in relation to others' using your work, namely the general public. Obviously, you could also create contracts and one-on-one relationships. But when you put out a product or something to the world, it is ideal to let them know how you feel about the rights and what they can or can't do with your work and in what situations. The rights statement with the copyright notice alerts the world as to the intentions of the copyright holder on what others can do. Sometimes there are additional words that communicate to the world permissible uses and restrictions on the use of the work. There are three basic kinds:

> *All Rights Reserved.* Copyright holder wants to control as much as possible. This is the default, even if you don't include the rights statement.
>
> *No Rights Reserved.* Copyright holder sends its work out into the world.
>
> *Some Rights Reserved, or a Creative Commons License.* This tells anyone that comes to the work what they can and can't do, without having to ask direct permission.

What is a Creative Commons License?

In the 21st century, with the rise of the Internet, people found that "All rights reserved" was a bit too restrictive--that there were many times where the copyright holder was okay with people further distributing/sharing the work, using the work to build new things (derivative work), and even using the work commercially. Creative Commons transformed how we think about rights statements. They allow a license from the copyright holder to be placed on the work--tagged, embedded--and so anyone coming to the work already knows the permission and limitations in using the work.

· **Attribution**: your name/company is included when someone else uses (posts, remixes, etc.) the work.
· **ShareAlike:** you allow people to use your work, but only if they share what they make, too.
· **No Derivatives:** you allow people to use your work, but they can't make different versions - they can't change or add anything to your work.
· **NonCommercial**: they can't sell your work or anything they make using your work, and they can't use it in a commercial context.
· **CCO "No Rights Reserved":** you disclaim all rights in the copyright and send it out into the world. No restrictions on how other people use the work.

You can create a Creative Commons license at their website and make a combination of these terms, or you can put them on your own works. www.creativecommons.com These tell the world what kind of license to the work you are giving them. You should still put the copyright notice in addition to these terms.

Creative Commons licenses are really great when you are OK with people further distributing and using your work. Free patterns, for example, would be great--they would include the right of attribution, would require others to share in the same manner (free) if they create a derivative work, and can even be used in a commercial context. But CC licenses are not for everyone, and that's okay.

Searching for Creative Common Images

Not only can you add a Creative Commons license to your work, you can also search and use Creative Commons works as inspiration or within your work, depending on the license. Here are ways to look for Creative Commons images, both at www.creativecommons.org, and also through Google, Flickr and other platforms. For instance, I did a Google image search for "butterfly quilts." I chose the dropdown option "Usage rights" under the "Tools" tab to limit my search. See how Creative Commons licenses are embedded. I chose "Labeled for reuse with modification." And I found this: Olga Kuba, Butterfly of Love on Flickr. https://www.flickr.com/photos/olgakuba/16333734340. On the right-hand side, there is information about the license. I clicked on the link. It took me to the CC License the creator had chosen.

Using Creative Commons works is an awesome way to add resources, and the rights statements are very helpful. In part 2 of this chapter, we will look at how to choose a CC license for your own works.

The © Notice Checklist

Making A Copyright Notice and Rights Statement

Mandatory Parts:

☐ Copyright or ©

☐ Name of Copyright Proprietor (person or company that holds the "rights" to the copyright holder at the time of publication.

☐ Year of first publication (and sometimes revisions)

Why include this?

- Puts the world on notice that you are planning to enforce your rights
- No "innocent infringer" defense available if there is a notice included

Rights Statement Choices

Rights statements help tell the world how you feel about your copyright. These are not mandatory. The default without a rights statement is that the copyright holder retains all the rights under Section 106 (reproduction, distribution, derivative work, public display, public performance). Note: these are not absolute rights, and a quilt show is not necessarily considered public display (according to one court). Including a rights statement is encouraged.

☐ **All rights reserved.** You want to control as many uses as possible.

This is the default protection. Any uses other than those permitted and fair uses, including library exceptions, first sale, etc.) are under the authority of the copyright holder. This usually means permission in the form of an exclusive license, a non-exclusive license or an assignment is needed for further uses.

☐ **No Rights Reserved.** The least control. You claim ownership but you don't care how people use it, even in a commercial context. This is also sometimes called CCo (Creative Commons Zero).

> ☐ Feel free to use this pattern, even for commercial purposes, without asking permission. You may make derivative works, make copies and distribute freely.
>
> ☐ Option: right of attribution. Please include "Original pattern by ______." when you use this pattern.

☐ **Creative Commons License**

> ☐ **Attribution**. Please include the following for any use of the pattern: "Original pattern created by Elizabeth Townsend Gard, Copyright 2019.
>
> ☐ **Derivatives Allowed.** You may create derivative works (your own version) of this pattern.
>
> ☐ **Sharealike.** You may use this pattern but are required to share your versions with others freely as well.
>
> ☐ **Commercial Uses.**
>
> > ☐ **Commercial Uses.** You may use this pattern for commercial use without additional fees.
> >
> > ☐ **Noncommercial Uses.** You may only use this for non-commercial and/or personal uses. No commercial activity is allowed. Please write for permission to any retail sale of the products created from or copies of the pattern itself.
> >
> > ☐ **Guilds or Groups.**

☐ **Permission Required.** If you are a group or guild and would like to use this pattern, please email the copyright holder, [name] [email].

☐ **Permission Granted.** Guilds and quilting groups may use this pattern without additional permission, even for fundraisers and charity events.

☐ **Registered.** This pattern has been registered with the U.S. Copyright Office, and any infringement could be up to $150,000 in damages.

☐ Nothing in the rights statement is meant to interfere with any exceptions or limitations under the U.S. Copyright law, including fair use, library exceptions, and the first sale doctrine.

Other options:

☐ **Charity Quilts.** Feel free to use the pattern for charity purposes.

☐ **Low Commercial uses.** You may obtain a license for commercial uses of the pattern on Etsy, your own website, and in situations where you are making less than $50,000 a year as a business. Please email __________.

☐ **Elements in the Public Domain.** Some elements used are in the public domain, as are the techniques. The expression of those elements took time and energy to create this pattern. Please respect the expression and make sure to purchase a pattern. Your purchase supports pattern-makers.

☐ **Underlying Work.** This work is based on a work by ________, Title, year.

☐ Permission by the copyright holder has been granted to use the underlying work within this new, derivative work. 17 U.S.C. Section 106.

☐ **No Warranty**: The author has in good faith believes the information is accurate, but no warranty is given for the results or information.

☐ **Digital Download.** "Digital pattern downloads are not for resale or transfer, and are a license to use the pattern for personal use only."

Copyright Registration

Copyright arises automatically upon fixation; when you make, write, or draw something, it has copyright. To have power, registration at the U.S. Copyright Office is necessary. Registration allows you to sue in court, and if you win a lawsuit, you may elect statutory damages (up to $150,000 for willful infringement) and attorney's fees may even be awarded in some cases. But more importantly, registration tells others in the world how to find you, in case they want to seek a license from you. And of course, registration allows the U.S. Customs to seize illegal copies of your work for you, too! Registration is important. It lets the world know that you care about your work –that you took the time to make a public record of its existence, and provide information about the work, including authorship.

A Short, Important Story

Paula Nadelstern is an important, famous quilter. She is also famous for a lawsuit she brought for copyright infringement, which she won in settlement! I interviewed her recently. She said the only reason she could even bring a lawsuit is that her publisher, C & T, had registered her book, which gave her the ability to file a lawsuit and attract an attorney to take her case. Now, she religiously registers each of her major quilts after she completes them. She said she gets them appraised and she registers them. Hers is the story about the importance of registration. We'll look at Paula's copyright infringement story in the next chapter. For now, the lesson is: if you care that someone might swipe your work, register it now.

Return on Investment: Set up a System

Another way to think about registration is the return on investment. A new decision from the U.S. Supreme Court, *Fourth Estate Public Benefit Corp. v. Wall-Street.com*, 586 U.S. ___ (2019), has confirmed how important registration is. First, a work must have a registration certificate, and not merely an application to file a complaint in court. Registration takes up to 18 months. So, think about registering *before the problem occurs.* You cannot file a lawsuit, have teeth related to sending a cease and desist letter or follow through on a notice-and-takedown through Internet Service Providers (ISPs) without registering your copyright. If you register within three months of publication, registration allows you to reach back to any infringement that occurred even before registration. Alternatively, you can do an expedited registration once there is trouble.

You do not get the benefit of statutory damages applying to infringement prior to registration, and only actual damages (which is harder to determine) for infringement occurring before registration. You are gambling on the need for registration. You will have to wait until the registration certificate is complete before filing a lawsuit.

Strategy

So, deciding when and how to register your copyrighted works is a strategy. And we see interesting trends. Book publishers consistently register works. Photographers often don't, but are doing so more in recent years. The recording industry regularly registers their works, as do content owners. Two very different approaches can be seen from different fabric companies: Jaftex and Michael Miller. Jaftex relies on expedited registrations. They have 50 to 60 lines of fabric, and so they find registering each design as unworkable. It's just not practical, said president Scott Fortunoff, for them to register each collection or each item in a collection. In contrast, fabric company Michael Miller registers *all of their designs*. So, think of the Copyright Registration as part of your business. Either keep it as part of your process (once you finish a work, you register it before you put it on sale), or you have a time that you regularly register (once a year, the 21st of every month, etc.) Or, expedite the registration (and pay more) when there is a problem. You do not need an attorney to register your works. You can learn to register them yourself.

Do you need to register everything? No. You are registering works you feel are valuable -- the ones that if someone swiped them you would be very unhappy about. The blog post you wrote this morning? Well, probably not. But maybe if that is really important to you, you will.

If you think you are going to pursue someone if they infringe, then you should register. If you are going to be a "let the chips fall where they may" kind of person, then you really don't need to register. But again, take note: the big companies register their works. They know that without registration, the copyright isn't very strong.

Choosing the Form

Once you choose the form, you will be asked for the type of work.

TX: literary
VA: visual arts

PA: performing arts
SR: sound recording

You choose the one that makes the most sense for the work.

So, how do you register a work?

It's easy. You go to the Copyright Office's website: www.copyright.gov. You have to choose a category to register the works: literary, visual, performing arts, or sound recording. Once your application is submitted, the full registration process takes around seven months.

The Deposit Requirement

The deposit requirement varies depending on what type of work is being registered.

Published work: two copies
Unpublished and foreign works: one copy

For artwork that is unpublished, has a limited edition, only one version, or it is an expensive item, you can send in a photograph.

Published artworks with circulating copies require a deposit of the object, and not a photograph.

Disclaiming pre-existing work

As part of the registration application, make sure to disclaim work that is not part of the copyright, that is public domain works, pre-existing works, etc. Here is an example from the Compendium:

> Theresa Tell creates a collage that combines her own artwork with logos from a number of famous companies. She files an application to register her "two-dimensional artwork." Depending on the facts presented, the registration specialist may ask the applicant to exclude the logos from the claim by stating, "pre-existing logos incorporated" in the Material Excluded field. In addition, the specialist may ask Theresa to limit her claim by stating, "selection and arrangement of preexisting logos with new two-dimensional artwork added" in the New Material Included field.

Filling Out the Registration Form

Once you are ready to file your own copyright registration, create an account at the U.S. Copyright Office.

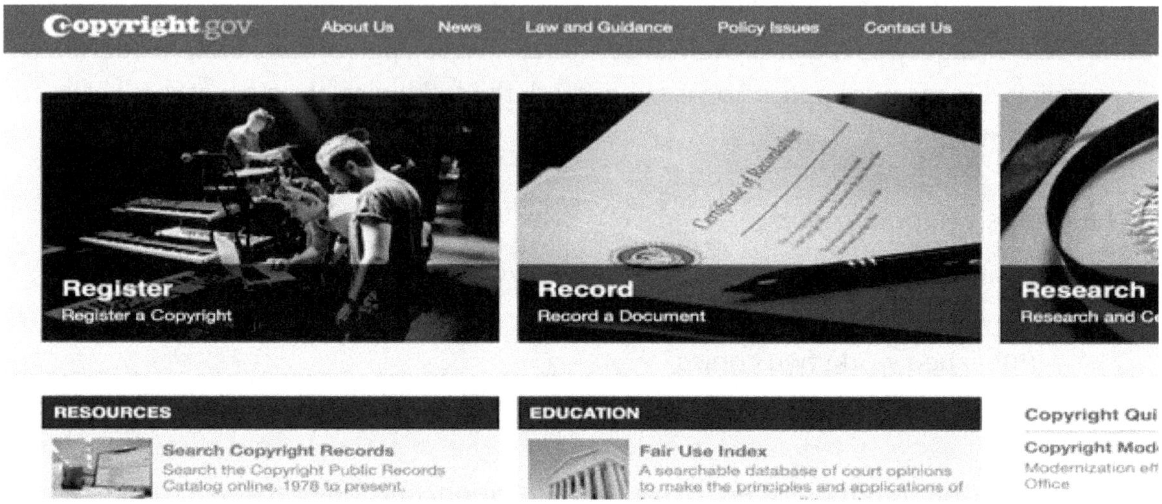

This screen (below) looks a bit intimidating. Never fear. We are here. The registration filing is based on both the type of work and also a few other factors. Let's walk through the choices.

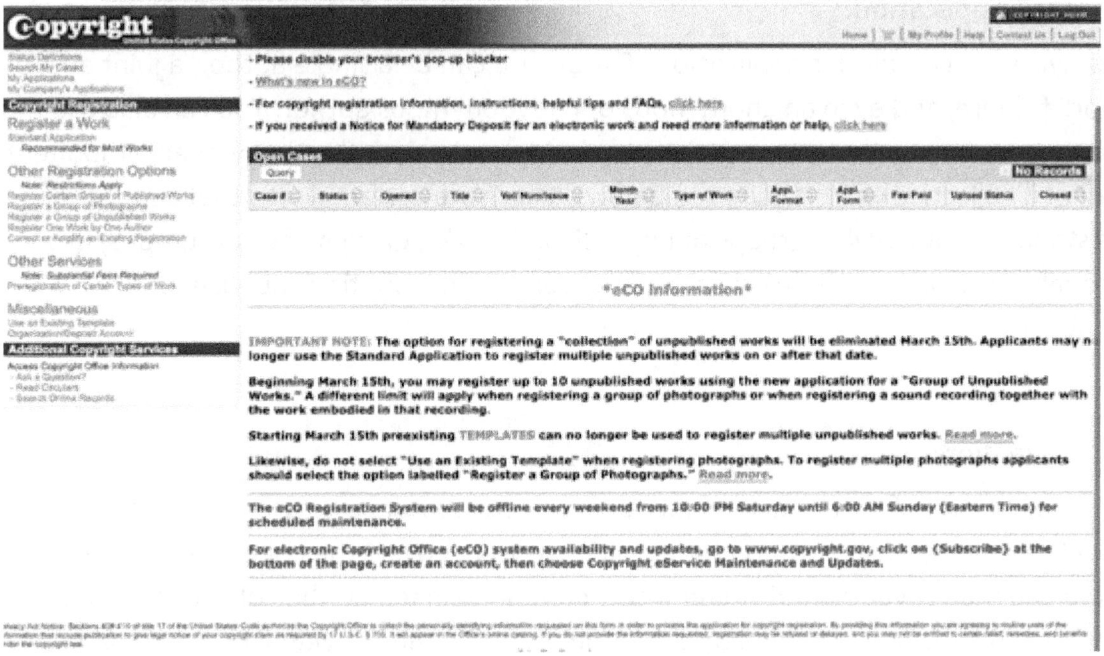

Look at the left-hand column. You have some choices:

Standard Application:

Most works fall under this application. The author can be a single author, a joint author, a work for hire, and even an anonymous or pseudonymous author. You can also use this form to register a collective work authorship (see below), and an individual component work of a collective work (again, see below). There are certain works that cannot use this standard application: groups of unpublished works, groups of photographs, groups of serials, newspapers, or newsletters, or groups of contributions published in a periodical.

Collective Works:

Where a number of separate and independent contributors are assembled into a collective whole. "A registration for a collective work covers the collective work as a whole and may cover the individual works contained in it if (1) the collective work and the individual works are owned by the same party, (2) the individual works have not been previously published or previously registered, and (3) the individual works are not in the public domain." Circular 34, Multiple Works, https://www.copyright.gov/circs/circ34.pdf.

The Copyright Office provides a list of what counts and does not count as a Collective Work for registration purposes.

For purposes of registration, representative examples of collective works include:

- ❑ A newspaper, magazine, or other periodical containing multiple articles, illustrations,
- ❑ and photographs
- ❑ An anthology containing multiple poems, short stories, or essays
- ❑ An online encyclopedia containing multiple articles, entries, or postings on various topics
- ❑ An album containing multiple sound recordings that embody multiple musical works
- ❑ A DVD containing a motion picture, theatrical trailers, deleted scenes, and audio commentary from the director

A collective work is not[8]

- a single unified work that contains separate parts or elements, such as
- a novel consisting of multiple chapters

[8] Circular 34, Multiple Works, U.S. Copyright Office, https://www.copyright.gov/circs/circ34.pdf

- a song with melody, harmony, and rhythm
- a drawing in pencil and ink
- a carpet design of overlapping figures and colors
- an architectural work or technical drawing with multiple illustrations of the same object
- an illustrated children's book created by one author
- a unified work created by multiple authors, such as
- a musical work created by a singer and songwriter in collaboration with each other
- a musical with script, music, and lyrics by two or more authors
- a motion picture with screenplay, soundtrack, directing, acting, cinematography, costume design,
- visual effects, or other production elements contributed by multiple authors
- a children's book created by a writer and illustrator in collaboration with each other
- a textbook
- a single contribution to a collective work

Contribution to a Collective Work:

You can register your contribution to a collective work separately. This includes an article within a periodical, a song on an album, or a photograph that appears in a newspaper or magazine.

Registration Options for Collective Works and Contributions to Collective Works:

You can register the collective work and the individual works under one application, but the individual works must also be from the author of the collective work, and the individual works cannot have been previously published or previously registered.

Damages consideration: If you register a collective work, it is considered one work for the purposes of damages.[9] If you register individual works within the collective work, each of those registrations is calculated separately, and so potentially more damages could be awarded.

[9] "Section 504(c)(1) of the Copyright Act states that a copyright owner may be entitled to recover "an award of statutory damages for all infringements involved in the [infringement] action, with respect to any one work," and "[f]or the purposes of this subsection, all the parts of a compilation . . . constitute one work." Circular 34, Multiple Works, U.S. Copyright Office, https://www.copyright.gov/circs/circ34.pdf.

One Work by One Author :

This application is for **one work**, by **one individual, an**d the work is not a **work for hire** and **does not include pre-existing materials.** For example, one poem, one song or one photograph. For instance, Ricardo Gonzalez's *Just Wanna Patent* qualifies as a single application. The current cost is $35, but will likely be raised to $45 in Spring 2020. The Copyright Office has a video to explain the process. See https://www.copyright.gov/eco/single.mp4. This video takes you step by step through the registration application. Note: you cannot use this application if the work contains pre-existing material, including materials created and included by others that you are excluding from the application.

Group Registration:

"Generally, you may only register one work per application but there are several exceptions to this rule." FAQ, Copyright Office, https://www.copyright.gov/help/faq/faq-register.html Some works can be registered in groups, which make it more affordable to register works. But be aware, it impacts on potential statutory damages. The collection, for award purposes, is treated as one work. So, what do people do? These are a group of related works that can be registered under one application and one filing fee. There are only a few types of works that qualify:

- Unpublished works
- Serials
- Newspapers
- Newsletters
- Contributions to periodicals
- Published photographs
- Unpublished photographs
- Database updates and revisions
- Questions, answers, and other items prepared for use in a secure test.

Unpublished Works: Unpublished works can be registered as a group of up to ten works. There are restrictions. They must all be unpublished, and created by the same author or joint authors, with the authors being the named copyright claimants, with the works being the same type (e.g. "unpublished illustrations," "unpublished musical compositions," or "unpublished jewelry designs"). Each work must have a title. You cannot register different types of works on the same application. The Copyright Office has provided a tutorial to walk you through the application of a group of unpublished works. Tip: if you are planning to publish works, you might think of registering them as unpublished under this grouping to save money. You do not need to re-register them when they are published to get the statutory benefits of registration. See the tutorial from the U.S. Copyright Office: https://stream-media.loc.gov/copyright/gruw.mp4. What is cool about this is you can file up to 10 unpublished works under one registration record. If you make substantial changes or want to re-register it when it is published, you can do that, too. The works are treated as individual works, not as a collection of works. Ten short stories, not an anthology of stories, UNLESS you claim the unpublished as an unpublished collective work, rather than a collection of works.

Bundled Physical Packages: this is a really interesting option. If you have a physical package that contains separately fixed works that have been bundled together for distribution to the public as a single, integrated unit, you can register it as a group registration. Here are the examples the U.S. Copyright Office gives:[10]

- A board game with playing pieces, game board, and written instructions
- A bound volume published with a dust jacket
- A book published with a CD-ROM
- A multimedia kit containing a book, a compact disc, and a set of stickers
- A compact disc containing multiple sound recordings packaged together with liner notes and cover artwork
- A box set containing multiple compact discs containing multiple sound recordings, packaged together with a booklet containing liner notes and photographs
- A multi-DVD package with a disc containing a motion picture, a disc containing trailers and deleted scenes from the motion picture, and a disc containing interviews with the director and the cast
- A physical package containing a computer program and a user's manual
- A physical package containing a video game, cover artwork, and written instructions for installing the game
- A package of greeting cards
- A jewelry set of a necklace and earrings that are sold to the public as a single unit.

[10] Circular 34, "Multiple Works," U.S. Copyright Office, https://www.copyright.gov/circs/circ34.pdf

What are the requirements? Each element must be a self-contained work, and must be first published as a single unit on the same date. The Copyright claimant must be the same on all units. It must be a physical copy and must be distributed to the general public. Important: "[The work] cannot be created solely for the purpose of registering the work with the Copyright Office."[11]

Contributions of periodicals: if you have created separate and independent work that has been published in a periodical, you can register your work as a contribution to a periodical. This includes newspapers, magazines, and journals.[12] You use the group registration form. This is called "GRCP". You will need to list the contributions in chronological order. The works can be in different periodicals and on different dates, with no limit on number of contributions. You have to have at least two contributions to use this form. All contributions must have been created by the author; the works must not be work for hire, the copyright claimant is the same person/entity for all contributions, and *each contribution was published within a twelve-month period, Jan-Dec of the particular year.* Here is a walkthrough tutorial for contributions to periodicals: *https://www.copyright.gov/eco/cp-transcript.pdf* and the accompanying video: https://www.copyright.gov/eco/grcp.mp4.

Newsletters: Newsletters can be registered with the U.S. Copyright office, as long as there are at least two issues, and neither of them have been previously published. They must be "fixed and distributed as a discrete, self-contained work."[13] The issues have to be published by the same claimant. Issues must be published within the same calendar month, and must bear issue dates within the month. You must submit one complete copy of each issue. This is a huge limitation. Ideally, it has an ISSN number for the newsletter.

Published photographs: You can register up to 750 photographs that have been published within the same calendar year created by the same author. Make up a title for the group, and sequentially number them, and you are good to go. You use a template that the U.S. Copyright Office provides. For more information, go to: https://www.copyright.gov/eco/help/group/grpph.html

[11] Id.
[12] Definition: periodicals are published on an established schedule (daily, weekly monthly). See https://www.copyright.gov/eco/grcp.mp4.
[13] Help: Daily Newsletters, U.S. Copyright Office, https://www.copyright.gov/eco/help-newsletters.html.

Unpublished photographs: this is up to 750 photographs in one application. Like published photographs, they must be by the same author, but there doesn't seem to be the one-year requirement.

On the next page is a handy table created by the U.S. Copyright Office.[14]

Registration Requirements	*Group Registration of Published or Unpublished Photographs*	*Group Registration of Contributions to Periodicals*	*Group Registration of Unpublished Works*
Type of work	Each work must be a photograph	Each work must be a visual arts or literary work	The application may be used for any type of work; however, each work in the group must be the same type
Application requirements	The applicant must use the online application	The applicant must use the online application	The applicant must use the online application
Number of photographs in the application	The applicant may include up to 750 photographs in the group	No limit on the number of works that may be included in the application	The applicant may include up to ten works in the group
Author	All the photographs must be taken by the same author	All the works must be created by the same author	All the works must be created by the same author or authors
Claimant	The claimant for all the photographs must be the same person or organization	The claimant for all the works must be the same person or organization	All of the authors must be listed as copyright claimant
Work made for hire	The photographs may be created as works made for hire	The works cannot be created as works made for hire	The works may be created as works made for hire
Publication	All the photographs in the group must be either published or unpublished. Unpublished and published works may not be combined on the same application.	All the works must be published	All the works must be unpublished

[14] Circular 62C, "Copyright Registration of Contributions to Periodicals,' U.S. Copyright Office, https://www.copyright.gov/circs/circ62c.pdf, p. 4.

As you work your way through the registration process, here are a few things to consider:

Author: Unless you are filling this out for someone else, or you have created the works in the course of your employment (and you are not for tax purposes an independent contractor), you are likely the author. You have to be either creating the work within the course of your employment, or it is a commissioned work that falls under the nine enumerated categories in 17 U.S.C Section 101.

Claimant: Unless you have assigned, transferred, sold, or licensed your rights to someone else, you are likely the claimant. If you have done any of the above, then the person controlling the copyright is the claimant.

Limitation of Claim: Here is where you disclaim anything for which you are not claiming copyright. So, if you recognize that some parts of what you are doing are in the public domain, for instance, or are based on another's work, you can place that info here.

Rights and Permissions: Who is allowed to give out rights and permissions? Usually this would be you, but you could put someone else down.

Correspondent: Who does the Copyright Office contact if they have questions?

Special Handling: If you check this box, you are expediting your application (in expectation of litigation), and you will pay a hefty fee. You would do this if you believe there has been infringement of your non-registered work, and you are planning to go to court. This would allow you to register the work quickly. It would not cover you for any infringement before the registration certificate issues. But it will quickly allow you to be able to go to court and collect (if you win) statutory damages. Special handling usually takes around five business working days and has an extra $800 cost.

You then pay the fees, and you also have to submit copies of the work. You can either upload them or mail them. You can upload lots of file types including .jpg, .gif, .pdf, .tif, .psd., and .bmp.

Costs

U.S. Copyright Office fees to register a work vary (as of July 2020):

Basic registration: $45 (single author, same claimant, one work, not for hire)
Standard: $65
Pre Registration for certain unpublished works: $200

There are a bunch of different types of group registration:

$35 Serials, per issue, minimum two issues.
$95 Newspapers (online) or newsletters
$85 Contributions to periodicals
$55 Published or unpublished photographs
$100 GATT form (for older foreign works)
$85 Ten unpublished works

Special Handling/Expedited service. Special handling is an expedited method of obtaining a copyright registration from the U.S. Copyright Office. You can only request special handling if there is "[a] pending or prospective litigation, [b] customs matter, or [c] contract or publishing deadline that necessitates the expedited issuance of a certificate." With special handling, the registration process takes about five business days. The fee for special handling starts at $800, as of 2020, but may change in the Spring.

What is the difference between registration or pre-registration? Most works are registered as either published or unpublished. The pre-registration category was designed for films, music, literary works, and other popular items that might get stolen before the release date, and so needed extra protection. If you are creating patterns and/or books, and want this extra protection, you qualify. However, pre-registration comes at a price: $140 along with the additional fee for actual registration fees. So, if you are not afraid of pirates on the Internet stealing your work before it is released to the public, you really don't need to do pre-registration.

The New Category: Group for Short Online Literary Works

The Copyright Office has a new category "group of short online literary works," which would cost $65. If it becomes an option, it will likely be defined as works that are 100 words to 17,500 words. Think poems, articles, blog entries, and social media posts. You would designate it a "literary work," and can upload 50 works with one application and filing fee But each application is for a three-month period.

Circular 67 guides us through the process: https://www.copyright.gov/circs/circ67.pdf.

- ❑ The designation is GRTX.
- ❑ Eligible works: short stories, articles, essays, columns, blog entries, and social media posts.
- ❑ *Not* eligible: emails, podcasts, audiobooks, and computer programs.
- ❑ Timeline: they all must be published online within a three-month period.
- ❑ All works must be written by the same individual author or the same co-authors.
- ❑ Each work must have a title, and the group of works must also have a title.
- ❑ You make include up to 50 works in one application
- ❑ Each work must be between 100 and 17,500 words

Each work is registered as a separate work, and are evaluated for copyright as individual works; one rejection does not ruin the whole application.

Regroup and Strategize

That was a lot to take in. Registration is important, in certain circumstances. And there are ways to strategize.[15]

[15] And what does the Compendium have to say? "As a general rule, it is not possible to register a group of pictorial, graphic, or sculptural works with one application, one filing fee, and a submission of identifying material. Instead, the applicant generally must submit a separate claim for each work. However, there are two limited exceptions to this rule. • If the works are unpublished it may be possible to register them as an unpublished collection. Photographs or illustrations of the two- or three-dimensional works may be used as identifying material in this situation, provided that the applicant asserts a claim in the works depicted in those images rather than the authorship involved in creating the images themselves. • If the works were physically bundled together for distribution to the public as a single, integrated unit and if all the works were first published in that integrated unit, it may be possible to register them using the unit of publication option. When a group of photographs are published in a catalog the works depicted therein are considered published, regardless of whether they are two- or three-dimensional. However, the fact that a group of works were published in the same catalog does not necessarily mean that the catalog constitutes a unit of publication or that the works may be registered together with the unit of publication option." Compendium III, Section 914

1. **Single Work**. A less expensive way than a standard application, and you are the only author, and it is not a work for hire.
2. **Unpublished works.** This is a great deal. Register up to ten of your works before you put them out, and they are protected even after they are published as individual works.
3. **Contributions published in a periodical.** This is a way to register a number of patterns and articles that were published in a periodical in the same year. Then, you could release them individually as patterns.
4. **Newsletters.** If your newsletters have material that you would like to protect, you can register them in a group every three months.
5. **Photographs:** unpublished allow you to register 750 at a time, but it protects the photograph and not the underlying work.
6. **Collective work.** You can register your works as a collective work -- register the patterns as a book, and then all of them are protected.
7. **Physical Bundle.** If you sell separately copyrightable works as a bundle, you can register them under one application.

What saved Paula Nadelstern is that the quilts that were infringed had been registered in the book, and the book is what was used to infringe. She had not registered the individual quilts. Now she does. If the quilts matter to you, register them. If the book about the quilt matters, register that. Think about what you need protected. There are lots of ways to register your works. Be clever. Protect your works.

The CASE Act

The CASE ACT, just passed in December 2020 into law, will likely greatly impact on the importance of registration, as registration is a requirement for bringing a claim. We will be looking more at the CASE Act in Chapter 12. For now, we want to note that the CASE Act requires application or registration with the U.S. Copyright Office to proceed. If the registration has not been completed, the claim will be paused until a certificate has been issued.

Fourth Estate v. Wall-street.com, 586 U.S. ___ (2019)

Finally, the U.S. Supreme Court in 2019 took up the question of copyright registration in the Fourth Estate case. Let's take a look at what it tells us.

Justice GINSBURG delivered the opinion of the Court.

Impelling prompt registration of copyright claims, 17 U. S. C. §411(a) states that "no civil action for infringement of the copyright in any United States work shall be instituted until . . . registration of the copyright claim has been made in accordance with this title." The question this case presents: Has "registration . . . been made in accordance with [Title 17]" as soon as the claimant delivers the required application, copies of the work, and fee to the Copyright Office; or has "registration . . . been made" only after the Copyright Office reviews and registers the copyright? We hold, in accord with the United States Court of Appeals for the Eleventh Circuit, that registration occurs, and a copyright claimant may commence an infringement suit, when the Copyright Office registers a copyright. Upon registration of the copyright, however, a copyright owner can recover for infringement that occurred both before and after registration.

Petitioner Fourth Estate Public Benefit Corporation (Fourth Estate) is a news organization producing online journalism. Fourth Estate licensed journalism works to respondent Wall-Street.com, LLC (Wall-Street), a news website. The license agreement required Wall-Street to remove from its website all content produced by Fourth Estate before canceling the agreement. Wall-Street canceled, but continued to display articles produced by Fourth Estate. Fourth Estate sued Wall-Street and its owner, Jerrold Burden, for copyright infringement. The complaint alleged that Fourth Estate had filed "applications to register [the] articles [licensed to Wall-Street] with the Register of Copyrights." App. to Pet. for Cert. 18a.[1] Because the Register had not yet acted on Fourth Estate's applications,[2] the District Court, on Wall-Street and Burden's motion, dismissed the complaint, and the Eleventh Circuit affirmed. 856 F.3d 1338 (2017). Thereafter, the Register of Copyrights refused registration of the articles Wall-Street had allegedly infringed.[3]

We granted Fourth Estate's petition for certiorari to resolve a division among U. S. Courts of Appeals on when registration occurs in accordance with §411(a). 585 U. S. ___ (2018). Compare, *e.g.*, 856 F. 3d, at 1341 (case below) (registration has been made under §411(a) when the Register of Copyrights registers a copyright), with, *e.g.*, *Cosmetic Ideas, Inc.* v. *IAC/Interactivecorp*, 606 F.3d 612, 621 (CA9 2010) (registration has been made under §411(a) when the copyright claimant's "complete application" for registration is received by the Copyright Office).

I

Under the Copyright Act of 1976, as amended, copyright protection attaches to "original works of authorship"—prominent among them, literary, musical, and dramatic works—"fixed in any tangible medium of expression." 17 U. S. C. §102(a). An author gains "exclusive rights" in her work immediately upon the work's creation, including rights of reproduction, distribution, and display. See §106; *Eldred* v. *Ashcroft*, 537 U.S. 186, 195 (2003) ("[F]ederal copyright protection . . . run[s] from the work's creation."). The Copyright Act entitles a copyright owner to institute a civil action for infringement of those exclusive rights. §501(b).

Before pursuing an infringement claim in court, how- ever, a copyright claimant generally must comply with §411(a)'s requirement that "registration of the copyright claim has been made." §411(a). Therefore, although an owner's rights exist apart from registration, see §408(a), registration is akin to an administrative exhaustion requirement that the owner must satisfy before suing to enforce ownership rights, see Tr. of Oral Arg. 35.

In limited circumstances, copyright owners may file an infringement suit before undertaking registration. If a copyright owner is preparing to distribute a work of a type vulnerable to predistribution infringement—notably, a movie or musical composition—the owner may apply for preregistration. §408(f)(2); 37 CFR §202.16(b)(1) (2018). The Copyright Office will "conduct a limited review" of the application and notify the claimant "[u]pon completion of the preregistration." §202.16(c)(7), (c)(10). Once "preregistration . . . has been made," the copyright claimant may institute a suit for infringement. 17 U. S. C. §411(a). Preregistration, however, serves only as "a preliminary step prior to a full registration." Preregistration of Certain Unpublished Copyright Claims, 70 Fed. Reg. 42286 (2005). An infringement suit brought in reliance on preregistration risks dismissal unless the copyright owner applies for registration promptly after the preregistered work's publication or infringement. §408(f)(3)–(4). A copyright owner may also sue for infringement of a live broadcast before "registration . . . has been made," but faces dismissal of her suit if she fails to "make registration for the work" within three months of its first transmission. §411(c). Even in these exceptional scenarios, then, the copyright owner must eventually pursue registration in order to maintain a suit for infringement.

II

All parties agree that, outside of statutory exceptions not applicable here, §411(a) bars a copyright owner from suing for infringement until "registration . . . has been made." Fourth Estate and Wall-Street dispute, however, whether "registration . . . has been made" under §411(a) when a copyright owner submits the application, materials, and fee required for registration, or only when the Copyright Office grants registration. Fourth Estate advances the former view—the "application approach"—while Wall-Street urges the latter reading—the "registration approach." The registration approach, we conclude, reflects the only satisfactory reading of §411(a)'s text. We therefore reject Fourth Estate's application approach.

A

Under §411(a), "registration . . . has been made," and a copyright owner may sue for infringement, when the Copyright Office registers a copyright.[4] Section 411(a)'s first sentence provides that no civil infringement action "shall be instituted until preregistration or registration of the copyright claim has been made." The section's next sentence sets out an exception to this rule: When the required "deposit, application, and fee . . . have been delivered to the Copyright Office in proper form and registration has been refused," the claimant "[may] institute a civil action, if notice thereof . . . is served on the Register." Read together, §411(a)'s opening sentences focus not on the claimant's act of applying for registration, but on action by the Copyright Office—namely, its registration or refusal to register a copyright claim.

If application alone sufficed to "ma[ke]" registration, §411(a)'s second sentence—allowing suit upon refusal of registration—would be superfluous. What utility would that allowance have if a copyright claimant could sue for infringement immediately after applying for registration without awaiting the Register's decision on her application? Proponents of the application approach urge that §411(a)'s second sentence serves merely to require a copyright claimant to serve "notice [of an infringement suit] . . . on the Register." See Brief for Petitioner 29–32. This reading, however, requires the implausible assumption that Congress gave "registration" different meanings in consecutive, related sentences within a single statutory provision. In §411(a)'s first sentence, "registration" would mean the claimant's act of filing an application, while in the section's second sentence, "registration" would entail the Register's review of an application. We resist this improbable construction. See, *e.g.*, *Mid-Con Freight Systems, Inc.* v. *Michigan Pub. Serv. Comm'n*, 545 U.S. 440, 448 (2005) (declining to read "the same words" in con- secutive sentences as "refer[ring] to something totally different").

The third and final sentence of §411(a) further persuades us that the provision requires action by the Register before a copyright claimant may sue for infringement. The sentence allows the Register to "become a party to the action with respect to the issue of registrability of the copyright claim." This allowance would be negated, and the court conducting an infringement suit would lack the benefit of the Register's assessment, if an infringement suit could be filed and resolved before the Register acted on an application.

Other provisions of the Copyright Act support our reading of "registration," as used in §411(a), to mean action by the Register. Section 410 states that, "after examination," if the Register determines that "the material deposited constitutes copyrightable subject matter" and "other legal and formal requirements . . . [are] met, the Register shall register the claim and issue to the applicant a certificate of registration." §410(a). But if the Register determines that the deposited material "does not constitute copyrightable subject matter or that the claim is invalid for any other reason, the Register shall refuse registration." §410(b). Section 410 thus confirms that application is discrete from, and precedes, registration. Section 410(d), furthermore, provides that if the Copyright Office registers a claim, or if a court later determines that a refused claim was registrable, the "effective date of [the work's] copyright registration is the day on which" the copyright owner made a proper submission to the Copyright Office. There would be no need thus to specify the "effective date of a copyright registration" if submission of the required materials qualified as "registration."

Section 408(f)'s preregistration option, too, would have little utility if a completed application constituted registration. Preregistration, as noted *supra*, at 3–4, allows the author of a work vulnerable to predistribution infringement to enforce her exclusive rights in court before obtaining registration or refusal thereof. A copyright owner who fears prepublication infringement would have no reason to apply for preregistration, however, if she could instead simply complete an application for registration and immediately commence an infringement suit. Cf. *TRW Inc.* v. *Andrews*, 534 U.S. 19, 29 (2001) (rejecting an interpretation that "would in practical effect render [a provision] superfluous in all but the most unusual circumstances").

B

Challenging the Eleventh Circuit's judgment, Fourth Estate primarily contends that the Copyright Act uses "the phrase 'make registration' and its passive-voice counterpart 'registration has been made' " to describe submissions by the copyright owner, rather than Copyright Office responses to those submissions. Brief for Petitioner 21. Section 411(a)'s requirement that "registration . . . has been made in accordance with this title," Fourth Estate insists, most likely refers to a copyright owner's compliance with the statutory specifications for registration applications. In support, Fourth Estate points to Copyright Act provisions that appear to use the phrase "make registration" or one of its variants to describe what a copyright claimant does. See *id.*, at 22–26 (citing 17 U. S. C. §§110, 205(c), 408(c)(3), 411(c), 412(2)). Furthermore, Fourth Estate urges that its reading reflects the reality that, eventually, the vast majority of applications are granted. See Brief for Petitioner 41.

Fourth Estate acknowledges, however, that the Copyright Act sometimes uses "registration" to refer to activity by the Copyright Office, not activity undertaken by a copyright claimant. See *id.*, at 27–28 (citing 17 U. S. C. §708(a)). Fourth Estate thus agrees that, to determine how the statute uses the word "registration" in a particular prescription, one must "look to the specific context" in which the term is used. Brief for Petitioner 29. As explained *supra,* at 4–7, the "specific context" of §411(a) permits only one sensible reading: The phrase "registration . . . has been made" refers to the Copyright Office's act granting registration, not to the copyright claimant's request for registration.

Fourth Estate's contrary reading of §411(a) stems in part from its misapprehension of the significance of certain 1976 revisions to the Copyright Act. Before that year, §411(a)'s precursor provided that "[n]o action or proceeding shall be maintained for infringement of copyright in any work until the provisions of this title with respect to the deposit of copies and registration of such work shall have been complied with." 17 U. S. C. §13 (1970 ed.). Fourth Estate urges that this provision posed the very question we resolve today—namely, whether a claimant's application alone effects registration. The Second Circuit addressed that question, Fourth Estate observes, in *Vacheron & Constantin-Le Coultre Watches, Inc.* v. *Benrus Watch Co.*, 260 F.2d 637 (1958). Brief for Petitioner 32–34. In that case, in an opinion by Judge Learned Hand, the court held that a copyright owner who completed an application could not sue for infringement immediately upon the Copyright Office's refusal to register. *Vacheron*, 260 F. 3d, at 640–641. Instead, the owner first had to obtain a registration certificate by bringing a mandamus action against the Register. The Second Circuit dissenter would have treated the owner's application as sufficient to permit commencement of an action for infringement. *Id.*, at 645.

Fourth Estate sees Congress' 1976 revision of the registration requirement as an endorsement of the *Vacheron* dissenter's position. Brief for Petitioner 34–36. We dis- agree. The changes made in 1976 instead indicate Congress' agreement with Judge Hand that it is the Register's action that triggers a copyright owner's entitlement to sue. In enacting 17 U. S. C. §411(a), Congress both reaffirmed the general rule that registration must precede an infringement suit, and added an exception in that provision's second sentence to cover instances in which registration is refused. See H. R. Rep. No. 94–1476, p. 157 (1976). That exception would have no work to do if, as Fourth Estate urges, Congress intended the 1976 revisions to clarify that a copyright claimant may sue immediately upon applying for registration. A copyright claimant would need no statutory authorization to sue after refusal of her application if she could institute suit as soon as she has filed the application.

Noteworthy, too, in years following the 1976 revisions, Congress resisted efforts to eliminate §411(a) and the registration requirement embedded in it. In 1988, Congress removed foreign works from §411(a)'s dominion in order to comply with the Berne Convention for the Protection of Literary and Artistic Works' bar on copyright formalities for such works. See §9(b)(1), 102Stat. 2859. Despite proposals to repeal §411(a)'s registration requirement entirely, however, see S. Rep. No. 100–352, p. 36 (1988), Congress maintained the requirement for domestic works, see §411(a). Subsequently, in 1993, Congress considered, but declined to adopt, a proposal to allow suit immediately upon submission of a registration application. See H. R. Rep. No. 103–338, p. 4 (1993). And in 2005, Congress made a preregistration option available for works vulnerable to predistribution infringement. See Artists' Rights and Theft Prevention Act of 2005, §104, 119Stat. 221. See also *supra,* at 3–4. Congress chose that course in face of calls to eliminate registration in cases of predistribution infringement. 70 Fed. Reg. 42286. Time and again, then, Congress has maintained registration as prerequisite to suit, and rejected proposals that would have eliminated registration or tied it to the copyright claimant's application instead of the Register's action.[5]

Fourth Estate additionally argues that, as "registration is not a condition of copyright protection," 17 U. S. C. §408(a), §411(a) should not be read to bar a copyright claimant from enforcing that protection in court once she has submitted a proper application for registration. Brief for Petitioner 37. But as explained *supra,* at 3, the Copyright Act safeguards copyright owners, irrespective of registration, by vesting them with exclusive rights upon creation of their works and prohibiting infringement from that point forward. If infringement occurs before a copyright owner applies for registration, that owner may eventually recover damages for the past infringement, as well as the infringer's profits. §504. She must simply apply for registration and receive the Copyright Office's decision on her application before instituting suit. Once the Register grants or refuses registration, the copyright owner may also seek an injunction barring the infringer from continued violation of her exclusive rights and an order requiring the infringer to destroy infringing materials. §§502, 503(b).

Fourth Estate maintains, however, that if infringement occurs while the Copyright Office is reviewing a registration application, the registration approach will deprive the owner of her rights during the waiting period. Brief for Petitioner 41. See also 1 P. Goldstein, Copyright §3.15, p. 3:154.2 (3d ed. 2018 Supp.) (finding application approach "the better rule"); 2 M. Nimmer & D. Nimmer, Copyright §7.16[B][3][a], [b][ii] (2018) (infringement suit is conditioned on application, while prima facie presumption of validity depends on certificate of registration). The Copyright Act's explicit carveouts from §411(a)'s general registration rule, however, show that Congress adverted to this concern. In the preregistration option, §408(f), Congress provided that owners of works especially susceptible to prepublication infringement should be allowed to institute suit before the Register has granted or refused registration. See §411(a). Congress made the same determination as to live broadcasts. §411(c); see *supra,* at 4.[6] As to all other works, however, §411(a)'s general rule requires owners to await action by the Register before filing suit for infringement.

Fourth Estate raises the specter that a copyright owner may lose the ability to enforce her rights if the Copyright Act's three-year statute of limitations runs out before the Copyright Office acts on her application for registration. Brief for Petitioner 41. Fourth Estate's fear is overstated, as the average processing time for registration applications is currently seven months, leaving ample time to sue after the Register's decision, even for infringement that began before submission of an application. See U. S. Copyright Office, Registration Processing Times (Oct. 2, 2018) (Registration Processing Times), https://www.copyright.gov/registration/docs/processing-times-faqs.pdf (as last visited Mar. 1, 2019).

True, the statutory scheme has not worked as Congress likely envisioned. Registration processing times have increased from one or two weeks in 1956 to many months today. See GAO, Improving Productivity in Copyright Registration 3 (GAO–AFMD–83–13 1982); Registration Processing Times. Delays in Copyright Office processing of applications, it appears, are attributable, in large measure, to staffing and budgetary shortages that Congress can alleviate, but courts cannot cure. See 5 W. Patry, Copyright §17:83 (2019). Unfortunate as the current administrative lag may be, that factor does not allow us to revise §411(a)'s congressionally composed text.

*   *   *

For the reasons stated, we conclude that "registration . . . has been made" within the meaning of 17 U. S. C. §411(a) not when an application for registration is filed, but when the Register has registered a copyright after examining a properly filed application. The judgment of the Court of Appeals for the Eleventh Circuit is accordingly

Affirmed.

12: State Copyright Sovereign Immunity

In the last few years, we have had a number of cases ask the question of whether or not a state or state institution can be sued for copyright infringement. We'll take a look at a recent case that examined the relationship between copyright and sovereign immunity. This will be important in understanding the boundaries of copyright. We also had a recent case on whether states can copyright their statutes, and how far that goes.

Georgia v. Public.Resource.Org, 590 U.S. ___ (2020)

The U.S. Supreme Court handed down their decision in Georgia v. Public.Resource.Org Inc. on April 27, 2020. 590 U.S. ____ (2020). The case concerned the Official Code of Georgia Annotated, which is a compilation of the laws of Georgia, plus annotations ""consisting of history lines, repeal lines, cross references, commentaries, case notations, editor's notes, excerpts from law review articles, summaries of opinions of the Attorney General of Georgia, summaries of advisory opinions of the State Bar, and other research references." The Code declared that the annotations were do not have the force of law. That will be important. Lexis prepared the annotations under an agreement with the State of Georgia. Public.Resource.Org (PRO), a non-profit, purchased a copy of the Code -- 186 volumes -- in print, scanned them, and then uploaded them to a free website, as well as distributing them to Georgia legislators, making them aware of the act. The State of Georgia sued for copyright.

The district court found that the annotations were not in the public domain, *because they do not have the force of law*. The 11th Circuit reversed, finding that because they are integrated with the official Code, they are in the public domain. The U.S. Supreme Court took up the question under the *government edict doctrine*: "Does the government edict doctrine extend to--and thus render uncopyrighrtable--the annotations in the Official Code of Georgia Annotated?" In a 5-4 majority, the U.S. Supreme Court found that under the government edicts doctrine, the annotations are ineligible for copyright protection. "No one can own the law." The case came down to who was the authors, and whether the work was created in the course of legislative duties. Two dissents were penned.

Note: this decision expands the public domain and what is not copyrightable.

Allen v. Cooper, 140 S.Ct. 994 (2020)

Allen v. Cooper was decided on March 23, 2020, which concerned the Copyright Remedy Clarification Act. The case concerned photographs and videos of a shipwreck off of North Carolina's coast. Frederick Allen had been hired to take footage in 1996 of the Blackbeard's Queen Anen's Revenge ship that sunk in 1718, and continued to document the shipwreck for twenty years. He registered his photographs and videos with the U.S. Copyright Office. The state of North Carolina at some point before October 2013 posted some of Allens' work on their website without permission. A settlement was reached for the infringing acts, but then shortly after that the state passed the "Blackbeard's Law" which converted Allen's work into "public record" materials that the state could freely use. Allen sued for copyright infringement. The state claimed sovereign immunity under the 11th Amendment of the U.S. Constitution. Allen responded that the Copyright Remedy Clarification Act abrogates state sovereign immunity for copyright infringement claims. In a 9-0 decision, the U.S. Supreme Court found that Congress lacked authority to abrogate state sovereign immunity from copyright infringement suits.

The Copyright Remedy Clarification Act (1990) amended Section 511(a) of the 1976 Copyright Act, and attempted to abrogate sovereign immunity of states for copyright infringement.

The statute reads:

> **(a) In General.—**
> Any State, any instrumentality of a State, and any officer or employee of a State or instrumentality of a State acting in his or her official capacity, shall not be immune, under the Eleventh Amendment of the Constitution of the United States or under any other doctrine of sovereign immunity, from suit in Federal court by any person, including any governmental or nongovernmental entity, for a violation of any of the exclusive rights of a copyright owner provided by sections 106 through 122, for importing copies of phonorecords in violation of section 602, or for any other violation under this title.

This had been a growing issue in appellate courts around the country, with most courts refusing to enforce the CRCA, but questions arose related to state universities and sovereign immunity related to copyright infringement. Following the ruling by the U.S.

Supreme Court, Congress in the form of Senators Tillis and Leahy requested that the U.S. Copyright office conduct a study on copyright infringement by state actors. The U.S. Copyright Office began that study on August 3, 2020 with a call for public comments, which were published in September 2020. "The Court's decision was based in part on the lack of evidence in the legislative record that states had intentionally infringed copyrights and had not provided adequate remedies for affected copyright owners under state law." https://www.copyright.gov/policy/state-sovereign-immunity/

The U.S. Supreme Court established a standard in which Congress could act regarding state copyright infringement. The Study by the Copyright Office sets out to assist by determining the "the degree to which copyright owners face infringement from state actors today, whether such infringement is based on intentional or reckless conduct, and what remedies, if any, are available to copyright owners under state law." Id.

Let's take a look at the comments and reply comments at the U.S. Copyright Office to understand what is at stake.
https://www.copyright.gov/policy/state-sovereign-immunity/

United States Senate
WASHINGTON, DC 20510

VIA ELECTRONIC TRANSMISSION

April 28, 2020

Maria Strong
Acting Register of Copyrights and Director
United States Copyright Office
101 Independence Avenue, SE
Washington, D.C. 20559

Dear Acting Register Strong:

The Supreme Court's ruling last month in *Allen v. Cooper* created a situation in which copyright owners are without remedy if a State infringes their copyright and claims State sovereign immunity under the Eleventh Amendment of the U.S. Constitution.[1] We are concerned about the impact this may have on American creators and innovators, and we would like for the Copyright Office to research this issue to determine whether there is sufficient basis for federal legislation abrogating State sovereign immunity when States infringe copyrights. We likewise are asking the Patent and Trademark Office to advise on the pervasiveness and patterns of States' infringements of patents and trademarks.

As you know, *Allen v. Cooper* involved a challenge to the constitutionality of the Copyright Remedy Clarification Act (CRCA),[2] which Congress enacted in 1990 to abrogate State sovereign immunity for copyright infringement and establish that a State would be liable "in the same manner and to the same extent" as a private party under copyright law. The Supreme Court found the CRCA was unconstitutional because it applied to all infringements of copyright by States, not just unconstitutional infringements.

But *Allen v. Cooper* provided Congress a blueprint for how to validly abrogate State sovereign immunity from certain copyright infringement claims. One element the court pointed to was the importance of Congress identifying a pattern of unconstitutional infringement before enactment. Though the Supreme Court found that the legislative record for the CRCA was insufficient despite a 1990 report from the Register of Copyrights titled *Copyright Liability of States and the Eleventh Amendment*, that report turned up only a handful of cases that alleged State infringements of copyright. It is on this point that we request the Copyright Office's expertise and advice.

---

[1] *See Allen v. Cooper*, No. 18-877 (Mar. 23, 2020).

[2] Pub. L. No. 101-553, 104 Stat. 2749 (1990).

We have heard from affected copyright owners that in recent years State infringements of copyright have become much more common. We ask that the Copyright Office study the extent to which copyright owners are experiencing infringements by state entities without adequate remedies under state law. As part of this analysis, the Office should consider the extent to which such infringements appear to be based on intentional or reckless conduct.

So that Congress can evaluate whether legislative action needs to be taken, please provide a public report summarizing the findings of your study, as well as the facts and analyses upon which those findings are based, no later than April 30, 2021. Thank you for your careful attention to this matter. If you have any questions, please do not hesitate to contact me.

Sincerely,

Thom Tillis
United States Senator

Patrick Leahy
United States Senator

Georgia v. Public.Resource.Org. Inc., 580 U.S. ___ (2020)

Chief Justice ROBERTS delivered the opinion of the Court.

The Copyright Act grants potent, decades-long monopoly protection for "original works of authorship." 17 U. S. C. §102(a). The question in this case is whether that protection extends to the annotations contained in Georgia's official annotated code.

We hold that it does not. Over a century ago, we recognized a limitation on copyright protection for certain government work product, rooted in the Copyright Act's "authorship" requirement. Under what has been dubbed the government edicts doctrine, officials empowered to speak with the force of law cannot be the authors of—and therefore cannot copyright—the works they create in the course of their official duties.

We have previously applied that doctrine to hold that non-binding, explanatory legal materials are not copyrightable when created *by judges* who possess the authority to make and interpret the law. See *Banks* v. *Manchester*, 128 U.S. 244 (1888). We now recognize that the same logic applies to non-binding, explanatory legal materials created *by a legislative body* vested with the authority to make law. Because Georgia's annotations are authored by an arm of the legislature in the course of its legislative duties, the government edicts doctrine puts them outside the reach of copyright protection.

I

A

The State of Georgia has one official code—the "Official Code of Georgia Annotated," or OCGA. The first page of each volume of the OCGA boasts the State's official seal and announces to readers that it is "Published Under Authority of the State."

The OCGA includes the text of every Georgia statute currently in force, as well as various non-binding supplementary materials. At issue in this case is a set of annotations that appear beneath each statutory provision. The annotations generally include summaries of judicial decisions applying a given provision, summaries of any pertinent opinions of the state attorney general, and a list of related law review articles and similar reference materials. In addition, the annotations often include editor's notes that provide information about the origins of the statutory text, such as whether it derives from a particular judicial decision or resembles an older provision that has been construed by Georgia courts. See, *e.g.*, OCGA §§51–1–1, 53–4–2 (2019).

The OCGA is assembled by a state entity called the Code Revision Commission. In 1977, the Georgia Legislature established the Commission to recodify Georgia law for the first time in decades. The Commission was (and remains) tasked with consolidating disparate bills into a single Code for reenactment by the legislature and contracting with a third party to produce the annotations. A majority of the Commission's 15 members must be members of the Georgia Senate or House of Representatives. The Commission receives funding through appropriations "provided for the legislative branch of state government." OCGA §28–9–2(c) (2018). And it is staffed by the Office of Legislative Counsel, which is obligated by statute to provide services "for the legislative branch of government." §§28–4–3(c)(4), 28–9–4. Under the Georgia Constitution, the Commission's role in compiling the statutory text and accompanying annotations falls "within the sphere of legislative authority." *Harrison Co.* v. *Code Revision Comm'n*, 244 Ga. 325, 330, 260 S.E.2d 30, 34 (1979).

Each year, the Commission submits its proposed statutory text and accompanying annotations to the legislature for approval. The legislature then votes to do three things: (1) "enact[ ]" the "statutory portion of the codification of Georgia laws"; (2) "merge[ ]" the statutory portion "with [the] annotations"; and (3) "publish[ ]" the final merged product "by authority of the state" as "the 'Official Code of Georgia Annotated.' " OCGA §1–1–1 (2019); see *Code Revision Comm'n* v. *Public.Resource.Org, Inc.*, 906 F.3d 1229, 1245, 1255 (CA11 2018); Tr. of Oral Arg. 8.

The annotations in the current OCGA were prepared in the first instance by Matthew Bender & Co., Inc., a division of the LexisNexis Group, pursuant to a work-for-hire agreement with the Commission. The agreement between Lexis and the Commission states that any copyright in the OCGA vests exclusively in "the State of Georgia, acting through the Commission." App. 567. Lexis and its army of researchers perform the lion's share of the work in drafting the annotations, but the Commission supervises that work and specifies what the annotations must include in exacting detail. See 906 F. 3d, at 1243–1244; App. 269–278, 286–427 (Commission specifications). Under the agreement, Lexis enjoys the exclusive right to publish, distribute, and sell the OCGA. In exchange, Lexis has agreed to limit the price it may charge for the OCGA and to make an unannotated version of the statutory text available to the public online for free. A hard copy of the complete OCGA currently retails for $412.00.

B

Public.Resource.Org (PRO) is a nonprofit organization that aims to facilitate public access to government records and legal materials. Without permission, PRO posted a digital version of the OCGA on various websites, where it could be downloaded by the public without charge. PRO also distributed copies of the OCGA to various organizations and Georgia officials.

In response, the Commission sent PRO several cease-and-desist letters asserting that PRO's actions constituted unlawful copyright infringement. When PRO refused to halt its distribution activities, the Commission sued PRO on behalf of the Georgia Legislature and the State of Georgia for copyright infringement. The Commission limited its assertion of copyright to the annotations described above; it did not claim copyright in the statutory text or numbering. PRO counterclaimed, seeking a declaratory judgment that the entire OCGA, including the annotations, fell in the public domain.

The District Court sided with the Commission. The Court acknowledged that the annotations in the OCGA presented "an unusual case because most official codes are not annotated and most annotated codes are not official." *Code Revision Comm'n* v. *Public.Resource.Org, Inc.*, 244 F. Supp. 3d 1350, 1356 (ND Ga. 2017). But, ultimately, the Court concluded that the annotations were eligible for copyright protection because they were "not enacted into law" and lacked "the force of law." *Ibid.* In light of that conclusion, the Court granted partial summary judgment to the Commission and entered a permanent injunction requiring PRO to cease its distribution activities and to remove the digital copies of the OCGA from the internet.

The Eleventh Circuit reversed. 906 F.3d 1229. The Court began by reviewing the three 19th-century cases in which we articulated the government edicts doctrine. See *Wheaton* v. *Peters*, 8 Pet. 591 (1834); *Banks* v. *Manchester*, 128 U.S. 244 (1888); *Callaghan* v. *Myers*, 128 U.S. 617 (1888). The Court understood those cases to establish a "rule" based on an interpretation of the statutory term "author" that "works created by courts in the performance of their official duties did not belong to the judges" but instead fell "in the public domain." 906 F. 3d, at 1239. In the Court's view, that rule "derive[s] from first principles about the nature of law in our democracy." *Ibid.* In a democracy, the Court reasoned, "the People" are "the constructive authors" of the law, and judges and legislators are merely "draftsmen . . . exercising delegated authority." *Ibid.* The Court therefore deemed the "ultimate inquiry" to be whether a work is "attributable to the constructive authorship of the People." *Id.*, at 1242. The Court identified three factors to guide that inquiry: "the identity of the public official who created the work; the nature of the work; and the process by which the work was produced." *Id.*, at 1254. The Court found that each of those factors cut in favor of treating the OCGA annotations as government edicts authored by the People. It therefore rejected the Commission's assertion of copyright, vacated the injunction against PRO, and directed that judgment be entered for PRO.

We granted certiorari. 588 U. S. ___ (2019).

II

We hold that the annotations in Georgia's Official Code are ineligible for copyright protection, though for reasons distinct from those relied on by the Court of Appeals. A careful examination of our government edicts precedents reveals a straightforward rule based on the identity of the author. Under the government edicts doctrine, judges—and, we now confirm, legislators—may not be considered the "authors" of the works they produce in the course of their official duties as judges and legislators. That rule applies regardless of whether a given material carries the force of law. And it applies to the annotations here because they are authored by an arm of the legislature in the course of its official duties.

A

We begin with precedent. The government edicts doctrine traces back to a trio of cases decided in the 19th century. In this Court's first copyright case, *Wheaton* v. *Peters*, 8 Pet. 591 (1834), the Court's third Reporter of Decisions, Wheaton, sued the fourth, Peters, unsuccessfully asserting a copyright interest in the Justices' opinions. *Id.*, at 617 (argument). In Wheaton's view, the opinions "must have belonged to some one" because "they were new, original," and much more "elaborate" than law or custom required. *Id.*, at 615. Wheaton argued that the Justices were the authors and had assigned their ownership interests to him through a tacit "gift." *Id.*, at 614. The Court unanimously rejected that argument, concluding that "no reporter has or can have any copyright in the written opinions delivered by this court" and that "the judges thereof cannot confer on any reporter any such right." *Id.*, at 668 (opinion).

That conclusion apparently seemed too obvious to adorn with further explanation, but the Court provided one a half century later in *Banks* v. *Manchester*, 128 U.S. 244 (1888). That case concerned whether Wheaton's state-court counterpart, the official reporter of the Ohio Supreme Court, held a copyright in the judges' opinions and several non-binding explanatory materials prepared by the judges. *Id.*, at 249–251. The Court concluded that he did not, explaining that "the judge who, in his judicial capacity, prepares the opinion or decision, the statement of the case and the syllabus or head note" cannot "be regarded as their author or their proprietor, in the sense of [the Copyright Act]." *Id.*, at 253. Pursuant to "a judicial *consensus*" dating back to *Wheaton*, judges could not assert copyright in "whatever work they perform in their capacity as judges." *Banks*, 128 U. S, at 253 (emphasis in original). Rather, "[t]he whole work done by the judges constitutes the authentic exposition and interpretation of the law, which, binding every citizen, is free for publication to all." *Ibid.* (citing *Nash* v. *Lathrop*, 142 Mass. 29, 6 N.E. 559 (1886)).

In a companion case decided later that Term, *Callaghan* v. *Myers*, 128 U.S. 617 (1888), the Court identified an important limiting principle. As in *Wheaton* and *Banks*, the Court rejected the claim that an official reporter held a copyright interest in the judges' opinions. But, resolving an issue not addressed in *Wheaton* and *Banks*, the Court upheld the reporter's copyright interest in several explanatory materials that the reporter had created himself: headnotes, syllabi, tables of contents, and the like. *Callaghan*, 128 U. S., at 645, 647. Although these works mirrored the judge-made materials rejected in *Banks*, they came from an author who had no authority to speak with the force of law. Because the reporter was not a judge, he was free to "obtain[ ] a copyright" for the materials that were "the result of his [own] intellectual labor." 128 U. S., at 647.

These cases establish a straightforward rule: Because judges are vested with the authority to make and interpret the law, they cannot be the "author" of the works they prepare "in the discharge of their judicial duties." *Banks*, 128 U. S., at 253. This rule applies both to binding works (such as opinions) and to non-binding works (such as headnotes and syllabi). *Ibid.* It does not apply, however, to works created by government officials (or private parties) who lack the authority to make or interpret the law, such as court reporters. Compare *ibid.* with *Callaghan*, 128 U. S., at 647.

The animating principle behind this rule is that no one can own the law. "Every citizen is presumed to know the law," and "it needs no argument to show . . . that all should have free access" to its contents. *Nash*, 142 Mass., at 35, 6 N. E., at 560 (cited by *Banks*, 128 U. S., at

253–254). Our cases give effect to that principle in the copyright context through construction of the statutory term "author." *Id.*, at 253.[1] Rather than attempting to catalog the materials that constitute "the law," the doctrine bars the officials responsible for creating the law from being considered the "author[s]" of "*whatever work* they perform in their capacity" as lawmakers. *Ibid.* (emphasis added). Because these officials are generally empowered to make and interpret law, their "whole work" is deemed part of the "authentic exposition and interpretation of the law" and must be "free for publication to all." *Ibid.*

If judges, acting as judges, cannot be "authors" because of their authority to make and interpret the law, it follows that legislators, acting as legislators, cannot be either. Courts have thus long understood the government edicts doctrine to apply to legislative materials. See, *e.g.*, *Nash*, 142 Mass., at 35, 6 N. E., at 560 (judicial opinions and statutes stand "on substantially the same footing" for purposes of the government edicts doctrine); *Howell* v. *Miller*, 91 F. 129, 130–131, 137–138 (CA6 1898) (Harlan, J., Circuit Justice, joined by then-Circuit Judge Taft) (analyzing statutes and supplementary materials under *Banks* and *Callaghan* and concluding that the materials were copyrightable because they were prepared by a private compiler).

Moreover, just as the doctrine applies to "whatever work [judges] perform in their capacity as judges," *Banks*, 128

U. S., at 253, it applies to whatever work legislators perform in their capacity as legislators. That of course includes final legislation, but it also includes explanatory and procedural materials legislators create in the discharge of their legislative duties. In the same way that judges cannot be the authors of their headnotes and syllabi, legislators cannot be the authors of (for example) their floor statements, committee reports, and proposed bills. These materials are part of the "whole work done by [legislators]," so they must be "free for publication to all." *Ibid.*

Under our precedents, therefore, copyright does not vest in works that are (1) created by judges and legislators (2) in the course of their judicial and legislative duties.

B

1

Applying that framework, Georgia's annotations are not copyrightable. The first step is to examine whether their purported author qualifies as a legislator.

As we have explained, the annotations were prepared in the first instance by a private company (Lexis) pursuant to a work-for-hire agreement with Georgia's Code Revision Commission. The Copyright Act therefore deems the Commission the sole "author" of the work. 17 U. S. C. §201(b). Although Lexis expends considerable effort preparing the annotations, for purposes of copyright that labor redounds to the Commission as the statutory author. Georgia agrees that the author is the Commission. Brief for Petitioners 25.

The Commission is not identical to the Georgia Legislature, but functions as an arm of it for the purpose of producing the annotations. The Commission is created by the legislature, for the legislature, and consists largely of legislators. The Commission receives funding and staff designated by law for the legislative branch. Significantly, the annotations the Commission creates are approved by the legislature before being "merged" with the statutory text and published in the official code alongside that text at the legislature's direction. OCGA §1–1–1; see 906 F. 3d, at 1245, 1255; Tr. of Oral Arg. 8.

If there were any doubt about the link between the Commission and the legislature, the Georgia Supreme Court has dispelled it by holding that, under the Georgia Constitution, "the work of the Commission; *i.e.*, selecting a publisher and contracting for and supervising the codification of the laws enacted by the General Assembly, including court interpretations thereof, *is within the sphere of legislative authority*." *Harrison Co.*, 244 Ga., at 330, 260 S. E. 2d, at 34 (emphasis added). That holding is not limited to the Commission's role in codifying the statutory text. The Commission's "legislative authority" specifically includes its "codification of . . . court interpretations" of the State's laws. *Ibid.* Thus, as a matter of state law, the Commission wields the legislature's authority when it works with Lexis to produce the annotations. All of this shows that the Commission serves as an extension of the Georgia Legislature in preparing and publishing the annotations. And it helps explain why the Commission brought this suit asserting copyright in the annotations "on behalf of and for the benefit of " the Georgia Legislature and the State of Georgia. App. 20.[2]

2

The second step is to determine whether the Commission creates the annotations in the "discharge" of its legislative "duties." *Banks*, 128 U. S., at 253. It does. Although the annotations are not enacted into law through bicameralism and presentment, the Commission's preparation of the annotations is under Georgia law an act of "legislative authority," *Harrison Co.*, 244 Ga., at 330, 260 S. E. 2d, at 34, and the annotations provide commentary and resources that the legislature has deemed relevant to understanding its laws. Georgia and Justice Ginsburg emphasize that the annotations do not purport to provide authoritative explanations of the law and largely summarize other materials, such as judicial decisions and law review articles. See *post*, at 3–4 (dissenting opinion). But that does not take them outside the exercise of legislative duty by the Commission and legislature. Just as we have held that the "statement of the case and the syllabus or head note" prepared by judges fall within the "work they perform in their capacity as judges," *Banks*, 128 U. S., at 253, so too annotations published by legislators alongside the statutory text fall within the work legislators perform in their capacity as legislators.

In light of the Commission's role as an adjunct to the legislature and the fact that the Commission authors the annotations in the course of its legislative responsibilities, the annotations in Georgia's Official Code fall within the government edicts doctrine and are not copyrightable.

III

Georgia resists this conclusion on several grounds. At the outset, Georgia advances two arguments for why, in its view, excluding the OCGA annotations from copyright protection conflicts with the text of the Copyright Act. Both are unavailing.

First, Georgia notes that §101 of the Act specifically lists "annotations" among the kinds of works eligible for copyright protection. But that provision refers only to "annotations . . . which . . . represent an original work of *authorship*." 17 U. S. C. §101 (emphasis added). The whole point of the government edicts doctrine is that judges and legislators cannot serve as authors when they produce works in their official capacity. While the reference to "annotations" in §101 may help explain why supplemental, explanatory materials are copyrightable when prepared by a private party, or a non-lawmaking official like the reporter in *Callaghan*, it does not speak to whether those same materials are copyrightable when prepared by a judge or a legislator. In the same way that judicial materials are ineligible for protection even though they plainly qualify as "[l]iterary works . . . expressed in words," *ibid.*, legislative materials are ineligible for protection even if they happen to fit the description of otherwise copyrightable "annotations."

Second, Georgia draws a negative inference from the fact that the Act excludes from copyright protection "work[s] prepared by an officer or employee of the United States Government as part of that person's official duties" and does not establish a similar rule for the States. §101; see also §105. But the bar on copyright protection for federal works sweeps much more broadly than the government edicts doctrine does. That bar applies to works created by all federal "officer[s] or employee[s]," without regard for the nature of their position or scope of their authority. Whatever policy reasons might justify the Federal Government's decision to forfeit copyright protection for its own proprietary works, that federal rule does not suggest an intent to displace the much narrower government edicts doctrine with respect to the States. That doctrine does not apply to non-lawmaking officials, leaving States free to assert copyright in the vast majority of expressive works they produce, such as those created by their universities, libraries, tourism offices, and so on.

More generally, Georgia suggests that we should resist applying our government edicts precedents to the OCGA annotations because our 19th-century forebears interpreted the statutory term author by reference to "public policy"—an approach that Georgia believes is incongruous with the "modern era" of statutory interpretation. Brief for Petitioners 21 (internal quotation marks omitted). But we are particularly reluctant to disrupt precedents interpreting language that Congress has since reenacted. As we explained last Term in *Helsinn Healthcare S. A.* v. *Teva Pharmaceuticals USA, Inc.*, 586 U. S. ___ (2019), when Congress "adopt[s] the language used in [an] earlier act," we presume that Congress "adopted also the construction given by this Court to such language, and made it a part of the enactment." *Id.*, at ___ (slip op., at 7) (quoting *Shapiro* v. *United States*, 335 U.S. 1, 16 (1948)). A century of cases have rooted the government edicts doctrine in the word "author," and Congress has repeatedly reused that term without abrogating the doctrine. The term now carries this settled meaning, and "critics of our ruling can take their objections across the street, [where] Congress can correct any mistake it sees." *Kimble* v. *Marvel Entertainment, LLC*, 576 U.S. 446, 456 (2015).[3]

Moving on from the text, Georgia invokes what it views as the official position of the Copyright Office, as reflected in the Compendium of U. S. Copyright Office Practices (Compendium). But, as Georgia concedes, the Compendium is a non-binding administrative manual that at most

merits deference under *Skidmore* v. *Swift & Co.*, 323 U.S. 134 (1944). That means we must follow it only to the extent it has the "power to persuade." *Id.*, at 140. Because our precedents answer the question before us, we find any competing guidance in the Compendium unpersuasive.

In any event, the Compendium is largely consistent with our decision. Drawing on *Banks*, it states that, "[a]s a matter of longstanding public policy, the U. S. Copyright Office will not register a government edict that has been issued by any state, local, or territorial government, including legislative enactments, judicial decisions, administrative rulings, public ordinances, *or similar types of official legal materials*." Compendium §313.6(C)(2) (rev. 3d ed. 2017) (emphasis added). And, under *Banks*, what counts as a "similar" material depends on what kind of officer created the material (*i.e.*, a judge) and whether the officer created it in the course of official (*i.e.*, judicial) duties. See Compendium §313.6(C)(2) (quoting *Banks*, 128 U. S., at 253, for the proposition that copyright cannot vest "in the products of the labor done by judicial officers in the discharge of their judicial duties").

The Compendium goes on to observe that "the Office may register annotations that summarize or comment upon legal materials . . . unless the annotations themselves have the force of law." Compendium §313.6(C)(2). But that broad statement—true of annotations created by officials such as court reporters that lack the authority to make or interpret the law—does not engage with the critical issue of annotations created *by judges or legislators* in their official capacities. Because the Compendium does not address that question and otherwise echoes our government edicts precedents, it is of little relevance here.

Georgia also appeals to the overall purpose of the Copyright Act to promote the creation and dissemination of creative works. Georgia submits that, without copyright protection, Georgia and many other States will be unable to induce private parties like Lexis to assist in preparing affordable annotated codes for widespread distribution. That appeal to copyright policy, however, is addressed to the wrong forum. As Georgia acknowledges, "[I]t is generally for Congress, not the courts, to decide how best to pursue the Copyright Clause's objectives." *Eldred* v. *Ashcroft*, 537 U.S. 186, 212 (2003). And that principle requires adherence to precedent when, as here, we have construed the statutory text and "tossed [the ball] into Congress's court, for acceptance or not as that branch elects." *Kimble*, 576 U. S., at 456.

Turning to our government edicts precedents, Georgia insists that they can and should be read to focus exclusively on whether a particular work has "the force of law." Brief for Petitioners 32 (capitalization deleted). Justice Thomas appears to endorse the same view. See *post*, at 4. But that framing has multiple flaws.

Most obviously, it cannot be squared with the reasoning or results of our cases—especially *Banks*. *Banks*, following *Wheaton* and the "judicial consensus" it inspired, denied copyright protection to judicial opinions without excepting concurrences and dissents that carry no legal force. 128 U. S., at 253 (emphasis deleted). As every judge learns the hard way, "comments in [a] dissenting opinion" about legal principles and precedents "are just that: comments in a dissenting opinion." *Railroad Retirement Bd.* v. *Fritz*, 449 U.S. 166, 177, n. 10 (1980). Yet such comments are covered by the government edicts doctrine because they come from an official with authority to make and interpret the law.

Indeed, *Banks* went even further and withheld copyright protection from headnotes and syllabi produced by judges. 128 U. S., at 253. Surely these supplementary materials do not have the force of law, yet they are covered by the doctrine. The simplest explanation is the one *Banks* provided: These non-binding works are not copyrightable because of who creates them—judges acting in their judicial capacity. See *ibid.*

The same goes for non-binding legislative materials produced by legislative bodies acting in a legislative capacity. There is a broad array of such works ranging from floor statements to proposed bills to committee reports. Under the logic of Georgia's "force of law" test, States would own such materials and could charge the public for access to them.

Furthermore, despite Georgia's and Justice Thomas's purported concern for the text of the Copyright Act, their conception of the government edicts doctrine has *less* of a textual footing than the traditional formulation. The textual basis for the doctrine is the Act's "authorship" requirement, which unsurprisingly focuses on—the author. Justice Thomas urges us to dig deeper to "the root" of our government edicts precedents. *Post*, at 5. But, in our view, the text *is* the root. The Court long ago interpreted the word "author" to exclude officials empowered to speak with the force of law, and Congress has carried that meaning forward in multiple iterations of the Copyright Act. This textual foundation explains why the doctrine distinguishes between some authors (who are empowered to speak with the force of law) and others (who are not). Compare *Callaghan*, 128 U. S., at 647, with *Banks*, 128 U. S., at 253. But the Act's reference to "authorship" provides no basis for Georgia's rule distinguishing between different categories of content with different effects.[4]

Georgia minimizes the OCGA annotations as non-binding and non-authoritative, but that description undersells their practical significance. Imagine a Georgia citizen interested in learning his legal rights and duties. If he reads the economy-class version of the Georgia Code available online, he will see laws requiring political candidates to pay hefty qualification fees (with no indigency exception), criminalizing broad categories of consensual sexual conduct, and exempting certain key evidence in criminal trials from standard evidentiary limitations—with no hint that important aspects of those laws have been held unconstitutional by the Georgia Supreme Court. See OCGA §§21–2–131, 16–6–2, 16–6–18, 16–15–9 (available at www.legis.ga.gov). Meanwhile, first-class readers with access to the annotations will be assured that these laws are, in crucial respects, unenforceable relics that the legislature has not bothered to narrow or repeal. See §§21–2–131, 16–6–2, 16–6–18, 16–15–9 (available at https://store. lexisnexis . com / products / official - code - of - georgia - annotated - skuSKU6647 for $412.00).

If everything short of statutes and opinions were copyrightable, then States would be free to offer a whole range of premium legal works for those who can afford the extra benefit. A State could monetize its entire suite of legislative history. With today's digital tools, States might even launch a subscription or pay-per-law service.

There is no need to assume inventive or nefarious behavior for these concerns to become a reality. Unlike other forms of intellectual property, copyright protection is both instant and automatic. It vests as soon as a work is captured in a tangible form, triggering a panoply of exclusive rights that can last over a century. 17 U. S. C. §§102, 106, 302. If Georgia were correct, then unless a State took the affirmative step of transferring its copyrights to the public domain, all of its judges' and legislators' non-binding legal works would be copyrighted. And citizens, attorneys, nonprofits, and private research companies would have to cease all copying, distribution, and display of those works or risk severe and potentially criminal penalties. §§501–506. Some affected parties might be willing to roll the dice with a potential fair use defense. But that defense, designed to accommodate First Amendment concerns, is notoriously fact sensitive and often cannot be resolved without a trial. Cf. *Harper & Row, Publishers, Inc.* v. *Nation Enterprises*, 471 U.S. 539, 552, 560–561 (1985). The less bold among us would have to think twice before using official legal works that illuminate the law we are all presumed to know and understand.

Thankfully, there is a clear path forward that avoids these concerns—the one we are already on. Instead of examining whether given material carries "the force of law," we ask only whether the author of the work is a judge or a legislator. If so, then whatever work that judge or legislator produces in the course of his judicial or legislative duties is not copyrightable. That is the framework our precedents long ago established, and we adhere to those precedents today.

*   *   *

For the foregoing reasons, we affirm the judgment of the Eleventh Circuit.

It is so ordered.

Notes

1 The Copyright Act of 1790 granted copyright protection to "the author and authors" of qualifying works. Act of May 31, 1790, §1, 1Stat. 124. This author requirement appears in the current Copyright Act at §102(a), which limits protection to "original works of *authorship*." 17 U. S. C. §102(a) (emphasis added); see also §201(a) (copyright "vests initially in the author or authors of the work").

2 Justice Thomas does not dispute that the Commission is an extension of the legislature; he instead faults us for highlighting the multiple features of the Commission that make clear that this is so. See *post*, at 16 (dissenting opinion).
3 Justice Thomas disputes the applicability of the *Helsinn Healthcare* presumption because States have asserted copyright in statutory annotations over the years notwithstanding our government edicts precedents. *Post*, at 11–12. In Justice Thomas's view, those assertions prove that our precedents could not have provided clear enough guidance for Congress to incorporate. But that inference from state behavior proves too much. The same study cited by Justice Thomas to support a practice of claiming copyright in non-binding *annotations* also reports that "many states claim copyright interest in their *primary* law materials," including statutes and regulations. Dmitrieva, State Ownership of Copyrights in Primary Law Materials, 23 Hastings Com. & Entertainment L. J. 81, 109 (2000) (emphasis added). Justice Thomas concedes that such assertions are plainly foreclosed by our government edicts precedents. *Post*, at 4. That interested parties have pursued ambitious readings of our precedents does not mean those precedents are incapable of providing meaningful guidance to us or to Congress.
4 Instead of accepting our predecessors' textual reasoning at face value, Justice Thomas conjures a trinity of alternative "origin[s] and justification[s]" for the government edicts doctrine that the Court *might* have had in mind. See *post*, at 5–7. Without committing to one or all of these possibilities, Justice Thomas suggests that each would yield a rule that requires federal courts to pick out the subset of judicial and legislative materials that independently carry the force of law. But a Court motivated by Justice Thomas's three-fold concerns might just as easily have read them as supporting a rule that prevents the officials responsible for creating binding materials from qualifying as an "author." Regardless, it is more "[ ]consistent with the judicial role" to apply the reasoning and results the Court voted on and committed to writing than to speculate about what practical considerations our predecessors "may have had . . . in mind," what history "may [have] suggest[ed]," or what constitutional concerns "may have animated" our government edicts precedents. *Ibid*.

Justice Ginsburg, with whom Justice Breyer joins, dissenting.

Beyond doubt, state laws are not copyrightable. Nor are other materials created by state legislators in the course of performing their lawmaking responsibilities, *e.g.*, legislative committee reports, floor statements, unenacted bills. *Ante*, at 8–9. Not all that legislators do, however, is ineligible for copyright protection; the government edicts doctrine shields only "works that are (1) created by judges and legislators (2) *in the course of their judicial and legislative duties*." *Ante*, at 9 (emphasis added). The core question this case presents, as I see it: Are the annotations in the Official Code of Georgia Annotated (OCGA) done in a legislative capacity? The answer, I am persuaded, should be no.

To explain why, I proceed from common ground. All agree that headnotes and syllabi for judicial opinions—both a kind of annotation—are copyrightable when created by a reporter of decisions, *Callaghan* v. *Myers*, 128 U.S. 617, 645–650 (1888), but are not copyrightable when created by judges, *Banks* v. *Manchester*, 128 U.S. 244, 253 (1888). That is so because "[t]he whole work done by . . . judges," *ibid.*, including dissenting and concurring opinions, ranks as work performed in their judicial capacity. Judges do not outsource their writings to "arm[s]" or "adjunct[s]," cf. *ante*, at 9, 11, to be composed in their stead. Accordingly, the judicial opinion-drafting process in its entirety—including the drafting of headnotes and syllabi, in jurisdictions where that is done by judges—falls outside the reach of copyright protection.

One might ask: If a judge's annotations are not copyrightable, why are those created by legislators? The answer lies in the difference between the role of a judge and the role of a legislator. "[T]o the judiciary" we assign "the duty of interpreting and applying" the law, *Massachusetts* v. *Mellon*, 262 U.S. 447, 488 (1923), and sometimes making the applicable law, see Friendly, In Praise of *Erie*—and of the New Federal Common Law, 39 N. Y. U. L. Rev. 383 (1964). See also *Marbury* v. *Madison*, 1 Cranch 137, 177 (1803) ("It is emphatically the province and duty of the judicial department to say what the law is."). In contrast, the role of the legislature encompasses the process of "making laws"—not construing statutes after their enactment. *Mellon*, 262 U. S., at 488; see *Patchak* v. *Zinke*, 583 U. S. ___, ___ (2018) (plurality opinion) (slip op., at 5) ("[T]he legislative power is the power to make law."). The OCGA annotations, in my appraisal, do not rank as part of the Georgia Legislature's *lawmaking process* for three reasons.

First, the annotations are not created contemporaneously with the statutes to which they pertain; instead, the annotations comment on statutes already enacted. See, *e.g.*, App. 268–269 (text of enacted laws are transmitted to the publisher for the addition of commentary); *id.*, at 403–404 (publisher adds new case notes on a rolling basis as courts construe existing statutes).[1] In short, annotating begins only after lawmaking ends. This sets the OCGA annotations apart from uncopyrightable legislative materials like committee reports, generated before a law's enactment, and tied tightly to the task of law-formulation.

Second, the OCGA annotations are descriptive rather than prescriptive. Instead of stating the legislature's perception of what a law conveys, the annotations summarize writings in which others express *their* views on a given statute. For example, the OCGA contains "case annotations" for "[a]ll decisions of the Supreme Court of Georgia and the Court of Appeals of Georgia and all decisions of the federal courts in cases which arose in Georgia construing any portion of the general statutory law of the state." *Id.*, at 403. Per the Code Revision Commission's instructions, each annotation should "accurately reflect the facts, holding, and statutory construction" adopted by the court. *Id.*, at 404. The annotations are neutrally cast; they do not opine on whether the summarized case was correctly decided. See, *e.g.*, OCGA §17–7–50 (2013) (case annotation summarizing facts and holdings of nine cases construing right to grand jury hearing). This characteristic of the annotations distinguishes them from preenactment legislative materials that touch or concern the correct interpretation of the legislature's work.

Third, and of prime importance, the OCGA annotations are "given for the purpose of convenient reference" by the public, §1–1–7 (2019); they aim to inform the citizenry at large, they do not address, particularly, those seated in legislative chambers.[2] Annotations are thus unlike, for example, surveys, work commissioned by a legislature to aid in determining whether existing law should be amended.

The requirement that the statutory portions of the OCGA "shall be merged with annotations," §1–1–1, does not render the annotations anything other than explanatory, referential, or commentarial material. See *Harrison Co.* v. *Code Revision Comm'n*, 244 Ga. 325, 331, 260 S.E.2d 30, 35 (1979) (observation by the Supreme Court of Georgia that "inclusion of annotations in [the] 'official Code' " does not "give the annotations any official weight").[3] Annotations aid the legal researcher, and that aid is enhanced when annotations are printed beneath or alongside the relevant statutory text. But the placement of annotations in the OCGA does not alter their auxiliary, nonlegislative character.

*   *   *

Because summarizing judicial decisions and commentary bearing on enacted statutes, in contrast to, for example, drafting a committee report to accompany proposed legislation, is not done in a legislator's law-shaping capacity, I would hold the OCGA annotations copyrightable and therefore reverse the judgment of the Court of Appeals for the Eleventh Circuit.

Notes

1 For example, OCGA §11–2A–213 was enacted, in its current form, in 1993. See 1993 Ga. Laws p. 633. The case notes contained in the OCGA summarize judicial decisions construing the statute years later. See §11–2A–213 (2002) (citing *Griffith* v. *Medical Rental Supply of Albany, Ga., Inc.*, 244 Ga. App. 120, 534 S.E.2d 859 (2000); *Bailey* v. *Tucker Equip. Sales, Inc.*, 236 Ga. App. 289, 510 S.E.2d 904 (1999)).

2 Suppose a committee of Georgia's legislature, to inform the public, instructs a staffer to write a guide titled "The Workways of the Georgia Legislature." The final text describing how the legislature operates is circulated to members of the legislature and approved by a majority. Contrary to the Court's decision, I take it that such a work, which entails no lawmaking, would be copyrightable.

3 That the Georgia Supreme Court described the Commission's work as "within the sphere of legislative authority" for state separation-of-powers purposes, *Harrison Co.* v. *Code Revision Comm'n*, 244 Ga. 325, 330, 260 S.E.2d 30, 34 (1979), does not resolve the federal Copyright Act question before us. Cf. *Yates* v. *United States*, 574 U.S. 528, 537 (2015) (plurality opinion) ("In law as in life, . . . the same words, placed in different contexts, sometimes mean different things."); Cook, "Substance" and "Procedure" in the Conflict of Laws, 42 Yale L. J. 333, 337 (1933) ("The tendency to assume that a word which appears in two or more legal rules, and so in connection with more than one purpose, has and should have precisely the same scope in all of them, runs all through legal discussions. It has all the tenacity of original sin and must constantly be guarded against.").

Justice Thomas, with whom Justice Alito joins, and with whom Justice Breyer joins as to all but Part II–A and footnote 6, dissenting.

According to the majority, this Court's 19th-century "government edicts" precedents clearly stand for the proposition that "judges and legislators cannot serve as authors [for copyright purposes] when they produce works in their official capacity." *Ante*, at 11. And, after straining to conclude that the Georgia Code Revision Commission (Commission) is an arm of the Georgia Legislature, *ante*, at 9–10, the majority concludes that Georgia cannot hold a copyright in the annotations that are included as part of the Official Code of Georgia Annotated (OCGA). This ruling will likely come as a shock to the 25 other jurisdictions—22 States, 2 Territories, and the District of Columbia—that rely on arrangements similar to Georgia's to produce annotated codes. See Brief for State of Arkansas et al. as *Amici Curiae* 15, and App. to *id.*, at 1. Perhaps these jurisdictions all overlooked this Court's purportedly clear guidance. Or perhaps the widespread use of these arrangements indicates that today's decision extends the government edicts doctrine to a new context, rather than simply "confirm[ing]" what the precedents have always held. See *ante*, at 5. Because I believe we should "leave to Congress the task of deciding whether the Copyright Act needs an upgrade," *American Broadcasting Cos.* v. *Aereo, Inc.*, 573 U.S. 431, 463 (2014) (Scalia, J., dissenting), I respectfully dissent.

I

Like the majority, I begin with the three 19th-century precedents that the parties agree provide the foundation for the government edicts doctrine.

In *Wheaton* v. *Peters*, 8 Pet. 591 (1834), the Court first regarded it as self-evident that judicial opinions cannot be copyrighted either by the judges who signed them or by a reporter under whose auspices they are published. Congress provided that, in return for a salary of $1,000, the Reporter of Decisions for this Court would prepare reports consisting of judicial opinions and additional materials summarizing the cases. *Id.*, at 614, 617 (argument). Wheaton, one of this Court's earliest Reporters, argued that he owned a copyright for the entirety of his reports. He contended that he had "acquired the right to the opinions by judges' gift" once they became a part of his volume. *Id.*, at 614 (same). The Court ultimately remanded on the question whether Wheaton had complied with the Copyright Act's procedural requirements. *Id.*, at 667–668. In doing so, it observed in dicta that "the court [was] unanimously of [the] opinion, that no reporter has or can have any copyright in the written opinions delivered by this court; and that the judges thereof cannot confer on any reporter any such right." *Id.*, at 668.

Fifty-four years later, the Court returned to the same subject, suggesting a doctrinal basis for the rule that judicial opinions and certain closely related materials cannot be copyrighted. In *Banks* v. *Manchester*, 128 U.S. 244 (1888), the state-authorized publisher of the Ohio Supreme Court's decisions, Banks & Brothers, sued a competing publisher for copyright infringement. The competing publisher reproduced portions from Banks' reports, including Ohio Supreme Court decisions, statements of the cases, and syllabi, all of which were originally prepared by the opinion's authoring judge. This Court held that these materials were not the proper subject of copyright. In reaching that conclusion, the Court grounded its analysis in its interpretation of the word "author" in the Copyright Act. It anchored this interpretation in the "public policy" that "the judge who, in his judicial capacity, prepares the opinion or decision [and other materials]" is not "regarded as their author or their proprietor, in the sense of [the Copyright Act], so as to be able to confer any title by assignment." *Banks*, 128 U. S., at 253. The Court supported this conclusion by stating that "there has always been a judicial consensus . . . that no copyright could[,] under the statutes passed by Congress, be secured in the products of the labor done by judicial officers in the discharge of their judicial duties." *Ibid.* (emphasis deleted). And the Court observed that this rule reflected the view that the "authentic exposition and interpretation of the law . . . is free for publication to all," which in turn prevents a judge from qualifying as an author. *Ibid.*

Importantly, the Court also briefly discussed whether the State of Ohio could directly hold the copyright. In answering this question, the Court did not suggest that States were categorically prohibited from holding copyrights as authors or assignees. Instead, the Court simply noted that the State fell outside the scope of the Act because it was not a "resident" or "citizen of the United States," as then required by statute, and because it did not meet other statutory criteria. *Ibid.* The Court felt it necessary to observe, however, that "[w]hether the State could take out a copyright for itself, or could enjoy the benefit of one taken out by an individual for it, as the assignee of a citizen of the United States or a resident therein, who should be the author of a book, is a question not involved in the present case, and we refrain from considering it." *Ibid.*

Finally, in *Callaghan* v. *Myers*, 128 U.S. 617 (1888), the Court addressed the limits of the government edicts doctrine. In that case, the Court settled another dispute between a publisher of court decisions and an alleged infringer. The plaintiff purchased the proprietary rights to the reports prepared by the Illinois Supreme Court's reporter of decisions, Freeman, including the copyright to the reports. Unlike in *Banks*, these reports also contained material authored by Freeman. *Callaghan*, 128 U. S., at 645. The alleged infringers copied the judicial decisions and Freeman's materials. In finding for the plaintiff, this Court reiterated that "there can be no copyright in the opinions of the judges, or in the work done by them in their official capacity as judges." *Id.*, at 647 (citing *Banks*, 128 U. S. 244). But the Court concluded that "no [similar] ground of public policy" justified denying a state official a copyright "cover[ing] the matter which is the result of his intellectual labor." *Callaghan*, 128 U. S., at 647.

II

These precedents establish that judicial opinions cannot be copyrighted. But they do not exclude from copyright protection notes that are prepared by an official court reporter and published together with the reported opinions. There is no apparent reason why the same logic would not apply to statutes and regulations. Thus, it must follow from our precedents that statutes and regulations cannot be copyrighted, but accompanying notes lacking legal force can be. See *Howell* v. *Miller*, 91 F. 129 (CA6 1898) (Harlan, J.) (explaining that, under *Banks* and *Callaghan*, annotations to Michigan statutes could be copyrighted).

A

It is fair to say that the Court's 19th-century decisions do not provide any extended explanation of the basis for the government edicts doctrine. The majority is nonetheless content to accept these precedents reflexively, without examining the origin or validity of the rule they announced. For the majority, it is enough that the precedents established a rule that "seemed too obvious to adorn with further explanation." *Ante*, at 6. But the contours of the rule were far from clear, and to understand the scope of the doctrine, we must explore its underlying rationale.

In my view, the majority's uncritical extrapolation of precedent is inconsistent with the judicial role. An unwillingness to examine the root of a precedent has led to the sprouting of many noxious weeds that distort the meaning of the Constitution and statutes alike. Although we have not been asked to revisit these precedents, it behooves us to explore the origin of and justification for them, especially when we are asked to apply their rule for the first time in over 130 years.

The Court's precedents suggest three possible grounds supporting their conclusion. In *Banks*, the Court referred to the meaning of the term "author" in copyright law. While the Court did not develop this argument, it is conceivable that the contemporaneous public meaning of the term "author" was narrower in the copyright context than in ordinary speech. At the time this Court decided *Banks*, the Copyright Act provided protection for books, maps, prints, engravings, musical and dramatic compositions, photographs, and works of art.[1] Judicial opinions differ markedly from these works. Books, for instance, express the thoughts of their authors. They typically have no power beyond the ability of their words to influence readers, and they usually are published at private expense. Judicial opinions, on the other hand, do not simply express the thoughts of the judges who write or endorse them. Instead, they elaborate and apply rules of law that, in turn, represent the implementation of the will of the people. Unlike other copyrightable works of authorship, judicial opinions have binding legal effect, and they are produced and issued at public expense. Moreover, copyright law understands an author to be one whose work will be encouraged by the grant of an exclusive right. See *Kirtsaeng* v. *John Wiley & Sons, Inc.*, 579 U. S. ___, ___ (2016) (slip op., at 6). But judges, when acting in an official capacity, do not fit that description. The Court in *Banks* may have had these differences in mind when it concluded that a judge fell outside the scope of the term "author." 128 U. S., at 253.

History may also suggest a narrower meaning of "author" in the copyright context. In England, at least as far back as 1666, courts and commentators agreed "that the property of all law books is in the king, because he pays the judges who pronounce the law." G. Curtis, Law of Copyright 130 (1847); see also *Banks & Bros.* v. *West Publishing Co.*, 27 F. 50, 57 (CC Minn. 1886) (citing English cases and treatises and concluding that "English courts generally sustain the crown's proprietary rights in judicial opinions"). Blackstone described this as a "prerogative copyrigh[t]," explaining that "[t]he king, as the executive magistrate, has the right of promulging to the people all acts of state and government. This gives him the exclusive privilege of printing, at his own press, or that of his grantees, all acts of parliament, proclamations, and orders of council." 2 W. Blackstone, Commentaries on the Laws of England 410 (1766) (emphasis deleted); see also *Wheaton*, 8 Pet., at 659–660. This history helps to explain the dearth of cases permitting individuals to obtain copyrights in judicial opinions. But under the Constitution, sovereignty lies with the people, not a king. See The Federalist No. 22, p. 152 (C. Rossiter ed. 1961); *id.*, No. 39, at 241. The English historical practice, when superimposed on the Constitution's recognition that sovereignty resides in the people, helps to explain the Court's conclusion that the "authentic exposition and interpretation of the law . . . is free for publication to all." *Banks*, 128 U. S., at 253.

Finally, concerns of fair notice, often recognized by this Court's precedents as an important component of due process, also may have animated the reasoning of these 19th-century cases. As one court put it, "[t]he decisions and opinions of the justices are the authorized expositions and interpretations of the laws, which are binding upon all the citizens. . . . Every citizen is presumed to know the law thus declared, and it needs no argument to show that justice requires that all should have free access to the opinions." *Nash* v. *Lathrop*, 142 Mass. 29, 35, 6 N.E. 559, 560 (1886) (cited in *Banks*, 128 U. S., at 253–254); see also *American Soc. for Testing and Materials* v. *Public.Resource.Org, Inc.*, 896 F.3d 437, 458–459 (CADC 2018) (Katsas, J., concurring).

B

Allowing annotations to be copyrighted does not run afoul of any of these possible justifications for the government edicts doctrine. First, unlike judicial opinions and statutes, these annotations do not even purport to embody the will of the people because they are not law. The General Assembly of Georgia has made abundantly clear through a variety of provisions that the annotations do not create any binding obligations. OCGA §1–1–7 states that "[a]ll historical citations, title and chapter analyses, and notes set out in this Code are given for the purpose of convenient reference and do not constitute part of the law." Section 1–1–1 further provides that "[t]he statutory portion of the codification of Georgia laws . . . is enacted and shall have the effect of statutes enacted by the General Assembly of Georgia. The statutory portion of such codification shall be merged with annotations . . . and other materials . . . and shall be published by authority of the state." Thus, although the materials "merge" prior to publication in the "official" code, the very provision calling for that merger makes clear that the annotations serve as commentary, not law.

As additional evidence that the annotations do not represent the will of the people, the General Assembly does not enact statutory annotations under its legislative power. See Ga. Const., Art. III, §1, ¶1 (vesting the legislative power in the General Assembly). To enact state law, Georgia employs a process of bicameralism and presentment similar to that embodied in the United States Constitution. See Ga. Const., Art. III, §5; Art. V, §2, ¶4. The annotations do not go through this process, a fact that even the majority must acknowledge. *Ante*, at 10; Ga. S. 52, Reg. Sess., §54(b) (2019–2020) ("Annotations . . . except as otherwise provided in the Code . . . are not enacted as statutes by the provisions of this Act").

Second, unlike judges and legislators, the creators of annotations are incentivized by the copyright laws to produce a desirable product that will eventually earn them a profit. And though the Commission may require Lexis to follow strict guidelines, the independent synthesis, analysis, and creative drafting behind the annotations makes them analogous to other copyrightable materials. See Brief for Matthew Bender & Co., Inc., as *Amicus Curiae* 4–7.

Lastly, the annotations do not impede fair notice of the laws. As just stated, the annotations do not carry the binding force of law. They simply summarize independent sources of legal information and consolidate them in one place. Thus, OCGA annotations serve a similar function to other copyrighted research tools provided by private parties such as the American Law Reports and Westlaw, which also contain information of great "practical significance." *Ante*, at 17. Compare, *e.g.*, OCGA §34–9–260 (annotation for *Cho Carwash Property, L. L. C.* v. *Everett*, 326 Ga. App. 6, 755 S.E.2d 823 (2014)) with Ga. Code Ann. §34–9–260 (Westlaw's annotation for the same).

The majority resists this conclusion, suggesting that without access to the annotations, readers of Georgia law will be unable to fully understand the true meaning of Georgia's statutory provisions, such as provisions that have been undermined or nullified by court decisions. *Ante*, at 17. That is simply incorrect. As the majority tacitly concedes, a person seeking information about changes in Georgia statutory law can find that information by consulting the original source for the change in the law's status—the court decisions themselves. See *ante*, at 17. The inability to access the OCGA merely deprives a researcher of one specific tool, not to the underlying factual or legal information summarized in that tool. See also *post*, at 4 (Ginsburg, J., dissenting).[2]

C

The text of the Copyright Act supports my reading of the precedents.[3] Specifically, there are four indications in the text of the Copyright Act that the OCGA annotations are copyrightable. As an initial matter, the Act does not define the word "author," 17 U. S. C. §101, or make any reference to the government edicts doctrine. Accordingly, the term "author" itself does not shed any light on whether the doctrine covers statutory annotations. Second, while the Act excludes from copyright protection "work[s] prepared by an officer or employee of the United States Government as part of that person's official duties," §101; see also §105, the Act contains no similar prohibition against works of state governments or works prepared at their behest. "Congress' use of explicit language in one provision cautions against inferring the same limitation" elsewhere in the statute. *State Farm Fire & Casualty Co.* v. *United States ex rel. Rigsby*, 580 U. S. ___, ___ (2016) (slip op., at 7) (internal quotation marks omitted); *Pacific Operators Offshore, LLP* v. *Valladolid*, 565 U.S. 207, 216 (2012). Third, the Act specifically notes that annotations are copyrightable derivative works. §101. Here, again, the Act does not expressly exclude from copyright protection annotations created either by the State or at the State's request. Fourth, the Act provides that an author may hold a copyright in "material contributed" in a derivative work, "as distinguished from the preexisting material employed in the work." §103(b); see also *Feist Publications, Inc.* v. *Rural Telephone Service Co.*, 499 U.S. 340, 359 (1991). These aspects of the statutory text, taken together, further support the conclusion that the OCGA annotations are copyrightable.

For all these reasons, I would conclude that, as with the privately created annotations in *Callaghan*, Georgia's statutory annotations at issue in this case are copyrightable.

III

The majority reads this Court's precedents differently. In its view, the Court in *Banks* held that judges are not "authors" within the scope of the Copyright Act for "whatever work they perform in their capacity as judges," 128 U. S., at 253, so the same must be true for legislators, see *ante*, at 8–9. Accordingly, works created by legislators in their legislative capacity are not "original works of authorship," §102, and therefore cannot be copyrighted. This argument is flawed in multiple respects.

A

Most notably, the majority's textual analysis hinges on accepting that its construction of "authorship," *i.e.*, all works produced in a judge's or legislator's official capacity, was so well established by our 19th-century precedents that Congress incorporated it into the multiple revisions of the Copyright Act. See *ante*, at 12–13. Such confidence is questionable, to say the least.

The majority's understanding of the government edicts doctrine seems to have been lost on dozens of States and Territories, as well as the lower courts in this case. As already stated, the 25 jurisdictions with official annotated codes apparently did not view this Court's precedents as establishing the "official duties" definition of authorship. See Brief for State of Arkansas et al. as *Amici Curiae*.[4] And if "our precedents answer the question" so clearly, *ante*, at 14, one wonders why the Eleventh Circuit reached its conclusion in such a roundabout fashion. Rather than following the majority's "straightforward" path, *ante*, at 5, the Eleventh Circuit looked to the "zone of indeterminacy at the frontier between edicts that carry the force of law and those that do not" to determine whether the annotations were "sufficiently law-like" to be "constructively authored by the People." *Code Revision Comm'n* v. *Public.Resource.Org, Inc.*, 906 F.3d 1229, 1233, 1242, 1243 (2018). The District Court likewise does not appear to have viewed the question as well settled. In a cursory analysis, it determined that the annotations were copyrightable based on *Callaghan*. *Code Revision Comm'n* v. *Public.Resource.Org, Inc.*, 244 F. Supp. 3d 1350, 1356 (ND Ga. 2017). It is risible to presume that Congress had knowledge of and incorporated a "settled" meaning that eluded a multitude of States and Territories, as well as at least four Article III judges. *Ante*, at 13. Cf. *Rimini Street, Inc.* v. *Oracle USA, Inc.*, 586 U. S. ___, ___–___ (2019) (slip op., at 9–10).

This presumption of congressional knowledge also provides the basis for the majority's conclusion that the annotations are not "original works of authorship." See *ante*, at 11–12 (discussing §101). Stripped of the fiction that this Court's 19th-century precedents clearly demonstrated that "authorship" encompassed all works performed as part of a legislator's duties, the majority's textual argument fails.

The majority does not confront this criticism head on. Instead, it simply repeats, without any further elaboration, its unsupported conclusion that "[t]he Court long ago interpreted the word 'author' to exclude officials empowered to speak with the force of law, and Congress has carried that meaning forward in multiple iterations of the Copyright Act." *Ante*, at 16. This wave of the "magic wand of *ipse dixit*" does nothing to strengthen the majority's argument, and in fact only serves to underscore its weakness. *United States* v. *Yermian*, 468 U.S. 63, 77 (1984) (Rehnquist, J., dissenting).[5]

B

In addition to its textual deficiencies, the majority's understanding of this Court's precedents fails to account for the critical differences between the role that judicial opinions play in expounding upon the law compared to that of statutes. The majority finds it meaningful, for instance, that *Banks* prohibited dissents and concurrences from being copyrighted, even though they carry no legal force. *Ante*, at 15. At an elementary level, it is true that the judgment is the only part of a judicial decision that has legal effect. But it blinks reality to ignore that every word of a judicial opinion—whether it is a majority, a concurrence, or a dissent—expounds upon the law in ways that do not map neatly on to the legislative function. Setting aside summary decisions, the reader of a judicial opinion will always gain critical insight into the reasoning underlying a judicial holding by reading all opinions in their entirety. Understanding the reasoning that animates the rule in turn provides pivotal insight into how the law will likely be applied in future judicial opinions.[6] Thus, deprived of access to judicial opinions, individuals cannot access the primary, and therefore best, source of information for the meaning of the law.[7] And as true as that is today, access to these opinions was even more essential in the 19th century before the proliferation of federal and state regulatory law fundamentally altered the role that common-law judging played in expounding upon the law. See also *post*, at 2 (Ginsburg, J., dissenting).

These differences provide crucial context for *Banks*' reasoning. Specifically, to ensure that judicial "exposition and interpretation of the law" remains "free for publication to all," the word "author" must be read to encompass all judicial duties. *Banks*, 128 U. S., at 253. But these differences also demonstrate that the same rule does not *a fortiori* apply to all legislative duties.[8]

C

In addition to being flawed as a textual and precedential matter, the majority's rule will prove difficult to administer. According to one group of *amici*, nearly all jurisdictions with annotated codes use private contractors that "almost invariably prepare [annotations] under the supervision of legislative-branch or judicial-branch officials, including state legislators or state-court judges." Brief for State of Arkansas et al. as *Amici Curiae* 16–17. Under the majority's view, any one of these commissions or counsels could potentially be reclassified as an "adjunct to the legislature." *Ante*, at 11. But the majority's test for ascertaining the true nature of these commissions raises far more questions than it answers.

The majority lists a number of factors—including the Commission's membership and funding, how the annotations become part of the OCGA, and descriptions of the Commission from court cases—to support its conclusion that the Commission is really part of the legislature. See *ante*, at 9–10. But it does not specify whether these factors are exhaustive or illustrative and, if the latter, what other factors may be important. The majority also does not specify whether some factors weigh more heavily than others when deciding whether to deem an oversight body a legislative adjunct.

And even when the majority does list concrete factors, pivotal guidance remains lacking. For example, the majority finds it meaningful that 9 out of the Commission's 15 members are legislators. *Ante*, at 9; see OCGA §28–9–2 (noting that the other members of the Commission include the State's Lieutenant Governor, a judge, a district attorney, and three other state bar members). But how many legislative members are needed for a commission to become a legislative adjunct? The majority provides no answers to any of these questions.

* * *

The majority's rule will leave in the lurch the many States, private parties, and legal researchers who relied on the previously bright-line rule. Perhaps, to the detriment of all, many States will stop producing annotated codes altogether. Were that to occur, the majority's fear of an "economy-class" version of the law will truly become a reality. See *ante*, at 17. As Georgia explains, its contract enables the OCGA to be sold at a fraction of the cost of competing annotated codes. For example, Georgia asserts that Lexis sold the OCGA for $404 in 2016, while West Publishing's competing annotated code sold for $2,570. Should state annotated codes disappear, those without the means to pay the competitor's significantly higher price tag will have a valuable research tool taken away from them. Meanwhile, this Court, which is privileged to have access to numerous research resources, will scarcely notice. These negative practical ramifications are unfortunate enough when they reflect the deliberative legislative choices that we as judges are bound to respect. They are all the more regrettable when they are the result of our own meddling. Fortunately, as the majority and I agree, " 'critics of [today's] ruling can take their objections across the street, [where] Congress can correct any mistake it sees.' " *Ante*, at 13 (quoting *Kimble* v. *Marvel Entertainment, LLC*, 576 U.S. 446, 456 (2015)).

We have "stressed . . . that it is generally for Congress, not the courts, to decide how best to pursue the Copyright Clause's objectives," *Eldred* v. *Ashcroft*, 537 U.S. 186, 212 (2003), because "it is Congress that has been assigned the task of defining the scope of the limited monopoly that should be granted to authors," *Sony Corp. of America* v. *Universal City Studios, Inc.*, 464 U.S. 417, 429 (1984). Because the majority has strayed from its proper role, I respectfully dissent.

Notes

1 See 1Stat. 124; 2Stat. 171; ch. 16, 4Stat. 436; 11Stat. 138–139; 13Stat. 540; 16Stat. 212.

2 The majority contends that, rather than seeking to understand the origins of our precedents, we should simply accept the text of the opinions that the Justices "voted on and committed to writing." *Ante*, at 16–17, n. 4. But that begs the question: What does the text of the relevant opinions tell us? The answer is not much. It is precisely this lack of explication that makes it necessary to explore the "judicial *consensus*" and public policy referred to in *Banks* v. *Manchester*, 128 U.S. 244, 253 (1888). Instead, the majority attempts to dissect the language of our prior opinions in the same way it would interpret a statute, an approach we have repeatedly cautioned against. See *St. Mary's Honor Center* v. *Hicks*, 509 U.S. 502, 515 (1993); *Reiter* v. *Sonotone Corp.*, 442 U.S. 330, 341 (1979). The proper approach is to "read general language in judicial opinions . . . as referring in context to circumstances similar to the circumstances then before the Court and not referring to quite different circumstances that the Court was not then considering." *Illinois* v. *Lidster*, 540 U.S. 419, 424 (2004); see also *Cohens* v. *Virginia*, 6 Wheat. 264, 399 (1821) (Marshall, C. J., for the Court) ("[G]eneral expressions, in every opinion, are to be taken in connection with the case in which those expressions are used. If they go beyond the case, they may be respected, but ought not to control the judgment in a subsequent suit when the very point is presented for decision").

3 As the majority explains, *ante*, at 9, the annotations were created as part of a work-for-hire agreement between the Commission and Lexis. See 17 U. S. C. §201(b). Because no party disputes the validity of the contract, I express no opinion regarding whether the contract established an employer/employee relationship or whether the Commission may be considered a "person" under §201(b).

4 According to one study published in 2000, approximately half of States owned copyright in official state statutory compilations, court reports, or administrative regulations. Dmitrieva, State Ownership of Copyrights in Primary Law Materials, 23 Hastings Com. & Entertainment L. J. 81, 83, 97–105 (2000). The majority attempts to undermine this study by emphasizing that some of these States owned copyright in primary law materials. *Ante*, at 13, n. 3. This misunderstands the point. I do not claim that this evidence demonstrates that the States necessarily interpreted the government edicts doctrine correctly. I merely point out that these divergent practices seriously undercut the majority's claim that its interpretation of "authorship" was well settled and universally understood. On this score, the majority has no answer but to insinuate that the lawmakers of over half the Nation's jurisdictions disregarded federal law and the Constitution to pursue their own agendas in the face of supposedly clear precedent.

5 The majority's approach is also hard to reconcile with the recognition in *Wheaton* v. *Peters*, 8 Pet. 591 (1834), that annotations prepared by the Reporter of Decisions could be copyrighted. Wheaton was paid a salary of $1,000, and it is difficult to say whether this salary funded his work on the opinions or his work on the annotations. See *id.*, at 614, 617 (argument).
6 For instance, this Court has not overruled *Lemon* v. *Kurtzman*, 403 U.S. 602 (1971), which pronounced a test for evaluating Establishment Clause claims. But a reader would do well to carefully scrutinize the various opinions in *American Legion* v. *American Humanist Assn.*, 588 U. S. ___ (2019), to understand the markedly different way that this precedent functions in our current jurisprudence compared to when it was first decided. Moreover, sometimes a separate writing takes on canonical status, like Justice Jackson's concurrence regarding the executive power in *Youngstown Sheet & Tube Co.* v. *Sawyer*, 343 U.S. 579, 634–638 (1952) (opinion concurring in judgment and opinion of the Court); see also *Katz* v. *United States*, 389 U.S. 347, 360–361 (1967) (Harlan, J., concurring) (reasonable expectation of privacy Fourth Amendment test). Still other times, the reasoning in an opinion for less than a majority of the Court provides the explicit basis for a later majority's holding. See, *e.g.*, *McKinney* v. *Arizona*, 589 U. S. ___, ___ (2020) (slip op., at 5) (discussing *Ring* v. *Arizona*, 536 U.S. 584, 612 (2002) (Scalia J., concurring)); *Estelle* v. *Gamble*, 429 U.S. 97, 102 (1976) (incorporating into the majority the Eighth Amendment "evolving standards of decency" test first announced in *Trop* v. *Dulles*, 356 U.S. 86, 101 (1958) (plurality opinion)). Even " 'comments in [a] dissenting opinion,' " *ante*, at 15, sometimes reemerge as the foundational reasoning in a majority opinion. See, *e.g.*, *Franchise Tax Bd. of Cal.* v. *Hyatt*, 587 U. S. ___ (2019) (discussing *Nevada* v. *Hall*, 440 U.S. 410, 433–439 (1979) (Rehnquist, J., dissenting)); *Lawrence* v. *Texas*, 539 U.S. 558, 578 (2003) ("Justice Stevens' [dissenting] analysis, in our view, should have been controlling in *Bowers* [v. *Hardwick*, 478 U.S. 186 (1986),] and should control here"). These examples, and myriad more, demonstrate that the majority treats the role of separate judicial opinions in an overly simplistic fashion.
7 *Banks* also stated that judicially prepared syllabi and headnotes cannot be copyrighted. 128 U. S., at 253. The majority cites these materials as further evidence of its broad rule, because the majority finds it beyond cavil that "these supplementary materials do not have the force of law." *Ante*, at 15. The majority feels it appropriate to assume—without any historical inquiry—that the words "syllabus" and "headnote" carried the same meaning, or served the same function, in 1888 as they do now. Without briefing on this issue, I am not willing to make that leap. See *Hixson* v. *Burson*, 54 Ohio St. 470, 485, 43 N.E. 1000, 1003 (1896) ("reluctantly overrul[ing] the second syllabus" of a previous decision); *Holliday* v. *Brown*, 34 Neb. 232, 234, 51 N.W. 839, 840 (1892) ("It is an unwritten rule of this court that members thereof are bound only by the points as stated in the syllabus of each case"); see also *Frazier* v. *State*, 15 Ga. App. 365, 365–367, 83 S.E. 273, 273–274 (1914) (clarifying the meaning of a court-written headnote and emphasizing that to understand an opinion's meaning, the headnote and opinion must be read together); *United States* v. *Detroit Timber & Lumber Co.*, 200 U.S. 321, 337 (1906) (acknowledging that some state statutes rendered headnotes the work of the court carrying legal force).
8 Although legislative history is not at issue in this case, the majority also contends that its rule is necessary to fend off the possibility that "[a] State could monetize its entire suite of legislative history." *Ante*, at 17. Putting aside the jurisprudential debate over the use of such materials in interpreting federal statutes, many States can, and have, specifically authorized

courts to consider legislative history when construing statutes. See, *e.g.*, Colo. Rev. Stat. §2–4–203(1)(c) (2019); Iowa Code §4.6(3) (2019); Minn. Stat. §645.16(7) (2018); N. M. Stat. Ann. §12–2A–20(C)(2) (2019); N. D. Cent. Code Ann. §1–02–39(3) (2019); Ohio Rev. Code Ann. §1.49(C) (Lexis 2019); 1 Pa. Cons. Stat. §1921(c)(7) (2016). Given the direct role that legislative history plays in the construction of statutes in these States, it is hardly clear that such States could subject their legislative histories to copyright.

Allen v. Cooper 589 US __ (2020)

Justice KAGAN delivered the opinion of the Court.

In two basically identical statutes passed in the early 1990s, Congress sought to strip the States of their sovereign immunity from patent and copyright infringement suits. Not long after, this Court held in *Florida Prepaid Postsecondary Ed. Expense Bd.* v. *College Savings Bank*, 527 U.S. 627 (1999), that the patent statute lacked a valid constitutional basis. Today, we take up the copyright statute. We find that our decision in *Florida Prepaid* compels the same conclusion.

I

In 1717, the pirate Edward Teach, better known as Blackbeard, captured a French slave ship in the West Indies and renamed her *Queen Anne's Revenge*. The vessel became his flagship. Carrying some 40 cannons and 300 men, the *Revenge* took many prizes as she sailed around the Caribbean and up the North American coast. But her reign over those seas was short-lived. In 1718, the ship ran aground on a sandbar a mile off Beaufort, North Carolina. Blackbeard and most of his crew escaped without harm. Not so the *Revenge*. She sank beneath the waters, where she lay undisturbed for nearly 300 years.

In 1996, a marine salvage company named Intersal, Inc., discovered the shipwreck. Under federal and state law, the wreck belongs to North Carolina. See 102Stat. 433, 43 U. S. C. §2105(c); N. C. Gen. Stat. Ann. §121–22 (2019). But the State contracted with Intersal to take charge of the recovery activities. Intersal in turn retained petitioner Frederick Allen, a local videographer, to document the operation. For over a decade, Allen created videos and photos of divers' efforts to salvage the *Revenge*'s guns, anchors, and other remains. He registered copyrights in all those works.

This suit arises from North Carolina's publication of some of Allen's videos and photos. Allen first protested in 2013 that the State was infringing his copyrights by uploading his work to its website without permission. To address that allegation, North Carolina agreed to a settlement paying Allen $15,000 and laying out the parties' respective rights to the materials. But Allen and the State soon found themselves embroiled in another dispute. Allen complained that North Carolina had impermissibly posted five of his videos online and used one of his photos in a newsletter. When the State declined to admit wrongdoing, Allen filed this action in Federal District Court. It charges the State with copyright infringement (call it a modern form of piracy) and seeks money damages.

North Carolina moved to dismiss the suit on the ground of sovereign immunity. It invoked the general rule that federal courts cannot hear suits brought by individuals against nonconsenting States. See State Defendants' Memorandum in No. 15–627 (EDNC), Doc. 50, p. 7. But Allen responded that an exception to the rule applied because Congress had abrogated the States' sovereign immunity from suits like his. See Plaintiffs' Response, Doc. 57, p. 7. The Copyright Remedy Clarification Act of 1990 (CRCA or Act) provides that a State "shall not be immune, under the Eleventh Amendment [or] any other doctrine of sovereign immunity, from suit in Federal court" for copyright infringement. 17 U. S. C. §511(a). And the Act specifies that in such a suit a State will be liable, and subject to remedies, "in the same manner and to the same extent as" a private party. §501(a); see §511(b).[1] That meant, Allen contended, that his suit against North Carolina could go forward.

The District Court agreed. Quoting the CRCA's text, the court first found that "Congress has stated clearly its intent to abrogate sovereign immunity for copyright claims against a state." 244 F. Supp. 3d 525, 533 (EDNC 2017). And that abrogation, the court next held, had a proper constitutional basis. *Florida Prepaid* and other precedent, the District Court acknowledged, precluded Congress from using its Article I powers—including its authority over copyrights—to take away a State's sovereign immunity. See 244 F. Supp. 3d, at 534. But in the court's view, *Florida Prepaid* left open an alternative route to abrogation. Given the States' "pattern" of "abus[ive]" copyright infringement, the court held, Congress could accomplish its object under Section 5 of the Fourteenth Amendment. 244 F. Supp. 3d, at 535.

On interlocutory appeal, the Court of Appeals for the Fourth Circuit reversed. It read *Florida Prepaid* to prevent recourse to Section 5 no less than to Article I. A Section 5 abrogation, the Fourth Circuit explained, must be "congruent and proportional" to the Fourteenth Amendment injury it seeks to remedy. 895 F.3d 337, 350 (2018). *Florida Prepaid* had applied that principle to reject Congress's attempt, in the Patent Remedy Act, to abolish the States' immunity from patent infringement suits. See 527 U. S., at 630. In the Fourth Circuit's view, nothing distinguished the CRCA. That abrogation, the court reasoned, was "equally broad" and rested on a "similar legislative record" of constitutional harm. 895 F. 3d, at 352. So Section 5 could not save the law.

Because the Court of Appeals held a federal statute invalid, this Court granted certiorari. 587 U. S. ___ (2019). We now affirm.

II

In our constitutional scheme, a federal court generally may not hear a suit brought by any person against a nonconsenting State. That bar is nowhere explicitly set out in the Constitution. The text of the Eleventh Amendment (the single most relevant provision) applies only if the plaintiff is not a citizen of the defendant State.[2] But this Court has long understood that Amendment to "stand not so much for what it says" as for the broader "presupposition of our constitutional structure which it confirms." *Blatchford* v. *Native Village of Noatak*, 501 U.S. 775, 779 (1991). That premise, the Court has explained, has several parts. First, "each State is a sovereign entity in our federal system." *Seminole Tribe of Fla.* v. *Florida*, 517 U.S. 44, 54 (1996). Next, "[i]t is inherent in the nature of sovereignty not to be amenable to [a] suit" absent consent. *Id.*, at 54, n. 13 (quoting The Federalist No. 81, p. 487 (C. Rossiter ed. 1961) (A. Hamilton)). And last, that fundamental aspect of sovereignty constrains federal "judicial authority." *Blatchford*, 501 U. S., at 779.

But not entirely. This Court has permitted a federal court to entertain a suit against a nonconsenting State on two conditions. First, Congress must have enacted "unequivocal statutory language" abrogating the States' immunity from the suit. *Seminole Tribe*, 517 U. S., at 56 (internal quotation marks omitted); see *Dellmuth* v. *Muth*, 491 U.S. 223, 228 (1989) (requiring Congress to "mak[e] its intention unmistakably clear"). And second, some constitutional provision must allow Congress to have thus encroached on the States' sovereignty. Not even the most crystalline abrogation can take effect unless it is "a valid exercise of constitutional authority." *Kimel* v. *Florida Bd. of Regents*, 528 U.S. 62, 78 (2000).

No one here disputes that Congress used clear enough language to abrogate the States' immunity from copyright infringement suits. As described above, the CRCA provides that States "shall not be immune" from those actions in federal court. §511(a); see *supra,* at 2–3. And the Act specifies that a State stands in the identical position as a private defendant—exposed to liability and remedies "in the same manner and to the same extent." §501(a); see §511(b). So there is no doubt what Congress meant to accomplish. Indeed, this Court held in *Florida Prepaid* that the essentially verbatim provisions of the Patent Remedy Act "could not have [made] any clearer" Congress's intent to remove the States' immunity. 527 U. S., at 635.

The contested question is whether Congress had authority to take that step. Allen maintains that it did, under either of two constitutional provisions. He first points to the clause in Article I empowering Congress to provide copyright protection. If that fails, he invokes Section 5 of the Fourteenth Amendment, which authorizes Congress to "enforce" the commands of the Due Process Clause. Neither contention can succeed. The slate on which we write today is anything but clean. *Florida Prepaid*, along with other precedent, forecloses each of Allen's arguments.

A

Congress has power under Article I "[t]o promote the Progress of Science and useful Arts, by securing for limited Times to Authors and Inventors the exclusive Right to their respective Writings and Discoveries." §8, cl. 8. That provision—call it the Intellectual Property Clause—enables Congress to grant both copyrights and patents. And the monopoly rights so given impose a corresponding duty (*i.e.,* not to infringe) on States no less than private parties. See *Goldstein* v. *California*, 412 U.S. 546, 560 (1973).

In Allen's view, Congress's authority to abrogate sovereign immunity from copyright suits naturally follows. Abrogation is the single best—or maybe, he says, the only—way for Congress to "secur[e]" a copyright holder's "exclusive Right[s]" as against a State's intrusion. See Brief for Petitioners 20 (quoting Art. I, §8, cl. 8). So, Allen contends, the authority to take that step must fall within the Article I grant of power to protect intellectual property.

The problem for Allen is that this Court has already rejected his theory. The Intellectual Property Clause, as just noted, covers copyrights and patents alike. So it was the first place the *Florida Prepaid* Court looked when deciding whether the Patent Remedy Act validly stripped the States of immunity from infringement suits. In doing so, we acknowledged the reason for Congress to put "States on the same footing as private parties" in patent litigation. 527 U. S., at 647. It was, just as Allen says here, to ensure "uniform, surefire protection" of intellectual property. Reply Brief 10. That was a "proper Article I concern," we allowed. 527 U. S., at 648. But still, we said, Congress could not use its Article I power over patents to remove the States' immunity. We based that conclusion on *Seminole Tribe* v. *Florida*, decided three years earlier. There, the Court had held that "Article I cannot be used to circumvent" the limits sovereign immunity "place[s] upon federal jurisdiction." 517 U. S., at 73. That proscription ended the matter. Because Congress could not "abrogate state sovereign immunity [under] Article I," *Florida Prepaid* explained, the Intellectual Property Clause could not support the Patent Remedy Act. 527 U. S., at 636. And to extend the point to this case: if not the Patent Remedy Act, not its copyright equivalent either, and for the same reason. Here too, the power to "secur[e]" an intellectual property owner's "exclusive Right" under Article I stops when it runs into sovereign immunity. §8, cl. 8.

Allen claims, however, that a later case offers an exit ramp from *Florida Prepaid*. In *Central Va. Community College* v. *Katz*, 546 U.S. 356, 359 (2006), we held that Article I's Bankruptcy Clause enables Congress to subject nonconsenting States to bankruptcy proceedings (there, to recover a preferential transfer). We thus exempted the Bankruptcy Clause from *Seminole Tribe*'s general rule that Article I cannot justify haling a State into federal court. In bankruptcy, we decided, sovereign immunity has no place. But if that is true, Allen asks, why not say the same thing here? Allen reads *Katz* as "adopt[ing] a clause-by-clause approach to evaluating whether a particular clause of Article I" allows the abrogation of sovereign immunity. Brief for Petitioners 20. And he claims that the Intellectual Property Clause "supplies singular warrant" for Congress to take that step. *Ibid.* That is so, Allen reiterates, because "Congress could not 'secur[e]' authors' 'exclusive Right' to their works if [it] were powerless" to make States pay for infringing conduct. *Ibid.*

But everything in *Katz* is about and limited to the Bankruptcy Clause; the opinion reflects what might be called bankruptcy exceptionalism. In part, *Katz* rested on the "singular nature" of bankruptcy jurisdiction. 546 U. S., at 369, n. 9. That jurisdiction is, and was at the Founding, "principally *in rem*"—meaning that it is "premised on the debtor and his estate, and not on the creditors" (including a State). *Id.*, at 369–370 (internal quotation marks omitted). For that reason, we thought, "it does not implicate States' sovereignty to nearly the same degree as other kinds of jurisdiction." *Id.*, at 362. In remaining part, *Katz* focused on the Bankruptcy Clause's "unique history." *Id.*, at 369, n. 9. The Clause emerged from a felt need to curb the States' authority. The States, we explained, "had wildly divergent schemes" for discharging debt, and often "refus[ed] to respect one another's discharge orders." *Id.*, at 365, 377. "[T]he Framers' primary goal" in adopting the Clause was to address that problem—to stop "competing sovereigns[ ]" from interfering with a debtor's discharge. *Id.*, at 373. And in that project, the Framers intended federal courts to play a leading role. The nation's first Bankruptcy Act, for example, empowered those courts to order that States release people they were holding in debtors' prisons. See *id.*, at 374. So through and through, we thought, the Bankruptcy Clause embraced the idea that federal courts could impose on state sovereignty. In that, it was *sui generis*—again, "unique"—among Article I's grants of authority. *Id.*, at 369, n. 9.

Indeed, *Katz*'s view of the Bankruptcy Clause had a yet more striking aspect, which further separates it from any other. The Court might have concluded from its analysis that the Clause allows Congress to abrogate the States' sovereign immunity (as Allen argues the Intellectual Property Clause does). But it did not; it instead went further. Relying on the above account of the Framers' intentions, the Court found that *the Bankruptcy Clause itself* did the abrogating. *Id.*, at 379 ("[T]he relevant 'abrogation' is the one effected in the plan of the [Constitutional] Convention"). Or stated another way, we decided that no congressional abrogation was needed because the States had already "agreed in the plan of the Convention not to assert any sovereign immunity defense" in bankruptcy proceedings. *Id.*, at 377. We therefore discarded our usual rule—which Allen accepts as applying here—that *Congress* must speak, and indeed speak unequivocally, to abrogate sovereign immunity. Compare *id.*, at 378–379 ("[O]ur decision today" does not "rest[ ] on any statement Congress ha[s] made on the subject of state sovereign immunity"), with *supra,* at 5 (our ordinary rule). Our decision, in short, viewed bankruptcy as on a different plane, governed by principles all its own. Nothing in that understanding invites the kind of general, "clause-by-clause" reexamination of Article I that Allen proposes. See *supra,* at 7. To the contrary, it points to a good-for-one-clause-only holding.

And even if *Katz*'s confines were not so clear, *Florida Prepaid*, together with *stare decisis*, would still doom Allen's argument. As Allen recognizes, if the Intellectual Property Clause permits the CRCA's abrogation, it also would permit the Patent Remedy Act's. See Tr. of Oral Arg. 9 (predicting that if his position prevailed, "ultimately, the Patent Remedy Act would be revisited and properly upheld as a valid exercise of Congress's Article I power"). Again, there is no difference between copyrights and patents under the Clause, nor any material difference between the two statutes' provisions. See *supra,* at 3, and n. 1, 6. So we would have to overrule *Florida Prepaid* if we were to decide this case Allen's way. But *stare decisis*, this Court has understood, is a "foundation stone of the rule of law." *Michigan* v. *Bay Mills Indian Community*, 572 U.S. 782, 798 (2014). To reverse a decision, we demand a "special justification," over and above the belief "that the precedent was wrongly decided." *Halliburton Co.* v. *Erica P. John Fund, Inc.*, 573 U.S. 258, 266 (2014). Allen offers us nothing special at all; he contends only that if the Court were to use a clause-by-clause approach, it would discover that *Florida Prepaid* was wrong (because, he says again, the decision misjudged Congress's authority under the

Intellectual Property Clause). See Brief for Petitioners 37; *supra*, at 6–7. And with that charge of error alone, Allen cannot overcome *stare decisis*.

B

Section 5 of the Fourteenth Amendment, unlike almost all of Article I, can authorize Congress to strip the States of immunity. The Fourteenth Amendment "fundamentally altered the balance of state and federal power" that the original Constitution and the Eleventh Amendment struck. *Seminole Tribe*, 517 U. S., at 59. Its first section imposes prohibitions on the States, including (as relevant here) that none may "deprive any person of life, liberty, or property, without due process of law." Section 5 then gives Congress the "power to enforce, by appropriate legislation," those limitations on the States' authority. That power, the Court has long held, may enable Congress to abrogate the States' immunity and thus subject them to suit in federal court. See *Fitzpatrick* v. *Bitzer*, 427 U.S. 445, 456 (1976).

For an abrogation statute to be "appropriate" under Section 5, it must be tailored to "remedy or prevent" conduct infringing the Fourteenth Amendment's substantive prohibitions. *City of Boerne* v. *Flores*, 521 U.S. 507, 519 (1997). Congress can permit suits against States for actual violations of the rights guaranteed in Section 1. See *Fitzpatrick*, 427 U. S., at 456. And to deter those violations, it can allow suits against States for "a somewhat broader swath of conduct," including acts constitutional in themselves. *Kimel*, 528 U. S., at 81. But Congress cannot use its "power to enforce" the Fourteenth Amendment to alter what that Amendment bars. See *id.*, at 88 (prohibiting Congress from "substantively redefin[ing]" the Fourteenth Amendment's requirements). That means a congressional abrogation is valid under Section 5 only if it sufficiently connects to conduct courts have held Section 1 to proscribe.

To decide whether a law passes muster, this Court has framed a type of means-end test. For Congress's action to fall within its Section 5 authority, we have said, "[t]here must be a congruence and proportionality between the injury to be prevented or remedied and the means adopted to that end." *Boerne*, 521 U. S., at 520. On the one hand, courts are to consider the constitutional problem Congress faced—both the nature and the extent of state conduct violating the Fourteenth Amendment. That assessment usually (though not inevitably) focuses on the legislative record, which shows the evidence Congress had before it of a constitutional wrong. See *Florida Prepaid*, 527 U. S., at 646. On the other hand, courts are to examine the scope of the response Congress chose to address that injury. Here, a critical question is how far, and for what reasons, Congress has gone beyond redressing actual constitutional violations. Hard problems often require forceful responses and, as noted above, Section 5 allows Congress to "enact[ ] reasonably prophylactic legislation" to deter constitutional harm. *Kimel*, 528 U. S., at 88; *Boerne*, 521 U. S., at 536 (Congress's conclusions on that score are "entitled to much deference"); *supra*, at 10. But "[s]trong measures appropriate to address one harm may be an unwarranted response to another, lesser one." *Boerne*, 521 U. S., at 530. Always, what Congress has done must be in keeping with the Fourteenth Amendment rules it has the power to "enforce."

All this raises the question: When does the Fourteenth Amendment care about copyright infringement? Sometimes, no doubt. Copyrights are a form of property. See *Fox Film Corp.* v. *Doyal*, 286 U.S. 123, 128 (1932). And the Fourteenth Amendment bars the States from "depriv[ing]" a person of property "without due process of law." But even if sometimes, by no means always. Under our precedent, a merely negligent act does not "deprive" a person of property. See *Daniels* v. *Williams*, 474 U.S. 327, 328 (1986). So an infringement must be intentional, or at least reckless, to come within the reach of the Due Process Clause. See *id.*, at 334, n. 3 (reserving whether reckless conduct suffices). And more: A State cannot violate that Clause unless it fails to offer an adequate remedy for an infringement, because such a remedy itself satisfies the demand of "due process." See *Hudson* v. *Palmer*, 468 U.S. 517, 533 (1984). That means within the broader world of state copyright infringement is a smaller one where the Due Process Clause comes into play.

Because the same is true of patent infringement, *Florida Prepaid* again serves as the critical precedent. That decision defined the scope of unconstitutional infringement in line with the caselaw cited above—as intentional conduct for which there is no adequate state remedy. See 527 U. S., at 642–643, 645. It then searched for evidence of that sort of infringement in the legislative record of the Patent Remedy Act. And it determined that the statute's abrogation of immunity—again, the equivalent of the CRCA's—was out of all proportion to what it found. That analysis is the starting point of our inquiry here. And indeed, it must be the ending point too unless the evidence of unconstitutional infringement is materially different for copyrights than patents. Consider once more, then, *Florida Prepaid*, now not on Article I but on Section 5.

In enacting the Patent Remedy Act, *Florida Prepaid* found, Congress did not identify a pattern of unconstitutional patent infringement. To begin with, we explained, there was only thin evidence of States infringing patents at all—putting aside whether those actions violated due process. The House Report, recognizing that "many states comply with patent law," offered just two examples of patent infringement suits against the States. *Id.*, at 640 (quoting H. R. Rep. No. 101–960, pt. 1, p. 38 (1990)). The appellate court below, boasting some greater research prowess, discovered another seven in the century-plus between 1880 and 1990. See 527 U. S., at 640. Even the bill's House sponsor conceded the lack of "any evidence" of "widespread violation of patent laws." *Id.*, at 641 (quoting statement of Rep. Kastenmeier). What was more, there was no evidence that any instance of infringement by States crossed constitutional lines. Congress, we observed, "did not focus" on intentional or reckless conduct; to the contrary, the legislative record suggested that "most state infringement was innocent or at worst negligent." *Id.*, at 645. And similarly, Congress "barely considered the availability of state remedies for patent infringement." *Id.*, at 643. So, we concluded, nothing could support the idea that States were more than sporadically (if that) "depriving patent owners of property without due process of law." *Id.*, at 646.

Given that absence of evidence, *Florida Prepaid* held, the Patent Remedy Act swept too far. Recall what the Patent Remedy Act did—and did not. It abrogated sovereign immunity for any and every patent suit, thereby "plac[ing] States on the same footing as private parties." *Id.*, at 647. It did not set any limits. It did not, for example, confine the abrogation to suits alleging "nonnegligent infringement or infringement authorized [by] state policy." *Ibid*. Neither did it target States refusing to offer alternative remedies to patent holders. No, it exposed all States to the hilt—on a record that failed to show they had caused any discernible constitutional harm (or, indeed, much harm at all). That imbalance made it impossible to view the legislation "as responsive to, or designed to prevent, unconstitutional behavior." *Id.*, at 646 (quoting *Boerne*, 521 U. S., at 532). The statute's "indiscriminate scope" was too "out of proportion" to any due process problem. 527 U. S., at 646–647. It aimed not to correct such a problem, but to "provide a uniform remedy for patent infringement" writ large. *Id.*, at 647. The Patent Remedy Act, in short, did not "enforce" Section 1 of the Fourteenth Amendment—and so was not "appropriate" under Section 5.

Could, then, this case come out differently? Given the identical scope of the CRCA and Patent Remedy Act, that could happen only if the former law responded to materially stronger evidence of infringement, especially of the unconstitutional kind. Allen points to a significant disparity in how Congress created a record for the two statutes. See Brief for Petitioners 7–10, 47–50. Before enacting the CRCA, Congress asked the then-Register of Copyrights, Ralph Oman, to submit a report about the effects of the Eleventh Amendment on copyright enforcement. Oman and his staff conducted a year-long examination, which included a request for public comments eliciting letters from about 40 copyright holders and industry groups. The final 158-page report concluded that "copyright proprietors have demonstrated they will suffer immediate harm if they are unable to sue infringing states in federal court." Copyright Office, Copyright Liability of States and the Eleventh Amendment 103 (1988) (Oman Report). Is that report enough, as Allen claims, to flip *Florida Prepaid*'s outcome when it comes to copyright cases against the States?

It is not. Behind the headline-grabbing conclusion, nothing in the Oman Report, or the rest of the legislative record, cures the problems we identified in *Florida Prepaid*. As an initial matter, the concrete evidence of States infringing copyrights (even ignoring whether those acts violate due process) is scarcely more impressive than what the *Florida Prepaid* Court saw. Despite undertaking an exhaustive search, Oman came up with only a dozen possible examples of state infringement. He listed seven court cases brought against States (with another two dismissed on the merits) and five anecdotes taken from public comments (but not further corroborated). See Oman Report, at 7–9, 90–97. In testifying about the report, Oman acknowledged that state infringement is "not widespread" and "the States are not going to get involved in wholesale violation of the copyright laws." Hearings on H. R. 1131 before the Subcommittee on Courts, Intellectual Property, and the Administration of Justice, 101st Cong., 1st Sess., 53 (1989) (House Hearings). Indeed, he opined: "They are all respectful of the copyright law" and "will continue to respect the law"; what State, after all, would "want[ ] to get a reputation as a copyright pirate?" *Id.*, at 8. The bill's House and Senate sponsors got the point. The former admitted that "there have not been any significant number" of copyright violations by States. *Id.*, at 48 (Rep. Kastenmeier). And the latter conceded he could not currently see "a big problem." Hearings on S. 497 before the Subcommittee on Patents, Copyrights and Trademarks, 101st Cong., 1st Sess., 130 (1989) (Sen. DeConcini). This is not, to put the matter charitably, the stuff from which Section 5 legislation ordinarily arises.

And it gets only worse. Neither the Oman Report nor any other part of the legislative record shows concern with whether the States' copyright infringements (however few and far between) violated the Due Process Clause. Of the 12 infringements listed in the report, only two appear intentional, as they must be to raise a constitutional issue. See Oman Report, at 7–8, 91 (describing a judicial finding of "willful" infringement and a public comment charging continued infringement after a copyright owner complained). As Oman testified, the far greater problem was the frequency of "honest mistakes" or "innocent" misunderstandings; the benefit of the bill, he therefore thought, would be to "guard against sloppiness." House Hearings, at 9. Likewise, the legislative record contains no informa- tion about the availability of state-law remedies for copyright infringement (such as contract or unjust enrichment suits)—even though they might themselves satisfy due process. Those deficiencies in the record match the ones *Florida Prepaid* emphasized. See 527 U. S., at 643–645. Here no less than there, they signal an absence of constitutional harm.

Under *Florida Prepaid*, the CRCA thus must fail our "congruence and proportionality" test. *Boerne*, 521 U. S., at 520. As just shown, the evidence of Fourteenth Amendment injury supporting the CRCA and the Patent Remedy Act is equivalent—for both, that is, exceedingly slight. And the scope of the two statutes is identical—extending to every infringement case against a State. It follows that the balance the laws strike between constitutional wrong and statutory remedy is correspondingly askew. In this case, as in *Florida Prepaid*, the law's "indiscriminate scope" is "out of proportion" to any due process problem. 527 U. S., at 646–647; see *supra*, at 13. In this case, as in that one, the statute aims to "provide a uniform remedy" for statutory infringement, rather than to redress or prevent unconstitutional conduct. 527 U. S., at 647; see *supra*, at 13. And so in this case, as in that one, the law is invalid under Section 5.

That conclusion, however, need not prevent Congress from passing a valid copyright abrogation law in the future. In doing so, Congress would presumably approach the issue differently than when it passed the CRCA. At that time, the Court had not yet decided *Seminole Tribe*, so Congress probably thought that Article I could support its all-out abrogation of immunity. See *supra*, at 6. And to the extent it relied on Section 5, Congress acted before this Court created the "congruence and proportionality" test. See *supra*, at 11. For that reason, Congress likely did not appreciate the importance of linking the scope of its abrogation to the redress or prevention of unconstitutional injuries—and of creating a legislative record to back up that connection. But going forward, Congress will know those rules. And under them, if it detects violations of due process, then it may enact a proportionate response. That kind of tailored statute can effectively stop States from behaving as copyright pirates. Even while respecting constitutional limits, it can bring digital Blackbeards to justice.

III

Florida Prepaid all but prewrote our decision today. That precedent made clear that Article I's Intellectual Property Clause could not provide the basis for an abrogation of sovereign immunity. And it held that Section 5 of the Fourteenth Amendment could not support an abrogation on a legislative record like the one here. For both those reasons, we affirm the judgment below.

It is so ordered.

Notes

1 The CRCA served as the model for the Patent and Plant Variety Protection Clarification Act (Patent Remedy Act), passed two years later (and repudiated by this Court in *Florida Prepaid*, see *supra,* at 1). Using the same language, the latter statute provided that a State "shall not be immune, under the [E]leventh [A]mendment [or] any other doctrine of sovereign immunity, from suit in Federal court" for patent infringement. §2, 106Stat. 4230. And so too, the statute specified that in such a suit, a State will be liable, and subject to remedies, "in the same manner and to the same extent as" a private party. *Ibid.*

2 The Eleventh Amendment reads: "The Judicial Power of the United States shall not be construed to extend to any suit in law or equity, commenced or prosecuted against one of the United States by Citizens of another State, or by Citizens or Subjects of any Foreign State."

Justice Breyer, with whom Justice Ginsburg joins, concurring in the judgment.

The Constitution gives Congress certain enumerated powers. One of them is set forth in the Intellectual Property Clause: Congress may "promote the Progress of Science and useful Arts, by securing for limited Times to Authors and Inventors the exclusive Right to their respective Writings and Discoveries." Art. I, §8, cl. 8. "And the monopoly rights so given," the Court acknowledges, operate against "States no less than private parties." *Ante*, at 6. States, in other words, have "a specific duty" not to infringe that "is assigned by law" and upon which "individual rights depend." *Marbury* v. *Madison*, 1 Cranch 137, 166 (1803). One might therefore expect that someone injured by a State's violation of that duty could "resort to the laws of his country for a remedy," *ibid.*, especially where, as here, Congress has sought to provide one. Or more concretely, one might think that Walt Disney Pictures could sue a State (or anyone else) for hosting an unlicensed screening of the studio's 2003 blockbuster film, Pirates of the Caribbean (or any one of its many sequels).

Yet the Court holds otherwise. In its view, Congress' power under the Intellectual Property Clause cannot support a federal law providing that, when proven to have pirated intellectual property, States must pay for what they plundered. *Ante*, at 6–10. To subject nonconsenting States to private suits for copyright or patent infringement, says the Court, Congress must endeavor to pass a more "tailored statute" than the one before us, relying not on the Intellectual Property Clause, but on §5 of the Fourteenth Amendment. *Ante*, at 16. Whether a future legislative effort along those lines will pass constitutional muster is anyone's guess. But faced with the risk of unfairness to authors and inventors alike, perhaps Congress will venture into this great constitutional unknown.

That our sovereign-immunity precedents can be said to call for so uncertain a voyage suggests that something is amiss. Indeed, we went astray in *Seminole Tribe of Fla.* v. *Florida*, 517 U.S. 44 (1996), as I have consistently maintained. See *College Savings Bank* v. *Florida Prepaid Postsecondary Ed. Expense Bd.*, 527 U.S. 666, 699–701 (1999) (dissenting opinion); *Federal Maritime Comm'n* v. *South Carolina Ports Authority*, 535 U.S. 743, 787–788 (2002) (same). We erred again in *Florida Prepaid Postsecondary Ed. Expense Bd.* v. *College Savings Bank*, 527 U.S. 627 (1999), by holding that Congress exceeded its §5 powers when it passed a patent counterpart to the copyright statute at issue here. See *id.*, at 652–664 (Stevens, J., dissenting). But recognizing that my longstanding view has not carried the day, and that the Court's decision in *Florida Prepaid* controls this case, I concur in the judgment. See *ante*, 9–10, 15–16; *Kimble* v. *Marvel Entertainment, LLC*, 576 U.S. 446, 455–456 (2015); *Franchise Tax Board of California* v. *Hyatt*, 587 U. S. ___, ___ (2019) (Breyer, J., dissenting).

Justice Thomas, concurring in part and concurring in the judgment.

I agree with the Court's conclusion that the Copyright Remedy Clarification Act of 1990, 17 U. S. C. §501 *et seq.*, does not validly abrogate States' sovereign immunity. But I cannot join the Court's opinion in its entirety. I write separately to note two disagreements and one question that remains open for resolution in a future case.

First, although I agree that *Florida Prepaid Postsecondary Ed. Expense Bd.* v. *College Savings Bank*, 527 U.S. 627 (1999), is binding precedent, I cannot join the Court's discussion of *stare decisis*. The Court claims we need " 'special justification[s]' " to overrule precedent because error alone "cannot overcome *stare decisis*." *Ante*, at 9–10. That approach "does not comport with our judicial duty under Article III." *Gamble* v. *United States*, 587 U. S. ___, ___ (2019) (Thomas, J., concurring) (slip op., at 2). If our decision in *Florida Prepaid* were demonstrably erroneous, the Court would be obligated to "correct the error, regardless of whether other factors support overruling the precedent." 587 U. S., at ___–___ (same) (slip op., at 8–9).

Here, adherence to our precedent is warranted because petitioners have not demonstrated that our decision in *Florida Prepaid* "is incorrect, much less demonstrably erroneous." *Gamble*, 587 U. S., at ___ (same) (slip op., at 17). The Court in *Florida Prepaid* correctly concluded that "Congress may not abrogate state sovereign immunity pursuant to its Article I powers," including its powers under the Intellectual Property Clause. 527 U. S., at 636 (citing *Seminole Tribe of Fla.* v. *Florida*, 517 U.S. 44, 72–73 (1996)). Petitioners' claims to the contrary are unpersuasive.[1]*

Second, I do not join the Court's discussion regarding future copyright legislation. In my view, we should opine on "only the case before us in light of the record before us." *Manhattan Community Access Corp.* v. *Halleck*, 587 U. S. ___, ___ (2019) (slip op., at 15). We should not purport to advise Congress on how it might exercise its legislative authority, nor give our blessing to hypothetical statutes or legislative records not at issue here.

Finally, I believe the question whether copyrights are property within the original meaning of the Fourteenth Amendment's Due Process Clause remains open. The Court relies on *Fox Film Corp.* v. *Doyal*, 286 U.S. 123 (1932), to conclude that "[c]opyrights are a form of property." *Ante*, at 11. But *Fox Film Corp.* addressed "property" in the context of state tax laws, not the Due Process Clause. 286 U. S., at 128. And although we stated in *Florida Prepaid* that patents are "property" for due process purposes, we did not analyze the Fourteenth Amendment's text, and neither of the cases we cited involved due process. 527 U. S., at 642 (citing *Brown* v. *Duchesne*, 19 How. 183, 197 (1857); *Consolidated Fruit-Jar Co.* v. *Wright*, 94 U.S. 92, 96 (1877)); see also Merrill, The Landscape of Constitutional Property, 86 Va. L. Rev. 885, 887 (2000) (noting that the "Court has not always been attentive to the 'property' threshold" of the Due Process Clauses). Because the parties agree that petitioners' copyrights are property, and because the Fourteenth Amendment does not authorize this statute's abrogation of state sovereign immunity either way, we need not resolve this open question today. I would, however, be willing to consider the matter in an appropriate case.

For these reasons, I join all of the Court's opinion except for the final paragraph in Part II–A and the final paragraph in Part II–B.

Notes

1 Because I adhere to our precedents regarding Article I and state sovereign immunity, I continue to believe that *Central Va. Community College* v. *Katz*, 546 U.S. 356 (2006), was wrongly decided. See *id.*, at 379–385 (Thomas, J., dissenting). The Court today rightfully limits that de-cision to the Bankruptcy Clause context, calling it a "good-for-one-clause-only holding." *Ante*, at 9. I would go a step further and recognize that the Court's decision in *Katz* is not good for even that clause.

13: The CASE Act

In December 2020, the CASE Act was signed into law, which for the first time would create a small claims court for copyright. So many elements are unknown, in part, because while the law itself is detailed, it still leaves a great deal up to regulations set by the Register of Copyright.

This is a short description of the CASE Act. The full title is the "Copyright Alternative in Small-Claims Enforcement Act of 2020" or the "CASE Act of 2020". The CASE Act adjudicates, according to Section 1504(c):

- A claim for infringement for an exclusive right in a copyrighted work (Section 106) by the legal or beneficial owner at the time of the infringement.
- A claim for a declaration of noninfringement of an exclusive right of a copyright work under section 106
- A claim under Section 512(f) for misrepresentation in connection with a notification of a acclaimed infringement or notification seeking to replace or remove disailed materials
- And counterclaims that arise under section 106 orr 512(f) and out of the same transaction or occurrence
- Legal or equitable defense in response to claim or counterclaim asserted.

The Register will be putting out regulations, and there is a lot of detail to the procedures under the CASE Act. A couple of key elements:

- You can opt out. All the way till before the final judgement
- Libraries can preemptively opt out with the Copyright office -- and it is a one-time opt out and there is no fee or renewal
- And there may be a mini-version of under $5000 that the Register can enact.
- You have to register, and if the registration is not complete, your claim will be paused until the registration goes through. So, encouraging registration before there is a problem.
- Monetary relief of either actual damages or statutory damages, with statutory damages a max of $7500 per work, and not more than $15,000 per proceeding. The Copyright Claims Board cannot find willful infringement. Attorney fees and costs up to $5000, and if pro se, up to $2500 for costs only.

- CCB can include a statement to cease certain activities
- Lawyers and certified law students, as long with pro se (no lawyer)
- Limits on number of cases and a mechanism (by Register) if bad faith claims are brought.
- Fees, not less than $100 but not more than district court filing fee (around $350).

What I am most surprised at is how complicated it is. We will be doing a deeper dive, especially once the Register of Copyright puts out the regulations.

This will be Chapter 15 in the 1976 Copyright Act, a new chapter. There are 11 parts:

- 1501. Definitions.
- 1502. Copyright Claims Board.
- 1503. Authority and duties of the Copyright Claims Board. "1504. Nature of proceedings.
- 1505. Registration requirement.
- 1506. Conduct of proceedings.
- 1507. Effect of proceeding.
- 1508. Review and confirmation by district court.
- 1509. Relationship to other district court actions.
- 1510. Implementation by the Copyright Office.
- 1511. Funding.

Because the law is not final, we've hesitated putting in more detail. A subsequent edition will include more information. But in short, this could be game changing for the entire copyright system.

We will be working through this new law throughout the semester. The questions that will arise include:

1. Is a work under copyright?
2. Who is the copyright holder? Is the person bringing the claim authorized to do so?
3. Under what claim is the suit being brought?
4. What are the defenses?
5. If someone wants to bring a claim, what must they do (requirements)?
6. What kinds of things should we be aware of when preparing a claim?
7. What are the alternatives (including the opt-out) that we should be aware of?

14: Usability Assessment

We started with the question, "can I use this work?" We learned that the answer is sometimes simple; other times it can get quite complex. But how do you begin your search? Let's take a look.

Finding the Right Traffic Cop

Where do you begin in your analysis of "Can I use this work"? We struggled with this question for over a year. We started saying that we need a sophisticated traffic cop, but we never figured out a definitive place to always start. So, here's some places:

1. The Date: If it is old or newer than 1989, this is a good place to begin.
2. The User: why are you wanting to use the work, and are there special exceptions or laws because of who you are (e.g. libraries, states).
3. The Use: what are you doing with the work
4. What is being used (think non-protectable elements or pd)
5. Commercial or Noncommercial Use? That's a big one.

Other Considerations: Section 107-122

The Copyright Act has a number of exceptions allowing for permissible uses during the lifetime of a copyrighted work. We have already looked at Section 108 - library uses. Many of you are likely familiar with Section 107 - fair use. But there are more. Section 109 includes the first sale doctrine. Section 110 includes exceptions for display and public performance, including classroom uses. Let's look a quick look at the list, Section 111-121.

- §111. Limitations on exclusive rights: Secondary transmissions of broadcast programming by cable
- §112. Limitations on exclusive rights: Ephemeral recordings
- §113. Scope of exclusive rights in pictorial, graphic, and sculptural works
- §114. Scope of exclusive rights in sound recordings

- §115. Scope of exclusive rights in nondramatic musical works: Compulsory license for making and distributing phonorecords
- §116. Negotiated licenses for public performances by means of coin-operated phonorecord players
- §116A. Renumbered §116]
- §117. Limitations on exclusive rights: Computer programs
- §118. Scope of exclusive rights: Use of certain works in connection with noncommercial broadcasting
- §119. Limitations on exclusive rights: Secondary transmissions of distant television programming by satellite
- §120. Scope of exclusive rights in architectural works
- §121. Limitations on exclusive rights: Reproduction for blind or other people with disabilities
- §121A. Limitations on exclusive rights: reproduction for blind or other people with disabilities in Marrakesh Treaty countries
- §122. Limitations on exclusive rights: Secondary transmissions of local television programming by satellite

Online

Section 512- notice and take down: when someone uses your work online without permission, you have to do a Section 512 analysis. Again, see *Just Wanna Create*. The CASE Act may also alter this relationship.

Section 1202 - prevents information -- metadata and the copyright information from being stripped from a work without penalty.

Custom: What role does our expectations and social customs play in the administration on justice with copyright on a daily basis? What is acceptable and what is not? We will also again see this alter potentially with the CASE Act.

Worksheet: Can I Use this Work?

In determining whether you can use a work, there are a number of questions that need to be asked. You can start in many different places, and as you learn more copyright, you will intuitively learn where to begin for yourself.

- Starting with the user:

  For libraries or patrons of libraries, for example, this is a good place to start.

- Starting with the use:

  For artists and scholars relying on fair use this is a good place to start, but quickly leads to a set of questions.

  - What exactly are you using? Is it protectable or unprotectable?
  - Is the work under copyright?
  - How much are you using?
  - Four-factor fair use test
    - Commercial or non-commercial use?
    - Market Replacement?
    - Transformative?
    - Nature of the original work?

      Among other questions.

- Starting with the venue

  Where is the work being displayed or used? On a social media platform? Sold online? This is more of a risk assessment approach.

- Starting with the work

  For most of the life of the Durationator, we began here. We saw the work as finite, and then we looked to the circumstances in which the question was being asked. This is still a good starting point.

- Start with registration

Is this work registered with the U.S. Copyright Office? Is there notice? Each of these steps are key to understanding the impact and seriousness of the copyright holder.

Why Do You Care?

Really, you need to ask yourself this question. Are you doing copyright clearance for your job? Are you creating a new product? Are you an artist and want to make sure you are within the customs and boundaries of your community? Or are you just nervous and don't know the law? Be smart about your approach. Many factors matter in why you care to know the answer.

www.ingramcontent.com/pod-product-compliance
Lightning Source LLC
LaVergne TN
LVHW082023200926
848481LV00010B/2910
* 9 7 8 1 7 3 4 1 2 7 1 7 1 *